The Taxation of Income from Business
and Capital in Colombia

The Taxation of Income from Business and Capital in Colombia

CHARLES E. MCLURE, JR.,   JOHN MUTTI,   VICTOR THURONYI,

AND GEORGE R. ZODROW

FISCAL REFORM IN THE DEVELOPING WORLD

DUKE UNIVERSITY PRESS   DURHAM AND LONDON 1990

© 1990 Duke University Press
All rights reserved
Printed in the United States of America
on acid-free paper ∞
Library of Congress Cataloging-in-Publication Data
The Taxation of income from business and capital in Colombia/
authors, Charles E. McLure, Jr. . . . [et al.].
p. cm.
Bibliography: p.
Includes index.
ISBN 0-8223-0925-4
1. Income tax—Colombia. 2. Business enterprises—Taxation—
Colombia. 3. Capital gains tax—Colombia. I. McClure, Charles E.
HJ4695.T39 1990
336.24'3'09861—dc20 89-11832

CONTENTS

**CHAPTER 5.   APPRAISAL OF COLOMBIAN TAXATION OF INCOME
                FROM BUSINESS AND CAPITAL**

CHAPTER 6.   THE NET WEALTH TAX

CHAPTER 7.   INFLATION ADJUSTMENT

To the good people of Colombia

FOREWORD

The repeated interaction between leading foreign scholars and Colombian tax officials has over the years proved to be peculiarly productive for both sides. Colombia has received the benefit of first-class advice from such leading economists as Richard Musgrave, Malcolm Gillis, and Charles McLure. In return these scholars—and indeed everyone concerned with development policy—have gained a great deal both from the unusual willingness of Colombians to consider new ideas in detail and from the hard-headed pragmatism that has led them to carefully adapt such ideas to local circumstances before attempting to put them into practice. The present book is the most recent example of what seems to have become a Colombian tradition of defining an interesting and important policy problem, asking some of the leading experts in the world to consider and to propose solutions for the problem and then, after full public discussion, drawing on the work of these experts to design a made-in-Colombia solution. In addition to setting an excellent example of how to use foreign expertise, this process has proven to be particularly valuable to the world as a whole because of the willingness—even eagerness!—of the Colombian authorities to put the work they have commissioned and paid for into the public domain so that other countries (and scholars) can also benefit.

This study by Charles McLure and his colleagues is thus a worthy addition to a tradition dating back to the first World Bank country report in 1949, with perhaps the most prominent prior example in the public finance field being the 1971 Harvard Tax Program volume by Musgrave and Gillis. Much more than that, however, the present book is an outstanding example of the kind of careful and systematic work that is needed to convert good theoretical analysis on what is required to attain the alternative goals of a comprehensive income tax and a consumption tax into policy designs that might work in the difficult practical circumstances of an open inflationary economy. The book discusses many important aspects of direct tax reform in a developing country—inflation adjustment under the income tax, the role of presumptive and net wealth taxes, the international aspects of income taxes, etc. Undoubtedly its most important contribution, however, concerns consumption taxes. No one, anywhere, has thought through with such care just how the so-called "simplified alternative tax" (essentially a direct personal consumption tax combined with a cash-flow corporate tax) might work in the real world. Since such taxes are increasingly being considered—if not yet adopted—all over the world, in developing and developed countries alike, this book should be high on the reading list of all those concerned with the design and implementation of efficient and equitable direct tax systems.

Richard M. Bird
University of Toronto
March 1989

PRESENTACION

La Dirección General de Impuestos Nacionales se complace en hacer entrega de la presente publicación, denominada «La tributación de la renta proveniente de los negocios y del capital en Colombia», la cual será editada en inglés y español.

La elaboración de este informe se inició por parte de un grupo de connotados expertos internacionales en las áreas fiscal y económica, liderado por el profesor Charles McLure, siendo Director de Impuestos el Doctor Santiago Pardo R., con miras a permitir al Gobierno Colombiano contar con mayores elementos de juicio, al desarrollar las facultades extraordinarias conferidas por el Congreso de la República en la Ley 75 de 1986 sobre los efectos de la inflación en la determinación del impuesto de renta.

El desarrollo de las mencionadas facultades constituye la tercera fase de la reforma tributaria, luego de las modificaciones de carácter sustantivo introducidas en la misma ley, como la reducción de tarifas y la eliminación de la doble tributación, y de la reforma procedimental puesta en marcha con la expedición del Decreto 2503 de 1987, que entre otras cosas simplificó drásticamente el cumplimiento de las obligaciones formales por parte de los contribuyentes, traspasó el recaudo y recepción de declaraciones a la red bancaria, eliminó el Certificado de Paz y Salvo, y en general estableció unas reglas de juego más claras y sencillas en la relación Estado-contribuyente.

Espera la Dirección de Impuestos que con este documento se inicie la discusión académica que permita tomar las decisiones tendientes a eliminar las inequidades que genera la inflación en la determinación del impuesto de renta, a equilibrar tributariamente las alternativas de financiamiento de las empresas, y en general a adoptar un sistema tributario que al tiempo que sea equitativo y de fácil administración, alcance los objetivos de estabilidad, distribución del ingreso y desarrollo económico.

LUIS FERNANDO RAMIREZ ACUÑA
Director General de Impuestos Nacionales

The English translation of this foreword is on the following page. Translations of other Spanish passages from the report can be found in the appendix on pages 387-388.

PRESENTATION

The General Directorate of National Taxes is pleased to make available this publication, entitled "The Taxation of Income from Business and Capital in Colombia," which is to be published in English and Spanish.

The preparation of this report began with a group of noted international experts in fiscal and economic areas, led by Professor Charles McLure, when Dr. Santiago Pardo R. was Director of Taxes, with a view to enable the Colombian government to rely on greater bases for judgment in carrying out the extraordinary faculties conferred by the Congress of the Republic in Law 75 of 1986 concerning the effects of inflation on the determination of income tax.

Carrying out these extraordinary faculties is the third phase of tax reform—following the substantive changes introduced in the same law—such as the reduction of rates and the elimination of double taxation, and the procedural reform set in motion by the publication of Decree 2503 of 1987 which, among other things, dramatically simplified the formal filing requirements for taxpayers, transferred the receipt of revenue and of tax returns to the banking system, eliminated the "Certificate of Peace and Safety" (tax payment certificate), and in general established clear and simple rules governing the taxpayer-government relationship.

The Directorate of Taxes hopes that this document will stimulate the academic discussion that will permit decisions to be taken that will tend to eliminate the inflation-generated inequities in determining the amount of income tax, to place alternative methods of financing businesses on an equal tax footing, and in general to adopt a tax system which, at the same time as being equitable and easily administered, advances the goals of stability, income distribution, and economic development.

Luis Fernando Ramírez Acuña
Director General of National Taxes

ACKNOWLEDGEMENTS

When Dr. Santiago Pardo Ramírez, then Director General of National Taxes in the Finance Ministry of Colombia, asked me to undertake this study of the taxation of income from business and capital in Colombia, I emphasized that the success of the project would depend on three key elements: his support for the project, my ability to gain the services of the four tax experts I had in mind to assist me with the analysis, and the availability of Dr. Jairo Lanao Alvarez to act as liaison between the research team and the Government. These three requirements were fully met.

Dr. Pardo gave us his full support, emphasizing in many ways the importance of the project. This was reflected in the valuable assistance we received from Dr. Jaime Duque Arbelaez on legal questions and from Dr. María Elisa Gálvez Velásquez on questions of data, as well as in the general spirit of cooperation and goodwill we experienced at the Ministry of Finance. Perhaps most important, Dr. Pardo devoted a substantial amount of his own very limited time to meeting with the research team, both to familiarize us with the relevant income tax provisions and their need for change and to consider our preliminary recommendations for reform. Dr. Luis Fernando Ramírez Acuña, who succeeded Dr. Pardo as Director General of National Taxes in July 1988, provided continued support for the project.

I was able to obtain the services of Professors Richard Bird, Jack Mutti, Victor Thuronyi, and George Zodrow, the four experts I had previously identified in my discussions with Dr. Pardo. My judgement in selecting them to collaborate on the project has been fully vindicated by their devotion to the project and the quality of their work on the report.

Finally, Dr. Lanao performed his duties at a level, and with a style, far beyond what we could have expected—and this despite a serious personal illness requiring surgery during the course of the project. The many services he cheerfully performed included assistance with administrative matters such as contracting, acquisition of data, and translation of the report.

Without his able assistance it would have been very difficult to complete the project on a timely basis.

The preparation of this report was, in many respects, a cooperative venture. The entire team participated in the planning of the project; it spent several weeks together in Bogotá during May 1987, gathering information and meeting with representatives of the private sector, as well as the public sector; and all members of the team exchanged views on virtually the entire manuscript as it was being prepared. Yet it is possible, as well as appropriate, to indicate which members of the research team were primarily responsible for preparing particular parts of the report.

Professor Victor Thuronyi prepared most of chapter 2 (Overview of Taxation of Income and Wealth), chapter 3 (Summary Description of Colombian Business and Capital Income), chapter 5 (Appraisal of Colombian Taxation of Income from Business and Capital), Chapter 6 (The Net Wealth Tax), and the appendix following chapter 6 (Technical Description of Proposals). Professor George Zodrow prepared most of chapter 4 (Marginal Effective Tax Rates), chapter 8 (Structural Differences between Income and Consumption Taxes), chapter 9 (The Simplified Alternative Tax), and chapter 10 (Comparison of the Two Proposals). I prepared most of chapter 7 (Inflation Adjustment) and chapter 1 (Overview of Objectives and Alternatives). Professor Jack Mutti prepared the portions of various chapters (especially chapters 3, 5, 7, and 9) dealing with international aspects of both the income tax and the Simplified Alternative Tax. Professor Richard Bird read the entire manuscript and provided useful comments to the primary authors of the various chapters, as well as participating in the preparatory field work in Bogotá.

Charles E. McLure, Jr.
Director, Tax Reform Project

PART ONE

Inflation Adjusting the Income Tax

1

An Overview of Objectives and Alternatives

An Overview of Objectives and Alternatives

I. Introduction

In December 1986 Colombia enacted Law 75, making fundamental changes in its income tax. Tax thresholds were raised, withholding was made a final tax for many taxpayers, and the top bracket rate paid by individuals was reduced from 49 percent to 30 percent. Especially important were the changes in the tax treatment of income from business and capital.

The taxation of corporations (sociedades anónimas) and limited partnerships (sociedades limitadas) was unified. This was accomplished by subjecting all the taxable income of both types of companies (sociedades) to the 30 percent rate and excluding dividends paid by corporations and partners' shares in the earnings of limited partnerships from the tax base of individuals. Interest income and expense are to be indexed for inflation; except in the case of interest income received by individuals from financial institutions and other payors subject to government regulation, which immediately qualifies for indexation, this inflation adjustment is to be phased in over a ten-year period, beginning in 1986. Inflation adjustment was not extended to depreciable assets or to inventory accounting, which already benefit from accelerated depreciation and the use of last-in, first-out (LIFO) accounting.

Law 75 of 1986 provides the Government of Colombia with «extraordinary faculties» (facultades extraordinarias) that allow it, among other things, to specify further changes in law needed to eliminate the effects of inflation from the measurement of taxable income.[1] The present Report is intended to provide guidance to the Government as it considers how best to satisfy that mandate.

The discussion of this Report goes beyond the narrow issue of whether and how the inflation adjustment scheme of Law 75 of 1986 might be improved. (Chapter 7 is devoted to an examination of that issue.) Rather, it takes the view that the rationale behind much of Law 75 — the achievement of equity and neutrality — requires the creation of a more accurate measure of real economic income for tax purposes. Since there may be little to be gained from making a highly defective tax system inflation-proof, the Report, especially in Chapter 5, examines fundamental issues of the taxation of income from business and capital that would arise even in the absence of inflation. Moreover, it recognizes that problems caused by the failure to make the tax system of Colombia inflation-proof extend beyond the income tax to include the measurement of net wealth; Chapter 6 thus examines the taxation of net wealth, and Chapter 5 also considers the measurement of presumptive income, which is based primarily on net wealth.[2] Finally, the examination of the tax system of Colombia contained in this Report goes beyond merely reforming the existing income and net wealth taxes. The Report also considers a more drastic reform of a type that in many ways is attractive in concept but that has not been implemented in any country, a system of direct taxation based on consumption, rather than income.

II. Alternative Solutions

Before the reforms adopted in December 1986, little systematic allowance was made for inflation in the measurement of income under the Colombian income tax. As a result, taxable income could be either understated or overstated, resource allocation was distorted by taxation as it interacted with inflation, and equity suffered. All these defects, which are explained further in the next section, were generally more important, the higher the rate of inflation.[3/]

There are two primary alternative means of dealing with this situation. One is to provide systematic inflation adjustment for crucial items of income and expense, including interest, capital gains, depreciation and similar allowances, and cost of goods sold from inventories.[4/] The result would be an «inflation-adjusted» income tax in which only real income would be taxed. This was the general approach followed in the 1986 reforms, although these reforms stopped short of the complete adjustments that would be required to make the measurement of real income accurate and independent of the rate of inflation. Consistent application of this approach would also produce a net wealth tax (and a measure of presumptive income) based on current values of assets and liabilities. The 1986 reforms made little progress on this front.[5/] Part One of this Report (Chapters 2-7) describes current law and the changes that would be required to convert the current system to one based more closely on real economic income and net wealth.

An alternative would be to adopt a system of direct taxation based on consumption, rather than on income. Such a system is described in detail in Part Two (Chapters 8 and 9) of this Report. A consumption-based tax has the considerable advantage that inflation adjustment is generally unnecessary, since all quantities relevant for the calculation of tax liabilities are measured on a cash flow basis in current-year pesos. (That is, payments are realized for tax purposes when cash is received, and deductions are allowed for expenses when cash is disbursed.) Under one variant of a consumption-based tax, businesses are allowed immediate deductions for all purchases, including those of depreciable assets and inventories; interest income of businesses is exempt, and dividends paid and interest expense are not deductible, while at the individual level interest income and dividends are exempt, and interest payments are not deductible.[6/]

A consumption-based tax enjoys another powerful administrative advantage over an income-based tax, because realization is tied to cash flow. The timing of cash flow is a relatively easily identifiable event. By comparison, under an income tax it is much less obvious when a taxable event occurs, that is, when income and expense should be recognized for tax purposes. For example, if taxable income is to reflect economic income, depreciation allowances for tax purposes must reflect economic depreciation, that is, the decline in the value of a depreciable asset (as measured by its ability to generate a future flow of income). It is, however, notoriously difficult to know the appropriate pattern of depreciation allowances to use for tax purposes. A large number of other difficult «timing» issues, sometimes called «time value of money» issues, must also be addressed in designing an income tax; these are discussed in detail in chapter 5.[7/] By comparison, virtually none of these issues arises under a consumption-based tax.

Compared to the largely unindexed pre-1986 income tax of Colombia, the policy reforms needed to establish an indexed income tax, including those of Law 75 of 1986, can be seen as either a final destination or an intermediate step toward the variant of a direct consumption-based tax offered in this Report for consideration by Colombia. This can be seen by considering the tax treatment of several key items of income and expense under the income and consumption-based regimes. The disallowance of the «inflation premium» contained in interest payments is required under an inflation-adjusted income tax. But this partial disallowance of interest income and expense can also be seen as a movement toward the full disallowance required under the consumption-based tax described above.[8/] Similarly, the exemption of dividends under the 1986 reforms can be seen as either a very ad hoc and inexact way to integrate the corporate and individual income taxes (though one that is appropriate for Colombia) or as a component of a consumption-based tax.

4

The consumption-based alternative described above is clearly simpler than an inflation-adjusted income tax; for this reason it is called the Simplified Alternative Tax in this Report. There are, however, other important considerations that must be weighed in choosing between these two alternatives. First, the Simplified Alternative Tax essentially exempts all income from business and capital from tax.[9] Thus, it raises severe equity concerns, especially in Colombia, which has a long tradition of attempting to achieve progressive taxation and in which the ownership of capital is highly concentrated.[10] Second, if Colombia is to retain its net wealth tax (impuesto de patrimonio), as recommended in the Report, the simplicity advantages the Simplified Alternative Tax enjoys over the inflation-adjusted income tax would be less than if there were no net wealth tax. This is true because many (but not all) of the complexities of the income tax that would be avoided under the Simplified Alternative Tax must be addressed in calculating net wealth. (See also Chapters 6 and 9.) Third, the calculation of presumptive income, an important anti-evasion «backstop» under the present income tax regime which is based primarily on net wealth, is simply inconsistent with adoption of a consumption-based tax. Finally, there is at least some uncertainty whether the Simplified Alternative Tax would be eligible for the foreign tax credit allowed by some capital-exporting countries, especially the United States.

The Report which follows describes more fully these two basic alternatives, examines the pros and cons of each in the Colombian context, and provides detailed proposals for the implementation of each approach, including transition measures. The choice between these two tax systems is a difficult one. It is not made easier by the fact that no country has practical experience with a tax such as the Simplified Alternative Tax. Nor are the Colombian data needed for a complete evaluation readily available. The decision on whether Colombia should take the path-breaking step of adopting the Simplified Alternative Tax must therefore be based largely on conceptual reasoning, rather than empirical analysis. Partly for these reasons, this Report makes no firm recommendation as to which of the two alternatives presented for consideration the Government of Colombia should adopt.

The remainder of this chapter describes briefly the objectives a tax system should achieve and applies the criteria used in this Report to provide an assessment of the two basic alternatives. Chapter 10 provides a more detailed comparison and evaluation of the pros and cons of the two systems in terms of these objectives and criteria. This discussion should be useful to those responsible for choosing between the two systems described in the remainder of the Report.

III. Objectives

The tax system of a country ideally should satisfy certain basic objectives. These include simplicity, fairness or equity, economic neutrality (or, more generally, economic efficiency), and consistency with economic development. In addition (or as aspects of these primary objectives), the tax system must yield adequate revenues, it must not needlessly discourage investment in the country, and it must not result in unnecessary sacrifice of tax revenues to foreign governments.

A. Simplicity

Simplicity is an important objective of tax policy in all countries; after all, little is gained from enacting an elegant system that theoretically meets the goals of equity and neutrality (as well as others to be described below), but in fact does not achieve either, because it cannot be implemented effectively. Simplicity is especially important in developing countries, where the expertise required for both taxpayer compliance and tax administration is extremely scarce. In many instances it may be necessary to sacrifice conceptually desirable refinements in the definition of the tax base in order to keep the system simple, economize on these scarce talents, and achieve rough justice.[11]

5

B. Fairness

Fairness or tax equity has two dimensions, the horizontal and the vertical. Horizontal equity requires that taxpayers with the same real income (if income is agreed to be the proper measure of ability to pay, an issue to be discussed further below) who are in similar circumstances in other relevant respects should pay roughly the same amount of tax. Knowledge that others of equal incomes are paying vastly different amounts of tax can undermine taxpayer morale and compliance. Horizontal equity may also be especially important from a political point of view. Horizontal equity is violated if certain forms of income are exempt or taxed at preferential rates or if extraordinarily high rates are applied to certain forms of income, if only some of the expenses of earning income are allowed as deductions, or if deductions or credits are allowed for expenditures that do not represent costs of earning income.[12/] Perhaps as important in a developing country, horizontal equity is not achieved if some sources of income more easily escape tax illegally than others.

The absence of precise inflation adjustment can cause severe horizontal inequities, even in a system that would be judged to be fair from the perspective of horizontal equity in the absence of inflation, because income from business and capital is mismeasured.[13/] For example, in a time of rapid inflation, interest income and capital gains are overstated in an unindexed but otherwise «ideal» income tax; by comparison, interest deductions are overstated, but depreciation allowances are understated. These and other problems caused by the failure to provide inflation adjustment in the measurement of taxable income are explained further in Chapters 2 and 7. One purpose of inflation adjustment is to prevent these horizontal inequities by producing a more accurate measure of real income. Similarly, timing issues must be handled adequately if income is not to be measured inaccurately.

Vertical equity involves the pattern of differentiation of tax burdens experienced at different income levels, or the progressivity of the tax system (tax as a percentage of income at various income levels). There is no scientific basis for judging the proper degree of progressivity in the tax system of a country or in any component of a tax system, such as the income tax. This is essentially a socio-political decision. It is generally agreed, however, that aggregate tax burdens should not fall as a percentage of income as income rises (that is, that regressivity is not appropriate); some believe that proportional taxation (taxation equal to a given percentage of income at all income levels) is appropriate, but the majority of observers probably agree that some degree of progressivity (an increase in the percentage of income taken by tax as income rises) is appropriate.

The above discussion has implicitly accepted income as the most appropriate measure of ability to pay to use in appraising horizontal and vertical equity. Very much the same conclusions would hold if consumption, rather than income, were chosen as the measure of ability to pay. But the issue goes deeper than is apparent at first glance.

Annual income has traditionally been accepted as the most satisfactory measure of ability to pay. Others have, however, argued that annual consumption is a better measure of taxpaying ability; this Report rejects that view. More recently it has been argued that income received over a lifetime is a better measure than either of these. Under certain idealized circumstances a tax based on consumption that includes the value of gifts and bequests in the tax base of the donor (as well as in that of the donee) approximates in present value terms a tax based on lifetime income.[14/] While these exact conditions are unlikely to prevail in actuality, it may be that a consumption-based tax (with transfers being included in the tax base of both donor and donee) approximates a tax on lifetime income closely enough to be preferable to a tax on annual income.[15/] This has important implications for both horizontal and vertical equity.

6

Perhaps the most important implication involves the interpretation of the exemption of income from business and capital under the Simplified Alternative Tax. Judged from the viewpoint that accepts annual income as the proper measure of ability to pay, this exemption appears to constitute a fundamental violation of both horizontal and vertical equity. By comparison, under the viewpoint that accepts lifetime income as the proper measure of taxpaying ability, the Simplified Alternative Tax (with inclusion of gifts and bequests in the tax base of both the donor and donee) is consistent with both aspects of equity.[16/] (This is explained further in Chapter 8.)

Another important issue of equity involves taxpayer perceptions. If taxpayers regard annual income as the proper measure of ability to pay, the Simplified Alternative Tax is likely to be perceived to be unfair, despite sophisticated arguments indicating that it is consistent with a lifetime income view of equity.

In Colombia there is an additional element in the debate over tax equity that is commonly not present in other countries. The Colombian net wealth tax provides an opportunity to augment the progressivity produced by graduated rates under the income tax. It might be thought that the existence of a net wealth tax is logically inconsistent with the consumption-based Simplified Alternative Tax, which exempts income from business and capital. Yet this Report proposes that if the Simplified Alternative Tax is adopted, the net wealth tax should be retained in order to prevent an unacceptable reduction in the progressivity of the Colombian tax system. This simply reemphasizes that the primary advantage of the Simplified Alternative Tax is its administrative simplicity. (The fact that it exempts income from business and capital means that it has the further advantage of being neutral toward the saving-consumption choice, to be discussed below; however, this is thought to be is a secondary consideration in the Colombian context.) As noted above, this simplicity advantage of the Simplified Alternative Tax is less important in Colombia than it might be in other countries, precisely because administration of the net wealth tax requires many of the complexities of a tax on real economic income that the Simplified Alternative Tax avoids. (This issue can also be seen from a somewhat different perspective; some would find the distributional effects of the Simplified Alternative Tax acceptable only because of the existence of the net wealth tax.)

It is assumed (without endorsing the existing distribution of tax liabilities) that the propriety of the existing distribution of tax burdens across income classes is not an issue that should be examined in this Report. The Report thus adopts as a working objective the maintenance of the existing distribution of tax liabilities across income classes; for convenience of future reference, this can be called distributional neutrality.[17/] This is not to say that the distribution of tax liabilities across income classes should not or will not be significantly modified by tax reform. Within limits the distribution of taxes can be changed by changes in tax rates, including those on net wealth. By comparison, it is taken as given that efforts should be made to reduce horizontal inequities. It seems likely that many of the horizontal inequities that occur may not be fully understood, especially if they result from the interaction of taxation and inflation.

C. Economic Neutrality

A tax system that is not neutral can do substantial damage to an economy by distorting choices about what to consume, what to produce, and how to organize and finance production. This is why economic neutrality and low tax rates are commonly high on the list of objectives for tax reform. For present purposes neutrality is interpreted as calling for uniform taxation, at relatively low rates, of all real economic income passing through the marketplace (or of all income used for consumption, gifts, and bequests under a consumption-based tax), regardless of its source or use.[18/]

Of course, in any given country there are market imperfections that raise questions about the case for economic neutrality and uniform taxation. Where such imperfections exist, some offsetting non-neutrality in the tax system might, in principle, be desirable; an obvious example would be relatively heavy taxation of activities which generate negative externalities such as pollution. Indeed, the theoretical case for differentiation in taxation goes even beyond that; the theory of optimal taxation suggests that economic welfare is maximized if the heaviest taxes are imposed on goods and services for which either supply or demand is relatively insensitive to price, or price-inelastic.

Practical considerations suggest, however, that the wisest policy is generally to attempt uniform taxation of all income or of all consumption. It is difficult to identify and quantify important non-tax distortions in the economy, to know which supplies and demands are least elastic, to determine the proper trade-off between the objectives of equity and efficiency, and to implement a system involving substantial differentiation across sources and uses of income. Beyond that, once differentiation is allowed for seemingly good policy reasons, it is difficult to withstand political pressures to provide preferential treatment for less deserving activities. Under these circumstances, there is much to be said for a policy of uniform taxation, even if, in principle, resource allocation could be improved by differentiation. Finally, meeting the mandates of optimal taxation almost inevitably involves violating the dictates of horizontal equity and simplicity. Besides being questionable in their own right from an equity point of view, deviations from uniform taxation of all income or consumption can undermine the faith in the basic fairness of taxation and encourage tax evasion.[19]

D. Revenue Neutrality

Analysis of the amount of tax revenue that should be collected by the Government of Colombia would go well beyond the scope of this Report. Accordingly, it is assumed (again without recommending it) that any tax reform should be «revenue neutral», that is, that the reformed system should yield roughly the same amount of revenue as the existing one. As with distributional neutrality, this objective can easily be modified, within limits, by changing tax rates.

E. Economic Development

To some extent, encouragement of economic development can be seen as merely an aspect of economic neutrality, albeit an especially important one. Seen in that light, a tax system that is neutral will be conducive to economic development, and one that is not neutral will inhibit development.[20] Particularly important in this regard is the neutrality of the Simplified Alternative Tax toward the choice between current consumption and saving for future consumption. Whereas the traditional income tax penalizes saving and thus encourages current consumption, a tax based on consumption is neutral in this regard.[21]

Depending on how it is structured, an income tax system can be either more or less conducive to economic development. High tax rates are likely to cause substantial disincentives for saving, investment, and work effort.[22] Perhaps more important, especially for saving and investment, are other structural features of the tax system. Rapid depreciation allowances and generous investment incentives encourage investment, but failure to allow for inflation in calculating depreciation allowances discourages investment. Domestic private saving may also be either encouraged or discouraged by structural tax policy. Particularly important in this regard is the fact that inflation erodes the principal amount of debt. Failure to take this into account encourages borrowing and discourages saving. Of course, it is almost certainly more effective to use a reduction in the budget deficit as a means of increasing aggregate saving than to rely on changes in the structure of taxation to boost private saving.[23] Moreover, it should be remembered that policies that increase domestic investment do not necessarily increase domestic saving, or vice versa. An increase in investment not matched by an increase in saving must be financed by inflows of foreign capital.

Particularly important in a relatively small, open, capital-importing country such as Colombia is the tax treatment accorded income from international investment. This involves both how the nation treats income earned by foreign investors in the country and how it treats income from foreign assets owned domestically. An important objective of tax reform is the improvement of the climate for investment in Colombia by both Colombians and foreigners. But it is important not to be over zealous in the pursuit of this objective, as has often happened in Colombia as well as elsewhere. Fairness and simplicity — not to mention revenues — must not be sacrificed needlessly for the sake of increased investment. Perhaps more important, it should be recognized that it is not always true in the investment field that «more is better».[24] Chapter 4 indicates that marginal effective tax rates on much debt-financed investment in Colombia are negative. This means that because of preferential tax treatment an attractive private return can be earned on investments that have a relatively low or even negative rate of return to the nation — clearly an undesirable state of affairs. Inflation adjustments of interest income and expense such as those enacted in 1986 can help remedy this situation. Chapter 7 examines how introduction of inflation adjustment of interest income and expense can be expected to change the cost of capital in Colombia.

F. Interaction with Foreign Taxes

The interaction between the income taxes of Colombia and those of other countries must be considered carefully. Many capital exporting countries, including especially the United States, the most important source of foreign investment in Colombia, allow foreign tax credits for income taxes paid to source countries. It might be a major mistake to introduce a change in Colombian tax law such as the Simplified Alternative Tax if that would jeopardize the foreign tax credit allowed by various home countries of foreign investors in Colombia. (The basic issues under U.S. law are whether a tax that allowed no deduction for interest expense would meet the test of being levied on «net income», whether immediate expensing of capital goods would provide adequate compensation for the failure to allow interest deductions, and whether credit would be allowed for withholding tax on foreign remittances if credit for the Simplified Alternative Tax were denied.) If American investors did not have access to this credit, they would be legally liable for both Colombian and American income taxes on income earned in Colombia; such an outcome could tend to make investment in Colombia unattractive.[25] (By comparison, investment in Colombia by residents of countries exempting income from foreign sources under so-called territorial systems might be adversely affected by an increase in the **level** of business taxation in Colombia, but be unaffected by a change in tax **structure** that collected the same amount of revenue from such investors.) One important objective of this Report is to examine (in Chapter 9) the importance of this issue, its possible resolution, and ways to structure a consumption-based tax or augment it with withholding taxes in order to assure continued collection of taxes on foreigners that would be creditable in their home countries.

G. Transition

Any changes in tax policy involve windfall gains and losses. For example, either total or partial disallowance of deductions for interest expense such as those contained in Law 75 of 1986 would cause substantial windfall losses if applied to outstanding debt, and exclusion of interest income on existing obligations creates windfall gains. Similarly, changing the tax treatment of depreciable assets and inventories could also generate gains or losses. Such windfalls are generally unfair, and they may cause undesirable economic disruptions, especially if they create financial hardships and the threat of widespread bankruptcies. Moreover, large windfall losses generate political opposition to tax reform that may be overwhelming, even if matched by windfall gains realized by others. For these reasons, introduction of tax reforms is frequently delayed or phased-in; for example, the inflation adjustments for interest income and expense introduced in the 1986 law (except for that on interest income of individuals) are to be phased in over a ten-year period. Even this has not stilled complaints from taxpayers.

The difficulties of designing a satisfactory scheme for transition may be greater for some alternatives than for others. Thus, transition to a consumption-based tax may be somewhat more difficult than that to an inflation-adjusted income tax, since the fundamental changes are greater. But, as indicated earlier, to some extent the difference is one of degree, rather than a difference in kind. This Report presents and evaluates (in Chapters 7 and 9) proposals for a fair and orderly transition from the present tax system to both the inflation-adjusted income tax and the consumption-based Simplified Alternative Tax.

H. Consistency and Conflicts

Some of the objectives just described are mutually consistent, but some are not. In the latter cases it may be necessary to choose among competing objectives in designing a system for the taxation of income from business and capital.

Horizontal equity and economic neutrality are generally quite compatible, since both require uniform and consistent taxation of all income (or all consumption). In a world without inflation both are also generally consistent with simplification, since non-uniform and inconsistent tax treatment of different types of income and expense is the source of much complexity, including complexity resulting from tax planning intended to avoid taxes. (In such a world the primary source of complexity under the income tax involves timing issues that must be resolved appropriately if income is to be measured accurately.) Inflation adjustment, while necessary in an inflationary environment for a fair and neutral income tax, also introduces considerable complexity. By comparison, the Simplified Alternative Tax reduces complexity because it eliminates the need for inflation adjustment, as well as most timing issues. But the calculation of the base for the net wealth tax — which this Report recommends should be retained regardless of whether income or consumption-based taxation is chosen — entails much of the complexity that would be eliminated by adoption of the Simplified Alternative Tax.

A consumption-based tax is simpler and more conducive to saving, investment, and economic growth than is an income-based tax, but it may not be acceptable on vertical equity grounds. Whether it would be eligible for foreign tax credits in capital-exporting countries is debatable, but this may not be an important issue. These points are explained further in the next section. Chapter 10 provides a more detailed analysis, building on the discussions of Chapters 2 through 9.

IV. Preliminary Appraisal of Alternatives

During the recent debate on tax reform in the United States, the following was often used as a shorthand description of the proximate objective of income tax reform: «uniform and consistent taxation of all real economic income at low rates, without regard to the source or use of such income». Analysis of key components of this definition of a good income tax system, in the light of the basic objectives set out in the previous section, is a useful starting point for the discussion of the reform of the taxation of business and capital income in Colombia; this is provided in parts A to D of this section. An analogous shorthand description of good tax policy could be applied to a consumption-based tax, which is analyzed in part E. Some — but not all — of the implications of attempting to implement this description of an ideal tax system suggest that a consumption-based tax may be preferable.

A. Taxing All Income (or All Consumption)

If horizontal equity is to be achieved, it is necessary — by definition — to tax all income (or all consumption, if that is the chosen measure of ability to pay). Similarly, economic neutrality requires uniform taxation of all income (or all consumption). Any deviations from uniform taxation will produce either horizontal inequities, economic distortions, or both.[26/] Whether the income tax or the Simplified Alternative Tax is preferable under this criterion depends in large part on whether annual or lifetime income is thought to be the better measure of taxpaying ability, since the latter effectively exempts income from business and capital. A further consideration is whether there are sectors of the economy that are political «sacred cows» that cannot be fully taxed. If there are, it may not be possible to achieve neutrality and horizontal equity under the income tax. It may, however, be possible to attain these objectives by adopting the Simplified Alternative Tax, which would lower the taxes on the other sectors to the level of taxes paid on real economic income in the favored sectors.

B. Taxing Real Income

In a world of significant inflation it is necessary to allow for the effects of inflation in the measurement of taxable income. Otherwise, taxation will be neither fair nor neutral. Unfortunately, inflation adjustment introduces an undesirable increase in complexity into an income tax system. The situation is, however, not as bad as it might seem. With an unindexed system there are generally numerous opportunities for tax-avoidance schemes that would not exist in an inflation-proof system. As a result of attempts to take advantage of these opportunities, economic relations, tax planning, compliance with the tax law, and tax administration are all more complicated than in a system with no such opportunities. On balance, considering distortions of economic decision-making, as well as difficulties of understanding the law and complying with it, economic life under an inflation-proof system, once established, may not be much more complicated than under one that is not indexed, and it may even be simpler.

One objective of this Report is to specify a system of inflation adjustment that reconciles (to the extent possible) the attractions of conceptual accuracy with simplicity of compliance and administration. Of course, no inflation adjustment is necessary under the Simplified Alternative Tax. But if the net wealth tax is retained, many of the complexities of inflation adjustment that plague the income tax cannot be eliminated.

C. Taxing Economic Income

As indicated earlier, taxation of economic income requires that rules for the realization of income and the timing of deductions match economic reality as closely as possible. Perhaps the most visible timing issue involves depreciable assets; depreciation allowances for tax purposes should track economic depreciation as closely as possible. There are, however, many other issues of the timing of recognition of income and expense. Among the timing issues that must be addressed to achieve a conceptually accurate measure of taxable income are depletion, amortization, the proper treatment of long-term contracts, installment sales, original-issue discount bonds, pre-production expenses, and methods of accounting (e.g., cash versus accrual). Some of these issues may be sufficiently unimportant in a particular country that they could be ignored without significant loss of revenue, equity, or economic neutrality. This is true to some extent even in Colombia, where the important problem is failure to comply with the tax law, especially through under-reporting of receipts, rather than sophisticated «tax fiddles» or «games» based on defects in the laws regarding timing of recognition of income and expense. But in certain sectors, even in developing countries, such issues are important and should be addressed. In

Colombia, for example, it would be desirable to consider conceptually correct tax treatment of pre-production expenses in agricultural industries (especially the important cattle and coffee sectors), as well as measures to improve the measurement of income in the advanced non-agricultural sectors. The administrative difficulties of handling these and other timing issues and the political problem of gaining acceptance of fair and neutral taxation of agriculture are important reasons to consider substitution of a consumption-based tax for income-based taxation.

D. Low Tax Rates

Avoiding high tax rates has several clear advantages. High income tax rates distort economic decision making, they discourage saving, investment, and work effort, and they encourage tax evasion. High tax rates under a consumption-based tax do not discourage saving and investment. But, depending on the relative size of the two bases, it may be that tax rates can be slightly lower — and the disincentives for work effort and other distortions correspondingly less — under the income-based tax than under the consumption-based tax. The difference in these two potential tax bases may not be as great as sometimes assumed, however, since under the Simplified Alternative Tax interest income is, in effect, taxed at the company level through disallowance of interest deductions, rather than at the individual level, as under the income tax, where evasion is widespread.[27]

E. Pros and Cons of the Simplified Alternative Tax

As the above discussion indicates, taxation based on consumption has substantial simplification benefits, relative to income-based taxation. Being based on cash flow, the business component of a consumption-based tax raises no issues of inflation adjustment or the timing of realization. The tax treatment of interest — no deduction and no taxation — is far simpler to administer than the treatment under a conventional income tax — deduction and taxation.[28] Moreover, because it does not penalize saving, the consumption-based tax is more nearly neutral (at least with regard to the saving-consumption choice) and more conducive to saving and economic growth than is the income tax.

Against these advantages must be ranged several offsetting considerations. The primary objections to a shift to consumption-based taxation involve concerns about vertical equity. A consumption-based tax is roughly equivalent to an income tax with an exemption for income from capital, that is, to a tax on only labor income.[29] Thus, for a given set of tax rates a comprehensive consumption-based system is less progressive than an equally comprehensive income-based system. It may be possible to achieve the same distribution of tax burden across income classes under either system by utilizing a more progressive rate structure under a consumption-based system than under an income-based system. An alternative would be to use somewhat higher net wealth tax rates to augment the progressivity of the Simplified Alternative Tax. Either of these has costs in terms of disincentives, distortions, and rewards for evasion. Moreover, in light of concerns of political acceptability and administration, there is a risk that, in practice, gifts and bequests may not be effectively included in the donor's tax base and that the net wealth tax may, in fact, not be sufficiently progressive. As a result, the consumption-based system may, in practice, be less progressive than the income-based system.

Although compliance and administration would generally be easier under the Simplified Alternative Tax, this approach is not without difficulties. The possibilities of fraud involving transactions in capital assets and the problems of policing business deductions for expenditures with an important non-business component would be somewhat greater than under the income tax.

12

A further risk is that the United States or other capital-exporting countries might not allow a foreign tax credit for a consumption-based tax such as the Simplified Alternative Tax. If they did not, there is some chance that credit might also not be available for the withholding tax on foreign remittances. Chapter 9 suggests that both the Simplified Alternative Tax and the remittance tax accompanying it should be creditable. But how the creditability issue would actually be settled in capital-exporting countries cannot be predicted with confidence. It should be recognized, however, that many U.S. corporations are expected be in an excess foreign tax credit position; that is, they will have paid more taxes to foreign governments than can be taken as credits (in part because of recent changes in U. S. tax law that reduced tax rates and restricted the availability of such credits). For an American firm in such a position there is little practical difference between creditable taxes and noncreditable taxes; in practice neither can be credited. As a result whether a particular Colombian tax is creditable may have substantially less practical importance for the choice between the income tax and the Simplified Alternative Tax than is commonly assumed.

FOOTNOTES

1/ See Article 90 of Law 75 of 1986. Although for the most part the extraordinary faculties have a duration of just over one year, until December 31, 1987, those relating to the elimination of inflationary effects from the calculation of taxable income are in effect until the end of 1988.

2/ Although Article 90 of Law 75 does not explicitly mention reform of the net wealth tax, it does refer to adjustments of financial statements, basing depreciation allowances on revalued assets, and modifying provisions covering presumptive income and assets and liabilities. It would be quite illogical to make changes in these areas for purposes of calculating taxable income without having them affect the base of the net wealth tax. The most extreme case is that of presumptive income, which for the most part has the same base as the net wealth tax.

3/ This is not necessarily true in particular cases. The calculation of marginal effective tax rates in Chapter 4 indicates that distortions of decisions on equity-financed investment under pre-1986 law were actually less at an inflation rate of 25 percent than at a zero rate of inflation. This is true because at a 25 percent rate of inflation the acceleration of depreciation allowances roughly offsets the failure to index such allowances for inflation. On the other hand, the distortion of financial decisions resulting from the failure to adjust interest income and expense for inflation increases monotonically with the rate of inflation. The sensitivity of marginal effective tax rates to variations in the rate of inflation is itself problematical.

The lack of indexing may mean that it is easier to raise public revenues when inflation accelerates. Seen from the point of view of counter-cyclical stability this is an advantage. But seen simply as a relatively costless means of raising the public share of command over resources this is not necessarily an advantage; certainly it reveals a rather dim view of democratic processes. Some argue that indexation for tax purposes increases the likelihood of inflation by reducing political resistance to it. The validity of this view is unclear, since the combination of inflation and an unindexed tax system creates winners as well as losers. It may also be worthwhile to note here that inflation-adjustment of the measurement of taxable income (and of monetary values specified in tax law) need not imply the indexation of wages, rents, etc., of the type that has been practiced in several Latin American countries (e.g., Brazil) in recent years.

4/ As noted in Chapter 7, one can either follow a «piecemeal» or ad hoc approach to inflation adjustment or one can adopt an «integrated» approach of the type employed in Chile. For the present purpose of describing the problem, this distinction is not important.

5/ Indeed, they represent retrogression in at least one respect; the 60 percent limit on the fraction of the cadastral value of real estate that can be included in the calculation of net wealth is clearly inappropriate.

6/ The description in the text pertains to what is called the «individual tax prepayment» (ITP) approach in Chapters 8 and 9. The distinction between the ITP and the alternative «individual cash flow» approach, also discussed there and judged to be inferior to the ITP approach for consideration by Colombia (for reasons explained in the appendix to Chapter 9), is not important for purposes of this introductory discussion.

7/ The resolution of these issues generally affects the timing of recognition of income and expense, but not the total amount of income. But how timing issues are resolved is not unimportant, to either taxpayers or the government, because of the «time value of money». Simply stated, if the relevant discount rate is 25 percent, a one year postponement of a tax payment of 100 pesos reduces the present value of the payment to 80 pesos.

8/ This characterization is more accurate for the «piecemeal» or ad hoc approach to inflation adjustment of interest income and expense that underlies Law 75 than for the integrated approach used in Chile. This point is discussed further in Chapter 7. The use of accelerated depreciation as a substitute for explicit indexation of economic depreciation may actually be closer to consumption tax treatment than is the conceptually more appropriate system of inflation adjusted allowances for economic depreciation.

9/ For marginal investments tax revenues are equal in present value to the tax reduction that resulted from prior expensing of investments, less the tax cost of deductions for current investments. The Simplified Alternative Tax may, however, actually yield revenues related to business and capital in a given year, since the government shares in infra-marginal profits in the same proportion it shares in the original investment via expensing. (In essence, the government is a «silent partner» in all private-sector investments under the Simplified Alternative Tax.) This is explained in detail in Chapter 8.

10/ For an appraisal of Colombia's success in actually achieving progressivity, especially via the 1974 reforms, see Gillis and McLure (1978). It should be noted that judging whether distributional neutrality has been achieved is an extremely problematical undertaking, in part because of the difficulties of knowing whose income is affected by changes in the taxation of companies.

11/ For a highly persuasive plea for keeping taxes simple in order to facilitate tax administration, see Bird (1987).

12/ Of course the fact that «equal treatment of equals» does not actually occur does not necessarily mean that a tax system is viewed as horizontally inequitable by taxpayers; that depends on taxpayer perceptions of whether particular instances of differential treatment are justified. The qualification that taxpayers should be «in similar circumstances in other relevant respects» allows wide latitude for inclusion of commonly employed features of individual income taxes such as personal exemptions and deductions for medical expenses.

13/ The failure to adjust magnitudes that are fixed in monetary (peso) values, such as personal exemptions, can also compromise both vertical and horizontal equity by allowing inflation to erode these nominal amounts. Most important nominal values in the Colombian income tax have been fully indexed for inflation since 1979 (and partially indexed since 1975). This Report does not consider this type of problem, which is really not one of accurate income measurement in any event. Rather, it focuses on how the lack of inflation adjustment distorts the measurement of real income from business and capital. For more on this distinction, see Aaron (1976).

14/ Some may object that taxing a gift or bequest when made by the donor, as well as taxing consumption financed by such a transfer, constitutes double taxation. The point is that this treatment is necessary to achieve taxation of the lifetime income of both donor and donee. For further discussion, see Chapter 8.

15/ It is worth mentioning that all member nations of the Organisation for Economic Co-operation and Development (OECD) that have recently considered the lifetime income alternative have rejected it; see OECD (1987). This need not be dispositive in Colombia, where administrative issues must be given greater weight than in the developed countries that belong to the OECD.

16/ For completeness it might be noted that the Simplified Alternative Tax, without inclusion of gifts and bequests in the tax base of the donor, would be consistent with a view of equity based on annual consumption. Since this view of equity is rejected in this Report, it is not discussed further.

17/ It might be noted that strictly speaking using this norm to evaluate vertical equity is consistent with acceptance of annual income as the proper measure of ability to pay, but not with acceptance of the lifetime income view of equity. Lack of information on patterns of tax liabilities across lifetime income classes would make it infeasible to use the latter standard in appraising vertical equity.

18/ Since it is not possible to tax leisure, it is impossible to achieve total uniformity in the taxation of everything that yields satisfaction — a list that would include leisure. Nor is it generally feasible to tax imputed income such as that from owner-occupied homes. Indeed, in a developing country it is often difficult to tax all market transactions. It is thus desirable to have low tax rates in order to minimize distortions. Perhaps it should be noted that neutrality in taxation does not necessarily lead to economic efficiency One of the prescriptions of the theory of optimal taxation is to levy differentially higher taxes on goods and services that are complementary to the consumption of leisure. (Examples might include yachts and sporting equipment.) This and other lessons from the theory of optimal taxation are disregarded, for reasons stated in the text.

19/ It may be worthwhile to emphasize that the case for uniform taxation of all income or consumption does not imply that a single rate should be imposed, without regard to the economic position of the taxpayer, as indicated by his taxable income or consumption. A single rate does have important administrative advantages, but it is generally agreed that these are outweighed by the vertical equity advantages of graduated rates.

20/ Of course, this proposition is not necessarily true. Even though production efficiency is generally desirable, it is easy to imagine taxes that are not neutral that would encourage saving, investment, and work effort and lead to faster development. But see also note 24 below.

21/ It should be noted explicitly that it is the consumption-based tax that is neutral. Whereas the income tax discourages saving, the consumption tax does not encourage saving; it is merely neutral.

22/ This proposition need not be true. If, for example, investment incentives structured as deductions (rather than as credits) are sufficiently generous, high tax rates may reduce the cost of capital rather than increasing it and may therefore provide greater incentives to investment. This is especially true for debt-financed investment where full deduction is allowed for nominal interest expense. In general the negative marginal effective tax rates reported in Chapter 4 would be even larger in absolute value if the statutory tax rate were higher.

23/ The aggregate domestic saving of an economy is comprised of private saving and public saving. Public saving is the excess of receipts over expenditures, that is, the budget surplus. (Under a conceptually accurate capital budget, the relevant surplus is that of receipts over current government expenditures, with public investment spending being added to private investment.) Funds available for investment consist of total domestic saving plus capital inflow from abroad.

24/ This statement may seem almost to be heresy in a country that desperately needs economic development. But to see its validity one need only contemplate the debt crises faced by the countries that ignored it.

25/ This may overstate the situation somewhat, since countries that employ the residence principle generally do not tax the income of foreign subsidiaries until repatriated. After-tax income earned abroad is thus allowed to accumulate free of home-country taxes until repatriation.

26/ If economic behavior were totally unresponsive to economic incentives, as reflected in prices and taxes, differences in tax treatment would only cause horizontal inequities. In fact, distortions occur as behavior adjusts to differences in taxation. Even so, adjustments often do not eliminate all inequities.

27/ The problem of evasion of tax on interest income can be addressed by requiring withholding or interest payments, as under current law in Colombia. Since withholding rates generally cannot be related closely to the personal circumstances of the taxpayer, as reflected in his marginal tax rate, either under or over withholding is almost inevitable. If the withholding rate is set below the top marginal tax rate applied to individual income, evasion is likely to occur. If tax is withheld at the top marginal rate the result is likely to be very nearly the same as under the Simplified Alternative Tax.

28/ Under an alternative approach to the taxation of consumption, borrowing and interest income would be subject to tax and repayment of loans and interest expense would be deductible. This approach was rejected in favor of the treatment mentioned in the text for reasons given in the appendix to Chapter 9.

29/ However, as described in Chapter 8, and explained briefly in footnote 9, some revenue would be raised from consumption-based taxation of businesses.

2

Overview of Taxation
of Income and Wealth

Overview of Taxation of Income and Wealth

This chapter provides an overview of the proposed reforms of the present Colombian system of taxing income and wealth. These reforms, which are discussed in detail in Chapters 3 to 7, are required to bring these taxes more closely into line with a system based on taxation of real economic income and real net wealth. An alternative approach based on replacing the current income tax with a consumption-based direct tax is discussed in Chapters 8 and 9. This chapter first sets forth a framework for assessing the proposed changes, in light of the criteria discussed in Chapter 1. It then considers highlights of the proposed changes, briefly setting forth their justification and relating them to each other.

I. Towards the Taxation of Real Economic Income

An individual's real economic income may be defined as the amount that the individual either did spend or could have spent on consumption during the year without diminishing the real value of the individual's net wealth.[1] Accordingly, it is usually defined as the change in value of the individual's net wealth during the year plus the market value of rights exercised in consumption by the individual.[2] (This is often called the «Haig-Simons» definition of income, after two of its best-known proponents.) Income tax advocates generally argue that this definition of income constitutes an appropriate measure of an individual's «ability to pay» taxes during a given time period.[3]

In an inflationary economy, taxation of real economic income would call for a system of income measurement that is adjusted for inflation. Otherwise, nominal income that is not real may be taxed, for example, through the full taxation of nominal interest income or nominal capital gains, without adjustment for either the loss of purchasing power of debt that is fixed in nominal terms or the basis of assets (in the case of capital gains).[4] Similarly, deductions may be allowed for interest expense that is not real. Finally, basing depreciation allowances on the historical cost of assets, without adjustment for inflation, prevents the tax-free recovery of capital. All these problems are explained briefly in the next section, as well as being discussed in detail in Chapter 7. In Law 75 of 1986 Colombia provided inflation adjustment for interest income and expense; but it did not extend inflation adjustment to depreciable assets or inventories.

A conceptually pure definition of income would take changes in net wealth into account even if they are not realized in identifiable transactions. Because such an accrual-based system would require annual valuation of all assets, it is not, in its pure form, suitable for implementation in an actual tax system. Annual valuation of all assets simply is not administratively feasible. Nevertheless, the concept of real economic income provides a useful benchmark against which to measure the tax system of a country, and tax rules can be structured so as to approximate it as closely as possible, given the constraints of administrability.

As noted in Chapter 1, one advantage of fully taxing real economic income is that all capital income would be subject to tax on the same basis, thereby eliminating tax-induced distortions of economic decision making that discourage particular forms of investment and encourage others. (It is, however, recognized that distortion against saving is inherent in the income tax. This distortion is accepted by advocates of income taxation as a reasonable price to pay for the equity benefits of taxing income, rather than consumption; see also Chapters 8 and 10.) Elimination of such distortions should improve the allocation of scarce economic resources. Moreover, it should simplify business decision-making, since tax considerations would play a greatly reduced role. These neutrality advantages of tax reform cannot be fully realized if some forms of economic income are not taxed as accurately as others. For example, even under the reformed system proposed in this Report, the imputed income from owner-occupied housing and consumer durables, as well as unrealized capital gains, would be taxed only to the extent that they are reflected in the taxation of presumptive income.[5/] This highlights the importance of reducing (if not eliminating) tax preferences (such as that for owner-occupied housing) where administratively feasible.

More consistent taxation of more types of economic income also contributes to the administrability of a tax system. If the instances of favorable treatment are reduced, the boundaries between favored items and fully taxed items generally become easier to police, as taxpayers have less incentive and opportunity to restructure transactions so as to receive more beneficial tax treatment. For example, if net capital gains are taxed as ordinary income, the need to police the distinction between capital gains and ordinary income largely disappears.[6/]

Another important advantage of moving closer to a tax on all economic income is that the tax base will be broader than under current law, thereby enabling the tax rates to be reduced. Lower rates have the considerable advantage of creating smaller disincentives and economic distortions than high rates.

Finally, more accurate taxation of real economic income serves to promote the equity of the tax system — the achievement of both the equal treatment of persons with equal amounts of ability to pay (horizontal equity) and the desired degree of progressivity of taxation among those with different ability to pay (vertical equity). Inaccurate taxation of real economic income often results in proportionately greater undertaxation of the wealthy, who can better manage to receive their income in tax-preferred forms (or take advantage of tax loopholes).

The changes proposed in Chapters 3 through 7 would move the Colombian tax system toward the taxation of real economic income from business and capital. The most important of these changes and the reasons for them are described briefly below.

II. Who Is Taxed

Translation of the ideal of taxing real economic income into an actual tax system requires the specification of what persons are to be subject to tax and at what rates. The taxation of these persons must also be coordinated.

Ideally the income earned by companies would be taxed as if earned by their owners, whether the company is a proprietorship, simple partnership, limited partnership, or corporation; it would not be subject to a separate tax at the company level. Otherwise, neither horizontal nor vertical equity will be achieved, and both investments and financial decisions will be distorted.

In light of the 1986 legislation, which integrated the taxation of all companies (corporations and limited partnerships) and their owners, no major changes are proposed for this aspect of the taxation of company income. The system of integration adopted in 1986 is simple and effective: the top tax rate paid by individuals is imposed at the company level, and shareholders (partners) are not taxed on dividends (income of partnerships). As a result, only one level of tax is generally imposed on company income.[7/]

Although the rate of tax may be higher than the rate that would apply to the income of some individual shareholders, this does not appear to be a major reason for concern, given the concentration of wealth in Colombia.

It is proposed to tax trusts and estates in a similar manner, in other words to impose the top individual tax rate on the income of the trust or estate, and to exempt the beneficiaries of the trust or estate from tax. As a technical matter, this treatment would not involve a major change from current law, which generally taxes trusts and estates as separate entities and does not attempt to flow trust or estate income through to the beneficiaries.

III. Inflation Adjustment

The need for inflation adjustment arises in at least four situations: interest income and expense, capital gains, depreciation, and cost of goods sold from inventories. Several of these also have important implications for the calculation of net wealth. The first three of these are explained briefly at this point; all are discussed in greater detail in Chapter 7.

Suppose that an asset is bought for $100 and is sold for $200. If there has been no inflation during the interim, it is appropriate that the full $100 gain be taxed. If, however, the price level has doubled, there is no «real» gain, and tax should not be levied, despite the nominal gain of $100. If there has been only 40 percent inflation, the real gain is $60 (the difference between the $200 sale price and the inflation-adjusted basis of $140); if, however, the price level has risen by 150 percent, there is actually a real loss of $50 ($250 — $200). The purpose of inflation adjustment of the basis of capital assets is to prevent the taxation of nominal gains that are not real.

Suppose that in the absence of inflation a given financial asset would yield a 10 percent rate of return. If the inflation rate is 20 percent, it can be expected that the nominal yield will be 32 percent (since 1.20 x 1.10 = 1.32).[8] If a tax of 30 percent is imposed on the full 32 percent nominal return, the net of tax nominal return will be reduced to 22.4 percent (the difference between 32 and 9.6, the result of multiplying 32 times 0.30); the net return after adjustment for inflation is only 2.4 percent (22.4 — 20), well below the 7 percent after-tax return that would be earned in the world without inflation. Stated differently, the effective tax rate on the real return of 10 percent would be 76 percent, rather than the statutory rate of 30 percent. The purpose of inflation adjustment of interest income and expense such as that introduced by Law 75 of 1986 is to assure that only the 10 percent «real» component of interest is subject to tax or allowed as a deduction.

Suppose finally that an asset with an economic life of four years is bought for $1,000. In the absence of inflation, straight-line depreciation (assumed for now to be economic depreciation, an issue to be addressed below) would be $250 per year. In order to prevent these allowances from being eroded by inflation it would be necessary to provide inflation adjustment for the basis from which allowances are calculated. If, for example, inflation were 20 percent, the amounts allowed for depreciation after the first year should be $300, $360, and $432 (120 percent of depreciation in the previous year). The calculation of net wealth should also reflect these adjustments.[9]

A fairly comprehensive system of inflation adjustment is proposed in Chapter 7. To meet the dual objective of taxing only real income and basing the taxation of net wealth on current values, it is proposed that explicit inflation adjustment replace the acceleration of depreciation allowances and that inflation adjustment be required as a part of inventory accounting, whether the taxpayer uses first-in, first-out (FIFO) or last-in, first-out (LIFO). Additional changes are proposed for the treatment of interest income and expense and for assets giving rise to capital gains.

The primary issue raised by inflation adjustment is its complexity. While the complexity costs of inflation adjustment are appreciable, it is the thesis of this Report that they are justified by the gains in equity and economic neutrality described above. Moreover, the complexity of inflation adjustment for companies may be justified in part by a non-fiscal need — both public and private — to keep more realistic accounts for financial reporting purposes. In the case of individuals, the problem of complexity is mitigated by the relatively high filing requirements, under which the bulk of taxpayers need not file returns.

IV. Timing issues

Most of the proposals relating to reform of the income tax, aside from those dealing with inflation adjustment, have to do with the timing of taxation. Concern about the timing of tax payments is appropriate because a given peso amount of tax revenue has a greater present value to both the government and the taxpayer, the sooner it is received. To the extent that income is not taxed at the right time, either over-taxation or under-taxation can occur, with consequent inequities and economic distortions. Particular attention must be paid to the design of timing rules in a country such as Colombia that has a significant inflation rate. The value of deferring income from one taxable year to the next is based on the nominal after-tax interest rate, which will be higher, the higher the rate of inflation.[10]

There would be no timing problems if changes in wealth could be taxed as they occurred, by means of annual valuation of assets. As a substitute for such annual valuation, various arbitrary events necessarily furnish the basis for taxation. These events are the various observable transactions by taxpayers, involving such things as the transfer of cash, the transfer of ownership of property, or the issuance of a bill. They are arbitrary in the sense that they are merely those events that are observable, and hence do not bear a simple, uniform relation to the accrual of economic income. An important objective of income tax design is to fashion rules based on these events specifying when income is to be recognized in such a manner as best to reflect economic income. Two examples help to clarify this. In the case of depreciation, the cost of an asset and the date when the asset is placed in service are known, but the actual pattern of decline in value of the asset is not known. Based on these known facts, rules must be devised for depreciation deductions that reflect the actual decline in value of depreciable property as closely as possible. This Report proposes to allow inflation-adjusted depreciation based on tables for particular classes of assets which are designed to reflect roughly the average economic depreciation for assets in the particular class.

Another example is the purchase of a debt obligation for cash, which is redeemable at a specified date for a greater amount of cash, with no payment of interest in the interim. Here, the observable phenomena are the amount of the purchase price, the terms of the instrument (which are observable at the time of purchase) and the amount paid at redemption (which is observable at the time of redemption and may be specified by contract). Between these two events economic income accrues (i.e., the taxpayer's wealth increases), but exactly when the increase in wealth occurs may not be observable. In this Report it is proposed to tax the holder of the debt instrument on the expected increase in value of the instrument, determined by applying the yield to maturity to the outstanding balance of the obligation (including accrued interest).

The ultimate goal is the same in all these cases of «timing» issues, namely the specification of rules that will approximate the taxation of economic income. However, the particular rules needed to achieve this goal differ according to the observable events of the particular type of transaction. Accordingly, the various proposals relating to timing may appear to be quite different in detail and structure.

Some of the proposals relating to timing are more important than others in terms of their consequences for tax revenues, equity, and economic neutrality. For example, the proposal relating to depreciation is of first importance, given the pervasiveness of the use of depreciable property. The proposal relating to production costs (including capitalization of interest) is probably the second most important, being applicable wherever taxpayers manufacture or produce property (including agriculture). Proposals relating to installment sales, original issue discount, publicly traded debt instruments, and long-term contracts are of some significance, although certainly less so than they would be in a country with a more industrialized economy or more sophisticated financial markets. Finally, the proposals related to deductions for amortization and for accrued but unpaid expenses and advance payments are essentially included for completeness; at present they would likely apply only very rarely, but it is desirable to include them in the tax law to cover those cases and preclude future taxpayer gimmickry.

One may ask whether it is necessary to provide complicated rules for transactions that are known to occur only rarely. The additional complexity of such rules should be judged not on the basis of the number of sections or words they add to the tax law, but on the basis of the compliance costs they actually cause for taxpayers — including those to whom they do not apply — and for the tax administration. The existence of relatively complicated rules for particular transactions is not likely to result in much complexity in this sense, as long as it can be ascertained relatively simply whether such rules apply to a given transaction. Under this criterion, the existence of rules that in themselves are complicated may actually simplify administration of, and compliance with the tax system, because such rules can serve to remove the tax advantage for particular types of complicated transactions that would be engaged in only rarely, if at all, in the absence of a tax benefit.

V. Occasional Gains

A comprehensive tax on real economic income would involve no special treatment of gains on capital assets. By comparison, current Colombian law provides special treatment for «occasional gains», which for the most part may be defined generally as gains from the sale of property other than inventory. The special treatment usually, although not always, leads to a lower rate of tax on a taxpayer's occasional gains than on ordinary income. It is proposed generally to eliminate the distinction between occasional gains and ordinary income; the primary exception is that occasional losses could be deducted only against occasional gains. Because the basis of assets would generally be indexed for inflation, full taxation of occasional gains would never result in taxing an amount of such gains in excess of real economic income.

Full taxation of gains only at the time of realization increases the potential problem of «lock-in» that results from the tax-induced disincentive to sell appreciated assets. However, the extent of «lock in» will be reduced by two factors, in addition to the mitigating effects of inflation adjustment of basis. First, because it is proposed that all gains be constructively realized for tax purposes at the time of a gift or bequest, there will be no incentive to hold property until death (beyond the advantage normally inherent in deferral of tax). Second, the benefits of deferral will be reduced because some unrealized gains will be taxed under the system of presumptive income. The extent to which such taxation takes place depends on whether the value of such assets for tax purposes is close to fair market value and on whether the taxpayer's ordinarily determined unearned income exceeds presumptive income. While income reflecting unrealized gains will not always be fully taxed because of problems of valuation, the number of cases where a substantial portion of a taxpayer's economic income consists of unrealized and untaxed gains should be significantly reduced.

VI. Presumptive Income and Net Wealth

The most significant method for calculating presumptive income in Colombia is based on the taxpayer's net wealth. Taxable income is presumed to be no less than a specified percentage of net wealth. This rule can catch taxpayers who understate business receipts or income from capital or who overstate deductions, but it generally is ineffective with respect to understated receipts from labor income and with respect to taxpayers who understate the value of their assets. Understatement of asset values is inevitably a problem for the net wealth tax and property taxes, as well as for the calculation of presumptive income. In addition to capturing understated receipts and overstated deductions, this wealth-based rule can serve (subject to inevitable and stubborn problems of valuing assets accurately) to tax unrealized appreciation in value of assets held by the taxpayer; to correct any deficiencies in application of the timing rules for taxing capital income not satisfactorily addressed by tax reform; and to tax imputed income on housing and other consumer durables. The proposed changes are designed to improve the functioning of presumptive income in achieving these objectives.

The basic principle behind the concept of presumptive income is that it is reasonable to assume that all wealth earns a minimum return, at least on average.[11/] Accordingly, if this return is applied to a base consisting of the net fair market value of a taxpayer's assets, one would expect that, on average, the taxpayer's economic income should equal or exceed this amount. For various reasons, the rules for tax accounting may not accurately capture economic income. (For example, accrued gains are not taxed until realized.) Moreover, the taxpayer may not fully report the entire amount of economic income for tax purposes. The purpose of the system of presumptive income is to make up for this shortfall, thereby placing a floor on the taxpayer's income in the amount of the minimum expected presumed return. In order for presumptive income to work properly, the base for calculating it must correspond as closely as possible to the net fair market value of the taxpayer's wealth.

A number of changes are proposed that would broaden the base for calculating presumptive income so as to make it as close as administratively possible to the fair market value of the taxpayer's net wealth. The most important of these changes relate to the determination of net wealth for purposes of the net wealth tax, and apply derivatively to the determination of presumptive income. All of these changes are geared toward conforming the base of the net wealth tax as closely as possible to the net fair market value of the taxpayer's assets — the most equitable base for a tax on net wealth.

Accordingly, it is proposed to repeal the exclusion for a portion of the assessed value of real property; to restrict deductible debts to the fair market value of such debts and allow a deduction only if the debt has been incurred to purchase an asset included in net wealth; and to value items such as depreciable property and inventories on a more realistic basis, in conformity with their proposed treatment for income tax purposes. Another important change would be to repeal the exclusions from the calculation of presumptive income for property used in cattle raising and for property in a nonproductive period .

In addition to modifying the base for calculating presumptive income, it is proposed to remedy a deficiency in the method for comparing presumptive income with ordinarily determined income. Under current law, wealth-based presumptive income is compared with the taxpayer's total income, including earned income. The proposal would segregate earned income from unearned income for purposes of this comparison, so that presumptive income would be compared only with unearned income. If presumptive income exceeded reported unearned income, then the taxpayer's taxable income would be the sum of earned income and presumptive income. The purpose for this change is to conform the actual application of presumptive income in Colombia with the above theory, which justifies presumptive income on the basis of a presumed rate of return on the taxpayer's net wealth. The theory for presumptive income relates only to capital income, not to earned income. That is, a taxpayer with a certain amount of earned income should be presumed to earn a minimum rate of return on his or her net wealth, over and above the earned income. Accordingly, the minimum amount of taxable income of such a taxpayer should be the amount of earned income plus the minimum presumed return on net wealth. Because of this change and because of the introduction of a comprehensive system of inflation adjustment, it is proposed that the rate of return used to calculate presumptive income be reduced from its current level.

In addition to wealth-based presumptive income, current law provides a presumption that income is no less than two percent of the taxpayer's receipts for the year. Unlike wealth-based presumptive income, receipts-based presumptive income is not grounded on economically meaningful assumptions. Certain sectors are known to have higher than average rates of return on sales, and others lower. (By comparison, it can be assumed that over the long run roughly the same rate of return will be earned on capital invested in all sectors, except to the extent that there are differences in risks.) To attempt to reflect these expected differences in profit margins in the calculation of presumptive income would be administratively impossible. It is thus proposed that the receipts-based measure of presumptive income be eliminated. However, temporary retention of the current receipts-based presumption may be justified as an interim measure pending correction of deficiencies in the base for calculating wealth-based presumptive income. Accordingly, it is proposed that the receipts-based measure of presumptive income be retained for a period of time, and then repealed.

When the analysis leading to this Report was first undertaken, there was no conscious intent to propose reforms of the net wealth tax. The proposed changes in the net wealth tax originated from a) the need for consistency of treatment of assets such as depreciable property and inventories under the inflation-adjusted income tax and the net wealth tax, and b) the importance of wealth-based presumptive income for the income tax. It would make no sense to base depreciation allowances on inflation-adjusted depreciable basis without reflecting the inflation adjustments in the calculation of net wealth. In order for the presumptive income rules to work properly, various changes in the net wealth base had to be made. These changes will also have an important effect on the functioning of the net wealth tax. The only change proposed for the net wealth tax that will not have an effect on presumptive income is the question of rates for taxation of the wealth of various members of the family. Again, these changes flowed from an examination of the analogous issue under the income tax, although no changes in this respect are being proposed for the income tax at this time.

VII. Compliance

Although further rationalization of timing rules and the definition of net wealth would help improve the Colombian tax system, a far more serious problem is noncompliance with the tax law. Some suggestions are offered with respect to the rules governing reconstruction of income on audit, but detailed consideration of this issue is essentially beyond the scope of this Report, since it would require an examination of current administrative and judicial practices in much greater detail than has been possible.[12/] The problem of noncompliance is addressed in this Report chiefly by proposals concerning presumptive income, which are discussed above. However, no system of presumptive income can deal with the chief manifestation of noncompliance, namely, the understatement of both assets and receipts, which are currently the bases for calculating presumptive income, as well as critical for the ordinary calculation of taxable income.

To a large extent, noncompliance is inevitable in a developing country such as Colombia, in which much of the economy remains «informal» (in the sense of being based largely on cash transactions with little or no accounting records) and the skills required for compliance and administration are scarce. But the problem of noncompliance is not only a problem with the technical details of the tax law or with tax administration as such; rather it reflects taxpayer attitudes in Colombia.

Even among taxpayers who have some respect for the government, there is apparently a widespread belief that substantial understatement of taxable income is permissible because such understatements are said to be so common. Under this view, a taxpayer who honestly reports all his or her income would be exposing himself or herself to an unfairly large liability, far out of line with that borne by others with the same amount of economic income. This taxpayer attitude can only be effectively dealt with by excising preferential treatment for particular types of income from the law and by proceeding through deliberate administrative actions to change attitudes about acceptable noncompliance. Needed reforms go beyond those recommended here and include, **inter alia**, those proposed by the Government in 1986, such as elimination of preferential treatment for legislators, civil servants, and members of the armed forces, a particularly visible and flagrant source of perceptions that the system is not fair. Strong administrative action of the type needed to show that tax evaders will be punished firmly, though fairly, is difficult, given scarce resources.[13/] But it may be possible if there is the requisite political consensus and adequate administrative support (such as a well-trained and adequately compensated staff and effective computerization of returns).

VIII. Conclusion

The proposed reforms would strengthen and coordinate the existing interlocking scheme involving ordinarily determined income, presumptive income, and the net wealth tax. Rules for ordinarily determined income would be changed so as to make the ordinary income tax conform as closely as administratively feasible to a tax on real economic income. The net wealth tax base would be changed so as to conform the tax as closely as feasible to a tax on the fair market value of net wealth. Presumptive income would then serve as the link between the two. Based on net wealth, it would provide a backstop to the ordinary rules for determining taxable income. Moreover, to the extent that presumptive income exceeds ordinarily determined taxable income, an adjustment would be made to net wealth. Thus, the rules for determining income, presumptive income, and net wealth would be coordinated and mutually supporting.

Additional mutual support would be provided through the effect on auditing and compliance. Because of the linkage of these three elements of the tax system, it would be more difficult to evade or avoid tax than if the system for taxing capital income were based on the income tax or the net wealth tax alone. This would be especially true if financial accounting were to be conformed to rules for the measurement of income and wealth for tax purposes.

FOOTNOTES

1/ For further discussions of this definition of income, see, for example, Goode (1977) or Bradford (1986), Chapter 2. Bradford repeats (p. 16) the following classical definition of income: «an individual's income is the sum of what he consumes during the year and the increase in his net wealth».

2/ See Simons, (1938), p. 50.

3/ For a discussion of the relative merits of annual income and lifetime income as the proper indicator of taxpaying ability, see Chapter 8. The present chapter discusses only issues that arise in the taxation of income; of course, many of the same issues arise in the taxation of consumption.

4/ «Nominal» amounts are those that are fixed in monetary (peso) terms, without adjustment for inflation. By comparison, «real» amounts reflect such adjustments; see also section III of the present chapter and, for a detailed discussion, Chapter 7

5/ Indeed, it is possible that a move from a system where all elements of economic income are undertaxed to a system where some are taxed fully but others continue to escape taxation would actually increase the aggregate level of distortion.

6/ This distinction would still be relevant for determining the deductibility of losses. Problems caused by deferral and the question of how to treat gains on assets transferred by gift or at death also arise, whether gains are taxed as ordinary income or preferentially.

7/ There would be an additional level of tax in those instances in which a) taxable income that is not fully distributed is reflected in share values and b) the gain is realized in a taxable transaction by the taxpayer.

8/ This is explained further in Chapter 7 and Appendix 7A. The posited relationship between the real rate of interest, the inflation rate, and the nominal interest rate (the unmodified version of Fisher's Law) is assumed for simplicity of exposition here and in footnote 10, even though, as explained in Chapter 7, it may not prevail in a world with taxes.

9/ This example and the implications for the taxation of net wealth are developed further in footnote [19] to Chapter 7.

10/ For example, suppose that the real interest rate is 4 percent and there is no inflation. A taxpayer in a 25-percent tax bracket who is able to defer $400 of income from one year to the next defers $100 of tax. If the $100 is invested for one year, until the tax payment comes due, the yield (after tax) is $3. The benefit of deferring income of $400 accordingly is a $3 payment received in the subsequent year, which has a present value of about $2.90. Now suppose that there is inflation of 20 percent, so that the nominal interest rate is 24.8 percent (1.20 x 1.04 — 1.00). If $100 of tax is deferred until the subsequent year, the tax saving can be invested and yields $24.80, less tax of $1 (assuming that the taxation of interest income is adjusted for inflation), or a net benefit of $23.80; this has a present value of about $19.20, which is over six times as great as the present value of the tax deferral under conditions of zero inflation. (In the absence of inflation adjustment of interest income for tax purposes, the results would be less dramatic — after tax income of only $18.60 — but the basic point remains valid.) What this example suggests is that even a one-year deferral, which may not be important in a country with a low inflation rate, may be cause for concern in a country such as Colombia, with a moderately high inflation rate.

11/ This minimum return is the return that is expected on assets with the lowest amount of risk. If a particular asset is expected to earn more or less than the normal rate of return, the price of the asset can generally be expected to adjust so as to conform the expected return to the minimal rate of return, plus an appropriate risk premium.

12/ It may, however, be appropriate to repeat the call in McLure (1982) for a national commission to examine tax administration, rather than continuing to study tax policy.

13/ To avoid becoming overwhelmed, a selective audit focus, whereby a particular area or areas can be covered thoroughly, may be appropriate. Such intensive auditing could also be coupled with appropriate public announcements.

3

Summary Description of Colombian Taxation of Business and Capital Income

Summary Description of Colombian Taxation of Business and Capital Income

The following description of current law aims at conveying a broad understanding of the current rules relating to the taxation of income from business and capital. It covers only those points of Colombian tax law that relate to the appraisal and options for change discussed elsewhere in this report. Details and qualifications that apply only in special cases are therefore omitted.

A statement that a certain treatment «generally» applies indicates that there are exceptions to this general rule. A statement that a certain treatment «apparently» applies indicates that there may be uncertainty as to what current law provides or how it is interpreted by taxpayers or by the Government.

References to amounts expressed in pesos are at 1986 levels, unless otherwise indicated. Under Colombian tax law, these amounts are adjusted annually for inflation.

The discussion begins with the income tax, starting with the rules for identifying the taxpayer and for taxing entities. It proceeds to the treatment of interest income and expense, timing issues, specially treated items and institutions (including withholding), and international issues. The chapter concludes with a discussion of presumptive income and of taxes that are complementary to the income tax (the tax on occasional gains and the net wealth tax).

I. Income Tax

The Colombian income tax is imposed on the net income of individuals, corporations, partnerships, estates, and trusts. The taxable income of companies is subject to a flat rate of 30 percent, although in the case of sociedades anónimas a transitional rate of 32 percent applies for 1987 and 31 percent for 1988.[1] Foreign corporations and other foreign entities are taxed at the same rate as domestic corporations.

Graduated rates apply to individuals, estates, and resident aliens. The rate schedule, which starts at $1,000,000 at a marginal rate of a fraction of one percent, reaches a marginal rate of 30 percent for taxable income in excess of $5,100,000.[2]

An individual is not required (or allowed) to file a return if:

(1) at least 80 percent of the individual's gross receipts for the taxable year consist of wages, salaries, or pensions;

(2) to the extent that withholding is required by law with respect to payments (except for the monetary correction portion of UPACs) received by the taxpayer, such withholding has in fact taken place; (**Note** from the editor: this requirement was repealed by Decree 2503 of 1987.)

(3) the taxpayer's gross wealth (i.e. wealth unreduced by debts) is $6,000,000 or less;

(4) the taxpayer is not liable for sales tax (Impuesto sobre las Ventas);

31

(5) the taxpayer's gross receipts do not exceed $4,000,000; and

(6) the taxpayer retains copies of withholding certificates.[3/]

For purposes of determining whether the taxpayer meets the 80-percent test set forth in (1) above and the gross receipts test of (5) above, gross receipts do not include proceeds from the sale of fixed assets or winnings from lotteries, etc. The tax liability of those not required to file a return is defined as the amount that has been withheld with respect to receipts of the taxpayer.[4/] Note that a taxpayer may qualify as a non-filer even though no tax has been withheld on certain receipts. In particular, fees or interest received from an individual are not subject to withholding (although if such amounts exceed 25 percent of the individual's employment income, the individual will not qualify as a non-filer). Proceeds from the sale of fixed assets are subject to a withholding rate of one percent. Lottery winnings are subject to a 20-percent withholding rate.

A. Persons to whom income is taxed

1. Corporations and Shareholders

Under the 1986 reform act, the tax treatment of corporations and domestic shareholders has been integrated by exempting dividends at the shareholder level, provided that the dividends correspond to taxable income of the corporation.[5/] The mechanism for exempting dividends is as follows:[6/] Dividends received by natural persons or by Colombian corporations or partnerships are not taxable to the extent of 7/3 of the corporation tax paid for the taxable year to which the dividends relate. Corporation tax for this purpose is the amount of income tax (before the CERT credit[7/]), plus the tax on occasional gains. For example, if the corporation has fully taxable income of 100 and pays tax of 30, then a tax-free dividend of 70 can be distributed. If, however, taxable corporate income is only 80, so that corporate tax is 24, only 56 can be distributed without subjecting the shareholders to tax on dividends. For purposes of the 7/3 rule, income tax paid is added to an account that can be carried over indefinitely. The amount of tax-free dividends is further limited to the after-tax financial accounting income of the corporation.

Premiums received by a corporation on the issuance of its stock are generally not taxable, but they are taxable to the corporation if the premium is subsequently distributed to the shareholders.[8/]

2. Partnerships

Starting with the 1986 Act, partnerships are taxed in the same manner as corporations.[9/] Thus, the partnership is subject to a 30-percent rate of tax, and the partners pay no tax on undistributed partnership profits. Partnership distributions are taxed in the same manner as distributions by corporations. Accordingly, distributions of partnership profits are nontaxable to the partners under the 7/3 rule described above. In determining the amount of taxable income at the partnership level, salaries, other payments for services, interest, rents, and similar payments made to partners, family members, or other persons are deductible as business expenses, subject to any applicable limitations on the deduction of business expenses. As a general rule, only a reasonable amount of business expenses is deductible.

3. Trusts and Estates

Trusts («bienes destinados a fines especiales» or «asignaciones y donaciones modales») and estates («sucesiones de causantes») are subject to tax on their income under the same rate schedule applicable to individuals.[10/] The income is taxed to the trust or estate whether or not distributed. Amounts received by beneficiaries are not taxed to them as income, but are subject to tax as occasional gains.

A commercial trust contract (contrato de fiducia mercantil) differs from a trust in that the contract must specify the beneficiary of the income and corpus without any discretion in the trustee. In the case of such a contract, the income is taxed to the person who receives it and the corpus is included in the net wealth tax base of the person who is to receive it. However, if the corpus is to revert to the grantor, the grantor is taxed on the income if the grantor is also a beneficiary of the income or if any beneficiary is related to the grantor (within the first degree of consanguinity or affinity).[11]

4. Husband, wife, and children

A husband and wife are taxed separately. There is no distinction in the rate schedules according to marital status.

Under the Civil Code, the parents enjoy an usufruct in the unearned income of their minor children.[12] Because of this usufruct, the unearned income of minor children is taxed to the parents. However, if the parents renounce the usufruct, such income is taxed to the children.[13]

B. Tax accounting

1. Taxable year

The taxable year of all persons and entities is the calendar year, with a few exceptions for short taxable years caused by liquidations and the like.[14] This rule precludes the opportunity to defer income by making payments in one taxable year to a person who will not include such payment in income until a later time because such person's taxable year ends later.

2. Methods of accounting

Both the cash and accrual methods are recognized, but corporations and financial institutions are required to be on the accrual method for regulatory reasons. An item of income accrues when the right to demand payment comes into being.[15] Deductions accrue when the obligation to pay comes into being, even though the payment may not currently be due.[16] Thus, for example, if a corporation incurs a liability to make payments on account of personal injury over a period of years, say $1,000,000 per year for 5 years, the entire $5,000,000 may be deducted in the year that the liability becomes fixed.

3. Intangibles

The cost of intangible items (patents, copyrights, goodwill and the like) is presumed to be 70 percent of the selling price.[17]

4. Deduction of Losses

Earned income may not be reduced by losses from any other source.[18] Agricultural losses incurred by individuals and estates may be deducted only against agricultural income; a five year carryover is allowed for this purpose.[19] The special deduction for investments in certain agricultural enterprises (see Section F(3)(b) below) is not treated as an agricultural loss for this purpose; that is, these deductions can be used to offset non-agricultural income, even if they produce an accounting loss from agricultural activity. Interest expense relating to a loss activity is considered as part of the loss from such activity.

Losses of partnerships and corporations may be carried over for five years.[20]

5. Accounting for costs incurred in foreign currency

When an expense is paid immediately in foreign currency, the amount of the expense for tax purposes is simply the peso equivalent of the amount of foreign currency paid. When debts are incurred in foreign currency, the treatment is more complicated. If inventory items are purchased by incurring debt payable in foreign currency, the amount of such debt outstanding at the end of the year is revalued in pesos according to the exchange rate prevailing at that time. The amount of exchange loss (less the portion of such loss treated as a nondeductible financial cost under the inflation adjustment rules discussed in section C(4) below) is treated as an additional cost of the inventory. This additional cost is deductible as cost of goods sold to the extent that the inventory items are deemed to have been sold during the year, and is included as a cost of closing inventory to the extent that the items are still on hand.[21/]

At the time that the loan is paid, any additional exchange loss (net of inflation adjustment) is similarly treated either as a cost of goods sold or as a cost of inventory on hand, depending on whether the inventory items to which the debt relates have been sold or are still on hand.

Foreign currency debt incurred to acquire property other than inventory, including depreciable assets, is treated in a similar manner. Thus, the exchange loss (net of inflation adjustment) is treated as an additional cost of the property. The exchange loss is taken into account at the end of each year. Moreover, any additional exchange loss is taken into account at the time that payments on the debt are made.

C. Interest Income and Expense

Interest income (after inflation adjustment) is generally taxed when received or accrued (depending on the taxpayer's method of accounting), and interest expense (after inflation adjustment) is deductible if the loan proceeds are used for business or investment. Financial costs that take the form of exchange losses are taken into account as they accrue annually, regardless of the taxpayer's method of accounting.

1. Original issue discount

Most obligations with original issue discount («OID») (títulos con descuento) in Colombia are short term. Important exceptions are coffee bonds (títulos cafeteros), issued by the Fondo Nacional de Café (the National Coffee Fund), and certificates (cédulas) of the Banco Central Hipotecario (The Central Mortgage Bank). Both of these longer-term obligations are issued by tax-exempt persons.

A cash method holder of a debt instrument is not taxed until he or she disposes of the instrument or the instrument is redeemed. An accrual method holder (such as a bank) accrues the interest income annually, apparently on a straight-line basis. An accrual method issuer may deduct the interest as it accrues.

Income tax is withheld with respect to OID obligations at the time of issuance. The amount subject to withholding is the difference between the redemption price and the issue price.[22/] The rate of withholding varies with the term of the instrument. The holder of the instrument may claim a credit for the withholding at the time that he or she is taxed on the income.

It would be difficult to apply the above-described rules to OID obligations that involve contingent terms. This does not appear to present a serious problem in Colombia, because OID obligations must be approved by the Superintendencia Bancaria, and generally are not allowed to be issued with contingent terms. The Central Bank does issue OID obligations payable in foreign currency, but these are generally issued to foreign persons, who would not be subject to Colombian tax on the interest income from such obligations.

2. Below-market loans to shareholders or partners

Loans made by sociedades (corporations or partnerships) to their shareholders or partners are presumed to earn a rate of interest at least equal to the rate of inflation.[23/]

3. Limitations on deduction

a. The deduction for interest paid to persons other than entities regulated by the Superintendencia Bancaria is limited to a rate specified by that agency.[24/]

b. A special rule allows a deduction for interest incurred to acquire a residence.[25/] Loans made to refinance old mortgages (up to the face amount of the mortgage) qualify as loans to acquire a residence. The deduction for home mortgage interest is limited to $1,000,000 per year.[26/] In the case of a husband and wife, if both are liable on a home mortgage, the total home mortgage interest deduction of the husband and the wife is limited to $1,000,000. However, if the husband and wife each pay interest with respect to separately owned houses, they may each deduct $1,000,000.[27/]

c. Interest incurred to finance the construction of property apparently must be capitalized as part of the cost of the property being constructed. As a result of such capitalization a deduction is allowed with respect to such interest only when the property is sold or (in the case of property constructed by the taxpayer for use in its business) after it is placed in service.[28/] (In the former case, the interest cost will reduce the gain upon sale of the property; in the case of self-constructed property, such cost will lead to increased deductions for depreciation.) Apparently, interest is treated as construction-period interest only if there is a direct relation between the borrowing and the construction. In other instances interest expense is deductible according to general rules. It is not clear whether the requirement to capitalize construction-period interest applies only to real property. The requirement to capitalize construction-period interest does not apply to those agricultural investments whose costs are currently deductible.

4. Inflation adjustment

Starting in 1986, part of the inflationary component of interest expense is not deductible. (Methods of calculating the inflationary component are described below.) This disallowance is phased in at 10 percent per year over a ten-year period beginning in 1986 (i.e., it is 20 percent for 1987). For taxpayers other than individuals, the inflationary component of interest received from any source is similarly excluded under a ten-year phase-in, 10 percent in 1986, 20 percent in 1987, and so on.

The disallowance and exclusion described in the preceding paragraph do not apply to loans to construction contractors made by savings and loan companies, or to financial intermediaries that are regulated by the Superintendencia Bancaria.[29/] Such disallowance and exclusion apply in the case of leasing (financial rental) contracts only to the extent provided in regulations, which have not yet been issued.

Starting in 1986, natural persons may exclude the entire inflationary component of net interest received with respect to: deposits with financial intermediaries regulated by the Superintendencia Bancaria, public debt, and debt of corporations issued under authorization of the Comisión Nacional de Valores. For purposes of this interest exclusion, net interest is computed by deducting all interest expense (including home mortgage interest) from the qualifying interest described in the preceding sentence.[30/]

The method of calculating the inflationary component of interest is as follows: In the case of qualifying net interest income received by individuals, the nontaxable portion is determined by dividing the inflation rate, as measured by the rate of monetary correction at the end of the year («correción monetaria», hereafter «CM»), by the annual rate of interest received by the taxpayer.[31/] If the current rate of interest equals the rate paid on the debt, this is equivalent to subtracting the rate of inflation from the nominal rate of interest, and taxing only the difference, and results in a fairly exact measurement of real interest income for tax purposes.

In the case of interest expense paid or accrued by persons other than natural persons, as well as net interest expense of individuals, the inflationary component is determined by dividing the CM as of the end of the previous year by the average rate of interest paid on bank loans at that time.[32/] (This average rate of interest paid is an economy-wide rate published by the Superintendencia Bancaria.) Under this method, the same fraction is applied to the interest paid by all taxpayers.

In the case of the financial cost of debt denominated in foreign currency, the nondeductible portion is determined by dividing the CM for the previous year by the average cost of external debt for the previous year for the currency in question, as determined by the Banco de la República.[33/] This average cost includes both the amount of interest paid and the change in the exchange rate.

In the case of interest income received by persons other than individuals, the excludable portion is determined by dividing the CM as of the end of the previous year by the average rate of interest paid by banks at that time.[34/] Since this rate will be lower than the rate of interest charged by banks, the excludable portion of interest received will be higher than the nondeductible portion of interest paid.

5. Exclusions

The following items of interest income are excluded from taxable income:

a. interest received by taxpayers other than natural persons on the debt of the Colombian central government and certain other Colombian governmental agencies issued before September 30, 1974.

b. interest on certificates issued by the Banco Central Hipotecario (Central Mortgage Bank) before September 30, 1974.[35/]

c. interest on local government bonds received by the original holder of such bonds.[36/]

D. Timing of Items of Income and Deduction Other Than Interest

1. Capital Cost Recovery

a. Depreciation

New tangible personal property (defined as personal property that has not previously been used in Colombia) may be depreciated at an annual rate of 40 percent of the original cost for the first year, 40 percent for the second year, and the balance for the third year. The first year's depreciation is prorated according to the number of months the property is in service. If the taxpayer does not specify the month of acquisition, 20 percent is allowed.[37/] Personal property previously used in Colombia may be depreciated over a 10-year period for equipment (5 years for vehicles), usually on a straight-line basis. Personal property is defined as property other than buildings.

The above-described allowances may be increased by 25 percent for each additional shift on which the property is used, until 100 percent of the basis is recovered.[38/] Thus, in principle, if new personal property is used on three shifts during the year in which it is placed in service, as much as 60 percent of the cost can be deducted in that year, and the rest in the subsequent year.

The rule for additional shifts does not apply to buildings.[39/] Buildings may be depreciated under the straight-line method over a 20-year period, or under a 10-percent declining-balance method.[40/]

Various investments in improving agricultural property (construction and repair of worker housing, land clearing, irrigation and drainage systems, construction of aqueducts, fences, and other investments in the improvement of farms) are deductible under the straight-line method over a five-year period.[41/] These include some investments that would be considered buildings or land. Presumably this special method is only used when buildings or land are involved, since otherwise the 40-40-20 method would be more favorable.

b. Amortization

Expenses subject to amortization include: organization expenses, development expenses, and mine or mineral exploration and development expenses. These expenses are to be recovered over a period of no less than five years, in the absence of justification for a shorter period of recovery.[42/] In principle, research and development («R&D») and advertising expenses may be required to be amortized under this rule, but it is likely that such expenses are deducted currently.

c. Depletion

Oil and gas exploration expenses are deductible at a rate of 10 percent per year, until production begins.[43/] At that point, percentage depletion is allowed in the amount of 10 percent of the value of the oil or gas that is produced. Percentage depletion ceases when the taxpayer's basis has been recovered.[44/] However, an additional special percentage depletion allowance is not limited by basis. This allowance is 15 or 18 percent of the value of oil or gas produced, depending on the location of the well.[45/] As an alternative to percentage depletion, the taxpayer may elect cost depletion.

In the case of minerals other than oil and gas, percentage depletion at a rate of 10 percent is allowed, not limited to basis.[46/]

2. Production Costs and Long Term Contracts

a. Long-term contracts

In the case of any contract involving deductible expenses, the income from which is received in more than one taxable year, the taxpayer may use the generally available methods of accounting (cash or accrual) or use one of the two special methods of accounting for long-term contracts specified by law, which for convenience may be called the percentage-of-completion and completed-contract methods.[47/] Under the percentage-of-completion method, the taxpayer must estimate total contract costs and the contract price as of the beginning of the contract. Each year, the amount to be included in gross income is the portion of the total estimated contract price that corresponds to the portion of the total estimated contract costs represented by the actual contract costs for the year. These actual costs may be deducted in the year incurred.

Under the completed-contract method, contract costs must be capitalized and deducted only when the income to which those costs correspond is realized. In cases where there are advance payments, it is not always clear whether the income is deemed to be realized at the time the payment is made or at the time the contract is completed. The tax treatment may depend on the terms of the contract (i.e. on whether the contract specifies a right to receive advance payments). The completed-contract method is apparently the most commonly used method for reporting income from long-term contracts. It is not restricted to construction contracts, but may also apply to service contracts.

b. Production costs

Costs incurred by a taxpayer in constructing property to be used in the taxpayer's business (e.g. as depreciable assets or inventories) must be capitalized, rather than deducted currently, but the law does not define which costs are considered construction costs. Presumably, only the most direct costs of construction or manufacture are in fact capitalized.

The following expenses relating to self-constructed agricultural assets are currently deductible: expenses of planting timber, coconuts, oil-producing palm trees, rubber, olives, cacao, fruit trees; and expenses of irrigation and drainage systems, wells, and silos.[48] Expenses of planting and cultivation of coffee must be capitalized and may be amortized over the expected productive life of the tree (on a straight-line basis), starting at the time the coffee tree becomes productive.

3. Inventories

Both last-in, first-out (LIFO) and first-in, first-out (FIFO) are available. Taxpayers must use LIFO for financial accounting purposes in order to use it for tax purposes. Farmers are apparently required to inventory costs of production.[49] As with self-constructed assets, there is no specification as to which production, manufacturing, acquisition, or carrying costs must be treated as costs of inventory.

4. Installment Sales

The installment method of accounting is available only for taxpayers using the accrual method of accounting who regularly sell property on installments.

5. Bad Debt Deductions

Business bad debts are deductible when the debt becomes wholly or partially worthless.[50] In addition, taxpayers may deduct additions to bad debt reserves under certain circumstances.

Accrual method taxpayers may take a deduction for bad debt reserves in the amount of 33 percent of debts that are one year past due, provided that a showing is made that the debts are hard to collect or that their collection is doubtful.[51] Entities that are regulated by the Superintendencia Bancaria may deduct 100 percent of debts whose collection is doubtful.[52]

As an alternative to taking this deduction for doubtful debts, the taxpayer may take a deduction for all debts, regardless of difficulty of collection, in the following amounts: 5 percent of debts 3 months past due, 10 percent for debts six months past due, and 15 percent for debts one year past due.

E. Pensions

A deduction is allowed for amounts set aside or paid for current or future pensions.[53] Under current regulations, the amount of this deduction is overstated, since a low interest rate is used to discount the deduction.[54] Pensions received by individuals are nontaxable, up to a monthly amount of $170,000. Virtually the entire amount of pensions paid is exempt from tax under this rule. Pension funds are exempt from tax, except on income derived from commercial activities.

F. Miscellaneous

1. Withholding

a. Dividends

The taxable portion of dividends paid to Colombian persons is apparently not subject to withholding under current rules. (Dividends may be taxable under the 7/3 rule or the financial accounting rule, or may be taxable because paid out of pre-1986 profits.) The withholding rate on dividends paid to foreign persons is 30 percent.

b. Interest

Withholding on UPAC (Unidades de Poder Adquisitivo Constante) accounts that constitute term deposits takes place at a rate of 7 percent of the CM plus interest paid. In the case of UPAC accounts that are currently available to the depositor, withholding is at a rate of 36 percent, but only on the interest portion (i.e. not on the CM). Accounts that pay daily interest (not including the CM) below $14 (at 1987 levels) are not subject to withholding.

Withholding on non-UPAC accounts that are under the control of the Superbancaria is at a 7 percent rate, but there is no withholding if the amount of daily interest paid (including the inflationary component of such interest) is below $53 (at 1987 levels).

Interest on certificates of deposit is withheld at a 7 percent rate.

Withholding on OID obligations (títulos con descuento) (which takes place at the time of issuance) is between 2 and 6 percent, depending on the term of the obligation (6% if less than 1 yr., 5% for 1-2 yrs., 4.2% for 2-3 yrs., 3.5-% for 3-4 yrs., 2.9% for 4-5 yrs., 2.4% for 5-6 yrs., and 2% for 6-7 yrs.)

c. Sales of Property

The notary public is to withhold one percent of the sales price in the case of any disposition of property (other than property sold in the ordinary course of the business). A seller of property who is required to file an income tax return may claim a credit for the amount withheld on the seller's return. There is a provision for lower rates of withholding in the case of dispositions of residences, depending on the holding period for the residence.

d. Corporate payments

Persons other than individuals making any payment or accrual which constitutes gross income for the recipient must withhold tax at the rate of one percent (one tenth of one percent for fuel), with the exception of payments under $23,000.[55/] This withholding requirement applies, for example, to purchases of property for more than $23,000.

Persons other than individuals making payments for services to persons who are not employees of the payor (including, for example, honorariums, commissions, payments to independent contractors, and rents) must withhold tax at rates varying from one to seven percent, depending on the type of payment.

e. Wages

Any person (including an individual) paying amounts to an employee[56/] must withhold tax if the payment exceeds a specified amount per month. The amount withheld depends on the amount of wages paid.

2. Credits

The following credits relate to capital income:

A credit is allowed for foreign taxes paid. This credit is limited to the amount of Colombian tax attributable to the taxpayer's foreign-source income.[57/]

A twenty-percent credit is available for reforestation expenses.[58/]

Subsidiaries of foreign corporations that are members of a consortium that is taxable in Colombia may claim a credit for 30 percent of dividends paid to them by the consortium.

Colombian enterprises engaged in air or sea transport may claim a credit for the portion of the tax attributable to their foreign-source transportation income.

A credit is allowed for donations to the «RESURGIR» Reconstruction Fund.[59/]

A 20-percent credit is allowed for donations to political parties.[60/]

3. Special rules for agriculture

a. Cattle raising

In computing gain on the sale of cattle, the cost is the actual cost, if acquired during the same taxable year, or the value on the preceding December 31.[61/] The gain on the sale of calves that are sold in the same year that they are born is not taxed.[62/]

b. Expensing for certain investments

Individuals and other taxpayers who invest in agricultural enterprises that are engaged in activities for which a current deduction for planting costs is allowed (i.e. coconuts, olives, fruit trees etc.) may currently deduct these investments. The deduction is limited to 10 percent of the taxpayer's taxable income, but it may be taken against nonagricultural income (including earned income).[63]

c. Gain on Timber

The taxpayer may elect to treat 80 percent of the value of timber sold as the cost of such timber, provided that the taxpayer did not claim any deductions for planting or cultivation expenses, including deductions for interest incurred for the purpose of raising timber.[64]

4. *Special enterprises*

a. Publishers and authors

Publishing companies are exempt from tax, provided that their sole activity is the publication of books, magazines or pamphlets that are of cultural or scientific character printed in Colombia.[65] The first $50 million of an individual's total investments in such companies are exempt from the net wealth tax.[66] An author's royalties are exempt from tax, up to $500,000 per year per book.[67]

b. Merchant Fleet

The Flota Gran Colombiana S.A. is exempt from income tax.[68]

c. Zonas Francas

The free trade zones (zonas francas) are considered as public agencies and accordingly are exempt from tax.[69] Corporations or partnerships conducting activities in these zones are exempt from income and complementary taxes with respect to receipts obtained from their industrial activities conducted in the zone.[70]

5. *Regional and touristic incentives*

New enterprises in the area affected by volcanic activity in the Nevado del Ruiz are exempt from tax for 1986 and 1987; this exemption phases out by 1992.[71] Similar treatment in the Departamento del Cauca phases out in 1987.[72]

There are special rules for foreign investment in specified areas, allowing tax-free repatriation of profits for a ten-year period.[73]

A special deduction for investment in Frontier Districts is allowed; it phases out in 1987 and 1988.[74]

Certificates of touristic development are available for investments in hotels or hostels; these certificates may be used for the payment of taxes.[75] Certain companies engaged in hotels, apartment buildings, etc. in San Andres and Providencia are exempt from tax until 1991.[76]

G. Foreign Investment Issues

1. *Taxation of Income*

Business-level taxation of most Colombian source income was unified at a rate of 30 percent under the 1986 Tax Reform Law.[77] With respect to the majority of foreign investment in Colombia the reduction in the statutory corporate rate from 40 percent to 30 percent was largely offset by the establishment of a single withholding tax on dividends paid to foreign entities.[78] For payments to foreign entities in non-tax haven countries this withholding tax rate rose from 20 percent to 30 percent; the tax on payments to entities in tax haven countries fell from 40 percent to 30 percent.

For the typical case of a parent company located in the United States and receiving dividends from a Colombian subsidiary, the two rate changes cited above resulted in the Colombian tax burden on $100 of pre-tax income falling from $52 to $51. In the pre-1986 situation $100 of before-tax income would have been subject to income tax of $40. If the entire amount of after-tax earnings, $60, were remitted to the U.S. parent as a dividend, an additional withholding tax of $12 would have been paid, giving a total Colombian tax burden of $52. Under current law, the income tax paid falls to $30, but the remittance of a $70 dividend to the parent causes a withholding tax of $21 to be paid. In that case, the total Colombian tax burden is $51.[79]

The 30-percent income tax rate at the business level also applies to other Colombian-source income paid to foreigners, such as interest, royalties, commissions, rents, and compensation for technical services, technical assistance or other payments to foreigners to obtain industrial know how.[80] Exceptions to this treatment of technical services performed outside of Colombia are possible when the services provided are not available within Colombia. The process of obtaining an exemption is time consuming and far from automatic; potential domestic entrants recognize the benefits from this protection and are likely to oppose the granting of exemptions.

Interest payments to foreigners are not regarded as generating Colombian-source income, and thereby are exempt from income tax, if they satisfy any of the following conditions:[81] that the interest payments are based on short-term credits to finance imports or exports; that Colombian financial institutions have obtained these foreign credits; or that businesses obtaining these credits carry on activities of special interest to Colombian development. At present, all debt service payments on officially registered foreign currency debt are exempt from income tax, as they meet the statutory requirements regarding eligible loans and project finance[82] or approved direct lines of commercial credit for international trade.[83]

The income tax imposed on royalty payments for movies and films is applied to a base equal to 60 percent of the gross payment made. No separate accounting of costs is made, as they are presumed to be covered by the 40-percent exclusion from the taxable base. In the case of rents and royalties for computer software, the applicable tax base is 80 percent of the payment made.

Capital gains are taxable to all foreign entities at a rate of 30 percent.[84] As explained previously, an inflation adjustment is applied in calculating the portion of foreign exchange losses or gains that will be recognized in calculating a firm's income tax liability.

2. Complementary Tax on Remittances

A Colombian company that pays dividends to foreign stockholders first must pay corporate income tax and then must withhold tax on the dividend payments. The withholding tax is imposed in lieu of the foreign recipient paying income tax in Colombia. In the case of branch profits or other situations where income is earned in Colombia by foreigners, the two-step process followed in the case of dividends is not applicable in exactly the same form. Two different taxes are levied on Colombian income received abroad, but in this case they are referred to as the income tax and the complementary remittance tax. Profits of foreign branches operating in Colombia are assumed to be remitted, unless the branch demonstrates that they have been retained in Colombia.[85] For the portion of branch income that is remitted abroad, a remittance tax of 30 percent is imposed in addition to the corporate-level income tax. This treatment is economically comparable to the withholding tax imposed on dividends paid to foreigners.[86/]

Payments to foreigners of interest, rents, royalties, commissions, and compensation for technical services and technical assistance are subject to a remittance tax of 12 percent of the value of the payment net of income tax.[87/] Given an income tax rate of 30 percent, the remittance tax on the gross flow is 8.4 percent. The exemption of interest payments and the special income tax bases for movies and computer software explained above apply here, too. As a result of tax changes adopted in 1974, remittances of profits by foreign oil companies essentially became exempt from the complementary remittance tax. Steps to end that special treatment were taken in 1983 and 1985, but those measures were declared unconstitutional by the Supreme Court. With the 1986 reform, oil company remittances have been subjected to the complementary remittance tax.[88/]

The taxable base in Colombia of turnkey projects and contracts is considered to be the value of the contract, without deductions. Such projects include engineering and construction contracts that result in a complete facility, such as a power plant or subway system, being delivered to the Colombian purchaser. Foreign contractors are subject to income and remittance taxes equal to one percent of the value of the contract.[89/] Other payments to foreigners not specifically mentioned in the law are also subject this one-percent rate.[90/]

3. Transactions with Related Parties

Payments of royalties, commissions, fees, compensation for technical assistance, and any other payment for the acquisition of intangibles are not deductible expenses when made to a foreign parent or other related company.[91/] Because such payments are taxed more favorably than dividends, foreign owners would otherwise have an incentive to receive any returns in such alternative forms. Also, the establishment of an appropriate arms-length price for royalties and related payments is generally difficult, because the underlying technology or expertise may not be available on an open market.

A related rationale lies behind the stipulation that debts of branches of Colombian corporations held by foreign parents or related parties are considered as net worth of the branch or Colombian corporation.[92/] This provision may affect the calculation of presumptive income; and in the case of mixed enterprises with some Colombian ownership, it also may alter the net wealth tax paid by Colombian owners; it also relates to the firm's calculation of taxable income. The Colombian tax administration has ruled that any interest payments or exchange losses attributable to debt owed to related foreign parties are not deductible business expenses.[93/] Consequently, foreign controlled firms have a strong incentive to arrange any debt financing through a financial institution and not to have it provided directly by the parent.

4. Other tax issues

Deductions for expenses incurred outside the country to generate Colombian-source income cannot exceed 10 percent of that income when such payments are not subject to Colombian withholding tax.[94/] To the extent that payments to foreigners for technical assistance or technical services are able to qualify for an exemption from Colombian income tax, the ability to treat them as deductible business expenses will be subject to this limitation.

To encourage exports other than coffee, petroleum and cattle hides, the income from such non-traditional exports may qualify for a tax credit under the CERT program.[95/] The rate at which this credit is available is set in accord with particular country and product market conditions.

With respect to income from Colombian investment abroad, the tax policy implications are minor because officially registered foreign investment is quite limited. Government approval is granted only in fairly restrictive circumstances, such as expenditures necessary to promote the distribution and sale of Colombian products abroad. Income from such investment is subject to Colombian taxation, with a credit granted for foreign taxes paid. The small amount of approved investment abroad has resulted in little need for extensive legal regulations governing such matters as the allocation of costs between domestic and foreign operations, the determination of the foreign tax credit limitations, or the tax treatment of foreign corporations controlled by Colombian persons. Foreign investment financed without recourse to foreign exchange provided by the Banco de la República is essentially outside the control of Colombian tax authorities.

Income earned in Colombia but received by a natural person residing abroad will be subject to income tax depending upon the proportion of the taxable year spent by the person in Colombia. Persons residing more than six months in Colombia face the graduated rate schedule applicable to Colombian residents, while those residing less than six months in Colombia face the maximum 30 percent rate.

II. Complementary Taxes and Presumptive Income

In addition to the tax on net income, Colombia employs a set of «complementary taxes», which are also reported on the income tax return. The complementary taxes consist of a tax on occasional gains (ganancias occasionales), a net wealth tax (impuesto de patrimonio), and withholding taxes on remissions abroad (impuesto de remesas). In addition, the separate computation of presumptive income (renta presuntiva) in effect operates as a complementary tax, although technically it is part of the income tax.

A. Tax on Occasional Gains

1. In general

The concept of occasional gain generally refers to gains on the sale of property held for at least two years and, for individuals, the amount of gifts or inheritances received. The net occasional gain of companies and foreign entities is subject to the same flat rate as ordinary income. The rate schedule for the net occasional gain of individuals, trusts, and estates is the same graduated schedule as for ordinary income of individuals, but the schedules are applied separately, so that a taxpayer who is subject to the top marginal rate for ordinary income might not be in the top rate bracket for occasional gains, and vice versa. In fact, the first $1,000,000 of net occasional gain is exempt from tax, even though the taxpayer's ordinary income might place that taxpayer in a high tax bracket.

The separate treatment of occasional gains also means that any net occasional loss may not be deducted against ordinary income. It is not clear whether net occasional losses may be carried forward to be offset against future occasional gains. (There is no provision specifically permitting this).

2. Types of Gains Included

The net occasional gain or loss is determined by subtracting occasional losses from occasional gains.[96] Occasional gains include gains from the sale of «fixed assets» (activos fijos), which are defined as property other than that which is sold in the ordinary course of the taxpayer's business, and which has been held for at least two years.[97] Gains on property held less than two years are treated as ordinary income. All depreciation is fully recaptured as ordinary income.[98]

Gain on the sale of a personal residence is treated as a taxable occasional gain; however, a transition rule excludes a portion of such gain depending on the year in which the property was acquired, up to a 100 percent exclusion for property acquired before 1978.[99/]

Gains on distributions in liquidation of companies that have been in existence for two years or more, and that do not constitute dividends or profits, are treated as occasional gains.[100/] In the case of corporations, the amount of the distribution not in excess of accumulated profits is treated as a dividend. In the case of partnerships, only the excess over the capital account is treated as an occasional gain. Liquidations in kind are not taxed at the corporate level but, in determining the shareholder's tax on a liquidating distribution, the fair market value of the property distributed is taken into account.

Gifts and bequests are treated as occasional gains. In general, the first $1,000,000 of bequests received by the taxpayer during the taxable year are exempt. (This exemption is in addition to the $1,000,000 exemption under the rate schedule).[101/] In the case of inter vivos gifts, 20 percent of the amount of the gift is exempt, up to a total exemption of $1,000,000 of gifts received by any one donee in any one year.[102/]

The value of the donated or inherited property taken into account for purpose of the tax on occasional gains is the value shown on the most recent return of the donor or testator for purposes of the net wealth tax. This will generally be the cost of acquisition, plus any adjustments, such as for inflation. It will sometimes, although not generally, correspond to the fair market value of the property. The donor or testator is not taxed on any difference between his or her adjusted basis and the fair market value of the gift or bequest. Thus, the donor's gain escapes tax completely. There is no estate or gift tax, so the inclusion in occasional gains of the donee is the only tax liability resulting from a gift or bequest.

Prizes from lotteries, raffles, etc. are treated as occasional gains, but are subject to a special 20 percent flat rate.[103/] Awards for scientific, literary, journalistic, artistic, or athletic accomplishment are exempt.[104/]

Gain from the sale of real property to government agencies is not taxable, provided that the sale is pursuant to negotiations that precede the commencement of a legal condemnation proceeding.[105/] There is also an exemption for sales to the «RESURGIR» Reconstruction Fund (Fondo de Reconstrucción «RESURGIR»).[106/]

In the case of property whose loss is reimbursed by insurance proceeds, the portion of the insurance proceeds in excess of basis is taxed as ordinary income to the extent of depreciation deductions previously taken, and any remaining gain is not taxable if the proceeds are reinvested in similar property.[107/] In the case where such an exemption applies, the basis of the old property is apparently not carried over.

3. Inflation Adjustment

In general, in determining the gain on the sale of fixed assets, the historic cost of the asset may be adjusted annually by up to 100 percent of the increase in the consumer price index.[108/] Making such an annual adjustment is not generally advantageous, since it leads to an increase in the net wealth tax and in presumptive income. If this adjustment is not made annually, the opportunity for making the adjustment is lost.

The preceding sentence does not apply in the case of real estate, partnership interests and stock held by individuals. Adjustments with respect to these assets may be made in the year of sale, even though adjustments had not previously been made. For this purpose, the cost of real estate is adjusted according to an index of real property prices, rather than the consumer price index.[109/] In addition, if real property is reassessed, the newly assessed value becomes the basis for all tax purposes, including the determination of gain upon sale[110/] (subject to provisions in the 1986 legislation reducing the percentage of the value of real estate taken into account for tax purposes to 60 percent, and 75 percent for certain rural property). In the case of stock or interests in partnerships (aportes), individuals may adjust the cost by the increase in the consumer price index between January 1 of the year of acquisition and January 1 of the year of sale.[111/]

B. Presumptive Income

1. In general

The rules for presumptive income apply to all taxpayers.[112/] The concept of presumptive income provides that taxable income is the greater of the taxpayer's presumptive income or the taxpayer's income as computed according to the ordinary rules.[113/] In general, the taxpayer's taxable income will be the greatest of the following amounts (the rules for determining which are explained below):

(a) taxable income computed without any presumptions;

(b) eight percent of net wealth;

(c) two percent of gross receipts; or

(d) the increase in net wealth for the year.

2. Wealth-based Rule

a. In general

Presumptive income as determined under the wealth-based rule equals a specified percentage (currently eight percent) of the taxpayer's net worth on the last day of the immediately preceding taxable year.[114/] For this purpose, net worth is determined in the same manner as for the net wealth tax (see below).[115/]

This amount is compared with the taxpayer's entire income, including earned income. Thus, taxpayers whose earned income exceeds eight percent of their net worth will not be subject to the presumptive income tax, even though they may fail to report substantial amounts of capital income.

b. Exclusions

The following items are excluded from the base that is used in computing presumptive income under the wealth-based rule:[116/]

i. Interests in a corporation or partnership

Stocks and partnership interests (aportes) in Colombian partnerships or corporations are excluded from the calculation of presumptive income.

ii. Cattle Raising

Sixty percent of the net value of property represented in cattle, breeding, and dairy cows is excluded.[117/]

iii. Assets in nonproductive period

The net value of assets invested in enterprises in a non-productive period is excluded. In the case of manufacturing, mining, construction, or the hotel industry, the nonproductive period includes the period for exploration, construction, and start-up.[118] In the case of agriculture, the non-productive period is specified according to the type of crop, and generally seems to be the average period before a marketable crop is produced.[119]

iv. Miscellaneous

The government may provide for lower rates for calculating presumptive income in the case of a specific economic sector or geographic area that is suffering from depressed incomes, but this power has not been exercised.

The net value of urban property that is subject to rent control or development restrictions is excluded. At the discretion of the Minister of Finance, property invested in economic activities that are affected by price controls or by regulations governing the preservation of historic sites or natural resources may be excluded, as may property that is subject to casualty or condemnation or economic abnormality.[120] This discretion has generally been exercised so as to deny this exclusion.

Real property affected by the volcanic activity of the Nevado del Ruiz is also excluded.[121]

3. Receipts-based rule

Presumptive income determined under the receipts-based rule equals two percent of the taxpayer's gross receipts for the taxable year.

4. Presumption Relating to Increase in Wealth

The taxpayer's income is presumed to be no less than the increase in the taxpayer's net worth, less any items of exempt income, such as exempt dividends.[122] For purposes of this rule, net worth is measured in the same manner as for the net wealth tax (impuesto de patrimonio). Unlike the wealth-based and receipts-based rules, this presumption is rebuttable (i.e. the taxpayer is given the opportunity to prove that the increase in net worth arose from nontaxable sources).[123]

C. Net Wealth Tax

1. In general

The net wealth tax (impuesto de patrimonio) is an important source of revenue, contributing about 30 percent of the revenue from the income and complementary taxes paid by individual taxpayers. The tax is imposed on individuals and estates under a graduated rate schedule, which begins at a marginal rate of a tiny fraction of one percent for net wealth in excess of $700,000, reaching a marginal rate of 1 percent at a net wealth of about $4,200,000, 1.2 percent at a net wealth of about $5,300,000, 1.55 percent at net wealth above $8,000,000 and 1.8 percent for net wealth above $15,300,000.[124]

The wealth tax base includes all property held by the taxpayer as of the last day of the taxable year, less debts of the taxpayer.[125] Personal-use property is included in the wealth tax base, although undoubtedly in practice much of it is not reported. In the case of Colombian residents, foreign assets are included in net wealth.

Nonresidents are taxed on property in Colombia. (Property in Colombia includes intangible property with a situs in Colombia, such as debt of Colombian residents and interests in Colombian corporations or partnerships.)[126/] Because the net wealth tax applies only to individuals, nonresidents may apparently avoid the tax by holding property in corporate or partnership form.

Debt of Colombian government agencies issued before September 30, 1974 is exempt from the net wealth tax.[127/]

Property taxes paid are creditable against the net wealth tax, but this credit may not exceed the portion of the net wealth tax that corresponds to the portion of the taxpayer's net wealth represented by such real property.

2. Valuation of assets

With the exceptions listed below, property is valued at its adjusted basis.[128/] In the case of stock that is listed on the Stock Exchange and is not stock in a family corporation, the value is the average value for the last month of the taxable year.[129/] For other stock, the value is obtained by dividing the adjusted basis of all corporate property by the number of shares outstanding.[130/] This rule applies in the case of multiple classes of stock, regardless of the relative value of the different classes of stock.

Interests in partnerships are valued at the greater of the partner's acquisition price or the partner's pro rata share of the adjusted basis of the partnership's assets (determined on the basis of the relative initial capital contributions of the partners).[131/]

Debt instruments are valued at their average Stock Exchange price for the last month of the taxable year or, if they are not listed on the Exchange, at their face value.[132/] Debt instruments with original issue discount that are not traded on the Stock Exchange are valued by adding the accrued discount (computed on a straight-line basis) to the acquisition price.[133/]

Personal use automobiles are valued at original cost.[134/]

Real property is valued at the greater of its cost or assessed value. Under the 1986 Reform Act, the assessed value for tax purposes is 60 percent of the actual assessment.[135/] The actual assessment is often far below fair market value, although some property is being revalued on a basis that is closer to fair market value.

Inflation adjustment is optional with the taxpayer.[136/] Such adjustment will reduce the amount of taxable gain upon disposition of the asset, but will result in a higher base for the net wealth tax, for calculating presumptive income, and, when the property is passed on, the tax on occasional gains of the donee or legatee of the property. As noted above, in the case of real property, stock, and partnership interests, an inflation adjustment may be made for purposes of the occasional gains tax in the year of sale, even though annual inflation adjustments had not previously been made.

3. Debts

In order to be able to deduct debts owed to foreign individuals from the patrimonio, the debtor must withhold the net wealth tax relating to the debt and includè the withholding receipt with his return.

The amount of tax withheld is determined by applying the rate schedule for the net wealth tax. The above rule requiring withholding on foreign debts does not apply to short term debts relating to imports or exports and debts approved and registered for purposes of exchange control.[137]

Debt in foreign currency is revalued each year according to the official exchange rate.[138]

FOOTNOTES

1/   Ley 75/86, art. 1.

2/   Ley 75/86, art. 4. This rate schedule, along with all other amounts expressed in pesos, is adjusted annually for inflation. Ley 75/86, art. 16.

3/   Ley 75/86, art. 63.

4/   Ley 75/86, art. 5.

5/   Ley 75/86, art. 21.

6/   Ley 75/86, art. 22.

7/   The CERT (Certificado de Reembolso Tributario) credit is described in Section G4 below.

8/   Ley 9/83, art. 13.

9/   Ley 75/86, art. 1, 21.

10/   Ley 75/86, art. 4.

11/   D.L. 2053/74, art. 36.

12/   D.L. 2820/74, art. 26.

13/   D.R. 187/75, art. 24.

14/   D.R. 187/75, art. 1.

15/   D.L. 2053/74, art. 16.

16/   D.L. 2053/74, art. 16.

17/   D.L. 2053/74, art. 25.

18/   Ley 9/83, art. 21.

19/   D.L. 2348/74, art. 8, inc. 3.

20/   Ley 9/83, art. 23.

21/   D.L. 2053/74, art. 30.

22/   D.L. 3803/82, art. 62.

23/   L. 9/83, art. 20. For this purpose, the inflation rate is measured by the tasa de correción monetaria del sistema de valor constante. This presumption applies both for purposes of the ordinary income tax rules and the presumptive income rules. D.R. 353/84, art. 16, par. 2. Thus, for example, if the taxpayer's ordinarily determined income is 200, presumed income with respect to shareholder loans is 75, and other presumptive income is 250, the taxable income will be 325 (rather than 275).

24/   D.L. 2053/74, art. 47.

25/   D.L. 2053/74, art. 47.

26/   Ley 75/86, art. 40.

27/   D. No. 3750 de 29 de diciembre, 1986, art. 8.

28/   D.R. 331/76, art. 4; Dirección de Impuestos Nacionales, División Legal, Oficio No. 06277, Abril 28, 1976.

29/   Ley 75/86, art. 28, 30.

30/   Ley 75/86, art. 27.

31/   Ley 75/86, art. 27.

32/   Ley 75/86, art. 29.

33/   Id.

34/   Ley 75/86, art. 28.

35/   Ley 75/86, art. 93.

36/   D.R. 1850/85.

37/   D.R. 1649/76, art. 1.

38/   D.R. 1649/76, art. 3.

39/   D.R. 1773/86, art. 3.

40/   D.R. 1649/76, art. 5; D.L. 2053/74, art. 59.

41/   Ley 26/59, art. 43; D. 1562/73, art. 109.

42/   D.L. 2053/74, art. 58.

43/   D.L. 2310/74, art. 10

44/   D.L. 2310/74, art.8.

45/   Ley 75/86, art. 45.

46/   D.L. 2310/74, art. 12.

47/   47 D.L. 2053/74, art. 69.

48/   Ley 9/83, art. 33.

49/   D.L. 2053/74, art. 22.

50/   D.L. 2053/74, art. 61.

51/   D.L. 2053/74, art. 60; D.L. 187/75, art. 74.

52/   D.R. 3883/85, art. 1.

53/   D.L. 2053/74, art. 51, 52.

54/   D.R. 331/76, art. 8.

55/   D.R. 1512/85, art. 5. This requirement does not apply to the sale of property described in the preceding paragraph.

56/   In technical terms, the withholding requirement applies to any payments made by reason of a «labor relationship, or legal and reglamentary relationship»; Ley 55/85, art. 38.

57/   D.L. 2053/74, art. 100.

58/   D.L. 2053/74, art. 98.

59/   D. 3406/85, art. 13; D. 3830/85, art. 1, 2.

60/   Ley 58/86, art. 13.

61/   Ley 20/79, art. 15.

62/   Ley 20/79, art. 16.

63/   Ley 75/86, art. 106.

64/   D.L. 2348/74, art. 12.

65/   Ley 34/73, art. 9; L. 32/83, art.1.

66/   Ley 32/83, art.2.

67/   Ley 32/83, art. 3.

68/   Ley 10/46.

69/   Ley 47/81, art. 1,2,7,37.

70/   Ley 109/85, art. 15.

71/   D.L. 3830/95, art. 11.

72/   Ley 11/83, art. 10.

73/   D.E. 3448/83, art. 17.

74/   D.E. 3448/83, art. 29.

75/   Ley 60/68, art. 7; D.R. 136/76, art. 1,2,3.

76/   Ley 2/81, art. 2.

77/   Ley 75/86, art. 1. Note that for sociedades anónimas this rate is 32 percent in 1987 and 31 percent in 1988 before falling to 30 percent in 1989.

78/   Art. 48 of Ley 9/83 and Art. 3 of Ley 75/86.

79/   With respect to the future remission of retained earnings that already were subject to the prior 40-percent corporate tax rate, the earlier 20-percent withholding rate will be applied.

80/ Art. 47 of Ley 9/83, Art. 11 of D.R. 2579/83, and Art. 10 of Ley 75/86. Earlier less inclusive language covered technical assistance, but not compensation for technical services. That distinction was eliminated by Article 14 of Ley 75/86.

81/ Art. 49 of Ley 9/83 and Art. 85, Ley 75/86).

82/ Art. 128, 131 of D.L. 444/67.

83/ Art. 132.

84/ Art. 1 of Ley 75/86.

85/ D.R. 2579/83.

86/ Art. 46 of Ley 9/83, Art. 11 of Ley 75/86.

87/ Art. 46 of Ley 9/83, Art. 14 of Ley 75/86.

88/ Ayala (1987), p. 16

89/ Art. 12 of Ley 75/86.

90/ Art. 13 of Ley 75/86.

91/ Art. 51 of Ley 9/83.

92/ Art. 87 of Ley 75/86.

93/ Concepto 5857/87. Subdirección Jurídica - Dirección General de Impuestos Nacionales.

94/ Art. 41 of Ley/75/86.

95/ Certificado de Reembolso Tributario.

96/ Ley 20/79, art. 6, par. 3.

97/ Ley 20/79, art. 6.

98/ D.L. 2247/74, art. 54.

99/ Ley 75/86, art. 64, par. 2.

100/ Ley 20/79, art. 6.

101/ Ley 20/79, art. 6.

102/ Ley 75/86, art. 72.

103/ Ley 75/86, art. 9.

104/ Ley 9/83, art. 44.

105/ Ley 9/83, art. 25; D. L. 3850/85, art. 14.

106/ D.L. 3850/85, art. 7.

107/ Ley 20/79, art. 32; D.R. 2595/79, art. 37,39.

108/ Ley 75/86, art. 16, par. 1.

109/ Ley 75/86, art. 64.

110/ Ley 14/83, art. 23.

111/ Ley 75/86, art. 64.

112/ Ley 9/83, art. 15. Although the tax on presumptive income is technically part of the income tax, it effectively functions as a separate, complementary tax.

113/ D.R. 353/84, art. 6.

114/ Ley 9/83, art. 15, inc.1.

115/ D.R. 353/84, art. 4.

116/ D.R. 353/84, art. 2.

117/ Ley 9/83, art. 15, parágrafo 2.

118/ D.R. 353/84, art. 7,8,9,10,11.

119/ D.R. 353/84, art. 12, 13.

120/ Ley 55/85, art. 50.

121/ D.L. 3830/85, art. 5, 7.

122/ D.R. 353/84, art. 18.

123/ D.L. 2053/74, art. 74.

124/ The calculation of marginal rates is based on the rate schedule for 1987, set forth in D. 59/87.

125/ Ley 9/83, art. 38; D.L. 2053/74, art. 106,107, 109.

126/ Ley 9/83, art. 38.

127/ D.L. 2053/74, art. 131.

128/ D.L. 2053/74, art. 112.

129/ D.L. 2247/74, art. 57.

130/ Id.

131/ D.L. 2053/74, art. 119.

132/ D.L. 2053/74, art. 120.

133/ D.R. 353/84, art. 33.

134/ D.L. 2053/74, art. 122.

135/ D.L. 2053/74, art. 116; Ley 75/86, art. 73.

136/ Ley 75/86, art. 16.

137/ D.L. 2053/74, art. 106, 124.

138/ D.L 2053/74, art. 114.

4

Marginal Effective Tax Rates on Capital Income in Colombia Before and After the 1986 Tax Reform

Marginal Effective Tax Rates on Capital Income in Colombia before and after the 1986 Tax Reform

I. Introduction

As noted in Chapter 1, economic neutrality is one of the essential criteria used in evaluating a tax system. A critical aspect of economic neutrality is the tax treatment of investment. Specifically, a neutral tax system provides for identical tax treatment of all types of investments, regardless of the type of asset, the business sector or industry, the source of finance, or the characteristics of the individual or institution providing the funds for the investment. In practice, no tax system achieves the goal of complete investment neutrality.

Much recent research in the economics of taxation has focused on measuring the extent to which tax systems deviate from investment neutrality. The most commonly used approach is the calculation of «marginal effective tax rates» on capital income. Such tax rates indicate the difference between the gross and net returns on alternative marginal investments, generally expressed as a percentage of the gross return. They thus provide an indicator of the relative tax burdens facing such investments.

Under a tax system characterized by investment neutrality, marginal effective tax rates would be identical for all types of investments.[1] Accordingly, the differentials in marginal effective tax rates across investments provide an indication of the extent to which the tax system deviates from economic neutrality and thus distorts investment decisions and the allocation of capital.

An example may help clarify the concept of marginal effective tax rates and its usefulness. Suppose that the before-tax real rate of return on a particular marginal investment is 10 percent and the after-tax return is 6 percent; clearly the marginal effective tax rate is 40 percent. If the effective tax rate on another marginal investment with the same before-tax real rate of return is only 20 percent, resources will be allocated away from the former investment and into the latter.

An even worse result occurs if the marginal effective tax rate is negative. Suppose, for example, that tax incentives are so generous that the after-tax real rate of return is 12 percent, even though the before-tax return is only 10 percent; in that case the marginal effective tax rate would be minus 20 percent. Incentives for misallocation of resources would be especially strong in this case.

This chapter reports the results of an analysis of marginal effective tax rates under the Colombian tax system. It presents three sets of results. First, it considers the tax system prior to the 1986 reforms. Second, it analyzes the effects of the 1986 reforms when they are fully phased-in; this is scheduled to occur in 1995. Finally, it describes the time path of marginal effective tax rates during the ten-year period specified by the 1986 reform for the phasing-in of inflation indexing of business interest income and expense. This provides a means of evaluating the effects of partial indexing of interest for inflation during this transition period, as well as during the alternative six-year transition period proposed in Chapter 7. In each of these three cases, marginal effective tax rates are presented for the four types of assets, eight business sectors, three types of finance, and three types of savers listed in Table 4.1.[2] The numerical results presented below provide an indication of the pattern of taxation of capital income in Colombia before and after the 1986 reforms. The large tax differentials across investment types and the negative marginal effective tax rates calculated for the pre-1986 tax structure, plus the sensitivity of marginal effective tax rates to variations in the rate of inflation, illustrate graphically why the 1986 reform was needed. The calculations under the 1986 law (when fully phased-in) indicate that, while substantial progress has been achieved in providing for uniform treatment of investment, further reforms are required to achieve additional gains in economic neutrality. The results for the phasing-in of inflation indexing for business interest income and expense provide a rough indicator of the allocative costs involved in delaying the movement to the new tax structure. These must be weighed against the inequities and distortions that would result from more rapid movement.

The following section provides a brief outline of the method of calculating marginal effective tax rates utilized in this Report; this methodology follows King and Fullerton (1984). Section III then describes the assumptions made in the calculation of marginal effective tax rates for Colombia and presents and evaluates the three sets of results described above. The appendix contains the mathematical details of the marginal effective tax rate methodology, as well as a discussion of several technical issues raised by the King-Fullerton methodology.

II. Marginal Effective Tax Rate Calculations for Colombia

A. *Marginal Effective Tax Rate Methodology*

The basic concept underlying a marginal effective tax rate calculation is straightforward. Nevertheless, a wide variety of methods of calculating marginal effective tax rates have appeared in the literature; each has its own advantages and disadvantages. Any calculation of marginal effective tax rates will inevitably be affected by the choice of the method of calculation, as well as a number of assumptions made in the method of calculation chosen. As noted above, this study generally follows the approach of King and Fullerton (1984), which has to some extent become the «standard» among public finance economists. The version of the King-Fullerton approach underlying this Report is summarized very briefly in the following discussion. Details are provided in the appendix, which also briefly discusses some criticisms of the King-Fullerton methodology and describes some alternative approaches.

In order to calculate the marginal effective tax rate on an investment, the tax «wedge» imposed on the income from the investment by the business and individual tax systems must be determined. This tax «wedge» is defined as the difference between the gross returns obtained by the firm that makes the investment and the net return (after all direct business and individual taxes) to the saver providing the investment funds to the firm. The marginal effective tax rate is defined as the tax wedge divided by the gross return. Investments are «marginal» in the sense that the after-tax cost of an asset is assumed to be equal in present value terms to the after-tax returns to the asset. Investments are characterized according to the type of asset, the business sector, the type of finance, and the type of saver providing the investment funds. Since the tax treatment of various types of investment differs, the tax wedge, and thus the marginal effective tax rate, generally varies across types of investments.[3/]

A comparison of marginal effective tax rates across types of investments requires that some rate of return in the economy be held fixed. The results presented below assume that all investments earn the same real gross rate of return (10 percent). This assumption results in marginal effective tax rates that are easy to interpret. For example, suppose the marginal effective tax rate for a particular investment is calculated as 30 percent. Since the investment is assumed to generate a total return of 10 percent, the 30 percent tax rate simply implies that the government receives 3 percentage points of the return in the form of business or individual income tax revenues, and the remaining 7 percentage points go to the individual or institution providing the funds to finance the investment.

This «fixed gross returns» approach provides a good description of the relative tax burdens facing alternative marginal investments, relative to an equilibrium without any business or individual income taxation. However, it should be noted that the assumption that all marginal investments yield the same gross return cannot be viewed as a realistic description of the actual pattern of gross returns in an economy that is in equilibrium. That is, in the presence of differentials in marginal effective tax rates, investors would be expected to reallocate capital toward relatively low-taxed types of investments and away from relatively high-taxed types; this reallocation would result in differentials in gross returns such that net returns were equalized, (rather than a uniform gross rate of return across all investments).[4] The tax rates calculated under this assumption should thus be viewed as «pre-adjustment» rates, that is, marginal effective tax rates that would prevail before adjustment to differentials in tax rates.[5] (This issue is discussed further in the appendix.)

Two benchmarks may be useful in evaluating the results of the marginal effective tax rate calculations for Colombia presented below. First, consider the case of a business income tax based on real economic income, which provides for indexed economic depreciation allowances, LIFO (or indexed-FIFO) inventory accounting, and complete indexation of interest income and receipts, coupled with individual taxation of dividends at the same rate as interest receipts but no capital gains or wealth taxes. In this case, the marginal effective tax rates (METR) for debt, new issues, and retained earnings, respectively, are

METR(debt) = t(int),

METR(new issues) = T + t(div(1-T),

METR(retained earnings) = T,

where T is the business tax rate, and t(int) and t(div) are the individual tax rates on interest and dividend income. These three marginal effective tax rate results under a system that taxes real economic income are interpreted as follows. First, income from debt-financed investment is taxed only at the personal tax rate on real interest income; this occurs because all returns on the marginal investment are assumed to be paid out as interest to the individual who provides the funds to the business and (real) interest payments are fully deductible at the firm level and fully taxed at the individual level. Second, income from investment financed with new issues is fully taxed at the firm rate T, and earnings after corporate taxes are subject to a second dividend tax at the individual level.[6] Third, income from investment financed with retained earnings is subject only to company tax; as will be explained below, the analysis follows the so-called «new view» of dividend taxation, which implies that dividend taxation does not affect marginal investment decisions financed from retained earnings.

The marginal effective tax rate results are quite different for a consumption-based tax (such as the Simplified Alternative Tax described in Chapter 9) that provides for expensing of investment and additions to inventories, exclusion of dividends, capital gains and interest receipts at the individual level, and non-deductibility of business interest payments. As demonstrated in Chapter 8, the marginal effective tax rate on capital income is zero irrespective of the method of finance under such a tax system.[7] Note that this implies that the allocation of investment is not distorted under the Simplified Alternative Tax; the marginal effective tax rate on capital income is zero regardless of the type of asset, the business sector, the source of finance, or the type of saver.[8] The calculations presented below demonstrate that such a result is in marked contrast to the differentials in marginal effective tax rates that will occur when the 1986 reform is fully phased in.

B. Assumptions Made in the Calculations

The marginal effective tax rate calculations presented below are based on a large number of assumptions and are subject to a variety of qualifications. These include the following.

The analysis is limited to capital investment made by companies in four assets — equipment, structures, inventories, and land. The marginal effective tax rates on investments in the two non-depreciable assets — inventories and land — are identical in all cases. This occurs because there are no depreciation deductions for either type of asset, because problems of inflation adjustment of business deductions do not arise because firms receive no deductions for land purchases and are assumed to use LIFO inventory accounting, and because taxation of income from investments in these assets at the level of the saver is assumed to be identical for both assets. As a result, marginal investments in inventories and land are taxed at the business level at the statutory rate if they are financed by new share issues or retained earnings, and at a zero (negative) rate if they are debt-financed and the inflation rate is zero (positive); any remaining tax burden on such investments, as measured by the marginal effective tax rate, reflects taxation at the level of the saver (which is assumed not to differ across these two assets).[9]

The business tax rate applied to corporations (and to mixed public-private enterprises) prior to the 1986 reform is 40 percent. Pre-1986 results are also presented for the cases in which individuals invest through limited partnerships; the income from investments made by these entities is subject to a business level tax rate of 18 percent. Under pre-1986 law, partnership income was «passed through» to the individual owners and subject to personal taxation; thus, for purposes of the marginal effective tax rate calculations, all equity finance is, in effect, treated as new share issues since retained earnings of limited partnerships do not benefit from the tax advantages of deferral.) Under the 1986 reform, corporations, mixed public-private enterprises, and limited partnerships are all subject to tax at a 30 percent rate.

Although the calculations account for most of the major aspects of the direct taxation of capital income in Colombia, certain features are ignored. In particular, no attempt is made to ascertain the effects of the taxation of presumptive income on a marginal investment, and features that provide special treatment to certain industries are ignored. For example, special rules for agricultural planting costs and for capital gains on the sale of cattle are described in Chapter 3; these rules are not considered in the calculations of marginal effective tax rates presented in this chapter. The calculations also apply only to national direct taxation of capital income; in particular, the Colombian value added tax and local property taxes are ignored. Perhaps as important, no allowance is made for other distortionary taxes, such as those on foreign trade.

The calculation of the marginal effective tax rates for investments financed by individuals requires an estimate of the average marginal tax rates applied to interest income, dividends, and partnership income received by individuals. For pre-1986 law (denoted as «1985» figures in the tables), these rates were set equal to the average marginal rates applied to such receipts in 1984. Personal income tax data for 1984 indicate that Colombian taxpayers are quite successful in arranging their affairs so that interest income is taxed at a relatively low marginal rate; despite a statutory maximum rate of 49 percent, the average marginal tax rate (weighted by the amount of interest received) applied to taxable interest income was 22.8 percent. All interest income on debt-financed investments was assumed to be taxed at this rate, irrespective of the form of business organization. Dividends were more concentrated in the higher income classes, as the average marginal rate applied to dividends in 1984 was 34.5 percent. This rate was assumed to be applied to both corporate dividends and partnership income. For 1986 law (including the fully phased-in version referred to as «1995» figures in the tables to reflect completion of the ten-year phase-in of inflation indexing for business interest income and expense), dividends and partnership income are untaxed at the individual level. For interest income, it is simply assumed that the reduction in the average marginal tax rate was proportional to the reduction in the top individual marginal tax rate, which fell from 49 to 30 percent; this results in an assumed average marginal tax rate of only 14.0 percent.

For foreign investors, interest income is effectively exempt from tax both before and after the 1986 reform. (See Chapter 3.) Dividends paid to foreigners are assumed to be subject to a 20 percent withholding tax prior to 1986 (the rate for dividends paid to residents of non-tax haven countries) and to the 30 percent rate prevailing after the 1986 reform. Foreign investors (other than individuals) are not subject to Colombian taxes on capital gains or net wealth.

Calculation of the marginal effective tax rate on capital gains is always difficult and to some extent arbitrary. A common procedure is to assume that the advantages of deferral and the exclusion (to the donor) of gains transferred at death imply that the effective tax rate on capital gains is equal to roughly one-fourth the maximum statutory rate on such gains.[10] In Colombia, capital gains have the additional advantage of being taxed as occasional gains and thus are subject to taxation under a separate rate schedule; this results in a lower rate of taxation if the taxpayer's ordinary income exceeds his occasional gains. (See Chapter 3.) Moreover, capital gains are probably seriously under-reported. The present analysis simply assumes that the effective marginal tax rate on capital gains is equal to one-eighth the maximum statutory tax rate on ordinary income. This results in an effective marginal tax rate on capital gains of 6.25 (3.75) percent prior to (after) the 1986 reform. Such an assumption is obviously only a rough attempt to capture the net effect of all of the aspects of the taxation of capital gains discussed above.[11] It is also assumed for simplicity that capital gains are fully indexed for inflation; as described in Chapter 3, the actual extent of inflation indexing varies with the type of asset.

Similarly, it is difficult to ascertain how the marginal effective tax rate on capital income is affected by the Colombian net wealth tax on individuals. The average tax rate on reported net wealth in 1984 was 1.07 percent. However, net wealth is presumably significantly under-reported, especially since the base of the net wealth tax is not indexed for inflation. The degree of under-reporting presumably varies across assets. For example, accelerated depreciation allowances result in significant understatement of the values of depreciable assets, and the use of LIFO inventory accounting has the same effect on the values of goods held in inventories. Land values are understated because of lags in revaluation and because as much as 40 percent of the assessed value of land is excluded from the net wealth tax base under the 1986 reform. (See Chapter 3.) In addition, the extent of evasion presumably varies across types of asset.. Rather than attempting to account for the effects of the net wealth tax on an asset-by-asset basis, it is simply assumed that under-reporting has the effect of cutting the effective tax rate on all net wealth in half to 0.535 percent.[12] Again, such an assumption is clearly arbitrary, and all results should be interpreted with caution.

The marginal effective tax rate calculations require an estimate of the rate of economic depreciation for all depreciable assets. The data needed to generate such estimates for Colombia are not available. The calculations assume simply that the rates of economic depreciation of particular types of assets are constant across sectors and are equal to 14 percent for equipment and 3 percent for structures. These depreciation rates are typical of those reported for the United States.[13] Although the application of these rates to Colombia is clearly tenuous, there is no obvious alternative in the absence of specific data.[14] For tax purposes, businesses are assumed to use the three-year write-off for equipment (40 percent in each of the first two years and 20 percent in the third) and the 10 percent declining balance method for structures described in Chapter 3. Depreciation allowances are not indexed for inflation.

The method of indexing interest income and expense currently used in Colombia is assumed to be accurate in that the inflationary component of such interest is assumed to be measured correctly. For individuals investing in UPACs (unidades de poder adquisitivo constante, an indexed financial asset of constant purchasing power), 60 percent of the inflationary component of interest income was non-taxable prior to 1986; for other indexed debt 40 percent of interest income could be excluded. By comparison, all interest income received by individuals was fully indexed for inflation under the 1986 reform. The marginal effective tax rate calculations for the cases of debt-financed investments when the source of funds is households assume that interest payments to the households qualify for either 60 percent (for pre-1986 calculations) or for complete (for post-1985 calculations) inflation indexing.[15]

For businesses, interest was fully deductible prior to 1986, but none of the inflationary component of interest expense will be deductible once the 1986 reforms are fully phased-in. The calculations of marginal effective tax rates during the phasing-in of inflation indexing for business interest assume that the ten-year, 10 percent per year, phase-in schedule specified in the 1986 reform is followed.

Firms are assumed to use LIFO accounting for tax purposes. This in turn is assumed to imply that the costs of goods sold from inventories are effectively fully indexed.

The calculations are based on the assumption that inflation is constant throughout the life of an investment. Results are presented for inflation rates of 0, 10, and 25 percent.[16]

Marginal effective tax rates are presented for the eight sectors of the Colombian economy listed in Table 4.1, and for the aggregation of these eight sectors, for each source of finance and each type of saver. To generate an industry tax rate, the marginal effective tax rates for each asset type must be weighted by the amount of net investment in that asset for the industry. Similarly, to generate the tax rate for the aggregation of these eight sectors (for each source of finance and each type of investor), the marginal effective tax rate for each industry must be weighted by the amount of net investment in that industry. To obtain these «net investment weights», it was assumed that the amount of net investment in each asset by each industry was equal to the difference in the total stock of that asset reported on 1984 and 1985 business income tax forms for purposes of the wealth-based component of the taxation of presumptive income.[17] In the absence of sufficient data regarding the ownership of assets and the sources of finance, no attempt was made to weight the aggregate eight-sector tax rates for each source of finance and type of saver in order to calculate a single marginal effective tax rate on all capital income for Colombia. Instead, results are presented for each possible combination of ownership and source of finance.

In summary, the marginal effective tax rates presented below provide an important and useful indicator of the taxation of capital income in Colombia before and after the 1986 reform, including the transition period during which inflation indexing for business interest expense is phased in. Nevertheless, the calculation of these rates involves a large number of assumptions and is subject to the various qualifications discussed above (and in the appendix). These limitations should be kept in mind in using the figures described below to evaluate tax policy in Colombia.

C. Marginal Effective Tax Rates for Colombia

The results of the marginal effective tax rate calculations for Colombia are provided in Tables 4.2-4.9. Results for the two types of equity finance (new share issues and retained earnings) are presented first, followed by the results for debt finance. For both equity and debt finance, results are first presented for the cases in which there is no taxation at the level of the saver, and then for the cases in which returns to the saver are subject to taxation. The marginal effective tax rates in the former cases thus reflect only taxation at the company level, while the tax rates in the latter cases reflect taxation at both the company and the saver level. For the cases in which the investments are financed by either debt or new share issues and the source of finance is households, the marginal effective tax rate on investments made by limited partnerships are presented in parentheses below the tax rate on the corresponding corporate investment. In the following discussion, pre-1986 law will be referred to as «old law» and the fully phased-in version of the 1986 reform will be referred to as «new law».

Table 4.2 presents results for equity-financed investments that bear no tax at the level of the saver; these are investments financed by retained earnings attributable to tax-exempt institutions or foreigners, as well as investments financed by new share issues purchased by tax-exempt institutions.[18], [19] In this case, the main change in the 1986 reform affecting the marginal effective tax rate calculations is the reduction in the statutory corporate income tax rate from 40 to 30 percent. (Note that under the new view of dividend taxation, withholding taxes paid by foreigners on dividends paid from earnings on investments financed out of retained earnings do not affect marginal effective tax rates).

The most striking feature of these results is that, at a 25 percent rate of inflation, the marginal effective tax rates on investment in all four types of assets are roughly equal to the statutory corporate rate. This result occurs because, at a 25 percent inflation rate, the real present value of the rapid tax depreciation allowances on both equipment and structures provided under Colombian law is roughly equal to the real present value of economic depreciation (and because in these calculations there is no taxation at the saver level). As a result, each of the sectoral marginal effective tax rates is also roughly equal to the statutory corporate rate. These results imply that, at a 25 percent inflation rate, the Colombian tax system (both before and after the 1986 reform) is quite close to satisfying the criterion of economic neutrality described in Chapter 1; that is, for the specific types of equity-financed investments analyzed in Table 4.2, the tax system does not distort the allocation of investment across assets or across business sectors at a 25 percent inflation rate.[20]

The result of investment neutrality does not obtain at lower rates of inflation. Although the present value of tax depreciation allowances under current Colombian law is roughly equal to economic depreciation at a 25 percent inflation rate, it is significantly higher than economic depreciation at lower rates of inflation. For both the new and the old law, there are dramatic reductions in marginal effective tax rates on income from depreciable assets (especially equipment) as the rate of inflation falls from the benchmark level of 25 percent.[21] This in turn implies significant tax differentials across industries at rates of inflation below 25 percent, as equipment-intensive (and to a lesser extent) structures-intensive industries are favored by the tax code, relative to land-intensive and inventory-intensive industries. (Note that, as explained above, the marginal effective tax rates on the two non-depreciable assets — inventories and land — are independent of the inflation rate.) As discussed in Chapter 1, such differentials in marginal effective tax rates imply an inefficient allocation of capital across investment assets and across industries; these tax differentials in turn imply a reduction in the productivity of investment and a reduction in the value of output produced by the Colombian economy. In addition, the variation of marginal effective tax rates with inflation rates introduces an undesirable element of uncertainty into the investment decision; such uncertainty is likely to reduce the level of investment.[22] Note, however, that the reductions in the overall level of taxation that occur as the inflation rate declines may increase the level of investment.

Results for investment financed by new share issues purchased by foreign investors are presented in Table 4.3. In this case, the main changes in the 1986 reform affecting the marginal effective tax rate calculations are the reduction in the statutory corporate income tax rate and the increase in the withholding rate on dividends paid to foreigners (in non-tax haven countries) from 20 to 30 percent. As suggested in Chapter 3, the net effect of these changes is to keep marginal effective tax rates roughly constant before and after the 1986 reform. At a 25 percent rate of inflation, marginal effective tax rates are roughly constant across all assets and sectors. Under (prior to) the 1986 reform, this reflects taxation at the statutory corporate rate of 30 (40) percent coupled with a withholding tax of 30 (20) percent. The tax system is once again roughly neutral with respect to the allocation of investment at an inflation rate of 25 percent, both before and after the 1986 reform. However, to the extent withholding taxes impose a burden on the foreign investor, the relatively high levels of taxation (under both the old and the new law) may reduce the level of investment and will favor retained earnings finance over the issuance of new equity shares to foreigners. (See Chapter 3 for a discussion of the conditions under which Colombian withholding taxes impose a tax burden on foreign investors.) In this case, lower marginal effective tax rates on retained earnings attributable to foreigners relative to the taxation of income from new issues purchased by foreigners will distort financing decisions and favor investment by firms already established in Colombia over new foreign enterprises.

For the reasons described above, the marginal effective tax rates on depreciable assets fall with a decline in the inflation rate relative to the benchmark inflation rate of 25 percent. Once again, this implies that equipment-intensive (and to a lesser extent) structures-intensive industries are favored by the tax code, resulting in tax differentials and tax-induced inefficiencies in capital allocation at inflation rates below 25 percent.

Table 4.4 presents results for investments financed by new share issues purchased by households. The returns to such investments are subject to tax at the corporate level since dividends are not deductible. They are also subject to dividend taxation at the individual level under the old law; this does not occur under the new law since dividends are exempt from individual taxation. In both cases, shares in companies are subject to the individual net wealth tax. Investments by limited partnerships are also subject to taxation at both the business and individual level under old law.

The results indicate that the 1986 reform dramatically reduced marginal effective tax rates on investments financed by new issues purchased by households. At a 25 percent inflation rate, marginal effective tax rates were reduced by roughly one-half as a result of the elimination of individual dividend taxation and the lowering of the statutory corporate tax rate; the marginal effective tax rates under the new law reflect the lower statutory tax rates at the corporate level coupled with net wealth taxation at the individual level. Once again, marginal effective tax rates are very nearly constant across assets and industries at a 25 percent inflation rate.

At inflation rates below 25 percent, the pattern of marginal effective tax rates is similar to that in the previous two cases. That is, at lower rates of inflation, marginal effective tax rates decline for depreciable assets due to the increase in the present value of tax depreciation allowances. In addition, tax differentials across assets and industries widen as the inflation rate falls below 25 percent.

The results also indicate that, under the old law, investments made by limited partnerships and financed by the issuance of new shares to households were tax advantaged relative to the same type of investments by corporations; this result reflects the preferential business tax rate applied to investments by limited partnerships. However, these tax rates on investments by limited partnerships should also be compared to the marginal effective tax rates on investments financed by retained earnings attributable to households (presented in Table 4.5 below); this comparison is relevant because under pre-1986 law investments financed with retained earnings made by limited partnerships do not benefit from deferral and thus face the same «new share issue» tax rates listed in Table 4.4. This comparison indicates that corporate investments financed with retained earnings attributable to households are subject to a lower marginal effective tax rate than the same type of investment made by a limited partnership. These results indicate a fairly complicated pattern of distortions of equity-financed investment under the old law, as investments financed with new share issues (retained earnings) by limited partnerships were tax advantaged (disadvantaged) relative to the same type of investment by a corporation. To the extent retained earnings finance is more prevalent than the issuance of new shares, the tax system under the old law actually favored equity-financed investments by corporations over those by limited partnerships; this result obtains despite the preferential business tax rate granted the latter form of business organization. In any case, the misallocation of resources induced by the differential tax treatment of investment by corporations and limited partnerships was eliminated by the 1986 reform since it eliminated such differential tax treatment.

The results for investments financed by retained earnings attributable to households are presented in Table 4.5. For retained earnings finance, the King-Fullerton methodology implies that dividend taxation at the individual level does not affect marginal effective tax rates on new investment; this so-called «new view» of the effects of dividend taxation is discussed at length in the appendix. The marginal effective tax rates in Table 4.5 thus reflect only income taxation at the business level and capital gains and net wealth taxation at the individual level. The 1986 reform resulted in lower marginal effective tax rates due to the reduction in the business tax rate and the reduction in individual tax rates (applied to capital gains). However, the reduction in rates is much smaller than it would be if the returns to investments financed by retained earnings were assumed to be subject to individual dividend taxation under the old law.[23], [24] Note that under the 1986 reform, marginal effective tax rates on retained earnings attributable to households are roughly equal to those on new issues purchased by households. This contrasts with the situation under pre-1986 law, when retained earnings were subject to a much lower tax rate than were new share issues. Thus, for funds provided by households, the 1986 reform eliminated a distortion favoring retained earnings finance over the issuance of new shares. This eliminates a distortion in business financing decisions as well as a tax preference favoring old established firms over new enterprises. Finally, for the same reasons as above, marginal effective tax rates are very nearly uniform across assets and sectors at an inflation rate of 25 percent; as the rate of inflation declines, marginal effective tax rates decline and tax differentials increase.

Table 4.6 presents results for debt-financed investments when the source of funds is tax-exempt institutions or foreign investors. Since neither of these types of savers is subject to Colombian withholding taxes on interest income, the results in this table reflect only changes in business taxes on debt-financed investment before and after the 1986 reform. Consider first the case of a 25 percent inflation rate under the new law. Since only the real component of interest expense is deductible to firms and tax depreciation approximates real economic depreciation, marginal effective tax rates are roughly zero on debt-financed investments for all assets and sectors. In marked contrast, full deductibility of nominal interest expense under the old law results in very large (and nearly uniform) negative marginal effective tax rates for these investors on all assets and all sectors. These results highlight the undesirable effect of full business interest deductibility when there is no offsetting taxation of nominal interest income received by the saver. In particular, the reduction in corporate rates under the 1986 reform is swamped by the effects of eliminating full deductibility of interest expense; thus, marginal effective tax rates on debt-financed investment when the source of funds is either tax-exempt institutions or foreign investors rise dramatically — though only to zero. Such increases in marginal effective tax rates are generally desirable; as noted above, negative marginal effective tax rates result in particularly serious misallocations of capital across assets and industries and distort financing decisions toward the tax-preferred source of finance.

Under the new law, marginal effective tax rates on income from depreciable assets again fall as the rate of inflation declines since the real present value of tax depreciation allowances increases. However, under the old law, this effect is swamped by the reduction in the value of full deductibility of business interest expense; thus, marginal effective tax rates rise dramatically as the rate of inflation declines. Moreover, the increases in tax differentials across assets and thus across industries as the rate of inflation declines is much more dramatic in the case of debt finance than in the equity finance cases analyzed above.

Table 4.7 presents results for debt-financed investment when the source of funds is households. The pattern of marginal effective tax rates is strongly affected by the tax treatment of interest income and expense.[25] Consider first the figures for a 25 percent inflation rate. As noted above, at such an inflation rate, the present value of tax depreciation allowed (for both equipment and structures) is roughly equal to the present value of economic depreciation. Under the new law, this implies approximately a zero rate of tax on debt-financed investment at the business level. (As noted above, the tax rate at the firm level would be exactly zero with deductions for real economic depreciation, because all returns on the marginal investment are paid out as interest to the saver, and real interest expense is fully deductible to the firm.) The marginal effective tax rates at a 25 percent inflation rate thus primarily reflect the taxation of interest income at the individual level under the income and wealth taxes.

As above, tax differentials across assets and thus across sectors are very small under the new law at a 25 percent inflation rate; thus, the new law is roughly neutral with respect to the allocation of investment across industries at rates of inflation in the neighborhood of — but somewhat below — current rates. The pattern of marginal effective tax rates under old law was also roughly neutral across assets and sectors at an inflation rate of 25 percent. However, the average rate of taxation was much lower (and negative) as a result of the full deductibility of nominal interest expense. As noted above, these negative tax rates result in serious resource misallocations and distortions of financing decisions. Moreover, a comparison of the marginal effective tax rates under old law with a 25 percent inflation rate in Table 4.7 with those in Tables 4.4 and 4.5 reveals a huge tax incentive favoring debt finance over retained earnings and new share issues when the source of funds is individuals. This tax incentive distorts firm financing decisions toward debt, and probably played an important role in the marked increase in debt finance in recent years in Colombia. (See Chapter 7). In addition, tax-induced increases in the proportion of investment that is debt-financed distort the allocation of risk-bearing in the economy and increase the likelihood that firms will incur a costly bankruptcy. One of the most important features of the 1986 reform is that these distortions of the financing decision were largely eliminated as a result of the provisions that provide for inflation indexing of business interest income and expense; that is, the differentials in marginal effective tax rates for a 25 percent inflation rate are smaller in Tables 4.4, 4.5, and 4.7 under the new law than they were prior to 1986.

Another comparison of relative tax rates is noteworthy. The large differences between the marginal effective tax rates on the income from debt-financed investments presented in Table 4.7 and those shown in Table 4.6 indicate clearly the necessity to limit the investment possibilities available to tax-exempt institutions (as was done in the 1986 reform)[26] In the absence of such limitations, taxpayers face a strong incentive to create entities that qualify for tax-exempt status and can be used as a tax avoidance device. Moreover, without such limitations, tax-exempt institutions (whether established for legitimate reasons or not) can compete unfairly with taxable businesses. Note that the tax differential favoring tax-exempt institutions on debt-financed investment is not eliminated under the new law. Tax-exempt institutions are almost always treated favorably relative to taxable businesses under an income tax; only under a consumption tax, such as the Simplified Alternative Tax described in Chapter 9, is this tax preference automatically eliminated.

As in all previous cases, the result of investment neutrality does not obtain at rates of inflation lower or higher than the benchmark rate of 25 percent. Under the new law, there are dramatic reductions in marginal effective tax rates on income from depreciable assets (especially equipment) as the rate of inflation falls. This in turn implies significant tax differentials across industries at rates of inflation other than 25 percent, as equipment-intensive (and to a lesser extent) structures-intensive industries are favored by the tax code.

Under the old law, tax differentials across assets and sectors also increase as the rate of inflation declines; however, the average marginal effective tax rate increases. Once again, larger real depreciation allowances have the effect of lowering marginal effective tax rates as the rate of inflation declines. However, this effect is outweighed by the reduction in the tax benefit attributable to full business deductibility of nominal interest expense, coupled with a 60 percent exclusion of the inflationary component of interest income for individuals. As a result, marginal effective tax rates for debt-financed investments by households increase with a reduction in inflation under old law. This is most clearly seen in the case of land and inventories, where tax rates are independent of inflation under the new law (as they are for all the equity-financed cases described above), but increase as the rate of inflation declines under the old law.

The results for the cases of investments made by limited partnerships financed with debt when the source of funds is individuals are also noteworthy. In each case, such investments face a higher marginal effective tax rate than the corresponding corporate investments, and the tax differential widens as the inflation rate increases. These results occur because the business tax rate applied to interest deductions (the limited partnership rate of 18 percent) is lower than the individual tax rate applied to interest receipts (which, as noted above, is roughly 23 percent). Accordingly, the use of debt finance is not as attractive as in the case of corporate investment (where business interest expense is deductible at a tax rate of 40 percent), especially as the rate of inflation increases and the magnitudes of nominal (and unindexed) interest deductions increase. Thus, corporate debt-financed investments when the source of funds is households were tax advantaged under the old law, relative to the same type of investment made by a limited partnership. The resulting misallocation of resources was corrected by the 1986 reform since it eliminated differential treatment of investment by corporations and limited partnerships.

Finally, results on marginal effective tax rates during the phasing-in of inflation indexing for business interest income and expense are presented in Tables 4.8 and 4.9. The results are based on an inflation rate of 25 percent. Table 4.8 considers the cases of debt-financed investments that are untaxed at the level of the saver, that is, those made with funds provided by either tax-exempt institutions or foreign investors. Table 4.9 considers debt-financed investments when the source of finance is households.[27]

The results are presented for the ten-year, 10 percent per year, phase-in of inflation indexing for corporate interest income and expense specified in the 1986 reform. The changes in the marginal effective tax rates between 1985 and 1987 reflect not only the elimination of deductibility of 20 percent of the inflationary component of interest expense, but also all of the other changes in the 1986 reform that were implemented immediately rather than being phased in. The further changes for the other years reflect only changes in inflation indexing of business interest income and expense; for example, the changes in marginal effective tax rates between 1987 and 1989 reflect only the effects of the increase in the fraction of the inflationary component of interest expense that is deductible from 20 to 40 percent.

These results indicate that after 1987 the phasing-in of inflation indexing of interest income and expense has a roughly linear effect on marginal effective tax rates. That is, the marginal effective tax rates shown in Table 4.8 (4.9) increase by a factor somewhat larger (smaller) than 20 percentage points for each increase of 20 percentage points in the fraction of the inflationary component of business interest expense that is not deductible. It is thus a straightforward matter to use this roughly linear relationship to approximate the effects on the time path of marginal effective tax rates of any proposal to phase-in interest indexing (for the type of investment and inflation rate analyzed), including the phase-in plan proposed in Chapter 7

APPENDIX

Details of the methodology used to generate the estimates of marginal effective tax rates in Colombia presented above are described in this appendix. As noted previously, the methodology generally followed is the approach of King and Fullerton (1984), which is arguably the standard in the public finance literature.[28] This appendix also considers briefly criticisms of the King-Fullerton methodology and describes alternative approaches utilized by other public finance specialists.

I. The Marginal Effective Tax Rate Methodology

For the calculation of a marginal effective tax rate on a particular investment project, the nature of the investment must be specified — the type of asset, the industry or sector, the source of finance, and the type of saver providing funds to finance the investment. To some extent, the choice of combinations considered in this Report is dictated by data considerations. In Colombia, the availability of data from business income tax returns and other sources suggests the breakdown presented below in Table 4.1.

Calculation of a marginal effective tax rate requires two basic assumptions. First, the marginal effective tax rate methodology does not include a general equilibrium modeling of the effects of tax policy; that is, all of the equilibrium rates of return to investment for a particular tax system are not calculated simultaneously in a model that describes an entire economy. Instead, a partial equilibrium approach is adopted, as some rate of return in the economy is held constant regardless of changes in the tax structure. Unfortunately, there is no general consensus in the literature regarding which rate this should be. The three prime candidates are gross returns (before-tax returns are constant for all investments), net returns at the business level (after-tax returns to all debt-financed investments by business are constant), and net returns at the saver level (after-tax returns on debt instruments are constant for some «marginal» saver).

The calculations in this Report consider the case of fixed gross returns to all investments. This approach provides an indication of the extent of differentials in marginal effective tax rates prior to the reallocation of investment that would occur in response to such differentials.[29] The numerical results obtained using the fixed gross returns approach are easily interpreted and provide a good indicator of the extent to which investment decisions are distorted by the tax system. Moreover, since this is the approach used in most other studies of marginal effective tax rates, the results detailed below can readily be compared to those presented elsewhere in the literature.[30]

Second, an assumption regarding the nature of arbitrage in the economy must be chosen. One possibility is «firm arbitrage», where the after-tax return to investment at the firm level is independent of the source of finance. Since the returns to debt, retained earnings, and new shares are subject to differing tax treatment at the individual level, this implies that after-tax returns to the individual will vary according to source of finance. An alternative possibility is «individual arbitrage», where individual after-tax returns are identical for all sources of finance; this assumption implies that firms earn different rates of return on investments financed with debt, new share issues and retained earnings.

These two assumptions are clearly inconsistent. Under firm arbitrage, returns after business taxes are identical for all types of investments, but returns after individual taxes vary according to the source of finance. In contrast, under individual arbitrage, after-tax returns to businesses vary according to the source of finance, but after-tax returns to the saver are independent of the source of finance. The latter assumption is more consistent with the view of the firm as a «conduit» for income that is ultimately distributed to the owners of the firm. Moreover, some empirical evidence in the U.S. indicates that rates

70

of return at the business level do in fact vary according to the source of finance. Accordingly, this Report follows King and Fullerton and assumes that Colombia is characterized by individual rather than firm arbitrage.[31]

Given these two assumptions, the calculation of a marginal effective tax rate requires a cost of capital calculation for an investment of the type specified. This calculation is based on the assumption that a profit-maximizing firm will invest to the point where, at the margin, the after-tax cost of an asset is equal in real present value terms to the after-tax returns to the asset; the calculation proceeds in three steps.

First, basic relationship between the fixed after-tax rate of return to the investment (p) and the firm's discount rate (d) is derived. This is done by equating the present value of the after-tax returns of the project to the after-tax cost of the investment, taking into account all relevant tax provisions, including depreciation allowances, investment credits or grants, wealth taxes, taxes on inventories, provisions for inflation indexing, and any other tax provisions which affect the investment. The units of investment are chosen so that a single unit costs one peso. The calculation of the present value of after-tax returns (V) assumes an infinitely-lived asset with a marginal rate of return (MRR) that falls over time at the rate of economic depreciation (D) but increases in nominal value with the rate of inflation (P). With a business tax rate (T), the present value of after-tax returns is

(4.1) $V = (1\text{-}T)\, MRR\, /\, (d + D\text{-}P)$.[32]

The cost of the investment (C) is

(4.2) $C = 1 - A$,

where A is the present value of the depreciation deductions allowed for tax purposes for an investment of one peso, discounted at the firm's discount rate (d).

By definition, the after-tax rate of return, net of depreciation, equals

(4.3) $p = MRR - D$.

Setting V equal to C and using (4.3) results in the basic relationship between the fixed after-tax rate of return (p) and the firm's discount rate (d)

(4.4) $p = (1\text{-}A)\, (d + D\text{-}P)\, /\, (1\text{-}T) - D$.

Second, the discount rate (d), which is equal to the after-tax opportunity cost of funds to the firm, must be specified as a function of the tax parameters and the nominal interest rate (i). As noted above, the assumption of individual arbitrage under the King-Fullerton approach implies that the discount rate used by the firm depends on the source of finance. In the case of debt finance (when the firm is taxable), the discount rate is simply the firm's after-tax nominal interest rate, or

(4.5) $d(debt) = (1\text{-}T)i + fTP$,

where d(debt) is the firm's discount rate for funds raised through the issuance of debt and f is the fraction of the inflationary component of business interest expense that is deductible; for example, f=0 prior to 1986, f=0.2 in 1987, and f=1 when the 1986 reforms are fully phased-in. This expression can be substituted into (4.4) to yield an expression for i as a function of known quantities.

Solving for the individual real after-tax return on debt-financed investment (s) yields

(4.6) $s = i - t(int) (i-eP) - w - P,$

where $t(int)$ is the individual income tax rate on interest receipts, e is the fraction of the inflationary component of interest income that is not taxed, and w is the wealth tax rate. As noted above, the assumption of individual arbitrage implies that this expression for s is the same for all individual investments, regardless of the source of finance. However, with a fixed gross rate of return, the actual numerical value for s will vary, since the nominal interest rate varies according to the source of finance. Note that the value of s also varies according to the saver, since the tax rate applied to interest income differs across savers.

The determination of the appropriate firm discount rate is somewhat more difficult for new issues and retained earnings finance. To isolate the taxation of new share issues, it is assumed that all real earnings are paid out as dividends at the end of the tax year, and the firm is then liquidated; with full indexing of capital gains, there would be no capital gain as a result of the liquidation.[33] Thus, individual arbitrage implies that the real after-tax return to the individual on the investment financed from new share issues must equal the after-tax return to a debt-financed investment (s), or

(4.7) $[d(ni)-P] [1-t(div)] - w = s,$

where $d(ni)$ is the firm's discount rate for new share issues, $t(div)$ is the individual tax rate on dividends (or the tax rate at the individual level on partnership income), and s is given by (4.6). This expression can be solved for $d(ni)$, which can in turn be substituted into (4.4) and solved for i and thus s.

In calculating the marginal effective tax rate on investment financed by retained earnings, the King-Fullerton approach follows the «new view» of the effects of dividend taxation, which implies that dividend taxes distort investment decisions financed with new issues but have no effect on marginal investment decisions financed with retained earnings.[34] Since this «new view» of the effects of dividend taxation is controversial, a brief description of its basic premises is in order. The basic assumption of the new view is that after-tax profits retained within a corporation must ultimately be paid out as taxable dividends. This proposition is obvious if the first-period returns to an investment financed with new issues are paid out as dividends. Suppose instead, however, that these returns are retained to finance new investment. For example, suppose the personal tax rate on dividends is 30 percent, and the return to the investment, after corporate taxes, is 10 percent. If returns of $1,000 were paid out as dividends, the individual would receive $700 and pay $300 in dividend taxes. If the first-period returns of $1,000 were retained and reinvested at the 10 percent rate of return, $1,100 could be paid out at the end of the second period. This would imply a return of $770 to the individual after dividend taxes of $330. Since the opportunity cost of the retained earnings investment to the individual was only $700, he realizes the full 10 percent return on the investment financed with retained earnings. The actual dividend tax paid in the second year is equal in present value terms to the tax that would have been paid at the end of the first year; that is, dividend taxes are either $300 in period one or $330 in period two.

In effect, there is no additional tax in present value terms on dividends paid from profits resulting from retained earnings, since the actual dividend tax paid merely offsets the benefit of deferring dividend taxes on the first-period returns. Since dividend taxes do not reduce the return to the individual from marginal investments financed with retained earnings, they do not affect the marginal effective tax rate calculation for such investments.[35]

The implications of the new view are two-fold. First, dividend taxes do affect marginal investments financed with new issues. The returns to such investments are subject to dividend taxes; these taxes are either paid at the end of the first period (if returns are paid out immediately), or deferred but ultimately paid (whenever dividends are paid out of returns on investment financed from retained earnings). Second, since any dividend taxes paid out of retained earnings simply represent the payment of a tax liability incurred during the first tax year following the issuance of new shares, dividend taxes have no effects on marginal investment decisions financed from retained earnings. Note that the above reasoning is not greatly altered if firms can distribute earnings without payment of a dividend tax at the individual level. For example, prior to 1986, Colombian firms effectively could distribute earnings through share repurchases or the purchase of shares of other firms; such distributions would be taxed as occasional gains rather than as dividends. As long as the same opportunities for avoiding the individual tax on dividends are available regardless of the form of finance, the only effect of such treatment is to lower the individual tax rate applicable to distributions.[36] Following King and Fullerton, this complication is neglected in the calculations of marginal effective tax rates for Colombia.

Although the «new view» of dividend taxes has much intuitive appeal, it is not universally accepted among economists; the primary reason is that empirical investigations of its implications have yielded mixed results. Nevertheless, adoption of the King-Fullerton methodology implicitly involves acceptance of the «new view» of dividend taxation. This assumption obviously has no effect on the marginal effective tax rate calculations for post-1986 law, since dividends are not taxed at the individual level; that is, first-period returns to new issues are taxed only at the firm level, and retained earnings are subject only to capital gains and net wealth taxes. However, the marginal effective tax rates for pre-1986 Colombian law on investment financed from retained earnings are lower than they would be if the calculations assumed that income from such investment were subject to dividend taxation at the individual level. See also note 24 above.

In light of this discussion, the firm discount rate used for investments financed with retained earnings can be calculated. Individual arbitrage implies that the real after-tax return to the individual on the investment financed from retained earnings must equal the after-tax return to a debt-financed investment (s), or

$$(4.7) \quad [d(re)-P][1-t(cg)]-w = s,$$

where $d(re)$ is the firm's discount rate for retained earnings, $t(cg)$ is the individual effective tax rate on capital gains, and s is given by (4.6). This expression can be solved for $d(re)$, which can in turn be substituted into (4.4) and solved for i and thus s.

The third and final step is the determination of the effective tax rates for any particular investment. Given the discount rate for any particular form of finance, substituting into (4.4) yields the equilibrium value for the nominal interest rate, which in turn yields the real after-tax return to the saver (s). The effective tax rate is then calculated as the difference between the gross real return to the investment and the real after-tax net return to the saver, divided by the former. That is, the marginal effective tax rate (METR) is simply

$$(4.8) \quad METR = (p-s)/p.$$

This procedure is used to calculate each of the separate marginal effective tax rates (based on combinations of assets, industries, sources of finance, and sources of saving) for the Colombian tax system estimated above.

Finally, the aggregate marginal effective tax rates for each of the sectors, as well as the aggregate marginal effective tax rate on capital income for a particular source of finance and type of investor, are simply weighted averages of the tax rates for single investments. For each combination of asset and business sector, the weights are the fraction of the national net investment accounted for by that particular combination.

II. Further Discussion of the King-Fullerton Methodology

As noted previously, a number of critical assumptions must be made in determining the methodology to be used in calculating marginal effective tax rates. Three major assumptions have already been discussed — the assumption of a fixed before-tax rate of return for all investments, the assumption of individual rather than firm arbitrage, and the adoption of the «new view» of the effects of dividend taxation. This section discusses five other critical assumptions or decisions implicit in adopting the King-Fullerton methodology utilized in this report. Again, additional details are provided in King and Fullerton (1984). Where relevant, alternative approaches to the calculation of marginal effective tax rates are discussed briefly.

First, «total» marginal effective tax rates are calculated in the sense that both business and individual tax burdens are considered. An alternative approach that is sometimes used is the consideration of only the tax burden at the business level.[37] However, since businesses generally can be assumed to make decisions considering the interests of their investors, the total tax burden approach arguably provides the better measure of the distortionary effects of an existing tax structure; this is especially likely to be the case in Colombia where much private business activity occurs in closely held or «closed» companies rather than publicly held corporations.

Second, the calculations consider only non-residential business investment by private corporations (and by mixed public-private firms that are taxed under the same rules as corporations under Colombian law) and by limited partnerships. Thus, calculations are not performed for owner-occupied housing.

Third, the treatment of assets upon disposition must be determined. The King-Fullerton approach assumes that assets are held to the end of their economic lives. In addition to being unrealistic, this assumption implies that the marginal effective tax rate calculations do not include the effects of capital gains taxes and recapture rules upon disposition. This is potentially an important issue if depreciation is highly accelerated and recapture rules are lenient so that there is a tax incentive for «churning» or selling assets after some or all of depreciation allowances for tax purposes are exhausted; in this case, the King-Fullerton approach would overstate effective tax rates, since at least some taxpayers would be expected to take advantage of the tax benefits of generous depreciation and recapture rules.[38] However, this does not appear to be a problem in Colombia, where the recapture rules provide for full taxation of gains on depreciable assets at ordinary tax rates. Accordingly, the calculations simply adopt the King-Fullerton assumption that assets are held until the end of their useful economic lives.

Fourth, the relationship between inflation and nominal interest rates must be specified. Two alternative assumptions are commonly made.[39] The first is «Fisher's Law», which specifies that the real before-tax interest rate is constant and that the nominal interest rate goes up point-for-point with the rate of inflation.[40] This assumption results in a constant real after-tax interest rate if interest income and expense are indexed for inflation, or if the marginal investor is a tax-exempt institution or a foreigner not subject to taxation on interest receipts. However, in the absence of inflation indexing, the real after-tax interest rate falls with inflation for taxable individuals, and sometimes becomes negative.

Accordingly, an alternative to Fisher's Law is to assume that the real after-tax interest rate is constant. This implies «Modified Fisher's Law», which specifies that the nominal interest rate goes up by the inflation rate divided by one minus the tax rate on the interest income of the marginal investor. Fisher's Law is assumed to hold for the results presented above. This assumption is clearly valid after the 1986 reform is fully in effect since interest income is fully indexed for inflation. Prior to 1986, it can be viewed as an approximation. An alternative interpretation is that the marginal investor is a foreigner who is not subject to Colombian taxes on interest income; in this case, both Fisher's Law and Modified Fisher's Law yield the same result — the nominal interest rate goes up point for point with the inflation rate.

Finally, the King-Fullerton approach is used above to calculate marginal effective tax rates for each sector of the economy, and for the economy as a whole, for each combination of source of finance and type of saver. These calculations are weighted averages of the marginal effective tax rates on each asset. King and Fullerton assume that the marginal investment occurs in proportion to existing capital stocks. In this case, for the sectoral calculations, the weights would be the fraction of the capital stock in the sector represented by each type of asset; for the economy-wide calculations, the weights would be the fraction of the capital stock in the economy represented by each type of asset. However, since a marginal investment is being considered, it is equally plausible to assume that the marginal investment occurs in proportion to current net investment flows; these two approaches are identical in a steady state but are likely to give different weights in any given year. Since the best data provide an approximation of net investment flows between 1984 and 1985 in Colombia, this Report adopts the investment flow approach for determining the weights in the calculation of aggregate marginal effective tax rates.

TABLE 4-1

Types of Assets, Business Sectors, Sources of Funds and Types of Savers Considered in the Calculations of Marginal Effective Tax Rates

Types of Assets:
1. Equipment
2. Structures
3. Inventories
4. Land

Business Sectors:
1. Agriculture
2. Mining
3. Manufacturing
4. Construction
5. Commerce
6. Transportation
7. Finance
8. Services

Sources of Funds:
1. Debt
2. New Share Issues
3. Retained Earnings

Types of Savers:
1. Households
2. Tax-Exempt Institutions
3. Foreigners

TABLE 4-2

Marginal Effective Tax Rates (Percent)

I. Type of Finance: Retained Earnings
   Source of Funds: Tax-Exempts, Foreigners

II. Type of Finance: New Share Issues
    Source of Funds: Tax-Exempts

	Inflation = 0		Inflation = .10		Inflation = .25	
	1985	1995	1985	1995	1985	1995
ASSET:						
Equipment	15.5	11.2	27.2	18.8	38.9	27.2
Structures	28.2	20.6	38.0	27.8	43.3	31.6
Inv./Land	40.0	30.0	40.0	30.0	40.0	30.0
SECTOR:						
Agriculture	37.3	27.8	39.4	29.4	40.7	30.3
Mining	24.5	17.9	33.9	24.5	41.2	29.7
Manufacturing	31.3	23.3	36.2	26.6	40.3	29.5
Construction	27.6	20.2	35.9	26.1	41.6	30.3
Commerce	37.8	28.3	39.0	29.1	40.1	29.9
Transportation	18.5	13.5	28.9	20.3	39.1	27.6
Finance	27.7	20.4	35.4	25.8	41.1	29.9
Services	30.8	22.7	38.2	28.1	42.4	31.1
TOTAL:	28.7	21.2	35.5	25.9	40.8	29.7

TABLE 4-3

Marginal Effective Tax Rates (Percent)

Type of Finance: New Share Issues

Source of Funds: Foreigners

	Inflation = 0 1985	Inflation = 0 1995	Inflation = .10 1985	Inflation = .10 1995	Inflation = .25 1985	Inflation = .25 1995
ASSET:						
Equipment	32.4	37.7	41.4	42.8	51.4	49.1
Structures	42.9	44.6	50.4	49.2	54.5	52.5
Inv./Land	52.0	51.0	52.0	51.0	52.0	51.0
SECTOR:						
Agriculture	49.9	49.5	51.5	50.5	52.5	51.3
Mining	39.8	42.6	47.0	46.9	53.0	51.0
Manufacturing	45.1	46.3	48.9	48.5	52.3	50.8
Construction	42.2	44.2	48.6	48.1	53.3	51.4
Commerce	50.2	49.8	51.2	50.4	52.1	50.9
Transportation	34.8	39.3	42.8	43.9	51.6	49.4
Finance	42.3	44.3	48.2	47.8	52.9	51.1
Services	44.9	46.0	50.6	49.5	53.8	52.1
TOTAL:	43.0	44.8	48.3	47.9	52.7	50.9

TABLE 4-4

Marginal Effective Tax Rates (Percent)

Type of Finance: New Share Issues*
Source of Funds: Households

	Inflation = 0		Inflation = .10		Inflation = .25	
	1985	1995	1985	1995	1985	1995
ASSET:						
Equipment	50.0	16.1	57.7	24.4	65.2	32.6
	(43.8)		(46.6)		(49.9)	
Structures	58.3	26.0	64.8	33.1	68.5	37.6
	(47.9)		(50.2)		(52.3)	
Inv./Land	66.0	35.4	66.0	35.4	66.2	35.4
	(51.6)		(51.6)		(51.6)	
SECTOR:						
Agriculture	64.2	33.2	65.6	34.8	66.7	35.8
	(50.7)		(51.2)		(51.7)	
Mining	55.9	23.1	62.1	29.9	66.9	35.4
	(46.7)		(48.9)		(51.3)	
Manufacturing	60.3	28.6	63.6	32.0	66.3	35.0
	(48.9)		(50.0)		(51.3)	
Construction	57.9	25.5	63.4	31.5	67.3	36.0
	(47.7)		(49.6)		(51.6)	
Commerce	64.5	33.6	65.4	34.5	66.2	35.3
	(50.9)		(51.2)		(51.5)	
Transportation	52.0	18.5	58.8	25.8	65.4	33.0
	(44.8)		(47.2)		(50.2)	
Finance	58.0	25.7	63.0	31.2	66.9	35.5
	(47.7)		(49.5)		(51.4)	
Services	60.0	28.1	64.9	33.5	67.9	36.9
	(48.7)		(50.5)		(52.1)	
TOTAL:	58.6	26.4	63.1	31.3	66.7	35.3
	(48.0)		(49.6)		(51.3)	

* Figures in parentheses and those for 1995 apply to limited liability companies; figures not in parentheses apply to corporations.

78

TABLE 4-5

Marginal Effective Tax Rates (Percent)

Type of Finance: Retained Earnings

Source of Funds: Households

	Inflation = 0		Inflation = .10		Inflation = .25	
	1985	1995	1985	1995	1985	1995
ASSET:						
Equipment	26.0	19.4	36.9	27.2	48.3	35.2
Structures	37.8	28.9	46.9	36.1	52.4	40.0
Inv./Land	49.2	38.0	49.2	38.0	49.2	38.0
SECTOR:						
Agriculture	46.6	35.9	48.6	37.5	49.8	38.4
Mining	34.4	26.2	43.2	32.8	50.4	37.9
Manufacturing	41.0	31.4	45.5	34.8	49.5	37.6
Construction	37.3	28.5	45.0	34.4	50.8	38.5
Commerce	47.1	36.3	48.2	37.2	49.3	37.9
Transportation	28.9	21.7	38.5	28.6	48.5	35.6
Finance	37.5	28.6	44.6	34.0	50.3	38.0
Services	40.3	30.9	47.2	36.4	51.5	39.4
TOTAL:	38.4	29.3	44.7	34.1	50.0	37.9

TABLE 4-6

Marginal Effective Tax Rates (Percent)

Type of Finance: Debt

Source of Funds: Tax-Exempts, Foreigners

	Inflation = 0		Inflation = .10		Inflation = .25	
	1985	1995	1985	1995	1985	1995
ASSET:						
Equipment	-41.0	-27.6	-88.6	-16.1	-169.0	-3.7
Structures	-19.4	-13.4	-70.1	-3.1	-161.0	2.9
Inv./Land	0.0	0.0	-66.7	0.0	-167.0	0.0
SECTOR:						
Agriculture	-4.5	-3.1	-67.7	-0.8	-165.8	0.5
Mining	-25.8	-17.5	-77.1	-7.9	-164.9	-0.1
Manufacturing	-14.4	-9.8	-73.2	-4.9	-166.5	-0.5
Construction	-20.6	-14.1	-73.7	-5.5	-164.0	0.8
Commerce	-3.7	-2.5	-68.4	-1.3	-166.9	-0.1
Transportation	-35.9	-24.2	-85.7	-14.0	-168.6	-3.1
Finance	-20.4	-13.9	-74.6	-6.1	-165.0	0.2
Services	-15.1	-10.4	-69.7	-2.6	-162.7	2.0
TOTAL:	-18.9	-12.8	-74.4	-5.9	-165.5	-0.1

TABLE 4-7

Marginal Effective Tax Rates (Percent)

Type of Finance: Debt*
Source of Funds: Households

	Inflation = 0 1985	Inflation = 0 1995	Inflation = .10 1985	Inflation = .10 1995	Inflation = .25 1985	Inflation = .25 1995
ASSET:						
Equipment	-3.5	-4.4	-31.1	5.5	-79.2	16.2
	(16.9)		(13.2)		(5.8)	
Structures	13.2	7.8	-16.9	16.7	-73.1	21.9
	(22.9)		(18.7)		(9.3)	
Inv./Land	28.1	19.5	-14.2	19.5	-77.7	19.5
	(28.1)		(20.3)		(8.6)	
SECTOR:						
Agriculture	24.6	16.8	-15.0	18.7	-76.8	19.9
	(26.9)		(19.9)		(8.7)	
Mining	8.2	4.3	-22.3	12.6	-76.1	19.4
	(21.1)		(16.7)		(7.8)	
Manufacturing	17.0	11.0	-19.2	15.2	-77.3	19.0
	(24.2)		(18.1)		(8.0)	
Construction	12.2	7.2	-19.7	14.6	-75.4	20.1
	(22.5)		(17.7)		(8.3)	
Commerce	25.2	17.3	-15.5	18.4	-77.6	19.4
	(27.1)		(19.7)		(8.4)	
Transportation	0.4	-1.4	-28.9	7.3	-78.9	16.7
	(18.3)		(14.1)		(6.2)	
Finance	12.4	7.5	-20.3	14.2	-76.2	19.6
	(22.6)		(17.5)		(8.1)	
Services	16.5	10.4	-16.6	17.1	-74.4	21.2
	(24.0)		(19.0)		(9.0)	
TOTAL:	13.6	8.4	-20.2	14.4	-76.6	19.3
	(23.0)		(17.6)		(8.0)	

* Figures in parentheses and those for 1995 apply to limited liability companies; figures not in parentheses apply to corporations.

TABLE 4-8

Marginal Effective Tax Rates During Phase-In

Type of Finance: Debt

Source of Funds: Tax-Exempts, Foreigners

Inflation Rate: Twenty-Five Percent

	1985	1987	1989	1991	1993	1995
ASSET:						
Equipment	-169.0	-90.0	-68.0	-46.9	-25.3	-3.7
Structures	-161.0	-82.7	-61.4	-39.8	-18.2	2.9
Inv./Land	-167.0	-85.3	-64.2	-42.5	-21.3	0.0
SECTOR:						
Agriculture	-165.8	-84.8	-63.7	-42.0	-20.7	0.5
Mining	-164.9	-85.9	-64.4	-42.9	-21.4	-0.1
Manufacturing	-166.5	-86.1	-64.7	-43.2	-21.8	-0.5
Construction	-164.0	-84.9	-63.5	-42.0	-20.5	0.8
Commerce	-166.9	-85.5	-64.3	-42.7	-21.4	-0.1
Transportation	-168.6	-89.3	-67.4	-46.2	-24.7	-3.1
Finance	-165.0	-85.6	-64.1	-42.6	-21.2	0.2
Services	-162.7	-83.5	-62.2	-40.6	-19.1	2.0
TOTAL:	-165.5	-85.8	-64.4	-42.9	-21.4	-0.1

TABLE 4-9

Marginal Effective Tax Rates During Phase-In

Type of Finance: Debt

Source of Funds: Households

Inflation Rate: Twenty-Five Percent

	1985	1987	1989	1991	1993	1995
ASSET:						
Equipment	-79.2	-57.9	-39.1	-21.0	-2.4	16.2
Structures	-73.1	-51.8	-33.5	-14.9	3.7	21.9
Inv./Land	-77.7	-54.0	-35.8	-17.2	1.0	19.5
SECTOR:						
Agriculture	-76.8	-53.6	-35.4	-16.8	1.5	19.9
Mining	-76.1	-54.5	-36.0	-17.6	1.0	19.4
Manufacturing	-77.3	-54.7	-36.3	-17.8	0.6	19.0
Construction	-75.4	-53.7	-35.3	-16.8	1.7	20.1
Commerce	-77.6	-54.2	-35.9	-17.4	0.9	19.4
Transportation	-78.9	-57.3	-38.6	-20.4	-1.9	-16.7
Finance	-76.2	-54.2	-35.8	-17.3	1.2	19.6
Services	-74.4	-52.5	-34.2	-15.6	2.9	21.2
TOTAL:	-76.6	-54.4	-36.0	-17.5	0.9	19.3

FOOTNOTES

1/ However, note that such a tax system may still be characterized by non-neutralities in other areas; for example, uniform tax treatment of investment does not imply tax neutrality with respect to individual choices among consumption commodities or between current consumption and saving or a neutral foreign trade policy. Moreover, because there are generally quite important non-tax distortions in the economies of most developing countries, including Colombia, a tax policy that is neutral toward investment will not necessarily result in overall neutrality throughout the economy.

2/ Colombian business income tax data are available by sector for nine sectors plus «Others». The data on the «Electrical» (utility) sector and the «Others» sector were suspect and were not used in the analysis. Thus, results are presented for the remaining eight sectors.

3/ The calculations assume «individual saver arbitrage» rather than the alternative assumption of «firm arbitrage»; definitions of these terms, as well as an explanation of the rationale for choosing individual saver arbitrage, are presented in the appendix.

4/ Note that all references to equalization of after-tax rates of return should be understood to refer to risk-adjusted returns.

5/ Unless indicated otherwise, subsequent references to «tax rates» in this chapter refer to marginal effective tax rates.

6/ As explained in the appendix, the marginal effective tax rate on new share issues is independent of whether dividends are paid out immediately or retained. Hereafter, all discussions of marginal effective tax rates on new share issues assume that dividends are paid out.

7/ Note that such a tax would raise revenue in present value terms, since the government would receive inframarginal returns on its «share» of the investment; this point is developed in detail in Chapter 9. Of course, a positive marginal effective tax rate would result if the individual wealth tax were maintained in conjunction with the Simplified Alternative Tax, as recommended in Chapter 9.

8/ This neutrality result obtains under the Simplified Alternative Tax only in the absence of preferential treatment for any type of investment. Preferential treatment of any type of investment implies a negative marginal effective tax rate on the income from that investment, which in turn gives rise to the severe allocational problems described above.

9/ As noted in Chapter 7, LIFO inventory accounting is not a perfect substitute for indexed FIFO if there are shifts in relative prices. This qualification is ignored here, since the methodology does not accommodate consideration of shifts in relative prices.

10/ See King and Fullerton (1984).

11/ To the extent this assumption implies that the marginal effective tax rate on capital gains is understated (overstated) by some number of percentage points, the marginal effective tax rate on the income from investments financed by retained earnings attributable to individuals will be understated (overstated) by a factor very roughly equal to the same number of percentage points.

12/ This assumption is probably conservative. Note that the effective net wealth tax rate of 0.535 percent is fairly small relative to the real before-tax rate of return, which is assumed to be fixed at 10 percent. Thus, if the effective tax rate on net wealth could be approximated as zero (or as the average rate on reported net wealth), the marginal effective tax rates in those cases where the saver is a household would be reduced (increased) by only about five percentage points. In addition, the level of net wealth taxation is sufficiently low that it is unlikely] that attempting to account for variations in effective net wealth tax rates across assets would have large effects on the marginal effective tax rate calculations presented below.

13/ See Hulten and Wycoff (1981).

14/ The most important general determinant of differences in economic depreciation across countries at very different levels of development is likely to be differences in relative costs of labor, capital, and other inputs. One could argue alternatively that depreciation is slower in Colombia because assets last longer or that it is faster because labor is less skilled and maintenance is less adequate. Strictly speaking, it would be appropriate to take account of differences in repair expenses as well as differences in asset lives.

15/ See Chapter 3 for a description of the conditions under which interest income received by individuals is eligible for inflation indexing.

16/ The 25 percent rate of inflation is a useful benchmark for two reasons. First, it is somewhat higher but roughly comparable to the current rate of inflation in Colombia; as noted in Chapter 7, the inflation rate in Colombia during the period 1983-86 varied from 16.6 percent to 22.5 percent. Second, the present values of the depreciation deductions for equipment and structures allowed for tax purposes — which were not changed in the 1986 reform — are roughly equal in present value terms to the deductions for real economic depreciation at a 25 percent inflation ratte. Specifically, the tax deductions for depreciation on equipment (structures) have a slightly higher (lower) real present value than would deductions for real economic depreciation. At somewhat higher inflation rates, tax depreciation would have a lower present value than would economic depreciation for both types of depreciable assets; this would imply higher marginal effective tax rates than those presented below. However, a rate of 25 percent seems like a reasonable upper bound for the expected Colombian inflation rate in light of recent experience.

17/ The stocks were adjusted for depreciation taken for book purposes, and the weights for corporations were assumed to be identical to those for all investment. An alternative to using differences in reported assets to calculate net investment weights would be to base the weights on the stock of each type of asset reported. If the year for which analysis was done was not typical, the use of capital stock figures would be preferable to the use of net investment flows as weights. (The weights calculated using net investment are equal to the capital stock weights in a steady state.) However, since the stock figures are much more likely to be distorted by the absence of inflation indexing than is the difference between the stocks over a single year, the net investment approach seems preferable in the Colombian context.

18/ Note that these results also apply to individuals in the zero tax rate bracket and to non-filers.

19/ ˙ The marginal effective tax rate calculations on the income paid to foreigners reflect only Colombian taxes on such income. The total tax burden on such income of course depends on the tax policies of the home country. See the discussion in Chapter 3.

20/ This result (and all similar neutrality results reported below) should of course be qualified by the fact that, as noted above, the marginal effective tax rate analysis in this Report ignores a number of relevant features of the tax structure in Colombia. For example, the marginal effective tax rates presented here do not capture the effects of the special preferences accorded to the coffee and cattle industries. The existence of these special preferences implies that the tax structure is not truly neutral with respect to the allocation of investment across industries even at an inflation rate of 25 percent. Moreover, it has been necessary to aggregate all structures and equipment into only two categories; by comparison, the best available evidence, as reported in the appendix of chapter 5, indicates that there is substantial variation in asset lives within these two aggregate categories. Of course, to the extent that the rate of economic depreciation of a particular asset differs from that assumed for the aggregate category, the calculations of marginal effective tax rates will be in error.

21/ The discussion in this chapter focuses on the effects of a reduction in inflation from the 25 percent rate. However, it should be noted in all cases that if inflation were to rise substantially above the 25 percent benchmark rate, marginal effective tax rates would also increase.

22/ Recall a) that the calculations of marginal effective tax rates are «ex ante» calculations, in the sense that they are the type that would be made in appraising a prospective investment and b) that the expected inflation rate is assumed to be constant over the life of the investment. Thus, the variation in marginal effective tax rates reflects only differences in the taxation of income from various types of investments at different expected steady state inflation rates; they take no account of unexpected changes in inflation after an investment in made. Thus, even if the inflation rate were 25 percent at the time of the investment, the calculated tax rates would not be the same as those actually experienced (so-called «ex post» rates) if the actual inflation rate were to vary over the life of the investment. Of course, such calculations could easily be performed for any specific time pattern of inflation rates.

23/ Thus, an interesting implication of the new view of the effects of dividend taxation is that capital gains taxes affect the marginal effective tax rate on investments financed from retained earnings while dividend taxes do not.

24/ Under the «old view» of the effects of dividend taxation, the existence of dividend taxes at the individual level would increase marginal effective tax rates. Thus, the tax rates under pre-1986 law would be higher than those listed in Table 4.5. The numerical values of such «old view» tax rates would depend on the assumptions made regarding the timing of the payment of dividends; they would lie between the values presented in Table 4.5 and those calculated for investments financed by new share issues purchased by individuals presented in Table 4.4.

25/ As noted above, personal income tax data indicate that the average marginal tax rate applied to individual interest income is 22.8 percent; the figures in Table 4.7 are based on this rate. For purposes of comparison, suppose that the average marginal tax rate on individual interest income were roughly 80 percent of the maximum statutory rate; this would yield average marginal rates of 39 percent prior to 1986 and 24 percent after the 1986 reform). In this case, the «total» marginal effective tax rates at a 25 percent inflation rate for a debt-financed investment when the source of funds is households would be -13.7 percent prior to 1986 and 29.4 percent after the 1986 reform.

26/ The same point can be made with respect to investments financed by new issues, as can be seen from a comparison of the marginal effective tax rates under old law for a 25 percent inflation rate in Tables 4.2 and 4.4.

27/ The marginal effective tax rates on equity-financed investments are not affected by the phasing-in of inflation indexing for business interest deductions.

28/ The treatment in this Report is specific to Colombian tax law. For a more general description of the marginal effective tax rate methodology, see King and Fullerton (1984). An additional source of information, especially on the treatment of inflation, is Fullerton (1987).

29/ In equilibrium, firms would reallocate capital from relatively high-taxed to relatively low-taxed types of investments until after-tax returns were equalized; this would imply higher (lower) gross returns for those types of investments with relatively high marginal effective tax rates.

30/ The alternative approach of assuming a fixed net return to some marginal saver has some appeal in the Colombian context; the obvious choice for the marginal saver would be a foreign investor, since it is reasonably safe to assume that Colombia can be characterized as a small open economy that is a «price-taker» in international capital markets. Moreover, since interest paid to foreigners is essentially untaxed under Colombian tax law, the assumption of fixed net returns to the saver on a debt instrument would imply fixed after-tax returns at the business level on all debt-financed investments. Unfortunately, this approach suffers from a severe drawback in the Colombian context. Specifically, marginal effective tax rates on debt-financed investments are commonly negative under pre-1986 law. As a result, the gross rate of return required to achieve a given after-tax return is commonly very small or negative. Since the gross rate of return is the denominator in the marginal effective tax rate calculation, the result is commonly tax rates that are extremely large or of the wrong sign; such results are very difficult to interpret. (This problem does not arise under the calculation approach used in this Report, since a constant gross rate of return to all investments is assumed.) Note that the problems caused by small or negative gross rates of return in the denominator of the marginal effective tax rate calculation could be eliminated by using the fixed after-tax return in the denominator. While the use of such «tax exclusive» marginal effective tax rates is logically beyond reproach, it would be somewhat unconventional and would result in relatively high tax rates that would be difficult to interpret. All things considered, it appears that the assumption of fixed gross returns is the most satisfactory of the available alternatives.

31/ It might appear that the assumptions of a fixed before-tax return and individual arbitrage resulting in the same after-tax return to the individual independent of the source of finance are inconsistent — or else that they imply that marginal effective tax rates cannot vary across sources of finance. As will be shown below, the assumption of individual arbitrage implies that the equation specifying the after-tax return to the saver is the same regardless of the source of finance. However, this expression is a function of the nominal interest rate, which is assumed to vary according to the source of finance. Thus, the numerical value for the after-tax return to the individual, as well as the marginal effective tax rate, vary across sources of finance.)

32/ This expression is obtained by integrating the after-tax return at each point in time — $(1-T) \, MRR \, \exp[-(d+D+P)]$ — from zero to infinity.

33/ This approach contrasts with King and Fullerton, who assume that inflationary earnings are paid out as dividends and subject to full taxation. At inflation rates typical of recent Colombian experience, the King-Fullerton approach results in extremely high tax rates on investments financed by new share issues if dividends are subject to individual taxation; these rates commonly exceed 100 percent. Moreover, under this approach, the marginal effective tax rate on new share issues increases dramatically with inflation even in a fully indexed tax system (where depreciation allowances, inventory valuations, capital gains, and interest income and expense are indexed for inflation). The assumption that firms pay out only real earnings as dividends seems to result in a more useful method of calculating the marginal effective tax rate on investments financed by retained earnings.

34/ See King (1977), Auerbach (1979), and Bradford (1981).

35/ Note that this reasoning is analogous to that presented in Chapter 8, where it is argued that an individual cash flow tax effectively exempts from tax the yield to capital income.

36/ The relevant tax rate would be a weighted average of the rates applicable to dividend and non-dividend distributions.

37/ See Gravelle (1985).

38/ See Gordon, Summers, and Hines (1986).

39/ See Bradford and Fullerton (1981).

40/ More accurately, one plus the nominal interest rate is assumed to equal the product of one plus the fixed real before-tax interest rate and one plus the inflation rate.

5

Appraisal of Colombian Taxation of Income from Business and Capital

Appraisal of Colombian Taxation of Income
from Business and Capital

This chapter offers an appraisal of specific provisions of the current Colombian system for taxing income from business and capital and suggests possible reforms of these provisions. The general thrust of the proposed reforms is discussed in Chapter 2.

Topics are discussed in the order in which they appear in the description of current law (Chapter 3).[1] Because familiarity with current law is assumed in this chapter, the reader may find it useful to consult Chapter 3 as this one is read.

I. Income Tax

A. Persons to whom income is taxed

1. Companies and their owners

a. Integration — in general

The 1986 reform had the objective of integrating the taxation of corporations (sociedades anónimas) and shareholders, as well as that of limited partnerships (sociedades limitadas) and their owners. It achieved this by taxing all company income (that of sociedades limitadas as well as that of sociedades anónimas) at a flat 30-percent rate and exempting distributions of after-tax company income from tax at the individual level. (For expositional convenience, the following discussion generally refers to corporations and shareholders, although the same rules also apply to limited partnerships and their owners. The treatment of limited partnerships is discussed in greater detail at (g) below.)

One of the principal defects of an unintegrated system that subjects income to tax at both the corporate and shareholder levels is the favoring of debt. Corporate debt enables the double corporate tax to be avoided, since interest is deductible. In troubled times, an excessive level of debt financing leads to financial disruption and, in some cases, to an increased risk of bankruptcy as firms have difficulty meeting interest payment obligations. This problem was one of the motivating factors for the 1986 reform:

> Tradicionalmente en el país se ha permitido la deducibilidad de intereses al paso que no se admite la deducibilidad de los dividendos, estribando en ello la incoherencia del sistema.

> Es obvio que el Estado ha venido subsidiando — en el caso de las sociedades anónimas — un 40% de los intereses en que incurren, al paso que con los dividendos es la propia sociedad la que tiene que atender el pago de los impuestos

> Como resultado de este fenómeno, en los últimos 20 años, la decisión que se tomó en el país — siempre que había que hacer aumentos de capital en las empresas — era hacerlos a través de endeudamiento.[2]

If the full amount of nominal interest is deductible because there is no inflation adjustment, the bias towards debt is further exacerbated. A key advantage of the 1986 reform is the establishment of tax neutrality vis-a-vis the form of corporate finance. It should be noted that corporate tax integration and inflation adjustment of interest do not create a **penalty** for debt finance, as has sometimes been claimed, but merely remove the substantial bias in **favor** of debt that existed before.

Integration is based on the premise that corporate income should be taxed like other forms of income earned, directly or indirectly, by individual investors. Accordingly, corporate income should not be taxed in the hands of the corporation; rather, each investor is appropriately taxed on the investor's share of the income of the corporation, whether distributed or not. The rationale for integration suggests that the appropriate rate to apply to corporate income is the investor's rate. The current Colombian method of integration is, of course, imprecise in this respect, since it imposes the flat 30-percent corporate tax rate on corporate income, regardless of the tax rate of the shareholder, and exempts dividends from tax at the shareholder level.

Despite this lack of theoretical precision, the current system has several important advantages, which make it an appropriate choice for Colombia. First, flowing retained corporate income through to the shareholder level is generally considered not to be administratively feasible. Thus, most actual integration schemes are limited to providing relief from double taxation of dividends. An approach to dividend relief such as a shareholder credit would involve much more paperwork than the existing Colombian system, since the credits would have to be claimed on individual returns, and the tax administration would have to verify that taxpayers were entitled to the credits claimed. This administrative cost is particularly significant because a shareholder credit system might call for some persons to file returns who, under the current rules, do not file.

Second, several factors suggest that the imprecision of current law is likely to be unimportant and that, on average, the current system may actually be more precise than a seemingly more exact method. This is the case because the validity of the shareholder credit approach depends on accurate reporting of the taxpayer's non-dividend income. It is likely that many Colombian shareholders with sufficient economic income to place them in the 30-percent bracket report taxable income that is far lower. (This shortfall between taxable and economic income can be due to deficiencies in the rules for measuring income, as well as to taxpayer fraud.) With respect to such shareholders, the current system of taxing all corporate income at a 30-percent rate is more accurate than a shareholder credit system would be. With respect to shareholders who report taxable income that places them at or near the 30-percent bracket, the current system results in no inaccuracy and is simpler than a shareholder credit system.

The current system does involve overtaxation of those shareholders who both are and should be in marginal rate brackets below 30 percent. This overtaxation either imposes an unfair burden on those persons or discourages them from corporate equity investments (or some combination of both). In light of the probable distribution of corporate share ownership in Colombia, however, such overtaxation should not be a serious problem, and its harm is outweighed by the benefits of the current method of integration, discussed above. Moreover, the relatively low corporate rate of 30 percent limits any inaccuracy resulting from the current method of integration, making such inaccuracy less problematic than it would be if the corporate rate were higher.

An alternative method of providing dividend relief, namely allowing a deduction for dividends paid at the corporate level, would require shareholders to report dividends as taxable income, thus raising concerns about administration and revenue loss even greater than those of the shareholder credit.

Some have raised the concern that the exemption of dividends at the individual level unduly benefits shareholders in the top tax bracket because it allows their other income to be taxed at marginal rates below 30 percent. This concern is misplaced. If dividends were included in income and a shareholder credit allowed, the shareholder's non-dividend income would still be taxed at the same rates as under current law. If the shareholder's non-dividend income were sufficient to place him or her in the 30-percent bracket, the dividends would be taxed at a 30-percent rate, and the resulting additional tax liability would be offset by the shareholder credit. Thus, the complaint that the system allows the wealthy to pay lower taxes than under a shareholder credit is unfounded.

b. The 7/3 rule

The mechanism for calculating the amount of dividend income that is exempt at the individual level (the «7/3 rule») has the effect of «stacking» preferred income last. [see McLure (1979)]. («Preferred income» is the difference between economic income and taxable income.) That is, dividends are in effect presumed to be paid first out of fully taxed corporate income. The 7/3 rule also has the effect of «washing out» preferences to the extent distributed. That is, to the extent that dividends exceed such fully taxed income, they are taxed at the shareholder level, thus negating the effect of any tax preferences that reduce the amount of corporate-level tax. This treatment of tax-preferred income has the effect of discouraging distribution of more than the amount of fully taxed corporate income. The rule is easy to administer, since it does not require the amount of tax-preferred income to be determined. Such a determination would be quite difficult, since it would require determining the corporation's economic income. The treatment of preferences under the 7/3 rule is in contrast to the flow-through of preference income that would occur under a completely integrated system, whereby corporate income, as reduced by preferences, would be taken into account by individual shareholders.

Tax-preferred income can arise not only from provisions consciously intended to reduce the corporate tax burden, but also from deficiencies in the rules for measuring taxable income (which may be due to administrative constraints) or from tax evasion at the corporate level. The treatment of tax preferred income under the 7/3 rule can be justified as a means of subjecting to individual income tax (albeit often on a deferred basis) income that has escaped tax at the corporate level. For these reasons, the 7/3 rule seems to be an appropriate manner of treating tax-preferred corporate income.

c. Financial accounting limitation

The financial accounting limitation on the amount of income that can be distributed as dividends that are exempt from tax at the shareholder level limits the exemption to the financial accounting income of the corporation. The justification for this limitation is not clear. Although the provision often applies in the case of corporations that pay tax on the basis of presumptive income, it cannot be defended as a means of disfavoring such taxpayers. The reason for this is that the rule does not apply solely to such taxpayers, but applies to any taxpayer whose financial accounting income happens to fall below its taxable income.[3/] Moreover, in the case of presumptive income taxpayers, the rule only has an adverse effect to the extent that financial accounting income is **less** than presumptive income. A concern for noncompliance might suggest less favorable treatment for taxpayers whose financial accounting income **exceeded** their presumptive income, but not the reverse.

Another possible rationale for the limitation is that, in its absence, individuals could in effect take credit for corporate payment of tax based on presumptive income in cases where the actual income of the corporation (as measured for financial accounting purposes) is less than its presumptive income. For example, if the corporation's financial accounting income and ordinarily determined taxable income are both $1,000,000, and its presumptive income is $10,000,000, then a payment of corporate tax of $3,000,000 would (in the absence of the financial accounting limitation) give the corporation the right to distribute tax-free dividends of $7,000,000. This situation gives rise to two potential concerns. First, the tax system would appear to be encouraging the distribution of corporate capital, which might not be good for the economy. Second, to the extent that presumptive income exceeds the corporation's real economic income, it might be considered inappropriate to give the shareholders credit for this tax. For example, such a credit could allow the distribution of pre-1986 accumulated income on a tax-free basis.

Neither concern is sufficient to justify the financial accounting limitation. To the extent that presumptive income exceeds the corporation's accurately reported economic income, the corporation is actually penalized by having to pay tax based on presumptive income. Allowing the shareholders to take credit for this tax via the exemption of dividends merely mitigates the penalty.

The concern about distribution of corporate capital is essentially a regulatory one, whereby the tax system is used to make corporations behave in a certain manner. The complexity involved in such a use of the tax system burdens tax administration and compliance. Only if excessive corporate distributions are considered to present quite a serious problem would it be advisable to use the tax system to police corporations in this respect. Any such policing would necessarily be somewhat arbitrary and imprecise, given that the calculation of financial accounting income is subject to manipulation and at best will in many cases not constitute a very good measure of the corporation's economic income, which is presumably the relevant criterion. Moreover, the impact of this rule can be expected to be quite uneven. It would be especially burdensome on companies with low ratios of accounting profits to either of the two bases for determining presumptive income — net wealth or gross receipts.

On balance, in the absence of a pressing need to discourage corporate distributions, it seems advisable to repeal the financial accounting limitation on the amount of corporate income that can be distributed tax free.

d. Treatment of premiums

Similar considerations suggest repeal of the rule taxing premiums on share issues as income at the corporate level in the event that the premium is distributed to shareholders. Such premiums are not income of the corporation in an economic sense; they merely constitute contributions to capital and do not become income if that capital is distributed. The only justification for taxing premiums is a desire to discourage such distributions. For the reasons discussed above in relation to the financial accounting limitation, it does not seem appropriate, in the absence of a pressing regulatory need, to use the tax system for this purpose.

e. Distribution of inflationary profits

The 7/3 rule for integration of the corporate and individual income taxes has the effect of taxing at the individual level distributed inflationary profits of the corporation. For example, suppose a corporation receives $30,000,000 of interest income, $25,000,000 of which consists of monetary correction. After full phase-in of the inflation adjustment relating to interest, only $5,000,000 will be taxed at the corporate level, giving rise to a tax liability of $1,500,000. If the corporation distributes the entire after-tax nominal profit of $28,500,000, only $3,500,000 will be exempt under the 7/3 rule, and the remainder will be taxable to the shareholders even though it represents a return of capital, rather than real income.

One possible response to this situation would be to adjust the 7/3 rule for inflation. Thus, the inflationary component of corporate taxable income, which is not taxed at the corporate level in an inflation-adjusted system, could be passed through tax-free to the shareholders. The mechanism for doing this would be to identify the net inflation adjustment made in calculating corporate income for the taxable year, and to add this amount to the result of the computation under the 7/3 rule.

The problem with this approach is that it is uneven. All distributions in excess of real taxable profits should be treated the same, regardless of whether they happen to correspond to inflationary profits. The treatment of distributions of inflationary profits should therefore depend on the general rule for nonliquidating distributions in excess of current taxable profits. Such distributions should be taxable to the extent that they are made out of tax-preferred real income, or real income that has not yet been subject to tax, or accumulated pre-1986 income; achievement of this effect is the purpose of the 7/3 rule. In principle, distributions made after exhaustion of these amounts could be treated as a nontaxable return of capital. However, this would be difficult to do, because it would require identifying the amount of pre-1986 accumulated profits, as well as the amount of post-1985 preference income. Accordingly, the most workable rule, which is the rule specified by current law, is that all non-liquidating distributions in excess of the amount specified by the 7/3 rule are taxable. This rule has the effect of allowing inflation adjustment only so long as amounts represented by such adjustments are retained by the corporation. This treatment is similar to the treatment of preference income, discussed above.

Any overtaxation of dividends resulting from characterization of returns of capital as taxable dividends will be corrected at the time of liquidation of the corporation.[4] To the extent that previous distributions of capital have been treated as taxable dividends, the shareholder's basis relating to such capital will not have been exhausted.[5] Accordingly, this basis would be available to offset the taxable portion of the liquidating distribution.[6] This conclusion depends on the assumption that the entire amount of the shareholder's basis could be deducted at the time of the liquidating distribution. Current law should be clarified, if necessary, to allow such a deduction. The simplest approach would be to treat the net taxable amount of the liquidating distribution (i.e. the taxable portion of the distribution minus the shareholder's basis) as capital gain or loss. It would be appropriate to do this, however, only if net capital gain is taxed as ordinary income, as is recommended below.[7] (The gain component of a liquidating distribution should be taxed as capital gain (instead of as ordinary income) so that the gain would be counted as capital gain in determining the amount of capital losses that could be deducted.)

f. Definition of dividend

Some consideration should be given to the definition of what is a dividend. Article 22 of Law 75 of 1986 states that distributions of financial accounting profits in excess of amounts determined under the 7/3 rule constitute taxable dividends. This suggests that a dividend is defined as any distribution to the extent of accumulated financial profits. Presumably, any distributions in excess of financial profits are treated as a return of capital and require the shareholder's basis to be reduced. This approach may be workable, although its reliance on financial reporting makes it depend on the vagaries of financial accounting. Moreover, the approach is complex, as it requires taxpayers to keep account of accumulated financial profits.

An alternative would be to specify that any distribution that does not constitute (1) a liquidating distribution, or (2) a qualifying redemption is taxable as a dividend, regardless of the corporation's accumulated profits. This approach would, of course, require liquidating distributions and qualifying redemptions to be defined with some specificity. At present, no recommendation is made on this point.

g. Treatment of limited partnerships

Under the 1986 reform, all companies are taxed in the same manner, regardless of whether they are corporations or limited partnerships, while the income of unincorporated partnerships or joint ventures is flowed through to the owners. This tax treatment of limited partnerships can be criticized on the basis that it can lead to overtaxation; the issues raised are essentially the same as for corporations, discussed above, and for the same reasons the treatment adopted in 1986 seems appropriate. This is particularly so in light of the important role that limited partnerships play in Colombia in the organization of large businesses and in the ownership of wealth by wealthy individuals. In the presumably rare case of limited partnerships with small numbers of partners who are individually in brackets below 30 percent, it is possible that the new rules will cause the business to be placed in the names of the individual partners, thereby sidestepping the entity-level tax. There should be nothing particularly disturbing about such a development, although it may lead to some revenue loss.

In the case of companies with a small number of owners, it would be possible to allow an option whereby the income of the company is flowed through to its owners, with no tax at the company level. The advantage of such treatment is that the income of the company will be taxed at the marginal rate of its owners, which is presumably the appropriate tax rate. However, such flow-through treatment also suffers from several disadvantages, which suggest that it is probably not appropriate for Colombia at this time. Flow-through treatment involves a greater amount of complexity than the current system. It raises the difficult conceptual issue of how to allocate company income to owners with varying ownership interests. Moreover, it can contribute to tax avoidance if the marginal rate of the company's owners does not reflect the true economic income of the owners, or if the owners simply fail to report their share of the company's income. On balance, a flow-through option for small companies does not appear desirable.

2. Trusts and Estates

Under the Haig-Simons concept of income, the income of trusts would be taxed to the beneficial owners of the income, or, in cases where the grantor has not really given up control over the trust, to the grantor. Achievement of this result would, however, be quite complicated. The correct result generally cannot be achieved by merely allocating trust income for tax purposes to the persons who receive it. For example, suppose that **A** is entitled for life to the income of a $1,000,000 trust that earns nominal interest income of 25 percent annually. Suppose that upon **A**'s death **B** will receive the corpus (i.e. $1,000,000). If the income of the trust were taxed to **A**, **A** would have $50,000 of taxable income every year until **A**'s death. Assume that the inflation rate is 20 percent, so 80 percent of interest income is excluded from taxable income; thus, taxable income is 5 percent of the trust corpus annually. At the time of **A**'s death, **B** would receive the corpus. At no point during the existence of the trust would **B** be taxed on any income of the trust, a result that may seem to make sense because **B** receives none of the trust's income. However a simple analysis shows that **B** does have substantial economic income during the term of the trust. Suppose that **A**'s life expectancy is 5 years. At a 25-percent interest rate, the present value of **B**'s interest in the trust is $327,680. Each year, the value of this interest increases by 5 percent in real terms. Thus, in the first year, **B**'s economic income is $16,384. By the same token, **A**'s interest is worth $672,320 at the inception of the trust (i.e., $1,000,000 minus $327,650), and each year this interest **decreases** in value, being worth zero by the end of the trust term. The portion of the cash payments that **A** receives which equals the decline in value of **A**'s interest is a return of capital, not income.

In this simple situation, it would be possible to measure **A**'s and **B**'s economic income reasonably closely for tax purposes, although this would involve some complexity. In the case of trusts involving contingencies or discretionary powers in the trustee, however, it would be impossible to accurately allocate trust income among the beneficiaries.

Under current law, the income of commercial trust contracts (contratos de fiducia mercantil) is taxed directly to the designated beneficiary or, in some cases, to the grantor. The income of other types of trusts, as well as that of estates, is currently taxed to the trust or estate under the rate schedule applicable to individuals; none of the income is allocated to the beneficiaries. This treatment gives an opportunity for substantial tax avoidance by placing property into one or more trusts, thereby benefiting from a much lower rate of taxation than if the grantor or the beneficiaries were taxed on the income. Similarly, the income of estates may be taxed at a lower rate than would be appropriate for the beneficiaries. For much the same reasons raised in the above discussion of integration, the appropriate response to this problem in Colombia appears to be to tax all trust and estate income, whether distributed or not, at a flat rate equal to the top marginal tax rate for individuals.

Taxation at the top marginal rate is administratively simpler than trying to attribute trust income to the grantor or to beneficiaries. Moreover, this approach will often achieve a more appropriate result than flowing the trust or estate income through to the beneficiaries, both because the declared taxable income of the beneficiary may not reflect the marginal rate bracket that would apply if economic income were used instead, and because income of trusts may often be more appropriately taxed at the rate of the person who established the trust (who will often be in a high bracket), rather than at the rates of the beneficiaries. It is recognized that applying a flat rate equal to the top marginal rate will sometimes be inaccurate, and may be perceived as harsh, but, in light of the above-discussed factors, it is the best available rule. As in the case of corporate income, the inaccuracy would be mitigated by the low top marginal rate and by the fact that many beneficiaries and grantors are (or should be) in the top tax bracket.

3. Husband, wife, and children

In a system with a progressive rate structure, it is necessary to determine what tax rate to apply to an individual's income. If the individual is a member of a family, the amount of income received by the individual alone may not be a good measure of that individual's economic well-being. Income received by other family members may in fact be available for consumption by that individual. (For example, a child with low income may benefit from the high income of his or her parents.) Moreover, a family each of the members of which receives the same amount of income is likely to enjoy a higher standard of living than an unmarried individual with the same per capita income. Much the same reasoning applies to the taxation of net wealth. The separate taxation of the unearned income of minor children (where the parents have renounced the usufruct of such income) can lead to significant tax avoidance by means of having capital income be received in the name of the child rather than by a parent in the top tax bracket. (The maximum amount of tax that can be saved annually in this manner is about $500,000 per child.[8/]) Accordingly, the marginal tax rate to be applied to income (or wealth) of family members should in principle be determined with respect to the entire income (or wealth) of the family.

Application of this norm may, however, lead to practical problems. For example, family members may not, in fact, have access to the income of other members of the family, but verifying this is difficult. Moreoever, some family members may file returns under current law and others may not. A family filing unit would increase the number of persons who must report their income on a tax return. In addition, it may be appropriate to impose lower rates on the earned income of secondary workers within the family unit, so as not to discourage employment.

Given the Colombian practice of separate tax treatment of family members, which is consistent with separate ownership of wealth under civil law, it may be premature to recommend aggregation of income of the family unit, even if such aggregation is confined to unearned income. However, the possibility of such aggregation should be kept in mind for the future. At the present time, it does seem appropriate to initiate a system whereby family wealth is aggregated for purposes of the net wealth tax. This proposal is discussed below in Chapter 6.

B. Tax Accounting

1. Methods of accounting

a. Future payments

(i) General statement of problem

Current law allows a business expense to be deducted by an accrual-method taxpayer in the taxable year in which the obligation to pay the expense comes into being, even though the expense may not be paid until some time in the future. In the case of expenses that remain unpaid as of the close of the taxable year, allowance of a current deduction for the undiscounted amount of the obligation understates the taxpayer's economic income. Economic income should reflect the change in a taxpayer's net worth, and a taxpayer who incurs a current obligation to pay a specified amount in the future suffers a decrease in net worth equal to only the present value of this amount.

Where future expenses are involved, the present value of the expense will always be less than the undiscounted amount. Accordingly, allowing a current deduction for this undiscounted amount, as under current law, results in an understatement of income for tax purposes. Allowance of an undiscounted deduction can even allow the taxpayer to recoup through tax savings an amount that exceeds the present value of the taxpayer's obligation. For example, if the after-tax interest rate is 25 percent, an obligation to pay $1,000,000 in six years has a present value of $262,000. If a taxpayer incurs such an obligation, for example as part of the settlement of a law suit, and is allowed to currently deduct the undiscounted obligation of $1,000,000, the tax saving resulting from the deduction will be $300,000, assuming a 30-percent tax rate. As a result, the taxpayer actually makes money when it is sued and agrees to pay damages, provided that the payment is deferred far enough into the future (or the interest rate is high enough) and a current deduction is allowed for the undiscounted amount of the obligation. Although this example is admittedly extreme, (and similar cases may occur rarely in Colombia), it should be noted that the problem exists (though to a lesser degree) in all cases where the undiscounted amount of a future obligation is deductible, not just in those cases where the tax saving from the deduction exceeds the actual burden of the obligation. Thus, a problem arises under current law in all cases in which an obligation to make a future payment accrues; such an obligation could represent payment for services rendered or goods already delivered (or, in the case of the law suit, extinguishment of a claim), or it could represent compensation for goods to be delivered or services to be performed in the future. In any of these cases, allowance of a current deduction prior to payment overstates the present value of the payment.

(ii) Methods of accounting for delayed payment

Explicit accounting for a delayed payment requires as an initial matter that the context of the transaction be identified. Where the transaction involves a payment for goods or services that have already been provided, it involves an interest-free loan from the seller to the taxpayer. In this case, the most accurate treatment of the transaction is to allow the taxpayer to deduct the present value of the payment, require the seller to include this amount in income, and similarly allow the taxpayer to deduct interest as it accrues and tax the seller on this interest.

Such explicit treatment of the transaction is complicated. An alternative is to provide matched treatment for the payee of the expense (i.e., require the payee to include in income the amount deducted by the payor). Premature accrual of a deduction has no net effect on the tax base if there is a corresponding inclusion in income by a taxpayer in the same tax bracket as the payor. Such matching treatment undertaxes the payor and overtaxes the payee, but any resulting inequity can be eliminated by bargaining between the parties. Under current Colombian law, the rule for accruing income matches the accrual of a deduction, so that an accrual-method payee will be required to include the amount that is deducted at the same time that the deduction is taken. This matching requirement means that premature accruals probably pose no problem in the vast majority of cases, provided that the payee complies with the income inclusion requirement. However, payees other than taxable Colombian businesses (individuals, tax-exempt entities, and foreign persons) do not provide matching. The accrual of deductions for future payments to such persons is likely to pose only a minimal problem. Nevertheless, it is appropriate to provide a rule for such transactions so that they are not given preferential treatment.

There are a couple of possible ways of dealing with accrued liabilities to make payments to such persons. One possibility is to delay the deduction for any accrued but unpaid expense payable to a person other than an accrual-method Colombian company until the expense is actually paid.[9] In present value terms, deferral of the deduction until the time of payment is equivalent to allowance of a current deduction for the present value of the payment. Because it is administratively simpler than allowing a deduction for the present value of the obligation, deferral of the deduction is the recommended course.[10] In the case of relatively small payments to persons other than accrual-method Colombian businesses, the identity of the payee may not be subject to effective audit, so that in practice this rule is likely to be important only with respect to significant international transactions.

Because of its present-value equivalence to allowing a deduction only for the present value of an obligation, deferral until the time of payment in effect denies a deduction for the interest that is implicitly paid by the taxpayer to the provider of the goods or services being purchased. The amount of this implicit interest is the difference between the amount of the future payment and its present value. Accurate implementation of the Haig-Simons concept of income would call for the payee to be taxed on the present value of the payment; and for such implicit interest to be deductible by the payor and includable in income by the payee as it accrues. However, the payee is not currently taxed on the payment or the interest income and it would be difficult or impossible to provide for such taxation, particularly in light of the fact that the payee may not even be identified. Denying a deduction for this implicit interest to the payor provides for taxation of this interest income to the payor as a substitute for taxing the payee.

Thus, for example, assume that the interest rate is 25 percent; the inflation rate is 20 percent; there is full inflation adjustment for interest; and both the payor and the payee are in the 30-percent tax bracket. If the payor incurs an obligation to pay 123.5 one year from now, in return for currently provided goods or services worth 100, it can set aside 70, which will amount to 86.45 in one year (including interest at the after-tax rate of 23.5 percent). Upon payment of the 123.5, the payor receives a tax saving of 37.05, so that the payor's out-of-pocket cost is 86.45. Because all that the payor needed to satisfy its obligation was a fund of 70, it is treated the same as if it had made a payment of 100 one year earlier. As far as the payee is concerned, when it receives the payment of 123.5, it has 86.45 left, the same as if it had been paid 100 one year earlier, and had invested the after-tax proceeds of 70 at an after-tax rate of 23.5 percent.

The above discussion applies only to obligations in the nature of currently deductible business expenses. In the case of other types of obligations, for example, obligations that give rise to a capital expense, delay of the deduction will not generally reach the result of substitute taxation of the interest income to the payor. In such cases, the remedy must be to tax the payee. For example, if **A** sells real property to **B**, but **B** delays payment, then **A** should be currently taxed on the sales price, and should be taxed on interest as it accrues. Presumably, this is the result under current law, at least as far as the sales price is concerned. Taxation of the interest income is desirable but may not be as critical, provided that the purchaser is not allowed to take an interest deduction in advance of the time that the seller is taxed.

b. Advance payments

Where goods or services are paid for in advance of their delivery, explicit accounting for the transaction would treat it as involving an interest-free loan from the purchaser to the seller or service provider. For example, suppose a taxpayer pays $1,000,000 for goods to be delivered in one year that are anticipated to be worth $1,250,000 at the time of delivery (at the price level anticipated to prevail at that time). This is equivalent to an arrangement whereby the taxpayer lends $1,000,000 to the seller, the seller pays $250,000 in interest to the taxpayer and repays the $1,000,000 of principal, and the taxpayer then pays $1,250,000 to the seller for the goods. Explicit accounting for the loan would require the taxpayer to include the $250,000 interest in income, and to deduct the $1,250,000 payment, thus leading to a net deduction of $1,000,000 at the time of delivery. The seller would obtain a $250,000 interest deduction, but would include $1,250,000 in income, for a net inclusion of $1,000,000.

In the absence of such explicit accounting, equivalent results can often be reached by the technique of (1) delaying the deduction or (2) allowing the deduction at the time of payment, but requiring the seller to include the payment in income. Such alternative approaches have the advantage of being simpler than explicit accounting for the interest free loan. However, their drawback is that they will generally be less accurate, particularly in an inflation-adjusted system, and will not work under certain circumstances (such as where the payment is for a capital good rather than a currently deductible item).

The same general effect as under interest-free loan accounting can be reached in the case of a one-year advance payment by delaying the deduction of the $1,000,000 payment until the time of performance (i.e. the time when the goods or services are provided).[11/] The effect of delaying the deduction until the time of performance is to indirectly tax the taxpayer on imputed interest income. (The taxpayer is indirectly taxed on imputed interest income because the amount of the deduction allowed is equal to the amount of the deduction that would have been allowed in the absence of an advance payment, less the imputed interest income received by the taxpayer.) The two approaches are not exactly equivalent in the case of a transaction that spans a longer period of time, since, under the approach of delaying the deduction, taxation of the imputed interest income would in effect be deferred until the time of performance. By the same token, the seller's interest deduction would be deferred.

An alternative to delaying the deduction until the time of performance would be to provide matched treatment for the payor and payee. Thus, the deduction could be allowed at the time of payment, but the seller or service provider could be required to include the payment in income at the time of payment. Under current law, in the case of an accrual-method seller, such inclusion is required if the seller submits a bill to the purchaser. Submission of a bill is also required in order for an accrual-method purchaser to take a deduction for the payment. Accordingly, there appears to be no problem in the case of an accrual method payor, since the payor can only deduct the payment if there is a bill, which condition also requires the payee to include the amount. However, a cash-method payor may be able to take a deduction in the absence of a bill. Accordingly, in the case of a cash-method payor who makes a payment to an accrual-method payee, matching could be provided in one of two ways. Under one approach, no deduction would be allowed until the issuance of a bill by the payee. Alternatively, it could be specified that accrual-method taxpayers would have to include advance payments in income when received.

Where a taxpayer makes a payment to a foreign person, a deduction relating to a payment made should be deferred until the time of «performance» to which the payment relates. In general, «performance» means the performance by the payee of whatever it is that the payee is being paid for. In most cases, the performance for which the taxpayer is paying consists of the provision of property or services to the taxpayer, and the time of performance is the time that the services or property are provided. In the case of property rented to the taxpayer, the property is considered as provided to the taxpayer as the taxpayer uses the property.

2. 70-percent rule for intangibles

The special rule that the cost of certain intangibles is presumed to be 70 percent of the selling price has no justification in general principles of tax accounting and should be repealed. In most cases, the taxpayer will have no basis in intangible items, since the costs of developing the intangible will either have been amortized or, more likely, will simply have been deducted as business expenses at the time incurred.

3. Deduction of losses

a. Reduction of earned income by losses

The rule prohibiting taxpayers from deducting losses against earned income is a crucial one. Although the rule may appear inconsistent with the Haig-Simons concept of income, which would allow a deduction for any business or investment loss, it is justified because in many cases losses reported for tax purposes do not reflect real economic losses. The discrepancy between economic and taxable income may be due to deficiencies in the rules for measuring taxable income, as well as to tax evasion. Prohibiting the deduction of losses against earned income is a crude response to this problem, since it does not preclude the deduction of fictitious losses against unearned income. Moreover, it can be harsh, since it precludes the deduction even where there is a real economic loss. On the other hand, the rule has the advantage of administrative simplicity. Given the extent of both defects in the tax law and non-compliance with the Colombian tax system, the benefits of the rule far outweigh its drawbacks. Any ambiguities or exceptions to application of this rule should be removed.

The current individual income tax return (Formulario Oficial No. 1 (1986), line 16) permits taxpayers to subtract items of exempt income from earned income. It is possible that some taxpayers are fraudently using this line to effectively reduce the items of taxable earned income included in line 9. In order to make it less likely that taxpayers are actually reducing taxable earned income, taxable earned income and exempt earned income should be stated on two separate lines, instead of being combined on line 9, so that the amount of taxable earned income appears on the form, thereby precluding even an accidental reduction of this item.

The only items that should be deductible from earned income (other than the qualifying portion of home mortgage interest) are the expenses that are directly related to earning such income that is subject to tax. To help assure this result, the income tax return should be modified so that expenses related to taxable earned income are stated separately from expenses related to other income.

The segregation of items related to taxable earned income will help to enforce the rule against reducing earned income by losses and is also required for purposes of the proposed reform dealing with the relation between earned income and presumptive income (see III (B)(1) below).

b. Agricultural losses

The special rule allowing a deduction for investments in certain agricultural enterprises should be repealed, as argued in Section F3 below; if, however, this deduction is maintained, it should be provided that such a deduction may be used to offset only agricultural income. There is no reason to treat this deduction more favorably than other deductions that give rise to agricultural losses.

c. Net Operating Losses

Deductions for net operating losses of companies that are carried over to future years should be increased by a reasonable rate of interest on a compound basis. In effect, the deferred tax saving represented by the carried over loss would be treated as a debt owed by the government to the taxpayer. For example, at a corporate tax rate of 30, a loss of $1,000,000 would represent a government debt of $300,000. Accrued interest on this debt should be treated as interest paid by the government to the taxpayer. For example, at an interest rate of 25 percent, a loss of $1,000,000 would be adjusted upwards to $1,250,000 in the year following the loss, thereby causing the debt of $300,000 to increase to $375,000. The taxpayer should be treated as having received interest of $75,000 representing a rate of 25 percent on its debt. The portion of such interest that would be taxable under the general inflation-adjustment rules should be included in the taxpayer's income for each year in which an adjustment to a net operating loss is made. For example, if under the general inflation-adjustment rules, 80 percent of nominal interest received is excluded from tax, then only $15,000 of nominal interest received would be taxable. Although this rule would include in taxable income the accrued interest on net operating losses before those losses are actually used to reduce tax, no tax would ever be due by reason of this rule, because a portion of the net operating loss could be used to offset the interest income. Thus, in the above example, the $15,000 of interest income would be offset by a portion of the loss, so that the net amount of the loss to be carried over to the subsequent year would be $1,250,000 less $15,000 or $1,235,000. This amount would again be adjusted upward, in like manner, to the extent not used to offset taxable income, until the carryover is exhausted.

The five-year carryover limitation should be repealed, unless administrative considerations preclude it. There is no economic reason why a loss should not be available to offset future income, no matter how much time has elapsed. Indeed, from an administrative point of view, repeal of the five-year limitation may constitute a simplification, since taxpayers and the government will no longer have to keep track of when the loss was incurred. It is assumed that if a loss is carried to a later year, the amount of the loss may be redetermined despite the running of the statute of limitations for the year in which the loss arose. Nevertheless, to prevent the facts relating to the year of the loss from becoming stale, losses to be carried to future years should be audited on a timely basis.

4. Accounting for costs incurred in foreign currency

Current law provides that in some cases the exchange loss on debts incurred in foreign currency is treated as part of the cost of goods acquired with the proceeds of the foreign currency loan. Although the result reached by this rule is generally appropriate (see discussion in Section C(5) below), there is no justification for treating foreign currency debt differently from debt incurred in pesos, except that accrued foreign exchange loss should be treated as additional interest paid for the year. In the case of debt (whether denominated in foreign currency or pesos) that is incurred to acquire property, uniform rules should apply in determining the extent to which the interest expense is treated as part of the cost of the property in question. A proposal for such uniform rules is discussed below at section C(5).

C. Interest Income and Expense

1. Original issue discount

In general terms, a debt obligation has original issue discount (OID) if the amount paid at redemption exceeds the amount lent. OID represents interest that is payable on a deferred basis. The current treatment of obligations with OID (títulos con descuento) is unduly favorable, in that a cash-method holder of the obligation need not include the interest in income until it is received, but an accrual-method issuer may currently deduct the interest as it accrues. This treatment constitutes a substantial subsidy for this type of obligation, although the extent of the subsidy is mitigated by the collection of a withholding tax at the time of issuance. The inconsistent treatment of borrower and lender can certainly be taken advantage of by economically related persons. For example, an accrual-method sociedad limitada (limited partnership) could borrow money from a cash method partner, issuing its OID obligation to the partner. The problem is not, however, peculiar to related persons. Since the loan can be issued at arm's-length rates, unrelated persons can take advantage of the current rules just as well. There are apparently no limitations on deducting interest incurred to finance the purchase of an OID obligation (other than the prohibition on deducting it against earned income), so that the holder need not even put up any money to participate in this tax shelter opportunity. As noted, the current withholding rules do limit the attractiveness of this abuse, by collecting some tax up front, but this is a crude response to this problem, since the withholding rate is independent of the rate of interest offered on the obligation and the marginal tax rates of the holder and issuer.

At the least, the issuer and holder should account for the interest consistently. The simplest way of doing so would be to put both on the cash method for purposes of reporting OID. However, such an approach would distort the income of both the holder and the issuer. It would undertax the holder, by delaying the taxation of interest income until the time of redemption, and would overtax the issuer by delaying the interest deduction. There is no reason to believe that the over- and under-taxation will balance out, since the holder and issuer may be in different tax brackets. For example, the issuer may be a government agency, as is frequently the case for OID obligations in Colombia. Given that issuers already accrue interest under current law, cash method treatment would be a regression from accuracy, at least as far as issuers are concerned. A more appropriate approach would be to require both holders and issuers to account for the interest as it accrues.

In addition, the current method of calculating accrued interest, which accrues the interest on a straight-line basis, should be modified to reflect the economic accrual of interest. The difference between straight-line and economic accrual can be illustrated by the following example. Suppose that the nominal interest rate is 25 percent, so that an obligation paying $1,000,000 at maturity in five years is issued for $327,680. Under straight-line accrual, $134,464 of interest accrues each year, for a total of $672,320 over the five-year period. Under economic accrual, the interest rate of 25 percent is applied to the outstanding balance of principal and interest each year. This method conforms more closely to the economic reality of the transaction. As a matter of economic substance, an OID obligation is an implicit contract whereby the lender agrees to relend interest to the borrower, and the borrower agrees to pay interest on this relent interest at a specified rate throughout the term of the instrument. Thus, in this example, each year's interest is in effect re-lent to the borrower, and interest on that amount is paid for subsequent years at the same 25-percent rate. The amount of interest determined under this method is shown in Table 5-1.

Interest under both methods adds up to $672,320, which is the difference between the issue price and the redemption price, but the timing differs. Because interest under the economic accrual method is calculated according to the outstanding cumulative balance of principal and interest, it grows over time, starting out lower than under the straight-line method and ending up at a higher amount per year. (In the above example, the interest is lower for the first three years and higher for the last two years.) Thus, it can be seen from the table that the straight-line method accelerates interest into the beginning of the period, thereby overstating the income of the holder and understating the income of the issuer. This acceleration will occur at any rate of interest and any term of maturity for an obligation that extends beyond the taxable year, although the effect will be more pronounced at higher interest rates and longer periods until maturity. Under the straight-line method the overstatement of the holder's income will always exactly compensate for the understatement of the issuer's income; however, the use of straight-line accrual will lead to a loss of tax revenue if the holder is in a lower tax bracket than the issuer. Moreover, the use of the economic accrual method will give a more accurate measure of both the holder's and the issuer's net wealth, which is desirable for purposes of the net wealth tax. The economic accrual method conforms exactly to Haig-Simons income if interest rates and the credit worthiness of the borrower do not change. However, if the fair market value of the obligation changes as a result of these factors, the economic accrual method will not reflect this change in value and accordingly will mismeasure the holder's and the issuer's income, as compared with the Haig-Simons benchmark. Except in the case of publicly traded obligations, however, there is no administratively feasible method that would fully reflect Haig-Simons income.

Calculation of economic accrual would be more complicated than straight-line accrual, but it should be a manageable complexity in that it does not involve keeping additional records, but merely involves applying a more sophisticated calculation on the basis of facts already at the taxpayer's disposal. The only facts needed to perform the calculation are the issue price, the redemption price, the maturity date, and the amounts and dates of any payments to be made prior to maturity. Presumably, the type of person who issues OID obligations is capable of performing this calculation (or having it performed) without hardship. The holders of the obligations would not have to perform any calculation, since they could rely on the information supplied by the issuer. The principal problem would be to get the information to the individual holders of the obligations.

To the extent that the holder's tax is simply paid through withholding, this need not be problematic. The current system of withholding, whereby tax is withheld at the time of issuance, should be changed in order to conform the timing of withholding to the timing of interest income. Thus, under the above proposal, tax should be withheld on interest as it accrues, at the withholding rate generally applicable to interest income. At the time of maturity, the taxpayer would receive the face amount of the obligation, less amounts that had been withheld.

In the case of some debt instruments, it will not be possible to calculate the economic accrual of interest because either the term of the instrument or the amount of principal or interest payments to be made are subject to contingency. In such a case, interest could be calculated by applying an imputed interest rate to the issue price. The imputed rate should be representative of rates on commercial debt instruments at the time of issuance, and should be a rate that is published by a government agency. At the time that contingencies are resolved, appropriate adjustments would be made to reflect any differences between the assumed and the actual amounts.

2. Publicly traded debt instruments

Under current law, debt instruments that are traded on the stock exchange are valued for purposes of the wealth tax according to their price during the last month of the year. This value could also be used to determine the amount and timing of income for income tax purposes. Under this approach, in the case of such an instrument, the amount of taxable income received by the holder would be the amount of interest received (including any interest that is due but unpaid, assuming that such interest in arrears would belong to the current holder rather than to a subsequent purchaser of the instrument) plus the increase in value of the instrument (or less any decline in value of the instrument). The issuer's deduction would be calculated in the same manner, and the issuer would report the amount of income to the holders and withhold tax on the income as so calculated.

The amount of income as determined above must be separated into interest and capital gain or loss. This separation is required because of the existence of separate rules related to interest (for example, capitalization requirements) and to capital gain (for example, the limitation on the deduction of capital losses). The amount of interest would be determined by applying a published rate of interest to the value of the debt instrument as of the close of the preceding year. The balance of the income related to the debt instrument would be treated as capital gain or loss.

The principal advantage of the market-based determination of interest is that it better reflects the economic income of the parties. With respect to both the borrower and the lender, the Haig-Simons concept of income calls for this change in wealth to be taken into account as it occurs. Just as with the accrual of original issue discount, the determining factor should be not the receipt of cash, but the occurrence of a readily determinable change in wealth. Such a market-based determination of interest income and deductions can be criticised on the basis that it involves taxing unrealized capital gains and losses resulting from interest rate fluctuations (and other causes) as ordinary income, and basing deductions on the same events. Moreover, applying such a market valuation rule only to one type of security might be considered inappropriate if competing securities were not similarly valued at market values (hereafter «marked to market»). Since publicly traded equity securities compete with untraded securities, this consideration presents a serious problem for proposals to mark such securities to market, if marking to market would involve a higher expected tax burden on the publicly traded securities. However, in the particular case of debt instruments, marking to market should neither encourage nor discourage the issuance of publicly traded instruments as compared with other securities. On an ex ante basis, the market-based rule should be expected to produce roughly the same timing for interest income and deductions as would be produced by the rules for non-publicly-traded debt instruments, since there is no systematic expectation (as of the time of issuance) that the security will go up or down in value during the time it is outstanding. Nevertheless, it is possible that the market would perceive marking to market as imposing a higher tax burden, even though this perception would be contrary to fact. The possible detriment of such market perception should be taken into account in deciding whether to adopt the rule.

If such a market-based determination of interest is adopted, it should be applied to all publicly traded debt instruments. In the case of obligations with original issue discount, this approach would actually be simpler than the general rule for original issue discount (particularly if contingent amounts are involved), since it requires no calculations or adjustments, just reference to published market values.

3. Below-market loans to shareholders or partners

To the extent that loans at below-market interest rates were in the past used as a means of paying disguised dividends, the new treatment of dividends removes this concern. (Because dividends are no longer taxable at the shareholder level, except when they exceed 70 percent of taxable company income, there is generally no longer any incentive to pay disguised dividends.) The remaining concern with such loans may be that the recipient of the loan will fail to pay tax on the income generated by investment of the loan proceeds, or will use the arrangement as a means of circumventing the disallowance of deductions for consumer interest. Given these concerns, the existing rule that imputes income on company loans to shareholders or partners and taxes this income at the company level is justifiable, if somewhat harsh. (The rule is harsh because there is apparently no deduction for imputed interest paid.) The harshness of the rule is mitigated, however, by the fact that the parties are always free to enter into a loan arrangement that calls for the payment of interest at market rates.

Given the inflation adjustment for interest, it may be appropriate to modify the below-market loan rules to provide for imputation of interest at the full market rate, the inflationary component of which would be excluded under the general inflation adjustment procedure.

4. Home mortgage interest

Under a comprehensive income tax, the imputed income from homeownership would be taxed and a deduction would be allowed for mortage interest paid. In systems where such imputed income is not taxed, the rationale for denying a deduction for home mortgage interest is that it is an indirect way of taxing the imputed income. Under current law, imputed income from homeownership may be taxed as part of presumptive income. However, because presumptive income is based on net wealth, there will never be a tax on the imputed income from the debt-financed portion of an owner-occupied home. Accordingly, it would be appropriate to deny any deduction for home mortgage interest.

Even if, for political reasons, the current allowance of a limited deduction for home mortgage interest cannot be repealed, the deduction with respect to mortgage interest on second homes should be eliminated. Currently, a family with only one home may deduct up to $1,000,000 of mortgage interest. However, a family with two homes that are owned separately by the husband and wife can deduct up to $2,000,000, provided that each spouse has sufficient income to absorb the deduction. This result is inequitable, in that a higher limit effectively applies for families that are wealthy enough to be able to own two homes. The problem can be dealt with by allowing a taxpayer to deduct mortgage interest only with respect to the taxpayer's principal residence.

5. Construction-period interest

If the expenses of constructing property are required to be capitalized on a comprehensive basis, a taxpayer who produces property for use in its business or for sale will have a basis in such property similar to the basis that it would have if such property had been purchased from another person. Comprehensive cost capitalization means that all costs of producing the property in question, including interest, would not be currently deductible but would instead be added to the basis of the property being constructed. Where the property is purchased from another, all the costs of producing the property will be included in the purchase price. A requirement to comprehensively capitalize costs therefore can be justified as a means of treating on an equal basis the taxpayer that constructs property and the taxpayer that purchases property.

A comprehensive capitalization requirement can also be justified in terms of the Haig-Simons concept of income, under which income would reflect the change in the taxpayer's net worth. Under a net worth approach, current deduction of the expenses of constructing or producing property not sold or used up during the accounting period should not be allowed, because these expenses give rise to an asset owned by the taxpayer that increases in value as expenses are incurred. Because the increase in the value of assets is not taxed during the production period, allowance of a current deduction for production costs would allow taxpayers to deduct such expenses against other income for tax purposes when there is no economic loss. Interest incurred during the construction period should be treated like other production costs.

Requiring construction-period interest to be capitalized can be seen as an indirect, albeit approximate, way of subjecting this increase in value[12/] to tax on a current basis. Thus, if the amount of interest that is required to be capitalized is not in excess of the expected increase in value of the property during the construction period, then interest capitalization is equivalent to taxing this increase in value (but not in excess of the construction period interest) and allowing the deduction for interest expense. For example, if property is worth 100, and construction-period interest is 25, requiring construction-period interest to be capitalized means that the taxpayer will get no deduction for the interest and will add the interest to the basis of the property, so that the basis will be 125. If the expected increase in value of 25 is taxed explicitly, and the interest deduction is allowed, the deduction will offset such increase in value, and basis will be increased to 125, the same result achieved by capitalization of the interest.

Both debt-financed and equity-financed property can generally be expected to increase in value during the production period because of the time value of money. Thus, for example, if $1,000,000 is spent to plant a stand of trees, the trees can be expected to be worth at least $9,313,000 after ten years (assuming a 25-percent interest rate), regardless of whether the $1,000,000 investment is financed through equity or by borrowing.

Where the the taxpayer finances construction through equity alone, there will be no interest payments to be capitalized, and the expected increase in value of the property due to the passage of time will not be taxed, unless it is explicitly taxed as imputed income. An alternative to interest capitalization, which would deal with such cases, would be to impute a current return, at the same rate for all taxpayers, on property under construction. The real (i.e. inflation-adjusted) portion of this return would be subject to tax, and the nominal amount of the return would be added to the basis of the property. However, given the high levels of debt in Colombia, it is unlikely that there exists a significant amount of equity-financed property under construction. Accordingly, imputation of a return on equity-financed property is probably unnecessary. For this purpose, property should be considered equity-financed only if the taxpayer has no debt outstanding. Thus, in capitalizing construction-period interest, all interest expense of the taxpayer should be treated as allocable to construction-period expenditures, to the extent of interest on debt not in excess of the amount of such expenditures. The justification for this approach is that money is fungible and, accordingly, construction expenditures can be said to be debt-financed if the taxpayer has any debt outstanding, even if the debt is totally unrelated to the construction. Interest expense on even unrelated debt could have been avoided if the funds used for construction had been used instead to pay off the debt.

It is proposed that the full amount of construction-period interest (unreduced for inflation) may be added to basis and that under the general rules for inflation adjustment the basis of property not be adjusted for inflation occurring during the construction period. For this purpose, «construction period interest» should be construed broadly, and should include interest expense incurred by a taxpayer purchasing property during the period before the property is placed in service or, in the case of inventory, before the property is sold. Under this scheme, after some point during the phase-in of the denial of the deduction for the inflationary component of interest, taxpayers will actually find it more advantageous to capitalize than to deduct construction-period interest. Capitalization will be advantageous because otherwise only the real portion of the interest will be deductible. For example, suppose that the interest rate is 25 percent, the inflation rate is 20 percent, and interest expense of 100 is incurred in 1988, so that 30 percent of the inflationary component of interest expense (i.e. 6 percentage points) is nondeductible.[13] If the taxpayer is treated as incurring the interest to construct a building, which is sold the following year, then capitalizing the interest gives the taxpayer a deduction against the sales price of 25 in the following year. Alternatively, if the interest is not capitalized, the taxpayer could deduct only 19 of interest in the current year. At an after-tax discount rate of 19.3 percent (assuming a tax rate of 30 percent), the deduction of 25 in the subsequent year is slightly more advantageous than a current deduction of 19. Accordingly, in this case the capitalization of construction-period interest is favorable for the taxpayer.

Implementation of a rule allowing (and in specified cases requiring) construction-period interest to be capitalized necessitates a definition of the construction period. Interest expense incurred after the construction period (including the future exchange loss on debt denominated in foreign currency) should be treated like any other interest expense, and should not be treated as part of the cost of the property being financed. In the case of property produced for use in the taxpayer's business, the construction period should end at the time the property is placed in service (which is when inflation-adjusted depreciation deductions would begin). In the case of property produced for sale, or acquired for resale, the period should end with the time when the property is actually sold.[14]

D. Timing of Items of Income and Deduction Other Than Interest

1. Depreciation

A comprehensive income tax based on economic income would allow an annual deduction for the real (i.e., inflation-adjusted) decline in value of assets used in the taxpayer's business. (Similarly, the calculation of net wealth should reflect adjustments to the original basis of assets for economic depreciation and for inflation.) Annual estimation of the actual decline in value of each taxpayer's assets is, of course, out of the question. Several alternatives are available as a substitute for this. In the case of each alternative, adjustment for inflation should be allowed explicitly, rather than only implicitly through accelerated depreciation allowances. Accelerated depreciation furnishes an inappropriate result at all rates of inflation but one. Moreover, it leads to an understatement of the taxpayer's wealth, which would be undesirable for the net wealth tax and for calculating presumptive income. (See also Chapter 7.)

One alternative for determining depreciation would be to allow taxpayers to estimate the useful lives of their assets and the pattern of decline in their value, and to deduct reasonable depreciation allowances based on those estimates. This system is subject to taxpayer manipulation and results in uneven treatment of taxpayers, depending on their aggressiveness and the success of audits. As a result, it is not recommended for Colombia.

A more administrable approach is to allow depreciation based on standard depreciation tables for particular classes of assets provided by statute or regulation. Current law takes this approach, although the number of asset classes used is not sufficient to accurately reflect economic depreciation. The weakness of using standard depreciation tables is that good data do not exist on the actual decline in value of particular classes of assets. Accordingly, the use of standard tables inevitably causes real economic income to be mismeasured to some extent for income tax purposes and involves some unknown amount of variance in the tax burden (as measured by marginal effective tax rates) on the income from particular assets and industries. On the other hand, the use of tables based on estimates of economic depreciation, combined with inflation adjustment of depreciable basis, would reflect real economic depreciation much more closely than current law, so that adoption of such a system, as described below, would be a substantial improvement over current law.

One alternative (hereinafter referred to as the «percentage-of-basis» method) for implementing a system of real economic depreciation would be a system whereby all depreciable tangible assets would be assigned to one of seven classes, each with a different depreciation rate. These classes are described in Appendix B. Depreciation deductions would be calculated by applying an invariant percentage rate of depreciation to the adjusted basis of each asset, reflecting the assumption, which is borne out by economic research, that such a pattern is more appropriate than straight-line depreciation. Provided that the depreciation rate is less than 100 percent, applying a fixed depreciation rate to the remaining basis of an asset would mean that an asset would never be fully depreciated. To simplify accounting, taxpayers would be allowed to close out their depreciation account for any asset in a particular class after a specified period of years. (The close-out year would not be an estimate of the economic useful life of the asset, but would be allowed simply as a matter of convenience.) The year in which depreciation allowances for an asset would be closed out would be the year in which 15 percent of the inflation-adjusted original cost remains to be depreciated. For example, an asset eligible for a 32-percent depreciation rate would be entitled to a 100-percent depreciation rate in the fifth year in which the asset is retained in service, because in that year the basis has been written down to less than 15 percent of the inflation-adjusted original cost. Retirement of an asset prior to the close-out year would be treated as a disposition, upon which a taxpayer would obtain full recovery of the asset's remaining basis and recognize gain or loss. Salvage value would not be taken into account.[15/]

Intangible assets would not be subject to this system, and would be amortized under rules similar to current law. The reason for excluding intangible assets is that such assets cannot conveniently be grouped into depreciation classes. In addition, assets that are currently depreciated under a depreciation method not measured in terms of years (such as the units-of-production or income-forecast method) would not be subject to the new system, since the existing depreciation methods are administrable and reasonably reflective of economic depreciation. Because the useful life of plants and animals varies substantially with the type of crop and climate, plants and animals (other than annual crops) would be depreciated on the basis of published tables geared specifically to Colombian agriculture.[16/]

As an alternative to calculating depreciation based on a percentage of remaining basis, straight-line depreciation could be used, based on a useful life that would give the same present value of depreciation as under the percentage-of-basis method (see Appendix B). Under this alternative, assets would be assigned to the same seven classes as under the percentage-of-basis alternative. Straight-line depreciation may not reflect economic depreciation as closely as the percentage-of-basis method. To the extent that it is less accelerated than economic depreciation in the beginning of an asset's life, it would provide an incentive for asset sales during this period (and would correspondingly discourage sales near the end of an asset's life), but this effect is not likely to be substantial. It would also cause net wealth to be overstated in early years. To be balanced against the slight inaccuracy of the straight-line method is the important factor that it is a simpler method for taxpayers to understand and apply, and would not distort investment choices, because it is equivalent to economic depreciation in present value.

Depreciation allowances would be adjusted for inflation by means of a basis adjustment. An asset's remaining unrecovered basis would be increased each year by the inflation rate and the fixed depreciation rate applicable to the asset's class would be applied against the resulting adjusted basis. In the case of the straight-line alternative, a pro rata portion of the remaining basis would be deductible, depending on the number of remaining years of the straight-line life of the asset. (For example, in the case of an asset with a straight-line life of 7 years, for the third year of the asset's life, one-fifth of the inflation-adjusted basis would be deductible.) The basis of depreciable property not subject to this system would be indexed for inflation in a similar manner. The inflation-adjusted basis of an asset would be used to compute gain or loss on the disposition or retirement of the asset and would also be used for purposes of determining the taxpayer's net wealth.

Under both the straight-line and percentage-of-basis alternatives, depreciation allowances and inflation adjustment for an asset's first year of service would be pro-rated, based on the length of time the asset was in service. Two alternative means of determining when an asset was placed in service are suggested, the mid-month convention and the half-year convention. Under the mid-month convention, depreciation allowances would be prorated based on the number of months the asset was in service. A mid-month convention means that assets placed in service in any given month would be deemed to be placed in service at the middle of that month. For example, an asset placed in service during October would receive 2-1/2 months' worth of allowance for depreciation and inflation adjustment for its first year of service. A similar pro-rating would be required in the year of disposition.

An alternative to this rule would be to apply a half-year convention, under which all assets are deemed to be placed in service on July 1. The half-year convention should be applied uniformly (i.e., taxpayers should not be given the option of using the half-year or the mid-month convention); otherwise the assumption on which the half-year convention is based, namely that property is placed in service relatively uniformly throughout the year, would be destroyed, because the half-year convention would tend to be used by taxpayers who placed property in service late during the taxable year.

Although the half-year convention is simpler than the mid-month convention, it furnishes a tax-avoidance opportunity for aggressive taxpayers. Under the half-year convention, the determination of the year in which an asset is deemed to be placed in service has substantial tax consequences. Taxpayers would accordingly have a substantial incentive to claim that assets were placed in service in November or December, as opposed to January or February. In many cases, particularly when large items are concerned, it is not clear exactly when an asset has been placed in service. Moreover, taxpayers can stretch or falsify the facts. The mid-month convention is salutary in this respect, since it reduces the stakes for disputes over when an asset was placed in service. If there is dispute as to which month the asset was placed in service, only one month's depreciation is involved, as opposed to as much as six months' worth with the half-year convention.

The current-law distinction between currently deductible repairs and expenditures that appreciably prolong an asset's useful life or materially add to its value (and thus must be capitalized) would be retained. Capitalized costs would generally be added to the adjusted basis of the underlying asset or, in some cases, would be depreciated separately. Each depreciation class would be assigned a safe-harbor repair allowance factor. The safe harbor would permit any expenses related to repair or improvement of an asset that are incurred after the asset is placed in service to be deducted without challenge, if such expenses incurred during the taxable year do not exceed the product of the asset's remaining inflation-adjusted basis and the repair allowance factor. Any repair or improvement costs incurred during the taxable year that are in excess of the repair allowance would have to be capitalized.

The new system would generally apply only to property placed in service after a specified date. Under current inflation rates, the present system of depreciation allowances is fairly close in real present value to the proposed system, at least in the aggregate, if not in detail. Thus, adoption of the new system should not greatly affect investment incentives, should not encourage churning of assets, and accordingly should not necessitate rules precluding the availability of the rules for used property acquired after the effective date of the new system. The new rules should apply without distinction as to whether or not property had been previously used in Colombia, since there is no basis for concluding that property previously used outside Colombia depreciates at a different rate.

Although the new system would be comparable to current law depreciation allowances in terms of real present value, the allowances would be spread out over a greater number of years. This will lead to a revenue gain for a period of time, followed by a revenue loss of roughly comparable present value.

The additional-shift rule provided by current law may be justified on the basis that it provides an incentive to utilize more efficiently scarce capital resources, which may otherwise be underutilized due to various distortions in the labor markets. However, provision of such an incentive is likely to be crude and overbroad, as it will not affect only those cases where the decision to use more than one shift is marginal. Many processes may use more than one shift in any event for other reasons. The additional-shift rule is crude because use of more than one shift is not only the way to utilize scarce capital more fully. In some cases, use of more than one shift may actually run counter to more efficient utilization of scarce capital, as it may accelerate breakdown of the asset. The preferable labor-intensive alternative may be to allocate more labor resources to maintenance. Moreover, this rule complicates the tax system, and requires administrative resources to be devoted to auditing compliance with the rule. To the extent that administrative resources are not devoted to such audits, the rule presents an opportunity for abuse, since the facts related to the utilization of property for more than one shift are likely to be murky in many cases and can be manipulated by taxpayers to their advantage, with little risk of being caught.

Although property that is used on more than one shift is often likely to depreciate faster, this is not always the case. Moreover, in the case of property that is customarily utilized for more than one shift, such usage should be reflected in the general rate of depreciation to be applied to such property. Thus, for example, because hotel equipment is invariably used on more than one shift, the depreciation rate for hotel equipment will reflect this customary usage, and it would be inappropriate to allow faster depreciation because of the additional shifts on which the equipment is used.

On balance, although there are justifications for the additional-shift rule, the complexity and opportunity for abuse created by the rule suggest that it should be repealed.

To sum up, because of the importance of simple rules in a country like Colombia, the best combination of alternatives appears to be the following: straight-line depreciation, with a half-year convention; repeal of the additional-shift rule; and provision of a repair allowance to eliminate most disputes over the deductibility of repair or improvement expenses.

2. Amortization

The straight-line five-year amortization that is provided by current law for intangible property such as organization and development expenses, and for mine or mineral exploration expenses is arbitrary but simple, and there is no reason to change the current approach, in the absence of evidence that it is inappropriate. The unrecovered basis should, however, be adjusted for inflation. Consideration should be given to whether five years is the appropriate recovery period.

In the case of an asset expected to produce a measurable benefit in each year of its life, such as a lease acquisition premium or finance charges on a loan, a better estimate of economic depreciation than straight-line can be made. Consideration should be given to requiring a more exact method of cost recovery in such cases, at least where there would be a substantial difference between such method and straight-line recovery.[17]

3. Depletion

Allowance of precentage depletion without regard to the basis of the mineral property cannot be justified as a means of correctly measuring economic income. An approach consistent with economic income would be to require exploration, drilling, and development costs to be capitalized and recovered as the minerals are depleted. An inflation adjustment to the cost basis of the property should be made each year, similar to the adjustment of depreciable basis.

4. Long-term contracts

Under a tax system that reflected economic income, profits from long-term contracts (contracts that are performed over more than one taxable year) would be taxed when they resulted in an increase in the taxpayer's net worth. It is difficult to translate this standard into an operational rule for an administrable tax system, because it is impossible to know when profits from long-term contracts accrue in an economic sense. A reasonable assumption is that such profits accrue as work is performed under the contract. This assumption provides the basis for the percentage-of-completion method of taxing long-term contracts,[18] and is probably the best that one can do. Nevertheless, in particular cases, profits may accrue earlier or later than actual performance of the work. For example, economic profit may accrue upon the signing of a contract with beneficial terms, even before any work is done. Alternatively, the uncertainty in a particular contract may be so great that no economic profit accrues until the work has been completed and the uncertainty has been resolved. Subjective distinctions such as these, based on unknown or speculative facts, cannot practicably be taken into account for tax administration purposes.

Keeping in mind that the rule will not always produce an accurate result, we will assume that profits on a long-term contract do accrue as the work is performed. We will also assume that the appropriate measure of work performed is costs incurred. This measure of completion is simple and is already the method used to determine the percentage of completion in Colombia. Under these assumptions, it can be shown (see Appendix A) that the percentage-of-completion method (which is available to taxpayers on an optional basis under current law) is appropriate for Colombia, because it approximately taxes economic income in many cases and is administrable.[19]

The option to use the completed-contract method, which is available under current law, permits an undue deferral of profits from long-term contracts and should be repealed. This method defers taxation of the entire profit until the contract has been completed. As noted above, although there may be individual differences, contract profits are most likely to be earned in an economic sense as the work is performed. Given the high level of nominal interest rates in Colombia, it is particularly important that deferral of income such as that allowed by the completed-contract method be eliminated. Thus, for example, consider a case where contract costs are equal in real terms over a five year period, and there is a markup of 10 percent. Because of inflation at a 25-percent rate, nominal costs and contract payments received are shown in Table 5-2.

Under the completed-contract method, the amount of profit taxed in Year 5 would be the difference between total contract payments received and costs incurred, or 8.21. At an after-tax discount rate of 28.5 percent (implicit in the nominal rate of 30 percent, less tax at a 30 percent rate on real interest of 5), the present value of the contract profits is 4.74 and the present value of the tax (30 percent of 8.21, or 2.46) is 0.90. Thus the marginal effective tax rate is 19 percent (0.90/4.74), as opposed to a marginal effective tax rate equal to the 30-percent statutory rate if the percentage-of-completion method were used.

If the percentage-of-completion method is generally mandated, should there be an exception for small contractors? Such an exception is likely to cause more complexity than it saves. The complexity would arise from defining «small contractor». A typical definition would require reference to the level of the taxpayer's gross receipts in prior years, and would require some scrutiny of ownership of the taxpayer to preclude avoidance of the rule by establishing separate small but related firms. By contrast, the complexity of applying the percentage-of-completion method is not great. The cost accounting data required to determine percentage of completion are the same as are required under the completed-contract method. The only additional information needed is the estimated contract price and the estimated contract costs. Small contractors could easily develop these estimates and need keep no extra cost accounting records to do so. In fact, cost accounting would be simpler under the percentage-of-completion method than under a properly applied completed-contract method. Under the completed-

112

contract method, it is important to identify all direct and indirect costs of contract performance, since these costs should not be deductible until the contract is completed. (See the next part of this section.) The cost accounting needed to identify all the indirect contract costs can be quite complex. By contrast, under the percentage-of-completion method, contract costs must be determined solely for purposes of determining the percentage of completion. For this purpose, it is not necessary to keep track of indirect costs, since direct costs should furnish an acceptable measure of contract completion.

5. Production Costs

In a comprehensive income tax, all costs of producing property, whether direct or indirect, would be added to the basis of the property and would not necessarily be currently deductible. When the costs would be recovered would depend on the taxpayer's use of the property. In the case of inventory, they would be recovered as part of the cost of goods sold. In the case of property used in the taxpayer's business, they would be recovered through depreciation allowances. The automatic allowance of a current deduction for such costs generally defers taxes on an interest-free basis and thereby provides a subsidy for investment in the affected areas, drawing investment from more productive uses.

Under current law, only the most direct costs of producing property are capitalized as part of the cost of such property. Many costs that economically represent costs of production are deducted currently. The effect of this treatment is to defer into the future on an interest-free basis the taxation of an amount of taxable income equal to such costs and to reduce the base of the net wealth tax. The length of this deferral depends on the type of property being produced. In the case of inventory, the deferral is for the period between the time the cost is incurred and the time the product is sold. The deferral will be less significant for taxpayers with rapid inventory turnover, and for taxpayers who use LIFO inventory accounting and are not adding to inventory (since such taxpayers recover costs that are treated as production costs very quickly for tax purposes).

In the case of property produced for use in the taxpayer's business (i.e. self-constructed property), the length of deferral depends on the applicable depreciation schedule. The current deduction of indirect production costs reduces the taxpayer's basis, thereby lowering the taxpayer's subsequent depreciation deductions (and also lowering the net wealth base). If depreciation is highly accelerated, current deduction of some production costs does not confer a large benefit. If, however, depreciation schedules reflect economic depreciation more closely, as proposed, then the failure to capitalize production costs becomes more significant.[20/]

While it is easy to state as a general matter that all costs of producing property should be capitalized on a comprehensive basis, it is more difficult to identify these costs. In principle, a cost incurred by a person producing a product for sale should be treated as a cost of producing that product to the extent that the cost may be expected to be recovered through the price of the product, as opposed to being absorbed as a loss or recovered through the price of some other product or service produced by the manufacturer. (For purposes of this standard, a person producing a product for use in its business should be treated as selling the product to itself at the fair market value of the product.) Under this standard, the question is whether as an economic matter the price of the product will reflect a particular cost. The «directness» or «remoteness» of the cost to the physical production process is irrelevant as such.

The Haig-Simons concept of income provides a benchmark in determining which costs are appropriately treated as production costs. Under this concept, the increase in the fair market value of the good being produced would be included in income and all costs would be deductible. For example, under the Haig-Simons concept, a manufacturer with no opening inventories and no sales during the year and whose

113

closing inventories were worth $10,000,000 would include the $10,000,000 in income and would subtract allr expenses incurred, whether identified as production costs or not. Suppose these expenses came to $9,000,000. In this case, the profit would be $1,000,000, even though the inventory had not yet been sold. (Under the Haig-Simons concept, increases in net worth are income even though not realized.)

By contrast, under current law, under which only direct costs are treated as production costs, perhaps only $7,000,000 of the taxpayer's expenses would be identified as production costs (the remaining $2,000,000 being treated as deductible overhead costs), with the result that closing inventory would be valued at $7,000,000 and the taxpayer would report a net loss of $2,000,000 for the year. Under an approach whereby only direct costs and those indirect costs that directly benefited production were treated as production costs, perhaps $8,000,000 would be treated as production costs, leading to a net loss of $1,000,000. Finally, if all expenses of the taxpayer were treated as production costs, closing inventory would be valued at $9,000,000 (still below its fair market value of $10,000,000), and there would be no net loss for the year. As this example demonstrates, as long as the costs identified as production costs do not exceed the fair market value of the product, the taxpayer's income will generally be understated as compared with the Haig-Simons benchmark.

The inventory cost capitalization rules adopted in the United States in 1986 require the identification of direct production costs, as well as indirect costs that directly benefit production activity.[21] For example, costs of a company's payroll department that are allocable to preparation of the paychecks of production employees must be treated as production costs. This approach requires a detailed analysis of the relation between various indirect costs and production activities.

An alternative to detailed inquiry as to the nature of particular cost items is to treat as production costs those costs that can easily be assigned to particular goods (i.e. direct costs), and to allocate all the taxpayer's remaining costs («indirect costs») among the various activities of the taxpayer in proportion to the direct costs of each activity, thereby treating an allocable portion of the taxpayer's indirect costs as production costs. The difference between this approach and the U.S. rule is that **all** indirect costs would be allocated to production activities and the allocation would be done without examining the relation of particular indirect costs to production. If production were the sole activity engaged in by the taxpayer, all of the taxpayer's costs would be treated as production costs, except for those costs that are otherwise of a capital nature, such as costs of acquiring equipment. (In the above example, this corresponds to the case where $9,000,000 of costs are capitalized.) The direct costs of producing goods would be allocated to the goods to which they were related, and all other costs incurred by the taxpayer would be allocated to goods in proportion to the direct costs of such goods.

If the taxpayer engaged in other activities besides production, for example, sales and advertising, then production costs would be determined as follows. First the total direct costs of the taxpayer's production activities and its non-production activities would be identified. All the remaining costs of the taxpayer would be allocated to production activities based on the direct costs of production divided by the total direct costs of the taxpayer's activities. Thus, for example, if the taxpayer had direct manufacturing costs of $6,000,000, direct sales costs of $2,000,000 and direct advertising costs of $2,000,000, then 60 percent of the taxpayer's indirect costs would be treated as indirect costs of manufacturing and would be allocated to the taxpayer's products in proportion to the direct costs of such products.

The above system for allocating indirect costs is comprehensive, in that all indirect costs are allocated to activities of the taxpayer. In this respect, it is preferable to the rule recently adopted in the United States, which treats only certain indirect costs as allocable to production activity and allows other costs to be currently deducted. For example, under the U.S. rule, general and administrative expenses that do not directly benefit production activities would not be allocated to such activities and accordingly would be deductible currently. A more comprehensive rule is proposed for two basic reasons. First, as an economic matter, it is generally more accurate to assume that all of the taxpayer's costs are recovered as part of the price of the various goods and services provided by the taxpayer. Second, it is simpler to deal with all the indirect costs of the taxpayer together than to allocate such costs to particular activities in a more detailed manner by specifically examining the relationship of particular costs to particular production activities. Under the comprehensive cost capitalization approach, the taxpayer's income for tax purposes will always be less than or equal to the taxpayer's economic income, provided that capitalized costs do not exceed the fair market value of the taxpayer's products.

The introduction of comprehensive cost capitalization rules is also important for purposes of wealth-based presumptive income and the net wealth tax. The capitalization rules of current law understate the value of inventory and property produced for use in the taxpayer's business.

The accounting system needed to implement the above rules must keep track of the direct costs of producing inventories and self-constructed property (which is already done under current law), and must in addition identify the direct costs of other income-producing activities of the taxpayer, such as the provision of services or sales activities. The latter requirement would be new, but it should be manageable, because only direct costs need be identified. All remaining costs would then be allocated in proportion to direct costs. Thus, no detailed records of indirect costs would have to be maintained, since the indirect costs to be allocated would be a residual amount, i.e. the taxpayer's total business expenses less total direct costs.

Because the above-described system does impose a significant new accounting burden, it would be appropriate to apply it, at least initially, only to the larger enterprises that are capable of maintaining the records needed to implement it. For this purpose, it is recommended that a «large» enterprise be defined according to an existing standard under current law, for example, the standard for requiring the taxplayer to submit a return signed by a public accountant. Alternatively, a large taxpayer could be defined as one whose average annual gross receipts for the three preceding taxable years did not fall below a specified amount. In determining a taxpayer's gross receipts for this purpose, the gross receipts of all trades or businesses which are under common control with the taxpayer would be taken into account, as well as the gross receipts of all members of any controlled group of companies of which the taxpayer is a member. This alternative approach suffers from the difficulty of indentifying commonly controlled companies. Once a taxpayer was treated as a «large» enterprise, it would be so treated forever, regardless of a subsequent decline in gross receipts, except as approved on a discretionary basis by the DIN. The reason for continuing to treat a taxpayer as a large enterprise is that the taxpayer would already have the necessary accounting methods in place; moreover, such a rule would avoid the complexity of accounting-method changes.

In principle, the requirement to capitalize production costs should apply to agricultural production in the same manner as to other types of production. However, under current law, the expenses of planting and cultivating certain trees during the preproductive period of those trees, as well as certain expenses related to irrigation, are deductible currently. These preproductive-period expenses raise the same issues as in manufacturing. In principle, the special rules allowing a current deduction for such expenses should be repealed. Planting and cultivation expenses during the preproductive period should be added to the basis of the tree, and recovered through amortization deductions when the tree becomes productive, or, in the case of timber, recovered when the timber is sold.

6. Installment Sales

The installment method as currently applied in Colombia allows certain businesses that regularly sell goods on an installment basis to defer a portion of the profit from the sale of those goods until the time that payments on the installment obligation are made. This method of accounting does not reflect the economic accrual of the income, which occurs at the time of the sale. Moreover, while the seller's income is deferred, a business purchaser can take an immediate deduction for the purchase (or, in the case of depreciable property, can immediately begin taking depreciation deductions). Neither does the installment method respond to concerns of administrative convenience, since the simplest approach would be to tax the profit (selling price less cost of goods sold) at the time of sale. Use of the installment method complicates the system, as it requires taxpayers and the tax administration to keep track of the profit ratios on various goods during the period that the installment obligations are outstanding.[22/]

The only valid justification for use of the installment method is in response to the taxpayer's lack of liquidity upon sale. But the liquidity argument is weakest when applied to the type of taxpayer allowed to use the installment method in Colombia, namely the taxpayer who regularly engages in installment sales. Such a taxpayer must have a means of financing the installment obligations (either internal or by borrowing), because a substantial portion of the face amount of such obligations must be used to pay the costs of production or acquisition of the goods. The installment method provides unduly favorable treatment for the affected taxpayers and complicates the system. It should be repealed, and the profit taxed at the time of sale.

7. Bad Debts

Taking the Haig-Simons concept of income as the benchmark again, a deduction for a bad debt should be allowed when the debt declines in value, that is, when the probability of collection declines. This may occur several times, as the chances of collection become increasingly bleak, until the debt becomes wholly worthless. A debt will decline in value as information becomes available about the status of the debtor. A decline in value may occur even if it is not certain that the debtor will not pay. An increase in the probability of nonpayment suffices to cause the value of the debt to decline.

The above principles do not lead to an obviously correct and administratively feasible rule to apply for tax purposes. The problem is that it is difficult to pinpoint the time or times when a debt actually loses value. Clearly, to delay the deduction for bad debts until the total worthlessness of the debt has been proven penalizes the taxpayer. On the other hand, to allow a current deduction of the entire principal amount of the taxpayer's outstanding debts that are expected to go bad in the future accelerates the deduction to the taxpayer's benefit.

The current rules allowing a deduction for specified fractions of bad debts depending on the amount of time the debt is past due take an appropriate general approach. Although these rules do not take into account the debt collection experience of the individual taxpayer, they are simple. The rules should be examined to determine whether the percentages of debts that are deductible reflect the typical actual experience of taxpayers, and should be adjusted if they do not. A fundamental change in approach is not, however, recommended.

E. Pensions

Under a comprehensive income tax, employer pension contributions would be deductible when made (and in the case of defined benefit plans the expected liability to make future payments would be deductible as it accrues), while the accrued value of pension rights (and any subsequent increase in that value) would be taxable to the employee. Many countries, including the United States, have adopted a much more liberal treatment of pensions whereby pension contributions are deductible, and pension payments are taxable to the recipient, but pension rights are not includable in income as they accrue, and pension funds are not taxable. This liberal treatment of pensions does not conform with general principles of taxing income, but accords a more favorable consumption tax treatment to pensions. Under certain assumptions, this treatment is equivalent to exempting from tax the income earned with respect to pension savings. (See Chapter 9).

The treatment of pensions in Colombia goes far beyond even the generous consumption-tax treatment accorded pensions in countries such as the United States. While pension contributions are deductible, pension receipts are generally not taxed, by reason of a large exemption amount. This treatment results in an even larger subsidy for this type of employee compensation that would consumption-tax treatment. The subsidy is most beneficial to employees with substantial income, because its value increases with the taxpayer's marginal tax rate, and because pensions are received disportionately by high-income workers in Colombia. Employees whose total income, including pensions, is below the taxable threshold derive no benefit from the pension exemption, and those whose income is not far above the threshold derive little benefit from it, but those with substantial taxable income derive substantial tax savings from the exemption.

It is recommended that Colombia reduce the size of the tax subsidy to private pensions by lowering the amount of pension income that is exempt from tax. In addition, the subsidy for pensions can be directed to those who are most in need of it by linking the nontaxable portion of the pension to the recipient's total income. Under such a rule, pension income would be fully taxable, but anyone receiving pension income would be entitled to a specified exemption amount not in excess of the amount of the pension income received. The exemption would be reduced by some fraction of the excess of the taxpayer's total income over a specified amount. Under this approach, an employee with substantial non-pension income would enjoy no exemption, while an employee who relied entirely on a modest pension could retain a total exemption.

Appropriate transition rules should be provided to phase in the proposed change.

F. Miscellaneous Provisions

A number of provisions have the effect of providing government subsidies to particular industries.[23/] In most cases, these subsidies appear to be unwarranted. Only if there is sound justification for government aid to the industry in question, and if the tax system constitutes a better means of furnishing such aid than a direct expenditure program, should these provisions be retained. The remainder of this Section discusses the tax rules that should apply to the affected industries if there is to be no government subsidization through the tax system (these are referred to as neutral tax rules).

1. Reforestation expenses

To achieve neutral tax rules, the credit for reforestation expenditures should be repealed. A tax subsidy for timber is particularly inappropriate in light of the negative marginal effective tax rate that likely applies to timber raising. In principle, the costs of planting and maintaining trees while they are growing (including real property taxes and interest) should be capitalized and recovered only when the trees are sold. In practice, many of such costs are likely to be deducted currently, while the income from timber sales is likely underreported. The exemption of 80 percent of the revenues from timber sales should also be repealed. Under current law, this exemption is conditioned on not claiming deductions for expenses while the trees were growing. However, such a restriction is probably difficult to enforce, and there is no guarantee that the costs for which a deduction was foregone are anything near 80 percent of the revenues from sale of the timber. A taxpayer should be allowed deductions only for those costs that are actually capitalized.

2. Cattle raising

Similar considerations apply to the special rules for determining the gain on sale of cattle. Neutral tax treatment would call for the costs of raising cattle to be capitalized as part of the cost of the cattle, until the cattle become productive or are sold. In no event should the taxpayer be given a basis in excess of actual costs that have been capitalized. Under the rules of current law, the gain on sales of calves born during the taxable year is exempt from tax, and the gain on sale of other cattle is computed by subtracting the fair market value of the cattle as of the end of the preceding taxable year. Because costs incurred with respect to newborn calves or other cattle (for example, feed, veterinary expenses, and expenses related to providing shelter) are likely deducted on a current basis, the current rules often result in a negative tax base for such activities. Particularly if such costs are currently deducted, favorable treatment upon disposition of the cattle is inappropriate.

3. Agricultural enterprises

Neutral tax rules would call for the current rule allowing immediate deduction for investments in certain agricultural enterprises to be repealed. Allowance of a current deduction for planting costs is sufficiently favorable treatment. If the concern is that a start-up enterprise may not be able to use the current deduction for planting costs, the appropriate remedy is to allow a carryover of that deduction, with interest, but to be used only against agricultural income.

4. Publishing

The special exemptions for publishing companies, investments in publishing companies, and author's royalties complicate the tax system and would be repealed under a neutral tax system. Direct government aid to publishing appears to be a more appropriate way to subsidize these activities. The government aid provided through the tax system under current law is directed only at profitable authors or enterprises; it does not help literary endeavors that cannot even cover their costs and which may be more deserving of government assistance than those that are profitable.

5. Export incentives

The current exemption for income earned through activities conducted in free trade zones as well as the tax credit for investment in hotels are inconsistent with a neutral tax system.

G. Foreign Tax Credit Aspects of Current Income Taxation.

Article 44 of the 1986 Colombian tax reform law specifically grants the government special power to reduce income and remittance taxes imposed on foreign taxpayers, in order to harmonize their Colombian tax payments with the foreign tax credits available to them. This section examines the advisability of making such adjustments. However, before any recommendations are made here regarding the way current tax policy might be changed, a brief discussion of foreign tax credit issues is provided. Then an overview is presented of several non-tax elements of Colombian foreign investment controls, in part to indicate which government entities are in a position to generate data on various aspects of the investment process and in part to suggest factors that may limit the response to any tax policy change. Following that summary, estimates are given of Colombian tax revenue derived from foreign investment income. Because this source of tax revenue appears to be an important share of total income tax collections, any policy changes must be considered with particular care. Finally, two recommendations are made regarding possible changes in current Colombian withholding tax rates.

1. Foreign Tax Credit Concepts

The ability of foreign investors to obtain a credit in their home countries for income taxes paid in Colombia can be quite important in determining the attractiveness of investing in Colombia. If a foreign tax credit is granted for Colombian taxes paid, the foreign investor avoids double taxation of Colombian source income. Furthermore, if the foreign parent firm owes additional tax at home on its Colombian income, the Colombian government may be able to raise revenue at the expense of the foreign treasury without creating a deterrent effect on foreign investors. In some cases foreign tax credit issues are not an important concern in policy formulation, but those exceptions do not appear very applicable to Colombia. Therefore, those possibilities are briefly reviewed at the outset of this discussion before attention is focussed on the more generally relevant interaction between the U.S. and Colombian tax systems.

Foreign investors from countries that utilize a source-based or territorial system of income taxation face no tax liability in their home country on Colombian source income. Rather, the tax levied where the income is produced is the only tax, and therefore the Colombian tax is the relevant one in determining the marginal effective tax rate on investment in Colombia. Source-based taxation is applied within the Andean Pact countries. Elsewhere in the world, Argentina, France, Switzerland, Belgium and the Netherlands utilize elements of the territorial system of income taxation.

A similar result is possible under an alternative setting, that of tax-sparing by a country employing a residence-based tax.[24] This alternative is of little economic significance to Colombia, but it merits a brief discussion. Investors from countries that use a residence-based system of taxation, where tax liability is imposed on worldwide income but a credit is granted for foreign taxes paid, still may have to pay an additional tax in their home country on foreign source income. This situation can arise when the tax rate in the home country exceeds that levied abroad on foreign income or where the host country has generous investment incentives. However, this additional tax may not be imposed in cases where a «tax sparing» privilege is granted to the foreign country; under such an arrangement, no additional tax is due to the home country even when the rate of taxation in the host country is less than in the home country. In essence, firms receive a credit greater than the amount of foreign tax actually paid, and any tax incentive made available to foreign investors by the host country will not be automatically transferred to the foreign treasury. Although this type of arrangement, or comparable treatment, has been included in tax treaties negotiated by countries such as Japan, Germany, the United Kingdom and Canada, Colombia has no such treaties in effect.

Even if Colombia were to negotiate tax treaties with those foreign countries, tax sparing would not be of major importance in this analysis, because the United States accounts for two-thirds of all registered direct foreign investment in Colombia; these figures exclude the petroleum sector and therefore probably understate the U.S. role. The United States applies a worldwide system of taxation and allows credits for taxes paid to source countries, but it does not grant tax sparing to developing countries. Therefore, Colombia traditionally has had to consider the extent to which U.S. investors will face a residual U.S. tax liability on Colombian source income, thereby reducing Colombia's ability to attract U.S. investment through lower tax rates or other forms of incentives.[25] Given the lower corporate rates provided by the 1986 tax reform in the United States, Colombian taxes now are more likely to determine the marginal effective tax rate on U.S. investment in Colombia. Therefore the Colombian government must assess whether any adjustment in its taxation of foreign investment is warranted. To provide a better understanding of both of these situations, a more complete explanation of U.S. foreign tax credit provisions is presented.

The major provisions of U.S. tax policy governing foreign tax credits are found in Sections 901 through 907 of the Internal Revenue Code. A basic principle is that foreign taxes must be levied on net income, excess profits, or war profits in order to be creditable. Royalties paid to foreign governments, production taxes, and sales taxes are not creditable, because their base is not income. In particular, they do not allow the recovery of significant costs and expenses attributable to the gross receipts taxed. A creditable tax also must require a compulsory payment that does not result in specific economic benefit to the taxpayer — some benefit that is not made available on substantially the same terms to the population in general (Sect. 901 and 902).

These distinctions have been controversial in recent years. One example of controversy involves the many high foreign taxes imposed on the oil sector. Not only are such taxes seldom levied on income generally, but in addition if the government owns the underlying mineral deposit, the taxpayer gains the right to extract this resource as a consequence of paying a tax that is differentially higher in the petroleum sector. Another example is Brazilian taxation of interest income, where high withholding taxes levied on foreign lenders were partially offset by rebates to Brazilian borrowers; such treatment can be expected to affect the interest rate Brazilian borrowers were willing to pay foreign lenders, even though the tax rebate was not provided directly to the foreign lender. In these cases the U.S. government has not allowed full crediting of the foreign taxes paid.

Taxes imposed in lieu of income taxes may be creditable, and foreign withholding or remittance taxes generally qualify under this provision. Again, the taxes must be broadly applied and not levied on residents of a specific country in order to «soak up» all of the foreign tax credit available in that particular country.

The United States imposes a limit on the available foreign tax credit to ensure that tax liabilities on U.S. source income are not reduced by taxes paid to foreign governments on foreign source income. This limit is calculated by determining the tentative U.S. tax liability on worldwide taxable income and then multiplying that figure by the ratio of taxable income from foreign sources to worldwide taxable income. The result shows the maximum amount of foreign taxes that can be credited against the U.S. liability that otherwise would be due. However, the numerator cannot exceed the denominator of this fraction, as may occur if there are domestic losses; in that situation the foreign tax credit claimed cannot exceed the U.S. tax liability on total taxable income.

The determination of allowable foreign tax credits often is described in terms of the U.S. versus the foreign average tax rate levied on foreign-source income; because that description pays inadequate attention to how domestic and foreign-source income are determined, it is a shortcut that can be misleading. In any event, if foreign taxes paid exceed the foreign tax credit limitation, no U.S. tax is collected on foreign-source income and the firm is said to be in an excess foreign tax credit position. Excess credits can be carried back two years or forward five years. Correspondingly, when foreign taxes paid are less than this limit, the firm is in a deficit credit position and owes a residual tax liability to the U.S. Treasury.

The tax credit limitation is made on an overall, rather than a per country basis; that is, all foreign income and all foreign taxes are considered as an aggregate. As a result, a firm's efforts to shift expenses from one foreign country to another are not of critical interest to U.S. tax authorities. However, this approach also implies that income from a high-tax country can be combined with income from a low-tax country to eliminate any U.S. tax liability on the latter income. To the extent that firms have substantial fixed assets in foreign countries where excess foreign tax credits are generated, those firms have an additional incentive to consider new investments in low-tax countries, because no additional U.S. tax will be due on earnings from the latter countries. Any U.S. liability will be offset by existing excess credits generated by income received from other (high tax) countries. For example, suppose a U.S. parent has two subsidiaries, one located in a country where the tax rate is 50 percent and the other in a country where the tax rate is 20 percent. If income of the first subsidiary is $500 and income of the second subsidiary is $100, the total foreign taxes paid by the firm are $270 (.5 x $500 + .2 x $100). Given a U.S. corporate income tax rate of 34 percent, the U.S. tax liability on the parent's foreign source income is $204 (.34 x $600). No residual U.S. tax liability must be paid. Furthermore, if the low-tax country were to reduce its corporate income tax rate to 10 percent, the U.S. parent firm's total foreign tax payments still would leave it in an excess foreign tax credit position ($260 of foreign taxes paid versus a $204 U.S. tax liability). Under these circumstances the low-tax country's tax incentive program benefits the U.S. investor, not the U.S. Treasury. Alternatively stated, the tax paid to the low-tax country does determine the marginal effective tax rate on investment there. That situation approximates the tax sparing arrangement described above, where host country taxes (eg. those paid in Colombia) also determine the marginal effective tax rate on foreign investment.

Another relevant principle in U.S. law is the creation of separate «baskets» or categories of foreign-source income for which separate foreign tax credit limitations will be calculated. An overall country limitation is still applied within a basket, but the ability for highly taxed foreign income to offset the U.S. liability on lightly taxed foreign income is more restricted to the extent that lightly taxed income is put in a separate basket from highly taxed income. As a result of the 1986 U.S. tax reform, several additional foreign income baskets were created, with the motivation of separating highly taxed and lightly taxed sources of income. Separate baskets now exist for shipping income, passive investment income, interest income subject to high withholding taxes, financial service income, foreign oil related income, and all other income. Regulations governing the allocation of deductions across these various categories are still being written.

From the standpoint of Colombian tax policy, one particular item that merits attention is the separate treatment of interest income that is subject to a high withholding tax, defined as greater than five percent. Previously, interest income bearing a high tax burden, as from Brazil, was combined with interest income bearing a low tax burden, as from Colombia, resulting in smaller U.S. tax revenue than if a per country limit were imposed. The new separate basket for interest payments subject to withholding taxes greater than five percent means that lenders will have less incentive to place funds in a country such as Brazil, since the excess foreign tax credits generated there cannot reduce the U.S. tax liability on interest income from Colombia. Alternatively, if the lender already has large long-term loans outstanding in countries that impose high withholding taxes, it no longer obtains any tax benefit from simultaneously making loans in countries that impose low withholding taxes. In particular, the Colombian tax exemption generally available to U.S. lenders is not as likely to benefit them as before U.S. passage of the 1986 Act. Rather, the U.S. Treasury will collect additional revenue at the expense of the Brazilian Treasury or the U.S. lender. This relationship represents an important change in U.S. policy that may call for a change in Colombian withholding rates.

An important aspect of determining taxable foreign income is the distinction between earnings of branches compared to earnings of U.S. controlled foreign corporations (CFCs). Branch income is directly taxable to the parent, whether it is repatriated or reinvested abroad. Income of the CFC is taxable to

121

the parent only when it is repatriated, unless it is Sub Part F income.[26/] This ability to defer payment of any U.S. tax liability until the income is repatriated constitutes a benefit which is less attractive than complete exemption or tax sparing but which nevertheless can favor investment in low-tax countries. That subject and the significance of future tax liabilities is discussed more fully later in this chapter.

A further aspect of the distinction between foreign branches and subsidiaries is the treatment of foreign losses. In the case of U.S. CFCs, foreign losses cannot reduce the U.S. liability on U.S. source income, because negative dividends cannot be declared. In the case of branches, if the net result from all foreign operations is a loss, the current tax liability on U.S. source income will be reduced, since branch losses flow directly through to be combined with the U.S. parent's income. This apparent asymmetry favoring branch operations is offset to some extent by the requirement that U.S. parents who have taken advantage of this provision must recharacterize a portion of their future foreign source income as domestic income, thereby reducing the allowable foreign tax credit in the future.

Rules for allocating expenses between U.S. and foreign sources were altered under the U.S. 1986 tax reform, an important change given the simultaneous reduction in the U.S. statutory corporate income tax rate. The statutory rate reduction means that U.S. firms are more likely to find themselves in an excess foreign tax credit position. Firms in such a position have an incentive to minimize the costs allocated to foreign source-income and thereby increase the creditable share of foreign taxes paid. For example, suppose a firm has $100 of foreign gross income, direct foreign costs of $40, domestic gross income of $100, direct domestic costs of $50, and overhead expenses of $50. First let all overhead expenses be allocated against U.S. income. If the U.S. tax rate is 34 percent, the firm's tentative U.S. tax liability is $20.40 (.34 x $60). For purposes of calculating the foreign tax credit limitation, foreign income is $60 and domestic income is $0. If the foreign tax rate is 50 percent, then foreign tax payments of $30 exceed the domestic liability of $20.40 and generate excess foreign tax credits of $9.60. If instead the U.S. government forces the firm to allocate the overhead expense of $50 in accord with gross sales at home and abroad, then foreign source income is regarded as $35 and domestic income as $25. The foreign tax credit limit now is (35/60) times the tentative U.S. liability of $20.40, or $11.90. An additional U.S. tax liability of $8.50 arises, and the total tax burden becomes $38.50 rather than the $30.00 when all overhead costs were allocated to the U.S. parent.

In the 1986 U.S. tax reform special provisions were included which will have the effect of forcing U.S. firms to allocate a greater share of their expenses to foreign source income. In particular, stricter rules for allocating both interest expenses and research and development expenses were part of these new provisions.

A final principle to note in the determination of foreign source income is that U.S. rules are applied in making this calculation. The discussion in Chapter 3 regarding the Colombian treatment of technical service income illustrates this complication: while Colombia may rule that technical services performed in the United States for Colombian entities are Colombian-source income, the United States is likely to regard that income as domestic source income and subject to U.S. income tax. The parent firm can treat the Colombian income tax paid as a creditable tax, but unless the parent is in a deficit foreign tax credit position initially, the additional credit is of no value, because it is not related to any additional foreign source income. The U.S. firm must treat all foreign income taxes paid as either creditable or deductible; but it can not choose some combination of the two practices. If the parent chooses to credit all foreign income taxes paid, but is in an excess foreign tax credit position, the technical service income taxed by Colombia appears likely to be subject to double taxation (U.S. Treasury, 1984).

2. Non-Tax Elements of Foreign Investment Controls

Colombian foreign investment policy has been consistent with Decision 24 of the Andean group's Commission of the Cartagena Agreement adopted in 1973. This decision was intended to restrict the role of investment from outside the Andean group to certain sectors of the member countries' economies and to control the ability of foreign firms to expand and exploit market advantages within the protected Andean market. Because of the adoption of a unified policy across member countries, foreign firms would be less able to play one country off against another in seeking the most favorable terms under which it might enter the market. Decision 220 of the Commission, adopted in 1987, takes a less restrictive stance toward foreign investment, especially regarding conditions for technology transfer. However, it is too early to summarize actual changes in practice among Andean countries that have resulted from the decision.

A general obligation under Decision 24 is that a foreign controlled firm must commit to converting itself, over a 15-year horizon, into a mixed company with 51 percent Colombian ownership.[27] Failure to meet this timetable results in the firm not receiving the benefit of tariff preferences accorded among Andean Pact countries. Such an incentive would appear to be relevant to a significant part of foreign investment, as 47 percent of the exports of manufacturing companies with foreign ownership are destined for other member countries of the Andean Pact.[28] Furthermore, after Decision 24 was adopted in 1973, real foreign investment in Colombia fell over the period 1974 to 1980.[29] Consequently, this requirement would appear to have an important effect on direct foreign investment inflows into Colombia, and Colombia's enforcement of this provision may be one reason that direct foreign investment plays a relatively smaller role in Colombia than in other Latin American countries. This deterrent effect seems particularly likely for smaller enterprises that find the information costs of acquiring compatible domestic partners to be high.

Under Colombian law direct foreign investment is to be registered with the government. The amount registered must be approved by the Planning Office and can be accounted for by new foreign funds being brought into the country, by machinery and equipment to be used in the enterprise, or by reinvested earnings.[30] Foreign firms have the automatic right to reinvest an amount equal to 7 percent of their registered capital in a year. Adding to their registered capital increases their ability to make remittances abroad in foreign currency; in 1986 few companies exhausted this ability, but in 1984 several companies did. In general twenty percent of registered capital can be remitted in any single year. This figure is somewhat higher in the case of investments in particular industries, or particular geographic areas of the country or for firms that derive over 50 percent of their earnings from exports.[31] Petroleum companies are not covered by these regulations and consequently registered investment data do not exist for them.[32] If a company does not choose to remit the 20 percent of registered capital allowed by law, it can request approval to reinvest these funds instead. Reinvested funds increase the firm's base of registered capital, and in addition they can be remitted at any time in the future.[33] If the firm experiences large fluctuations in its earnings, it may find that in years of high earnings the 20 percent limitation on remittances is a binding constraint. In those years the firm is forced to consider the less attractive options described below.

A firm can request approval to capitalize its earnings up to an amount equal to 20 percent of its registered capital. In this case it increases the base against which future remittances may be made, but it loses the right to remit the capitalized funds unless the company is liquidated. For funds to be capitalized in this category, foreign firms must buy at least an equal amount of bonds from the Instituto de Fomento Industrial (IFI), or meet an obligation to increase exports or invest in certain agro-industrial enterprises.[34] Because IFI bonds generally yield a below-market rate of return, this provision is generally seen as

123

indirectly imposing a tax on excess profits. Such a policy has been justified on the grounds that any profits in this amount would appear to be the result of the firm's monopoly power in the Colombian market. In any event companies have found themselves in this position in the past, and cumulative purchases of IFI bonds by foreigners under this provision were $6,226 million in 1986.

Finally, if a firm does not register a new investment at all, but simply adds to its working capital with no corresponding right to make remittances abroad, that action will not appear in statistics of the Departamento Nacional de Planeación or the Banco de la República.

3. Empirical Measures of Tax Credit Concepts

It is difficult to establish very precisely the importance to Colombia of tax revenues collected from foreign controlled corporations and branches or the likelihood that such taxes come at the expense of foreign treasuries, either on average or at the margin. Yet, that information is critical in designing appropriate Colombian tax policy in this area. Therefore, various incomplete measures are assembled in this section of the report in order to provide some background for the later policy discussion.

Two types of Colombian data are available: tax revenue data available from the National Tax Administration (Dirección de Impuestos Nacionales — DIN); and remittance and withholding tax data from the Central Bank (Banco de la República — Banco). The DIN information gives income and taxes paid by branches of foreign firms operating in Colombia. In theory all taxable activity is covered, and presumably there is little incentive for foreign controlled firms to report fraudulent data if they face a residual tax liability in their home country on Colombian-source income. The disadvantage of these tax data is that foreign controlled companies incorporated in Colombia, which are presumably much more important than branches, are not separated from domestically owned corporations, and their activities do not appear in the DIN figures shown in Table 5-3. For this reason alone the role of foreign activity and tax payments in Colombia is greatly understated in the DIN data. A further aspect of this understatement is that foreign activities that will ultimately be incorporated in Colombia are often operated initially as branches of foreign firms when the parent wants start-up losses to flow through it for use in calculating its income tax liability at home. Once the branch generates taxable income, the parent is likely to incorporate it in Colombia. Thus, income reported per dollar of capital invested in a given industry would likely be lower for branches than for mature corporations.

Colombian income taxes paid by foreign branches in both 1984 and 1986 represented approximately 10 percent of all Colombian income tax revenues, including individual net wealth tax payments. The implicit Colombian tax rate paid by foreign branches was 34 percent. The 10 percent figure is much higher than the share of foreign branch income in total taxable income in Colombia, where the latter term includes the income of individuals and companies (sociedades). This result is not surprising given the higher tax rate imposed on capital income than on labor income. However, the figure is somewhat surprising when compared to the estimated role of all foreign investment as a share of total investment in the economy (2 percent). That result implies that a considerable amount of Colombian investment is devoted to activities that yield little reported taxable income,[35/] that foreign investment is much more productive than domestic investment, or that the observed change in registered foreign capital understates the true level of investment activity of foreign entities in Colombia.

The DIN figures, reported in Table 5-3, do not include remittance tax revenue, and a more complete compilation of amounts remitted and taxes paid is available from the Banco data. However, because foreign petroleum producers are not subject to the Bank's foreign exchange restrictions in registering invested capital or making remittances, comparable data on payments to foreigners by the petroleum

124

sector are not available. Regarding the remaining, non-petroleum sectors of the economy, information in Table 5-3 indicates that remitted profits of branches are significantly smaller than for foreign controlled firms incorporated in Colombia; branch profits remitted are roughly 15 percent of dividends remitted by Colombian corporations. As explained in Chapter 3, D.R. 2579 of 1983 allows branches to retain earnings in Colombia without an immediate remittance tax liability. Nevertheless, this branch income is subject to tax in the United States when it is earned, even if it is retained in Colombia. Therefore, foreign branches seem more likely than foreign subsidiaries to remit profits. Thus the relative importance of subsidiaries is understated by these remittance figures. The significance of all foreign controlled companies operating in Colombia, including those incorporated in Colombia, is likely to be much greater to Colombian tax authorities than the figure cited earlier suggests, i.e., foreign branches account for 10 percent of all Colombian income tax payments. Therefore, special concern over this segment of the economy, as reflected in the special faculties granted in Article 44 of Law 75/86, appears quite warranted.

An additional indirect inference can be drawn from the branch income reported by the Banco, which excludes petroleum, in comparison with the global figures reported by DIN. The wide gap between these two figures (US$ 17 million versus US$ 317 million) suggests either that: (1) a large share of branch income is retained and therefore does not result in foreign currency remittances through the Banco; or (2) the petroleum sector has become a very significant part of the foreign presence in Colombia. The latter factor can be partially documented from U.S. data which give the U.S. direct investment position in Colombia: in both 1985 and 1986 the petroleum sector's share of total direct U.S. foreign investment in Colombia was 47 percent (**Survey of Current Business**, June 1987).

A further aspect of interest in these figures is that just as the United States accounts for over two-thirds of registered foreign capital invested in Colombia, the United States was the destination for more than 70 percent of total dividends, branch profits, royalties, and technical service payments to foreigners.

A final point of comparison is provided by U.S. Internal Revenue Service (IRS) data from tax returns filed by U.S. firms claiming a credit for foreign taxes paid. The income and tax revenue figures are expected to be smaller than the overall tax figures reported by DIN, which include foreign income from other sources besides the United States, but they could well exceed the data reported by the Banco because petroleum operations are excluded from the latter figures. The U.S. data are only available with a considerable lag; for example, the 1982 data were released in the fall of 1986. Also, U.S. data correspond to corporate fiscal years, not calendar years. Therefore, direct data comparisons are difficult to make, but the U.S. data do provide different insights.

A simple comparison of the 1980 and 1982 IRS data show much greater volatility than the Colombian data regarding the amount of branch income reported and the implicit withholding tax rate imposed by Colombia on royalties and service income. The large swing in branch income, from a significant positive figure in 1980 to a negative figure in 1982, perhaps may be attributable to the fact that the U.S. figures combine gains and losses by branches operating in Colombia. In contrast, the Banco figures presumably include only branches that are making positive profits which they want to remit home. Of the US$29 million of Colombian taxes that are reported by the IRS as being paid by branches in 1982, no division between remittance taxes and income taxes is given; such a distinction would allow a more direct comparison with DIN data on income taxes or with Banco data on remittance taxes. Foreign branch income reported by DIN for 1984 does appear quite large relative to the earlier income and tax figures given in the U.S. data. This difference is most likely the result of a marked increase in profits earned by foreign petroleum producers in the more recent period, although it also may reflect the fact that branch income reported to the IRS has been restated on the parent's U.S. tax return on the basis of U.S. tax law, which may allow more deductions than does Colombian law.

Another example of volatility in the IRS statistics is the implicit Colombian tax rate paid by U.S. controlled corporations in Colombia. The implicit Colombian corporate tax rate faced in 1980 was 33 percent while in 1982 it was 18 percent. Presumably this difference is not the result of any Colombian policy change. With respect to the 1980 figure, allowing for withholding tax paid, as well as the income tax, would yield a ratio for taxes paid to grossed up dividend income of 47 percent, a figure that suggests Colombian tax policy essentially exhausted the U.S. foreign tax credit available at that time on this source of income.

The IRS data also indicate that other sources of income are not necessarily taxed more lightly than dividends, and that Colombian tax authorities may not always have to be concerned over efforts to characterize payments as royalties or technical service income rather than dividends. For example, gross payments from Colombia to U.S. firms of rents and royalties were US$ 22.4 million in 1982, and Colombian withholding tax revenue of US$ 3.2 million was collected. However, deductions directly allocable against this income were US$15 million, implying a tax rate on net income of 43 percent. Thus, characterizing payments to the United States as royalties rather than dividends does not appear to be an effective avenue for a firm to use to avoid generating excess foreign tax credits.

4. Policy Aspects of Foreign Tax Credits

The data reported in Table 5-3 regarding income and withholding tax revenues collected from foreign controlled operations in Colombia do not allow unambiguous conclusions to be drawn about the effects of prospective Colombian tax policy changes on the cost of capital to those enterprises. A major reason for this ambiguity is that the overall foreign tax credit position of the parent firm making an investment in Colombia is not known. At the outset of this discussion it is worth analyzing the primary alternative cases that may arise and then assessing which of these outcomes is most likely. Because of the dominant role played by direct foreign investment from the United States, the discussion particularly centers on factors relevant to a U.S. parent firm investing in Colombia.

If the U.S. parent firm is in an overall deficit credit position and must pay a residual U.S. tax on foreign income it receives, then the argument for lowering Colombian taxes on foreign investment income is less compelling than when the parent is in an excess credit position. In the deficit credit situation, the benefit from a Colombian tax reduction would accrue primarily to the U.S. Treasury, without reducing the cost of capital to the U.S. firm investing in Colombia. That extreme result, where the foreign investor receives no benefit from a Colombian tax incentive, may not hold, because of the opportunity for U.S. subsidiaries to defer the repatriation of their profits from a low-tax country. However, the potential benefits from deferral depend upon the relative after-corporate-tax returns available in the host country and the home country.

To understand the potential implications of deferral, consider a line of reasoning suggested by Hartman (1984), which indicates that the Colombian withholding tax and any subsequent U.S. tax liability on remitted dividends will not enter into the firm's decision whether to reinvest its foreign earnings in Colombia. The reason is that in present value terms no new U.S. tax liability is created on the amounts earned by retaining earnings in Colombia. The liability already exists, and whether it is paid now or later, the discounted present value of this payment will be the same. This line of reasoning is similar to the explanation of the new view of dividend taxation given in Chapter 4, where the rate of dividend taxation at the individual level does not enter a corporation's decision to retain earnings or pay out dividends.

This argument can be illustrated with the following example, where the U.S. parent firm is assumed to have a residual U.S. tax liability on its earnings from an investment in Colombia. If a U.S. parent

126

repatriates $1 of after-Colombian-tax earnings from a Colombian subsidiary, and if all of the Colombian tax is creditable in the United States, it will have $[\$1/(1-t_c)](1-t_{us})$ to invest in the United States, where t_c is the Colombian company income tax rate, t_{us} is the U.S. corporate income tax rate, and withholding taxes are ignored. As a more complete explanation of this expression, the before-tax profits of the Colombian affiliate are $\$1/(1-t_c)$, and the total tax obligation is $t_{us}(\$1)/(1-t_c)$, leaving the amount shown above to invest in the United States. The firm's subsequent return from this investment will be

$$[\$1/(1-t_c)](1-t_{us})[1 + r_{us}(1-t_{us})],$$

where r_{us} is the before-tax return earned in the United States. If those funds instead are retained abroad, the firm will invest $1, earn the Colombian before-tax rate of return, r_c, on which it must pay the Colombian income tax (again assumed to be creditable). Once it repatriates those earnings it pays the residual U.S. tax liability and is left with $\$1[[1 + r_c(1 - t_c)]/[1 - t_c]](1 - t_{us})$.

Note that this example assumes the firm will not be able to convert this income into a form that receives preferential tax treatment, such as capital gains. Rather, the same U.S. tax rate is applied in each of the two investment scenarios above. Also, the possibility of avoiding U.S. tax by having the parent borrow against the increased value of the foreign subsidiary, rather than remit profits directly to the parent, is ignored. As a result, in deciding where to make its investment, the firm will compare the real after-tax returns in each country, $r_{us}(1-t_{us})$ versus $r_c(1-t_c)$. The additional U.S. liability does not affect the right hand side of this comparison, as long as this rate is expected to be constant through time. The same reasoning applies in the case of a Colombian withholding tax on remittances to foreigners. Such taxes simply represent «toll gate» charges on payments of funds to the United States; for funds already in Colombia they do not affect the criteria for retaining or remitting those earnings. Correspondingly, a reduction in such a toll gate charge would not cause a major outflow of funds from Colombia, unless investors felt the rate change was likely to be reversed in the future and wished to take advantage of a temporary opportunity to remit earnings at a lower tax rate.

Consider a numerical example of this relationship, where t_{us} is .34, t_c is .20, r_{us} is .097 and r_c is .08. The Colombian affiliate is assumed to have earnings of $100, which result in a Colombian income tax payment of $20. If the affiliate remits those earnings to the United States now, they become subject to the U.S. tax liability of $34, against which the $20 payment in Colombia can be credited. At the end of the succeeding year it receives the after-tax U.S. return of 6.4 percent (.097x.66), giving a total return over two periods of $70.22. Alternatively, if the affiliate retains the $80 in Colombia and receives the after-tax return of $r_c(1-t_c)$, or 6.4 percent (.08x.80), it has $85.12 to remit at the end of the succeeding year. The U.S. liability on this foreign-source income is $36.18 (.34 x $106.40), leaving an after-tax return over two periods of $70.22. The returns are identical under the two alternative strategies, as long as the after-tax return available in each country is the same (6.4 percent here). Furthermore, the comparison of these two after-tax rates of return is quite independent of the U.S. tax rate eventually imposed on Colombian-source income.[36/]

In terms of tax policy principles, there are tax-favored forms of structuring foreign affiliate operations such that Colombian withholding taxes can be avoided. Even when these taxes cannot be avoided, variations in the Colombian withholding tax rate will not affect the choice of U.S. firms whether to retain subsidiary earnings in Colombia. That judgment holds regardless of whether the parent is in a deficit or excess foreign tax credit position. The Colombian withholding tax also does not directly affect the marginal effective tax rate on new equity investment in Colombia when the U.S. parent is in a deficit foreign tax credit position and a residual U.S. tax is due.[37/] However, in the case of new equity investment by a parent firm in an excess foreign tax credit position, the Colombian withholding tax can be avoided, and it does determine the marginal effective tax rate on investment in Colombia.[38/] With respect to the rationale for modifying current remittance tax rates, the potential for Colombia to attract more foreign investment occurs in this latter case of new equity investment by parents in an excess foreign tax credit position. That contrast to the other situations described here is summarized in Figure 5.1, which shows schematically how the marginal effective tax rate paid on income in Colombia by foreign investors depends on the income tax treatment accorded such income in the home country and (under certain circumstances) whether the firm is in an excess foreign tax credit position. The proportion of Colombian investment that falls in the category where it is influenced by withholding tax changes cannot be determined very precisely. Before the 1986 U.S. tax reform, roughly 25 percent of U.S. manufacturing firms were in an excess foreign tax credit position. The lower U.S. statutory tax rate is expected to result in 69 percent of such firms being in an overall excess credit position (Grubert and Mutti, 1987). Additionally, the many separate foreign income baskets established by the 1986 reforms, to be used in calculating separate foreign tax credit limitations, imply that firms are less able to make effective use of any excess credits they may have, because lightly taxed income and heavily taxed income can less easily be combined.[39/]

With respect to the importance of new equity investment relative to retained earnings, registered foreign investment figures reported by the Banco de la República for 1983 indicate that retained earnings were roughly 88 percent of the amount attributable to new equity. Since 1983, Colombian experience is particularly influenced by the large Cerrejón coal project, which has resulted in new equity being the dominant source of funding in more recent years. Retained earnings are likely to assume relatively greater importance in the future, but how soon this result will be observed cannot be easily forecast. The significance of this factor is that the larger the role played by new equity, the more likely will any reduction in Colombian withholding taxes be to attract foreign investment.

Of course, the alternative policy of reducing the Colombian company income tax rate would increase the attractiveness of U.S. investment out of retained earnings as well as from new equity. Such a policy change would have much broader tax revenue implications, however, because it would affect both domestic and foreign firms. Perhaps differential treatment of domestically controlled and foreign controlled firms under the company tax would be thought appropriate, on the grounds that these firms already are differentially affected by current withholding taxes. For foreign controlled firms, a reduction in the company tax, rather than a reduction in the withholding tax, would provide a greater incentive for investment out of retained earnings per peso of tax revenue given up by the Colombian government. If such a differential approach is not judged to be feasible politically, then it is important to evaluate the response of domestic firms to a reduction in the company income tax rate. To the extent that domestic firms produce more for the domestic market where product demand is less price responsive than in international markets, the policy would likely result in a windfall gain to current capital owners without substantially increasing investment. Granting such windfalls to capitalists would be controversial politically, given that no relief to labor income would be provided at the same time.

5. Policy Proposals Relating to Foreign Tax Credits

Two proposals are made here, one regarding the withholding tax rate applied to interest income earned by foreigners in Colombia, and another regarding the withholding tax rate applied to dividends and remitted branch income.

a. Withholding taxes on interest payments to foreigners

With respect to the first issue, of particular relevance is the earlier discussion of post-1986 changes in the way that the U.S. foreign tax credit limitation is calculated. To understand why these changes are significant, first consider the effect of Colombian withholding taxes on the cost of funds to Colombian borrowers. Interest payments made to U.S. entities appear likely to face some U.S. tax liability when received, but are subject to little Colombian tax. The U.S. tax liability represents a cost which must be covered to yield a competitive after-tax return to U.S. investors. The greater this tax liability, the higher the cost of funds faced by Colombian borrowers. A policy issue arises because Colombia potentially is giving up tax revenue by exempting this income without achieving the goal of reducing Colombian costs of borrowing. If instead Colombia were to tax this income, and the Colombian tax were creditable against the U.S. tax liability, Colombian borrowers would see the same cost of funds, but the Colombian Ministry of Finance would gain the tax revenue, rather than the U.S. Treasury or some foreign treasury.[40/]

This simplified representation may be somewhat misleading because it treats the supply curve for foreign funds as if all funds came from the United States. As shown in Table 5-4 approximately 40 percent of private foreign borrowing comes from the United States. Some of the other lenders also are subject to taxation on world-wide income, with a credit granted for foreign taxes paid. To the extent that non-U.S. lenders face no tax liability at home, though, the imposition of a Colombian withholding tax gives them an incentive to lend elsewhere. Unless U.S. lenders are willing to expand their lending at the initial interest rate to replace the other foreign funds, the Colombian tax will cause some increase in the cost of borrowing for Colombians. If the cost of funds rises and results in larger deductible business expenses, the net gain in tax revenue is smaller than projected from the increase in withholding tax receipts.

Even in the case of funds from U.S. sources, choosing the appropriate withholding rate to avoid generating excess foreign tax credits is not easy. Any Colombian withholding tax would be levied on the gross interest payment to the foreign creditor, but the U.S. tax liability against which the Colombian tax would be credited instead is determined on the basis of net interest income. In the case of loans by U.S. financial intermediaries, interest expenses paid to attract deposits must be deducted from gross interest receipts from loans. Therefore, the tentative U.S. tax liability on foreign source interest income may be smaller than the foreign withholding tax on gross interest paid. In that case, the withholding tax drives up the cost of funds to Colombian borrowers, because the Colombian tax does not simply result in a transfer from the U.S. Treasury to the Colombian Treasury.

These constraints can be represented with the following example. Suppose the interest rate charged Colombian borrowers of U.S. dollars is 12 percent and the interest rate paid depositors by the U.S. financial intermediary is 10 percent. If US$1 million is lent, then the income earned through this margin is US$20,000. If the applicable U.S. income tax is 34 percent, then the lender's U.S. tax liability is US$6,800. That figure, divided by the gross interest payment of US$120,000, suggests that a withholding rate greater than 5.7 percent will generate excess foreign tax credits for the U.S. lender. If the margin were lower or other costs were allocated against this income, the appropriate threshold withholding tax rate would be lower. Additionally, if the U.S. lender experienced domestic losses, as the U.S. banking sector has in recent years, then even this lower threshold withholding tax rate would not be fully creditable. For example, if the U.S. lender has foreign source income of US$20,000 and domestic losses of $10,000, the maximum allowable foreign tax credit would be 34 percent of worldwide taxable income, or US$3,400. For that situation a foreign withholding tax payment of US$6,800 generates excess foreign tax credits.

Colombian withholding taxes applied to interest payments to foreigners should be modified. The current statutory rate of 12 percent in fact is not applied to any currently registered foreign debt. We recommend that a much lower withholding tax rate be applied, but that the current exemptions granted to private lenders be rescinded. Such a policy change would allow the Colombian government to collect tax revenue that currently flows to foreign treasuries. However, this policy change may increase the cost of borrowing in Colombia, if lenders from low-tax or territorial countries provide fewer funds and this decline is not offset by greater lending from U.S. entities and others subject to world-wide taxation. Based on these considerations, a withholding tax of four or five percent is recommended.

This treatment of interest payments leads to a related recommendation, that Article 87 of Law 75/86 be replaced by an alternative provision to govern debt between related parties. Article 87 stipulates that debt owed to a related foreign party must be treated as equity. This provision is not as necessary if a withholding tax is imposed on interest payments, because there is less incentive for foreign parents to attempt to avoid income tax by characterizing their funding as debt rather than equity. Furthermore, irrespective of the withholding tax levied, current law represents a very strong «thin capitalization» rule, designed to avoid the revenue loss that occurs when funding from a related party is treated as debt rather than equity. However, debt is a legitimate form of finance, and in some cases direct loans from the parent may be more efficient than relying on external funding. An example of a less extreme policy measure is Canadian practice, which limits intracompany debt to no more than three times the firm's equity. It is recommended that a similar measure be adopted in Colombia. Such a rule addresses the concerns that led to the inclusion of Article 87 in Law 75/86. If administrative problems arise in determining the potential interrelationship between foreign intermediaries and Colombian subsidiaries, then perhaps this limitation should more appropriately be applied to all foreign debt in relation to registered capital.

b. Withholding taxes on profits of subsidiaries and branches

A more general issue pertains to the tax treatment of branch profits and dividends paid by subsidiaries of foreign parents. One way of conceptualizing the consequences of any change in the Colombian withholding tax rate is in terms of Figure 5.2, where the demand by foreigners to make equity investments in Colombia is shown. The before-tax return appears on the vertical axis. The position of the curve (that is, the attractiveness of making investments in Colombia) depends upon factors such as current technology, input costs and demand conditions where output is to be sold. The availability of improved technology, lower input costs, or higher output prices would cause the curve to shift to the right. The curve slopes downward, indicating that more projects will be undertaken in Colombia when the required return is lower. In the case of a multinational corporation, this required return can be thought of as a benchmark used in an internal budgeting process in which the parent firm assesses its pay-off from investing in Colombia relative to alternative uses of its funds.

As a starting point for analyzing the consequences of a Colombian tax reduction, ignore the role of taxation in the foreign investor's home country. Consider some arbitrary after-tax benchmark return from investment in Colombia of i_0. If a 51 percent tax (combining income and withholding taxes) is levied on foreigners, the before-tax return must be i_1 in Colombia in order to yield the same alternative benchmark return shown at i_0. Areas $a+c$ in Figure 5.2 represent the tax revenue collected by the Colombian government. If the Colombian tax rate is reduced, the before-tax return necessary to yield an after-tax return of i_0 falls to a level such as i_2. This reduction in the before-tax cost of capital from i_1 to i_2 encourages greater investment in Colombia. The impact effect of the rate reduction causes Colombian tax revenue to fall by rectangle a, but new investment attracted by the Colombian policy change generates additional tax revenue, represented by rectangle b. Whether the new amount of revenue collected exceeds the initial amount depends upon the responsiveness of investment demand to a change in the required rate of return.

If the parent firm is from a country that taxes worldwide income and is in an excess foreign tax credit position, this analysis applies directly, as it also would for parent firms from countries with territorial tax systems. The shift from i_1 to i_2 is determined by the change in Colombian tax policy. A contrary situation arises when the parent firm is in a deficit foreign tax credit position. Under those circumstances the change in the Colombian tax rate would alter the amount of tax revenue collected by the Colombian government, but it would not affect the marginal cost of capital; the necessary return from investment in Colombia to yield i_o would not change and there would be no movement downward along the demand curve. As a result of the U.S. 1986 tax reform, the excess foreign tax credit situation is the generally relevant one to consider.

The sensitivity of foreign investment to the rate of return available in Colombia is particularly crucial: the more elastic the demand by foreign investors, the greater the likelihood that box a, the loss in revenue collected from existing capital, will be less than box b, the gain in revenue from attracting an inflow of capital into Colombia. Aspects of this relationship are discussed again in Chapter 7 from the standpoint of the economy as a whole in evaluating potential employment impacts of a change in the cost of capital. The present context is somewhat different, because the demand for investment by foreign controlled firms is not necessarily determined by the same factors as investment in the economy generally. In particular, factor input requirements and substitution possibilities in the sectors where foreign investment occurs, as well as output demand conditions, may differ from those observed in many sectors of the economy in which domestically-owned capital dominates.

One important factor is the elasticity of demand for the output produced. In some cases this elasticity will be small because the output is sold in the protected domestic market, and therefore the elasticity of demand for capital by those producers will be small. That is, quotas and other trade restraints may create considerable market power for those serving the home market and allow them to earn monopoly profits. Under those circumstances, a reduction in the withholding tax rate would not necessarily result in a large increase in investment, because existing firms would not want to expand output so much that price reductions would erode the initial above average profits earned. Indeed, higher taxes might be absorbed primarily by reduced profits, rather than reduced output.

The extent of this local market power depends importantly on the degree of competition faced, either from other domestic producers or from imports. For products where transport costs are high and the fixed costs of entering the industry represent a substantial share of the cost of production, a small number of existing firms may face little potential competition from other domestic or foreign producers. As a result, they have a large degree of market power, which makes their production decisions relatively insensitive to tax policies.

Another situation where economic rents may exist, or returns may exceed the level necessary to guarantee continued production, is mineral production. The development of mineral resources, including oil, gas, coal, gold and nickel, has become an increasingly important part of foreign investment in Colombia. Because mineral deposits are not a movable resource that companies can take with them elsewhere in the world, the public reaction often is that economic rents exist and that a country such as Colombia must have significant market power in dealing with multinational exploration and production firms. A corollary conclusion is that a high Colombian tax will simply reduce the monopoly profits or economic rents of those exploiting the resource.

This conclusion may be accurate with respect to existing deposits already in production, where an additional tax incentive may have little effect on the amount produced and instead may confer a windfall gain on the current owner of the resource. In the case of additional exploration and development, though, the firm must anticipate a high enough return to recover those expenditures, and not just enough revenue to justify continued operation of an existing mine or well. At this stage of the decision process, Colombian alternatives must compete with options all over the world, and correspondingly, the demand for investment in Colombia would appear to be fairly elastic or responsive to the rate of return required.

Thus, those setting Colombian tax policy must weigh the loss in revenue from existing operations that would result from any reduction in current income taxation versus the gain in revenue from new or expanding operations. The more responsive this new investment is to the required return, and the smaller existing production is compared to potential, the more likely that a reduction in the withholding tax on foreign investment would increase rather than decrease Colombian tax revenue.

In the case of many protected import competing industries, potential competition still may exist in the form of production elsewhere within the Andean Pact countries. Earlier in this chapter figures were cited showing the high share of exports from foreign controlled companies that are destined for other Andean countries. This pattern suggests that many foreign firms choose a production location somewhere within the Andean community and use it as an export base in serving the markets of other member countries. To the extent that all Andean countries impose the same regulations and taxes on this activity, and any policy change in one country is simultaneously followed by all other countries, a reduction in the Colombian withholding tax would not result in it becoming a more attractive location for foreign controlled production. On the other hand, if a Colombian tax reduction is not mirrored by the other Andean countries, investment in Colombia would become relatively more attractive. While the goal of various Andean Commission decisions has been to avoid such competition over the location of activity within the region, it cannot be expected that all decisions on tax policy will be identical. Thus, fiscal incentives available across different countries will continue to be important as long as the relatively closed regional market provides profitable opportunities for particular industries. This element of foreign investment would appear to be fairly responsive to reductions in the local tax burden.

The distinction between the responsiveness of output from new versus existing capital is what has caused some countries to provide more favorable tax treatment to new investment. Investment tax credits granted for new investment are one example. Such an approach might be considered in the case of withholding taxes. However, such a differentiated tax structure would be complex administratively and would appear less likely to qualify as a creditable tax in foreign countries; the potential loss of creditability would make this strategy unattractive. Therefore, a general adjustment of the withholding tax is the only policy considered here. Again, the change in the tax base will depend upon the incentive to substitute capital for labor and the potential to generate greater demand for output in response to lower costs of production. The likelihood that a tax reduction will generate more revenue also depends upon the new tax rate that will be applicable to any new investment.

Consider the following simplified example of how these factors are interrelated. Suppose the initial before-tax income earned by foreign capital is $100, represented in Figure 5.2 by 100 units of capital that yield an annual return of $1 per unit. Let the composite tax rate be 51 percent, the result of a company tax rate of 30 percent and a withholding tax rate of 30 percent. The demand for capital is assumed to be determined by the following conditions: the elasticity of substitution between capital and other inputs is 0.75, capital accounts for 25 percent of the value of output, and the elasticity of demand for output is -2.0. In this aggregate formulation the elasticity of demand for capital is -1.06, a weighted average of the incentive to substitute labor for capital and the incentive to reduce output when the cost of capital rises; the weights in this calculation are the share of other inputs in production and the share of capital in production, respectively.

Under those circumstances, a reduction in the withholding tax rate from 30 percent to 29 percent reduces the cost of capital by 1.4 percent. The loss in tax revenue from existing investment attributable to this rate reduction is $1.41 (box a in Figure 5.2), while the gain in tax revenue from the additional capital invested is $0.75 (box b in Figure 5.2). The net decline in tax revenue, from $51.00 to $50.34, suggests that for these values, the tax break given to old capital is not offset by greater tax collections from new capital.

132

Whether tax revenue rises or falls depends upon the size of the tax change and the responsiveness of the demand for capital to changing returns. The greater the elasticity of demand for output, the more responsive the demand for capital, and the more likely that tax revenue will rise if withholding rates are reduced. Greater elasticity of demand in the output market may be relevant when foreign investment is directed to export market segments where demand is more elastic than in home markets for nontraded goods.

Leaving all other values as specified in the preceding example but letting the output demand elasticity be -10 gives the results shown in Table 5-5. The larger the tax reduction, the greater this product market elasticity must be in order to result in a revenue neutral change, because with each further reduction in the new tax rate, the smaller the amount of additional tax revenue collected per unit of new investment. That tendency is shown in line 3 of Table 5-5; as bigger rate reductions are considered, the rate at which total revenues rise diminishes.

Line one of Table 5-5 represents a case where product demand is assumed to be relatively inelastic. In that situation, revenue collections fall much more rapidly than on line two, because the tax reduction essentially represents a windfall gain to existing capital, but does not attract much new investment.

The conditions for a withholding tax reduction to be advisable may not be as stringent as implied by the revenue neutrality constraint imposed above. The additional output or employment generated by a capital subsidy might argue in favor of such a policy, even if a direct loss in tax revenue raised from foreign capital income results. That is, the additional tax revenue generated by putting previously unemployed labor to work or the reduction in public welfare expenditures made possible by an increase in employment would alter the budgetary outlook calculated above. Furthermore, if reducing unemployment is a separate social goal, achieving it through such investment incentives may be more efficient than other alternative policies. However, all tax and expenditure policies generate direct and indirect multiplier effects, and focussing on them only in this particular case would give an unbalanced view of the desirability of government action here. A broader consideration of those possibilities is well beyond the scope of this report.

The analysis to this point has assumed that the only directly relevant policy consideration is a reduction in the Colombian withholding tax rate. However, tax changes in the United States and elsewhere should influence the way in which the Colombian government might use the special powers granted in Article 44 of Law 75/86. The 1986 U.S. tax reform reduced the statutory corporate income tax rate from 46 percent to 34 percent, a change that has increased the after-tax profitability of existing investment. However, other measures included in the 1986 reform, including the elimination of the investment tax credit and the alteration of accelerated depreciation schedules, increased the tax burden on new investment. The net result of the many changes made appears to be an increase in the marginal cost of capital in the United States (Fullerton, Mackey and Gillette, 1987). Therefore, in spite of the commonly expressed view that the reduction in the U.S. corporate income tax rate will draw capital out of other countries, the other changes made simultaneously with that rate reduction have reduced the attraction of investment in new capital in the United States. On balance capital is expected to flow out of the United States.

Nevertheless, the U.S. policy changes may result in two possible adverse effects on the Colombian economy. While capital may flow out of the United States in the aggregate, Colombia will not necessarily experience a capital inflow. In particular, before the U.S. 1986 reform, most U.S. parent firms with investments abroad (75 percent of all manufacturing parents) were in deficit foreign tax credit positions. As a consequence, the marginal tax rate on income from U.S. investment abroad tended to be the statutory 46 percent corporate income tax rate, regardless of whether the investment took place in high-tax or low-tax foreign countries. In other words, income earned in high-tax countries where excess credits were generated was only subject to a marginal tax rate of 46 percent, because sufficient income from low tax countries also was repatriated to the United States.[41]

The combination of the reduction in the U.S. statutory rate and the shift to a situation where most U.S. parent firms are in excess foreign tax credit positions alters that balance. No longer are earnings from high-tax countries shielded from the consequences of those high taxes. Rather, investment is likely to flow out of those countries. Beneficiaries of this shift will be countries with tax rates below 46 percent. Leaving aside the possibility of deferral again, U.S. investors previously did not benefit on the margin from those lower rates, but now the marginal effective tax rate on foreign investment in those countries will fall. In oversimplified terms, for those countries with tax rates between 46 and 34 percent, the METR will fall to the foreign tax rate, while in low-tax countries it will fall to 34 percent.

Some investment that previously was made in Colombia is likely to take place elsewhere now. In terms of the earlier analysis based on Figure 5.2, the additional element considered here is the change in the benchmark return available to investors outside of Colombia, which has occurred for reasons quite independent of any Colombian tax policy change. Even in the absence of a Colombian policy change, the demand curve for foreign investment shifts inward as a result of the U.S. policy change. In terms of the tax revenue analysis, areas a + c, the amount of Colombian income tax revenue collected from foreign investment, is smaller. Consequently, the effect of a Colombian tax reduction will be measured from a smaller base. The gain in tax revenue from new investment, shown as area b, is more likely to offset the loss in revenue from existing investment, shown as area a, than if the analysis were based on the pre-1986 situation. Any assessment of this possibility cannot be too precise, but for the central case reported in Table 5-5 (which shows the likely revenue consequences of a reduction in the Colombian withholding tax) this additional factor appears likely to cut the revenue loss in half, but it is not sufficient to result in a large gain.[42]

However, the Colombian government is re-evaluating its stance toward foreign investment on a much broader basis, as exemplified by Decree 220 of the Cartagena Commission. That decree in part recognizes that Colombia and other Latin American countries may have cut themselves off from new technologies and wider market opportunities, and may have lost a potential catalyst toward development by stringently controlling the foreign investment process. If measures to encourage greater foreign investment in Colombia are to be considered, a reduction in the withholding tax on foreign profit remittances is a logical option to be evaluated. The discussion above has addressed the trade off of providing a windfall gain to current foreign investors relative to the incentive created to promote additional foreign investment.

Any reduction in the current withholding should be limited to a small change, in order to avoid a large potential revenue loss. Colombia admittedly must run some risk of losing tax revenue if it wants to attract more foreign capital. But, given the significant tax revenue collected from existing foreign capital in Colombia, taking the risk of a radical change in policy is not appropriate. Therefore, we propose that any reduction in the withholding rate on dividends and branch income be limited to 5 to 10 percentage points. Lowering it sufficiently to eliminate all the excess foreign tax credits generated under current Colombian law would probably be a mistake.[43]

6. Summary

The preliminary parts of this discussion were devoted to explaining U.S. foreign tax credit provisions and Colombian non-tax regulations governing foreign investment, and to presenting the limited empirical information available regarding the importance of the foreign sector in accounting for Colombian income tax revenue collected. Background in all three of these areas is necessary in order to evaluate the consequences of altering Colombian tax provisions that affect foreign investment.

Two policy proposals are made to modify current withholding tax rates. The proposal to raise the effective withholding tax rate on interest payments to foreigners is motivated by the opportunity for Colombia to collect tax revenue from this Colombian source income without having an effect on foreign investment that would be as detrimental as in the case of increases in other withholding tax rates. An important reason for this distinction is the new basis in the United States for calculating the foreign tax credit limitation, especially the creation of a separate basket for interest income from countries with high withholding taxes.

The creation of separate baskets for calculating the foreign tax credit limitation means that the overall excess or deficit credit position of a U.S. parent with income in several baskets no longer determines whether an increase in Colombian taxation also increases the marginal effective tax rate faced by foreign investors. By way of contrast, for foreign firms who have no income in these special baskets the overall excess or deficit credit position still does determine whether an increase in Colombian taxation also increases the marginal effective tax rate faced. Calculations by the U.S. Treasury suggest that as a result of the 1986 U.S. tax reform, well over two-thirds of U.S. parent firms with foreign operations will be in excess foreign tax credit positions. Therefore, a reduction in the Colombian withholding tax rate on foreign profit remittances is likely to raise the marginal return to new equity investment for a large majority of firms considering an investment in Colombia. This potential to attract additional investment motivates the proposed reduction of the withholding tax imposed on profit remittances to foreigners.

II. Capital Gains Tax

A. In general

The distinction between capital gains and ordinary income has little economic significance under the Haig-Simons definition of income. Income is income, no matter what its source. The feature of the current tax system that creates a distinction is that gains are not taxed until they are realized. Capital gains tend to be realized at the taxpayer's option, while ordinary income is usually realized on a current basis. Preferential tax treatment for capital gains is based at least partly on this factor. (Treatment of gifts and bequests as capital gains is based on different considerations, which are discussed in section D below.) It is argued that without low rates for capital gains, taxpayers would refuse to realize their gains and tax revenue would suffer. Moreover, taxpayers would become «locked in» to their investments in appreciated assets, thereby impeding the free flow of capital. In addition, it is asserted that, in the absence of a relief provision, taxpayers realizing gains bunched in one or a few years would be penalized because the gains may put them into an unusually high tax bracket.

Preferential treatment for capital gains is also sometimes justified on the basis that a large component of gains is inflationary, so that taxation at ordinary income rates would be confiscatory. However, the problem of inflation does not justify treating capital gains more favorably than other kinds of income from capital. Moreover, the mechanism for providing preferential treatment of capital gains is typically unrelated to the actual inflationary component of the gain. Thus, an exclusion for a portion of the nominal gain favors highly appreciated property, compared with property that has not substantially appreciated or that has gone down in value. Moreover, the preference is available even if the inflation rate is low. The proper remedy for a concern about inflation is explicit adjustment of the basis of property for inflation. (See Chapter 7.)

A desire to provide incentives to encourage investment in new ventures and entrepreneurship is another reason often cited for favorable treatment of capital gains. However, the availability of capital gain treatment is not targeted to venture capital and entrepreneurship, and it would be difficult to define capital gains so as to target these activities. Moreover, it is not clear why the tax system should give preferential treatment to venture capital, particularly in light of the vertical and horizontal equity implications of any such favored treatment.

A principal problem with preferential treatment for capital gains is that, although a distinction between capital gains and ordinary income can be envisaged in general terms, it is difficult to specify how the line is to be drawn in practice. As a result, substantial amounts of effort may go into recharacterizing ordinary income as capital gain, with adverse effects on equity, neutrality, and revenues. These difficulties arise from the basic point that capital gains and ordinary income are both income, without any fundamental differences other than that arising from the realization rules. Drawing any line between the two is arbitrary and substantially complicates the tax system.

Many of the problems with capital gain taxation would vanish if gains could be taxed as they accrued, i.e. before they were realized by sale or disposition of the asset. Accrual taxation would eliminate the lock-in and bunching problems that result from taxation on a realization basis. Accrual taxation would, however, involve substantial administrative costs with respect to most assets, since it would depend on periodically ascertaining the fair market value of property. The current rules whereby income is presumed to be no less than a specified percentage of net wealth in effect result in taxation of anticipated accrued gains to a certain extent. The proposals relating to the presumptive income and net wealth taxes would lead to a greater taxation of accrued gains, thereby bringing the Colombian system closer to realizing the benefits of accrual taxation.

The current Colombian system for taxing capital gains (involving the application of a separate rate schedule to such gains) represents an uneasy compromise between treating capital gains the same as ordinary income and according them preferential treatment. The current system accords preferential treatment to capital gains in a very haphazard manner, which depends on the mix between the taxpayer's ordinary income and capital gain (and the characterization of such income for tax purposes), and which sometimes results in higher rates on capital gains than on ordinary income. Table 5-6 illustrates the haphazard nature of current law for taxpayers that each have a total income of $7,000,000, consisting of various combinations of ordinary income (in excess of personal deductions and exemptions) and capital gain.[44]

As can be seen from the table, it is possible for a particular taxpayer to face a marginal rate on capital gains that is 30 percentage points higher than the marginal rate on ordinary income, roughly equal to the rate on ordinary income, or substantially lower, by as much as 30 percentage points in the case of a taxpayer with very high ordinary income and capital gains below the taxable threshold. Moreover, taxpayers with the same total income pay different amounts of tax, depending on the composition of the income. This scheme cannot represent a rational means of dealing with capital gains.

The argument that some kind of special treatment is required for capital gains because such gains result in bunching of income suffers from several serious weaknesses. First, many recipients of capital gains realize them on a regular basis, without any bunching. Second, many recipients of capital gain income are (or should be, if all their economic income were reported) continually in the top tax bracket. Even if their income were bunched, they would suffer no adverse consequences as far as the marginal rate of tax is concerned. Third, the reduction in the top marginal rate to 30 percent has substantially mitigated any deleterious effects of bunching. Fourth, many other types of income may be received

136

in an irregular manner, yet no special relief is considered appropriate. Fifth, the bunching of taxable gains will be substantially reduced by the proposals to strengthen the presumptive income tax and allow a basis adjustment for excess presumptive income. (See the discussion in section III below and in Chapter 6). Finally, because the bulk of bunched gains tend to be inflationary gains, inflation adjustment substantially relieves the bunching problem.

For the above reasons, it is recommended that net real capital gains be taxed as ordinary income. Such a reform would substantially simplify the tax system, making the distinction between capital gain and ordinary income relevant only for purposes of the limitation on the deduction of capital losses. In this respect the Colombian tax system would be going down the same path being followed by the United States, which has recently eliminated the rate preference for capital gains. Indeed, the Colombian system would represent an even closer measurement of economic income, since the measurement of capital gains would be adjusted for inflation, unlike in the United States.

The current-law exemption for certain sales to governmental entities should be replaced by a provision whereby gain on such sales is not recognized, but the basis of property purchased with the sales proceeds is a substituted basis. However, for the purpose of determining net wealth, the basis of the replacement property should be its actual cost.

Although it is recommended that the separate rate schedules for occasional gains and ordinary income be eliminated, so that net occasional gain would be taxed as ordinary income, for institutional reasons the separate treatment for lottery winnings will probably remain in the tax system. The separate scheme for such income, with its 20-percent withholding rate, could accordingly be preserved.

The current exemption of awards for scientific, literary, journalistic, artistic or athletic accomplishment should be repealed. Such awards constitute income for the recipient, and neither the recipient's meritorious accomplishments nor his or her lack of solicitation of the award vitiates this fact. For the same reason, the United States repealed its tax exemption for such awards in 1986.

B. Losses

As under current law, capital losses should be deductible only against capital gains.[45/] Taxpayers should be allowed to carry any net capital losses forward to future years. The reason for allowing capital losses to be deducted only against capital gains is to prevent taxpayers from reducing their income by claiming fraudulent losses. Moreover, even if a loss is bona fide, there may be an offsetting unrealized capital gain. Deduction of the loss is accordingly appropriately deferred until the gain is realized. If immediate deduction of the loss against ordinary income were allowed, taxpayers could eliminate or reduce their tax liability on ordinary income even though they had suffered no net economic loss, while deferring tax on gains.

This reasoning also leads to the conclusion that interest should not be allowed on capital losses that are carried forward. For example, suppose that the taxpayer owns two identical shares of stock, both worth 100, one with a basis of 200 and the other with a basis of zero. If the taxpayer realizes the loss of 100 on the share with the high basis, but continues to hold the low-basis share, it is not appropriate to allow an immediate deduction for the realized loss, since, in light of the offsetting gain on the other share, the taxpayer has suffered no net economic loss. Deferral of the deduction for the capital loss without interest is equivalent in present value terms to constructively taxing the offsetting gain in the same year that the loss is realized. Considering that allowance of interest on capital loss deductions would also complicate the system, it is recommended that current law be retained in this respect, and that no interest on unused capital losses be allowed.

C. Basis

The basis for computing gain or loss would be adjusted for inflation. (See discussion in Chapter 7).

If the value of an asset is increased for purposes of the net wealth tax, other than by reason of inflation adjustment, this increase in value should not change the basis for purposes of calculating gain or loss on disposition. For example, if a parcel of real property is reassessed, the reassessed value should be included in the patrimonio, but the original basis (adjusted for inflation) should be used to determine gain on sale of the parcel. The reason for this rule is simply that otherwise a certain amount of gain will escape the income tax.

D. Assets transferred by gift or bequest

When a taxpayer disposes of appreciated property by gift or bequest, the gain accrued up to the time of disposition will escape tax in the taxpayer's hands unless it is taxed at that point. There will be no other chance to impose the tax, unless the donor's basis is carried over to the donee. However, a carryover basis would be complicated, and would exacerbate the lock-in effect. The integrity of the system for taxing gains requires a final reckoning upon disposition of property. Accordingly, it is recommended that gifts or bequests (other than to charity[46/]) constitute realization events. It should be noted that the proposal relating to «unallocated basis» arising from presumptive income (see Chapter 6) would reduce the amount of gains subject to tax under this realization requirement.

Another important reason for taxing gains at the time of disposition by gift or bequest is to discourage the retention of property for the purpose of avoiding tax on accrued gains. Because gains are taxed only when realized, in the absence of a provision taxing gains at death, taxpayers would have an incentive to retain appreciated property until death. Such retention of assets is undesirable for the free flow of capital and leads to substantially reduced revenues from the taxation of realized gains.

Treating dispositions by gift or bequest as taxable events would require valuation of the property. This raises obvious administrative concerns, especially in the case of closely held businesses. The amount of administrative resources that would have to be devoted to auditing the fair market value of gifts or bequests would depend to some extent on the distribution between inter vivos gifts and bequests. Bequests are easier to deal with because they are by definition found only on returns of decedents, and such returns are limited in number and are easily identified. Regardless of whether the transfer is a gift or a bequest, the determination of fair market value will often be problematic. Nevertheless, the strong policy interest in taxing gains at the time of disposition argues in favor of trying to overcome the administrative obstacles.

The heavy reliance of the Colombian tax system on the net wealth and presumptive income taxes provides an additional powerful argument in favor of constructive realization at the time of gift or bequest. The integrity of the net wealth determination depends on the valuation of property being as close to fair market value as possible. If there is never a requirement to determine the fair market value of property, the net wealth valuation of particular assets can seriously deviate from fair market value. Constructive realization at the time of gift or bequest helps to insure that the valuation of property for purposes of determining net wealth is checked against fair market value at least once every generation. This is the minimal amount of checking required to make the net wealth tax function in a reasonably effective manner.

Except for an exemption for small amounts received, the fair market value of property received by gift or bequest should be included in the income of the donee or legatee, since it constitutes an accession to wealth and hence is income. In addition, the denial of a deduction for the gift or bequest to the transferor implicitly presumes a finding that the gift or bequest constitutes a personal use of funds on the part of the transferor. (The theory of the tax treatment of gifts and bequests is discussed in greater detail in Chapter 9). Although the proposed rule differs from current law, it does not represent a substantial departure in principle. Under current law some donees may pay a lower tax rate because a gift or bequest is treated as an occasional gain, and most donees include in income an amount less than fair market value, since under current law the amount included is equal to the transferor's basis.

The net tax paid by a particular donee may be higher or lower than under current law, depending on offsetting changes in the rate structure. But the proper approach to this issue is not to focus on whether the burden on donees is higher or lower. Rather, it is to look at the treatment of different donees relative to each other. Why should a donee receiving stock worth $100,000,000 but with a (donor's) basis of only $10,000,000 be allowed to include only $10,000,000 in income, the same as a donee who receives $10,000,000 in cash? Once the principle is accepted (as it apparently has been in Colombia) that a donee should include gifts and bequests in income, then equal treatment of donees calls for inclusion in income of the fair market value of the property received, regardless of the donor's basis. After all, the donor's prior basis in the property should relate only to the tax treatment of the donor and has no relation to the equitable treatment of the donee.

III. Presumptive Income Tax

A. In General

Quite apart from the inherent merits of net wealth as a tax base (discussed in Chapter 6), net wealth plays an important role in the Colombian tax system as the principal basis for the calculation of the minimum income tax base known as presumptive income. The taxable income of all taxpayers, individuals and companies alike, is the greater of eight percent of net wealth at the end of the previous year, two percent of gross receipts (excluding occasional gains) for the current taxable year, or the amount of taxable income reported.[47] The inclusion of limited liability companies in the scope of these provisions in 1983, rectifying a change made a few years earlier, substantially strengthened the importance of the presumptive income tax.

The importance of these «minimum tax» provisions is suggested by the fact that in 1984 one-third of all companies were taxed on a presumptive basis, with the proportion being as high as 43 percent in the financial sector and 39 percent in the agricultural sector. Slightly less than 13 percent of company taxes were assessed on this basis in that year. Two-thirds of those assessed on the presumptive basis were taxed on the basis of net wealth and the remainder on gross receipts, with the former basis being most important in the agricultural and financial sectors and the latter in the manufacturing and commerce sectors. The presumption based on gross receipts was introduced in 1983 largely in the belief that firms in these latter sectors were substantially underreporting inventories and hence net wealth.[48] Although comparable figures are not available for individual taxpayers, studies for earlier years suggest that perhaps as much as 30 percent of all income taxes are based on presumptive assessments, particularly those based on net wealth.[49] Even these figures may substantially understate the importance of the presumptive provisions if, as has been suggested, many taxpayers deliberately report ordinary income a little larger than that which would otherwise be presumed in order to reduce the likelihood of being investigated.

The current presumptive income tax originated in 1974, following several earlier, and not particularly successful, attempts to apply such minimum taxes in the agricultural sector, where it was felt that the underreporting of taxable income was particularly chronic and widespread. It is thus rather ironic that a number of specific provisions favoring agriculture, and in particular the cattle industry, have crept back into the law in recent years, notably the outright exclusion from the net wealth basis for calculating presumptive income of 40 percent of the net value of property used for cattle raising and the inclusion of only 75 percent of the value of rural land.[50] Other important exclusions include the value of urban property subject to rent control and (since 1986) stocks and partnership interests in Colombian corporations. Similarly, receipts affected by price controls are excluded for purposes of the presumption based on gross receipts.[51]

Viewed as part of the Colombian income tax system, the presumptive income tax has undoubtedly been a major success in the sense of maintaining a certain minimal degree of integrity in the system and in particular in ensuring that most of the better-off sectors of society contribute to the cost of government at least roughly in proportion to their ability to pay.

B. *Wealth-based presumptive income*

The rule (hereinafter referred to as the «wealth-based» rule) that the taxpayer's taxable income is presumed to be no less than a specified percentage (currently eight percent) of the taxpayer's net wealth as of the beginning of the year serves two principal functions. First, the rule makes it more difficult to avoid tax on income from capital. For example, if a taxpayer owns an apartment building and includes the value of the building in net wealth, the taxpayer will obtain a benefit from failing to declare rental income, only to the extent that net income from the building exceeds eight percent of the net declared value of the building. Second, in cases where the rules relating to the timing of the taxation of income from capital fail to tax such income currently, the wealth-based rule effectively imputes such income, thereby making it currently taxable. For example, if the taxpayer holds property that is appreciating in value, but does not sell the property, the realization requirement defers the taxable income until the time of realization, but the wealth-based rule in effect taxes the appreciation currently (to the extent of eight percent of the net declared value of the property). Both of these functions are of great importance as a back stop to the income tax. The wealth-based rule should be rationalized and strengthened so as to better fulfill these objectives. (The appropriateness of continuing to use an eight-percent imputation rate is discussed below.)

1. *Earned Income*

As currently applied, the wealth-based rule does not distinguish between the taxpayer's earned and unearned income. This is a serious flaw. There is no reason to expect a close relationship between a taxpayer's **earned** income and his or her prior wealth. The wealth-based rule should rather presume that the taxpayer's **unearned** income is at least equal to a given percentage of the taxpayer's net wealth. Such an assumption is reasonable on an ex ante basis. A given amount of wealth, no matter what form it takes, can be presumed to earn, on average, a given rate of return (assuming that the taxpayer invests the wealth in a rational manner). Accordingly, the taxpayer's earned income should be segregated from unearned income in applying the wealth-based rule.

Thus, in comparing the taxpayer's presumptive income with the taxpayer's income as determined through ordinary methods, earned income should be subtracted from ordinarily determined income. If the presumptive income exceeds the amount of unearned income calculated in this fashion, then the taxpayer's taxable income would be the presumptive income plus the taxpayer's earned income. For example, if the taxpayer's net wealth is $10,000,000, earned income is $1,000,000, and the taxpayer reports no unearned income, then under current law the wealth-based rule would not increase the taxable income beyond the $1,000,000 that is reported; but under the proposal the presumptive income of $800,000 would be compared with the taxpayer's unearned income (0), and so total taxable income would be $1,800,000.

For this purpose, earned income would be defined as wages, salaries, and any other income received for personal services rendered, less any deductions directly related to the earning of such income.

In the case of income received on account of both capital and services (i.e. income from a business in which the taxpayer works and in which the taxpayer has also invested his or her capital), a rule is needed to divide the ordinarily determined business income into earned and unearned income. The most appropriate way of doing this seems to be to treat as earned income all the income of the business that is not accounted for by imputing a return to capital invested in the business. That is, the amount treated as earned income would be the total amount of ordinarily determined income from the business reported by the taxpayer, less the presumed percentage (currently eight percent) multiplied by the amount of the taxpayer's net wealth that is used to produce income in the business.[52/] This approach is consistent with the calculation of presumptive income from capital and for that reason is a simple approach, since it is based on a calculation that needs to be performed in any event in determining presumptive income.

One effect of this proposed rule for dividing business income into earned and unearned income is that extraordinary returns to capital are effectively treated as earned income and therefore taxed in addition to presumptive income. By contrast, a taxpayer who earns extraordinary returns on capital invested in an enterprise in which the taxpayer does not work will not be taxed on such extraordinary returns under the presumptive income calculation. If it is desired to remedy this, it could be provided that, in determining the portion of mixed capital and labor income from a business that is attributable to capital, the presumptive return used would be higher than the rate of return used generally for the presumptive income calculation. For example, if the general presumptive rate of return were five percent, a six percent rate of return could be used in determining the amount of earned income. This approach is not, however, recommended, due to its added complexity and to the fact that any rule will necessarily be somewhat arbitrary.

2. Exclusions

The exclusions for property used in cattle raising and for property in a nonproductive period should be eliminated. The exclusions are not justified as a matter of principle, and also serve to complicate administration and perhaps furnish an opportunity for evasion. Cattle raising should not be accorded preferential treatment. Plants and animals that are not currently income-producing are precisely the type of asset that should be included in the taxpayer's wealth in determining presumptive income, in order to deal with the issue of the proper timing of income for tax purposes. Even though such assets do not yet yield a crop, they can be presumed to earn an economic return, in the form of an increase in their value. Thus, a two-year-old coffee tree is worth more than a one-year-old tree, even though it has not yet borne a crop. The same reasoning applies to the exclusion for non-agricultural assets in an improductive period, such as real property under construction. Inclusion of assets in a nonproductive period in the calculation of presumptive income can result in taxation of this increase in value, depending on the general relation between the taxpayer's ordinarily determined and presumptive income. Where this increase in value is effectively taxed, because presumptive income exceeds ordinarily determined income, this imputed increase in value could be added to the basis of the property and recovered after the property becomes productive. (This is explained in greater detail in Chapter 6.)

Similarly, exclusions for property subject to rent control or development restrictions and real property affected by volcanic activity should be repealed. There is no reason not to expect such properties to yield the same rate of return over the long run as other properties. An event such as the imposition of rent control or a volcanic eruption may diminish the fair market value of property. If the fair market value consequently falls below the value used for net wealth tax purposes, the taxpayer should be allowed to petition for revaluation of the property to its fair market value. Because most property is substantially undervalued, such a petition procedure is not likely to be used frequently and accordingly should be administrable. (Specification of the details of the petition procedure, in particular its interaction with valuation for purposes of the real property tax, is beyond the scope of this report.)

3. Fluctuations in income

The presumption that a taxpayer earns, on average, a minimum return on its capital is likely to prove fairly accurate in the vast majority of cases, provided that the presumed rate of return is a realistic reflection of the prevailing risk-free return. This flows from the proposition that owners of capital generally do not choose to invest their capital in ways that earn a return that is below the risk-free return. Only if a taxpayer consistently takes risks and loses will its rate of return be below this level. However, there is no reason to believe that the income of a particular year will correspond to this average return. One year's income may be higher and another year's income lower than the average. If the taxpayer is taxed on its actual income in years when it exceeds the average, but on presumed income when the actual income falls below the average, overtaxation may result.

This problem is taken care of to some extent by the proposal to allow the excess of presumptive income over regular income to be used to offset capital gains realized in the future. This proposal responds to the fact that the presumptive income calculation in effect taxes unrealized gains, and that a credit for such tax should accordingly be available at the time of realization. However, the realization of capital gains is not the only factor that can cause regular income to exceed presumptive income. Tax accounting rules can also cause such an excess to occur. (For example, the expensing of research and development expenditures can reduce regular income below presumptive income in one year and cause it to exceed presumptive income in the years when the research bears fruit.) In addition, regular income can exceed presumptive income because of the earning of an extraordinary return on one project, which might be offset by a reduced return on some other project, either in the past or the future.

To remedy this situation, it seems appropriate to allow a carryover of the excess of regular income over presumptive income, to be used in a future year against the excess, if any, of presumptive income over regular income. It is recommended that, for reasons of simplicity, interest not be allowed on such carryforward. Because the carryforward is only a crude measure to begin with, no precision will be lost by failing to allow an interest adjustment. In this respect, the carryover differs from the allowance of a net operating loss. In the case of a net operating loss, allowance of the loss in future years with interest is necessary for the proper measurement of income. The same cannot be said for the carryover of the excess of regular income over presumptive income. Such excess may represent simply the earning of a risk premium on a successful investment, which will not be offset by lower earnings on other investments in the future. Thus, while allowance of a carryover seems appropriate to mitigate the hardship of a taxpayer whose regular income fluctuates as compared with presumptive income, taking this relief measure to an extreme via the allowance of interest seems inappropriate, in light of the additional complexity that interest adjustment would involve and the approximate nature of the measure to begin with.

Depending on the timetable for implementation of the recommended changes in the net wealth base, it may be appropriate to delay implementation of the carryover described above. During the transition to a net wealth base that more closely reflects fair market value, the net wealth base of many taxpayers is likely to be substantially below fair market value. To allow such taxpayers to take credit for the excess of regular over presumptive income in such circumstances would be to open the door to tax evasion in the future. Accordingly, such a credit should be allowed only when the proposed reforms have fully come into effect, so that it is possible to say with reasonable confidence that the net wealth base generally does not seriously deviate from fair market value.

4. Conforming changes

a. Coordination with filing requirement

Taxpayers receiving primarily earned income and whose gross wealth is $6,000,000 or less generally do not have to file tax returns under current law. It is possible that such a taxpayer would have presumptive income under the proposal for segregating earned income. An administrative determination will have to be made as to whether to maintain the current filing requirements or to require taxpayers whose presumptive income exceeds their unearned income to file returns. One possibility would be to provide that taxpayers who under current rules do not have to file would only have to file if their presumptive income exceeds their unearned income by more than a specified amount, but only if their total income exceeds the filing threshold. Under such an approach, very few additional returns would have to be filed, while at the same time nonfiling taxpayers would not be treated on a substantially more favorable basis than taxpayers required to file.

b. Presumed Rate of Return

If the suggested reforms relating to the taxation of net wealth (see Chapter 6); constructive realization of gains with respect to gifts and bequests (see Section IID above); and excluded assets (Section IIIB 2 above) are adopted, the net wealth base will be much closer to fair market value than under current law. On the assumption that presumptive income is only unearned income and that the base for calculating presumptive income is roughly equal to net wealth at current market values, an eight percent real presumed yield is excessive. Four or five percent is more realistic. However, given that transition to the new system will likely not be immediate and that there may be a considerable understatement of net wealth due to fraud and other reasons, a reduction of the presumed rate of return should be made with care, so as not to lose revenue, worsen equity, and unintentionally reduce the role of presumptive income. One possible approach would be to reduce the presumed rate from eight percent to five percent by one percentage point per year, starting in the year in which changes in the presumptive income tax base first become effective.

c. Deposits in financial institutions

During the transition to a lower presumption rate, the rate would likely exceed the real rate of return on interest-bearing deposits. It may be desirable to exclude from the presumptive income base deposits in financial institutions, provided that interest received with respect to such deposits is subject to adequate information reporting. For example, as a condition of excluding a financial deposit, the taxpayer may be required to attach the information return from the financial institution to his or her return, and report the interest shown as taxable income. If this is done, the income from such accounts should of course be subtracted from ordinarily determined (unearned) income in comparing ordinarily determined income with presumptive income.

d. Principal residence

The proposed reform segregating earned income from the wealth-based presumptive income comparison would likely lead to a substantial increase in the number of taxpayers taxed on a presumptive basis. For example, completely honest taxpayers whose only taxable income consisted of wages and salaries and whose only wealth consisted of home equity and personal-use property would be taxed on presumptive income based on this wealth (assuming that they were required to file a return). This result would not be inappropriate, since imputed income from owner-occupied housing and consumer durables is part of a taxpayer's economic income. However, such taxation of imputed income may be politically unpopular. One possibility for avoiding political problems would be to exempt from the wealth-based rule a specified peso amount of the net patrimonial value of the taxpayer's principal residence and personal-use property (automobile, home furnishings, etc.).

C. Receipts-based presumptive income

In contrast to the wealth-based rule, which is based on a reasonable assumption of a minimum rate of return on net wealth, the presumption that net income is at least equal to two percent of gross receipts does not correspond to economic reality. The receipts-based rule is based on net receipts,[53/] which are defined as gross receipts, less returns and discounts.[54/] Accordingly, the cost of goods sold is included in net receipts. Different firms will have different profit margins on their receipts, even within the same industry, depending on their level of integration. For example, if Firm A manufactures a product at a cost of 90, sells it to Firm B for 100, which further manufactures it at a cost of 90 and sells the finished product for 200, Firm A's profit would be 10 percent of gross receipts, while Firm B's profit would be only 5 percent of gross receipts. If instead Firm B were to complete the entire manufacturing process itself, it would have a profit of 10 percent of gross receipts. Moreover, the amount of profit margin on gross receipts will vary from industry to industry.

One undesirable effect of the receipts-based rule may be to encourage mergers, thereby increasing economic concentration. A taxpayer that is unfairly treated by the rule has an effective avenue of self-help: it can merge with a company with a high ratio of profits to sales (or enter such a line of business without merging with an existing company). By reason of such self-help measures, the revenues from the receipts-based rule are likely to erode over time.

Moreover, the receipts-based rule is difficult to justify as a means of controlling evasion, since by hypothesis it only operates if the taxpayer includes a substantial level of receipts in income. By contrast, the wealth-based rule can catch a taxpayer who reports its wealth but underreports its receipts.

The receipts-based rule may be justified under the current scheme of things to deal with taxpayers who can avoid the wealth-based rule because their net wealth is understated. Such understatement can result from a number of factors, including: the failure to adjust asset values for inflation; the use of LIFO; failure to fully capitalize production costs; and the use of accelerated depreciation. The proposed reforms of the net wealth tax, including those for inflation adjustment (see Chapters 6 and 7), should ameliorate this problem. The receipts-based rule could be retained for a transitional period for this purpose, as the net-wealth base of companies approaches more closely to fair market value.

For the above reasons, it is recommended that the receipts-based rule for determining presumptive income be repealed, but retained for a transition period as the changes to the net wealth base come into effect.

D. Comparison of net wealth

The current rule providing a presumption that the taxpayer's income is no less than the increase in the taxpayer's net wealth over the preceding year is quite deficient. Under this rule there would be no presumed income if the taxpayer's unreported income were consumed during the year.

One alternative to this rule would be to give flexible authority to the DIN (Dirección de Impuestos Nacionales) to reconstruct the taxpayer's income according to bank accounts, allowances for personal consumption, and any other available information. The granting of such flexible authority might, however, be problematic, in that such authority could be abused or applied in an uneven manner. Nevertheless, such a flexible approach should be considered, in light of the serious compliance problems in Colombia.

Under such an approach, the DIN could be given the authority to reconstruct the taxpayer's income on the basis of bank accounts and other assets. For example, if the taxpayer's bank accounts showed gross receipts of $10,000,000 over the year, these could be presumed to constitute taxable income, absent a contrary showing by the taxpayer. Accounts that are in the name of persons related to the taxpayer or that are in joint names with another person could be considered as belonging to the taxpayer for this purpose, absent a showing that deposits were actually made by the nominal owner from the nominal owner's separate funds. The taxpayer's acquisition of consumer durable items paid for from unknown sources could also be presumed to reflect taxable income, absent a contrary showing. If withdrawals from the taxpayer's bank accounts were not adequate to finance personal consumption (food, lodging, etc.), a reasonable allowance for such expenses, based on the taxpayer's apparent standard of living, could be presumed to reflect taxable income, again subject to rebuttal. The increase in the taxpayer's net wealth over the course of the year would be a factor in the reconstruction of the taxpayer's income, but would not be the sole means of performing the reconstruction. The taxpayer would be given the opportunity to rebut the DIN's determination, but would be required to offer detailed and probative evidence in order to prevail. Because such approach would necessarily vary in application from case to case, it would not be possible to specify completely mechanical rules that would preclude differences in result depending on who was conducting the audit.

An alternative to such a flexible approach would be to provide fixed rules based on readily available information that do not depend on the exercise of administrative discretion. For example, under such an approach, the taxpayer's income could be presumed to be no less than the cost of the taxpayer's car multiplied by a specified factor, plus the assessed value of the taxpayer's residence, also multiplied by a specified factor, and so on. Additional indices to be used for this purpose could include such items as energy consumption, rent paid, credit card purchases, and school tuition for family members. There should probably be an opportunity to rebut this presumption in a judicial determination, but in order to do so the taxpayer should be required to provide clear and convincing evidence and the burden of proof should be on the taxpayer. The advantage of this approach would be that it would give rise to less concern about potential administrative abuse; the examining agent would simply apply a mechanical formula. The disadvantage is that the multipliers would have to be set so as not to inadvertently catch honest taxpayers, thereby letting some dishonesty escape.

Because the Colombian institutions that would administer rules such as those described above have not been fully evaluated, no recommendations in this respect are being made at this time. The Government might consider appointing a special high level commission to examine how best to improve taxation of so-called «hard-to-tax» groups.

FIGURE 5-1

Host Country Withholding Taxes and

Their Effect on the Cost of New Equity Investment*

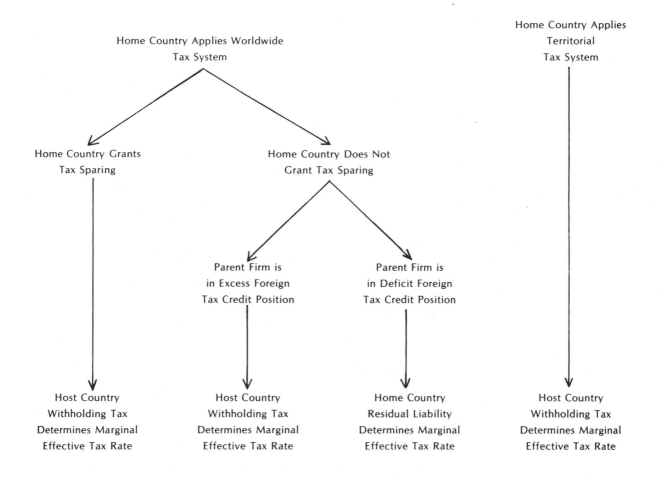

* As discussed in the text, investment out of retained earnings generally will not be affected by the host country withholding tax. Investment in foreign branch operations, whose income is taxed by the home country as earned, is subject to the same treatment as new equity investment.

APPENDIX A:

LONG-TERM CONTRACTS

Under the assumptions that profits on a long-term contract accrue as the work is performed, and that the appropriate measure of work performed is costs incurred, it is straightforward to calculate the income of a contractor who is currently paid on a cost-plus basis as the contractor's costs are incurred (assuming that the rules for determining the contractor's costs for tax purposes, such as the depreciation rules, conform to economic income). The income will simply be the difference between the payments received and the contractor's costs. There is no need for inflation adjustment in this simple case, because the contractor is reimbursed currently for all its expenses. For example, assume that the following costs are incurred at the end of each of the four years of the contract: $100, $60, $200, and $50. Suppose that the contract calls for the following payments to be made at the end of each year from the customer to the contractor: $120, $72, $240, and $60, and that these payments are in fact made. Under the percentage-of-completion method, taxable income for the four years of the contract will be as follows, 20, 12, 40, and 10. For example, at the end of year one, the percentage of completion would be 100/410, and the total contract price would be 492, so the amount of the price included in income is 49200/410 = 120, and the year's costs of 100 are deducted. Note that this calculation achieves a correct result in this simplified example regardless of the rate of inflation. At a different rate of inflation, both the nominal costs and the nominal payments for each year would be different from the above figures, but their ratio, and the amount of real profit taxable in each year, would be the same.

Accurate taxation of the more general case when contract payments are made earlier or later than completion of the work is more complicated. To illustrate, suppose that the pattern of payments differs from the above example, although the pattern of costs is the same as above. Thus, suppose that the payments are: 160, 22, 210, and 97.5. In order to compare these payments with the contract costs, we need to calculate the present value (or future value) of both. For convenience, the future value of both payments and costs will be calculated as of the end of the contract. Thus, interest on each payment and cost up to the final year of the contract will be calculated. This calculation requires the appropriate interest rate to be known.

Assuming that the interest rate is 25 percent (representing a real interest rate of 4.2 percent and inflation of 20 percent), the values of the above payments (including interest) as of the end of the contract are as follows: 312.5, 34.38, 262.5 and 97.5, for a total of 706.88. Similarly, the restated amount of the contract costs will be: 195.31, 93.75, 250, and 50, for a total of 589.06. The percentage markup on contract costs can now be calculated by dividing the total future value of the payments by the total future value of the costs: 706.88/589.06 = 1.2. Thus, the markup is 20 percent, as in the earlier example. (This markup may arise because the contract is a cost-plus contract, with an explicit markup of 20 percent, or may simply result from the payments specified under the contract and the actual amounts of contract costs.) We can now calculate the gross contract price attributable to each year of the contract, which will be 120 percent of contract costs for the year, as follows, noting also the difference between the actual payment received and the gross contract price.

The last column of Table 5-A1 shows the difference between the actual payments received and the amount that would have been paid if costs plus profit had been paid for currently. There is a prepayment of $40 in year 1 which has a year 2 value of $50. There is a delayed payment of 30 for year 3 which constitutes 37.5 paid in year 4. (For convenience, this example is constructed so that there is no carryover of excess or deficiency from year 2 to year 3.)

Now the total nominal contract profit of $79.50 (difference between total payments of $489.5 and total costs of $410) can be allocated over the contract period. Of the first payment of 160, 120 represents contract costs plus profit for year 1, and so is taxable for that year. (The 100 of contract costs are deductible, so the net taxable income is 20.) The remaining 40 of this first payment represents a prepayment of year 2 costs. Thus, if the 40 is restated in year 2 values (50) and added to the actual year 2 payment of 22, the total of 72 entirely satisfies the year 2 costs plus profit.

The taxable income for year 2 is computed by adding the prepayment of 40 made in year 1 to the payment actually received in year 2 (22), for a total of 62, and subtracting the year 2 contract costs (60), for a net taxable income of 2. Note that the amount added to the year 2 payment is only 40, rather than 50. This is because it is assumed that the contractor has invested the prepayment of 40 and is already separately taxed on any investment income earned. Because this investment income is presumably already inflation-adjusted, there is no need for inflation adjustment in computing the contract profits.

For year 3, the actual payment of 210 falls short of the 240 costs plus profit for that year, so that 30 must be brought forward from year 4 to cover the gap. Of this 240, the excess over contract costs, 40, is taxable.

The remainder of the year 4 payment, 67.5 (payment of 97.5 less the 30 relating to year 3), is taxable in year 4, less the 50 of contract costs, for a net taxable income in year 4 of 17.5. Of this amount, 10 represents the profit for year 4 and 7.5 is in the nature of interest on the delayed payment from year 3. Accordingly, a system of inflation adjustment would call for 6 to be exempt as the inflationary component of this interest.

If contract profits have already been taxed under the percentage-of-completion method as the contract was being performed, an adjustment will have to be made to reflect this retroactive allocation of profits. Thus, amounts can be added or subtracted from taxable income, as the case may be, and interest charged (or paid) on the resulting deficiency (or refund) for each year. Depending on the timing of these adjustments there will be a net amount of interest due to or from the contractor.

The above calculation, which may be called a look-back calculation because it looks back over the record of the contract when it is completed, can be summarized as follows:

1. Restate contract costs and payments in end-of-contract values by using an assumed nominal pre-tax interest rate.

2. Obtain the markup by dividing the total restated payments by the total restated costs.

3. Multiply each year's costs by the fraction obtained in (2), yielding the cost plus profit for each year.

4. Compare the first year's payment with the cost plus profit (amount in (3)) for that year. If the payment is less than the cost plus profit, bring back a portion of the next year's (or, if inadequate, a later year's payment) to make up the difference. If the payment exceeds the cost-plus-profit, carry the excess over to the next year. Subtract the contract costs; this is the taxable amount.

5. Repeat (4) above for each year. If an amount has been carried back from that year (or from a subsequent year), an amount of that year's (or a subsequent year's) payment representing interest on the amount should be treated as taxable in that year, and subject to the generally applicable inflation adjustment for interest. In comparing the year's payment to the cost plus profit for that year, interest must be added to amounts carried over from preceding years, but such interest is not taxable.

6. The amount of contract profit that is allocated to each year of the contract under the above calculation is to be compared to the amount that has already been subject to tax under the percentage of completion method. The increase or decrease in income should be added to the taxpayer's return, as adjusted in any previous audits, for the year in question, and interest is to be paid on any resulting change in tax liability.

Some assumption needs to be made as to when during the year contract costs were incurred. A half-year convention could be used for this purpose (i.e., it could be assumed that all costs incurred during one year are incurred on July 1 of that year).

Although the above method results in a fairly accurate inflation-adjusted measure of the income from long-term contracts, it is obviously fairly complicated and requires the reopening of prior years' returns. While it may not be practicable for these reasons, it does represent a useful benchmark against which alternative methods of taxing long-term contracts can be judged.

In particular, comparison with the above benchmark reveals that use of the percentage-of-completion method, without any adjustment for the time value of money or inflation, may be an appropriate alternative for Colombia. In cases where the contractor is paid for its costs plus profit on a fairly current basis, the percentage-of-completion method would yield the same result as the more complex look-back method described above. This is an important point, because it means that contractors would always have the option of obtaining accurate tax treatment by arranging to be paid on a fairly current basis. In the case of contracts involving prepayments that are made no more than one year in advance, the percentage-of-completion method reaches approximately the same result as the lookback method, because the income earned by the contractor by investing the prepaid amounts is taxed in the same year that it would have been taxed as contract profit. Thus, for example, suppose that the customer has $100 at the beginning of the year. The customer could pay the contractor $106 at the end of the period, (which is what the customer would have from investing the fund at an after-tax rate of 6 percent), leaving the contractor $63.60 after tax. Alternatively, assume that because the customer is required to capitalize construction-period interest, it is prepared to pay the contractor only $96.40 up front. At a pre-tax rate of return of ten percent, this comes to $106, roughly the same as the first case. Whether the $3.60 burden due to the interest-capitalization requirement assumed above is accurate depends on the length of the construction period and the use of the property by the customer. It is likely that this burden is not so high in most cases, so that prepayment will usually be advantageous. Inflation adjustment of interest income further increases the advantage of prepayment, because in this case not all of the contractor's income from investing the prepayment is taxed. Despite the ability to gain an advantage from prepayment, it is doubtful if it is worth the administrative complexity to eliminate the advantage, particularly since repeal of the completed-contract method would eliminate most of the tax advantages for long-term contracts. Where the prepayment is more than one year in advance, the contractor may achieve some deferral under the percentage-of-completion method, but the difference between the two methods will not be significant unless the contract term is very long.

Contractors that receive delayed payments (i.e., payments that are made after the time of performance to which they relate) may be overtaxed by the percentage-of-completion method in two ways. First, the delayed payment causes some acceleration of tax. Because the delayed payment contains an element of implicit interest income to compensate for the delay, the apparent amount of contract profit is greater than if the payment had been made at the time of performance, thereby causing what is in effect interest income that should be taxed in later years to be taxed as contract profits as the contract is completed in earlier years. Unless the bulk of the contract is completed early, this distortion should not be significant. More important is the fact that under the percentage-of-completion method as currently applied there is no inflation adjustment. Thus, the portion of delayed payments representing interest will be fully taxable, as compared with the more sophisticated look-back calculation that explicitly accounts for the interest element of delayed payments, thereby allowing such interest to be adjusted for inflation.

On balance, the complexity of the look-back approach does not seem justified for Colombia, given that fairly close results can be obtained in many cases by the percentage-of-completion method.

Accordingly, it is recommended that the income from all long-term contracts (i.e. contracts involving costs spanning more than one taxable year) be taken into account under the percentage-of-completion method. The percentage of completion would be calculated as under current law, that is by reference to contract costs incurred as a percentage of total contract costs. As discussed above, it would not be necessary to provide for any inflation adjustment in applying the percentage-of-completion method.

APPENDIX B

The seven proposed depreciation classes would be defined in the following manner. A table would be developed according to which every type of depreciable asset would be assigned to a depreciation class. The table would employ two classification methods. Certain assets, generally those that are commonly used in most industries, for example cars, office furniture and equipment, and computers, would be assigned to a class based on the characteristics of the asset, without regard to the industry in which the asset is used. All other assets would be assigned to a class based on the industry in which the asset is used; in some case there would be subdivisions for a particular industry, but there would usually be no more than two subdivisions. (For example, depreciable property used in the assembly of motor vehicles would be divided into special tools and all other assets.)

The depreciation rate and close-out year for the seven classes would be as follows: Alternatively, under the straight-line method, each asset would be assigned one of seven tax lives as set forth in Table 5-B1. The straight-line lives set forth above are determined so as to equate the present value of straight-line depreciation (using a 4-percent real discount rate) with the present value of depreciation under the percentage-of-basis method. This equivalence will generally hold if the tax system is fully adjusted for inflation. The present values of depreciation under the two methods (for an investment of $1,000) are shown in Table 5-B2. The present values differ only because the straight-line lives have been rounded to the nearest year.

Table 5-B3 shows the assignment of assets to classes. The table is based on the classification of assets by the U.S. Internal Revenue Service for purposes of the U.S. depreciation system (see Revenue Procedure 83-35, 1983-1 Cumulative Bulletin 745, for a detailed description of each asset class), and reflects how assets would have been classified under the depreciation system proposed by the U.S. Treasury Department in 1984. Because this classification was developed for the United States, it may be appropriate to make some changes in the classification for Colombia to reflect differences in the two economies. Nevertheless, the attached table should furnish a good starting point for a Colombian depreciation system. If the straight-line method is chosen, the table could be revised to show directly the straight-line life, there being no particular need to refer to an asset class, as well as simplified by combining different classes. Such a simplified table is set forth in Table 5-B4.

150

TABLE 5-1

Comparison of Economic Accrual and Straight Line Accrual

| | Economic Accrual | | Straight-line Accrual |
	Issue price plus interest at beginning of year	Accrued Interest	Accrued Interest
Year 1	327,680	81,920	134,464
Year 2	409,600	102,400	134,464
Year 3	512,000	128,000	134,464
Year 4	640,000	160,000	134,464
Year 5	800,000	200,000	134,464
Year 6	1,000,000	—	—
Total	—	672,320	672,320

TABLE 5-2

Hypothetical Example of Costs and Payments

	Costs	Payments	Profit	Present Value
Year 1	10.00	11.00	1.00	1.00
Year 2	12.50	13.75	1.25	.97
Year 3	15.62	17.19	1.56	.95
Year 4	19.53	21.48	1.95	.92
Year 5	24.41	26.85	2.44	.90
Total	82.07	90.27	8.21	4.74

TABLE 5-3

Foreign Investment Income and Taxes Paid in Colombia
(All figures in Millions of U.S. Dollars)

Source and Item	Year			
	1980	1982	1984	1986
Dirrección de Impuestos Nacionales[1]				
Taxable Income of Foreign Branches	NA[4]	NA	$317	$343
Income Taxes Paid by Foreign Branches	NA	NA	$107	$116
Banco de la República[2]				
Branch income remitted, total	$9.3	$15.3	$17.3	$16.1
Remittance tax, total	$1.8	$2.6	$3.2	$2.7
Dividends paid to foreigners, total	$59.6	$88.7	$115.4	$116.0
Dividends paid to foreigners, to U.S.	$37.2	$53.5	$82.0	$82.0
Withholding tax, total	$11.6	$17.4	$24.3	$23.3
Royalties paid, total	$9.3	$7.4	$6.6	$5.7
Royalties paid, to U.S.	$3.6	$4.4	$4.6	$3.0
Technical service payments, total	$16.5	$34.4	$71.2	$95.8
Technical service payments, to U.S.	$9.8	$23.8	$55.5	$66.9
Internal Revenue Service[3]				
Gross branch income in Colombia	$21.4	-$2.0	NA	NA
Colombian income taxes paid	$19.6	$29.2	NA	NA
Dividends received by U.S. corporations	$46.4	$102.4	NA	NA
Deemed paid credit	$23.0	$22.2	NA	NA
Colombian withholding taxes claimed	$9.9	$12.1	NA	NA
Gross royalties received	$26.0	$22.5	NA	NA
Specific deductions	$15.6	$14.9	NA	NA
Colombian withholding taxes claimed	$3.2	$6.6	NA	NA
Service income received	$18.9	$88.1	NA	NA
Specific deductions	$8.8	$22.8	NA	NA
Colombian withholding taxes claimed	$2.9	$3.2	NA	NA
Interest income received	$85.0	$113.8	NA	NA

1/ DIN revenue estimating worksheets
2/ Banco de la República worksheets, exclude petroleum
3/ IRS, Statistics of Income Bulletin, Fall 1986 and Winter 1984-1985
4/ NA denotes not available

TABLE 5-4

Current Private External Debt, by Geographic Source
(millions of dollars)

Description	1982	1983	1984	1985	1986
North America	875.4	880.3	880.8	921.2	918.9
Canada	2.9	2.6	10.2	9.3	7.4
United States	872.5	877.7	870.6	911.9	911.5
South America	15.7	14.0	11.3	12.3	14.2
Andean Pact	12.8	11.7	9.3	10.3	12.1
Other Countries	2.9	2.3	2.0	2.0	2.1
Central America	608.6	505.8	405.8	386.4	427.5
Central American Common Market	0.8	0.8	0.8	0.1	0.1
Mexico	28.1	21.2	19.5	24.0	29.1
Panama	579.7	483.8	385.5	362.3	398.3
Antilles	122.6	112.0	131.5	208.4	274.8
Europe	261.5	301.3	496.4	532.3	541.7
EFTA	15.8	16.0	13.7	11.2	9.3
EC	217.5	247.4	365.6	396.6	446.6
Rest of Europe	28.2	37.9	117.1	124.5	85.8
Other Countries	21.0	18.2	19.9	21.0	22.6
International Organizations	7.2	7.2	4.7	4.7	4.7
Total	1.912.0	1.838.8	1.950.4	2.086.3	2.204.4

(1) Includes private sector debts backed by government guarantees and also direct lines of credit. Excludes debt contracted through the financial sector or credits from suppliers.
Source: Banco de la República — Oficina de Cambios

TABLE 5-5

Hypothetical Change in Tax Revenue From Withholding Tax Reductions
(Pesos: Initial Revenue Collected Is $51)

Product Demand Elasticity	Withholding Tax Rate			
	.29	.25	.20	.056
−1	50.17	46.89	42.91	32.15
−2	50.34	47.70	44.35	34.62
−10	51.79	54.77	57.95	62.84

Example assumes company income tax rate of 30 percent, initial withholding tax rate of 30 percent, elasticity of substitution between labor and capital of 0.75, and capital's share in national output of 25 percent.

TABLE 5-6

Comparison of Taxation of $7,000,000, Depending on Its Characterization as Ordinary Income or Capital Gain

Ordinary Income	Capital Gain	Marginal Tax Rate		Tax
		Ordinary Income	Total Capital Gain	
1,000,000	6,000,000	0	30	1,207,250
6,000,000	1,000,000	30	0	1,207,250
3,500,000	3,500,000	25	25	1,074,500
7,000,000	— 0 —	30	0	1,537,250

TABLE 5-A1

Illustration of Look-Back Method

	Cost	Gross Price	Payment	Difference
Year 1	100	120	160	40
Year 2	60	72	22	(50)
Year 3	200	240	210	(30)
Year 4	50	60	97.5	37.5
Total	410	N/A	489.5	N/A

TABLE 5-B1

Alternative Depreciation Schemes

	Depreciation Rate	Close-out Year	Straight-line Life
Class 1	32 percent	5 years	4 years
Class 2	24 percent	8 years	6 years
Class 3	18 percent	12 years	9 years
Class 4	12 percent	17 years	13 years
Class 5	8 percent	25 years	20 years
Class 6	5 percent	38 years	31 years
Class 7	3 percent	63 years	49 years

TABLE 5-B2

Present Value of $1,000 Depreciation Allowance
Under Alternatives Proposals

	Percentage-of-Basis Method (a)	Straight-line Method (b)
Class 1	924	926
Class 2	888	891
Class 3	847	843
Class 4	781	783
Class 5	697	693
Class 6	582	579
Class 7	445	444

TABLE 5-B3

Depreciation Classes

Specific Depreciable Assets Used in all Business Activities

Asset Type	Class
Office Furniture, Fixtures, and Equipment	2
Computers and Peripheral Equipment and Data Handling Equipment	2
Airplanes (airframes and engines)	3
Automobiles, Taxis	1
Buses	2
Light General Purpose Trucks	1
Heavy General Purpose Trucks	2
Railroad Cars and Locomotives	5
Tractors Units for Use Over-the-Road	1
Tractors — other	3
Trailers and Trailer-Mounted Containers	2
Vessels, Barges, Tugs, and Similar Water Transportation Equipment	5
Land Improvements, Structures	7
Engines and Turbines	5
Industrial Steam and Electric Generation or Distribution Systems	4

Depreciable Assets (Other than Specific Assets Listed Above) Used in the Following Activities

Activity	Class
Agriculture (including cattle, horses, sheep, and goats)	4
Cotton Ginning Assets	4
Hogs, Breeding	1
Farm Buildings	7
Mining	3
Offshore Drilling, Drilling of Oil and Gas Wells, Exploration for and Production of Petroleum and Natural Gas Deposits	3
Petroleum Refining	4
Construction	3
Manufacture of Grain and Grain Mill Products	4
Manufacturing of Sugar and Sugar Products	4
Manufacturing of Vegetable Oils and Vegetable Oil Products	4
Manufacturing of Other Food and Kindred Products	4
Manufacturing of Food and Beverages — Special Handling Devices	1
Manufacturing of Tobacco and Tobacco Products	4
Manufacturing of Knitted Goods	4
Manufacturing of Yarn, Thread, and Woven Fabrics	4
Manufacturing of Carpets, and Dyeing, Finishing, and Packaging of Textile Products and Manufacturing of Medical and Dental Supplies	4
Manufacturing of Textured Yarns	4
Manufacturing of Nonwoven Fabrics	4
Manufacturing of Apparel and other Finished Products	4
Cutting of Timber	4
Sawing of Dimensional Stock from Logs	4
Manufacture of Wood Products, and Furniture	4
Manufacturing of Pulp and Paper	4
Manufacturing of Converted Paper, Paperboard, and Pulp Products	4
Printing, Publishing, and Allied Industries	4
Manufacturing of Chemicals and Allied Products	4
Manufacturing of Rubber Products	4
Manufacturing of Rubber Products — Special Tools and Devices	1
Manufacturing of Finished Plastic Products	4
Manufacturing of Finished Plastic Products — Special Tools	1
Manufacturing of Leather and Leather Products	4
Manufacturing of Glass Products	4
Manufacturing of Glass Products — Special Tools	1
Manufacturing of Cement	4
Manufacturing of other Stone and Clay Products	4
Manufacturing of Primary Nonferrous Metals	4

Manufacturing of Foundry Products	4
Manufacturing of Primary Steel Products	4
Manufacturing of Fabricated Metal Products	4
Manufacturing of Fabricated Metal Products — Special Tools	1
Manufacturing of Electrical and Non-Electrical Machinery and other Mechanical Products	4
Manufacturing of Electrical Components, Products, and Systems	4
Manufacturing of Motor Vehicles	4
Manufacturing of Motor Vehicles — Special Tools	1
Manufacturing of Aerospace Products	4
Ship and Boat Building Machinery and Equipment	4
Manufacturing of Locomotives	4
Manufacturing of Railroad Cars	4
Manufacturing of Athletic, Jewelry and other Goods	4
Railroad Equipment	5
Motor Transport	4
Water Transportation	4
Air Transport	4
Pipeline Transportation	4
Telephone Communications	4
Radio and Television Broadcasting	4
Telegraph, Ocean Cable, and Satellite Communications	4
Cable Television	4
Electric Utility Hydraulic Production Plant; Electric Utility Steam Production Plant; Electric Utility Transmission and Distribution Plant; Gas Utility Distribution Facilities; Gas Utility Manufactured Gas Production Plants; Water Utilities; Central Steam Utility Production and Distribution	6
Other Public Utility Property	4
Distributive Trades and Services and Recreation	3
Theme and Amusement Parks	6

TABLE 5-B4

Simplified Table Showing Straight-Line Lives

Specific Depreciable Assets Used in All Business Activities

Asset Type	Life (Years)
Office Furniture, Fixtures, and Equipment,Computers and Peripheral Equipment and Data Handling Equipment	6

	Life (Years)
Airplanes (airframes and engines)	9
Buses, Heavy General Purpose Trucks and Trailers and Trailer-Mounted Containers	6
Automobiles, Taxis, Light General Purpose Trucks, Tractor units for use over-the-road	4
Tractors — other	9
Vessels, Barges, Tugs, and Similar Water Transportation Equipment	20
Land Improvements, Structures	49
Engines and Turbines	20
Industrial Steam and Electric Generation or Distribution Systems	13

Depreciable Assets (Other than Specific Assets Listed Above) Used in the Following Activities

Activity	Life (Years)
Hogs, Breeding	4
Farm Buildings	49
Mining, Offshore Drilling, Drilling of Oil and Gas Wells, Exploration for and Production of Petroleum and Natural Gas Deposits	9
Construction	9
Manufacturing of Food and Beverages Special Handling Devices	4
Special Tools Used in Manufacturing of: Rubber Products, Finished Plastic Products, Glass Products, Fabricated Metal Products, or Motor Vehicles	4
Railroad Equipment	20
Electric Utility Hydraulic Production Plant; Electric Utility Steam Production Plant; Electric Utility Transmission and Distribution; Plant; Gas Utility Distribution Facilities; Gas Utility Manufactured Gas Production Plants; Water Utilities; Central Steam Utility Production and Distribution	31
Distributive Trade and Services and Recreation	9
Theme and Amusement Parks	31
All Other Activities	13

FOOTNOTES

1/ Chapter 2 contains a list of proposals classified according to the priority of their enactment.

2/ Pardo, in ANDI, (1987) at 23.

3/ This can occur for a number of reasons. For example, if depreciation is accounted for under the straight-line method for financial accounting purposes, but under an accelerated method for tax purposes, a taxpayer who has recovered for tax purposes the costs of a recently undertaken investment program, and whose current investment level is low, may have taxable income that exceeds financial accounting income.

4/ Of course, in present value terms, the ultimate correction does not fully compensate for the overtaxation, because of the delay in correction.

5/ If such distributions had been treated as returns of capital, they would not have been taxable, but would have required the recipient shareholder to reduce his or her basis by the amount of the distribution.

6/ I.e. the amount of the distribution, less any amount treated as nontaxable dividends under the 7/3 rule.

7/ If the distinction between capital gain and ordinary income is retained, the portion of the distribution that corresponds to accumulated profits of the corporation should be treated as ordinary income to the extent that it does not qualify for tax exemption under the 7/3 rule.

8/ This is the difference between the tax on $5,100,000 of income at a 30-percent rate, and the tax on such income under a separate rate schedule.

9/ For purposes of this rule, in the case of an expense that will be paid in kind (i.e. by the taxpayer's provision of property or services to another person), the payment would be considered made at the time that the property or services are provided by the taxpayer. Where a taxpayer incurs indebtedness in satisfaction of an obligation, the incurrence of the debt should be treated as a payment, provided that the debt bears adequate stated interest. The reason for treating such a debt as a payment is that the present value of such an obligation equals the face amount of the debt. Because this amount is fixed as a result of the debtor-creditor relationship, the above-described administrative concerns relating to allowance of a deduction for the present value of an obligation do not arise.

10/ Allowing a current deduction for the present value of a future obligation would be complex. In some cases, the time that the payment is to be made may not be known. In addition, the determination of the appropriate discount rate would be controversial, since the discount rate to be used should be the after-tax discount rate, which depends on the taxpayer's marginal tax bracket for each year until the expense is paid, as well as on the taxpayer's credit rating. Finally, if the actual amount of the future obligation turns out to differ from the estimated amount, complicated adjustments (involving calculations of interest) would have to be made, requiring reference to prior returns. (Current law presents a similar problem, in that excess deductions taken must be recaptured, but there is no interest calculation.)

11/ Inflation adjustment of interest leads to a different result than the result reached under explicit accounting for interest. Suppose that because of inflation adjustment only $50,000 of the $250,000 interest were taxable. In this case, accounting for the transaction as an interest-free loan would lead to a $50,000 inclusion for the purchaser and a $1,250,000 deduction for the cost of the good, for a net deduction of $1,200,000. Similarly, the seller would have net income of $1,200,000 ($1,250,000 less interest deduction of $50,000). Thus, delaying the deduction understates the amount of the deduction but also understates the income of the seller.

12/ It should be noted that any scheme for imputing income or capitalizing interest (or, indeed, any other expense) depends on the validity of the assumption that the property is actually increasing in value by the amount in question. On average, actual increases in value will exceed the amount of expenses to be capitalized, because the taxpayer will expect to earn a profit in excess of these expenses. Accordingly, it is reasonable to assume that the property is expected to increase in value at least by the amount of such expenses. Of course, in some cases, the actual increase in value will be less than expected. In these cases, if the taxpayer is taxed on the expected increase in value, he or she will be overtaxed. Ultimately, this overtaxation will be compensated for, since the taxpayer's basis in the property is increased in the amount that is taxed, although the delay in such compensation results in a net burden on the taxpayer in present value terms.

160

13/ This example is on the basis of current law, without modification for changes in the transition rules relating to inflation adjustment of interest that are proposed in Chapter 7.

14/ An argument can be made that interest should be capitalized only up to the point when property is included in inventory, on the basis that there is no reason to expect inventory to increase in real value over time. If interest capitalization were to stop at the point at which property is added to inventory, however, inflation adjustment should be allowed between that point and the time of sale. The administrative complexity of such an adjustment system argues in favor of a rule that would capitalize interest incurred to finance inventory up to the time of sale.

15/ The basic structure of this depreciation system would be substantially the same as that proposed by the U.S. Treasury Department in 1984, since this system represents the most up-to-date attempt to conform tax depreciation to economic depreciation. The description of the system is adapted from the General Explanation of the proposal issued by the U.S. Treasury Department (1984, Vol. 2, pp. 152-72), with some modifications.

16/ As discussed in Section D4, it is recommended that agricultural production costs be required to be capitalized. However, to the extent that the costs of planting and cultivation for the period before the plant or animal becomes productive continue to be deducted currently, there would be no depreciation deductions, since the taxpayer's basis would be zero.

17/ Thus, for example, suppose that a prospective lessee acquires a premium lease (i.e. a lease with below-market rentals) that runs for five years, and that the premium is worth $100 per year. If there is no inflation and the interest rate is 5 percent, then the present value of the lease is as follows:

	Premium	Present Value
Year 1	100	95.2
Year 2	100	90.7
Year 3	100	86.4
Year 4	100	82.3
Year 5	100	78.4
Total	—	433.0

Thus, the lessee will pay $433 for the lease. After one year, the lease will decline in value by 78.4. This decline in value represents 18 percent of the cost of the investment. By contrast, under straight-line recovery 20 percent of the cost (i.e. 86.6) could be recovered in each year. (In subsequent years, amortization deductions based on the decline in the present value of the premium would be 82.3, 86.4, 90.7, and 95.2.) Note that straight-line cost recovery will always be more accelerated than cost recovery based on the present value of the property, assuming that the property is of a type that furnishes an equal benefit for each year of its useful life.

The same relationship between straight-line cost recovery and a present-value calculation will hold where there is inflation. The calculation is more complicated, however, since basis must be adjusted for inflation each year.

Accordingly, where a cost is amortized over an ascertainable useful life, the amortization deductions could be calculated on the assumption that the investment generates an equal real benefit in each year of its life, unless a basis for an alternative assumption exists. The amortization deduction for each year would equal the decline in the present value of the investment between the beginning and end of the year, using a published nominal interest rate. The basis of the investment would be adjusted for inflation in making this calculation. Because of the complexity of this approach, we recommend that it apply only to those cases where the difference between economic and straight-line amortization is substantial, for example, investments with a recovery period of more than three years. Moreover, the rule need not apply to assets amortized under the five-year schedule provided by current law, since there is no evidence as to the actual economic depreciation of such assets. So limited, the rule would apply only to a small number of cases, and its only purpose would be to prevent an unduly fast cost recovery in such cases. In the absence of such a rule, taxpayers may have an incentive to structure transactions so as to benefit from the straight-line cost recovery rule.

18/ The percentage-of-completion method taxes a proportionate part of the contract profit in each year of performance, based on the percentage of the work that has been performed.

19/ This is demonstrated in Appendix A.

20/ Even though the current-law depreciation schedule is accelerated, it is not indexed for inflation, and is accordingly close to inflation-adjusted economic depreciation in present value terms at a rate of inflation of 25 percent. Therefore, under current law, the possibility of deducting currently the costs of producing depreciable property to be used in the taxpayer's business is approximately as serious a problem as it would be under a regime providing for indexed economic depreciation.

21/ See section 263A of the U.S. Internal Revenue Code.

22/ Account of profit ratios must be kept in order to determine the portion of each principal payment received with respect to an installment obligation that is taxable as profit.

23/ For a general discussion of the use of tax provisions to furnish government subsidies, see Surrey (1973) and Surrey and McDaniel (1985).

24/ This outcome also holds if the lender is exempt from taxation in his home country, even though the country applies a residence-based principle in taxing worldwide income. Exempt entities such as pension funds and non-profit foundations often are constrained from making such loans to foreigners, and that possibility is not considered further in this report.

25/ Given the absence of tax treaties discussed above, this same concern over residual foreign tax liabilities applies to foreign investment from other countries with residence based tax systems.

26/ Sub Part F provisions attribute passive, tax-haven income directly to the parent as if it were repatriated.

27/ Article 30.

28/ Proyecto, p. 15.

29/ Proyecto, p. 9.

30/ Art. 106 of D. 444/67.

31/ Res. 36 of CONPES/83, Dec. 3448/83.

32/ Art. 2 of Res. 17 CONPES/72.

33/ Art. 118 of D.L. 444/67.

34/ Res. 29 of CONPES/78, Res. 41 of CONPES/85.

35/ Because housing falls in this category, tax evasion or fraud need not account for all of this difference. Housing represented 16 percent of gross fixed investment in 1985 (Revista del Banco de la República, Marzo 1987, p. 1170).

36/ There is an advantage to retaining earnings abroad if the return after company tax is greater in Colombia than in the United States. One explanation of such a divergence in returns is the situation where Colombian returns are determined on the margin by foreign investors providing new equity funding. The return to new equity must exceed the return to retained earnings, because for funds not yet located in Colombia, the toll gate type taxes discussed above may be avoided by investing elsewhere. The return in Colombia must be high enough to compensate for the additional tax that will be due there but not elsewhere. Similar logic holds in the case of a residual U.S. tax liability when the U.S. rate applied to foreign earnings differs from the rate applied to other investments. For example, prior to 1986 U.S. domestic investment benefitted from the investment tax credit, while investment by foreign subsidiaries did not. Returns from foreign investment must be high enough to offset this less favorable tax treatment. Enterprises retaining earnings abroad benefit from the fact that the foreign marginal return must be high enough to cover the avoidable toll gate taxes.

37/ Even in the case where there are benefits from deferral, the Colombian withholding tax rate is not particularly relevant in determining how large they may be. That is, the Colombian withholding tax rate does not determine the gap between U.S and Colombian returns that generates the benefits from deferral.

38/ Because the relevant tax burden is greater for new equity investment than in the case of retained earnings a firm would be expected to fund any investment by first exhausting its retained earnings and only then providing new equity; it would not pay out dividends if its planned investment otherwise would require the provision of new equity by the parent.

39/ In the absence of more precise information, these average figures appear applicable to U.S. investment in Colombia. Most firms operating in Colombia have operations elsewhere in the world, and their foreign tax credit position is likely to be determined by worldwide average conditions rather than conditions in Colombia alone. If a sample of major U.S. firms operating in Colombia were selected and their U.S. 10-K reports analyzed, a measure of the parent's excess credit position might be developed that is more specific to Colombia. However, the drawback of such a procedure is that the 10-K figures generally refer to income from foreign operations, and do not necessarily include passive income from royalties, interest received, etc.

40/ As discussed earlier in this chapter, the foreign tax credit changes adopted by the United States in 1986 make it more likely that the U.S. Treasury will benefit from the current tax exemption for foreign lenders provided by Colombia.

41/ Because this example ignores the potential benefits from deferral, it gives only an approximate assessment of changes in the marginal effective tax rate on foreign investment. Nevertheless, it does provide a conceptual basis for distinguishing countries likely to experience capital outflows.

42/ A second consequence of the U.S. tax reform is to encourage the migration of the tax base, if not the relocation of real economic activity. U.S. affiliates may attempt to borrow in high-tax locations and lend to the parent, or charge higher prices on intracompany import by subsidiaries in high tax countries or charge lower prices on intracompany exports from high tax countries to transfer profits to lower tax jurisdictions. Although borrowing in Colombia may be discouraged by the nondeductibility of interest payments, the adoption of a thin capitalization rule, discussed above, should be pursued. Vigilance in auditing transfer pricing practices also will grow in significance due to U.S. tax policy changes.

43/ Given the U.S. tax rate of 34 percent, and a Colombian income tax rate of 30 percent, the withholding tax on dividends paid to a U.S. parent would have to fall to 5.7 percent from the current 30 percent rate in order that all Colombian taxes paid to be creditable against the U.S. tax liability. The latter outcome is particularly undesirable because such a loss in tax revenue requires higher taxes on domestic activity to make up the shortfall, a result that would be considered highly unfair and contrary to Colombian development strategy.

44/ Table 5-3 is based on the rate schedule for 1987.

45/ However, in light of the proposal to require realization of accrued gains at death, a deduction for capital losses should be allowed without restriction in the case of the final return of a deceased taxpayer.

46/ Under current law, gifts to charity give rise to a tax credit of 20 percent, but this credit is calculated with reference to the basis of the property, rather than its fair market value. In the case of appreciated property, this scheme is equivalent to allowing a credit for 20 percent of the taxpayer's basis, requiring realization of the gain, and allowing a charitable contributions deduction for the excess of the fair market value of the property over its basis. For example, if property with a basis of 20 and fair market value of 100 is contributed to charity, a credit of 4 is allowed. In addition to allowing the 20-percent credit with respect to the portion of the fair market value of the property equal to its basis (i.e. 20), the current rule can be said to implicitly require the taxpayer to realize the gain of 80 and to allow a deduction for a charitable contribution in the same amount (i.e. 80). In the case of taxpayers in brackets above 20 percent, this approach gives somewhat more preferential treatment for appreciated property contributions, as compared with cash. (If instead, the gain were required to be realized, but the credit were limited to 20 percent, there would be a net tax due on the appreciation.) On balance, however, the current rule seems appropriate, given the administrative considerations. The administrative advantage of this approach is, of course, that there is no need to value the property. Accordingly, the tax treatment of gifts and bequests to charities need not change: the tax credit would be determined by the basis of the property, and no gain would be recognized. If it is not clear already, it should be made clear that if the fair market value of the property is less than its basis, then the tax credit should be based on this lesser amount. This rule does, of course require valuation of the property (if the property has depreciated); for this reason it may rarely apply in practice, but it should be stated as a matter of principle.

47/ In addition, the tax administration may, if it wishes, treat any increase in net wealth over the course of the year (less any exempt income) as taxable income. Unlike the measure discussed in the text, however, this provision is not applied automatically and, more importantly, is rebuttable by the taxpayer. It appears that in practice this provision is hardly ever used.

48/ Such underreporting can be due either to a misstatement as to the quantity of inventory, or to undervaluation due to incomplete cost capitalization rules or the use of LIFO.

49/ See, e.g., Perry (1986).

50/ Ley 75/86, art 73. This 75-percent inclusion now applies only to rural properties not yet revalued under Law 14 of 1983; those that have been revalued are subject to the general 60-percent inclusion rule mentioned above.

51/ For 1984, the fiscal cost of this last exclusion alone was estimated at $5.2 billion (about eight percent of total assessed company taxes). (Comisión del Gasto Público, 1987).

52/ For this purpose, capital not invested in the business would not be used to reduce the amount of earned income presumed to be earned in the business.

53/ Ley 9/83, art. 15.

54/ D.L. 2053/74, art. 15.

Note from the editor: This Figure follows the above Figure 5-1.

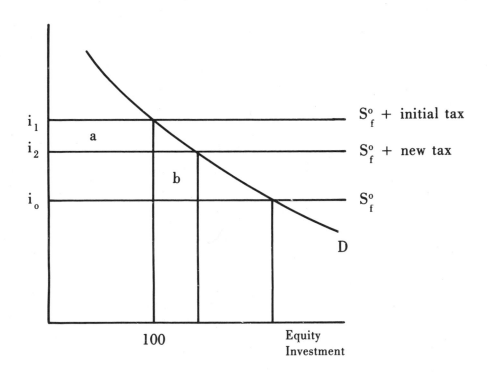

FIGURE 5-2

Revenue Effects of Withholding Tax Reduction

6

The Net Wealth Tax

The Net Wealth Tax

I. Introduction

The major problem in the administration of direct taxes in developing countries is the underreporting of income. Although Colombia has as many difficulties in this respect as most developing countries, over the years it has nonetheless managed to maintain the relative importance and to some extent the progressivity of its system of income and complementary taxes largely through the net wealth tax (impuesto de patrimonio) and the concept of presumptive income (renta presuntiva).

This chapter first outlines the rationale and effects of the net wealth tax in the context of the current Colombian income tax. The appropriate role and design of this tax under an income tax that approximates more closely to a tax on real (inflation-adjusted) income is then discussed. (The appropriate design of the net wealth tax under the Simplified Alternative Tax is discussed in Chapter 9.) Issues concerning inflation adjustment of the net wealth base are discussed in Chapter 7.

The role and design of presumptive income are discussed in detail in Chapter 5. Presumptive income plays the role of a minimum tax, in that it puts a floor under the income tax and hence limits the extent to which the income tax can be evaded. This role will become even clearer if the proposal for comparing presumptive income only with unearned income, offered in Chapter 5, is adopted. Presumptive income is closely related to the net wealth tax because the more important base for calculating presumptive income is net wealth. Accordingly, the proposals discussed in this chapter should be considered not only for their effect on the net wealth tax but also for their implications for presumptive income.

II. Rationale for the Net Wealth Tax

A tax on net wealth in essentially its present form has existed in Colombia since 1935, although both its rates and its base have been altered several times since then. The original purpose of this tax was explicitly to impose a heavier tax on income from capital than on income from labor, apparently on the ground that capital income had a greater «ability to pay» than labor income because it constituted a «purer» form of net income (perhaps on the theory that the provision of capital services involves less disutility than working). A net wealth tax, rather than a higher tax rate on capital income, was chosen to accomplish this goal in recognition of the fact that it is generally easier to identify taxable assets than to locate the income to which they give rise.

Additional arguments for the net wealth tax have frequently been made in Colombia. First, in view of the obvious difficulty in any developing country in taxing capital income effectively, it may be argued that a tax on wealth is needed not so much to tax such income more heavily than labor income but in many cases just to tax it at all. Secondly, the possession of wealth, whether it produces taxable income or not, may be thought to imply an ability to pay over and above that shown by any measurable income flow. Wealth can confer power, social acclaim, or peace of mind, quite apart from any income it may generate or any consumption it may finance. By expanding the options for consumption available to the taxpayer, wealth can bestow a further benefit. If wealth gives rise to such extra benefits, a tax on net wealth is needed simply in order to achieve horizontally equitable treatment of taxpayers who are in essentially the same position in terms of their ability to pay. Thirdly, since the concentration of wealth is greater than the concentration of income in every country, even a proportional tax on wealth will increase or at least preserve the progressivity of the fiscal system, a goal generally considered desirable.

Fourthly, achieving any given degree of progressivity with the combination of a moderately progressive income tax and a tax on net wealth may create fewer disincentives to saving and investment than would a more steeply progressive income tax. Fifthly, as has often been noted in Colombia with respect to rural land in particular, a tax on wealth may provide a useful stimulus to employ capital more productively in order to generate a flow of funds with which to pay the tax.

Finally, in light of the difficulty of taxing intergenerational wealth transfers as they occur, a net wealth tax may play the role of reducing the inequality of wealth distribution that could otherwise be played by a smoothly functioning transfer tax. Under current law, there are no wealth transfer taxes, but gifts and bequests are taxed as occasional gains of their recipients. The value used for this purpose is not fair market value, but is the value as reported on the donor's previous wealth tax return. Chapter 5 discusses proposals to tax the fair market value of gifts and bequests as ordinary income. The net wealth tax performs a complementary function to the taxation of gifts and bequests as income, since it too reduces the inequality in the distribution of wealth. Some gifts and bequests escape the net of the income tax, as such transfers may simply not be reported or may be undervalued. By contrast, a net wealth tax may be more difficult to avoid or evade, since it needs to be avoided or evaded every year, not only in the year of the transfer.[1/] Moreover, since there is no special tax on generation-skipping transfers, the income tax burden on gifts and bequests can also be reduced by making transfers that skip generations. The net wealth tax does not suffer from this problem, since the wealth would be subject to tax regardless of which generation owned it.

On its own, each of the arguments noted above may be vulnerable to attack on various grounds. In combination, however, these arguments provide a compelling case for taxing net wealth in any country, particularly in developing countries such as Colombia in which it is always difficult to bring the full weight of the income tax to bear on some of the most affluent sectors of society. The fact that the net wealth tax accounts for almost one-third of the total income and complementary tax paid by individuals, with most of this revenue almost certainly coming from higher-income individuals, suggests the importance of the tax in the present Colombian fiscal system. Moreover, the continued endurance of the net wealth tax through more than a half century of huge social, economic, and fiscal changes in Colombia suggests that the rationale for this tax is well accepted.

When coupled with the importance of net wealth as a basis for determining presumptive income (see discussion in Chapter 5), the case for the continued existence and indeed the strengthening of the net wealth tax as a key component of the Colombian tax system thus seems overwhelming. The balance of this chapter outlines the nature of the changes that seem necessary to strengthen the net wealth tax base.

III. The Measurement of Net Wealth

A. Debts

1. Allocation of debts to assets

If all assets were valued at fair market value and there were no taxpayer fraud, debts would not be a cause for concern under the net wealth tax. Net wealth would be properly measured by subtracting debts from assets. The actual net wealth tax is, however, plagued by problems of valuation and fraud. As a result, debts can become an avenue of tax avoidance or evasion. Such avoidance or evasion can occur in two ways: borrowing against appreciated property, and concealment of the proceeds of borrowing.

Consider first the taxpayer who reports all of his or her assets and debts. All of the debts will of course be stated in current pesos. But many of the assets may be valued (either legally or illegally) at less than fair market value.[2] By borrowing against the appreciated value of property, the taxpayer could substantially reduce and in some cases eliminate his or her net wealth for tax purposes. In the case of debt denominated in pesos, accomplishment of this result may require periodic borrowing as the taxpayer's assets appreciate in value. In the case of debts denominated in foreign currency, the taxpayer need not even take out additional debt, since the peso amount of such debts for net wealth tax purposes is adjusted upward each year according to the exchange rate, while the value of the corresponding asset is generally not adjusted to reflect the rise in its fair market value.

The taxpayer who is willing to conceal assets has an even easier time. If there are certain assets that the taxpayer cannot conceal (for example, the taxpayer's residence or a business operated by the taxpayer in Colombia), the taxpayer can simply borrow up to the value of those assets, and conceal assets purchased with the loan proceeds, thereby totally eliminating reported taxable net wealth. (Of course, if total elimination would be regarded as suspicious, the taxpayer may exercise restraint, and refrain from entirely offsetting his or her reported wealth with debt.)

Both types of abuse can be addressed by limiting the debts that are deductible in computing net wealth to those debts the proceeds of which were used to acquire an asset that is listed in the taxpayer's net wealth, and by limiting the deductible amount of such a debt to the taxable value of such asset for net wealth tax purposes.

Restricting deductible debts to those used to acquire an asset would have the effect in some cases of including in the tax base amounts that represent prior purchases of nondurable goods, thereby causing the tax base to exceed the net wealth of some taxpayers. Nevertheless, the advantages of the rule outweigh the potential inequity of any such overtaxation. There would be no such inequity in two types of cases where debt proceeds are used for personal purposes. First, there would be no overtaxation to the extent that loan proceeds are used to purchase consumer durables that are still in existence but are not reported on the taxpayer's return. Second, in the case of debt that was used to purchase nondurable consumption items, to the extent that the debt takes the form of borrowing against appreciation in value of the property that is not included in the net wealth base, the taxpayer has no cause for complaint.

For purposes of the recommendation described above, debt would be treated as incurred to acquire an asset if it was incurred to refinance debt incurred to acquire the asset. In the case of loans incurred to improve property, the improvement should be treated as an asset acquired with the proceeds of the loan. This will allow the loan to be fully deducted from net wealth, provided that the improvement is included in net wealth at a value at least equal to the amount of the loan.

If debt was incurred to acquire an asset that was initially listed as part of the taxpayer's net wealth, it may be that the asset is no longer so listed for legitimate reasons. For example, the property could have been destroyed or given to a family member. The property could also have declined in value or could have been sold, so that limiting the deduction for the debt to the value listed for net wealth tax purposes (i.e. the amount of the sales proceeds) would be unreasonable. In such special cases, the taxpayer should be allowed to deduct the debt, provided that the special circumstances are stated on his or her return. Any such claims should, of course, be audited as appropriate.

In order to restrict application of the above-described limitations, thereby simplifying compliance and administration, a de minimis amount of debt that is otherwise deductible in determining net wealth, would be deductible without a requirement to allocate it to particular assets.

One method of implementing the proposed denial of a deduction for debt that is not related to the acquisition of reported assets would be to establish rules for the tracing of loan proceeds. This approach would involve some complexity, but the complexity should not be great in most cases. Usually, a debt incurred to acquire an asset will be secured by that asset, and the debt will be paid off if the taxpayer disposes of the asset. Only when the debt is unsecured (or if security is substituted), and the loan proceeds are invested in assets that are subsequently sold and the sales proceeds are used to purchase other assets in succession will there be difficulty in tracing. In such cases, account must be kept of how asset sales proceeds are used.

The simplest approach to determining the use of loan proceeds would be to allow the taxpayer to allocate a debt to any asset purchased during the year in which the debt was incurred. Thus, debt newly incurred during the year and still outstanding at the end of the year could be allocated, at the taxpayer's option, to (1) any asset included in net wealth that was purchased during the year, (2) any asset to which was allocated any debt that was retired during the year, or (3) any asset purchased or debt retired in a subsequent year, if the debt is traceable to such transaction in a subsequent year. For example, suppose that on January 15 of Year 1 the taxpayer purchases an investment asset for $1,000,000 in cash, and takes out a bank loan for $1,000,000 on June 1. The loan could be allocated to this asset. Suppose that the loan is paid off on April 1 of Year 2, and that another loan of $1,000,000 is taken out on November 1 of Year 2. The new loan could be allocated to the asset purchased in Year 1, since the debt allocable to such asset was retired during Year 2.

The rationale for allowing flexibility in allocating debt is that it does not require the taxpayer to keep track of the use of debt proceeds, unless the related asset is purchased in a subsequent year. Assets newly acquired during the year will be known (because these are not listed as part of the previous year's net wealth), as will the net amount of new debt. All the taxpayer has to do is arbitrarily allocate the debts to the assets (any debts in excess of assets will not be deductible for net wealth tax purposes). Such flexibility is appropriate because a well-advised and careful taxpayer could have arranged for the physical use of debt proceeds in any manner, and there is no reason to constrain taxpayers to actually do this, since their financial affairs might be disrupted by such a requirement. (For example, in the above case, the taxpayer could have taken out the bank loan before purchase of the asset, and used the loan proceeds to make the purchase. In Year 2, the taxpayer could have taken out the new loan earlier and used the loan proceeds to retire the old loan.) Flexibility in allocation simply recognizes that any allocation is necessarily arbitrary, because of the fungibility of money. Once the allocation is made, however, it should be irrevocable for future years.

Taxpayers should be required to state on the net wealth tax return which assets are being treated as having been acquired with the proceeds of the debts that they seek to deduct. A mechanism should be devised to prevent the taxpayer from altering this story on future returns. This would require the prior year's return to be compared with the current year's return, a process that could be performed on audit or by requiring the current year's return to be filled in on a form that shows the taxpayer's assets and debts for the prior year, which could be mailed to taxpayers. The ability to make such comparisons effectively could greatly improve enforcement in the case of debts taken out after the effective date of the change. Such a debt would be deductible only if related to the acquisition of an asset reported as part of the taxpayer's net wealth. It will be clear from the face of the return (as compared with the return for the preceding year) whether the asset being claimed is a new one or was already listed on the prior year's return.

In the case of debt already in existence at the time of enactment of the new regime, the taxpayer should be required to show that the debt proceeds are traceable in some reasonable manner to the acquisition of a particular asset or assets included in net wealth. Claims that existing debt can be so allocated should be audited selectively, particularly in the case of heavily leveraged taxpayers. Debt that cannot be so allocated should not be deductible in determining net wealth.

However, a further measure seems necessary in the case of such nondeductible debt currently in existence. Merely denying a deduction for such debt would not preclude taxpayers from turning such nondeductible debt into qualifying debt by selling an asset, using the proceeds to retire the old (nondeductible) debt, and purchasing a new asset with newly incurred debt. The new debt would qualify for the deduction, since it was incurred for the purpose of acquiring an asset. To preclude this abuse, it should be presumed that the proceeds of existing debts that cannot be traced to assets included in net wealth were used to acquire assets that are unreported. This presumed amount should be added to the taxpayer's net wealth and adjusted for inflation, and should be removed only if the taxpayer reports a previously unreported asset, or demonstrates that the debt had been incurred to purchase property transferred to another person or property that was lost or destroyed.

The proposed rule requiring allocation of debt could be applied to individuals alone, or also to companies. Concealed assets may not be as large a concern with companies (particularly large companies with independently audited accounts), but the problem of borrowing against appreciated property may be just as significant for companies as for individuals, if not more so. Such borrowing is likely to be significant in light of the historical combination of the highly leveraged position of most Colombian businesses and the rapid depreciation and LIFO inventory accounting rules, which greatly understate the value of the assets of many companies. For example, large amounts of company debt were presumably incurred to finance the acquisition of equipment, which may have a zero basis for income tax and net wealth purposes, while its fair market value may be substantial. On top of the undervaluation of such property, allowance of a deduction for this debt permits the company to reduce the value of other assets in determining its net wealth, thus reducing its presumptive income and, for some companies, the net wealth tax of the company's owners.

2. Debts with below-market interest rates

Under current law, the full face amount of a debt is deductible in determining net wealth, even though the debt calls for the payment of interest at a rate below the current market rate. This treatment results in an understatement of the taxpayer's net wealth, since the true burden of the debt (i.e. the present value of all payments to be made) is less than the face amount.

To correct this problem, if the present ovalue of all payments to be made under a debt (discounted according to a rate of interest published by the government) is less than the face amount of the debt, then such present value should be substituted for the face amount of the debt in determining the taxpayer's net wealth. To minimize the number of instances in which this rule applies, the published rate could be set at a relatively low level, particularly for the first year or so that this rule is in effect, so that this rule would apply only in cases where there is a substantial difference between the face amount of the debt and its present value. Taxpayers should be required to report the interest rate applicable to debt, as well as its face amount.

Original issue discount obligations issued after the effective date of the proposal should generally be valued for net wealth purposes in conformity with their treatment for income tax purposes. This will result in a valuation that will generally be close to full market value. Accordingly, the above rule will almost never apply to such obligations. The rule would apply to obligations that are originally issued at a below-market interest rate or that bear an interest rate that is below the current market rate.

B. Real Property

Under the 1986 law, only 60 percent of the assessed value (avalúo catastral) of real property is included in the tax base for purposes of all national taxes, namely the net wealth tax and the presumptive income tax. This provision is especially important because in practice real property is undoubtedly the single most important component of the net wealth tax base. The history of the last few decades in this respect consists of a largely unsuccessful struggle to keep these assessed values from falling too far behind the pace of inflation. Indeed, it was only with the introduction of an automatic inflation adjustment system in 1983 that the real value of assessed property ceased to decline, for the first time in over a decade. This improvement in the local property tax base was, however, achieved at the price of allowing the property tax to be credited against the net wealth tax. The 1986 reduction of this important component of the net wealth tax base marked a considerable step backward in terms of strengthening the scope and effectiveness of both the net wealth and presumptive income taxes.

The value assigned for real property is particularly important in this context because it is almost the only value that can be readily checked by the tax administration. Other elements of the net wealth tax base — both assets and the liabilities set against them — are for the most part in effect self-assessed and difficult to audit. Even with respect to publicly quoted shares, it has been claimed that the market is so thin and closely controlled that prices are commonly depressed at the end of the year in order to keep the net wealth tax base low. The strong suspicion that commercial firms substantially underreported the value of their inventories[3/] was the reason for the introduction of the receipts-based presumptive income rule in 1983. The decline in bank balances and other visible evidence of wealth at the end of the year, when their value is supposed to be taken into account for purposes of calculating net wealth, is a well-known phenomenon. Fictitious debts are reportedly widespread, despite the existence of provisions intended to check this practice. All in all, it is difficult to think of any measure that would do more to improve the effectiveness and equity of the net wealth tax than the inclusion of the full assessed value of real property in the base, and the continued adjustment of that value in accordance with inflation. The concession already given in 1983 with respect to the crediting of property taxes against the net wealth tax seems more than adequate to deal with any legitimate concerns with respect to the overtaxation of real property, especially given the very low levels of even adjusted cadastral values.

Full inclusion of real property in net wealth is necessary to achieve a rational net wealth tax. This tax can never be satisfactory if some elements of the base are included at fair market value and others are substantially discounted. Moreover, the integrity of wealth-based presumptive income depends on full inclusion of all assets in the base for calculating the presumed rate of return.

C. Inflation Adjustment

Another major problem with the net wealth tax is the failure to adjust the base for inflation. This failure causes the valuation of different assets for wealth tax purposes to fall short of fair market value to varying degrees, thereby in effect imposing substantially different tax rates on different assets in a rather haphazard manner. (For further discussion, see Chapter 7.) It is clear that if a system of general inflation adjustment for fixed assets is introduced for purposes of the income tax, the increased values of depreciable assets and inventories must form part of the net wealth tax base unless the system is to lose all logic.

In general, it would be desirable from the point of view of simplicity and administration to use the same method of inflation adjustment, including the same price index, for all income tax and net wealth measurement purposes. Real property constitutes an exception. Under current law, a special index is used to revalue real property for purposes of determining cadastral values, which are in turn used for purposes of the net wealth tax. In this case, conformity with the property tax argues in favor of using the cadastral values, which are adjusted by a special real property price index, for purposes of the net wealth tax.

Inflation adjustment should apply to all assets other than assets that are valued at fair market value on a current basis (i.e. cash, securities traded on a stock exchange, and debt instruments denominated in Colombian pesos), since valuation at fair market value already implicitly takes inflation into account.

D. Excluded Assets

Pre-1974 assets that are currently excluded from taxable net wealth would remain exempt, but should be taken into account for purposes of determining the rate of taxation for the net wealth tax. Mechanically, this could be done by including these assets for purposes of determining the net wealth tax and then giving the taxpayer a credit for the amount of wealth tax liability that the taxpayer would have if such assets were taxable and were the sole assets of the taxpayer. The rationale for this treatment is that the excluded asset should not bear any net wealth tax itself, but still should be taken into account in determining how wealthy the taxpayer is for purposes of determining what rate to apply to the taxpayer's non-exempt wealth.

E. Financial Accounting Revaluations

If the assets of a business were revalued for financial accounting purposes, the new valuation should be used for purposes of determining the taxpayer's net wealth, but only if the new valuation exceeds the old valuation. The justification for this rule is that if the taxpayer itself declares that its assets have increased in value, it cannot object if that value is used for tax purposes.

IV. Coordination with Presumptive Income

A taxpayer's presumptive income can exceed taxable income as ordinarily determined for a number of reasons. First, the taxpayer may receive income in cash and fail to report it, or he may overstate deductions. Second, the income accounting rules may allow income to be deferred (for example, the taxpayer may take a current deduction for advertising expenses even though part of such expenses are really capital in nature). Third, there may be an unrealized appreciation in value of an asset of the taxpayer. Fourth, the taxpayer's income as measured for tax purposes may accurately reflect the taxpayer's economic income, but may simply fall below presumptive income because business was bad. Fifth, the presumptive income could constitute imputed income from consumer durables, which is not taxed for regular tax purposes.

It is proposed that the excess of the taxpayer's presumptive income over income as ordinarily determined should be presumed to reflect an increase in value of some asset or assets of the taxpayer, and so should be added to the taxpayer's wealth as of the beginning of the next taxable year. This assumption is in line with the third possibility (unrealized appreciation) discussed above. It is also consistent with the first possibility (unreported income), on the assumption that the unreported income is converted into an unreported asset. Where the unreported income is consumed, the taxpayer would be penalized by the presumed addition to wealth, but this case should attract little sympathy, because it involves taxpayer fraud. Moreover, the taxpayer can avoid the problem by accurately reporting income.

The second case above (legal deferral of income) is sympathetic, since the accrued increase in wealth may not take the form of a capital asset, but may result in additional taxable income in subsequent years. A taxpayer in the position of having potential presumptive income tax liability can often, however, take advantage of the flexibility inherent in accounting methods to eliminate this problem, by increasing income as measured for tax purposes up to the amount of presumptive income in the earlier year. (Income in later years would be correspondingly lower.) In such a case, there would be no excess of presumptive over ordinarily determined income in the earlier year. For example, such a taxpayer could amortize advertising expenditures that are capital in nature over the five-year period prescribed by law, rather than immediately deducting such expenditures. Only the taxpayer in the fourth case (temporarily depressed business), where the presumptive income tax is unfair in the first place, would be unfairly disadvantaged by the proposed rule. It is difficult to do anything about this case because the problem is inherent in the notion of presumptive income; there will always be taxpayers whose economic income is less than presumed, and relief cannot be accorded to them without abandoning the presumptive income tax altogether. The best that can be done is to make sure that the rate of presumed income is not so high that many taxpayers are caught in this bind.

In order to deal with the fifth case identified above, the amount of presumptive income that is attributable to owner-occupied housing and other consumer durables would be excluded from operation of the above rule. Such presumptive income reflects imputed income that is consumed by the taxpayer and that accordingly does not become part of the taxpayer's wealth. Accordingly, the net value of consumer durables and owner-occupied housing that is included in net wealth, multiplied by the presumed rate of return, should be subtracted from the excess of presumptive income over ordinarily determined income, and the balance should be added to net wealth. For this purpose, consumer durables should be restricted to personal-use items that are subject to depreciation (i.e decline in value) by reason of wear-and-tear. (Thus, items such as jewelry and paintings would be treated as investment items rather than as consumer items.)[4]

The amount added to net wealth under the rule described above will be referred to as «unallocated basis», since it reflects tax basis that has not yet been allocated to a specific asset. The effect of this rule would be to increase both the net wealth tax liability and the amount of presumptive income for subsequent years. Upon sale or disposition of a capital asset in a transaction in which gain is realized, the taxpayer would be allowed to use any such unallocated basis to reduce or eliminate the taxable gain. (Any capital losses carried over from a prior year would have to be exhausted first.)

In addition, in the case of assets in a nonproductive period (defined in the same way as under current law), the taxpayer would be allowed to add unallocated basis to the basis of such assets once they became productive (i.e. were used in the taxpayer's business or were sold) and recover such basis through depreciation deductions or as an offset to gain on sale of the property. The amount of unallocated basis that could be so added would be limited to the amount of presumptive income attributable to such asset during its nonproductive period. For example, if property with a basis of $100 were in a nonproductive period for one year, and the presumptive rate of return were eight percent, then $8 could be added to the basis of the property.

An alternative to allowing unallocated basis to be used fully against any realized capital gain would be to allocate the basis among the assets of the taxpayer on a pro rata basis. This would be difficult or impossible to do, however, since it would require the fair market value of the taxpayer's assets to be determined. Allowing unallocated basis to reduce realized gain is a simple rule; is favorable to the taxpayer; and has the salutary effect of reducing (and in some cases eliminating) the tax bias against selling appreciated property.

The application of the unallocated basis rule can be illustrated by the following example. Suppose that the taxpayer has net wealth of $50,000,000, ordinarily determined unearned income of $3,000,000, earned income of $5,000,000, and presumptive income of $3,500,000 (assuming, for purposes of this example, that the presumptive rate has been reduced to 7 percent). Taxable income would be $8,500,000. The $500,000 excess of presumptive income over unearned income as ordinarily determined would be added to the taxpayer's wealth, so that wealth for the subsequent year would be $50,500,000 (plus other additions to wealth and any adjustments, such as for inflation). If in a subsequent year the taxpayer sold for $800,000 an asset with a basis of $400,000, then the taxpayer could use up $400,000 of the $500,000 unallocated basis to wipe out the gain.

V. Coordination with Income Tax

Besides being appropriate for the proper measure of income, a number of the proposed changes to the income tax also have the effect of conforming the tax basis of assets more closely to their fair market value. Use of the income tax basis of an asset for net wealth tax purposes accordingly will help to rationalize the net wealth tax base, leading to more equal treatment for various types of assets. The changes involved are as follows.

The value of depreciable property for purposes of determining the taxpayer's net wealth would be its basis for income tax purposes. This basis would reflect economic depreciation and inflation adjustment. (See Chapters 5 and 7.) It will generally be higher than the basis of property under current rules, which involve fast write-offs and no inflation adjustment, and will in general correspond more closely to the fair market value of the property, thereby improving the accuracy of the net wealth and presumptive income taxes.

Indexed FIFO accounting for the cost of inventories (as proposed in Chapter 7) would also cause inventories to be valued closer to fair market value, and should accordingly be used for net wealth tax purposes.

The proposed rules for capitalizing indirect costs in the case of inventories and self-constructed property to be used in the taxpayer's business would also tend to bring the tax basis of this type of property closer to fair market value.

In the case of original issue discount obligations that are valued for net wealth tax purposes under current law on the basis of cost plus accrued discount, the same method of accruing original issue discount that is used for income tax purposes (i.e. economic accrual) should be used for net wealth tax purposes.

Bad debts should be written down at the same time that a deduction is allowed for income tax purposes.

Accrued but unpaid expenses that are not currently deductible for income tax purposes probably should not be deductible in computing net wealth, given that the corresponding accounts receivable are probably not included in the net wealth of another taxpayer. This lack of inclusion in another taxpayer's wealth is not necessarily due to fraud; it may be that no particular taxpayer has recognized these accrued amounts for income tax purposes, for example, because the recipient of the expense has not yet been identified.

VI. Treatment of the Family

The graduated rates for the net wealth tax imply a judgment that taxpayers with a higher amount of net wealth should pay higher rates of tax on their wealth than those with smaller wealth. For this purpose, a taxpayer's wealth should be determined by aggregating the wealth held by all family members, meaning the husband, wife, and minor children. Family wealth should be aggregated because the various benefits of owning wealth are in practice shared by family members, although in light of the intangible nature of these benefits the extent of such sharing in particular cases cannot be precisely determined. Under current law, a father with a net wealth of $10,000,000, whose wife and five children have no property, pays a net wealth tax of the same amount as a two-year-old with net wealth of $10,000,000 whose parents and siblings are quite wealthy. This simply makes no sense.

Moreover, the taxation of wealth can be shifted to lower-bracket family members under circumstances where it is not clear that the effective economic ownership of property (as opposed to its legal ownership) has actually been transferred. For example, a parent could execute a promissory note to a child. This action would reduce the wealth of the parent and increase the wealth of the child, even though the child may not in fact be aware of the arrangement or be able to enforce the obligation as a practical matter. Moreover, under such an arrangement, the parent would retain control over the property owned by the parent, since none of it, other than the note, would be transferred to the child.

The situation can be remedied by limiting a husband and wife to one graduated rate schedule for purposes of the net wealth tax, and by taxing the net wealth of minor children at the top marginal wealth tax rate, in the absence of an assignment of unused rate brackets from a parent of the child. A parent could assign an unused rate bracket to a child if the net wealth of the parent (combined with that of the spouse) fell below the top marginal rate bracket. The net wealth of trusts and estates should also be taxed at the top marginal rate, with rate bracket assignment allowed from the grantor of the trust.

VII. Treatment of Foreign Persons

Under current law, individuals are the only foreign persons taxed on their net wealth owned in Colombia. This rule is easily avoided by holding the wealth in the name of a corporation or partnership. In the case of net wealth owned by Colombian persons, the reason for imposing the net wealth tax only on the wealth of Colombian individuals is to prevent a double tax. This rationale does not, however, apply to foreigners, since there is generally no net wealth tax in the country of residence. Thus, in the absence of a net wealth tax on property held in Colombia by a corporation or partnership, there will be no net wealth tax at all, since the indirect owners of the property will not be subject to net wealth tax. To remove this anomaly of current law, the net wealth tax on nonresident foreign individuals should be repealed.

VIII. Tax Rates

The rate of the net wealth tax rises gradually to a maximum marginal rate of 1.8 percent on taxable net wealth over $15.3 million for the 1987 taxable year. When the tax was first introduced in 1935, the maximum marginal rate was only 0.8 percent, but it was raised to 1.1 percent in 1944, 1.5 percent in 1960, and 2 percent in 1974, before being reduced to 1.8 percent in 1985. Although unfortunately data are not available, it does not seem unreasonable to assume that the average rate of tax even on reported taxable capital is probably one percent or less. Moreover, since the reported tax base is undoubtedly much less than the real value of even taxable wealth, the real effective rate of the wealth tax in Colombia is no doubt much less.

Even with these low effective rates, the net wealth tax undoubtedly makes a critical contribution to the presumed goal of obtaining at least a modest degree of progressivity in the distribution of the fiscal burden among Colombians. In these circumstances, the present level of net wealth tax revenue seems warranted. Should the simplified alternative tax system, which essentially exempts most capital income at the individual level, be adopted, the maintenance of the present level of revenues from the net wealth tax seems even more necessary, at least in terms of generally accepted standards of equity.

If the reforms suggested herein are adopted, the base of the net wealth tax will be considerably broadened. This will enable the rates of tax to be reduced without diminishing the current level of revenue.

APPENDIX

Technical Description of Proposals

This appendix contains a technical description of the proposals discussed in Chapters 5 and 6, in the order in which they appear. It is intended to serve as a guide for those interested in the technical details of the proposals and those involved in drafting the legislation recommended for enactment in this Report. To avoid becoming unwieldy, this appendix does not describe alternative proposals that are discussed in these chapters; rather, only the alternative that seems at this point to be most appropriate is described. In some cases, the chapters discuss instances in which current law may require clarification or matters to which further consideration should be given, without recommending a specific proposal. These items are not treated in this appendix.

This appendix should be considered as only a first step for legislative drafting of the proposed changes; not all of the necessary details are discussed, and conforming amendments are generally not considered.

Income tax

1. Financial accounting limitation. The limitation on the amount of corporate income that can be distributed tax free to the shareholders, based on the financial accounting income of the corporation, would be repealed. This could be done by amending article 22, num. 2 of Law 75/86 by repealing the phrase «el cual en ningún caso podrá exceder de la utilidad comercial después de impuestos obtenida por la sociedad durante el respectivo año gravable».

2. Premiums on corporate shares. The taxation to the corporation of premiums received on the issuance of corporate shares in cases where the premium is subsequently distributed to the shareholders would be repealed. This could be done by amending art. 13 of Law 9/83 by inserting a period after «ganancia ocasional» and striking out the remainder of the article.

3. Trusts and estates. Provide that the income of trusts and estates (sucesiones de causantes colombianos, sucesiones de causantes extranjeros residentes en el país, bienes destinados a fines especiales, en virtud de donaciones o asignaciones modales, y contratos de fiducia mercantil) is taxed at the top marginal tax rate applicable to individuals. Trusts and estates would be treated as separate taxpayers for net wealth tax purposes and would be taxed on their net wealth at the top marginal rate applicable to individuals. In addition, perhaps it should be provided that the income of any «trust equivalent» is to be taxed at the top marginal rate. A trust equivalent would be defined as any arrangement that has the same effect as a trust (An example of a trust equivalent would be a legal life estate, with a remainder to another person.) As under current law, distributions from trusts or estates would not be taxable to the beneficiaries.

The fair market value property transferred to a trust or estate would be taxable to the trust or estate (see item 26(f) below). Again, this taxation of gifts or bequests would be in lieu of imposing a tax on the beneficiaries. In cases where property transferred in trust reverts to the donor, the trust should be allowed a deduction for the fair market value of the property at the time of the reversion (and, to the extent unused, the deduction should carry over to the donor).

4. Future payments. In the case of an accrual method taxpayer, no deduction would be allowed for any accrued but unpaid expense payable to any person other than an accrual-method Colombian taxpayer until the time of payment. For purposes of this rule, an expense that will be paid by means of providing property or services to another person would be considered as paid at the time that the property or services are provided by the taxpayer. Where the taxpayer incurs indebtedness in satisfaction of the obligation, the incurrence of the debt would be treated as payment, provided that the debt bears adequate stated interest (determined according to a published interest rate).

5. Advance payments.

a. In the case of a cash-method payor who makes a payment to an accrual-method payee, no deduction would be allowed for a payment in advance of the issuance of a bill by the payee.

b. A person making a payment to a foreign person could deduct the payment only at the time of «performance» to which the payment relates. In general, «performance» means the performance by the payee of whatever it is that the payee is being paid for. Where the payee is paid to provide property or services, performance consists of the provision of the property or services. In the case of property rented to the taxpayer, the property is considered as provided to the taxpayer as the taxpayer uses the property.

6. Intangibles. The special rule that the cost of certain intangibles is presumed to be 70 percent of the selling price (art. 25, D.L. 2053/74) would be repealed.

7. Reduction of earned income by losses. Revise Formulario Oficial No. 1 by requiring taxable earned income and exempt earned income to be listed on separate lines. Also require the expenses of earning taxable earned income to be listed separately from other expenses.

8. Agricultural losses. If the deduction for investments in certain agricultural enterprises provided by art. 106 of Law 75/86 is not repealed, provide that such deduction may not be used to offset non-agricultural income. This could be done by treating the deduction as an agricultural loss for purposes of art. 8, D.L. 2348/74.

9. Net operating losses. Repeal the five-year limitation in art. 23, Law 9/83. Provide that when a loss is carried over to a subsequent year, the amount of the loss shall be increased each year by the nominal rate of interest (determined according to a published government figure). In each year that a loss carryover is so increased, the amount of such increase shall be treated as interest income received by the taxpayer.

10. Foreign currency losses. Amend art. 30, D.L. 2053/74 to remove references to adjusting the cost of goods with reference to exchange losses. These provisions are to be replaced by a general rule concerning interest capitalization.

11. Original issue discount.

a. In general. The proposal would apply to obligations with original issue discount, defined as the excess of the redemption price at maturity over the issue price. In the case of such obligations, the amount of interest would be determined by multiplying the adjusted issue price by the yield to maturity, the adjusted issue price being the issue price plus amounts of interest previously taken into account.

b. Contingencies. In the case of obligations involving a contingency, the amount of interest income and expense would be determined by applying a published rate of return to the issue price. However, if the rate of return that would obtain if all contingencies were resolved in favor of the maximum payment is lower than such published rate, then such lower rate would be used. If there is only one contingency, the amount of interest would be adjusted to reflect resolution of the contingency at the time that the contingency is resolved. If there is more than one contingency, an adjustment would be made at the time that a sufficient number of these contingencies were resolved so as to render the assumed rate incorrect.

12. Publicly traded debt instruments. Both interest income and expense on debt instruments that are publicly traded would be computed by applying a published interest rate to the price of the instrument on the relevant stock exchange as of the end of the preceding year. Such price would be determined in the same manner as under art. 120, D.L. 2053/74. In addition, any increase or decrease in the value of the instrument, measured as of the close of the current year, would be taken into account by both the holder and the issuer as capital gain or loss.

For example, suppose that an instrument with OID yielded $200 in interest paid in cash and also increased in value from $15,000 to $20,000. Suppose that the published interest rate were 25 percent. The amount of interest would then be 25 percent of $15,000, or $3,750. Accordingly, since $200 of interest is paid in cash, $3,550 of the increase in value of the instrument would be treated as interest and the remainder ($1,450) would be treated as capital gain for the holder and capital loss for the issuer.

For this purpose, any accrued but unpaid interest that would not be included in the stock exchange valuation (i.e. that would not belong to a purchaser of the instrument) would be treated as paid. This rule for determining interest would override the OID rules (that is, a publicly traded obligation with OID would not be subject to the OID rules).

Because capital gains and losses would be taken into account every year under the above rule, taxpayers would not have the opportunity to selectively realize losses while deferring gains. Accordingly, the above-described gains and losses should not be taken into account in determining the limits on the deduction for capital losses (i.e. the losses should be allowed without limitation and the gains should not enter into the amount of realized gains for purposes of determining the limitation).

13. Below-market loans. Amend art. 20, Law 9/83 to provide for presumed interest at a market rate, determined according to a published government figure. Such presumed interest should be made eligible for the general rules relating to the inflation adjustment of interest income.

14. Mortgage interest. The deduction allowed by art. 47, D.L. 2053/74 for home mortgage interest should be eliminated. If this is not done, the deduction should at least be limited to interest relating to the taxpayer's principal residence. Where the taxpayer lives in more than one residence during the taxable year, the taxpayer's principal residence would generally be defined as the residence where the taxpayer spends the longest period of time during the taxable year. (Such an objective test is designed to prevent taxpayer claims that, for example, the city home is the husband's principal residence, while the country home is the wife's principal residence, even though both the husband and the wife spend the majority of their time in the city home.) Thus, in general, a taxpayer could have only one principal residence for any one taxable year. However, where the taxpayer moves during the taxable year to a new residence, both the old principal residence and the new residence (but only one at any given time) would be considered to be the principal residence of the taxpayer for the year of the move.

15. Preproductive-period interest.

a. Definition. Preproductive-period interest is interest expense incurred during the preproductive period of property that could have been avoided if the property had not been purchased or produced, as the case may be. The amount of interest expense that could have been avoided is determined with respect to the average rate of interest on all outstanding debt of the taxpayer; it is presumed that any production expenditures could have been used to retire such debt. The preproductive period of property begins when the taxpayer first incurs costs for producing, manufacturing, constructing, planting, raising, etc. the property. In the case of property purchased or produced for use in the taxpayer's business, the preproductive period ends at the time the property is placed in service. In the case of property held for sale, the preproductive period ends when the property is sold.

b. Capitalization. A taxpayer may elect to capitalize preproductive-period interest. If such interest is capitalized, current deduction for payment or accrual of the interest is not allowed, but the full amount (including the inflationary component of the interest) is added to the basis of the property for all tax purposes, including depreciation allowances, amortization, depletion, etc. and for calculation of the value of inventories and cost of goods sold. Preproductive period interest must be capitalized in the case of real property and property with a construction period of two years or longer.

c. Property constructed under contract. A taxpayer who contracts with another to construct property for the taxpayer will be treated as incurring construction expenses with respect to that property to the extent of any payments made to the contractor.

16. Depreciation.

a. Classification. Assets would be classified for depreciation purposes into seven classes. Each class would be assigned a useful life; salvage value would be ignored. A preliminary description of the assets contained in each class is set forth in Appendix B to Chapter 5. Intangible assets would not be subject to this system, and would be amortized under rules similar to current law. In addition, assets that are currently depreciated under a depreciation method not measured in terms of years (such as the units-of-production or income-forecast method) would not be subject to the new system. Plants and animals would be depreciated on the basis of published tables geared specifically to Colombian agriculture.

b. Method. Assets would be depreciated according to the straight-line method. That is, in each year, the amount to be deducted is the adjusted basis divided by the number of remaining years of the asset's life. For purposes of this calculation, the basis of the asset would be adjusted annually for inflation. The inflation-adjusted depreciated basis would be used to compute gain or loss on the disposition or retirement of the asset and would also be used for purposes of determining the taxpayer's net wealth.

c. Convention. All taxpayers would be required to use the half-year convention for assets included in one of the seven depreciation classes. Thus, for the first year only one-half year's worth of depreciation would be allowed, and the basis of assets would be adjusted upward for one-half year's worth of inflation.

d. Repair allowance. An annual repair allowance would be specified for each class. The level of the allowance should be set according to a reasonable level of repairs for the particular type of property in Colombia. Any expenses related to repair or improvement of an asset that do not exceed this annual allowance would be deductible; the balance of such costs would have to be capitalized.

e. Additional-shift rule. The rule allowing additional depreciation if an asset is used for more than one shift would be repealed.

17. Long-term contracts. The income from long-term contracts would be taken into account under the percentage-of- completion method. That is, the method described in num. 1 of art. 69, D.L. 2053/74 would be made the sole acceptable method of accounting for long-term contracts.

18. Production costs. Large enterprises would have to account for indirect costs in capitalizing the costs of producing property to be used in the taxpayer's business or to be sold. Indirect costs would be capitalized as follows: First, the taxpayer's total direct costs of manufacturing and other production activities would be determined. Second, the direct costs of the taxpayer's non-manufacturing or non-production activities (such as service, research and development, and sales and advertising activities) would be determined. Third, the taxpayer's indirect costs would be determined by subtracting the total direct costs identified above from the total business expenses of the taxpayer. These indirect costs would be allocated to manufacturing and other production activities in proportion to the direct costs of such activities as a percentage of the taxpayer's total direct costs. Finally, the indirect costs allocable to manufacturing and other production activities would be allocated to specific goods in proportion to the direct costs of producing such goods.

Taxpayers engaged in purchasing products for resale would determine their cost of such products by accounting not only for the direct cost of the goods, but also for the indirect costs of acquiring the goods.

The above rules would only apply to «large» enterprises. These would be defined as taxpayers currently required to submit a return signed by a public accountant. Once a taxpayer is treated as a large enterprise for this purpose, it would continue to be so treated, absent consent from the DIN.

19. Installment method. The installment method would be repealed. Accordingly, taxpayers who sell property on installments would recognize the entire income in the year of sale, even though they do not receive the cash until later.

20. Pensions. The current-law exemption for a specified peso amount of pension income would be modified by reducing the exempt amount by a specified fraction of the excess of the taxpayer's total income (including the pension income) over a specified amount. Thus, the law would specify that an amount of pension income equal to $x would be exempt from tax, but that the exempt amount would be reduced by y percent of the excess (if any) of the taxpayer's total income (including total pension benefits received) over $z. During the transition period, z could be set at a high level, and could eventually phase down to x. In addition, y could be increased over time and x could be reduced to zero.

21. Timber.

a. The reforestation credit (D. L. 2053/74, art. 98) would be repealed.

b. The expenses of planting and maintaining trees while they are growing (including interest expense) would be required to be capitalized.

c. The election to exempt 80 percent of the proceeds of timber sales (D.L. 2348/74, art. 12) would be repealed.

22. Cattle raising.

a. The exemption for cattle sold in the year they were born would be repealed.

b. Repeal the last sentence of art. 15 of Law 20/79 (construing the cost of cattle to be no less than the fair market value as of the beginning of the year).

c. Require the costs of raising cattle to be capitalized (determined under published tables, so that the farmer would not have to keep track of the exact cost of each animal).

23. Agricultural investments. The deduction for investments in certain agricultural enterprises (art. 106, Law 75/86) would be repealed.

24. Publishing. The exemption for publishing income; the exemption of publishing company investments from the net wealth tax; and the exemption for author's royalties would be repealed.

25. Exports and Tourism. Repeal the exemption for income earned in free trade zones. Repeal the tax credit for investment in hotels. Repeal the CERT credit.

26. Occasional gains.

a. The special rate schedule for occasional gains (ganancias occasionales) would be repealed. The taxpayer's net occasional gain (i.e. the excess (if any) of occasional gains over occasional losses) would be added to ordinary income in determining the taxpayer's tax liability.

b. Occasional losses (perdidas occasionales) could be deducted against occasional gains of a later year. Such losses could be carried over for an indefinite period, but no interest would be allowed on the loss.

c. The current-law treatment of winnings from lotteries, etc. would be maintained.

d. The basis of property for purposes of calculating gain or loss would be its adjusted basis (i.e. cost, adjusted for items such as depreciation, amortization, and depletion, and for inflation. Any valuation changes made for purposes of the net wealth tax (other than basis adjustments such as those described above) would accordingly not affect the basis for income tax purposes.

e. The exemption for awards for scientific etc. accomplishment (Law 9/83, art. 44) would be repealed. Such awards would be taxed as ordinary income (not as occasional gain).

f. The fair market value of property received by gift, bequest, legacy, or inheritance would be treated as ordinary income (not as occasional gain). In the case of transfers in trust, the trust would be taxed on the gift or property received from the decedent.

g. The donor or decedent would recognize gain (measured with respect to the fair market value of the property transferred) upon making a gift or a transfer at death.

h. The exclusion for gain on property sold to a government agency (Law 9/83, art. 25) would be modified to provide for nonrecognition treatment, with a carryover of the taxpayer's basis for income tax purposes.

27. Wealth-based presumptive income.

a. The amount of wealth-based presumptive income would be compared with ordinarily determined unearned income, which would be defined as total ordinarily determined income, less earned income. (For this purpose, earned income means taxable earned income less the expenses of earning such income). If presumptive income exceeds ordinarily determined unearned income, the taxpayer's taxable income would be the sum of (1) presumptive income and (2) earned income. In the case of income derived from a business in which the taxpayer works and in which capital of the taxpayer is invested, the amount of earned income would be determined by subtracting from the total taxable income attributable to the business the amount of presumptive income attributable to the taxpayer's capital invested in the business (i.e. the net wealth of the taxpayer invested in the business multiplied by the presumed rate of return (currently eight percent)).

b. The exclusions for property in a nonproductive period, property used in cattle raising, property subject to rent control or development restrictions, and real property affected by the volcanic activity of the Nevado del Ruiz would be repealed. These exclusions would be replaced by a general rule that a taxpayer may petition for a revaluation of an item of property, on the basis that the valuation of the property exceeds its fair market value.

c. The excess of regular income over presumptive income would be allowed to be carried over to be used in a future year against the excess, if any, of presumptive income over regular income. No interest on this carryforward would be allowed. This rule would be phased in. For example, in the first year, a carryover could be allowed to the extent that regular income exceeds 200 percent of presumptive income, 180 percent in the second year, and so on down to 100 percent.

d. Filing requirement. Taxpayers who under current rules do not have to file a return would only have to file if their presumptive income exceeds their regular income by more than a specified amount, but only if their total income (including presumptive income) exceeds the filing threshold.

e. A specified peso amount of the net patrimonial value of the taxpayer's principal residence and personal-use property (automobile, home furnishings, etc.) would be exempt from the base for calculating wealth-based presumptive income. This exemption could be phased out in real terms by providing that the specified amount will not be adjusted for inflation.

f. The presumed rate of return would be reduced from 8 percent to no more than 5 percent over a period of years, under an appropriate schedule. The schedule for the phase down should be adjusted as appropriate, depending on revenues and experience with the new system.

g. Deposits in financial institutions would be excluded from the presumptive income calculation (i.e. they would be excluded from the base for computing presumptive income, interest on such deposits would be subtracted from ordinarily determined income in comparing such income with presumptive income; and the taxpayer's total income would be the sum of: earned income, presumptive income, and interest on deposits in financial institutions). To qualify for this exclusion, the taxpayer would have to attach the information return from the financial institution to his or her return, and report the interest shown on the information return as part of taxable income (subject to any applicable inflation adjustment).

28. Receipts-based presumptive income.

The receipts-based rule for determining presumptive income would be repealed, but retained for a transition period as the changes to the net wealth base come into effect.

Net Wealth Tax

29. Limitation of Debts to Value of Related Asset.

a. Debts would be deductible only if used to purchase an asset that is listed in the taxpayer's net wealth, and only to the extent of the taxable value of such asset as shown on the net wealth return.

b. With the approval of the DIN, a taxpayer could deduct a debt even if not allowed to do so under the above rule, upon an appropriate showing as to what became of the asset purchased with the debt proceeds. For example, the taxpayer would be allowed to deduct the debt if he or she shows that the asset was stolen, destroyed, or given away, or is valued at an amount below the amount of the debt because of a decline in value since the time of acquisition.

c. In determining whether the proceeds of a debt were used to acquire an asset, the taxpayer would be allowed to elect to treat any asset acquired during a particular year as having been acquired with the proceeds of any debt incurred during that same year. In addition, any debt incurred during the year could be allocated, at the taxpayer's option, to the asset to which was allocated any debt that was retired during the course of that year. Once debt is allocated to á particular asset, that allocation could not be changed in subsequent years.

d. In the case of debts outstanding as of the effective date, the taxpayer would be required to show that the debt proceeds are traceable in some reasonable manner to the acquisition of a particular asset or assets included in net wealth. The amount of existing debt that is nondeductible under this rule would be presumed to reflect assets that are not reported as part of net wealth (or appreciation in value of assets that are reported). Thus, the debt would be fully deductible but an amount equal to such debt would be added to net wealth. Such amount added to net wealth could be reduced only if: the taxpayer reports a previously unreported asset; demonstrates that an asset acquired with the debt in question was stolen, destroyed, or transferred to another person; or realizes appreciation in value of assets included in net wealth.

e. A specified peso amount of debt that is otherwise deductible in determining net wealth would be deductible without a requirement to allocate it to particular assets under the rules described above.

30. Below-market debts.

In the case of debt owed by a taxpayer where the present value of all payments to be made, discounted at a specified published rate, is less than the face amount of such debt, the amount of the debt that is deductible for purposes of determining the taxpayer's net wealth would be such present value. The published discount rate could be set at a relatively low level, at least for the first year that this rule is in effect.

31. Real property.

The exclusion of a percentage of the assessed value of real property (Law 75/86, art. 73) would be repealed.

32. Inflation adjustment.

The value of property (other than property that is valued at fair market value, such as property listed on the stock exchange), would generally be adjusted for inflation using a general price index. The value of real property would be adjusted for inflation using the same real property price index as is used for purposes of the real property tax. In general, the value of real property for net wealth tax purposes would be the greater of its assessed value for property tax purposes and the inflation-adjusted basis of the property.

33. Excess presumptive income.

a. The excess of the taxpayer's presumptive income over income as ordinarily determined would be added to net wealth as of the beginning of the taxable year following the year of such excess. Such amount would be adjusted for inflation in subsequent years and would become part of the net wealth base for purposes of determining presumptive income in the future. Such excess is hereinafter referred to as «unallocated basis».

b. Unallocated basis would be used to reduce or elimi(nate any subsequent taxable gain on the disposition of property by the taxpayer (but could not be used to create a loss).

c. Unallocated basis could also be added to the basis of property in a nonproductive period, thereby generating additional depreciation deductions with respect to such property when it is placed in service, or reducing the gain upon disposition of the property. The amount that can be so added would be limited to the amount of presumptive income attributable to the property during the property's nonproductive period.

d. Presumptive income attributable to owner-occupied housing and other consumer durables would be subtracted from presumptive income in applying the rule set forth in a. above. For purposes of this rule, consumer durables would be restricted to items that are subject to depreciation by reason of wear and tear. (Thus, items such as gold, jewelry, and paintings would be treated as investment items rather than as consumer durables.)

34. Treatment of family.

a. The wealth of a married person would be taxed under a rate schedule whose brackets were half as large as the brackets applicable to single persons. A spouse could assign unused rate brackets to the other spouse, as described below.

b. The wealth of minor children would be taxed at the top marginal net wealth tax rate, absent a rate bracket assignment from a parent. The rate bracket assignment would operate as follows: the parent would determine his or her net wealth. If the parent's net wealth falls into the top marginal rate, there would be no rate brackets to assign. If either parent's wealth falls below the top rate, he or she (or both) could assign to his or her (or their) children, in any combination, the rate brackets taxable at rates below the top marginal rate that the parent has not used, and the amount of tax payable by the assignee would be determined according to the rate for the assigned bracket or brackets, to the extent of the width of such brackets. The assignment of brackets would have to be made at the time the parent files his or her return and would be irrevocable. For purposes of any subsequent adjustments to the net wealth of the assignor, the assignor's rate schedule would be determined by deleting the assigned unused brackets. (Thus, for example, if the parent's net wealth is subsequently increased on audit, and all brackets below the top rate have been assigned to the children, then the adjustments will be taxed at the top rate).

The net wealth of trusts would also be taxed at the top rate bracket, and the grantor of a trust would be allowed to assign unused rate brackets to the trust.

Absent a rate bracket assignment from a parent or a grantor, a trust or minor child would have no unused rate brackets to assign to another person, since trusts and minor children would be taxed at the top rate. A trust or minor child that receives a rate bracket assignment and is the grantor of another trust could reassign the bracket to such trust.

35. Excluded assets.

Pre-1974 assets that are excluded from the net wealth tax under current law would continue to be excluded, but would be taken into account in determining the rate of net wealth tax to be applied. The mechanism for this would be to include the valuation of such assets in applying the rate table, but then to subtract the tax that would apply under the rate table to the amount of such assets alone. (It should also be noted that, as a corollary of no. 29 above, debt incurred to purchase excluded assets could not be subtracted in determining the taxpayer's net wealth.)

36. Financial accounting revaluation.

If the assets of a business are valued in financial reports of the business at an amount in excess of the valuation used in determining net wealth, the financial accounting value would be used for tax purposes.

37. Foreign persons.

Foreign persons not resident in Colombia would be exempt from the net wealth tax.

FOOTNOTES

1/ Evasion of tax on a transfer takes the form of one-time concealment of the asset transferred, while evasion of the net wealth tax requires concealment not only of the assets, but also of future income from the asset. It is often easier to conceal the existence of the asset for one year than to conceal it and the income it produces indefinitely. Moreover, avoidance of tax on a donative transfer often takes the form of understating the fair market value of the asset. There is often a colorable basis for such understatement, such as reasonable uncertainty as to valuation, minority discounts, blockage discounts, splitting of interests via «estate freezing» transactions, and the like. While peculiar circumstances may facilitate undervaluation at the time of the transfer, these circumstances may not continue forever, and may therefore preclude subsequent undervaluation for net wealth tax purposes. Thus, for example, if the heir subsequently sells the asset, its fair market value will be less subject to dispute.

2/ The proposals set forth in this chapter and in Chapter 7 would reduce the extent to which assets would be valued below fair market value for net wealth tax purposes, but would not eliminate this problem. Thus, even if these proposals are adopted, undervaluation will be a problem due to taxpayer fraud or aggressive positions taken at the time of a gift or bequest. Moreover, rules for valuing property other than at the time of gift or bequest will not always produce taxable values that correspond to fair market value. For example, small businesses would continue to be valued by reference to the adjusted basis of their assets (instead of their fair market value as a going concern), and real property assessments are not likely to keep up with fair market value, even if the revaluation of real estate provided on Law 14 of 1983 is fully implemented.

3/ Such underreporting can result from the use of LIFO; the failure to fully capitalize production costs; or the failure to adjust asset values for inflation; as well as from underreporting of physical levels of inventories.

4/ This distinction is admittedly somewhat arbitrary, in that items such as jewelry and paintings involve the possibility of real appreciation in value and provide consumption benefits. An alternative solution would be to exclude an arbitrary fraction, say, one-half, of the value of such nondepreciable items from the calculation.

7

Inflation Adjustment

Inflation Adjustment

I. Introduction

The income tax of Colombia, like that of virtually all countries, was originally designed for a world of stable prices. In such a world, it is quite reasonable to base depreciation allowances for tax purposes on historical costs, to base deductions for costs of goods sold on the assumption that inventory is handled on a first-in, first-out basis, to allow deduction for the full amount of interest expense, and to tax all interest income and all realized capital gains.[1/] Providing problems of income definition, including especially those involving timing issues (such as those discussed in chapter 5 above), are handled appropriately, income for tax purposes should closely resemble real economic income. Moreover, in such a world, accounting calculations of net wealth based on historical costs should provide a reasonable basis for both a net wealth tax and a wealth-based presumptive income tax of the type employed by Colombia.[2/] In a world of substantial inflation, on the other hand, a tax system based on historical values that would be satisfactory in an inflation-free world creates serious problems.[3/] Because taxable income under such a system does not accurately reflect real economic income, inequities and distortions of economic decisions occur.[4/] Moreover, the base of the net wealth tax is seriously understated.

This chapter is devoted to an examination of the problems in the measurement of income and net wealth created by inflation.[5/] It is relevant for the consideration of comprehensive income tax reform and reform of the net wealth tax (under both income and consumption based strategies compared in chapter 10), but not for introduction of the Simplified Alternative Tax. As noted in chapter 10, one of the primary advantages of the Simplified Alternative Tax described in Chapter 9 is that there is no need for inflation adjustment, since all monetary quantities that are relevant for tax purposes are reported in values of the current year. The potential administration and compliance advantages of the Simplified Alternative Tax are somewhat less in Colombia than in other countries, because of the existence of the net wealth tax. On the other hand, some observers would argue that it is acceptable for Colombia to consider the Simplified Alternative Tax only because it does employ the net wealth tax. This Report thus proposes that the net wealth tax should be retained and strengthened, even if Colombia should choose to adopt the Simplified Alternative Tax. (See chapters 6, 9, and 10 for further discussion.) If the net wealth tax were used to supplement the Simplified Alternative Tax, reforms of the net wealth tax base would presumably be less ambitious than if the tax continues to supplement the income tax. Even so, improvement of the net wealth tax would require at least a few basic reforms that would guarantee that its base approximates actual net wealth more closely — essentially indexation of the basis of depreciable assets and more realistic valuation of inventories.

Section II provides a general description of the problems created by the interaction of inflation and a tax system based on historical values. Section III presents evidence that the economy of Colombia does indeed exhibit some of the symptoms of such problems. Section IV describes briefly the system of inflation adjustment introduced in Law 75 of 1986 to deal with these problems and notes that it is not sufficiently comprehensive in its coverage.

Section V presents an appraisal of an especially important issue, whether Colombia should continue to utilize the type of partial and ad hoc adjustments to particular items in an income statement based on unindexed historical costs envisaged in the 1986 law or should move to an integrated system such as that employed in Chile, in which the balance sheet is adjusted for inflation and these adjustments are reflected in income for tax purposes. (The basic details and rationale of an integrated system of the type used in Chile are provided, but only in appendix A to this chapter, in order to avoid interrupting the flow of the argument of the text.) The existence of the net wealth tax (and the presumptive income tax based on net wealth) in Colombia provides a strong argument for adoption of an integrated system that is not found in most countries. After all, even under an ad hoc approach adjustments should be made to many balance sheet items in order to provide an improved measure of net wealth, as well as to measure income more accurately. None the less, the section concludes that moving all the way to a Chilean-type integrated system at this time would probably not be advisable, despite the manifest advantages of such a system.

Section VI provides further conceptual background for the appraisal of the Colombian system of inflation adjustment. The most important issue is whether inflation adjustments should be based on changes in general price levels or on changes in prices of particular assets or other measures of replacement costs. Included in this section is a discussion of the inflation adjustment that is appropriate for imports of capital goods financed by debt denominated in foreign currencies.

Section VII examines in detail the particular inflation adjustments contained in the 1986 law (other than provisions for transition) and makes proposals for their improvement; it also indicates complementary changes that should be made, especially in the tax treatment of depreciable assets and inventories. Of course, much of this discussion is more applicable to businesses than to individuals.

Section VIII examines in greater depth than section II the economic effects of not providing inflation adjustment and the effects of doing so, especially on the cost of capital experienced by businesses operating in Colombia. Reflecting the fact that Colombia acquires funds on world capital markets at terms that are essentially beyond its control, this section emphasizes the role played by international capital flows in determining these effects.

Section IX contains proposals for transition to the proposed treatment of depreciable assets and inventories and an appraisal of the transition rules for phasing in interest indexing (the exclusion from income and the disallowance of deduction of the inflationary component of interest payments) contained in the 1986 law. It recommends changes that should better accomplish the two-fold objective of easing the burden on those who would be affected particularly adversely by the 1986 provisions for interest indexing, while simultaneously increasing the speed with which improved measurement of income for tax purposes resulting from inflation adjustment would come into effect. Mitigating these adverse effects should reduce political opposition to inflation adjustment and hasten the improvement of decision-making at the margin.

The final section draws together the conclusions of the chapter in one readily accessible place.

II. The Nature of the Problem

The problems caused by the interaction of inflation and a tax system based on unadjusted historical costs are somewhat different, depending on whether or not inflation is anticipated and therefore reflected in economic decisions. Moreover, the mere fear that the rate of inflation may change significantly can cause problems, by affecting economic decisions. The problems associated with inflation (whether actual, expected, or only feared) may be serious enough to justify resort to measures to offset the effects of inflation in causing mismeasurement of taxable income and net wealth. Whether this is true depends on the rate of inflation that is currently being experienced, the rate that is expected to prevail in the future, and the degree of uncertainty about future inflation.

A. Unexpected Inflation

If inflation is unanticipated, the problem caused by the mismeasurement of income resulting from a tax system based on historical values is primarily one of tax equity. Creditors experience windfall capital losses equal to the product of the inflation rate and the amount of money owed them, and debtors experience windfall gains of the same amount; however, a tax law based on historical costs takes account of neither of these windfalls in the measurement of income. Similarly, capital gains taxes are paid on gains that are purely inflationary, capital losses are understated, and capital gains taxes may even be levied when the taxpayer experiences a real loss, rather than a gain.[6] Finally, those who have invested in physical assets such as depreciable assets or inventories are unable to recover their capital (or to maintain a given level of investment) tax-free.[7]

The lack of inflation adjustment poses problems for the net wealth tax as well as for the income tax. The basis of depreciable assets is understated, and if LIFO is used for inventory accounting the value of inventories is also artificially low. To the extent that other capital assets increase in price as a result of inflation, their values are also understated. Of course, these understatements reduce presumptive income artificially, in addition to depressing the base of the net wealth tax.[8]

There is also likely to be an undesirable element of vertical inequity in the pattern of taxation that results from the interaction of unexpected inflation and a tax system based on historical costs. The understatement of net wealth is especially important in this regard; given the pattern of ownership of assets and the structure of the net wealth tax, the understatement of assets for purposes of the net wealth tax and the calculation of presumptive income is likely to reduce the progressivity of the tax system. The pattern of overtaxation and undertaxation across income classes created by unexpected inflation is somewhat more difficult to predict for the income tax. To the extent that those with greater income or wealth are more sophisticated and therefore more able to predict inflation, to protect against its effects, or to avoid paying taxes on fictitious income they are less likely than lower income taxpayers to be harmed by the interaction of inflation and a tax system based on historical values.[9] But these differences are generally more relevant for the discussion of the effects of anticipated inflation. Finally, to the extent that inflation causes mismeasurement of income it interferes with both vertical and horizontal equity in yet another way, by subjecting taxpayers to marginal tax rates that are not appropriate to their levels of real income.

B. Anticipated Inflation

Inflation that is not expected can cause little distortion in the allocation of resources or in financial decisions, though it may create expectations (or fears) that inflation will occur in the future. Except for such effects on expectations, the gains and loses from unanticipated inflation are truly windfall gains and losses that by their very nature can have little effect on economic decisions. (Uncertainty about the course of future course of inflation can affect economic decisions, for example, by causing investors to prefer real investments over financial investments and causing both borrowers and lenders to prefer debt obligations with short maturities.)

The situation is generally quite different in the case of anticipated inflation. The economic effects produced by the combination of expected inflation and an unindexed tax system are discussed briefly here, without systematically taking into account the important fact that Colombia is a very «open» economy, i.e., an economy that acquires capital on world capital markets at terms that are largely beyond its control. These effects and the effects of inflation adjustment, especially on the cost of capital in Colombia, are considered further in section VIII.

Consider first the special and unrealistic case in which debt-financed investment is made only in land or other non-depreciable assets whose income tax treatment is not affected by inflation; this allows attention to be focussed first on the effects of inflation working through the taxation of interest-bearing obligations.[10/] If borrowers and lenders have the same expectations about the future course of inflation and are subject to the same marginal income tax rate, equilibrium solutions in an inflationary world can be expected to be quite similar to those in a world without inflation, in terms of real (inflation-adjusted) after-tax interest rates, resource allocation, and financial decisions.[11/] In such a world, the failure of the tax system to allow for inflation would have little real effect on either the equity of taxation or economic decisions. Nor would net wealth be misstated, except to the extent that inflation-induced increases in land values would not be reflected in its calculation.[12/]

Of course, borrowers and lenders do not necessarily have the same expectations about the future course of price levels, and they certainly are not necessarily in the same marginal tax brackets. (Lenders, including tax-exempt organizations, are commonly subject to lower marginal tax rates than borrowers.) Even more important, significant amounts of real investment — in depreciable assets, inventories, other capital assets — occur in assets that also are not treated «correctly» under the income tax in a time of inflation. Nor are debt obligations treated correctly. (Correct treatment is defined below.)

It can be expected that taxpayers will respond to the incentives created by the combination of inflation and a tax system based on historical costs in such a way as to earn the same (risk-adjusted) after-tax real rate of return from all investments. As a result, the equity effects of failure to index the tax system may be much less important than in the case of unexpected inflation. (One potentially important source of inequity results when income is taxed at the wrong tax rates under a graduated rate schedule — say that of the lender, rather than that of the borrower — in inflationary times.) But taxes levied on an income base calculated from data on historical costs can cause important distortions of investment decisions and financial structures. In a sense, the inequities that result when inflation is unanticipated are converted to inefficiencies when inflation is anticipated.[13/] Moreover, the failure to provide inflation adjustment in the measurement of taxable income and net wealth can create important perception problems, even if there are no real inequities. In fact, in most real world cases the undesirable effects of inflation almost inevitably include some combination of inequities caused by unexpected changes in the rate of inflation and distortions caused by expected changes.

The inability to recover or maintain capital under these circumstances discourages investment in physical assets. Capital is diverted from investments in which fictitious gains, as well as real ones, are subject to tax. Saving is discouraged, and borrowing is encouraged. Debt is favored over equity as a source of finance, with adverse effects on the vulnerability of the economy to a cyclical downturn. Equity-financed investment in depreciable assets is discouraged. But the benefits to debtors of full deduction of nominal interest expense can easily dominate the costs resulting from the failure of depreciation allowances to reflect inflation, so that marginal effective tax rates paid by companies on debt-financed investment in depreciable assets are well below statutory rates, or even negative. The calculations of marginal effective tax rates presented in chapter 4 indicate the magnitude of the divergence from the statutory tax rate that can be caused by relatively low rates of inflation, even in a system that would be economically neutral in the absence of inflation.[14/] Of course, it is these divergences in marginal effective tax rates that create distortions in resource allocation and financial decisions.

C. Ad Hoc Approaches

As long as the rate of inflation remains relatively low (say, below 10 percent), or is expected to return to a low level after a temporary spurt, most governments are ordinarily quite reluctant to adopt, as a permanent part of their tax systems, explicit measures intended to offset the effects of inflation. This is true in large part because of the great complexity of such measures.[15/] To prevent the erosion of capital-consumption allowances, many countries adopt ad hoc approaches such as acceleration of depreciation allowances, first-year investment allowances, investment tax credits, and various other investment-related incentives, and some allow the use of LIFO accounting for inventories. Partial exclusion of nominal capital gains is also sometimes justified as a means of offsetting the effects of inflation.[16/]

While ad hoc steps such as these may prevent the adverse effects on capital formation that result from an unindexed tax system, they cause problems of their own. Acceleration of depreciation allowances and other investment incentives can properly correct for only one rate of inflation; at any other rate a given combination of depreciation allowances and investment incentives will be either too generous or not generous enough. Thus, as a technical matter it is extremely difficult to provide ad hoc increases in capital-consumption allowances intended to compensate for inflation that do not cause distortions of resource allocation because the resulting pattern of marginal effective tax rates is not uniform across economic activities. Moreover, once real economic depreciation is cast aside as a guide for policy in this area, political power is often left as the primary determinant of depreciation schedules.[17/]

The problems with using partial exclusion of nominal capital gains to offset inflation are generally even worse. As with accelerated depreciation allowances (and other investment incentives), a particular exclusion rate is appropriate only for particular combinations of inflation rates and real gains; other combinations can cause the exclusion rate to be either too high or too low. Moreover, excluding part of nominal capital gains from tax cannot rectify the fact that tax is collected when real losses occur.[18/]

A final difficulty with such ad hoc approaches is especially relevant for Colombia. Acceleration of depreciation allowances intended to compensate for the effects of inflation in eroding the real value of depreciation allowances based on historical costs causes the value of such assets (as indicated by adjusted basis or book value) to be understated for purposes of determining the net wealth of the taxpayer. This, in turn, causes an understatement of liability for the net wealth tax and the calculation of presumptive income. This understatement occurs for two reasons: first, the use of historic costs, rather than inflation-adjusted costs, in the calculation of depreciated basis; and second, the acceleration of depreciation allowances. By comparison, if depreciation allowances were based on application of estimated rates of economic depreciation to the inflation-adjusted basis of assets, as proposed below (and in greater detail in chapter 5), both income and net wealth would generally be measured more accurately (at least to the extent depreciable assets are at issue).[19/]

Similarly, the use of LIFO for purposes of inventory accounting gives a more accurate measure of cost of goods sold than does FIFO in a world of inflation. But it results in a chronic understatement of the value of inventories, since the value assigned to ending inventories is the cost of the oldest stock.

It is useful to reemphasize this last point — that the goals of calculating real economic income and calculating net wealth on the basis of current values of assets are sometimes in conflict and sometimes in harmony, depending on the exact method used to allow for the effects of inflation. Where conflicts in these two objectives (accurate measurement of real income and of net wealth) are irreconcilable, perhaps for administrative reasons, it is suggested that priority be given to accuracy in the measurement of income. It seems that more tax revenue is likely to be at stake and that both equity and neutrality are more likely to be compromised by defects in the measurement of income than by defects in the measurement of wealth.

The measurement of income requires that historical costs incurred in previous periods be indexed for inflation using a general price index. (On the choice of a general price index rather than replacement cost or a specific index of asset prices for this purpose, see the discussion of section VI.) By comparison, the measurement of net wealth requires that assets be valued at their current market value. In the absence of shifts in relative prices, this dual objective is achieved automatically by inflation adjustment of the basis of depreciable assets and either indexed FIFO or indexed LIFO accounting for inventories, but not under unindexed depreciation schemes or under either unindexed LIFO or unindexed FIFO.[20]

Objectives are more likely to conflict when there are changes in relative prices. Using a general price index to adjust the basis of depreciable assets results in proper allowances for depreciation in the measurement of income (provided the time pattern of allowances reflects economic reality); by comparison it does not produce an accurate measure of net wealth, to the extent that the price of the fixed asset does not change at the same rate as the general price level. On the other hand, using replacement costs or a specific index for the price of capital goods may give a better measure of net wealth, but it is not appropriate from the point of view of income measurement. (This distinction is explained further below.)

Indexed FIFO produces accurate measures of both cost of goods sold and ending inventories, at least if FIFO accurately portrays the physical movement of goods. The cost of goods sold is based on the indexed historical cost of the goods acquired earliest, and ending inventories are valued at the price of the most recently acquired inventories. By comparison, under these assumptions about the movement of goods, indexed LIFO mismeasures both the cost of goods sold and the value of ending inventories, to the extent that the goods in question rise in price at a rate different from the general rate of inflation.[21] Both these errors work either for or against the taxpayer, depending on how replacement costs move in relation to the general price level; that is, if costs of goods acquired for inventory rise faster (slower) than the general price level, both income and net wealth are understated (overstated). Of course, if LIFO more accurately describes the physical flow of goods, indexed LIFO is more accurate than indexed FIFO in the calculation of income, but indexed FIFO more accurately reflects the value of ending inventories.

Table 7-1 summarizes the conclusions of the preceding discussion of inflation adjustment of non-monetary or real assets. It indicates, for example, that indexed FIFO and a system of indexed economic depreciation provide reasonably accurate measures of both taxable income and net wealth. By comparison, such alternatives as accelerated depreciation based on historical costs and inventory methods other than indexed FIFO result in the mismeasurement of income, net wealth, or both.

Finally, ad hoc measures such as these do nothing to correct the distortions that result from the full deduction of nominal interest expense and the taxation of nominal interest income. Employing ad hoc measures for capital-consumption allowances, inventories, and capital gains, without also disallowing deductions for the inflation component of interest expense, can create serious inequities and can distort decisions on resource allocation and methods of finance, as demonstrated by the calculations of marginal effective tax rates in chapter 4. Failure to exclude the inflation component of interest income can also cause inequities and adversely affect saving incentives.[22] The net effect on tax revenues depends on the relative importance of these deviations of taxable income from real economic income and the choice among various means of attempting to deal with them.

D. Options for Colombia

Despite these problems, as long as a high rate of inflation is not expected, it may be better to accept the inequities and distortions inherent in ad hoc adjustments than to pay the administrative and compliance costs of explicitly indexing the tax system for inflation. But in some countries in which relatively high rates of inflation are deemed to be a more or less permanent fixture of the economy, as in several Latin American countries and in Israel, policy-makers have judged the advantages of an explicit system of inflation adjustment to outweigh the disadvantages. Thus Argentina, Brazil, and Chile (among others) have long had quite far-reaching systems of inflation adjustment for the calculation of income for tax purposes.[23] In such systems, indexation commonly extends to financial assets and liabilities, as well as to physical assets such as depreciable assets and inventories.

The most refined of the Latin American systems of inflation adjustment — and the one that is generally agreed to be the most sophisticated in the world — is that used in Chile. The Chilean system involves an «integrated» approach in which a) the value of real assets and net worth in the balance sheet are corrected for the change in the general price level and presented in real terms in currency of the current accounting period, and b) these balance sheet adjustments are reflected in the income statement. This approach produces inflation-adjusted measures of both income and net wealth. (Moreover, in Chile the same concepts must be employed in the calculation of both taxable income and income for financial accounts. Section VI below considers the propriety of such a «conformity» requirement.) A more detailed explanation of the approach used in Chile is provided in appendix A to this chapter; the advisability of Colombia's adopting that approach is appraised in section V.

Less sophisticated systems simply make ad hoc adjustments for the loss of purchasing power of certain financial assets and liabilities, as well as adjusting depreciation allowances (and perhaps the basis used in determining capital gains) for inflation in calculating income for tax purposes; they may or may not also require adjustment of balance sheets. LIFO inventory accounting is commonly provided as a means of dealing with the potential understatement of cost of goods sold; inflation adjustment seldom extends to indexation of the value of inventories, under either LIFO or FIFO. Mismeasurement of real income is not totally eliminated, and the balance sheet does not reflect economic reality, to the extent it is based on income tax accounting concepts that reflect historical costs.

The approach adopted by Colombia in Law 75 of 1986 falls in this category. Ad hoc adjustments are made for the inflationary component of interest income and expense in the calculation of taxable income, without any attempt to create a consistent set of inflation-adjusted financial statements. LIFO is allowed for inventory accounting, without indexing of stocks. No explicit inflation adjustment is allowed for depreciable assets, but depreciation is quite accelerated. Inflation adjustment is generally allowed for purposes of calculating capital gains (which are taxed as «occasional gains»). In principle, these adjustments to the basis of assest should be made every year and employed for purposes of the net wealth tax; under current law, however, inflation adjustment for the most important assets can be made in the year of sale, even if no adjustment has been made previously. As a result of this approach to inflation adjustment, the value of fixed assets and inventories on the balance sheet tends to be understated; this has important implications for the net wealth tax and for the calculation of presumptive income tax, as noted above.[24]

III. Symptoms of the Problem in Colombia

Chapter 4 presents estimates of the marginal effective tax rates applicable to various types of investment in Colombia, depending on the source and type of financing and the rate of inflation. There is no need to repeat that evidence here; in summary we can note that in general, before passage of Law 75 of 1986, and considering only taxation at the entity (company) level, at an inflation rate of 25 percent marginal effective tax rates on income from equity-financed investments (whether in depreciable assets, land, or inventories) approximated the statutory rate, but those on income from debt-financed investments were decidedly negative. As noted there, the near equality of statutory rates and marginal effective tax rates in the case of both equity financed structures and equipment is largely coincidental, reflecting the mutually offsetting effects of acceleration of depreciation allowances and the absence of inflation adjustment.

This pattern of marginal effective tax rates resulting from the historical combination of a tax system based on unindexed historical costs and fairly rapid and variable inflation creates strong incentives for firms to borrow to finance investment, rather than using equity finance. Moreover, because the tax treatment increases the risk inherent in variations in the rate of inflation, both borrowers and lenders may prefer short-term debt rather than long-term obligations. Both of these tendencies can be observed in the Colombian economy.[25]

Colombian companies have increased substantially their reliance on debt finance over the past 35 years.[26] Table 7-2 provides estimates of the debt ratios (indebtedness as a percentage of the sum of debt and equity) for all Colombian corporations and for Colombian manufacturing corporations during the period from 1950 to 1983. Column (a) shows that, starting from a level of just under 25 percent in 1950, this ratio for all corporations rose fairly steadily to the neighborhood of 45 percent for the period 1964-70, and by 1980 had risen to over 70 percent. Much the same story can be told for the manufacturing portion of the corporate sector. (See column (b) of Table 7-2.) Indebtedness rose from below 35 percent of the sum of debt plus net worth in 1960 to about 45 percent by the end of the decade and to more than 60 percent by 1979.

The shortening of the period of credit can be seen from the figures on the term structure of debt of Colombian manufacturing corporations presented in Table 7-3. The use of short-term credit (that with a term of less than 2 years) fell from 31 percent of total credit in 1970 to 21 percent in 1972 and has since risen to 50 percent. By comparison, the use of long-term credit (that with a term of more than 5 years) fell from 54 percent in 1972 to only 23 percent in 1980. Medium-term (3 to 5 year) credit has been relatively stable, but has generally shown the same tendencies as long-term credit.

These changes in the way in which companies have chosen to finance themselves have been reflected in the asset holdings of households. During each year from 1977 through 1982 shares of companies held by households actually fell.[27] In the early 1960s only about 14 percent of the assets of households were held as deposits in credit institutions and almost 70 percent were in «investments», including shares of companies.[28] By 1975 the former figure exceeded 27 percent and the latter had fallen to just over 50 percent.

These changes — and others not documented here — are troublesome. They present a picture of an economy that is much more vulnerable to cyclical downswings or financial stringency than before. That they have occurred partly as a result of flawed tax policy has been asserted forcefully as follows:

> Entre 1953, cuando se establece la doble tributación, y 1985, el nivel de endeudamiento de las sociedades organizadas del país pasó de un 25% a un 85%; la concentración accionaria lógicamente aumentó enormemente y se fueron cerrando gradualmente las sociedades....[N]o era ni conveniente ni útil financiar las sociedades a través de capitalización. Era indiscutiblemente mejor financiarlas a través de deuda, entre otras cosas no solamente por la existencia del gravámen a la empresa y a los socios o accionistas, y plena deducibilidad de los intereses, sino porque el fenómeno se agravó más aún por la aceleración de la inflación que ocurre en Colombia después de los años 70....De allí que la proporción del

financiamiento que se hace con crédito sea absolutamente anormal en Colombia en los últimos años con relación a países de ingresos percápita similares. Y la razón es muy lógica, no era negocio aportar capital sino endeudarse, por el problema de las dobles cargas tributarias y por el manejo de la inflación que se hacía a través de la deducción plena de los intereses con su contenido inflacionario. (Urdinola, 1987, p. 58-59).

Another Colombian observer of these developments offers the following similar assessment:

La sociedad anónima colombiana ha registrado un proceso de descapitalización y endeudamiento progresivos desde por lo menos comienzos de los años cincuenta, acompañado, especialmente durante los años setenta, por un desarrollo de los intermediarios financieros...Estos captaron los recursos de los hogares para prestárselos a las empresas, sustituyendo así la modalidad de inversión directa a través de acciones.... Las estimaciones realizadas para el caso Colombiano muestran un costo sistemáticamente más bajo de la alternativa de endeudamento, la cual se hace progresivamente más favorable que la alternativa de emisión de acciones, en razón de la creciente carga de la tributación directa. (Carrizosa, 1986, p. 19).

Although the inflation rate in Colombia has not been as high as in the Latin American countries mentioned earlier, it has been (and can be expected to be) high enough to justify introduction of a system of explicit inflation adjustment. This is especially true given the role played by the net wealth tax and the vulnerability of the calculation of net wealth to both inflation and ad hoc measures to compensate for inflation in the calculation of taxable income. Following a brief description of the actions taken in 1986, the remainder of this chapter provides an assessment of the best way to make the tax system of Colombia relatively immune to inflation, taking into account administrative realities.

IV. The Colombian System

A. Non-interest Provisions

The ad hoc system of inflation adjustment adopted by Colombia in 1986 applies only to the financial costs of borrowing and the income from lending. No adjustment is allowed for either depreciable assets or inventories, although extremely rapid depreciation of equipment and structures and the availability of LIFO tax accounting for inventories serve as imperfect substitutes for indexing, at least as far as the income tax treatment of those assets is concerned. (See also chapter 3 for a more complete description of these provisions and chapter 4 for calculations of the marginal effective tax rates applicable to income from investments in such assets).

In addition, the basis of assets for purpose of calculating capital gains (subject to tax as «occasional gains») can, at the option of the taxpayer, be adjusted annually by as much as 100 percent of the increase in the consumer price index. In the case of certain types of assets, if such adjustments are not made annually, the opportunity to make the adjustment is lost. Since the adjusted basis must also be employed for purpose of the net wealth tax and the presumptive income tax, it is often not in the taxpayer's interest to take advantage of this provision for optional indexing of basis.[29] However, important statutory exceptions exist for real estate, corporate shares, and partnership interests; adjustments for inflation since the time of acquisition of such assets can be made at the time of disposition, even if no adjustment has previously been made.

The base of the net wealth tax is not adjusted automatically to reflect inflation, except in the case of UPACs (Unidades de Poder Adquisitivo Constante, debt instruments of constant purchasing power), other indexed debt instruments, and assets that have been adjusted at the taxpayer's discretion, as described in the preceding paragraph. Real estate is generally seriously undervalued both because revaluation for property tax purposes is not kept on a current basis and because only 60 percent of the cadastral value of real property is included in the base of national taxes, including that of the net wealth tax.[30/] The taxable basis of machinery and equipment is systematically understated because such assets are not revalued to reflect inflation and because they are eligible for rapidly accelerated depreciation. While the use of LIFO accounting for inventories generally results in a relatively satisfactory measure of taxable income, it produces a systematic understatement of business inventories for purpose of the net wealth tax and the calculation of presumptive income. This systematic understatement of the value of depreciable assets and inventories is an important reason acceleration of depreciation allowances and LIFO are not acceptable substitutes for indexation in the Colombian context, where the net wealth tax is an important source of revenue and progressivity, and it and the net wealth-based taxation of presumptive income are accepted parts of the fiscal landscape intended to prevent widespread evasion of the income tax.

B. Interest Indexing

The adjustments for interest income and expense provided by the 1986 law have been described in Chapter 3. That description is repeated here, to facilitate reading of this chapter, especially the part dealing with interest indexing and transition provilsions. Once fully in effect, interest indexing will consist of the following elements:[31/]

1. For individuals receiving interest income from certain sources, 100 percent of the inflationary component of such income is exempt from tax. This provision, unlike those described below, is effective immediately; that is, it has been applied fully, beginning with the 1986 tax year. To benefit from this exclusion, interest income must be paid by entities supervised by the Superintendent of Banking (Superintendencia Bancaria), by Colombian governments (on public debt), or by corporations on issues authorized by the National Securities Commission (Comisión Nacional de Valores). Moreover, interest expense must be deducted from interest income before the exclusion factor, calculated as described below, is applied.[32/] Thus, although mortgage interest remains fully deductible up to $1 million (an amount to be indexed for inflation occurring after 1986) of interest annually, the requirement that interest expense must be offset against interest income before application of indexation to the latter implies that indexation effectively applies to deductible mortgage interest (that below the $1 million limit), as well as to other deductible interest, to the extent it is offset by interest income of the taxpayer.[33/]

In this case the inflationary component of interest income is calculated as the ratio of the monetary correction (corrección monetaria, a measure of the loss of purchasing power of debt that has been used for indexation of UPACS since [1974]), for the tax year to the interest rate received by the individual during that year. (By comparison, under prior law 60 percent of the monetary correction on UPACs and 40 percent of that on other inflation-adjusted debt was exempt from tax.) Thus the exclusion factor is different for each taxpayer; indeed, it apparently could be different for each debt instrument held by the taxpayer. The borrower is obligated to inform the lender of the amount of interest that is not taxable.

2. For companies, the exclusion factor applied to determine the inflationary component of interest income is the ratio of the monetary correction for the year immediately prior to the taxable year to the interest rate paid by banks («tasa de captación») in that year.[34/] This exclusion factor, which is to be phased in over ten years beginning in 1986, is thus the same for all companies in a given year.

3. In the case of interest expense paid by both individuals and corporations on debt to domestic lenders (except for that on home mortgages, which remains fully deductible, subject to the $1 million limit and the requirement for offsetting against interest income before application of inflation-adjustment for the latter, described above), a fraction of said expense is non-deductible; this fraction, to be phased in over ten years, is equal to the ratio of the monetary correction to an interest rate («tasa de colocación») analogous to the prime rate in the previous year. In the case of leasing contracts, the government is to specify non-exclusion rules during the year following passage of the 1986 law.[35/]

4. On foreign debt the exclusion factor is the ratio of the monetary correction to the cost of external indebtedness published by the Central Bank (Banco de la República), both for the year immediately prior to the taxable year in question. The cost of external debt reflects both the interest rate on foreign debt and the change in the exchange rate.[36/]

The above provisions dealing with the inflation adjustment of interest income and expense of companies do not apply to leasing companies, to construction credits issued by savings and housing corporations (Corporaciones de Ahorro y Vivienda), and to financial intermediaries subject to supervision by the Superintendent of Banking which regularly borrow and lend large amounts of money in transactions with the public.[37/]

To soften the impact of the introduction of inflation adjustment on those with outstanding indebtedness at the time of passage of this legislation, a ten-year phase-in was provided for the disallowance of interest expense; thus only 10 percent of the full inflation adjustment is in effect for 1986, 20 percent for 1987, etc., with inflation adjustment not fully in effect until 1995.[38/] The exclusion of interest income of companies (but not of individuals) is also phased-in according to the same ten-year schedule.[39/] This phase-in rule is analyzed in section IX.

C. Remaining Issues

The discussion to this point makes it clear that Colombia should replace its system of accelerated depreciation with a system of real economic depreciation and that inflation adjustment should be provided for inventories. That is, the partial system that covers only interest income and expense should be expanded to cover depreciable assets (and similar assets, such as those subject to depletion and amortization) and to inventories.

This ad hoc approach to inflation adjustment raises several other issues that are discussed in the remainder of this chapter. These include the choice between an ad hoc approach and an exact approach such as that used in Chile; whether to use a general price index or specific indices for the inflation-adjustment of particular assets; the decision (under the ad hoc approach) to employ an approximate method based on application of a fractional exclusion rate to interest income and expense, rather than making an exact adjustment based on the product of the principal amount of debt and the inflation rate; the choices of the elements to be employed in the calculation of the exclusion and non-deduction factors; the use of figures for monetary correction and interest rates for the prior year rather than for the taxable year in question in these calculations; whether conformity between accounting methods used for tax purposes and for financial reporting should be required; and the nature of the phase-in that should be used during a transition period a) to protect those with outstanding obligations from the capital losses that would result from immediate application of the provisions for disallowance of deductions for the inflationary component of interest expense and b) to hasten introduction of the system of inflation-adjusted depreciation and inventory accounting. The first of these (the comparison of the ad hoc and Chilean approaches) is the subject of section V and appendix A to this chapter. The last (transition provisions) is discussed in section IX. The remaining issues are the subjects of sections VI and VII.[40/] Section VIII examines the effects on the cost of capital in Colombia that can be expected to result from the introduction of inflation adjustment.

V. Integrated Versus Partial and Ad Hoc Approaches

The system of inflation adjustment included in Law 75 of 1986 is partial and involves ad hoc adjustments of various items of income and expense. It is partial in the sense that there is no inflation adjustment of either depreciation allowances or inventories; rather, depreciation for tax purposes is quite accelerated and LIFO accounting for inventories is allowed. The 1986 system is ad hoc, in that there is no attempt to provide an integrated and comprehensive approach to inflation adjustment. There is no requirement of conformity between income for tax purposes and that reported for financial purposes, except that taxpayers using LIFO for tax purposes must also use it for financial accounting. The inflation adjustments allowed for income tax purposes have no necessary consequences for the calculation of net wealth for purposes of either financial accounting or determination of the net wealth tax, except in the case of indexed debt and inflation adjustment for certain assets yielding capital gains (those for which adjustments to the value of capital assets must be reflected in the calculation of taxable net wealth if they are made annually).

This approach, which is called the partial and ad hoc approach in what follows, stands in marked contrast to the system employed in Chile, which is sometimes referred to as an «integrated» approach. In the Chilean system «real» or «non-monetary» assets and liabilities in the balance sheet, including net wealth, are adjusted for inflation, so that the balance sheet is based on indexed historical costs. These adjustments are also reflected in the calculation of taxable income, and income statement entries such as depreciation allowances are based on the indexed amounts in the balance sheet, rather than on unindexed costs. The result is an accounting system which measures real (inflation adjusted) income accurately. This system must be used for financial accounting in Chile, as well as tax purposes. (The key elements of this approach and their rationale are described in considerable detail in the appendix to this chapter, which is based on Casanegra (1984) and Harberger (1982); these details, though important for an understanding of the Chilean system and its advantages and disadvantages, are omitted from the text for the convenience of the general reader).

The partial and ad hoc approach incorporated in Law 75 of 1986 has certain well-known defects. First, as noted in part C of the next section, inflation adjustment for financial or «monetary» assets is based on interest payments, rather than on the principal of debt. As a result, no adjustment is made for the loss of purchasing power of cash balances or other debts paying no interest. More generally, the fractional disallowance of interest deductions and the partial exclusion of interest income do not compensate exactly for inflation, except in the rare cases in which the nominal interest rate on a particular debt actually reflects the current rate of inflation; of course, interest rates on debt instruments with maturities of several years generally will not pass this test in a period of variable inflation. As argued in part C of section VI, this defect may not be critical, as long as most debt is relatively short term.

Second, the use of accelerated depreciation as a substitute for explicit adjustment of the depreciable basis for inflation (combined with depreciation allowances that reflect economic depreciation) can be appropriate only for a single rate of inflation. Nor does the balance sheet used for the calculation of net wealth accurately show the value of assets that receive such treatment. Of course, these defects of a partial approach are not inherent in the ad hoc approach, which can easily accommodate a system of real economic depreciation allowances of the type proposed in chapter 5 and discussed in section VII of the present chapter. Even such an ad hoc system can produce satisfactory measures of both real economic depreciation and inflation-adjusted basis. Similarly, the use of LIFO for inventory accounting, in the absence of indexing, produces a figure of cost of goods sold that is satisfactory, but understates the value of inventories; as noted earlier, either indexed FIFO or indexed LIFO is a superior alternative.

An integrated system of inflation-adjusted financial statements of the type required in Chile has obvious advantages over the ad hoc system recently introduced in Colombia. Perhaps the most important of these — an advantage that is virtually unique to Colombia — is the fact that the Chilean system automatically produces an inflation-adjusted calculation of net wealth, as well as an accurate measure of real income (provided, of course, that the underlying reporting is accurate).[41] Yet the ad hoc system can be tailored to provide substantially similar information. A system such as that used in Chile is substantially more complicated for both taxpayers and the tax administration than is the type of ad hoc approach included in the 1986 Colombian tax reforms, even if the latter is modified as proposed in this Report.

Moreover, the ad hoc system has the considerable advantage of policy flexibility in one sense. The adjustments of interest income and expense that are necessary under it can be seen as «way stations» on the road to the treatment of interest income and expense (complete exclusion and no deduction) that are appropriate under the Simplified Alternative Tax. By comparison, the integrated system used in Chile follows a quite different approach from the Simplified Alternative Tax.

All things considered, it may be unwise for Colombia to attempt to move in one giant step from a tax system based on historical costs to a highly sophisticated system involving integrated inflation adjustment, especially given the moderate rates of inflation prevailing in Colombia in recent years.[42],[43] That seems to be the conclusion to be drawn from the following assessment of Chilean experience by an expert from the International Monetary Fund:

> It is doubtful whether the private sector and the tax administration
> would have been able to cope with this sophisticated mechanism if they
> had not previously had lengthy experience with simpler profit adjustment
> schemes. (Casanegra, p. 29).

An appropriate income tax based strategy for Colombia would seem to be to proceed in stages along the path toward an integrated system of inflation adjustment. The first and most important stage is to modify the present partial and ad hoc system to correct certain readily identifiable faults; the following two sections provide recommendations along those lines. Besides providing significant gains in equity and neutrality, this will allow the country to gain important experience in operating an inflation-adjusted system. It may be that no further progress along the road to a more exact system will be required; that depends on both the expected and the actual course of future inflation. But if it seems desirable at a later date to move to a system based on adjustment of net wealth statements, or even to a fully integrated system, that can be done, building on experience gained in the meantime. Again the wisdom of such a strategy is borne out by the following appraisal:

> The Chilean experience shows that comprehensive profits adjustment
> schemes can be administered, provided the tax service and the private
> sector have had previous experience with such schemes and they are
> based on indexation of assets and liabilities rather than on indexation
> of income and expense flows. (Casanegra, p. 4).[44]

VI. Methodological Issues

The possibility of modifying and extending the ad hoc system of inflation adjustment contained in Law 75 of 1986 raises several interesting general issues that must be addressed in designing tax policy in this area.[45/] This section discusses several of these.

A. Replacement Costs versus Inflation Adjustment[46/]

A common source of contention in discussions of income tax adjustments of income statements for the effects of inflation is whether such adjustments should be based on a general price index such as the consumer price index (CPI) or on replacement costs or indices specific to particular assets and liabilities such as an index for the cost of capital goods or the exchange rate.[47/] This issue has been encountered above in the discussion of the distinction between indexed FIFO and LIFO as measures of cost of goods sold. It also arises in terms of the choice of index to be used to calculate the inflation adjusted basis on which to base depreciation allowances. It is important because it is, of course, possible that prices for particular assets do not move at the same rate (or even in the same direction) as prices in general.[48/] The debate over the choice between a general index and replacement costs or specific indices goes to the very heart of the basic purpose of income measurement for tax purposes.[49/]

The standard by which income tax proposals are commonly judged is the Haig-Simons definition of income: consumption plus change in net worth.[50/] This definition leads directly to the conclusion that inflation adjustment for income tax purposes should be based on a general price index.

This can be seen most easily by considering a single non-depreciable asset. Leaving aside the use of income for consumption during the accounting period (or concentrating on the measurement of business income, where consumption is not an issue), Haig-Simons income can be defined simply as the change in net worth of the taxpayer. According to this definition, a shift in relative prices that caused the productive assets of a firm to become more valuable, at a time when the general price level was stable, would constitute taxable income. Inherent in this view is the belief that the increase in net worth represented by the increase in the value of the productive asset should be counted as part of income, whether or not the income is realized (for example by selling the asset).[51/] Of course, if a shift in relative prices of the type just discussed did occur, use of an asset-specific index for inflation adjustment would reveal no increase in net worth and no income. Use of an asset-specific index underlies what can be called replacement-cost accounting. For example, it is sometimes suggested that depreciation allowances should be based on replacement costs, rather than either historical costs or inflation-adjusted historical costs (that is, historical costs adjusted for the change in the general price level, the concept advocated in this Report as being the most appropriate for the measurement of real income for tax purposes).[52/]

Income measurement based on replacement costs sees a shift in relative prices from a different perspective than that of Haig-Simons, that of a **going concern**.[53/] It argues that a shift in the relative prices of productive assets should not be treated as giving rise to income, since the firm owning the asset in question could not continue in business without the asset (or must replace the asset at an equal cost, if it were to dispose of it).[54/] The use of replacement costs for tax purposes would help prevent the problem of decapitalization, since depreciation allowances and deductions for cost of goods sold from inventories would be large enough to allow their tax-free replacement.

The going-concern argument for replacement cost accounting may have considerable appeal from the point of view of financial accounting. Many authorities suggest, for example, that it may give a better picture than inflation-adjusted historical cost accounting of the ability of management to earn profits for stockholders in the future.[55/] But its use for the measurement of income for tax purposes is vulnerable on several grounds.[56/]

First, there is little doubt that the hypothesized increase in asset value under examination constitutes income; that the owner (or owners) of the firm owning the asset chooses not to realize the increase in value or chooses to reinvest in another asset in order to continue as a going concern does not change that fact.[57/] An extreme version of the replacement-cost accounting argument — and one that shows clearly the basic problem with the approach — would use the replacement cost of publicly-traded securities in measuring gains from such securities; of course, by definition income is eliminated by the use of such a convention, even if real gains are realized.

Nor is the argument that use of replacement costs is necessary to prevent decapitalization convincing. Adjustment based on the general rate of inflation is adequate to achieve the proper objective of protecting tax-free recovery of the value of existing assets from the effects of general inflation; further protection against changes in relative prices is not required for the accurate measurement of real income. Whether funds should be invested in an industry in which asset prices have risen is a question of investment strategy, not a matter of income measurement.

Second, a particular asset may or may not be essential for the continuation of the firm as a going concern; that depends on the possibilities of substituting for the productive services of the asset in question other productive services that have not risen in price.[58/] Perhaps more important, the cost of replacing an existing asset may be largely irrelevant, because of technological progress. If the relevant alternative is acquisition of a technologically superior but more (or less) expensive replacement, rather than merely replacement of the existing asset, it may be necessary to make an adjustment for saving in (or greater expenditures on) the costs of other inputs (e.g., other capital goods, labor, and energy), in order to avoid the over-statement of costs.[59/] Since such adjustments involve hypothetical situations, rather than the actual experience of the taxpayer, they entail substantial discretion on the part of those responsible for making them and are inevitably controversial. While such adjustments may be useful and appropriate if financial accounting is to give an accurate picture of the profit-making potential of a firm, they are clearly out of place in the measurement of income for tax purposes.[60/]

Clearly the most telling arguments against replacement cost accounting and the use of indices specific to particular assets are practical ones. Attempting to base deductions on replacement costs would be an administrative nightmare and would open the door to evasion.[61/] In addition, even if one wanted to use specific indices despite the criticisms just expressed, it would generally be impossible to do so. Specific indices are generally unavailable, especially in certain industries, even in developed countries; of course, price indices for specific assets are even less likely to be available in developing countries.[62/], [63/] This being the case, it might be thought unfair to allow (or require) the use of specific indices in the few cases in which they exist. Of course, there is no alternative to using a general index in the case of financial assets and liabilities. (See also the discussion below of changes in net wealth resulting from changes in the exchange rate).

There are several notable exceptions to the general proposition that is impossible to use replacement costs and specific indices in calculating income for tax purposes. These involve the valuation of real estate, the use of LIFO accounting for inventories, and the use of changes in exchange rates for the adjustment of the value of capital assets imported from abroad. Related to the last issue is whether the rate of devaluation or the change in the general domestic price level should be used in adjusting the financial costs of borrowing denominated in foreign currency. These issues are discussed in the remainder of this subsection.

It would be possible to employ a specific index for the valuation of real estate in Colombia; indeed, such an index has been employed for that purpose since 1983. While the use of this specific index has clear advantages so far as the calculation of net wealth is concerned, it has no place in the calculation of income. Compounding the problems in the income measurement context discussed before is the fact that real estate is a mixture of land and capital (improvements); unless it is assumed that both components rise in value at the same rate the use of a single index for the indexation of depreciable real property will generally yield incorrect results. The presumption is that a general index should be used for this purpose as well as for others. The primary questions to be answered are a) whether the potentially greater accuracy of measurement of net wealth justifies over-riding the general view reflected in this Report that priority should be given to income measurement (which requires use of the general index), and b) if so, whether the property index should be employed for the measurement of income as well as net wealth.

LIFO accounting for inventories essentially uses replacement cost accounting for goods sold from inventory. If LIFO accurately portrays the movement of inventories through a firm, its use for income tax purposes is beyond reproach. As noted earlier, however, LIFO also results in the understatement of the value of inventories for purposes of the net wealth tax, unless they are indexed. If, however, as generally seems more likely, inventory movement is more accurately described by FIFO, it is more appropriate to employ indexed FIFO (with indexing based on a general index). The use of LIFO in such a case is tantamount to employing FIFO and a specific index to calculate the cost of goods sold, rather than a general index. While the use of indexed LIFO in the latter situation, rather than indexed FIFO, is not totally consistent with a system otherwise based on a general price index, this practice seems generally non-controversial and is widely accepted; moreover, many Colombian firms presently employ LIFO. Accordingly, indexed LIFO is proposed as an alternative to indexed FIFO.

A substantially more important issue in a country such as Colombia is the treatment of imported capital goods. Even if no price index exists for capital goods, it can be argued that the cost in pesos of imported assets should be adjusted to reflect changes in the exchange rate, rather than simply being adjusted by the rate of domestic inflation.

The differences between the Haig-Simons and going concern concepts of income can be seen clearly in this case. The Colombian who imports an asset (and has already paid for it or owes a debt denominated in pesos) just before a major devaluation clearly experiences an increase in net worth, measured in pesos; but he may not feel much richer, if the asset must be used in his business and must be replaced at the new higher exchange rate. (On the other hand, few would disagree that a Colombian with outstanding debt denominated in foreign currency would experience a loss as a result of devaluation, even if it is anticipated that such debt would be rolled over indefinitely — as in the going-concern scenario — rather than being retired.) However, to allow depreciation allowances based on the adjustment of asset values for the rate of devaluation, without also requiring recognition of this increase in wealth, would be overly generous.[64] Basing depreciation allowances on asset values indexed for domestic inflation is the most satisfactory compromise in the situation, in part for additional reasons akin to those described in the remainder of this subsection.

Another extremely important issue in a capital-importing country such as Colombia is the treatment of debt denominated in foreign currencies. (Since exactly the same issues are raised by the quantitatively less important cases of foreign indebtedness to Colombians denominated in foreign currencies, they are not discussed explicitly. All references to foreign debt in the remainder of this section refer to obligations denominated in foreign currencies. Obligations to or from foreigners denominated in Colombian pesos would pose no issues other than those already discussed.)

A basic proposition in the theory of international trade, is the so-called «purchasing-power parity» (PPP) theorem. This theorem, to be explained more fully in section VIII, suggests that changes in exchange rates fundamentally must have their origin in differences in expected domestic rates of inflation.[65] This has important implications for the design of a system of inflation adjustments for foreign obligations. Devaluation of the Colombian peso increases the peso cost of repaying a given foreign obligation; but to the extent devaluation merely reflects the internal rate of inflation in Colombia, relative to that in the capital-exporting nation, as the PPP theorem suggests, the debtor neither gains nor loses from the combination of devaluation and inflation.

Suppose, for example, that a Colombian incurs a debt of 1,000,000 at a time the exchange rate is 2 yen per peso; that is, the value of the loan in pesos is $500,000. If the peso depreciates by 20 percent relative to the yen, $600,000 will be required to repay the loan. But if the rate of domestic inflation is also 20 percent, the Colombian debtor will experience no real loss, since this figure is exactly equal in real terms to the $500,000 initially borrowed.

Reflecting this line of reasoning, the 1986 tax reform provides for the disallowance of a fraction of the financial cost of foreign debt (the sum of the interest rate and the change in the exchange rate) equal to the ratio of the monetary correction to the financial cost of such debt. If the rate of monetary correction (assumed for purposes of tnhis discussion to be a reasonable measure of the rate of inflation) exactly equals the rate of change in the exchange rate, only the real component of financial costs of foreign borrowing is deductible under this rule.[66]

It may be argued that this approach is inappropriate because the relationship between exchange rates and the relative rates of inflation in Colombia and creditor nations does not precisely follow the relationship specified by the PPP theorem.[67] According to this reasoning, where extraordinary devaluations break the link between the relative rates of domestic inflation and movements in exchange rates, it may be appropriate to allow adjustments based on such unusual changes in exchange rates, rather than merely on movements in domestic prices. (That is, the change in the exchange rate would be substituted for the rate of inflation in the calculation of the fractional disallowance.) But, as noted below, caution should be used in pursuing this strategy; it seems unlikely to be appropriate in Colombia, as long as the value of the peso is allowed to vary with little official intervention.

Others may argue that it is appropriate to use the change in the exchange rate in which debt is denominated, rather than the monetary correction, in making this adjustment. However, this would greatly complicate matters. In the absence of strong evidence of failure of the PPP theorem, it should be avoided; certainly it should be employed only in the case of extraordinary devaluations. Harberger (1982) offers the following advice on this issue:

> One must be **extremely careful** not to extend the principle ...to assets and liabilities generally. This is the sure road to making the indexing system unbearably complicated. One must recall clearly that in a non-indexed system with flexible exchange rates, obligations and assets expressed in different currencies are all going to change in value by different percentages. It is not a part of the task of an indexing system to correct for the variation of the mark relative to the pound, the pound relative to the yen, or the yen relative to the dollar. One correction at most should be applied to all these currencies....The peril is to extend the principle of a special adjustment so as to have separate adjustments for the different principal currencies-and even, ultimately, for differential movements in commodity prices. The key to simplicity in an indexation system is to recognize that inflation is a

movement of the **general** price level. It therefore calls, in principle, **for one** adjustment, and one adjustment only. Multiplying the bases in which different adjustments are made is thus to be avoided at all costs.

B. Exact versus Approximate Adjustments

The conceptually correct way to calculate the inflation-induced loss of purchasing power of financial assets fixed in nominal terms (commonly called the inflationary component of interest expense or financial costs) is to multiply the principal amount of debt by the rate of inflation.[68] An exact adjustment of this type is easy to implement if either the principal or the interest rate on a loan is constant over the course of a year. However, it is extremely cumbersome in the case of financial obligations that have both a principal amount and an interest rate that varies during the year, as is often the case. Banks and other large financial institutions, most large non-financial institutions, and others with ready access to computers could probably handle the task of calculating average daily principal during the year. But there would be enough exceptions to that rule that it seems unwise to attempt to base inflation adjustment on this «exact» approach. It is also generally inappropriate to provide exact adjustments in some cases, but allow or require approximate adjustments in others. Besides being questionable on equity grounds, such a mixed strategy would create administrative difficulties and might open the way to manipulation by taxpayers who could take advantage of differences in the two systems to earn arbitrage profits.

The alternative contained in the 1986 law seems to be an appropriate compromise with reality, although some suggestions are made for its improvement. Under this approach, as noted in section IV above, a fraction of nominal interest income and expense is either excluded from income or disallowed as a deduction, depending on the ratio of the monetary correction to the interest rate (either on the debt of the taxpayer or for the country as a whole, as the case may be).

This inexact approach has the disadvantage that it understates the adjustment that would be appropriate in the case of debt bearing an interest rate below that on which the exclusion/non-deduction fraction is based and overstates the adjustment for debts carrying a higher interest rate.[69] The problem is especially important in the case of cash balances, which are eligible for no inflation adjustment, although their real value is eroded by inflation. Otherwise, given the generally short term structure of debt in Colombia, this does not seem to be a major problem, since it can be expected that the inaccuracies inherent in the approximate approach will be greatest for debt with relatively long terms.[70] All things considered, the basic approach of exempting a portion of interest adopted in Law 75 of 1986 seems appropriate, unless Colombia is to shift to an integrated system of inflation-adjusted financial statements. (Since exact compensation automatically occurs implicitly under the latter type of system, the issue does not arise.)

C. Conformity of Tax and Financial Accounting

Both income tax returns and financial accounting (including net wealth statements in both cases) appear to have the same purpose: to determine the income and net wealth of the taxpayer. In order to obtain an accurate indication of real income and wealth it is necessary to answer the same basic questions, including those involving the timing of various items of income and expense and adjustments for inflation. It is therefore natural to ask whether it is appropriate to require conformity of accounting standards for tax and financial purposes. Such conformity could be quite limited, as it is in Colombia (as in the United States), where a taxpayer using LIFO for tax purposes must also use it for financial accounting, but there are few other important «conformity» requirements. Or it could be quite comprehensive, as it is in Chile, where the same accounting rules must be used for both purposes. This section examines the issue of conformity in the context of reform of the income tax and the net wealth tax, especially as it relates to inflation adjustment. It is assumed that conformity would generally not exist if Colombia were to adopt the Simplified Alternative Tax discussed in chapter 9, which involves immediate deductions for all purchases, including those of capital assets and inventories, and disallowance of deductions for interest expense. Of course, the issue of inflation adjustment does not arise under that form of taxation.

There are arguments on both sides of the conformity issue. Those in favor of conformity generally involve a mixture of tax and non-tax objectives. Suppose, for example, that there is widespread belief that taxpayers are revaluing assets for purposes of negotiating loans with bankers or to be able to pay dividends out of the revaluation profits, but they (and their owners, in the case of companies) are not paying net wealth tax or calculating presumptive income on the basis of the revaluation.[71] If the revaluation is realistic, then conformity would serve the tax objective of assuring that the base of the net wealth tax is also realistic. If, on the other hand, the revaluation is unrealistic, no tax revenue that should be collected is at stake; rather, the apparent objective of a conformity requirement would be the non-tax one of preventing the borrower from overstating the value of assets and thereby being able to obtain credit on false pretenses or pay what are effectively liquidating dividends to shareholders without saying so. The most likely scenario probably involves both appropriate and inappropriate revaluations and both tax and non-tax objectives.

An additional argument for conformity involves costs of compliance and administration. It is clearly easier for the taxpayer to comply with the tax law and for the tax administration to guarantee compliance if the same accounting standards must be used for tax and financial purposes. Considerations such as these are especially important where such complicated issues such as timing problems (discussed in chapter 5) and inflation adjustment are concerned. In the absence of conformity, compliance and administration will have been made considerably more complicated by the introduction of interest indexing, and adoption of the other proposals regarding timing and inflation adjustments contained in this Report will further accentuate that problem if conformity is not required.

There is a temptation to argue that non-tax objectives should play little role in the determination of the conformity issue. This matter is, however, clouded by the fact that neither the accounting profession nor the government of Colombia has developed a system of «generally accepted accounting principles» to serve as guidelines in the preparation of financial accounting reports.[72] In such a context the tax authorities may be left to develop such a system as a matter of default. Indeed, in many of the controversial areas covered by generally accepted accounting principles in other countries, the Colombian tax administration has been forced to adopt specific rules in order to protect the public revenue, prevent inequities and economic distortions, and provide some degree of certainty for taxpayers; such areas include installment sales, reserves for bad debts, and long-term contracts. Proposals being made in this Report would modify some of these in the interest of more accurate measurement of income and provide statutory guidance for income tax purposes in yet other areas.

If the measurement of income for tax purposes were based on the best available estimates of real economic income, the notion of conformity of tax and financial accounting would be quite attractive. But if the definition of taxable income is distorted by various provisions intended to stimulate or discourage certain types of activities, the case for conformity is substantially weaker. Financial accounts, to be useful for their intended purpose, would need to be qualified to show the effects of such special provisions that deliberately cause income for tax purposes to be mismeasured.[73] Moreover, it is not proposed that an integrated system be adopted for purposes of tax accounting; rather, it is proposed that a system of ad hoc adjustments be applied to selected income statement and balance sheet items.

All things considered, it does not seem appropriate to recommend in this Report that Colombia institute a requirement for the conformity of tax and financial accounting. Given the substantial advantages of conformity the issue does, however, deserve further study by the government, the private sector, and the accounting profession.

VII. Analysis of Particular Problems Under Current Law

The discussion to this point sets the stage for the detailed examination of the system of indexation used in Colombia following enactment of Law 75 of 1986. This section provides such details; much of it is relevant only if a decision is made to continue with the ad hoc approach inherent in that law, as suggested, rather than to move to an integrated system of the type used in Chile.

The greatest need for modification in the present system of inflation adjustment lies in the treatment of depreciable assets and assets subject to depletion or amortization. As noted repeatedly in this Report, the acceleration of depreciation allowances is not a satisfactory substitute for explicit inflation adjustment of allowances that would more closely approximate true economic depreciation. Nor would it be appropriate to provide inflation adjustments in the context of the existing system of highly accelerated allowances. For this reason, it is recommended in chapter 5 that a system of real economic depreciation allowances be introduced. Since the proposed system is described in detail there, it is not described here. Such a system (or an analogous system tailored to the particular problem) should be extended to all assets subject to depreciation, depletion, or amortization.

Inflation adjustment of such assets should not affect only the calculation of taxable income. Rather, the inflation-adjusted basis of assets should be employed in calculating the base of the net wealth tax and presumptive income. In the case of real estate it would be appropriate to utilize the greater of this figure and that from the cadastral survey. The provision of present law that allows only 60 percent of the cadastral value of real estate to be included in taxable net wealth should be repealed; taxable net wealth should include the full value of real estate.

Taxpayers should be given the option of using indexed FIFO for inventory accounting; as noted in section II it is the conceptually correct measure of both cost of goods sold and net wealth. The present taxpayer option to employ LIFO should probably also be maintained, provided indexing of beginning stocks is required. As noted earlier, LIFO treatment of inventories in the calculation of taxable income is generally not as appropriate as indexed FIFO (because of the treatment of changes in relative prices), but LIFO generally provides a reasonable approximation to indexed FIFO for inventory accounting.

The implications of these two options for the calculation of net wealth are, however, quite different. As noted above, under indexed (or unindexed) FIFO the accounting value of inventories can be expected to approximate true value rather closely, except in times of quite rapid inflation or inventory accumulation. By comparison, under unindexed LIFO balance sheet figures understate the true value of inventories accumulated before inflationary periods. Accurate measurement of the value of inventories for purposes of both the net wealth tax and the presumptive income tax under a LIFO system of accounting requires inflation-adjustment of stocks held in inventories.

The systems of inflation adjustment applied to financial costs and income under Law 75 of 1986 seem generally satisfactory, except as noted below. The use of the «monetary correction» in the adjustment formulas seems generally appropriate, at least in principle, since that index was originally constructed for just such a purpose.[74] Whether the monetary correction is properly constructed to meet this objective is beyond the scope of this Report; given the increased importance of this issue it may be worthwhile to have the National Statistical Office (Departamento Nacional de Estadística — DANE) undertake a re-examination of this matter.

The formulas used to calculate the exclusion factors also seem to be generally appropriate, except in one regard.[75/] There seems to be no good reason that the adjustments for interest income of companies and for interest expense of both individuals and companies should be based on the comparison of inflation rates and interest rates for the prior year. Certainly there is no administrative reason that variables for the tax year in question should not be used, given that the relevant exclusion rates are to be announced by the government. Nor should the fact that use of the prior year's figures provides greater certainty for the taxpayer be controlling. Perhaps the best argument for this lagged approach is that most loans extend over several years and that a one year lag provides a kind of rough averaging of the fraction of interest that should be disallowed or excluded. These advantages, such as they are, are bought at some cost, since this procedure yields inaccurate measures of the impact of inflation on newly negotiated interest rates. All things considered, it seems best to base adjustment factors on the actual experience during the taxable year. Though there is much to be said for basing the exclusion factor on an interest rate specific to the taxpayer, administrative realities suggest that it is better to retain the present system under which the same exclusion rate is generally used for all taxpayers in a given group.

It would be desirable to clarify the proper tax treatment of such costs incurred to finance acquisition of depreciable assets and inventories, whether through purchase from third parties or self-construction. (As should be clear from the discussion of chapter 5 and section VI of the present chapter, the same treatment should be accorded exchange-rate losses on debts incurred to acquire assets abroad as for debt incurred to acquire assets domestically.) As indicated more fully in chapter 5, such costs should not be deducted currently, since they are «production costs»; rather, they should be capitalized and be recovered either through depreciation allowances or as costs of goods sold from inventories. But the entire amount of financial costs incurred in acquiring such assets should be capitalized, without disallowance of the inflationary component. (To see that this is the appropriate treatment, one need only consider the tax treatment of the economically equivalent transaction in which assets are bought from third parties who incur analogous expenses and recover them as part of the price of the asset in question; the full purchase price would be capitalized and recovered, either through depreciation allowances or deductions for costs of goods sold.) Financial costs incurred after the asset has been placed in service or added to inventories should be treated according to the regular rules for the disallowance of deductions for the inflationary component of interest. For further discussion of this issue, see chapter 5.

This clarification should reduce the grounds for one of the most commonly heard complaints about the system of inflation adjustment. It has been noted that banks and other financial institutions have an advantage over non-financial institutions in that they are exempt from the rules for interest indexing. Rather than importing raw materials or fixed assets directly and being unable either to deduct or to capitalize the full amount of financial costs (which generally would include an important component of exchange loss), under current law a non-financial firm has an incentive to have a bank or other financial institution exempt from the indexation scheme do the importing, since it could deduct the full amount of financial costs. The proposed change would reduce the competitive advantage of financial institutions, by allowing non-financial institutions to capitalize the full amount of financial costs they incur in transactions of the type described. The problem cannot be fully eliminated unless interest indexing is extended to the financial sector, as is recommended below.

Leases pose one of the thorniest problems for the theory and practice of inflation adjustment. The proper treatment is relatively clear in two polar cases, those of leases involving no long-term commitment and leases that are essentially commitments for installment purchases.[76/] In the first of these cases there is clearly no fixed monetary obligation on which an inflationary gain or loss can be experienced, and thus no case for inflation adjustment; this is true regardless of the expected period which will actually be covered by the lease, as long as there is no contractual agreement to make future lease payments. On the other hand, inflation adjustment should be allowed in the second case, in which the lease is simply (but clearly) a form of installment purchase in which the obligation to make future payments is clear and binding. In short, where a payment is treated as «rent» for tax purposes, no inflation adjustment is appropriate; where it is treated as a payment on a purchase, interest indexing should be allowed, but only for the interest component. (How this is to be done is discussed after the next paragraph).

The problem of definition, of course, lies in the intermediate range in which obligations are subject to contingencies or options. It appears that it is not possible to construct bright-line tests of when a commitment is sufficiently certain to justify treating a lease as a monetary liability on which inflation gain (loss) must (can) be recognized for tax purposes. There seems to be no alternative to considering the facts and circumstances in each particular case.

Where a lease is tantamount to an installment purchase an additional complication arises. It is clearly incorrect to treat the entire lease payment as eligible for inflation adjustment. To see this it is useful to think of the lease payments as installment payments on the purchase of the leased asset. Rather than simply deducting lease payments currently, it is appropriate to capitalize them and deduct the implied depreciation allowances and interest expense, as in the case of a true purchase. In an inflationary environment the depreciable basis and the interest implicit in the lease payment should be eligible for inflation adjustment under the same rules applicable to other assets and interest payments.[77/]

Inflation adjustment should be extended to the financial sector. Failure to do so sacrifices potential gains in equity and neutrality. This is highlighted by both the unfair competition that has been mentioned earlier in this section and the fact that financial institutions are active in the leasing business.

It would probably be appropriate to apply an exact method of inflation adjustment to financial institutions. Such institutions should have no difficulty in calculating the average daily balances of loans and deposits needed for implementation of this approach. While there is some conceptual inconsistency between the methods applied to such institutions and their customers, this does not appear to be a practical cause for concern.

In many respects the present tax treatment of capital gains is appropriate. The basis of assets whose value is not set in nominal (monetary) terms should be adjusted for inflation that occurs between the time of acquisition and the time of disposition, so that only real gains are taxed. In the case of depreciable assets the basis to be used in calculating gain or loss upon disposition would ordinarily be the inflation-adjusted depreciated original cost of the asset.

The primary issue in this area is whether the indexed basis of assets should constitute their value for purposes of the net wealth tax and the calculation of presumptive income. (It has been argued that no attempt should be made to include unrealized gains in taxable income, except via the presumptive income tax). The discussion above has argued strongly that such is the case for real estate, depreciable assets and inventories; otherwise these forms of business assets would be grossly understated following a period of rapid or substantial inflation.[78/] If the inflation-adjusted basis of any of these types of assets is not used for this purpose, severe inequities or distortions can occur. (For example, those who buy assets prior to inflation pay relatively less taxes than those who buy similar assets after inflation, and the lack of inflation-adjustment in the calculation of net wealth tends to discourage present owners from selling assets.) For the same reason it would be appropriate to extend inflation adjustment of basis to non-business assets (especially owner-occupied housing) included in the calculation of net wealth. It makes little sense to allow inflation adjustment in the calculation of capital gains, without also including the inflation adjustment in the basis of the net wealth tax on a current basis.

It may be argued that it is unfair to include the inflation adjusted value of assets in the calculation of net wealth, since the value of a particular asset may not have kept up with inflation. (Recall from the earlier discussion that the conceptually correct value to use for this purpose is the actual value or replacement cost, not the inflation-adjusted original cost.) But this argument is generally not telling, for a quite similar argument can be made in a world without inflation; after all, in a world of stable prices shifts in relative prices can cause the value of some assets to be more than their book value normally original cost (adjusted for depreciation, where appropriate) and the value of others to be less. In the absence of a far-reaching system of appraising all assets periodically — clearly an administrative impossibility, except in the case of real estate, where appraisals are notoriously inaccurate — there is no real alternative to a system in which calculations of net wealth are based on original cost, adjusted for inflation as well as depreciation. To fail to reflect inflation in the base of the net wealth tax simply because the results may not be exactly correct in some cases would result in a large systematic bias toward understatement of asset values. Using the general price index admittedly gives incorrect values in some cases. Yet, as argued earlier, there is no alternative to its use. Even so, there may be cases in which inflation-adjusted values are clearly out of line with true values. Some of the more important of these deviations of inflation-adjusted book valuations from economic values can be corrected, for example, by using market values of securities traded on stock exchanges and cadastral values of real property assessed for property tax purposes. For similar reasons provision was made in Chapter 6 for the possibility of taxpayer petitions for revaluation in such cases.

VIII. Economic Effects of Inflation Adjustment

A. Inflation Adjustment and the Cost of Debt-Financed Capital

The primary inflation adjustment measure included in the 1986 Colombian reform is the nondeductibility as a business expense of the inflationary component of interest expense and the corresponding exemption from income taxation of the inflationary component of interest received. Analysis of this measure in this section of the Report illustrates graphically how tax policy changes often have different cost of capital effects in an open economy than in a closed economy that is isolated from international capital markets. The following presentation is related to the earlier discussion of marginal effective tax rates and the cost of capital given in Chapter 4, but it does not include any consideration of simultaneous adjustment in depreciation allowances, another important determinant of the cost of capital to a firm. The approach taken here assumes that the inflation adjustment of interest payments, to be phased in through 1995, is being made in the context of a system in which real economic depreciation already is provided, as proposed in Chapter 5 and earlier in this Chapter. Under those circumstances no further change in tax provisions for depreciation are needed for reasonably accurate measurement of real income.[79]

1. Analysis for a Closed Economy

Begin by considering the market for loanable funds in a closed economy where all investment is financed with debt. While this framework may be less satisfactory from a macroeconomic perspective than a model of interest rate determination through money market equilibrium, for expository purposes it provides a useful way of incorporating the tax policy changes to be addressed in the present

211

discussion.[80/] Figure 7.1 represents this situation diagrammatically; the horizontal axis shows the quantity of loanable funds and the vertical axis indicates the nominal before-tax rate of return. The domestic supply of and demand for loanable funds are assumed to be functions of this nominal interest rate, but also of other factors that determine the real after-tax rate of return. One way of summarizing this relationship is the following expression, referred to by economists as «modified Fisher's Law»:

$$i\,(1 - t) - \pi = r,$$

which can be written as:

$$(7.1) \qquad i = (r + \pi)\,/\,(1 - t)$$

where i is the nominal rate of return, r is the real after-tax rate of return, π is the expected inflation rate and t is a proportional income tax rate.[81/] This formulation can be interpreted as indicating that the real after-tax rate of return is equal to the after-tax nominal rate of return minus the inflation rate; it assumes that the tax system is not inflation adjusted. Depending on the tax rate chosen, that of the borrower or the lender, this condition is relevant in explaining either the demand for or supply of loanable funds.

Equation (7.1) shows the relationship between four different economic variables, yet only one of these variables, the nominal interest rate, appears in Figure 7.1. Furthermore, economic responses of lenders and borrowers are determined by the real after-tax interest rate received or paid. For example, the supply of funds made available by lenders might be represented in simple linear form as $S = a + br = a + b[(1-t)i - \pi]$, where **b** indicates the responsiveness of lenders to changes in the real rate of return and **a** summarizes the influence of all other variables that determine the volume of funds lent. This formulation shows that a supply (or demand) curve such as that in Figure 7.1 is based on given values of π and t. Whenever there is a change in the value of either of these variables, the position of the curve must change. In the case of the supply curve, start from a given real after-tax rate of return that lenders expect to receive, r. It is straightforward to determine the nominal interest rate that must be earned to yield that real after-tax return, given the values of t and π. When a higher tax rate is imposed or a higher inflation rate erodes the value of the currency in which the loan is repaid, lenders will require a higher nominal return to earn the same real after-tax return.

A numerical illustration may further clarify this point. Suppose the real after-tax return is 5 percent, the inflation rate is 25 percent, and the relevant tax rate is 30 percent. Under those circumstances, the nominal interest rate must be 43 percent in order to yield a real after-tax return of 5 percent [.428 = (.05 + .25)/.7 or 0.05 = (.70 x .428) − .25]. The higher nominal return is necessary not only because inflation implies that a loan will be paid back in pesos that are worth less than at present, but also because tax is levied on both the real and inflationary components of interest.

If the tax and inflation rates are unchanged, the real after-tax return and the nominal before-tax return move together. Thus, if the underlying economic behavior in the economy results in the supply of loanable funds increasing when the real after-tax rate of return increases, the supply curve in Figure 7.1 will be upward sloping. In the case of the demand curve, the lower the real after-tax cost of borrowing funds, the more potential projects that become economically feasible. At a given inflation rate and a given tax rate for borrowers, a lower required real after-tax return corresponds to a lower nominal return, and therefore the demand curve in Figure 7.1 slopes downward.

If some portion of interest income becomes exempt from taxation, the supply curve for loanable funds will shift to the right, indicating that at any given nominal interest rate, the supply of loanable funds will be greater. Or, correspondingly, the initial level of loanable funds will now be available at a lower nominal interest rate, because this lower rate still allows lenders to earn the same after-tax real return as originally.

The demand for loanable funds shifts to the left if part of nominal interest expense is made non-deductible. Although the significance of taxes faced by borrowers is omitted from many academic analyses of the Fisher equation, that omission may generally be inappropriate. (See Feldstein, 1976). If the nominal interest paid by a borrower is a fully deductible expense, but the inflation-induced increase in the price of the real asset acquired by the borrower escapes taxation, then an increase in the tax rate applied to income against which interest expense can be deducted or an increase in the rate of inflation makes borrowing more attractive. (Such a situation generally holds for borrowers such as homeowners, but much more broadly, too, when evasion of capital gains taxes is widespread.) The partial nondeductibility of interest payments means that borrowers will choose to borrow a smaller amount of funds at a given nominal interest rate, because the real after-tax cost of borrowing rises and marginally profitable projects now are rejected. Or, correspondingly, borrowers will take out the same level of loans as initially only if the nominal interest rate falls enough to restore the initial real after-tax cost of funds.

The importance of the adjustment for the inflationary component of interest payments in determining tax liabilities can be shown in the analytical framework used above. The relationship between nominal before-tax returns (i), and real after-tax returns (r), becomes:

$$(i - \pi)(1 - t) = r,$$

which can be rewritten as:

$$(7.2) \qquad i = r / (1 - t) + \pi$$

Thus the after-tax real rate of return is equal to $(1 - t)$ multiplied by the before-tax real rate of return. Subtracting equation (7.2) from equation (7.1) indicates that the failure to provide inflation adjustment results in taxation of the inflation premium, since the difference is $(t)(\pi)$.

In other words, without inflation adjustment the real after-tax return falls by $(t)(\pi)$ at any nominal return. As a result the supply curve shifts inward and the demand curve shifts outward, with the amount of the shifts depending on the responsiveness of lenders and borrowers to changes in real returns (parameter **b** in the simple supply curve illustrated above) multiplied by $(t)(\pi)$.

Another way of viewing the consequences of adopting inflation adjustment is that a given real return can be earned with a lower nominal interest rate. In terms of the variables shown in equations (7.1) and (7.2), the difference in the nominal interest rate is $\pi \, t/(1 - t)$. That is, the higher the inflation rate and the higher the tax rate, the bigger the decline in the nominal interest rate that will be acceptable to lenders when the inflation adjustment is adopted. In terms of the numerical example given above, for the same inflation rate, tax rate, and real rate of return, the nominal return now is only 32 percent instead of 43 percent [.32 = .05/.7 + .25].

The policy adopted by Colombia in Law 75 of 1986 applies an average correction factor to business sector interest payments and receipts; that is, all firms are allowed to deduct the same fraction of interest expense, rather than the fraction inflation represents of the interest rate they actually pay. In this case, the expression for the vertical shift in the demand curve for loanable funds represents an average result. Firms whose nominal cost of borrowing is less than the average will benefit from being able to deduct more than their real interest cost; thus, they will have less incentive to reduce borrowing. The opposite conclusion holds for firms whose cost of borrowing exceeds the average; because they cannot deduct all of their real interest costs, they will face an even greater incentive to cut back their borrowing. Firms in this latter category are likely to include all firms with debt-equity ratios that are high for their industries, smaller enterprises for whom accurate accounting information is difficult to assemble, and other borrowers for whom lenders perceive a high degree of risk. Such borrowers are charged an above-average rate of interest, but they will not be able to deduct all of the risk premium they pay.

Because the demand curve for loanable funds shifts inward and the supply curve shifts outward, the primary effect of such a policy change is to reduce the nominal interest rate, with relatively little effect on the quantity of loans and investment. If the tax rates faced by borrowers and lenders are the same, then the total level of borrowing would remain unchanged, as shown in Figure 7.1. The same result would hold if the demand for loanable funds were assumed to be vertical and the downward shift of the supply curve determined the new nominal interest rate. The latter situation corresponds to the conclusions drawn from models in which the demand for money is not responsive to the interest rate. (See Peek, 1982, for a survey of this literature).

Over a longer time horizon a wider set of responses appears likely, as implied by the diagrammatic treatment here. Of course, knowing the relevant tax rates of the marginal borrowers and lenders in any economy with a complex tax law and a progressive income tax structure is problematic. In Colombia, the most likely case would seem to be that borrowers face higher tax rates than lenders. Tax returns showing net wealth for shareholders in corporations and partners in limited partnerships (socios) and for others (no socios) allow a rough comparison. Socios tend to be wealthier and presumably fall in higher tax brackets than no socios. This wealthier group reports somewhat more debt relative to net wealth than do the no socios (47 percent compared to 42 percent). In addition, tax-exempt entities are generally net debtors. If this generalization is appropriate, it implies the qualitative situation shown in Figure 7.2. Because the vertical shift of the demand curve exceeds the vertical shift in the supply curve, the nominal interest rate falls by less than the vertical shift in the demand curve. Lenders are satisfied with what borrowers are willing to pay them only if the total amount of borrowing in the economy declines and a smaller amount of saving is generated.

2. Analysis for an Open Economy

The principal prediction above, that nominal interest rates will fall substantially when the inflationary component of interest payments is made nontaxable and nondeductible, is much less certain in the case of an open economy. Consider the simple situation in which foreign and domestic assets can be treated as perfect substitutes, and as a result the same rate of return is earned on all assets; the more complete case of differentiated assets is discussed later in this chapter. Figure 7.1 can be modified in a straightforward way to show why the market return will depend on more than the supply and demand conditions of a single country. To do so, though, two additional relationships must be added to the above characterization of the economy.

First, a portfolio balance equation is assumed to hold, to ensure that a foreign citizen or company investing in Country C (denoting Colombia) earns the same after-tax return there, after allowing for any change in the exchange rate, as he does from investing at home in Country R (denoting the rest of the world):

(7.3) $i_R = i_C + e,$

where e is the expected change in the value of Country C's currency, the peso, expressed in terms of dollars. This equation appears especially simple because an individual in Country C is assumed to face the same tax rate on interest income earned in Country C as in Country R.[82/] It also must be true that the tax on exchange rate gains or losses is the same as on ordinary income and that the lender has sufficient capital gains to allow all losses to be claimed. While the first of these conditions is broadly consistent with U.S. tax law, cases in which one or both of the conditions are violated could be considered without changing the thrust of the argument that follows.

Equation (7.3) indicates that if the nominal interest rate in the rest of the world i_R is 10 percent and the peso is expected to depreciate by 20 percent relative to the dollar, then the nominal interest rate in Colombia i_C must be 30 percent to provide a comparable return. If the Colombian interest rate were less than 30 percent, a capital outflow would occur, until capital had become sufficiently scarce in Colombia that its return rose to 30 percent.

Second, the way in which the exchange rate is expected to change must be specified. For the longer run horizon being considered here, that is, beyond the completion of the phased-in inflation adjustment in 1995, a long-run representation of exchange rate determination is appropriate. As noted above, a common long-run explanation of exchange rate movements is the purchasing power parity theorem, which implies that any change in the exchange rate depends on differences in the expected inflation rates in the two countries. For example, if at a given exchange rate the Colombian inflation rate exceeds that in the rest of the world, Colombian goods will become less competitive on world markets. As Colombian imports rise and exports fall, the quantity of dollars demanded internationally rises while the quantity supplied declines. In the absence of Central Bank intervention, the value of the peso will fall or depreciate while the dollar appreciates. Starting from an equilibrium position, the relation between the expected rates of inflation in the two countries, π_r and π_c, and the expected change in the exchange rate between their countries is:

$$(7.4) \qquad e = \pi_R - \pi_C.$$

When the two inflation rates are the same, the exchange rate does not change.

Equations (7.3) and (7.4) together imply that in the long run the same real before-tax rate of return will be earned in each country:

$$(7.5) \qquad i_C - \pi_C = i_R - \pi_R.$$

When this condition is not met, capital is expected to flow out of the country offering lower returns into the country offering higher returns.

Return now to the link between nominal before-tax returns and real after-tax returns given in equation (7.1), which was used to explain the graphical representation of the demand and supply curves for loanable funds. The domestic saving and borrowing relationships discussed above hold in an open economy, but the determination of the equilibrium interest rate differs. In a closed economy the equilibrium nominal before-tax return is determined by the intersection of the domestic supply and demand curves, as shown at i_0 in Figures 7.1 and 7.2. At any return below i_0, there is more demand for loanable funds than domestic savers want to supply. However, if domestic borrowers can obtain funds from foreign savers, the equilibrium return can be less than i_0. To determine this value, the domestic and foreign supply curves must be added together, giving a total or aggregate supply of funds which intersects the domestic demand curve at the new equilibrium.[83/]

In one important case, though, this aggregation is not necessary. If the borrowing country is smalll in relation to the world economy, and its demand for funds on world financial markets is such a small share of the total that it is a price taker, the foreign supply surve can be represented as a horizontal line. A country the size of Colombia is commonly regarded as playing a small enough role in world capital markets that any change in its borrowing or lending will not significantly alter international rates of return. Such a relationship implies that if Colombia were to offer a return below this market rate, no international lender would be willing to provide it funds, since the lender could always get a higher return somewhere else in the international capital market. By the same token it need not pay a higher rate of return. Thus, the interest rate facing Colombian borrowers is determined almost entirely by foreign supply conditions and will not be significantly influenced by changes in available domestic savings. That situation is shown in Figure 7.3 with a horizontal foreign supply curve. If the country is large enough that its level of borrowing or lending affects interest rates internationally, then the new equilibrium instead tends more towards the closed economy example in Figure 7.1, with some response to inflation adjustment occurring through nominal interest rate changes and less through the level of borrowing. However, most countries, including Colombia, are more likely to experience an outcome closer to Figure 7.3 than to Figure 7.1 because the elasticity of supply of foreign funds is likely to be much greater than the elasticity of supply of domestic saving. Because of that difference in supply elasticities, even if the initial share of foreign borrowing in the economy is relatively small, the large potential inflow (or outflow) of funds keeps the market interest rate from changing significantly in response to a tax change.

At the equilibrium nominal before-tax return shown in Figure 7.3, total domestic borrowing is OP. The portion of domestic borrowing financed by foreign lenders is MP and the portion financed domestically is OM.

The position of the foreign supply curve is determined by factors identified in equations (7.1) and (7.5). Those equations can be used to calculate the nominal before-tax return required in Country C for any given real after-tax return sought by lenders in Country R. First, recall from equation (7.5) that to satisfy U.S. lenders who face the same total tax burden on Colombian income as on U.S. income, the long-run equilibrium relationship between Colombian and U.S. returns must be $i_C = i_R - \pi_R + \pi_C$. This equation indicates that the nominal return in Colombia must rise point-for-point with Colombian inflation, but not by some larger proportion, as might be inferred for a closed economy from the modified Fisher equation (7.1). (This result has been noted by Hansson and Stuart, 1986).

Specifying how the nominal returns for the rest of the world, i_R, are determined suggests additional relationships. For example, if the change in i_R depends on the Fisher equation (7.1), as specified for the lender (a result that follows when the demand curve for loanable funds is vertical), then the expression above can be rewritten as:

$$(7.6) \qquad i_C = \frac{r_R}{1-t_R} + \frac{t_R \pi_R}{1-t_R} + \pi_C,$$

where t_R refers to the tax rate of the lender in the rest of the world. In addition to the result above regarding an increase in the Colombian inflation rate, equation (7.6) shows that if the tax rate in the rest of the world increases, the current supply of loanable funds will be available only if the nominal return abroad and in Colombia rises. Also, if foreign inflation increases, that requires a higher nominal return in Colombia; when there is no inflation adjustment abroad, foreign inflation requires a large enough rise in foreign nominal before-tax returns that this effect dominates the tendency for foreign inflation to cause peso appreciation and a consequent reduction in Colombian nominal returns.[84/]

With respect to Figure 7.3, recall that the initial amount of foreign borrowing is shown by the amount MP, the difference between the quantity of loanable funds demanded at the market rate of interest and the quantity supplied domestically at the same interest rate. Even if foreign borrowing represents a small share of total loanable funds in the economy, the foreign sector plays a pivotal role as the marginal source of funds. For example, if there is an increase in Colombian demand for loanable funds, the fixed nominal interest rate faced in international markets implies that the extra demand for credit will not drive up the Colombian interest rate and thereby generate more domestic saving. Instead, the primary response will be greater borrowing from foreign sources. Conversely, an increase in Colombian saving will not appreciably drive down Colombian interest rates. Rather, the extra Colombian saving replaces foreign lending, which shifts elsewhere in the world without any appreciable tendency for Colombian returns to fall.

When inflation adjustments of nominal interest payments and receipts are introduced, the demand curve for loanable funds shifts inward and the domestic supply curve shifts outward, as in the closed economy case. As long as there is no change in the combined Colombian-foreign tax burden on foreign funds, the result of this policy shift is to leave the nominal rate of return in the economy unchanged.[85/] Nevertheless, because of the shifts in the domestic demand and supply curves, the policy will increase domestic saving by MN, decrease total borrowing by the amount QP, and reduce net foreign borrowing by Colombia to the amount NQ. Because the after-tax cost of borrowing rises, debt-financed investment in Colombia will decline over time, but due to the higher after-tax return from lending, a larger share of this investment will be financed domestically.

The extent of this reduction in net foreign borrowing depends upon the vertical shifts of both the domestic supply and demand curves, and also on their interest elasticity, or responsiveness to changes in the interest rate. The vertical shift in either curve is given by the relationship between real and nominal returns, tax rates and inflation rates, as determined by equation (7.1). The change in quantity supplied or demanded will depend on the relevant elasticity, as well as on this shift. That relationship, which indicates the sensitivity of supply and demand to the relative rate of returns, is shown in Figure 7.4, where the same vertical shift is shown for two supply curves. The supply curves shown with solid lines (S^{Low}) represent an economy with a small degree of interest elasticity, while the supply curves shown with dotted lines (S^{High}) represent an economy with a larger degree of interest elasticity. Starting from the same initial level of loanable funds, LF_0, and adopting a policy change that gives the same vertical shift from S_0 to $S1$, the new level of loanable funds provided by the economy represented with dotted lines is much larger due to a higher interest elasticity of savings.

The significance of such elasticity comparisons is that for greater elasticities of domestic supply and demand, the effect of inflation adjustment will be a larger reduction in net foreign borrowing and (in the case of demand alone) in a larger decline in the debt-financed capital stock. With respect to the appropriate value of the elasticity of saving supply, no consensus has been reached even in countries such as the United States, where substantial econometric efforts have been made to measure it. Estimates have proven sensitive to the measurement of saving and the choice of the real after-tax rate of return, and little more can be confidently stated beyond that the response seems to be positive.

With respect to the domestic demand for loanable funds, total borrowing will decline more in response to the nondeductibility of interest expense when that demand is more sensitive to interest rate changes. Although a precise assessment of this sensitivity or elasticity is beyond the scope of this project, several generally important factors can be identified. First, this demand elasticity will be greater when other inputs such as labor can be substituted easily for capital. A recent critique by two economists, Betancourt and Clague (1981), of efforts to estimate this production relationship suggests that an elasticity of substitution between 0.5 and 1.0 would be an appropriate general figure in the industrial sector of a developing country such as Colombia. Using the midpoint of this range implies that a 10 percent increase in the cost of capital relative to labor will reduce the capital-labor ratio by 7.5 percent. Because estimates of this elasticity for agriculture and the service sector of the economy often tend to be higher, and these sectors play a larger role in the Colombian economy, the overall response is likely to be somewhat larger

A second important factor is the elasticity of demand for domestic output. The value of the dominant Colombian export, coffee, depends on export quotas assigned by the International Coffee Organization, as well as on fluctuations in world coffee prices. World demand for the product is inelastic, and the demand elasticity facing Colombia alone is not much greater, due to the existence of country quotas that rule out price competition among alternative suppliers. However, coffee exports account for less than half of Colombian merchandise export earnings. Growing exports such as oil, coal, and gold are characterized by markets in which the Colombian share is relatively small, and the demand elasticity faced is significantly greater than in the case of coffee. For domestically produced goods sold in international markets where demand is sensitive to price changes, the derived interest elasticity of demand for capital will be greater. Therefore, the inflation adjustment adopted by Colombia in 1986 appears likely to cause some reduction in the debt-financed capital stock, due to the ability to substitute away from capital in production and to the potential reduction in national output.

B. Implications of Changes in the Cost of Capital

The nondeductibility of the inflationary component of interest payments makes borrowing more expensive in Colombia and is likely to cause the cost of capital faced by Colombian firms to rise. The latter outcome cannot be stated with certainty, because the 1986 tax reform also gave more favorable treatment to equity investment. As noted in Chapter 4, no projection regarding these two conflicting tendencies is made in this Report, as data limitation preclude the calculation of weighted average marginal effective tax rates for aggregate investment. Nevertheless, the very pronounced negative marginal effective tax rates for debt-financed investment, together with the high reliance on borrowing in the Colombian economy, suggests that inflation adjustment of interest payments may result in somewhat less capital investment, as many investment projects will no longer be profitable without their previous tax subsidy.

If a reduction in the capital stock occurs, that result may suggest to some a failure of economic policy. Such a judgment would be quite incorrect in this case. Eliminating investments where the return to society is less than the cost of borrowing funds should strengthen, not weaken, that economy's performance. Simply stated, borrowing at a market rate of 10 percent in order to make investments that yield only 6 percent is economic folly that no private investor would consciously undertake, in the absence of a sizeable subsidy. Yet, private investors will take advantage of tax subsidies that make ventures appear profitable to them even though these same ventures represent a waste of resources from the viewpoint of the economy as a whole. For the country, negative marginal effective tax rates are just such a tax subsidy to economic inefficiency, because overutilization of certain tax-favored types of capital is encouraged.

Such a policy plants the seeds of a major debt crisis in the future. When funds are borrowed from foreigners to invest in projects that yield less to society than the cost of those funds, a country can service its debt in the future only by imposing higher burdens on others in the economy. In particular, higher taxes and other deflationary policies must commonly be utilized to reduce domestic income and purchasing power, retard imports, and promote exports over domestic sales in order to obtain or preserve foreign exchange for debt service; a trade surplus often emerges only at a high cost to the domestic standard of living.

Another way of viewing this same situation is in terms of the difference between gross domestic product and gross national product. The former measure indicates the value of output that is produced within a country, while the latter measure indicates the value of production that is available to residents of the country. Encouraging high levels of capital formation in Colombia through large negative marginal effective tax rates on debt-financed investment may well allow gross domestic product to rise. But if this higher level of activity is financed with greater foreign debt, gross national product will rise only if that investment yields a higher return to society than the rate of interest that must be paid to foreign lenders. The negative marginal effective tax rates cited above suggest that this was not the case with respect to much investment in Colombia under pre-1986 law. Debt-financed investments could yield returns below the cost of borrowing abroad and still be profitable for private firms, because borrowers received a tax benefit in addition to the market return. The very large negative marginal effective tax rates cited earlier imply that the market return could be very low (or even negative) because the tax benefit from such investment was so great. As a consequence, a great deal of tax-favored investment activity was encouraged, which likely resulted in a higher gross domestic product than would have otherwise been produced, but also yielded a smaller gross national product.

A further factor is relevant in evaluating the consequences of a higher cost of debt-financed investment. It might be argued that if a decline in the capital stock also implies a decline in employment, then perhaps the situation is more serious than an examination of the market for loanable funds alone might imply. Yet, even if the higher cost of capital causes a decline in output as the international competitiveness of Colombian goods declines, this is not the entire story; it also implies an incentive to substitute labor for capital. As discussed above, in most developing countries there is a significant potential to substitute away from capital into labor, in both the traditional and the industrial sectors of the economy. This positive substitution effect on employment will partially offset, and may even dominate, the tendency for higher capital costs to result in reduced output and employment. In short, focusing on output effects alone is highly misleading.

C. Additional Factors Relevant in Determining the Cost of Capital

1. Creditability of the Colombian Income Tax

If inflation adjustment of the Colombian income tax were to cause it to be judged noncreditable in the United States, or in other countries that tax income on a worldwide basis, the cost of capital would be even more likely to rise than suggested above. Such a ruling may seem unlikely, but a strict interpretation of U.S. law might regard the Colombian inflation adjustment as disallowing a significant business expense, because interest is a significant expense and in many countries the inflationary component accounts for most of nominal interest paid. The Economic Council of Canada (1987, p. 20) cites this potential problem with creditability as a reason why full indexation of the corporate tax system is not a viable policy to pursue. If the Canadian concerns are correct, post-1986 Colombian law will be challenged by the U.S. Internal Revenue Service or by tax administrators in other countries.

Such an interpretation seems overly pessimistic, because it can also be argued that a system attempting to tax real income should only allow real expenses to be deducted. That a large adjustment must be made to reduce nominal interest paid to the real interest expense simply indicates that there is a large initial distortion in measuring real income. The inflationary component of nominal interest payments represents a return of capital to the lender; because the purchasing power of the principal eventually returned will have fallen as a result of inflation, a higher nominal interest payment is necessary to maintain the same real value of the amount lent. This reasoning has been accepted by the U.S. Treasury Department itself in a different context. In its 1984 report on tax reform to President Reagan, the Treasury Department proposed an adjustment to make the inflationary component of interest payments nondeductible and the inflationary component of interest receipts nontaxable. The Treasury explained the rationale for the proposal in the following terms: «The proposed inflation adjustment will assure that taxpayers no longer pay tax on fictitious income from capital that merely reflects inflation; similarly interest deductions subject to the inflation adjustment will not be bloated by inflation premiums that do not represent real costs» (U.S. Treasury, Vol. I, p.99). Although this should not be read as indicating what the official U.S. policy would be on a tax that provided inflation adjustment for interest expense, it at least shows that the rationale for inflation adjustment is understood in Washington.

Although the loss of creditability does not appear likely, if the Colombian form of inflation adjustment creates problems in this regard, it might be appropriate to consider more carefully the comprehensive or integrated inflation adjustments adopted by Chile and other Latin American Countries. Because the comprehensive approaches generally do not explicitly disallow deductibility of the inflationary component of interest payments, but instead adjust other income and balance sheet items upward to take account of inflation, on cosmetic grounds they appear less susceptible to challenge.

2. Domestic and Foreign Assets as Imperfect Substitutes

The ease of showing domestic and foreign influences on the cost of capital all in a single diagram justified the simplifying assumption above that domestic and foreign assets were perfect substitutes. That unrealistic assumption is not necessary for the validity of the analysis under more general circumstances. Let Colombian and foreign assets be treated in two separate markets. Under this approach, there can be a gross outflow of capital from Colombia to the rest of the world, in addition to the larger gross inflow into Colombia. The fact that there is a net inflow of capital into Colombia is not altered. However, in this framework it is important to distinguish between the tax treatment of the two assets. For example, suppose income from Colombian holdings of assets abroad was not effectively taxed, either before or after the 1986 reform, while the taxation of interest income in Colombia is reduced by the reform. This differential change in tax incentives likely causes Colombian savers to lend relatively more funds at home rather than abroad. The supply curve of loanable funds in the Colombian market shifts out, while the supply curve of loanable funds in the foreign market shifts in. A smaller net inflow of funds into Colombia still holds, just as in the simplified model, although the nominal interest rate in Colombia may decline to some extent. To implement this more complete market representation requires that sufficient information be available about the degree of substitution between domestic and foreign assets, a trade-off determined by risk, liquidity, and other relevant characteristics.

3. The Foreign Supply of Funds

The diagrammatic analysis above illustrates the effects of an inflation adjustment policy, assuming that all other factors are unchanged. Of course, the tendencies identified there may not be observed if other factors do change. An additional influence evaluated in Chapter 4 was the corporate tax reduction introduced in the 1986 reform. Another influence addressed here is the role of events and policy choices outside Colombia that affect the cost of funds within Colombia. Several of these factors have resulted in an upward shift in the supply curve of foreign funds. One of the more important elements in this scenario has been a changing balance of saving and investment in the rest of the world. A decline in net saving in the United States and a rise in U.S. investment has resulted in an international reallocation of capital.

Contributing to that reallocation was the U.S. decision in 1984 to eliminate its withholding tax on portfolio interest income paid to foreigners, which has the effect of making the taxation of income from loans to borrowers in the United States more nearly comparable to that on holdings in tax haven countries or in European bearer bonds.[86/] As a result of the higher U.S. return available, the United States became more attractive to savers from all over the world. To the extent that after-tax returns available to foreigners investing in the United States rose, countries such as Colombia experienced smaller net inflows of capital (as well as larger gross outflows of funds since capital flight was encouraged) and were forced to pay a higher rate of return to attract those funds.[87/] Furthermore, as noted in Chapter 5, the 1986 U.S. tax reform may cause U.S.-owned capital to flow out of high-tax countries and into low-tax countries.

IX. Transition Rules

Some Colombian taxpayers have argued that the provisions for the non-deductibility of interest expense contained in the 1986 reform of the income tax are unfair because they apply retroactively to interest on debt already in existence at the time the law was passed. The government has expressed concern about problems such as these and has acknowledged from the beginning of the tax reform process that the provisions of the 1986 law might need to be modified to compensate for this effect.[88/] It is appropriate to re-examine the transition rules for interest indexing contained in Law 75 of 1986, because it is important that they be fair, while leading as quickly as possible to a system that is economically neutral. It is important at a practical political level that transition be seen to be fair, for if transition is perceived to be unduly harsh the 1986 tax reform could be jeopardized.[89/] It is important that they achieve economic neutrality quickly to reduce tax-induced misallocation of resources during the transition period.

A solution to this problem that is frequently discussed in Colombia is inflation-adjustment of depreciation allowances on existing assets.[90/] This approach is unsatisfactory for several reasons.[91/] Adjusting existing fixed assets for inflation does not target relief specifically to those who would be most affected by the non-deductibility of interest on existing debt. For example, an owner of equity-financed investments in depreciable assets would benefit from transitional relief provisions of this type, despite the fact that he would not be adversely affected by the enactment of interest indexing. On the other hand, adjusting fixed assets for inflation is of little or no benefit to those who commonly utilize no (or few) depreciable assets, including the service sector, or to those who have benefited from extraordinarily rapid write-off of investments, such as agriculture, even though they might be highly leveraged.[92/] Thus this type of adjustment would not even eliminate political opposition to indexing from these quarters. The second part of this section describes a more satisfactory method of dealing with the problem of windfall losses created by the introduction of interest indexing. It will be useful to consider first the transition rules that are appropriate for other (non-interest) provisions.

A. Non-interest Provisions

As has been argued in the preceding section and explained more fully in chapter 5, inflation adjustment should be provided for depreciable assets as part of a system of real economic depreciation allowances. Transition to an inflation-adjusted system for depreciation allowances on assets other than real estate is probably best handled by continuing present-law treatment of existing assets, and applying the new system only to assets acquired after enactment of the law.[93/] Net wealth invested in such assets would continue to be understated, but it would seem inequitable, as well as economically disruptive and politically unacceptable, to attempt to include the true market value of previously depreciated assets in net wealth for tax purposes. Of course, to the extent that such assets are sold, they should be covered by the new system. It would also be inappropriate to provide inflation adjustment of the remaining basis in the case of existing assets that have not been fully depreciated; since chapter 4 indicates that the acceleration under current law can be seen as a rough surrogate for such adjustment at current inflation rates, also allowing explicit adjustment would be overly generous.

The change from the present system of accelerated depreciation to one based on real economic depreciation should cause no churning of assets, because accelerated depreciation claimed under the existing system would be recaptured upon disposition. If anything, there may be some disincentive for disposition of used assets, relative to current law, since the present value of the net wealth tax attributable to such assets would be increased. This does not appear to be a significant problem.

In the case of land (and perhaps all real estate) it seems appropriate to attempt a transition to a system in which valuation for purposes of the net wealth tax is the greater of the cadastral value of the land or the historical value of land, indexed for inflation (and for depreciation, in the case of structures) since the time of acquisition. (As noted earlier, the full cadastral value of land should be used for this purpose, rather than the 60 percent of valuation specified in Law 75 of 1986.) This might be achieved, for example, under a schedule that by 1995 would eliminate any shortfall of valuation for net wealth tax purposes below the greater of these two figures.[94/]

Transition from unindexed systems of inventory accounting to indexed systems can be handled relatively simply, provided a change from LIFO to FIFO (or vice-versa) does not occur simultaneously.[95/] In the case of the transition from FIFO to indexed FIFO no change need be made in the treatment of existing inventories. Leaving aside shifts in relative prices and inflation that occurs between the date of acquisition and the end of the year, inventories are valued correctly for purposes of the net wealth tax under indexed FIFO. If inflation adjustment is applied only to inventories acquired after enactment of tax reform, cost of goods sold will gradually cease to be understated; as this occurs, taxpayers will experience neither a gain nor a loss.

The transition from LIFO to indexed LIFO poses greater problems because of the existence of inventories carried on books at their historical costs, which in many cases may be far below current market values. It would be desirable to eliminate this undervaluation both because net wealth is understated and because the prospect of being forced to include such goods taken from undervalued inventories in costs of goods sold (and thus pay taxes on the inflationary gains involved) can seriously distort decision-making for firms that for business reasons might otherwise wish to draw down inventories. The choice of method to be used to eliminate the undervaluation is critical because it involves substantial amounts of revenues and large potential windfall losses for taxpayers.

A particularly harsh viewpoint is that taxpayers should be forced to include some portion of the increase in the nominal value of inventories in taxable income, as well as including the adjusted value of inventories in net wealth. This would be much less generous than the proposed treatment of taxpayers using FIFO or the proposed treatment of depreciable assets; it would not be equitable, and it is not proposed.

Under an alternative view existing inventories would be written up immediately, with tax consequences only for the future calculation of taxable income and net wealth. This position relies on the viewpoint that taxpayers accumulated the inventories in question under current law, expecting never to have to pay income tax on the inventory gains because stocks would be maintained. An extreme version of this attitude would even question whether existing inventories should ever be revalued, even for purposes of the net wealth tax. This last view should be rejected because it would create complexity and would continue the undervaluation of inventories and the artificial barrier to depletion it implies.

An intermediate position would require that existing inventories be written up over a period of time (say five or ten years, perhaps using the scheme described in note 94 for land), in order to phase in the impact of the net wealth tax. Since the revaluation of inventories would not be subject to income tax, this proposal would have no income tax consequences except when inventories are depleted; then cost of goods sold would be greater than under current law. All things considered, this seems to be the preferred approach.

Rules described thus far would apply to calculation of the value for net wealth tax purposes for the following types of assets: real estate, depreciable assets, and inventories. In the case of publicly traded securities there is generally no transition problem since it is appropriate to continue to base the net wealth tax on current market values. In all cases it would be appropriate to calculate gains on dispositions by deducting inflation-adjusted cost (or other basis) from the proceeds of sale.

B. Interest Indexing

The ten-year phase-in of the non-deductibility of the inflationary component of interest expense provided by Law 75 of 1986 fails to deal satisfactorily with the windfall losses that would result from immediate non-deductibility for at least two reasons.[96] First, those who incurred debt obligations under pre-1986 law presumably expected to be allowed to deduct the full nominal amount of interest expenses. Windfall losses would result, to the extent that non-deductibility applies to the inflationary component of interest on such indebtedness.[97] While such losses are reduced in present value terms by the phasing-in of the disallowance of deductions, they are not eliminated.

Second, the phase-in applies to all interest paid during the phase-in period, without regard to whether the debt in question existed at the time of enactment of the 1986 reforms. As a result, revenue is lost unnecessarily, and throughout the long (ten year) phase-in period incentives for uneconomic borrowing continue, with consequent adverse effects such incentives have on financial decisions and resource allocation. (See also chapter 4 for calculations of negative marginal effective tax rates on debt-financed investments under pre-1986 law and during the phase-in period if the transition is implemented as prescribed under current law).

It is possible to construct many alternatives for the transition to a system in which the inflationary component of interest is not deductible. Several are presented here in order to illustrate their relative strengths and weaknesses. All are composed of the following key features which can be varied to achieve various purposes: a) continuation for ten years of at least partial deduction of an amount of net interest expense equal to that claimed as a deduction in 1985 (hereafter called the base-period amount of interest), b) some degree of indexing (within the range of zero to 100 percent) of this base-period amount for inflation since 1985, c) phase-out of the deductibility of the inflationary component of interest expense in excess of this (partially indexed and phased out) base-period amount.[98]

For example, one proposal (one that is probably less generous than is appropriate, for reasons to be enxplained below) would allow full deduction of the nominal amount of interest paid in 1985, but would provide no inflation adjustment of this amount; deduction for the inflationary component of interest payments exceeding that base-period amount of interest would be phased out over six years. During 1986-91 partial deduction would be allowed for the inflationary component of net interest expense in excess of the base-period amounts according to a phase-out schedule that after 1987 would be somewhat faster than that contained in the 1986 law for the entire inflation component of interest expense. Specifically, deduction of the inflationary component of interest payments exceeding the base-period interest would be phased out over a six-year period, with 90 percent deductible in 1986, 80 percent deductible in 1987, 60 percent deductible in 1988, 40 percent deductible in 1989, and 20 percent deductible in 1990. Beginning in 1991, the phase-out of the inflationary component of the excess of interest over the base-period levels would be complete. However, the interest not in excess of the base-period amount would continue to be deductible during the full ten-year period; after that only the inflation component of the base-period amount would be deductible. In what follows this scheme is identified as Alternative I.[99]

The effects of this scheme are compared to those of current law in Table 7-4, which is constructed on the «base-case» assumptions that the interest rate is 25 percent and that nominal indebtedness grows at the rate of inflation (assumed for purposes of this example to be 20 percent) so that the real value of debt remains constant.[100] Under this scheme interest deductions are greater in eight of the years 1986-95 than under current law, but slightly smaller in two years. As a result, Alternative I is somewhat more generous than current law. This can be seen from the summary statistics in Table 7-5, which shows a) the percent of the present value of nominal interest expense incurred during the ten year period that would be allowed as deductions under various transition schemes, for various assumptions about the growth of indebtedness, and b), in parentheses, the fraction of the present value of interest payments during the ten year period that would be allowed as deductions during the first five years. Under the assumptions of Table 7-4 the present value of the interest deductions that would be allowed under alternative I are 64 percent of the present value of interest expense during the ten year period in question; the comparable figure for current law is 59 percent.[101] Perhaps equally important, the greater present value of interest deductions available during the first five-year period (46 percent of the present value of interest expense during the ten year period, compared to 42 percent) indicates that windfall losses during this early period when adjustment to the use of relatively less debt finance would be difficult would be less dramatic than under current law.

If indebtedness grows somewhat more rapidly, at the assumed rate of interest used in constructing these examples, the benefits of Alternative I over current law are rather modest, 58 versus 56 percent of deductions (41 versus 38 percent in the first five years) remain deductible in present value terms. (See the last column of Table 7-5.)

Even though Alternative I would be preferable to current law, it does not appear to be generous enough, especially in its treatment of base-period interest. An unindexed base-period amount would rapidly lose real value in an inflationary environment. (At an inflation rate of 20 percent, a fixed nominal deduction of $100,000 would be worth only $64,000 in real terms in two years and $32,768 in five.) Moreover, as a political matter it may be necessary to provide more relief than that under Alternative I. Thus some inflation adjustment of the base-period amount seems appropriate.

An alternative proposed for more serious consideration (Alternative II) is to allow taxpayers to continue for a period of ten years (1986-95) to deduct the full amount of net nominal interest expense, up to the base-period level after adjustment for one-half the inflation since 1985; at the end of the ten-year period, the full deduction for the inflation component of partially indexed base-period interest would be eliminated. Deduction for the inflationary component of interest expense in excess of this inflation-adjusted base-period amount would be phased out over six years, according to the schedule given above for Alternative I. This alternative is also illustrated (for the same set of assumptions used to illustrate Alternative I) in Table 7-4, and its effects are summarized in Table 7-5. Deductions under this alternative are greater in each of the ten years than under current law, and the present value of interest deductions is 77 percent of that of interest payments (at constant real levels of debt). During the first five years deductions with a present value equal to 50 percent of the value of interest payments during the ten year period are allowed, compared to 42 percent under current law. If indebtedness grows at a 25 percent rate, interest deductions during the ten years are only 68 percent (44 percent in the first five years) as great in present value as interest payments.

The partial (50 percent) inflation adjustment of 1985 level interest payments in Alternative II is allowed in recognition of the fact that inflation would rapidly erode fixed base-period amounts. This erosion of the base-period amount explains why under Alternative I only 64 percent of the present value of interest expense incurred over the ten year period is allowed as a deduction, in comparison to 77 percent under Alternative II, in the case of constant real debt under examination here.

Complete adjustment of the base-period amount for inflation is not suggested because it would entail too much loss of revenue, because it is important to move quickly to reduce incentives for firms to rely on debt finance (including those provided by the continuation of deductions for the base-period amounts in some cases), and because the eventual elimination of the full deduction of the inflation component of the inflation-adjusted 1985 amount would be less problematical if it were phased-out over time, that is, if full adjustment were not allowed in the interim. The revenue consequences of complete adjustment of the base-period amount can be seen from the entries for Alternative III in Table 7-5. By definition, if indebtedness grows at the rate of inflation that is used to index the base-period amount, no interest deductions are disallowed. Even if indebtedness grows somewhat more rapidly than the rate of inflation, little interest is non-deductible under this rule; in the case of 20 percent inflation and a 25 percent rate of interest and growth rate of indebtedness, the present value of interest deductions is 86 percent of the present value of interest payments (48 percentage points of this occurring in the first five years). While some taxpayers may contend (correctly, when this measure is considered in isolation) that allowing only partial indexation of the base-period amount imposes windfall losses, this approach none-the-less seems like a reasonable compromise between the various objectives of equity, revenue, and incentives for rational decision making, subject to the proviso of the next few paragraphs.

There is no reason that the fraction of the inflation rate used to adjust base-period interest payments should be the same (e.g., either zero, 50 percent, or 100 percent, as in the three alternatives described above) in all years. It might, for example, be thought appropriate to provide full adjustment of the base-period amount for inflation occurring during the first few years and then phase it down to zero. (The phase-out of the deductibility of the inflation component of interest expense in excess of the indexed base-period amount of interest expense might follow the same schedule as above, in any event, but need not.) This would allow firms more time to adjust their financial structures in response to the projected pattern of incentives provided by future tax law, without inflicting heavy windfall losses in the short term when it is difficult to adjust to the new fiscal realities.

Another objection that can be made to Alternative II and especially to Alternative III is that deductions for the inflation component of partially indexed base-period interest are suddenly eliminated in 1995. It is true that by 1995 these deductions for the inflation premium will be relatively insignificant in real terms under Alternative II (but not under Alternative III), as seen from the perspective of 1985 (or 1987, when this Report is being prepared). But it can be expected that as 1995 nears there would be opposition to their being eliminated as scheduled. It may thus be worthwhile to consider alternatives that would avoid or further reduce the problem posed by this sudden elimination of the indexed base-period deduction. For example, full inflation adjustment might be allowed for base-period interest expense for several years; then the fraction of the inflation rate used to index the base-period deduction could be reduced to zero over several more years; finally the base-period amount could be phased out over several years.

Alternative IV, described in Table 7-6 and summarized in Table 7-5, provides an example of such a more sophisticated adjustment scheme. During the first three years the base-period amount is adjusted for the full amount of inflation, in the second three-year period adjustment is allowed for only 50 percent of inflation, the indexed base-period amount is held constant in nominal terms in the seventh year, and during the last three years this indexed amount is phased out; the treatment of interest payments that exceed this indexed base-period amount is the same as in Alternatives I-III.

In both the cases of constant real debt and of growth of debt at a rate equal to the rate of interest, the present values of interest deductions are almost exactly the same as under Alternative II, in which the base-period amount is indexed by a fixed 50 percent of inflation. But because of the difference in the way the adjustments of the base-period amounts are structured, significantly more of the total deductions (in present value terms) occur in the first five years under Alternative IV than alternative II. Indeed, if indebtedness grows at the interest rate the present value of interest deductions during the first five years are almost as great as under Alternative III (46 versus 48 percent), even though they are substantially less over the full ten-year period (68 versus 86 percent).

It can be expected that at least some firms will want to respond to the 1986 reforms by reducing indebtedness during the ten-year period 1986-95 to the point that interest payments fall below the indexed level of base-period interest payments. In such a case, it will be desirable to have a rule that prevents such firms from losing the benefits of the full deduction of partially indexed pre-1985 interest expense. Otherwise incentives to reduce indebtedness will be blunted, and there will be a tendency for firms to merge in order to be able to take full advantage of the deductions.

Two possible ways of achieving this objective would be to allow firms either to carry forward (with interest) unused deductions of this type to future years or to sell them to other firms who could use them immediately to augment their own deductions for partially-adjusted pre-1985 interest expense and thereby offset taxable income. The first alternative has the disadvantage of adding some complexity and of reducing somewhat the incentive to decrease indebtedness, since amounts carried forward could be fully utilized only if the firm did not reduce future interest expense to below the partially indexed 1985 level, minus the amount carried over. The second alternative of allowing unused deductions to be sold to other taxpayers would also add undesirable complexity, as well as reducing incentives of the taxpayer buying the excess deductions to decrease reliance on debt.

For these reasons, a third alternative is offered. Taxpayers could be allowed a special deduction equal to the partially indexed amount of 1985 interest expense. If post-1985 interest expense fell below this special deduction, the full amount of the special deduction might none-the-less be allowed as an «interest»deduction. If post-1985 interest expense exceeded the special deduction, the excess would be treated as described above.

The basic approach to the introduction of interest indexing just described has the substantial advantage of dealing directly with the windfall losses that would otherwise result from introduction of interest indexing; it largely avoids the windfalls by guaranteeing full deduction of partially indexed 1985 interest payments. As a result, it essentially avoids providing relief where it is not required or appropriate (that is, on post-1985 increases in real debt). This improved targeting of relief reduces the revenue costs of providing transitional relief. Moreover, it allows depreciation policy to be determined on the basis of economic principles, rather than as an ad hoc offset for the inflation adjustment of interest. Finally, and perhaps most importantly, it allows full disallowance of the inflationary component of interest expense in excess of partially indexed 1985 interest deductions to be achieved more quickly than under current law. As a result the unfortunate incentives provided by current law to rely excessively on debt finance and to invest in uneconomic activities characterized by negative marginal tax rates can be eliminated more quickly.

Of course, providing transition relief will entail the loss of revenue. While no revenue loss is welcome, and must be compensated with other measures, the losses are probably a reasonable price to pay to maintain — and, indeed, to accelerate — the indexation of interest expense introduced in the 1986 law.

C. Economic Effects of Adjustment: 1986 to 1995

Several important short-run issues may arise as the inflation adjustment of interest payments is phased in through 1995. Some of these issues are related to macroeconomic factors, others are related to microeconomic efficiency issues, and still others are related to equity considerations. Many of these adjustment issues are discussed elsewhere in the report, and the ones included here relate most directly to the international perspectives presented above.

One issue discussed in Chapter 3 is the asymmetric nature of the phase-in of the inflation adjustment. The taxable base of borrowers is expanded by phasing in the nondeductibility of the inflationary component of interest payments by progressively allowing 10 percent fewer of these payments to be deducted each year from 1986 through 1995. The same treatment applies to the taxable portion of interest payments received by businesses. However, natural persons are immediately able to exclude the inflationary component of net interest received from the following sources: financial intermediaries regulated by the Superintendencia Bancaria; public debt; and the debt of corporations issued under authorization of the National Securities Commission (Comisión Nacional de Valores). Such a situation implies that the immediate supply or saving response will be greater than the decline in demand for loanable funds. Therefore, in the early years of the phase in, the potential retarding effect on capital formation will not be as visible as the favorable domestic saving response. As the demand for loanable funds falls over time, net foreign borrowing will decline more than in the initial period.

Another aspect of the phase-in period is that macroeconomic factors determining the exchange rate tend to be different in the short run than in the long run. That is important, in the context of Figure 7.3, because an expected depreciation of the peso causes the supply curve of foreign funds to shift upward. The inflation adjustment being considered here causes an increase in Colombian saving, leading to a smaller net inflow of foreign funds. A smaller net inflow of funds, in turn, can give rise to a short-run deterioration of the balance of payments and require a depreciation of the nation's currency. This scenario implies that in the short-run exchange rate expectations may deviate from levels suggested by the purchasing power parity condition of equation (7.4); nor will the equality of real before-tax returns shown in equation (7.5) necessarily hold. Those conditions assume a long-run perspective, in which exchange rates are essentially determined by trade in goods. In the short run exchange rates may be influenced much more by asset flows. For that time horizon, the portfolio balance condition given in equation (7.3) may be a more appropriate indicator of whether the supply curve of foreign funds will shift up or down. Given that condition, though, it is still necessary to specify whether or not a policy change is anticipated in order to predict the effect on nominal interest rates.

If a future Colombian policy change that reduced the net inflow of foreign capital were to occur as a complete surprise, holders of Colombian assets would experience an immediate windfall loss from an unanticipated currency depreciation. However, they then would expect the exchange rate to appreciate, as the economy moved to the long-run position where the exchange rate again was determined by relative inflation rates. Because the exchange rate is expected to rise, the nominal interest rate in Colombia declines. Such a pattern of exchange rate adjustment has been suggested by Dornbusch (1980) and by Blejer (1984).

227

When the policy change instead is anticipated, as seems more appropriately the case under the 1986 Colombian reform which phases in the inflationary adjustment over ten years, lenders might expect the peso to depreciate, given their recognition that a smaller capital inflow implies a smaller demand for pesos. As a consequence, equation (7.3) suggests there must be a temporary rise in nominal interest rates to offset the expected exchange loss. In that case the upward shift in the foreign supply curve of loanable funds implies a further short-run negative impact on capital formation.

While the possibility of a temporary increase in nominal interest rates may appear to cause additional adjustment problems in the economy, the short-run result of an exchange rate depreciation is related to the resolution of one aspect of these problems. Some commentators have argued that a higher cost of capital in Colombia might have a disproportionate impact on capital-intensive import competing industries. To offset this negative effect, one reaction might be to consider greater tariff protection for these producers. However, any acceptance of such a policy should be recognized primarily as an income distribution issue and a political response to a change in the pattern of national output, not as a way of significantly affecting the level of national output. Any effort to go beyond a general exchange rate adjustment, to impose tariffs on imports where domestic competitors are especially impacted by inflation adjustment, would be a mistake. A policy to offset exactly any competitive disadvantage from inflation adjustment faced by import-competing industries would dissipate the efficiency gains from tax reform and lock the economy back into a wasteful pattern of capital utilization and production.

X. Summary

The conclusions of this chapter can be summarized briefly. First, if Colombia is to continue to employ the income tax, rather than adopting the Simplified Alternative Tax, it should extend the system of inflation adjustment to include depreciable assets (and assets subject to amortization, depletion, and similar schemes for allocating costs across years) and inventories. The failure to do so would result in the continuation of undesirable inequities and distortions of economic decisions.

Under either the income or the consumption-based strategy inflation adjustment should be employed in the calculation of net wealth. (For further discussion of this issue, see Chapters 6 and 10.) Though it would be desirable for financial accounting to follow a similar system of inflation-adjusted accounts, this Report does not propose that conformity between tax and financial accounting be required.

Despite the advantages of the Chilean system of integrated inflation adjustments, it is suggested that Colombia should not adopt that approach; rather, it should continue to employ ad hoc adjustments of the type contained in the 1986 tax reform. In particular, the basis of depreciable assets should be adjusted for inflation for purposes of calculating both depreciation allowances and net wealth; the best available estimates of economic depreciation should then be employed to calculated depreciation allowances. Similarly, inflation adjustment should be extended to inventories; although indexed FIFO is clearly the preferable approach, taxpayers might reasonably be allowed the option of using indexed LIFO. For all purposes a general index of inflation should be used, rather than either replacement costs or indices specific to particular assets or industries.

Inflation adjustment of interest income and expense should continue to be implemented by disregarding a fraction of such income and expense equal to the ratio of the inflation rate to the relevant interest rate; it does not seem appropriate to apply the conceptually preferable approach of disregarding an amount of income or expense equal to the product of the principal of debt multiplied by the inflation rate, except in the case of financial institutions. (Inflation adjustment should be extended to the financial sector and to leases that are, in effect, purchase agreements.) These fractions should be calculated from contemporaneous inflation and interest rates, rather than those for the prior year, as in Law 75.

It is important that transition rules be sufficiently generous to avoid undue economic hardships and forestall political opposition. This is particularly true in the case of inflation adjustment of interest expense. In order to meet this objective while achieving the benefits of interest indexing as soon as possible, it is suggested that interest expense be split into two parts: the amount claimed in 1985 (perhaps partially adjusted for inflation and then phased out) and the excess over this «indexed base-period amount». The first would be fully deductible; deductions for the inflation component of interest expense in excess of the fully deductible amounts would be phased out over a period of years.

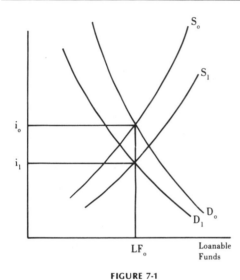

FIGURE 7-1

Inflation Adjustment in a Closed Economy

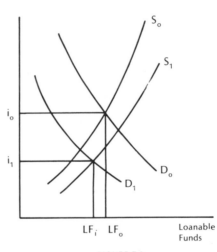

FIGURE 7-2

Asymmetric Effects of Inflation Adjustmment in a Closed Economy

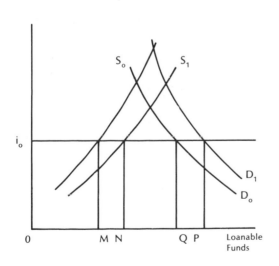

FIGURE 7-3

Inflation Adjustment in an Open Economy

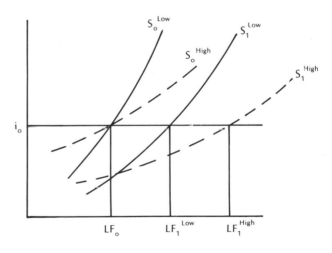

FIGURE 7-4

The Role of Saving Responsiveness in an Economy

TABLE 7-1

Accuracy of Alternative Measures to Compensate for Inflation on Non-monetary Assets

	Measurement of Income	Measurement of Net Wealth
Ad Hoc Approaches Accelerated	Potentially satisfactory in present value terms; vulnerable to changes in inflation rate	Understates net wealth
FIFO inventory accounting	Overstates income	Roughly accurate; depends on changes in relative prices and changes in inventory
LIFO inventory accounting	Roughly accurate; depends on changes in relative prices and changes in inventory	Understates net wealth
Partial Exclusion of Capital Gains	Generally inaccurate, except by accident	Understates net wealth unless basis is inflation adjusted or revalued
Indexed Approaches Indexation of Depreciable Basis (General Prices)	Accurate	Roughly accurate; depends on changes in relative prices
Indexed FIFO inventory accounting	Accurate	Roughly accurate; depends on changes in relative prices and inventory accumulation
Indexed LIFO inventory accounting	Roughly accurate; depends on changes in relative prices	Roughly accurate; depends on changes in relative prices
Indexed basis of capital assets	Accurate, if gains taxed on realization basis; income deferred if not	Roughly accurate, if assets are revalued each year

TABLE 7-2

INDEBTEDNESS OF COMPANIES
(Debt as percent of debt plus equity)

Year	All Companies (a)	Manufacturing Companies (b)
1950	24.0	— —
1951	27.0	— —
1952	27.0	— —
1953	32.0	— —
1954	31.0	— —
1955	29.0	— —
1956	32.0	— —
1957	32.0	— —
1958	34.0	— —
1959	35.0	— —
1960	37.0	34.2
1961	37.0	35.9
1962	40.0	37.9
1963	40.0	40.0
1964	43.0	42.5
1965	43.0	42.8
1966	45.0	45.7
1967	44.0	44.1
1968	44.0	44.5
1969	46.0	— —
1970	43.9	42.5
1971	47.4	46.8
1972	49.8	49.0
1973	53.7	52.7
1974	57.0	57.0
1975	60.5	59.9
1976	62.1	61.5
1977	61.6	60.4
1978	61.1	59.4
1979	65.1	63.5
1980	73.0	— —
1981	71.2	— —
1982	71.7	— —
1983	71.2	— —

Sources: Column (a): Carrizosa S., Mauricio., **Hacia la Recuperación del Mercado de Capitales en Colombia**. (Bogotá, Colombia: Editorial Presencia, Ltda., 1986), p. 32. Carrizosa's Primary Sources: 1950-1980: Restrepo, J.C., «La Economía Colombiana y el Desarrollo de la Sociedad Anónima en los Ultimos Treinta Años», en Comisión Nacional de Valores. Boletín Mensual, Mayo de 1983, p. 14: 1981-1983: Superintendencia de Sociedades Anónimas, Boletín Mensual, Nos. 3, 4, y 6.

Column (b): Chica, A., Ricardo. «La Financiación de la Inversión en la Industria Manufacturera Colombiana: 1970-1980», in **Desarrollo y Sociedad**, Centro de Estudios sobre Desarrollo Económico, Vol. 15-16 (Septiembre 1984-Marzo 1985), pp. 232-33.

TABLE 7-3

TERM STRUCTURE OF DEBT OF MANUFACTURING COMPANIES

Year	Short Term (a)	Medium Term (b)	Long Term (c)
1970	30.95	28.19	40.86
1971	27.21	28.03	44.76
1972	21.00	24.84	54.16
1973	27.51	21.87	50.62
1974	31.89	20.70	47.41
1975	32.26	21.24	42.50
1976	43.74	21.40	34.86
1977	45.83	26.06	28.11
1978	46.01	27.40	26.59
1979	47.59	25.53	26.88
1980	49.94	26.98	23.08

Source: Chica, Ricardo A. «La Financiación de la Inversión en la Industria Manufacturera Colombiana: 1970-1980», in **Desarrollo y Sociedad**, Centro de Estudios sobre Desarrollo Económico, vol. 15-16 (Septiembre 1984, Marzo 1985), p. 220.

TABLE 7-4

Effects of Alternative Transition Rules for Disallowance of Interest Expense
(Assumptions: inflation rate = 20%; interest rate = 25%)
(Rate of growth of debt equals inflation rate)

A. 1986 Law

Year	Debt	Interest.	Inflation Component	% Non-Deductible	Non-deduct. Interest	Deductible Interest
1985	1000	250	200	0	0	250
1986	1200	300	240	10	24	276
1987	1440	360	288	20	58	302
1988	1728	432	346	30	104	328
1989	2074	518	415	40	166	353
1990	2488	622	498	50	249	373
1991	2986	746	597	60	358	388
1992	3583	896	717	70	502	394
1993	4300	1075	860	80	688	387
1994	5160	1290	1032	90	929	361
1995	6192	1548	1238	100	1238	310

B. Alternative I: No Indexation of Base-period Interest

Year	Excess over 1985 Ineterest	Inflation Component of Excess	% Non-Deductible Interest	Non-Deductible Interest	Interest Deduction	Increase in Deduction
1986	50	40	10	4	296	20
1987	110	88	20	18	342	40
1988	182	146	40	58	374	45
1989	268	215	60	129	390	37
1990	372	298	80	238	384	11
1991	496	397	100	397	349	-39
1992	646	517	100	517	379	-15
1993	825	660	100	660	415	28
1994	1040	832	100	832	458	97
1995	1298	1038	100	1038	510	200

C. Alternative II: 50% Indexation of Base-period Interest

Year	Adjusted 1985 Interest	Excess over Adj. 1985 Interest	Inflation Component of Excess	Non-Deductible Interest	Interest Deduction	Increase in Deduction
1986	275	25	20	2	298	22
1987	303	58	46	9	351	48
1988	333	99	79	32	400	72
1989	366	152	122	73	445	93
1990	403	219	176	140	482	108
1991	443	304	243	243	504	115
1992	487	409	327	327	569	175
1993	536	539	431	431	644	257
1994	589	700	560	560	730	368
1995	648	899	720	720	828	519

TABLE 7-5

**Comparison of Effects of Alternative Transition Rules
for Interest Indexing for Three Different
Growth Rates of Indebtedness**

**(Percent of present value of 1986-95 interest
deductions allowed under alternative rules)**

(Assumptions: Inflation rate = 20%; Interest rate = 25%)

	Zero (a)	Inflation Rate (b)	Interest Rate (c)
	Growth Rate of Indebtedness		
A. Current Law	70	59	56
(Of which, first five years)	(60)	(42)	(38)
B. Alternative I: (No indexing of base-period interest)	100	64	58
(Of which, first five years)	(75)	(46)	(41)
C. Alternative II: (50% indexing of base-period interest)	100	77	68
(Of which, first five years)	(75)	(50)	(44)
D. Alternative III: (100% indexing of base-period interest)	100	100	86
(Of which, first five years)	(75)	(75)	(48)
E. Alternative IV: (Declining indexing and phase-out of base-period interest)	100	77	68
(Of which, first five years)	(75)	(54)	(46)

TABLE 7-6

Effects of Alternative IV Transition Rules
for Disallowance of Interest Expense
(Assumptions: inflation rate = 20%; interest rate = 25%)

1. Rate of growth of debt equals inflation rate

Year	Interest Expense	Adjusted 1985 Interest	Excess over Adj. 1985 Intrerest	Inflation Component of Excess	Non-Deductible Interest	Interest Deduction
1986	300	300	0	0	0	300
1987	360	360	0	0	0	360
1988	432	432	0	0	0	432
1989	518	465	43	35	21	498
1990	622	523	99	79	64	558
1991	476	575	172	137	137	609
1992	896	575	321	257	257	639
1993	1075	383	692	553	553	522
1994	1290	192	1098	879	879	411
1995	1548	0	1548	1238	1238	310

2. Rate of growth of debt equals interest rate

Year	Interest Expense	Adjusted 1985 Interest	Excess over Adj. 1985 Intrerest	Inflation Component of Excess	Non-Deductible Interest	Interest Deduction
1986	313	300	13	10	1	312
1987	391	360	31	25	5	386
1988	488	432	56	45	18	470
1989	610	475	135	108	65	545
1990	763	523	240	192	154	609
1991	954	575	379	303	303	651
1992	1192	575	617	494	494	698
1993	1490	383	1107	885	885	605
1994	1863	192	1671	1337	1337	526
1995	2328	0	2328	1863	1863	466

APPENDIX 7A

Integrated versus Ad Hoc Approaches to Inflation Adjustment

As Colombia considers ways to improve the partial and ad hoc system of inflation adjustments introduced in 1986, it is instructive to examine the integrated system used in Chile, which is widely regarded as the most sophisticated system of inflation adjustment in the world. This is done in this appendix through a series of examples which contrast a stylized system based on the Chilean approach and an ad hoc approach.[102/] In its treatment of interest expense this stylized ad hoc approach resembles the newly enacted Colombian system, except as noted later in this introduction. It incorporates inflation-adjusted depreciation allowances of the type proposed in chapter 5 in the calculation of taxable income. Whether adjustment is also made to the basis of depreciable assets for the calculation of net wealth is a policy matter; such an adjustment is easily incorporated in an ad hoc system and in the examples. A depreciation system that is based on historical costs, without any adjustment for inflation, is included for the sake of comparison.[103/]

The examples are presented for two states of the world: zero inflation and an inflation rate of 20 percent. The real interest rate is assumed to be 10 percent; thus in the case of 20 percent inflation the nominal interest rate is 32 percent (1.10 x 1.20 = 1.32).[104/]

To focus attention on other fundamental similarities and differences between the integrated and ad hoc approaches, these examples assume that inflation adjustment for interest income and expense under the ad hoc approach is exact, rather than approximate, as in the 1986 Colombian law. That is, the ad hoc inflation adjustment for debt used in the examples is the inflation rate times the outstanding principal, rather than a fraction of nominal interest expense. It has been argued in section VI.C of the text that it would be quite difficult to implement these exact adjustments under an ad hoc system. By comparison, the Chilean approach in effect produces exact adjustments, although there is no explicit adjustment of interest, per se; see the discussion below of the case of debt finance for an explanation of why this occurs. Thus to the extent that the fractional disallowance of interest deductions actually employed in Colombia produces results different from the exact adjustments under the stylized ad hoc approach used in these illustrations, the Colombian system departs even further from the system used in Chile than the examples suggest.

To concentrate attention on the important issues of inflation adjustment, it is assumed that the figures for monetary magnitudes other than those on which attention is focussed (e.g., sales, labor, and material costs) increase at the rate of inflation. For simplicity the examples are based on a 50 percent tax rate and a depreciation rate of 30 percent, which is assumed to be the economic rate of depreciation on an asset that has a beginning basis equal to its initial purchase price of $1,000.

In the initial examples it is assumed that there are no beginning inventories and that all materials purchased in the year in question are resold, perhaps after further processing; thus there are no changes in physical inventories, and issues of valuing both goods sold from inventories and ending inventories during an inflationary period are avoided; of course, there is no difference in LIFO and FIFO under these special assumptions. These assumptions are relaxed in the discussion of inventories that follows later in the appendix.

Each example consists of two tables that present information from the balance sheet and income statement of a hypothetical firm. The first column of the balance sheet provides the basic data on the structure of assets, liabilities, and net worth (capital and surplus) at the beginning of the year.[105/] The remaining columns of the balance sheet are relevant for the explanations of both the Chilean and ad hoc systems, though with somewhat different interpretations. The four columns of the income statement report calculations of taxable income for (1) the world of zero inflation, (2) historical cost accounting in the world of 20 percent inflation, (3) the Chilean system of inflation adjustment, and (4) the ad hoc approach.

Equity finance. Case 1 presents the simple case in which a depreciable asset is financed with equity. (See Tables 7-A1 and 7-A2.) In the absence of inflation taxable income (gross profit) is $400. If inflation is 20 percent, taxable income must be $480 (120 percent of $400) to be equal in real terms to the $400 in the world of zero inflation. Tax accounting based on historical costs produces an overstatement of taxable income, $540 rather than $480, because of the failure to adjust depreciation allowances for inflation.

In the integrated system of inflation adjustment used in Chile the following adjustments would be made in this example. Both the basis of depreciable assets and net worth (capital and surplus), as reported on the balance sheet before preparation of the income statement, are increased by the rate of inflation; see column (2) of Table 7-A1. Depreciation allowances are then calculated from this inflation-adjusted figure for the depreciable basis. Finally, these balance sheet adjustments are recognized in the calculation of income for tax purposes; that is, the adjustment of assets is included as a positive income item and the adjustment of net worth is included as a deduction from income; see column (3) of Table 7-A2. (The rationale for these adjustments is explained in the discussion of case 2, which includes debt finance, where the rationale is more easily appreciated.) In this simple case the two adjustments exactly offset each other in the calculation of income, so the only net difference in the calculation of income between this case and that of historical-cost accounting is the use of the inflation-adjusted basis of assets to calculate depreciation allowances. Taxable income is calculated as $480, which is equal in real value to the $400 calculated in the absence of inflation. Of course, the inflation adjustment of fixed assets and net wealth is an important additional difference in a country that relies on a tax on net wealth.

The ad hoc system reaches exactly the same figure for taxable income in this case simply by allowing inflation-adjustment of depreciation allowances; see column (4) of Table 7-A2. If the calculation of net wealth under the ad hoc system is based on historical costs, without adjustment of the basis for depreciation, net wealth is understated. In that case the figure for the value of depreciable assets in the calculation of net wealth is the same as in the «no inflation» case in Table 7-A1. Failure to make this adjustment results in understatement of ending net wealth by $140, the amount of the proper inflation adjustment, reduced by one year's depreciation on that amount. This is a potentially important advantage of the integrated system, which automatically produces an inflation adjusted figure for net wealth.[106] Under the ad hoc approach information on the inflation-adjusted basis of depreciable assets is needed for fair and effective implementation of the Colombian tax on net wealth and the calculation of presumptive income. Of course, there is no reason not to adjust the depreciable basis for inflation under the ad hoc approach. In that case, net wealth would be calculated as a residual, by subtracting debt (assumed to be non-existent in this first example) from the value of assets (which in this simple example consists only of the inflation-adjusted basis of a fixed asset). With that modification (and reinterpretation) the result under the ad hoc approach in this simple example (shown in the last column of Table 7-A1) would be identical to that under the integrated system.

Debt finance. Case 2 modifies the facts assumed in the previous example to allow for the existence of debt finance. (See Tables 7-A3 and 7-A4.) In the zero-inflation case, taxable income (gross profit) is only $340, because of the payment of interest at a rate of 10 percent on borrowing of $600. With a rate of inflation of 20 percent and an interest rate of 32 percent, nominal interest expense is $192 and income calculated on a historical-cost basis is $348, well below the real equivalent of $340, or $408. This shows how the failure to provide inflation adjustment for interest expense can cause understatement of income, even if there is also no inflation adjustment of depreciation, and produce marginal effective tax rates below the statutory rate.

As in Case 1, the inflation adjustment for depreciable assets in the integrated system is $200, and depreciation allowances are based on the inflation-adjusted basis of $1,200. But the adjustment for net worth is only $80, since the beginning net worth (capital and surplus) is only $400 in this example. Taxable income is $408, which is 20 percent more in nominal terms than in the case of no inflation, but the same in real terms. As before, net wealth is measured accurately.

The ad hoc approach to the inflation adjustment of interest expense patterned after the 1986 Colombian law and the tax treatment of depreciable assets proposed in chapter 5 reaches this same figure for taxable income through the combination of indexed depreciation allowances and the inclusion of $120 in inflation gain (20 percent of the $600 of debt) in the tax base. As before, the inflation-adjusted basis of depreciable assets can also be employed in the calculation of net wealth under the ad hoc approach.

It is readily apparent why the results for the calculation of income in these two cases are the same under the integrated approach and under the ad hoc approach. In the ad hoc approach the inflation gain (loss) realized by debtors (creditors) because inflation erodes the real value of debt is added to (subtracted from) income otherwise determined in order to calculate real income for tax purposes. (For this purpose and for the calculation of taxable income under the integrated approach, depreciation allowances are calculated from indexed basis). The same result is achieved under the integrated system because of the following simple accounting identity: real assets + financial assets = financial liabilities + net worth.[107] Rearrangement of terms in this equation indicates that increasing income by the effects of inflation on the real value of net financial liabilities (financial liabilities less financial assets) under the ad hoc approach is equivalent to adding to income the product of the inflation rate and the nominal value of real assets and subtracting the product of the inflation rate and net worth, the procedure under the integrated Chilean system.[108]

It must be stressed that this identity of results between the Chilean and ad hoc approaches holds only if there are no cash balances or other financial assets or liabilities that carry nominal interest rates that do not reflect the current rate of inflation. This important qualification is explained further in the discussion of case 5 below entitled «cash holdings». It is also important to keep firmly in mind the fact that the identity of results in these examples is predicated on the unrealistic assumption that exact inflation adjustments are possible under the ad hoc approach; since exact adjustments are not generally feasible, the difference between the results for that system and the Chilean system are greater than may appear from these examples.

Real assets and liabilities. It should be noted that the terms «financial assets» and «financial liabilities» are used in the previous section as a shorthand way of denoting assets and liabilities the principal of which is not explicitly indexed for inflation. A more accurate term might be «monetary» assets and liabilities. Of course, in countries that experience substantial rates of inflation it is fairly common for indexed debt securities to be issued. The most common type of indexed debt in Colombia are the UPACs (Unidades de Poder Adquisitivo Constante).

If the principal of assets is indexed exactly for inflation, such assets increase in nominal value with inflation; that is, they are «real» or «non-monetary» assets Under the integrated system of inflation adjustment, the product of the inflation rate and the principal of the obligation should be added to income, in the same way as the inflation adjustment to the basis for depreciable assets. (Similarly, the increase in the nominal value of indexed liabilities must be subtracted from income.) More generally, the amount of the contractual increase in principal can simply be added to (subtracted from) income; this accommodates partial indexing, as well as exact indexing. (Of course net wealth should be adjusted for inflation, in any event).

Tables 7-A5 and 7-A6 illustrate this approach for a holder of indexed bonds financed through the issuance of equity. These tables are constructed on the assumption that the adjustment for inflation (200) is added to principal. Since the economics of the matter are quite straightforward, the example is not discussed in detail. (This approach is discussed further in Harberger, 1982.) It is to be noted that under the integrated method, taxable income is the same in real terms when inflation is 20 percent (interest income of 120) as when inflation is zero (interest income of 100). Of course, net wealth is calculated correctly because of the contractual adjustment to the principal of the debt.

The figures in the columns for «no adjustment» and «ad hoc adjustment» require further explanation. These examples are constructed on the convention that in the «no adjustment» case tax is levied on the inflation adjustment as well as on the interest payment. By comparison, the convention in the «ad hoc adjustment» case is that the inflation premium is excluded from tax via an inflation adjustment, so that only the real interest rate is subject to tax. This interpretation setems to be consistent with the spirit of Law 75 of 1986, although the wording of the law leaves some doubt.[109] Under these interpretations real interest income is taxed too heavily under the «no adjustment» scenario, but correctly under the ad hoc approach. Provided the nominal increase in principal is included in net wealth, both the Chilean and ad hoc systems produce the correct statement of net wealth.

Though not shown explicitly here, it is worth noting that the integrated system automatically deals correctly with partial inflation adjustment. The ad hoc system also deals relatively well with debt that is only partially indexed, provided it is applied with care. The primary requirement is that all payments or increases in principal, whether called interest or monetary correction, must be subject to adjustment.[110]

Inventories. In the example of Table 7-A1 and 7-A2 it was assumed that there are no initial inventories and that all materials purchased during the year are resold; thus there was no change in physical inventories and no issue of valuing either goods sold from inventories or ending inventories. Under these special assumptions there is no distinction between FIFO and LIFO.

These assumptions are now relaxed to allow examination of issues of valuing goods sold from inventory, the valuation of ending inventories, and cases of inventory accumulation and depletion. For this purpose the results of Tables 7-A1 and 7-A2 serve as a useful benchmark.

Section II of the text of the present chapter noted the important conceptual differences between unindexed FIFO, indexed FIFO, unindexed LIFO, and indexed LIFO. (See also the discussion of footnote 21 to the text of this chapter.) These need not be reviewed in detail. Briefly, indexed FIFO produces the correct figure for cost of goods sold, but may mismeasure the value of remaining inventories if there have been shifts in relative prices. Indexed LIFO provides a reasonable approximation for both, except to the extent of shifts in relative prices; if, for example, the price of the inventoried good in question is rising faster (less rapidly) than the general price level, indexed LIFO understates (overstates) both real income and net wealth. Finally, unindexed FIFO overstates income, while measuring net wealth more or less accurately, and unindexed LIFO understates net wealth; whether it measures income correctly depends on how relative prices change. Indexed accounting for inventory is thus essential to the measurement of both income and net wealth in an inflationary economy.

In principle the integrated system could be based on either indexed FIFO or indexed LIFO; presumably the unindexed options would not be considered. In fact the Chilean system is based on indexed LIFO, so only that system is examined here. An ad hoc system based on the same methodology as the integrated system would produce identical results for both the measurement of income and the calculation of net wealth.

There is no need to consider explicitly cases in which physical inventories are constant. Results in those cases are suggested adequately by the results of footnote 21. Tables 7-A7 and 7-A8 and Tables 7-A9 and 7-A10, respectively, present case 4A of inventory accumulation and case 4D of inventory depletion (as well as depreciation of fixed assets) by a business financed by equity. It is convenient for expositional purposes in examining LIFO to use the «materials» entry in the income statement to denote total purchases of materials, including those added to inventories. (Thus amounts of goods that are drawn from inventories do not appear here.) Net additions to inventories are then handled as a positive adjustment to income, and net depletions of inventories are treated as negative adjustments. (The net result of these two entries for «materials» and «accumulation of inventories», in a time of stable prices, would thus be the cost of goods sold. It can be seen that in the example of Table 7-A7 half of goods purchased in the period are added to inventory; thus the net deduction for cost of goods sold is only the remaining half of purchases.) A comparison of these tables with Tables 7-A1 and 7-A2 indicates that, for a given amount of purchases, in the case of adjustment for 20 percent inflation, as in the zero-inflation case, taxable income differs from that for constant inventories by the amount of inventory accumulation or depletion, as it should if real economic income is to be measured accurately. (Income differs by this amount because, by assumption, all figures except the change in inventories are the same as in the case of constant inventories. An increase or decrease in inventories indicates that income is greater or less than in the case of constant inventories by the amount of the change.) By comparison, if there is no inflation adjustment for inventories or if the ad hoc approach makes no allowance for changes in price levels that have occurred since acquisition of inventories depleted during the year the results will not reflect real economic income.

Depletion of inventories raises the issue of the value that should be assigned to materials drawn from inventories accumulated in previous periods when prices were lower. This problem arises even under LIFO, although it is generally less troublesome than under FIFO. (For a sufficiently large reduction in inventories LIFO may give a quite misleading measure of the cost of goods sold, by deeming sales to be made from goods long held in stock. By comparison, FIFO generally becomes increasingly accurate, the larger the reduction of inventories.) The conceptually correct approach is to inflation adjust the balance sheet entry for inventories each period so that they will always be valued at historical costs, adjusted for inflation. Then when inventories are drawn down the adjustment for inventory depletion in the income statement will be appropriate. This is the procedure adopted in the Chilean approach to inflation adjustment. It can be seen from Tables 7-A9 and 7-A10 that the real values in both income statements and balance sheets are identical for the zero inflation scenario and for exact adjustment for 20 percent inflation.

Capital Gains. The exact adjustment approach can easily accommodate capital gains simply by treating assets on which gains are realized as though they were placed in inventory when bought and taken from inventory when sold. (Of course, such assets would not actually be placed in inventory accounts; but the tax accounting has the same effect.) Thus the balance sheet reflects inflation-adjusted historical costs, and the income statement reflects real gains on such assets when they are realized. To the extent such assets cannot be identified, the reasoning is exactly the same as for inventories. For assets that can be separately identified, each purchase and each sale is automatically treated as an addition to or a depletion of inventories, without the necessity of an ordering convention.

Cash holdings. Those who hold cash balances in a time of inflation experience losses of purchasing power that do not occur in a world without inflation. The existence of cash holdings breaks the equality of results (as indicated by equality of real taxable income) between the zero-inflation world and the world with inflation and perfect indexation. The Chilean system captures the loss of purchasing power experienced by those who hold cash balances in the face of inflation — a loss that does not occur in the absence of inflation.

The existence of cash balances destroys the equivalence of results under the Chilean and ad hoc approaches. Case 5 shows this for the case of initial cash holdings of $500. (See Tables 7-A11 and 7-A12.) In this case the ad hoc approach gives a figure for taxable income that is clearly wrong, even though (by coincidence) the $408 that is reported is equivalent in real terms to the $340 figure for taxable income in the zero-inflation case. Income is seen correctly to be only $308 in the case of perfect indexing under the integrated system. The difference between this figure and that reported by the ad hoc system reflects the fact that a loss of $100 (20 percent of $500) in real value is suffered on cash holdings. The ad hoc approach fails to capture this loss, since it is based on indexing of interest expense, and cash holdings pay no explicit interest. By comparison, the Chilean system would indicate accurately that this loss in the purchasing power of cash occurs, since it is based on the separate indexation of real assets and net worth, rather than the indexing of debt.

The discussion to this point has noted that the Colombian system of indexation of interest income and expense for inflation is based on an approximate fractional approach, rather than on the exact approach underlying these examples. The fractional approach clearly cannot give the correct result for cash balances; since there is no interest, there is nothing to adjust. Much the same conclusions hold in the case of debt paying a rate of interest that does not adjust to reflect current inflation — a common occurrence when there are unexpected changes in the rate of inflation. Debtors gain and creditors lose from unexpected increases in the rate of inflation. These gains and loses would be reported accurately by the integrated system; they would not be reported accurately by an ad hoc fractional system of the type recently enacted in Colombia.[111] This is potentially a very important point, since it implies that ad hoc inflation adjustments will generally be inaccurate for an extended period following an unexpected change in the rate of inflation.

Foreign obligations. The discussion in the text of this chapter argues that debt denominated in foreign currency should be adjusted for domestic inflation, rather than for the rate of devaluation. The result of such a policy is illustrated in Tables 7-A13 and 7-A14. Consistent with the purchasing-power parity theorem explained in the text, it is assumed that 20 percent domestic inflation results in 20 percent appreciation of the dollar, relative to the peso, thereby increasing the peso equivalents of both principal and interest on foreign obligations by this amount. In real terms both the integrated adjustment approach and the ad hoc approach produce the same result in real terms in the inflationary situation as in the zero-inflation world.

Conclusions. These examples lead to several important conclusions. First, the integrated and ad hoc systems can produce accurate and comparable results, so far as depreciable assets, inventories, and other «real» assets and liabilities are concerned, provided the results of inflation adjustment under the ad hoc system are reflected in the calculation of net wealth.

Second, inflation adjustments based on interest income and expense (or similar items of financial income and expense) cannot generally produce totally accurate measurement of real income for tax purposes. At the very least the lack of indexing for cash balances causes mismeasurement of income. The problem is compounded if inflation adjustments are based on a fractional approximation of the erosion of real purchasing power of debt, as under the new Colombian system, rather than on exact calculations of the loss in purchasing power. By comparison, an integrated system of the type used in Chile automatically produces an accurate (or at least more accurate) measure of income, because it is based on adjustments for real assets and net worth, rather than on items of income and expense. An important question is thus whether this difference in the precision of the measurement of income and net wealth justifies the added complexity of the integrated system.

It seems that Colombia, a country in which there is both a relatively low rate of inflation and little experience with inflation adjustment, should adopt a more comprehensive but admittedly ad hoc approach. Such a strategy would be preferable to moving all the way at this time to an integrated system of the type used in Chile, a country with both a much higher rate of inflation and considerably more experience with inflation adjustment. As noted in the text, this judgement seems to be borne out by experience in other countries.

TABLE 7-A1

COMPARISON OF INTEGRATED AND AD HOC APPROACHES TO INFLATION ADJUSTMENT: BALANCE SHEET

Case No. 1: Depreciable Asset Financed by Equity
Balance Sheets, before and after Income Statement

	Balance Sheet before Income Statement				Balance Sheet after Income Statement
Item	Beginning Balance (1)	Inflation Adjustment (2)	Adjusted Balance (3)	From Income Statement (4)*	(5)
			Zero Inflation Case		
ASSETS					
Machinery	1,000	n.a.	1,000	(300)	700
Cash	0	n.a.	0	500	500
Total	1,000	n.a.	1,000	200	1,200
LIABILITIES & NET WORTH					
Capital &					
Surplus	1,000	n.a.	1,000	200	1,200
Total	1,000	n.a.	1,000	200	1,200
			20 % Inflation Case		
ASSETS					
Machinery	1,000	200	1,200	(360)	840
Cash	0	0	0	600	600
Total	1,000	200	1,200	240	1,440
LIABILITIES & NET WORTH					
Capital &					
Surplus	1,000	200	1,200	240	1,440
Total	1,000	200	1,200	240	1,440

* Entries in column (4) reflect the following income statement entries: **Machinery:** depreciation, calculated as 30% of the beginning inflation adjusted balance; **Cash:** net (after tax) cash flow reported in the income statement; **Capital and surplus:** net profits reported on the income statement in Table 7-A2.

TABLE 7-A2

COMPARISON OF INTEGRATED AND AD HOC APPROACHES TO INFLATION ADJUSTMENT: INCOME STATEMENT

Case No. 1: Depreciable Asset Financed by Equity
Income Statement, with and without Inflation, without Inflation Adjustment and with Exact and Ad Hoc Adjustment.

| Item | Zero Inflation (1) | 20 % Inflation | | |
		No Adjustment (2)	Exact Adjustment (3)	Ad Hoc Adjustment (4)
CASH RECEIPTS				
Sales	1,500	1,800	1,800	1,800
Total	1,500	1,800	1,800	1,800
CASH DISBURSEMENTS (except income tax)				
Labor	(600)	(720)	(720)	(720)
Materials	(200)	(240)	(240)	(240)
Total	(800)	(960)	(960)	(960)
NON-CASH ALLOWANCES AND ADJUSTMENTS				
Depreciation	(300)	(300)	(360)	(360)
Inflation Adjustments:*				
Assets	n.a.	n.a.	200	n.a.
Liabilities	n.a.	n.a.	(200)	n.a.
GROSS PROFITS	400	540	480	480
INCOME TAX	200	270	240	240
NET PROFIT	200	270	240	240
NET CASH FLOW	500	570	600	600

* Inflation adjustments in column (3) are from column (2) of the Balance Sheet in Table 7-A1.

TABLE 7-A3

COMPARISON OF INTEGRATED AND AD HOC APPROACHES TO INFLATION ADJUSTMENT: BALANCE SHEET

Case No. 2: Depreciable Asset Financed with Debt and Equity
Balance Sheets, before and after Income Statement

	Balance Sheet before Income Statement				Balance Sheet after Income Statement
Item	Beginning Balance (1)	Inflation Adjustment (2)	Adjusted Balance (3)	From Income Statement (4)*	(5)
Zero Inflation Case					
ASSETS					
Machinery	1,000	n.a.	1,000	(300)	700
Cash	0	n.a.	0	470	470
Total	1,000	n.a.	1,000	170	1,170
LIABILITIES & NET WORTH					
Debt	600	n.a.	600	0	600
Capital & Surplus	400	n.a.	400	170	570
Total	1,000	n.a.	1,000	170	1,170
20 % Inflation Case					
ASSETS					
Machinery	1,000	200	1,200	(360)	840
Cash	0	0	0	444	444
Total	1,000	200	1,200	84	1,284
LIABILITIES & NET WORTH					
Debt	600	0	600	0	600
Capital & Surplus	400	80	480	204	684
Total	1,000	80	1,080	204	1,284

* Entries in column (4) reflect the following income statement entries: **Machinery:** depreciation, calculated as 30% of the beginning inflation adjusted balance; **Cash:** net (after tax) cash flow reported in the income statement; **Capital and surplus:** net profits reported on the income statement in Table 7-A4.

TABLE 7-A4

COMPARISON OF INTÉGRATED AND AD HOC APPROACHES TO INFLATION ADJUSTMENT: INCOME STATEMENT

**Case No. 2: Depreciable Asset Financed by Equity
Income Statement, with and without Inflation,
without Inflation Adjustment and with Exact and Ad
Hoc Adjustment.**

		20 % Inflation		
Item	Zero Inflation (1)	No Adjustment (2)	Exact Adjustment (3)	Ad Hoc Adjustment (4)
CASH RECEIPTS				
Sales	1,500	1,800	1,800	1,800
Total	1,500	1,800	1,800	1,800
CASH DISBURSEMENTS (except income tax)				
Labor	(600)	(720)	(720)	(720)
Materials	(200)	(240)	(240)	(240)
Interest	(60)	(192)	(192)	(192)
Total	(860)	(1,152)	(1,152)	(1,152)
NON-CASH ALLOWANCES AND ADJUSTMENTS				
Depreciation	(300)	(300)	(360)	(360)
Inflation Adjustments:*				
Assets	n.a.	n.a.	200	n.a.
Liabilities	n.a.	n.a.	(80)	n.a.
Interest	n.a.	n.a.	n.a.	120
GROSS PROFITS	340	348	408	408
INCOME TAX	170	174	204	204
NET PROFIT	170	174	204	204
NET CASH FLOW	470	474	444	444

* Inflation adjustments in column (3) are from column (2) of the Balance Sheet in Table 7-A3.

TABLE 7-A5

COMPARISON OF INTEGRATED AND AD HOC APPROACHES TO INFLATION ADJUSTMENT: BALANCE SHEET

Case No. 3: Holding of Indexed Bonds Financed by Equity
Balance Sheets, before and after Income Statement

	Balance Sheet before Income Statement			From Income Statement (4)*	Balance Sheet after Income Statement (5)
Item	Beginning Balance (1)	Inflation Adjustment (2)	Adjusted Balance (3)		
		Zero Inflation Case			
ASSETS					
Bonds	1,000	n.a.	1,000	0	1,000
Cash	0	n.a.	0	50	50
Total	1,000	n.a.	1,000	50	1,050
LIABILITIES & NET WORTH					
Capital &					
Surplus	1,000	n.a.	1,000	50	1,050
Total	1,000	n.a.	1,000	50	1,050
		20 % Inflation Case			
ASSETS					
Bonds	1,000	200	1,200	0	1,200
Cash	0	0	0	60	60
Total	1,000	200	1,200	60	1,260
LIABILITIES & NET WORTH					
Capital &					
Surplus	1,000	200	1,200	60	1,260
Total	1,000	200	1,200	60	1,260

* Entries in column (4) reflect the following income statement entries: **Machinery:** depreciation, calculated as 30% of the beginning inflation adjusted balance; **Cash:** net (after tax) cash flow reported in the income statement; **Capital and surplus:** net profits reported on the income statement in Table 7-A6.

TABLE 7-A6

COMPARISON OF INTEGRATED AND AD HOC APPROACHES TO INFLATION ADJUSTMENT: INCOME STATEMENT

Case No. 3: Holding of Indexed Bonds Financed by Equity Income Statement, with and without Inflation, without Inflation Adjustment and with Exact and Ad Hoc Adjustment.

		20 % Inflation		
Item	Zero Inflation (1)	No Adjustment (2)	Exact Adjustment (3)	Ad Hoc Adjustment (4)
CASH RECEIPTS				
Interest**	100	320	120	320
Total	100	320	120	320
CASH DISBURSEMENTS (except income tax)				
Labor	n.a.	n.a.	n.a.	n.a.
Materials	n.a.	n.a.	n.a.	n.a.
Total	n.a.	n.a.	n.a.	n.a.
NON-CASH ALLOWANCES AND ADJUSTMENTS				
Depreciation	n.a.	n.a.	n.a.	n.a.
Inflation Adjustments:*				
Assets	n.a.	n.a.	200	200
Liabilities	n.a.	n.a.	200	0
GROSS PROFITS	100	320	120	120
INCOME TAX	50	160	60	60
NET PROFIT	50	160	60	60
NET CASH FLOW	50	160	60	60

* Inflation adjustments in column (3) are from column (2) of the Balance Sheet in Table 7-A5.
** Interest receipts in columns (2) and (4) include amount of inflation adjustment added to principal; column (3) excludes it.

TABLE 7-A7

COMPARISON OF INTEGRATED AND AD HOC APPROACHES TO INFLATION ADJUSTMENT: BALANCE SHEET

Case No. 4A: Inventory Accumulation and Depreciable Asset
Financed by Equity
Balance Sheets, before and after Income
Statement

| Item | Balance Sheet before Income Statement | | | From Income Statement | Balance Sheet after Income Statement |
| | Beginning Balance | Inflation Adjustment | Adjusted Balance | | |
	(1)	(2)	(3)	(4)*	(5)
Zero Inflation Case					
ASSETS					
Machinery	1,000	n.a.	1,000	(300)	700
Inventory	1,000	n.a.	1,000	100	1,100
Cash	0	n.a.	0	450	450
Total	2,000	n.a.	2,000	250	2,250
LIABILITIES & NET WORTH					
Capital &					
Surplus	2,000	n.a.	2,000	250	2,250
Total	2,000	n.a.	2,000	250	2,250
20 % Inflation Case					
ASSETS					
Machinery	1,000	200	1,200	(360)	840
Inventory	1,000	200	1,200	120	1,320
Cash	0	0	0	540	540
Total	2,000	400	2,400	300	2,700
LIABILITIES & NET WORTH					
Capital &					
Surplus	2,000	400	2,400	300	2,700
Total	2,000	400	2,400	300	2,700

* Entries in column (4) reflect the following income statement entries: **Machinery:** depreciation, calculated as 30% of the beginning inflation adjusted balance; Accumulation of inventories calculated as 10% of the beginning inflation adjusted balance; **Cash:** net (after tax) cash flow reported in the income statement; **Capital and surplus:** net profits reported on the income statement in Table 7-A8.

TABLE 7-A8

COMPARISON OF INTEGRATED AND AD HOC APPROACHES TO INFLATION ADJUSTMENT: INCOME STATEMENT

Case No. 4A: Inventory Accumulation and Depreciable Asset Financed by Equity
Income Statement, with and without Inflation,
without Inflation Adjustment and with Exact and Ad
Hoc Adjustment.

		20 % Inflation		
Item	Zero Inflation (1)	No Adjustment (2)	Exact Adjustment (3)	Ad Hoc Adjustment (4)
CASH RECEIPTS				
Sales	1,500	1,800	1,800	1,800
Total	1,500	1,800	1,800	1,800
CASH DISBURSEMENTS (except income tax)				
Labor	(600)	(720)	(720)	(720)
Materials*	(200)	(240)	(240)	(240)
Total	(800)	(960)	(960)	(960)
NON-CASH ALLOWANCES AND ADJUSTMENTS				
Depreciation	300	300	360	360
Accumulation of Inventory*	100	100	120	100
Inflation Adjustments:**				
Assets	n.a.	n.a.	400	n.a.
Liabilities	n.a.	n.a.	(400)	n.a.
GROSS PROFITS	500	640	600	580
INCOME TAX	250	320	300	290
NET PROFIT	250	320	300	290
NET CASH FLOW	450	520	540	550

* The figure for materials is the amount actually purchased; depletion and accumulation of inventories are shown as adjustments.
** Inflation adjustments in column (3) are from column (2) of the Balance Sheet in Table 7-A7.

TABLE 7-A9

COMPARISON OF INTEGRATED AND AD HOC APPROACHES TO INFLATION ADJUSTMENT: BALANCE SHEET

Case No. 4D: Inventory Depletion; 100% Equity Finance
Balance Sheets, before and after Income Statement

	Balance Sheet before Income Statement				Balance Sheet after Income Statement
Item	Beginning Balance (1)	Inflation Adjustment (2)	Adjusted Balance (3)	From Income Statement (4)*	(5)
Zero Inflation Case					
ASSETS					
Machinery	1,000	n.a.	1,000	(300)	700
Inventory	1,000	n.a.	1,000	(300)	700
Cash	0	n.a.	0	650	650
Total	2,000	n.a.	2,000	50	2,050
LIABILITIES & NET WORTH					
Capital &					
Surplus	2,000	n.a.	2,000	400	2,400
Total	2,000	n.a.	2,000	400	2,400
20 % Inflation Case					
ASSETS					
Machinery	1,000	200	1,200	(360)	840
Inventory	1,000	200	1,200	(360)	840
Cash	0	0	0	780	780
Total	2,000	400	2,200	60	2,460
LIABILITIES & NET WORTH					
Capital &					
Surplus	2,000	400	2,400	60	2,460
Total	2,000	400	2,400	60	2,460

* Entries in column (4) reflect the following income statement entries: **Machinery:** depreciation, calculated as 30% of the beginning inflation adjusted balance; **Depletion of inventories:** calculated as 30% of the beginning stock; **Cash:** net (after tax) cash flow reported in the income statement; **Capital and surplus:** net profits reported on the income statement in Table 7-A10.

TABLE 7-A10

COMPARISON OF INTEGRATED AND AD HOC APPROACHES TO INFLATION ADJUSTMENT: INCOME STATEMENT

Case No. 4D: Inventory Depletion; 100% Equity Finance Income Statement, with and without Inflation, without Inflation Adjustment and with Exact and Ad Hoc Adjustment.

		20 % Inflation		
Item	Zero Inflation (1)	No Adjustment (2)	Exact Adjustment (3)	Ad Hoc Adjustment (4)
CASH RECEIPTS				
Sales	1,500	1,800	1,800	1,800
Total	1,500	1,800	1,800	1,800
CASH DISBURSEMENTS (except income tax)				
Labor	(600)	(720)	(720)	(720)
Materials*	(200)	(240)	(240)	(240)
Total	(800)	(960)	(960)	(960)
NON-CASH ALLOWANCES AND ADJUSTMENTS				
Depreciation	(300)	(300)	(360)	(360)
Depletion of Inventories*	(300)	(300)	(360)	(300)
Inflation Adjustments:**				
Assets	n.a.	n.a.	200	0
Liabilities	n.a.	n.a.	(200)	0
GROSS PROFITS	100	240	120	180
INCOME TAX	50	120	60	90
NET PROFIT	50	120	60	90
NET CASH FLOW	650	720	780	750

* The figure for materials is the amount actually purchased; depletion and accumulation of inventories are shown as adjustments.
** Inflation adjustments in column (3) are from column (2) of the Balance Sheet in Table 7-A9.

251

TABLE 7-A11

COMPARISON OF INTEGRATED AND AD HOC APPROACHES TO INFLATION ADJUSTMENT: BALANCE SHEET

Case No. 5: General ilustration, with Cash Holdings and Debt and Equity Finance Balance Sheets, before and after Income Statement

	Balance Sheet before Income Statement				Balance Sheet after Income Statement
	Beginning Balance	Inflation Adjustment	Adjusted Balance	From Income Statement	
Item	(1)	(2)	(3)	(4)*	(5)
Zero Inflation Case					
ASSETS					
Machinery	1,000	n.a.	1,000	(300)	700
Cash	500	n.a.	500	470	970
Total	1,500	n.a.	1,500	170	1,670
LIABILITIES & NET WORTH					
Debt	600	n.a.	600	0	600
Capital & Surplus	900	n.a.	900	170	1,070
Total	1,500	n.a.	1,500	170	1,670
20 % Inflation Case					
ASSETS					
Machinery	1,000	200	1,200	(360)	840
Cash	500	0	500	494	994
Total	1,500	200	1,700	134	1,834
LIABILITIES & NET WORTH					
Debt	600	0	600	0	600
Capital & Surplus	90	180	1,080	154	1,234
Total	1,500	180	1,680	154	1,834

* Entries in column (4) reflect the following income statement entries: **Machinery:** depreciation, calculated as 30% of the beginning inflation adjusted balance; **Cash:** net (after tax) cash flow reported in the income statement; **Capital and surplus:** net profits reported on the income statement in Table 7-A12.

TABLE 7-A12

COMPARISON OF INTEGRATED AND AD HOC APPROACHES TO INFLATION ADJUSTMENT: INCOME STATEMENT

Case No. 5: General Illustration, with Cash Holdings, Debt, and Equity Finance Income Statement, with and without Inflation, without Inflation Adjustment and with Exact and Ad Hoc Adjustment.

| | | 20 % Inflation | | |
| | Zero Inflation | No Adjustment | Exact Adjustment | Ad Hoc Adjustment |
Item	(1)	(2)	(3)	(4)
CASH RECEIPTS				
Sales	1,500	1,800	1,800	1,800
Total	1,500	1,800	1,800	1,800
CASH DISBURSEMENTS (except income tax)				
Labor	(600)	(720)	(720)	(720)
Materials	(200)	(240)	(240)	(240)
Interest	(60)	(192)	(192)	(192)
Total	(860)	(1,152)	(1,152)	(1,152)
NON-CASH ALLOWANCES AND ADJUSTMENTS				
Depreciation	(300)	(300)	(360)	(360)
Inflation Adjustments:*				
Assets	n.a.	n.a.	200	n.a.
Liabilities	n.a.	n.a.	(180)	n.a.
Interest	n.a.	n.a.	n.a.	120
GROSS PROFITS	340	348	308	408
INCOME TAX	170	174	154	204
NET PROFIT	170	174	154	204
NET CASH FLOW	470	474	494	444

* Inflation adjustments in column (3) are from column (2) of the Balance Sheet in Table 7-A11.

TABLE 7-A13

COMPARISON OF INTEGRATED AND AD HOC APPROACHES TO INFLATION ADJUSTMENT: BALANCE SHEET

Case No. 6: Foreign Exchange Loss on Debt of ¥1,000 Financed by Equity
Balance Sheets, before and after Income Statement

	Balance Sheet before Income Statement				Balance Sheet after Income Statement
Item	Beginning Balance (1)	Inflation Adjustment (2)	Adjusted Balance (3)	From Income Statement (4)*	(5)
Zero Inflation Case					
ASSETS					
Indexed					
Bonds	1,000	n.a.	1,000	0	1,000
Cash	0	n.a.	0	25	25
Total	1,000	n.a.	1,000	25	1,025
LIABILITIES & NET WORTH					
Foreign					
Debt**	500	n.a.	500	0	500
Capital &					
Surplus	500	n.a.	500	25	525
Total	1,000	n.a.	1,000	25	1,025
20 % Inflation Case					
ASSETS					
Indexed					
Bonds	1,000	200	1,200	0	1,200
Cash	0	0	0	30	30
Total	1,000	200	1,200	30	1,230
LIABILITIES & NET WORTH					
Foreign					
Debt**	500	100	600	0	600
Capital &					
Surplus	500	100	600	30	630
Total	1,000	200	1,200	30	1,230

* Entries in column (4) reflect the following income statement entries: **Cash:** net (after tax) cash flow reported in the income statement; **Capital and surplus:** net profits reported on the income statement in Table 7-A14.

** Foreign Debt is peso equivalent of ¥1,000 debt denominated in yen, paying interest rate of 10 percent. Entry in inflation adjustment column is the effect of 20 percent devaluation of peso.

TABLE 7-A14

COMPARISON OF INTEGRATED AND AD HOC APPROACHES TO INFLATION ADJUSTMENT: INCOME STATEMENT

Case No. 6: Foreign Exchange Loss on Debt ¥ 1,000
Income Statement, with and without Inflation, without Inflation Adjustment and with Exact and Ad Hoc Adjustment.

Item	Zero Inflation (1)	20 % Inflation		
		No Adjustment (2)	Exact Adjustment (3)	Ad Hoc Adjustment (4)
CASH RECEIPTS				
Interest	100	120	120	120
Total	100	120	120	120
CASH DISBURSEMENTS (except income tax)				
Interest**	50	60	60	60
NON-CASH ALLOWANCES AND ADJUSTMENTS				
Inflation Adjustments:***				
Assets	n.a.	n.a.	200	n.a.
Liabilities	n.a.	n.a.	(200)	n.a.
GROSS PROFITS	50	60	60	60
INCOME TAX	25	30	30	30
NET PROFIT	25	30	30	30
NET CASH FLOW	25	30	30	30

* See the text for explanation of column (4).
** Interest expense is peso cost of interest payments denominated in yen.
*** Inflation adjustments in column (3) are from column (2) of the Balance Sheet in Table 7-A13.

APPENDIX 7B

Realization versus Accrual Treatment of Inflation Adjustments

The way in which inflation adjustment is handled in the measurement of income for tax purposes involves important issues of realization versus accrual accounting. This can perhaps be seen most clearly in the case of capital gains.

Chapter 5 noted that capital gains can be taxed either as they accrue (the conceptually correct approach) or when they are realized (commonly the only feasible alternative). Inflation adjustment of the basis of assets used to calculate capital gains could also be handled in either of two ways, to be consistent with the underlying income tax treatment of capital gains.[112/] Under what can be called the realization approach to inflation adjustment, the basis of capital assets would be adjusted for inflation only at the time of realization of gain or loss. This is, in effect, the approach utilized in Colombia for purposes of both the income and net wealth taxes for gains on stock and ownership shares in companies and on real estate. (It is also effectively employed for income tax purposes in the case of other assets, for which inflation adjustments can be made annually at the taxpayer's discretion, even though gains on such assets are taxed only upon realization. Though inflation adjustments are made annually, they have no income tax consequences until gain or loss is realized. Such optional inflation adjustments must be reflected in the base of the Colombian net wealth tax; that is, the accrual approach is used for net wealth purposes).

By comparison, under the accrual approach, gains and losses would be recognized annually as they accrued, and inflation adjustments would also be made on an annual basis, so that only real accrued gains would be subject to tax. As indicated in Chapter 5, the accrual method is rarely used because of administrative and cash flow problems. It is not suggested that Colombia attempt to implement accrual taxation of capital gains.

The disallowance (and the exclusion) of the inflationary component of interest expense (income) can also be handled on either an accrual or a realization basis.[113/] One interpretation of the treatment of interest income and expense provided by Law 75 of 1986 is that the inflationary components of nominal interest payments are properly seen as repayments of principal that should not be allowed as a deduction (and should be excluded from taxable income). This «accrual» interpretation implies that the gain of the debtor (the loss of the creditor) that results from inflation and that is represented by the inflation component of interest payments should be accrued and subject to tax (excluded from taxable income) currently, rather than being handled on a realization basis (to be explained below).

The accrual approach is fully consistent with the Haig-Simons definition of income. Yet it could pose cash flow problems for some taxpayers who are debtors, since they must make payments based on nominal interest rates, but are allowed deductions only for the real component of interest. Even so, this seems to be more of a problem during transition to an inflation-adjusted system than a steady-state (long-term) problem, since in steady state, debts would be incurred with full awareness of their tax and cash flow consequences.[114/] The transition provisions proposed in the text of this chapter should reduce any concerns of this type.

Moreover, the cash-flow consequences for creditors under the alternative «realization» approach seem to be even more unacceptable. This «realization» interpretation would allow current deduction of the full amount of nominal interest expense, with a reduction of basis for income tax purposes equal to the inflationary component of interest. (For creditors it would require that tax be paid on the entire nominal amount of interest income, with an increase in basis for the inflation component of interest).[115] Under this interpretation, the debtor would not pay tax on the inflation gain currently (and the creditor would not be allowed to exclude from income the loss of purchasing power due to inflation), but would experience a capital gain for income tax purposes (loss, in the case of the creditor) equal to the total accrued loss in purchasing power resulting from inflation at the time the debt is repaid.

The cash-flow problem in this case would afflict the creditor, who would be forced to pay taxes currently on the full nominal amount of interest income, even though he would have a later deduction for the same nominal amount. Bunching capital gains and losses in the year of repayment of debt could be disadvantageous to both borrowers and lenders, the former because gains are taxed at graduated rates and the latter because income from other sources may be inadequate to absorb accumulated inflation losses realized in a given year when debt is repaid.[116] It would be extremely complicated to implement a realization system for those with small amounts in savings accounts, even if it were thought appropriate to do so; since fluctuations in account balances would presumably be interpreted as realization events, realization could be achieved for tax purposes simply by moving funds between commonly owned accounts. Of course, it would be inappropriate to employ the accrual approach for these items, but not for interest expense. To do so would create opportunities for arbitrage and other abuses that would undermine both equity and neutrality.

The realization approach would probably be more vulnerable to abuse than the accrual approach. Under the realization approach the government would be taking a substantial gamble that it could tax the inflation gains of debtors at the time of retirement of debt. It would, in principle, have information on such gains from the reported losses of creditors reported in the same year, but widespread experience in many countries suggests that little reliance should be placed on this avenue of cross-checking.

All things considered, the accrual approach to the inflation adjustment of interest income and expense adopted in Law 75 of 1986 seems appropriate.

Under the accrual approach the value of depreciable assets shown in the balance sheet would reflect inflation since the time of acquisition and depreciation allowances would be based on this inflation-adjusted cost (or other basis) of assets. In this case net wealth as shown on the balance sheet would provide an appropriate base for the net wealth tax. By comparison, the realization approach would allow only deductions based on the historical cost of the asset, which is the figure that would be reflected in the balance sheet, with a deduction for the accrued loss in value of the original basis of the asset resulting from inflation being allowed only at the time an asset is retired. The cash-flow consequences of the realization approach would be quite unattractive to businesses contemplating investments in depreciable assets. Use of this approach would create strong incentives for the «churning» of depreciable assets (resale to another user) in order to be able to benefit from accrued but unrealized inflation adjustments. Moreover, the balance sheet would understate the true value of depreciable assets. In short, there seems to be little to recommend the realization approach in this case.

Indexed FIFO raises more subtle questions of accrual versus realization. That is, inflation adjustment could be made on an accrual basis each year, or it could be done only when inventory is sold. The former approach would probably be simpler and would have the advantage of improving the measurement of net wealth in the balance sheet.

LIFO can be seen as either an accurate portrayal of the movement of goods in process through a firm or as a substitute for indexed FIFO; since there is ordinarily no explicit adjustment for inflation if LIFO is employed, the issue of accrual versus realization does not arise. Since the use of LIFO results in an understatement of the value of inventories for purposes of the net wealth tax, it may be thought desirable to employ explicit inflation adjustment, even with LIFO. Little would be gained from indexing beginning inventories unless the indexing were done on a current (accrual) basis, as proposed in the text of this chapter.

The difference in the timing of inflation adjustments under the realization interpretation and the accrual interpretation can generally be quite significant. The total amount of taxable income would be the same under the two interpretations (provided capital losses could be offset against other income at the time of realization, differences in tax treatment of inventories eventually washed out, etc.), but the present value of taxable income would differ, as in all cases involving issues of accrual versus realization.[117] Of course, differences in the marginal tax rates faced by the taxpayer at various points in time further complicate this question and create opportunities for manipulation of transactions to avoid taxes. An even more important difference is that net wealth is consistently understated if the realization approach is used.

It seems that the accrual approach is the only one that makes sense in the case of interest income and expense and of depreciable assets. It is clearly the only one that is consistent with the Haig-Simons definition of income for tax purposes. Practical considerations point in the same direction, especially in the case of depreciation allowances and interest income. It would be extremely difficult to justify treating either of these items on the realization basis described above. As indicated above, it does not seem advisable for Colombia to attempt to tax capital gains on an accrual basis, except to the extent this is achieved by the taxation of presumptive income under the proposals of Chapter 5; thus for income tax purposes inflation adjustment of the basis of capital assets must be done at realization. This does not, however, imply that inflation adjustment should not be made currently for purposes of the net wealth tax. There may be some difficulty in employing the realization approach in adjusting the basis of assets giving rise to capital gains, while using the accrual basis for the indexation o f indebtedness; though these do not seem to be important, they may deserve further attention. All things considered, there seems to be no alternative to the basic approach underlying Law 75 and the proposals of this Report.

The most compelling argument that can be made against the use of the accrual method in the case of interest expense involves transition issues — the fact that those who have incurred debt expecting interest expense to be fully deductible would be even more adversely affected by sudden introduction of an accrual-based indexation scheme than by introduction of a realization-based scheme. By comparison, it seems that once transition has been completed, complaints against use of the accrual system would have little force. The generous transition rules proposed in section VIII of the text, under which issuers of debt outstanding at the end of 1985 would suffer relatively little as a result of the introduction of inflation adjustment, should deal effectively with arguments against use of the accrual approach that can be traced to transition problems. Transition problems should not be allowed to stand in the way of adoption of the accrual approach for interest income and expense. The discussion in the text is based on the assumption that the accrual approach should be used for all aspects of inflation adjustment except the taxation of capital gains.

FOOTNOTES

1/ The two most commonly discussed methodologies for inventory accounting are FIFO (first-in, first-out) and LIFO (last-in, first out). As the terms imply, these methodologies are based on assumptions about the physical flow of goods through the production-distribution process. In a world of zero inflation it makes relatively little difference whether FIFO or LIFO is used for inventory accounting. The two differ only to the extent that relative prices change during the time inventories are held. See also the discussion in sections II and VI below.

2/ This is not to say that the value of some assets may not be understated and others overstated by their book values.

3/ For expositional convenience, the discussion of this chapter is framed in terms of the differences between a world of zero inflation and one in which the rate of inflation is positive. Of course, the more relevant comparison will often be between states of the world characterized by two different rates of inflation. Unexpected changes in inflation rates can create distortions or inequities, even if economic decision-makers have accommodated to a positive expected rate of inflation.

4/ Two observers have described the problem in the following similar terms:

> As computed for purposes of income taxation, profits, rents, and income from unincorporated businesses do not measure income in current prices; in fact, they do not measure income in prices of **any** date. Instead they are numbers that defy definition except by reference to the method of calculation. Taxes levied on income so measured contain a random, irrational element. (Denison, 1976, pp. 233-34)

> Inflation destroys the assumption that money is stable which is the basis of classic accountancy. In such circumstances, historic values registered in accountancy books become heterogeneous amounts measured in different units. The use of such data under traditional accountancy methods, without previous correction, makes no sense and leads to results which are void of meaning. (Massone, 1981a, p.6)

5/ This chapter deals only with the type of inflation adjustment that is required for the accurate measurement of real income; it does not concern itself with inflation adjustment of nominal (peso) amounts stated in the tax law. On this distinction, see Aaron (1976). It is taken for granted that such nominal amounts will continue to be fully indexed for inflation, as they should be, except in those cases in which it is recommended that nominal values be fixed or only partially indexed as a means of phasing out undesirable provisions.

6/ This statement is predicated on the assumption that the capital gains tax is actually implemented effectively — an assumption that is generally not accurate in Colombia. as well as in many other developing countries. The overtaxation of reported gains that results from the failure to allow inflation adjustment in the measurement of capital gains is not an appropriate response to the practical difficulties of implementing taxation of capital gains.

7/ This statement is true especially under FIFO inventory accounting. LIFO accounting for inventories avoids this income measurement problem to a large degree, since costs of goods sold are based on the most recent purchases. But it does so at the cost of systematically understating the inventory component of net wealth and recognizing shifts in relative prices, as well as inflation, in calculating costs of goods sold. See also footnote 21 and the discussion of the choice between general and specific price indices in section VI below. It should be noted that recovering capital tax-free and maintaining a given level of investment are not necessarily the same thing; this important distinction is also discussed further in section VI.

8/ Since the presumptive income tax applies primarily in the case of substantial understatement of income, the understatement of net wealth is likely to have a greater proportionate effect on taxable presumptive income (the excess over income as ordinarily determined) than on net wealth, per se.

9/ For evidence from the United States that high-income taxpayers do better than low-income taxpayers in avoiding paying capital gains taxes on fictitious gains, see Feldstein and Slemrod (1978).

10/ With proper indexation, other assets could be added to this example, making it more realistic; they have been ignored in order to focus on the effects of the lack of inflation adjustment for interest-bearing obligations.

11/ Suppose that the interest rate is 10 percent in a world without inflation. A taxpayer subject to a marginal tax rate of 50 percent would receive a net return of 5 percent and a borrower in the same tax bracket would face a 5 percent after-tax cost of funds. In a world in which a 10 percent inflation rate is expected by both borrowers and lenders, the nominal interest rate should rise to 30 percent, but the after-tax real rate of interest should remain unchanged at 5 percent. (Deduction and taxation of nominal interest would reduce both the after-tax nominal cost of borrowing and the after-tax return to lending to 15 percent. Subtracting the 10 percent rate of inflation would result in a net real rate of interest of 5 percent, as in the case without inflation.) This proposition is demonstrated more rigorously in section VIII, which deals with the international implications of inflation adjustment for the cost of capital in Colombia.

12/ This is true regardless whether the principal amount of the debt in question is fixed in nominal terms or indexed for inflation; in either event net wealth includes the current nominal value of the debt. Of course, for the statements in the text to be true, the inflation adjustment of debt must be included in taxable income; if it is not, the tax treatment of interest is, in effect, indexed.

13/ In drawing the distinction between the equity effects of unanticipated inflation and the distortions created by adjustments to expected inflation, one commentator has said, «...no longer is society trying to protect unknowing fools against random inflation-induced inequities; rather, it is trying to prevent the adverse economic implications of the measures knowing smarties take to protect themselves against inflation». See Gramlich (1975), p. 607.

14/ Economic depreciation calculated on the basis of historical costs would be less generous than appropriate, since it is not adequate to allow tax-free recovery of capital. By comparison, full deduction of nominal interest expense would be more generous than appropriate, because it involves deduction for what is essentially a repayment of principal. Which effect would dominate in a particular case depends on the facts in that case.

The marginal effective tax rates calculated in chapter 4 reflect the effects of the extremely rapid depreciation allowed under current Colombian law (a feature which was not changed by the 1986 reforms), as well as those of full deductibility of nominal interest payments. Of course, accelerated depreciation is often allowed as an ad hoc means of adjusting for the reduction of the real value of such allowances caused by inflation. By coincidence, the acceleration of depreciation allowances in current Colombian law approximately offsets the effects of a 25 percent rate of inflation; see chapter 4.

15/ Many countries, including developed ones, have, however, in the wake of inflationary episodes, adopted schemes for one-time revaluation of assets for purposes of calculating depreciation allowances; see Lent (1975) or (1976). The present chapter is concerned solely with permanent provisions intended to compensate for continued inflation. Thompson (1982) pp. 512-19 provides a survey of provisions employed by a number of countries to adjust for inflation in the measurement of income. No developed country provides for permanent and comprehensive inflation-adjustment, even on an ad hoc basis. In its 1984 report to President Ronald Reagan the United States Department of the Treasury (1984) proposed a far-reaching system of inflation adjustments that contained elements similar to the provisions adopted in Colombia in 1986. They included a proposal for inflation-adjusted depreciation allowances similar to that described in chapter 5, as well as a system of partial disallowance of interest deductions and exclusion of interest income similar in spirit to that contained in Law 75 of 1986. These proposals did not receive much support in either the business community or the U.S. Congress and were not adopted. Among the reasons commonly cited were complexity, revenue loss, adverse economic impacts on particular sectors (due especially to the inadequacy of the transition provisions), and the belief that inflation adjustment is not needed at the rates of inflation now prevailing in the United States.

16/ Thompson (1982) provides a description of the techniques that can be interpreted as offsetting inflation that are employed by various countries.

17/ This is not to say that economic depreciation can be known with a high degree of certainty; as noted in chapter 5, data on rates of economic depreciation are extremely unreliable, even in developing countries. But anchoring tax policy to the best available data on economic depreciation and allowing explicitly for inflation adjustment is likely to be preferable to choosing arbitrary accelerated depreciation rates that are known to bear no resemblance to economic reality, as was done in the United States in 1981. It is widely believed that much recent misallocation of investment in the United States (for example, in commercial real estate) can be traced to overly generous tax treatment.

18/ Even an indexed system of taxing capital gains is likely to be overly generous to the taxpayer. In Colombia, as in virtually all countries that tax such gains, capital gains are recognized for tax purposes only when realized through the sale or other disposition of an asset. As a result, taxation of accrued gains may be deferred for long periods, providing substantial benefits to the taxpayer. Because heirs of appreciated property take as their basis the basis of the decedent, the problem of undertaxation created by deferral is further aggravated.

The alternative — which is implied by a strict interpretation of the Haig-Simons definition of income — would be to tax capital gains on an accrual basis; this would require valuing assets and paying tax on gains accrued during the year. This approach would dovetail nicely with a conceptually pure net wealth tax, which requires that assets be valued annually. By comparison, under the realization basis there may be a tendency to use historical costs as the basis for wealth taxation;

this generally results in systematic understatement of net wealth during a period of inflation. The accrual basis is rarely used for income tax purposes, in part because of the administrative difficulties of valuing many types of property (especially equity interests in closely-held businesses) and the cash flow problems that would arise from the requirement to pay tax on accrued but unrealized gains. (Again, this problem may be particularly acute in the case of closely-held businesses.) Accrual taxation is generally not recommended in this Report, though constructive realization at death is.

19/ The problem can be illustrated in the case of a piece of equipment falling in class 1 (and therefore qualifying for write-off over four years, the most rapid straight-line depreciation rate) under the classification scheme proposed in chapter 5, for a 20 percent rate of inflation. The value of the asset for purposes of the net wealth tax at the beginning of each year and depreciation allowances for the year under the current Colombian tax law and the treatment proposed in this Report would be as shown in the following table:

| Year | Existing Law | | Proposed Law | |
	Beginning Value	Depreciation Allowance	Beginning Value	Depreciation Allowance
1	1,000	400	1,000	250
2	600	400	900	300
3	200	200	720	360
4	-0-	-0-	432	432

The year-2 values under the proposed law were calculated as follows: The unindexed value at the end of year 1 of $750 is written up by 20 percent, to $900. One-third of that amount (one year's straight-line depreciation over the remaining three-year useful life used for tax purposes) is allowed as depreciation.

20/ Under indexed FIFO (which Aaron, 1976, p. 14, calls «current-price FIFO») or indexed LIFO the cost of goods in inventory would be written up by the change in a general price index since the time of acquisition of the goods. The example in the table in footnote 21 illustrates these techniques.

21/ The following table helps to clarify the nature of the problem in the case of inventories. The first column indicates that purchases of 100 physical units are added to beginning inventories of 100 and that sales of 100 also occur, leaving ending inventories of 100. (For the sake of simplicity this example assumes no inventory depletion.) In the remaining four columns of this table, beginning inventories, purchases, sales (as measured by cost of goods sold) and ending inventories are valued as they would be for purposes of the income and net wealth taxes, under four different methods of inventory accounting; unindexed FIFO, unindexed LIFO, and indexed variants of the same two systems. In constructing this table it is assumed that the price of the good in question rises from $1.00 to $1.30 during the year, while the general price level rises by 25 percent. The following appraisals of the four systems are based on the usual assumption that physical inventories actually follow a FIFO pattern.

Comparison of Alternative Indexed and Unindexed Approaches to Inventory Accounting

| | Physical Units | Value Units | | | |
| | | Unindexed FIFO | Options LIFO | Indexed FIFO | Options LIFO |
	(1)	(2)	(3)	(4)	(5)
Beginning inventories	100	100	100	125*	125*
Purchases	100	130	130	130	130
Sales (cost of goods sold)	100	100	130	125*	130
Ending inventories	100	130	100	130	125*

* Amounts which have been indexed for inflation.

261

The example in the table shows that unindexed FIFO overstates income, because sales (cost of goods sold) are valued at their historical cost of $100, rather than at their indexed value of $125; but FIFO gives an accurate picture of the ending value of inventories. By comparison, unindexed LIFO gives a reasonably satisfactory measure of cost of goods sold for purpose of calculating taxable income; it is deficient for this purpose to the extent that the price of recent purchases ($130) differs from the indexed costs of inventories carried over from previous years, $125. A crucial defect of unindexed LIFO in the Colombian context is that, by assigning ending inventories the historical value of inventories carried over from the previous year ($100) it seriously understates both their true value ($130) and their indexed historical cost ($125) in the calculation of net wealth. (There is, of course, no reason in principle that the historical value of inventories must be less than replacement cost, even in an inflationary economy. In fact, however, it is likely to be).

Under LIFO, if inventories decline, costs of some goods sold are based on the price of goods purchased earlier, possibly subjecting long-deferred gains to tax. By comparison, under FIFO, if inventories are depleted, costs of goods sold reflect the prices of inventories acquired more recently. See also Aaron (1976b, p. 13), who notes that this result would not occur under a system that calculated the cost of all goods sold using the price of those purchased most recently, a system which he calls «strict LIFO». While strict LIFO may result in the more accurate measurement of income, it does not automatically overcome the problem of understatement of the value of ending inventories unless ending inventories are valued in the same way.

Aaron (1976b, p. 13) states the issue this way:

> The two accounting conventions embody different views of the impact of inflation on the value of the firm and of the time and circumstances under which gains or losses due to changes in the relative prices are realized. FIFO accounting treats the change in the element of business profit subject to tax in the same way historical-cost depreciation does. If the average price level is stable, FIFO accounting treats as profit (or loss) any increase (or decrease) in the price of the firm's inventory relative to the general price level. In effect, the change in liquidation value of the firm is made subject to tax. By contrast, LIFO accounting treats any change in the value of inventories as unrealized and not subject to tax so long as the holdings of each category of inventory do not decrease. In this case, replacement cost is used for measuring the value of materials used. ... If inventories are maintained, LIFO functions very much like replacement-cost depreciation in its domain.

22/ Statements such as this are most appropriate in countries in which credit markets are relatively free from government intervention, at least in the determination of interest rates. Where interest rates are kept below equilibrium market rates by government fiat, such intervention may be a more important source of inequity and economic distortions, including adverse effects on saving, than the failure to exclude the inflation component of nominal interest expense. In theory it is often impossible to know whether removing one distortion will improve resource allocation, if there are other distortions which cannot be elminated simultaneously. In the present case there is little doubt that extending interest indexing will improve matters, since the failure to provide indexing and limitations on interest rates reinforce each other. Of course, it would be even better is interference in credit markets could be reduced as well.

23/ For relatively recent discussions of the systems of inflation adjustment used in Argentina, Brazil, Chile, and Israel, see international Fiscal Association (1984). Massone (1981a, b) provides information that is slightly more out-of-date on a larger group of Latin American countries. Lent (1975) also contains (somewhat dated) descriptive material. Appendix A to this chapter provides a description of the general approach used in Chile; this description is based on Casanegra (1984) and Harberger (1982).

24/ Interestingly, the time pattern followed in Colombia in enacting explicit provisions for inflation adjustment differs from the usual historical sequence of enactment of such provisions followed in other countries; ordinarily adjustment is allowed first for depreciable assets, then for inventories, and finally for interest. This progression is emphasized in Massone (1981a, b). The Colombian pattern is not difficult to understand; since LIFO and highly accelerated depreciation allowances (as well as partial indexation of interest on UPACs and other indexed debt and indexation of basis for capital gains purposes) were already allowed under pre-1986 law, a generally applicable system of inflation adjustment for interest income and expense was the primary item still needed.

25/ This phenomenon is sometimes referred to as the «decapitalization» of the Colombian economy. On this issue, see generally Carrizosa (1986) and Chica (1985).

26/ Though there is no reason to question the estimates reported here, it should be noted that the calculation of debt-equity rates is inevitably difficult, both because of conceptual and methodological issues and because of difficulties in obtaining exactly the type of data needed to make the conceptually preferred calculations. Resources do not allow careful analysis of the methodology and data used to calculate these ratios and other indicators of indebtedness reported here. But even large errors could not mask the overwhelming impression given by the data cited.

27/ See Carrizosa (1986), p. 38, for figures based on flow of funds data.

28/ See Carrizosa (1986), p. 34. A small and slowly growing — from 16-17 percent to 19 percent — fraction was held in bills of the Central Bank (Banco de la República) and reserves of life insurance companies.

29/ For an analysis of the interaction of these conflicting incentives under the 1974 reforms, see Gillis and McLure (1975), pp. 79-83.

30/ Art. 73 of Law 75 of 1986.

31/ For ease of reference these adjustable items will usually be called simply interest income and expense, although the more inclusive technical terms will occasionally be used; for example, «financial costs» is the more accurate term, since adjustment is applied to such items as exchange rate gains and losses, as well as to interest expense, per se.

32/ Art. 27 of Law 75 of 1986.

33/ This indexation of the deductible amount of mortgage interest is not necessarily exactly correct, because of possible differences in interest rates on such mortgages and on debt held by the taxpayer.

34/ Art. 28 of Law 75 of 1986.

35/ Art. 29 of Law 75 of 1986.

36/ Art. 29 of Law 75 of 1986.

37/ Art. 30 of Law 75 of 1986.

38/ Art. 29 of Law 75 of 1986.

39/ Art. 28 of Law 75 of 1986.

40/ Appendix B discusses yet another issue, the interaction between inflation adjustments and the choice between accrual and realization accounting.

41/ This issue is likely to be important only in countries that both employ net wealth taxes and experience relatively high rates of inflation. Thus it is important in Chile, which has a high rate of inflation as well as a net wealth tax, but much less so in Sweden, another country with a net wealth tax, but a relatively low rate of inflation. Indexation is also important for the property tax, a much more wide-spread form of taxation, the great bulk of which is levied on real estate. Historically the Colombian property tax has been based on direct assessments, which often have rapidly become out-dated, especially during inflationary periods. In 1983 an important change in the law provided for indexation of property values.

42/ Chile adopted the basic system of inflation adjustment still in effect in 1974, after «a gradual evolution extending over more than four decades.» (Casanegra, 1984, p. 25) After running at an annual rate of 17 to 35 percent during the period from 1965 to 1971, inclusive, Chile's inflation rate, as measured by the change in the consumer price index (CPI), during the five-year period 1972 to 1976 was 163.4, 508.1, and 375.9, and 340.7, and 174.3 percent. (Casanegra, 1984, p. 100) These figures are well above the rates of inflation experienced recently in Colombia; for the four years 1983-86, the annual changes in the CPI for Colombia were 16.6, 18.3, 22.5, and, 20.9 percent. (**Revista del Banco de la República**, Febrero 1987, p. 112) Massone (1981a), p. 4 notes:

> It is not, therefore, surprising that Chile was . . . a leading country in introducing measures to adjust law and taxation for inflation and to shift from partial adjustment of income to more sophisticated methods, namely the global adjustment and the integral adjustment.

The following similar assessment has been given by Casanegra (1984), p. 28:

The new revaluation scheme ... [was] enacted in late 1974 during a period of hyperinflation, when only a fully comprehensive system could be expected to correct grossly unrealistic income statements. Moreover, the lengthy previous experience with less comprehensive systems had shown that they gave rise to a host of administrative problems and inequities.

43/ It may be appropriate to explain why the novelty of a Chilean-style integrated system of inflation adjustment is deemed to be too high a hurdle to pass, whereas the novelty of the Simplified Alternative Tax described in Chapter 9 is not. The point is that introduction of the Chilean-style system would involve a substantial increase in complexity, whereas moving to the Simplified Alternative Tax would involve a reduction in complexity.

44/ This judgement is echoed in the following assessment by Massone (1981b), p. 60:

It is worthwhile to point out that some countries first used partial adjustment measures and then shifted to a global or intermediary system. ... Those countries which introduced the global system earlier ... underwent several years of experience with it and then introduced a complete adjustment system.

This kind of experience, where simpler methods are first used and then more accurate methods are introduced, should be taken into account by those countries which are considering the introduction of adjustment methods. Under this approach, the tax administration, tax advisers and taxpayers gradually become acquainted with the adjustment techniques.

... Although the complete method is not so excessively complex as to exclude its introduction, its widespread use by taxpayers demands a period of development, spreading and training because in most developing countries it is known to a few experts only.

Even in those countries where the integral adjustment method is better known there are issues for which an agreement has not been reached or which are still being discussed. It is therefore, inconvenient to introduce directly integral methods in countries where adjustment is just beginning to be used. In these countries the complete adjustment can be a final target to be reached gradually after going through partial and intermediary levels of adjustment.

45/ See Shoven and Bulow (1975) and (1976) and the related comments by Gramlich (1975 and 1976) for a provocative discussion of many of the issues covered in this section.

46/ Siegel (1981) provides an excellent discussion of the mechanics of, and differences in, constant purchasing power accounting and current-cost accounting, as well as references to literature on this subject. Other references include Davidson, Stickney, and Weil (1976) and Largay and Livingstone (1976). None of these works concentrates on the use of inflation adjusted financial accounts for tax purposes.

47/ A third alternative, based on real current costs, involves the combination of replacement cost accounting and inflation adjustment to account for the change in the general price level; see Siegel (1981). In the United States, the Financial Accounting Standards Board (FASB) in its Statement No. 33, entitled «Financial Reporting and Changing Prices,» requires that large firms report both historical costs in constant dollars and current costs in constant dollars. See Swanson (1984) for an overview of issues that have concerned FASB in this area and Thompson (1982) for a similar assessment for Canada. The alternative of real current-cost accounting is not discussed further here because it is unlikely to be considered seriously in the tax policy arena, and should not be. While potentially useful as a management tool, this concept is not appropriate for the measurement of taxable income, for reasons described below in the discussion of current-cost (replacement-cost) accounting. Moreover, it is far too complicated to be a realistic candidate for use in the calculation of taxable income, especially in a developing country such as Colombia.

48/ For example, because of rapid technological progress, in the United States in recent years an index for the prices of high-technology electronic equipment such as computers would have fallen or risen relatively slowly at the same time the general price level was rising. In the Colombian context this phenomenon would manifest itself in a rate of price increase for high-tech products lower than that for the general price level. Of course, most such equipment is imported; it can be expected that its prices would rise less rapidly than those of other more traditional equipment in which technological progress has been less rapid. Moreover, there are likely to be differential movements in exchange rates (e.g., between the United states and Japan), depending on the relative importance of such high-tech exports.

49/ It is interesting that the author of one recent survey of Latin American experience in this area (Massone, 1981a, b) does not acknowledge the importance of this issue. Though Massone appears to favor the use of replacement costs rather than a general price index, he tends to use the two concepts almost interchangeably, as in the following two consecutive paragraphs:

> Real profits exist only if the effective purchasing power of the enterprise is increased and a balance of receipts is left after deducting all expenses, **such amounts being calculated in accordance with their real values and measured with currency of the same purchasing power**.
>
> No real profits exist if consumption of tangible assets during production is measured incorrectly and the enterprise is deprived of fixed assets and inventories and put into a position where **it is unable to replace them**. (Massone, 1981a, pp. 6-7; emphasis added)

50/ Chapter 2 briefly discusses the Haig-Simons concept of income, its importance, and difficulties in its implementation. See Bradford (1986) for a more thorough discussion of the Haig-Simons concept of income and for references to prior literature. Chapter 5 of this Report examines difficulties other than inflation adjustment in implementing the Haig-Simons definition of income for tax purposes. It is interesting to note that Henry Simons, for whom the concept is named, did not actually favor inflation adjustment, although he did some of his most important work on the definition of income for tax purposes during the Second World War, when inflation rates in the developed countries were at historically high levels. See, for example, Simons (1950, pp. 134-36) for a discussion that is ironic in retrospect because it suggests that inflation adjustment of basis for calculating capital gains should not be made because, **inter alia**, no one would seriously propose similar adjustments for depreciable assets and for interest income and expense.

51/ It is recognized that taxation must generally be based on identifiable vents; see chapter 2. But it must also be realized that selling an asset is not the only way to realize an increase in its value. For example, a firm owning an asset that can be duplicated by its competitors only at a higher price can, under certain conditions, be expected to earn quasi-rents from that asset; thus the increased relative value of the asset can be realized over time without selling the asset.

52/ Of course, taxpayers holding assets whose replacement prices are expected to rise less rapidly than the rate of inflation can be expected to be quite content with inflation adjustment based on a general price index. It should be noted that replacement cost is only one of several concepts that could be used to measure current costs. Two alternatives, liquidation value and economic value, both have serious shortcomings for this purpose. The former, sometimes called exit values, would seem to be appropriate only if liquidation were the most relevant alternative to continued operation — an assumption totally foreign to the going-concern view that underlies the use of current cost accounting; of course, liquidation values may be substantially below both replacement costs or economic value (to be defined below), especially in the case of unique or highly specialized assets. The economic value of an asset is the present discounted value of the future income stream it produces. It is, of course, necessary to deduct from the income stream to be discounted the amount of revenue contributed by other productive inputs. It is, however, virtually impossible to know the economic value of particular assets that are used in conjunction with many other assets and non-capital inputs to produce a stream of revenue. For more on this issue, see Siegel (1981), pp. 311-13 and references cited there, as well as the text at footnote 59.

53/ Shoven and Bulow (1976), pp. 561-62, attribute this view to Pigou (1941), who in turn credits Marshall. See also Hicks (1946), pp. 171-81.

54/ In actuality current-cost accounting can be used to distinguish between profit and loss resulting from operations (operating gains and losses), gains and losses resulting from the holding of assets that are realized through operations (realized holding gains and losses), and unrealized gains and losses that result from holding of assets. For further discussion, see Siegel (1981) and the references cited there.

55/ Much of the available literature on this question concentrates on this issue. Thus Thompson (1982, pp. 498-99) notes in commenting on the relevance for tax purposes of recommendations by the Canadian Institute of Chartered Accountants for a system of current cost accounting:

> The dominant emphasis is on the maintenance of operating capacity. In other words, the costs to be matched against revenue in the year are current costs; they are not historic costs or indexed historic costs. The resulting measure of income is therefore more indicative of the real income realized as a going concern and of the income likely to be realized in the future than is the case with historic cost accounting. Relatively little literature addresses the question of measurement of income for tax purposes or even recognizes that the question exists and is important.

For important exceptions, see Aaron (1976a) and Shoven and Bulow (1975) and (1976) and the discussions thereof.

56/ A Canadian authority (Thompson, 1982, p. 503) gives the following assessment of the issue:

> ...the concept of maintenance of operating capability may lead to the exclusion of holding gains from income, including not only the nominal gain arising from inflation, but also the real gain arising from changing market values. It is debatable whether the latter should be excluded from the tax base. In terms of operating capability, such a «real gain» is not a gain, in the sense that it represents additional capital required for carrying on the particular business. On the other hand, in terms of equity between taxpayers, it is more likely to be viewed as a measure of additional ability to pay tax.

Basically the same conclusion is reached by John Kay (1982, p. 527), an expert from the United Kingdom: «It is impractical to think of CCA (current cost accounting) profits as a possible company tax base, and this has always been obvious to most people who have considered the issue».

57/ Shoven and Bulow (1976), p. 562, usefully describe this controversy in terms of the «purchasing opportunity set» of the firm. If it «is going to maintain indefinitely the same portfolio of physical assets, regardless of events, then one can argue that changes in the value of, say, depreciable assets do not constitute income. On the other hand, if the relevant purchasing opportunity set of the firm is represented by the total domestic sales of new products reflected in the domestic spending deflator, then real capital appreciation should be included in income.» The Haig-Simons definition of income underlying this Report clearly requires the latter interpretation.

Combining the reasoning of accrual-based taxation with depreciation allowances based on replacement costs would require recognition of the accrued capital gain represented by the increase in the value of the depreciable asset, together with allowing deduction of depreciation allowances based on this higher figure. Aaron (1976b, pp. 10-11) provides the following example of what he describes as the Samuelsonian rule (a rule that specifies that depreciation is best measured by the loss in value of an asset): «If in 1975 new widgets cost 100 and the depreciated value of one-year-old widgets is 80 while in 1976 new widgets cost 120 and the depreciated value of one-year-old widgets is 96, the Samuelson rule would permit the owner to take 4 in depreciation, the difference between the purchase price in 1975 and the value of one-year-old widgets in 1976. In effect, the owner is required to deduct 20 in depreciation and report a gain of 16 on his one-year-old widgets». Thus deduction for the loss in real market value of a depreciable asset is equivalent to taxieng accrued capital gains currently as ordinary income. Of course, most advocates of replacement cost depreciation do not also advocate taxation of accrued gains on the asset in question that result from movements in relative prices. It might be argued that taxpayers should be allowed to defer taxes on such gains when proceeds of realization are reinvested; but that is a question of tax policy that does not necessarily imply belief that the gains are not real.

58/ This argument is suggested by Gramlich (1976), p. 605-606.

59/ See the discussion of economic value in footnote 52, as well as Swanson (1984) p. 80.

60/ John Kay (1982, p. 527) states the matter as follows: «The two questions of how best to report a company's annual activities and how to determine its tax liability are not ones that obviously have the same answer».

61/ In this regard, the following observation by Massone (1981a), p. 9 is instructive:

> The auditing and control problems are greater for inventory adjustment, where the replacement cost is normally used, than for fixed assets, which are corrected in conformity with fixed indexes.

62/ It is noteworthy that the Financial Accounting Standards Board in the United States has found it necessary to issue separate guidelines for such specialized assets as timberland and growing timber, mineral-ore bodies, proved oil and gas reserves, and income-producing real estate; see FASB Statements No. 39-41 and 69.

63/ In many instances it may be more appropriate to use indices for prices of used goods, rather than of new assets, especially in developing countries; but even in the United States price indices are available only for a few types of used assets, such as computers, airplanes, and automobiles.

64/ See the discussion of footnote 57 above.

65/ For further discussion of the purchasing-power parity theorem, see section VIII on international capital flows and the cost of capital.

66/ A similar result would be achieved under the integrated system by treating foreign debt as a «real» or «non-monetary» obligation. That is, the peso value of foreign debt would be written up by the internal rate of inflation. See also Appendix A and Harberger (1982).

67/ A further objection, that the domestic currency is so closely linked to that of the creditor nation that the exchange rate, in effect, does not change, is sufficiently unrealistic in the Colombian context to deserve no further consideration. Harberger (1982) indicates that in this case debt denominated in foreign currency should simply be treated like domestic debt.

It can also be argued that it is inappropriate that no allowance is made for inflation in the capital-exporting nation. (This argument is most likely to be made by those who report net interest income from assets denominated in foreign currencies; since many of those who hold such obligations are unlikely to report the income for tax purposes, little concern may be expressed openly about this issue. Those with debts denominated in foreign currencies would oppose disallowance of the part of financial expenses represented by inflation in the creditor country.) According to this reasoning, a further adjustment should be made for the portion of the nominal rate of interest paid on foreign debt that reflects inflation in the creditor country. (This point is most easily understood in the context of a country in which the foreign currency is actually the circulating medium of exchange. Failure to allow for the effect of inflation in eroding the real value of foreign debt in such a case is obviously equivalent to allowing a deduction for the full nominal amount of interest on domestic debt.) While this argument is clearly correct conceptually, inflation rates are probably low enough in capital-exporting countries that this defect is not a major cause for concern. If at a later date, after the effects of the first round of inflation adjustment have been absorbed, this is seen to be problematical, perhaps because of an increase in the rate of inflation in major capital-exporting countries, further adjustment can be made.

68/ If the rate of inflation is highly variable, it may be appropriate to apply interest indexing over a period shorter than a year, for example, on a monthly basis. Recent experience with inflation in Colombia does not suggest that this further complication would be justified. To be completely accurate, inflation adjustment should also apply to cash balances and deposits in bank accounts that do not pay interest. (Note that cash balances, like demand deposits that pay no interest, are simply interest-free loans — to the government or to the financial institution holding the deposit, respectively.) This conceptually correct solution is implicit in what is done in the integrated system used in Chile, although adjustment is not actually applied to financial assets and liabilities, per se; see the discussion of the integrated system in Appendix A. Such adjustments are impossible in an ad hoc system based on fractional adjustments to interest income and expense.

69/ From an economic point of view this approach is, however, likely to be far superior to the approach proposed in the United States in 1985. Under it the exclusion/non-deduction factor would be calculated as the ratio of the inflation rate to the sum of that rate plus 6 percent; see U.S. Department of the Treasury (1984), vol. 2, pp. 193-200. The Colombian approach is somewhat more complicated administratively in the case of exclusion-disallowance rates that vary by taxpayers, but not in those cases in which these rates are published by the government. Even in the former case, the problem is minimized because the exclusion rate must be calculated by the borrower (commonly a financial institution).

70/ It should be recognized, however, that debt may have relatively short maturities precisely because there had been little interest indexing in Colombia before 1986; see also section III above.

71/ Nor are they likely to report the revaluation profits for income tax purposes, since current law does not provide for income taxation of such profits. The conclusion stated in Chapter 5 and repeated in Appendix B that it would not be appropriate to tax unrealized gains might appropriately be modified to allow taxation of inflation-adjusted gains resulting from voluntary revaluations made by the taxpayer for financial accounting purposes.

72/ On this, see Ayala (1986).

73/ An alternative would be to adopt a policy of taxing real economic income and limiting tax expenditures to tax credits and preferential rates, so that the measurement of income would not be distorted and could, with a conformity requirement, appropriately be employed for financial purposes. While such an objective might be laudable, it seems to be utopian, for there seems to be no practical way to restrict the latitude of future tax legislation in this way.

74/ Clearly the use of the CPI is to be preferred over the GDP deflator, even though the latter is a more comprehensive index. As indicated earlier, the purpose of inflation adjustment is to reflect the change in well-being of the owners of capital and business assets. It is thus inappropriate to employ a deflator such as that for GDP that includes changes in the prices of capital goods and intermediate goods. For further discussion along these lines, see Sterling (1970), pp. 335-44.

75/ It may be worthwhile to stress that indexing probably should not be extended generally to all interest income of individuals; certainly this should not be done a) if the exclusion of the inflationary component of interest income is complete, while the disallowance of the inflationary component of interest expense is phased in or b) if the disallowance factor is based on the previous year's relation of the inflation rate to the interest rate, but the exclusion factor for interest income of individuals is based on the current year relation of the inflation rate to the interest rate. To see the possibilities for arbitrage in the latter case suppose that from one year to the next the inflation rate increases from 15 percent to 25 percent and the interest rate rises from 20 to 30 percent. (For purpose of this example it is assumed that there is only one interest rate; of course, the legislation provides for the exclusion factors and the disallowance factors to be based on different interest rates.) If an individual were to loan funds to a company he or she owned, 5/6 of the interest income (25/30) would be excluded from taxable income, but only 3/4 of the interest expense (15/20) would be allowed as a deduction. (If the inflation rate and interest rate were to fall the scheme could not be operated in reverse, provided that the adjustment factors for both interest expense of companies and interest expense of individuals would both depend on prior year variables, as under current law.) The difference in these factors (only 1/12) may seem like a small amount, but it is not; 2.5 percentage points of the «loan» would be available to reduce the taxable income of the company without increasing the taxable income of the owner. Moreover, this excessive tax deduction can be earned on a riskless transaction, either between the taxpayer and his or her own company or by the use of mirror transactions in which two friends loan funds to each others companies. This opportunity for abuse could be prevented by basing both the exclusion factor and the disallowance factor on variables in the tax year in question, as would be appropriate in any case.

76/ Even in the second of these cases the proper treatment may not be as clear as one might think; see also the text paragraph that follows.

77/ For example, in the simple case of a two year lease requiring payments of $1,000 per year the capitalized value would be $1,800, assuming a discount rate of 25 percent. Depreciation would be calculated on this amount and the year two deductions for depreciation and implicit interest expense of $200 would be eligible for inflation adjustment.

78/ In general, except for long-lived assets, it is the rapidity, as well as the aggregate amount of inflation since acquisition of the asset that matters in the case of depreciable assets. In the case of unindexed LIFO inventory accounting it is not even necessary for there to have been recent inflation for a significant problem to exist.

79/ As discussed in Chapter 4, accelerated depreciation measures under current Colombian tax law do appear to be roughly equivalent in present value terms to economic depreciation at an average annual inflation rate of 25 percent, which is just above the rate experienced in recent years. Because this outcome is not guaranteed to hold in the future, modifications of current depreciation practices are proposed in Chapter 5 and the present chapter.

80/ Equity finance is not considered in the analysis presented here, because it is not directly affected by inflation adjustment provisions under a hypothetical income tax that already provides real economic depreciation. Equity financed investment is promoted by the company tax rate reductions made in the 1986 Colombian reforms; that topic is treated in Chapter 4.

81/ In a world with no capital income taxes, «Fisher's Law» is simply $i = r + \pi$, indicating that the nominal interest rate equals the real rate of return plus the expected rate of inflation. When taxes on capital income must be paid but there is no indexation of the tax system for inflation «modified Fisher's Law», shown as equation (1) in the text, is the equilibrium condition. A higher nominal return must be earned to compensate for the tax levied on both the real return and the inflationary component of the nominal return. If the tax system is indexed for inflation, so that tax is not due on the inflationary component of interest received, nor is the inflationary component of interest paid a deductible business expense, then the equilibrium condition is $i = \pi + r/(1 - t)$. That relationship appears as equation (7.2) in the text; for given values of r, π and t, it implies a lower nominal return than required under «modified Fisher's Law».

82/ For foreign lenders from countries that tax worldwide income, this condition appears appropriate, except in-so-far as they channel investments through countries using the territorial system in order to escape (or at least defer) taxation in their country of residence. In the case of Colombians lending abroad, compared to lending at home, this may be less true. Colombians may pay no foreign tax on interest income earned abroad, due to tax exemptions available in many markets such as the United States; furthermore, due to tax evasion they may pay no Colombian tax, either, in spite of Colombia's statutory residence-based system. The present formulation assumes that the equilibrium relationship between Colombian and rest-of-world returns is determined by the essentially completely elastic supply of funds to Colombia. To the extent that Colombian and foreign assets are seen by Colombians to be good substitutes and there is no constraint on the ability of Colombians to acquire foreign assets, Colombians have an opportunity to earn arbitrage profits by concentrating their portfolios in foreign assets.

83/ Again, because this representation assumes assets in Colombia and the rest of the world are perfect substitutes, only net financial flows are represented. The net capital inflow into Colombia is the relevant situation to address. For disparate views of the empirical validity of the view that investors see investments in different countries as nearly perfect substitutes, see Harberger (1980) and Feldstein and Horioka (1980).

84/ This interpretation of equation 7.6 demonstrates the determination of nominal returns in Colombia; the implications of international capital flows further depend on the responses of Colombian lenders and borrowers when the real after-tax interest rate changes even as the nominal return remains constant. For example, when the Colombian inflation rate rises, and the nominal return in Colombia rises on a point-for-point basis, without inflation adjustment the real after-tax rate of return in Colombia must fall. As a consequence, the Colombian supply of funds shifts inward and the demand curve shifts outward, implying a larger inflow of funds from abroad. Papers that consider in more detail the potentially divergent movements in real after-tax returns across countries include Howard and Johnson (1982) and Blejer (1984). Both papers consider cases in which exchange rates are not necessarily determined by purchasing power parity, and the latter one addresses differential taxation of domestic income, foreign income, and exchange gains and losses.

85/ The inflation adjustment of interest payments has no implications for foreign lenders, who are currently exempt from Colombian taxation and whose tax liability in their home country on interest income received from Colombia is not affected by inflation adjustment. Therefore, for a given real return and inflationary expectations, the nominal return required in Colombia is unchanged. That before-tax cost of funds to Colombian borrowers translates into a higher after-tax cost of borrowing given the nondeductibility of the inflationary component of interest payments.

86/ Portfolio interest is that received from investments in marketable debt securities. The U.S. has long exempted bank interest paid to foreigners. The current U.S. tax treatment of interest on privately placed debt (taxable or exempt like interest on portfolio debt) is the subject of some controversy.

87/ For extensive discussion of this issue, see McLure, (1987).

88/ In the «Exposición de Motivos» the government noted:

> Es necesario iniciar la corrección de algunos fenómenos descritos, limitando la deducibilidad del componente inflacionario de los intereses en un lapso amplio, de forma que no se causen traumatismos en la actividad productiva del país. (p. 10).

See also, for example, the following statement by Santiago Pardo, then General Director of National Taxes:

> [E]s necesario hacer referencia a las facultades que tiene el Gobierno en materia de inflación....Me parece que como resultado de estas facultades, a partir del año gravable de 1987 o del año gravable de 1988, existirán en el país, para efectos del impuesto de renta, ajustes por inflación en las cuotas de depreciación, ajustes por inflación a los inventarios que sean susceptibles de deducirse en el respectivo año, en que se generan. Esto va a permitir una compensación absolutamente total de la eliminación de la deducibilidad del componente inflacionario de los intereses. (Pardo, 1987, p. 29).

89/ Bossons (1984, p. 960) notes: «...[T]he major problems that arise in attempting to implement tax base indexation are associated with the interest deductibility problem. The key problem is to find ways to avoid unacceptable transitional windfall losses that would occur through disallowance of the deductibility of interest on existing borrowings».

90/ It usually is not clear whether it is thought that inflation adjustment for depreciation allowances that is intended to compensate for the adverse effects of interest indexing should be allowed a) only for «new» assets — those acquired after the time of enactment of inflation adjustment for interest expense, b) for both new assets and the remaining basis of assets existing at that date as well, or c) even for assets existing at the time of enactment of inflation adjustment, regardless of their remaining basis. Since only the second of these alternative interpretations makes any sense, the discussion in the text of defects of such an approach concentrates on that interpretation. (See also the following footnote with regard to the first interpretation and footnote 92 with regard to a particularly outrageous version of the third interpretation, the view that depreciation allowances should be allowed for land, conventionally regarded as a non-depreciable asset).

91/ The first interpretation is not attractive as a means of offsetting the adverse effects of inflation adjustment on issuers of existing debt. Depreciation allowances on newly acquired assets should be adjusted for inflation as a matter of policy based on principle; it should not be a mere side-effect of an attempt to offset the windfall losses of debtors resulting from inflation-adjustment of interest expense. More to the point, it would share most of the problems of the second interpretation described in the text, but like the third alternative, be even less well-targeted to the groups claiming relief.

92/ Thus the agricultural sector has argued that it should be allowed to write off the purchase price of land as compensation for the adverse effects of inflation adjustment, even though land is not exhausted by exploitation. The real reason that agriculture cannot be treated as generously as other sectors in an attempt to inflation adjust depreciation to compensate for inflation adjustment of interest expense is that under current law its capital expenditures are already treated much more generously than those in other sectors (and more generously than is appropriate). In addition, it should be noted that many sectors would be unable to benefit significantly from inflation adjustment of existing assets because depreciation is so rapid that little basis remains. It would be inappropriate, as well as ineffective (for reasons stated earlier) to allow «depreciation» of assets that are not depreciable or that have already been fully depreciated as an offset to the disallowance of deductions for the inflationary component of interest expense.

93/ A distinction is made between real estate and other assets because, on average, the economic life of real estate exceeds that of other assets. If no distinction were made among types of depreciable assets, the most troublesome problems of undervaluation that would result from failure to apply inflation adjustment to existing assets for purposes of the net wealth tax would involve structures. Of course, attempting to draw this type of line entails undesirable issues of definition, creates administrative problems, and opens an avenue for evasion. Adoption of the proposal to include the full assessed value of real estate in the tax base (plus improvement in assessment practices) would mitigate the problem of undervaluation.

94/ For example, in the first year of implementation of this plan 10 percent of the difference between the value that would otherwise be declared for net wealth tax purposes and the target value (the greater of indexed cost or assessed value) could be eliminated. In the second (third) year one-ninth (one-eighth) of the difference remaining at that time could be eliminated, etc. In this way the entire difference could eventually be eliminated, even if the target value was increasing over time.

95/ Such changes are the only ones examined here; it seems relatively unlikely that many firms would be induced to switch systems simply because of the introduction of inflation adjustment; if anything tax considerations should create less pressure on that choice than under current law.

96/ It appears that the asymmetric phase-in rules of 1986 law may create an opportunity for tax arbitrage. Interest income received from individuals on deposits with financial institutions benefits immediately from full exclusion of the inflationary component of interest. By comparison, disallowance of the inflationary component of interest expense is phased in over 10 years. There may be instances in which it would be worthwhile for a company to borrow funds and relend them to its individual owner, who would then deposit them in a financial institution in order to take advantage of this disparity in tax treatment. Even so, it is not proposed that the exclusion of the inflationary component of interest income of individuals also be adjusted to prevent windfall gains. It may have been appropriate to include a phase-in strategy in the 1986 legislation; however, since that was not done, it does not seem appropriate to do so at this point. The faster phase-in of the disallowance of the inflationary component of interest expense would hasten elimination of this problem. In the interim it may be worthwhile to place a limit on the amount of interest income that can benefit from the interest exclusion.

97/ Some may argue that no relief is necessary, because many of the same taxpayers that lose from the non-deductibility of interest expense also gain from provisions that result in windfall gains, such as lower statutory rates on income of individuals and companies, elimination of taxation of dividends and income from partnership shares, and the full exclusion of interest income of individuals. But these benefits are available to all taxpayers, not merely those who incurred debt before 1986. A more telling objection to the provision of transition relief is that taxpayers have had ample warning that interest indexing would eventually be introduced, as it had been decreed temporarily in 1982.

98/ The basic idea behind this type of scheme is presented in Bossons (1982 and 1984). He notes that it is not feasible to make distinctions in the tax treatment accorded interest on «old» and «new» debt instruments. Bossons (1982, p. 489; 1984, p. 962) notes: «...[T]he allowance approach has the advantage of making the tax system neutral in its impact on most decisions regarding the use of debt. For most taxpayers, the debt financing decision would involve choices between alternative levels of debt which were all in excess of the allowable debt limit. The distinction between old and new debt would thus be irrelevant to the decision making of most taxpayers. In such cases (presumably the vast majority), the only purpose of the distinction would be to prevent losses that are pure windfalls».

Bossons would base allowable deductions on the amount of principal outstanding at the time of enactment of indexation and would simply freeze that amount, reducing it by a given percentage each year until it is eliminated. Basing the non-indexed amount on principal would be more complicated than basing it on interest payments, as proposed here. Moreover, simply freezing the fully deductible nominal amount may be too harsh at inflation rates prevailing in Colombia.

270

99/ An even faster phase-out might be desirable in order to reduce incentives for debt finance more rapidly. While defensible on equity grounds, a faster phase-out might be unwise on economic grounds, despite the arguments of Chapter 4 that negative marginal effective tax rates are undesirable. The rapid elimination of the deduction for the inflationary component of interest expense can be expected to cause the cost of debt capital to rise rapidly, exerting a short-run unsettling influence on the investment plans of business. Beginning in 1991 the deduction for the base-period amount of interest could also be eliminated, either abruptly or by phasing it out.

100/ The case in which debt remains constant in real terms seems to be the most relevant one for analysis. It is under those circumstances (or at lower rates of growth of debt, which signify declining real debt) that the taxpayer complaint about windfall losses seems most compelling. While it can be argued that windfall losses should be avoided on the existing level of real debt, it is more difficult to argue convincingly that there is any obligation to allow full deduction of real debt in excess of 1985 levels. Of course, if the use of debt declines as a result of interest indexing, a falling real level of debt is likely. Table 7-5 provides summary statistics of the effects for a constant nominal amount of debt and a growth rate of debt equal to the interest rate (assumed to be 25 percent for illustrative purposes).

101/ In the unlikely event of constant nominal debt, the interest deductions disallowed under current law are equal in present value to 70 percent of interest payments during the ten year period. By comparison the proposal to allow deduction for the base-period amount of interest, even without adjustment of that amount for inflation, would in this case result in the allowance of deductions for all interest expense incurred between 1986 and 1995. The same result occurs under any alternative that provides for partial adjustment of the base-period amount, as long as indebtedness does not grow more rapidly than the product of the inflation rate and the adjustment factor applied to 1985 interest. This is illustrated by the entries in the lower left-hand portion of Table 7-5.

102/ This description of the Chilean system draws heavily on the description in Casanegra (1984) and the examples in Harberger (1982). The examples are meant to be illustrative of the approach used in Chile; they are not intended to be a totally accurate description of actual Chilean law in all respects.

103/ Of course, in the absence of inflation adjustment, depreciation for tax purposes might be accelerated, as under current Colombian law. Chapter 4 indicates that the acceleration found in current law in Colombia roughly offsets the lack of inflation adjustment in the measurement of income at an inflation rate of about 25 percent. It compounds the problem of understatement of net wealth.

104/ Note that the multiplicative relationship between the nominal interest rate, the real before-tax interest rate, and the rate of inflation (commonly known as Fisher's law) employed in these examples is the exact equivalent of the approximations used in the text of the chapter. Strictly speaking the assumption that this relationship holds, without modification, is inconsistent with the discussion in sections II and VIII of the text and in footnote 81, where it is shown that in an economy with taxes and no inflation adjustment the nominal interest rate rises more than point-for-point with inflation. In a system with perfect inflation adjustment for income tax purposes, Fisher's law holds, as shown in section VIII of the text and in footnote 81. It is likely, therefore, that the posited relationship between the rate of inflation, the real before-tax rate of interest, and the nominal rate of interest would hold at least approximately under the Chilean system. In order to assure comparability between the systems examined in these illustrative examples this same relationship is assumed for all systems, even though the failure of Fisher's law may be quite pronounced in a system that is only weakly indexed. Fisher's law will also hold if foreigners are the marginal investors in the economy and all Colombian taxes can be credited against liabilities to their home countries (or if interest income earned in Colombia is tax-exempt in the home country). This requirement is, of course, rather strong; thus primary reliance is not placed on it.

105/ Net worth for this purpose need only be defined as the sum of paid-in capital and accumulated retained earnings. Casanegra notes (1984, p. 92) that «Net worth is defined as the difference between the firm's assets (less all accounts that do not represent actual investments) and liabilities». She goes on to note, «The beginning-of-the year net worth for a given fiscal year is in practice equal to the end-of-year net worth of the previous fiscal year and includes the profits of that year».

106/ It may be argued that the balance sheet does not accurately indicate the closing financial position of the firm, because it is based on inflation-adjusted historical costs, rather than on current costs; see also the discussion of section II of the text. While there is something to be said for this viewpoint, it is doubtless true that the inflation-adjusted balance sheet generally gives a far more accurate picture than one based on unadjusted historical costs. In her appraisal of the Chilean system, Casanegra (1984, p. 29) makes the following observations:

> In spite of the advantages of the current system, it is by no means perfect. Its main problems
> arise from the fact that adjustment indices, whether general or special, can at best

result in adjusted costs that approximate true current costs but, in many instances, give rise to book values that differ widely from current costs....[The] cost of fixed assets fluctuates according to factors that have little relation to consumer price changes....[T]he adjustment of all fixed asset costs by the change in the consumer price index has resulted in unrealistic costs that have distorted financial statements....Consideration has been given to the idea of using special indices for adjusting fixed assets.... Unfortunately each possible solution adds to complexity or may create new inequities. The general consensus seems to be that the current system, as it now stands, is a reasonable solution to the problem of profits adjustment, and has the great advantage of having proved administratively feasible.

Of course, in the absence of a requirement for conformity between tax and financial accounting (which exists in Chile), the accuracy of balance sheet figures is relevant only if they are being used for the calculation of net wealth for purposes of a net wealth tax. As argued in greater detail in the text, the use of replacement cost accounting for the purpose of calculating taxable income is generally not appropriate.

107/ This discussion draws heavily on Harberger (1982).

108/ It is important to notice what this approach does not say. There may be a tendency to think that gains on real assets (such as depreciable assets) are being taxed on an accrued basis, because of the adjustment just described. In fact this is not the case. Realization-based taxation would require taxation of any increase (deduction of any decrease) in real value of assets on a constructive basis, as if the asset had been sold. As indicated in the text, the adjustment under discussion is necessary simply as the asset-side counterpart of the adjustment of equity and real debt in order to leave the residual, net nominal indebtedness or financial assets, unchanged.

109/ Article 27 of Law 75 of 1986 refers only to excluding a fraction of financial yields equal to the ratio of the monetary correction to the rate of interest corresponding to the yield received by the taxpayer. The discussion of «Exposición de Motivos» for this provision makes it quite clear that the intent is to exclude the inflationary component of financial returns from the tax base, whether these returns are called interest, monetary correction, or adjustment of principal. If the intent is not sufficiently clear, the wording of the law should be modified to provide the appropriate description.

110/ Under the exact approach to ad hoc inflation adjustment there should be no problem in achieving the correct result; all such payments are included in taxable receipts (expenses) and an amount equal to the product of the inflation rate and the outstanding principal is implicitly allowed as a deduction. Under the approximate approach underlying the current Colombian system it makes more difference whether a particular payment is called interest, increase in indebtedness, or return of principal; see also footnote 109.

111/ One easy way to appreciate this is to think of the cash balances in Case 3 as representing the principal of an outstanding interest-free loan originally made during a period of zero inflation. The ad hoc approach, in which inflation adjustment is applied to interest expense, could never give the correct result unless the inflation adjustment to interest expense were allowed to exceed nominal interest expense. (In the example of Case 3, a deduction for 20 percent of cash balances or debt would be required, even though there is no interest income. In the example of Case 2, nominal interest on $600 of debt paying 10 percent at a time of 20 percent inflation would be $60, but an inflation adjustment of $120 would be required in order for income to be measured accurately).

112/ One could imagine systems in which inflation adjustment was made on an accrual basis, even though gains were taxed only upon realization, and vice versa. Under the accrued inflation adjustment/realized gain approach, inflation adjustments would result in current deductions for the nominal increase in the value of the asset, but the full nominal amount of capital gains would be subject to tax when realized. This hybrid approach produces results that few would find appropriate and so is therefore not considered further. The other hybrid approach (accrued gain/realization-based inflation adjustment) produces results that are even more bizarre: nominal capital gains would be taxed on an accrual basis, with inflation adjustment (and the capital losses for tax purposes it would produce) occurring only at the time of realization.

113/ Aaron (1976b) distinguishes yet another alternative, which he terms «complete accrual», to distinguish it from the «partial accrual» system (Aaron's term) described in the text. This alternative would involve taxing on an accrual basis capital gains and losses resulting from variations in the present value of outstanding indebtedness that result from changes in interest rates. For discussion of such a proposal, to be limited to debt securities traded on securities markets, see chapter 5. This issue is not central to the present discussion, and so is not pursued further.

114/ Thus, for example, debtors anticipating a cash-flow problem could pay some (or all) of the interest on a deferred basis through resort to original issue discount.

115/ Yet another alternative would be to trace debt financing to the asset being financed and allow inflation adjustment for depreciable assets only to the extent such assets are equity-financed. The administrative difficulties of such an approach seem to rule it out. Moreover, it would be appropriate to allow inflation adjustment for debt that is incurred for reasons other than to finance fixed investments.

116/ Taxpayer discretion over when to repay debts might alleviate this problem somewhat, but it would not eliminate it.

117/ In principle it would be possible to allow for an inflation factor that would eliminate the difference in the present value of income and deductions under the two approaches. The discussion of chapter 5 confirms that such a scheme would be extremely complex and cannot be proposed.

PART TWO

A Simplified Alternative Tax

Thus far, the analysis in this report has focused solely on taxation on the basis of income. The principles of income taxation have been described, and the reforms required in the Colombian tax system to make it conform to those principles have been specified.

In Part Two of this report, an entirely different approach to reform of the Colombian tax system is considered. This approach provides for a tax structured to conform with the principles of taxation on the basis of consumption rather than of income; as will be explained below, another interpretation is that it follows the principles of taxation on the basis of «lifetime» income rather than annual income. The primary advantage of such a consumption-based approach is that it is, in many respects, much simpler than taxation on the basis of income. These simplicity advantages arise because the multitude of problems associated with accurate measurement of capital income under the income tax largely disappear under the consumption-based approach. The consumption tax approach is also arguably superior to an income tax in terms of the other criteria commonly used to evaluate a tax system – neutrality or efficiency, equity, and the promotion of economic growth. However, the relative merits of consumption and income taxes in these areas constitutes one of the more contentious issues among tax economists. In the absence of an obvious name for the consumption-based tax system considered in this report, it is referred to as the «Simplified Alternative Tax».

The Simplified Alternative Tax is described in this part of the report. The discussion proceeds as follows. Chapter 8 begins at a very general level by discussing the basic structural differences between taxation on the basis of consumption and of income. Both the taxation of businesses and of individuals is considered, as well as two alternative approaches to consumption-based taxation of individuals.

The features of the Simplified Alternative Tax are described in Chapter 9. The discussion begins by identifying the major structural issues that must be resolved in the construction of a consumption-based tax. The resolution of these issues in the Simplified Alternative Tax is explained, and detailed rationales are provided for the recommendations made in the report. Additional details of the Simplified Alternative Tax are then described. The discussion covers problems that would arise in the implementation of the Simplified Alternative Tax in Colombia, including avoidance problems, the relationship of the Simplified Alternative Tax to the net wealth tax and the taxation of presumptive income under current law in Colombia, and transitional issues.

Chapter 10 compares the two proposals in terms of the standard tax criteria of equity, simplicity, neutrality or efficiency, and consistency with economic growth.

8

Structural Differences Between Income and Consumption Taxes

Structural Differences Between Income and Consumption Taxes

As noted above, the Simplified Alternative Tax is a tax system based on consumption rather than on income.[1/] Accordingly, a knowledge of the differences between the income and consumption tax approaches is essential to an understanding of the effects of this proposed alternative to income tax reform. This chapter provides a general description of the basic structural differences between consumption-based and income-based tax systems.[2/] Business and individual taxes are considered in turn.

I. Business Taxes

A «consumption-based» business tax is distinguished from an «income-based» business tax in primarily two ways. The first is the tax treatment of business-related receipts and expenditures. As explained in Chapter 2, business expenses incurred in a given year are deductible under an income tax in that year only to the extent that they result in business receipts in the same year. Expenses that give rise to receipts in later years must be capitalized and deducted in those years; that is, the deduction of expenses must be «matched» with the inclusion of the related receipts on a year-by-year basis. Thus, under an income tax, expenses that give rise to receipts in later years are capitalized and recovered through subsequent deductions such as those for depreciation, depletion, amortization and cost of goods sold from inventory. In marked contrast, under a consumption tax, all business-related expenditures are fully deductible in the year they are made.

The second major difference between a «consumption-based» and an «income-based» business tax is in the tax treatment of debt and interest. In both cases, the proceeds of a loan are not included in the tax base, and repayment of the principal is not deductible. However, under an income tax, the real component of business-related interest payments is a fully deductible business expense, while the inflationary component is non-deductible.[3/] In contrast, under a consumption tax, both the real and the inflationary components of interest expense are not deductible.[4/]

The first of these two issues is the focus of the following subsection as the treatment of equity-financed purchases is discussed; the subsequent subsection considers the effects of debt finance. An alternative means of implementing a consumption-based business tax, which is referred to as present value expensing, is described briefly in the appendix to this chapter.

A. Cash Flow Accounting for Receipts and Expenditures

Under a consumption-based business tax, all gross sales receipts (including those from exports and sales of fixed assets) and all business-related expenditures are treated on a cash flow basis; that is, receipts are included in the tax base in the year the firm receives cash payment, and deductions for expenditures are allowed from the tax base in the year cash outlays are made.[5/] For this reason, such a tax is also commonly referred to as a business «cash flow» tax.[6/] Equity contributions are not included in the tax base, and dividends are not deductible. Symmetrically, business purchases of the stock of another firm are not deductible and dividends received are not included in the tax base of the firm owning the stock.

Cash flow treatment of sales receipts and business-related expenditures contrasts sharply with the treatment of these transactions under an income tax, where accrual accounting is required.[7/] (The appropriate treatments of various transactions under an accrual accounting system are described in Chapter 5.) Indeed, the use of cash flow rather than accrual accounting gives rise to many of the simplicity advantages of a consumption-based tax, relative to an income-based tax. In particular, all of the multitude of troublesome timing problems under an income tax, discussed in Chapter 5, disappear because all receipts and expenditures simply enter the tax base on a cash flow basis. Moreover, the problems of inflation adjustment under an income tax, discussed in Chapter 7, also disappear under a consumption-based tax; all receipts and expenditures are simply measured in monetary values of the current year.

Included among the expenditures treated on a cash flow basis under a consumption-based business tax are all purchases of inventories and of depreciable assets, as well as all other expenditures which, under an income tax, should be capitalized and amortized over several years or give rise to depletion deductions. (To simplify exposition, the term «depreciable asset» will hereafter refer to all such assets and the term «depreciation allowances» will refer to all the associated methods of cost recovery). Again, cash flow treatment or «expensing» of expenditures on inventories and depreciable assets is much simpler than the inventory accounting and depreciation allowances required under an accrual-based income tax. The advantages and disadvantages of consumption taxes, relative to income taxes, in terms of the simplicity criterion, are discussed in Chapter 10.

The most striking difference between an income-based and a consumption-based business tax is in the differing treatments of depreciable assets. The traditional Haig-Simons definition of the individual tax base under an income tax is annual consumption plus the change in net wealth. Ideally, changes in the net wealth of businesses would be attributed to individuals and taxed at the individual level. In practice, most countries that tax income at the individual level also tax business income, commonly with a corporate income tax; the extent to which the business and individual income taxes are integrated varies widely. If a business tax is used to supplement an individual income tax, the Haig-Simons definition of income suggests that the business tax base should equal the change in the net wealth of the business. (In addition, any individual consumption expenditures that are disguised as business expenses should be included in the tax base of either the business or the individual).

Consider the application of this definition to a firm making an investment in a depreciable asset which costs $1,000. The purchase of the asset, in and of itself, has no effect on the tax base of the firm; the cash outlay of $1,000 (a reduction in cash assets) is exactly offset by the firm's claim on an asset worth $1,000 (an increase in fixed assets). A deduction for income tax purposes should theoretically be allowed only to the extent of the physical or «economic» depreciation of the asset during the year. For example, if the asset depreciates 10 percent per year, a deduction of $100 would be allowed in the first year of ownership, with subsequent deductions similarly based on actual economic depreciation.

In contrast, under the consumption-based business tax, deductions are allowed for all cash outlays, and changes in net wealth by definition have no effect on the tax base. Thus, the firm would receive a deduction of $1,000 in the year of investment, and no further deductions would be allowed.

The effects of the alternative treatments are summarized as follows. With deductions for economic depreciation under the income tax, the entire return to the capital investment — the economic income resulting from the investment — is subject to taxation at the statutory rate. With expensing under the consumption tax, the effect depends on the nature of the investment. Define a «marginal» investment as one with a return equal to the firm's discount rate or opportunity cost of funds, and an inframarginal investment as one with a higher rate of return.[8] Under a consumption tax, the returns to a marginal investment bear a zero rate of tax in present value terms. If the investment is inframarginal, the inframarginal or above-normal returns to the investment are subject to taxation at the statutory tax rate, while the marginal or normal returns are untaxed.

A more instructive way of thinking about these results is to note that allowing expensing rather than deductions for economic depreciation implies that the government is a «silent parther» in the investment, sharing in both the risk and the return. Under this interpretation, the government gets a rate of return on its investment (the tax revenue deferred by allowing expensing rather than deductions for economic depreciation) equal to the difference between the actual return and the normal rate of return. That is, the government gets no revenue in present value terms on a marginal investment, but earns a share of any inframarginal returns on the investment in the form of an increase in the present value of future tax revenues. This interpretation implies that both marginal and inframarginal returns to the business share of the investment are untaxed, while the government share of the investment results in higher revenues in present value terms only to the extent that inframarginal returns are earned.

Since these results are not intuitively obvious, they are illustrated with some simple two-period examples of the treatment of investment under income-based and consumption-based business taxes. The examples are highly stylized; nevertheless, they illustrate all of the essential differences between the two alternative tax treatments. This analysis considers only the tax burden at the business level; consideration of individual taxes on dividends, capital gains, or interest payments is deferred to the following section.

In the model, a firm purchases an asset on the last day of Year 1 for $1,000. The asset lasts exactly one year and has no salvage value. The internal rate of return on the asset is assumed to be 10 percent; thus, the asset generates gross receipts of $1,100 in Year 2.[9] The internal rate of return is also the discount rate used by the firm to calculate present values of future cash flows; thus, the investment is a marginal one (as defined above).

This two-period model obviously includes monetary values in both years. Accordingly, in order to compare these monetary values, they must be converted into present values of one of the years. The standard approach is to convert all monetary values into present values in Year 1. However, in the examples to be analyzed, all returns and deductions except the deduction for expensing occur in Year 2. As a result, it is much more convenient to measure all monetary quantities in present values of Year 2; this approach is followed throughout the analysis. Of course an analysis in Year 1 present values would yield identical qualitative results; all Year 2 present values would simply be divided by one plus the interest rate.

The marginal tax rate faced by the firm is assumed to be 30 percent. The firm is assumed to have other sources of income that may be offset by the deductions generated by the investment; alternatively, it could be assumed that losses may be carried forward indefinitely with interest. Expensing under the consumption tax alternative results in a Year 1 deduction of $1,000, which has a Year 2 value of $1,100. Economic depreciation allowances under the income tax alternative result in a Year 2 deduction of $1,000.

The results for the income-based and consumption-based taxes are as follows. For the income tax, gross receipts in Year 2 of $1,100 less a deduction of $1,000 for economic depreciation result in taxable income of $100. Taxable income thus equals economic income, which is equal to the internal rate of return of 10 percent times the investment of $1,000. The tax paid in Year 2 is $30. Thus, the effective tax rate, defined as the tax paid divided by economic income, is equal to the statutory income tax rate of 30 percent $(0.30 = 30/100)$.

The results are quite different in the consumption tax case where expensing is allowed. The Year 2 value of expensing ($1,100) equals the value of gross receipts. Thus, the present value of the business tax base under the consumption tax is zero, which in turn implies a zero marginal effective tax rate.

This simple example also illustrates another significant difference between an income-based and a consumption-based business tax. In the year of the investment, expensing unambiguously reduces the firm's tax burden by an amount equal to the product of the tax rate and the amount of purchase. However, the firm's tax burden in subsequent years is uncertain at the time of the investment, since it depends on the gross receipts generated by the investment. As a result, the government shares in the risk and in the return of the investment. As noted above, the government effectively becomes a «silent partner» in the investment.

To see this, note that expensing has a revenue cost to the government of $300 in Year 1 since the firm's taxes are reduced by that amount; this is the amount of the government's «share» of the investment. In Year 2, the government receives $330 in tax revenue. This «tax revenue» is in fact simply a return on the government's share of the investment purchased through the reduction in the firm's taxes in Year 1. On a marginal investment such as the one analyzed, the present value of taxes on gross receipts generated by the investment exactly equals the present value of the foregone revenue; that is, the government's share of the investment earns the same 10 percent return earned by the investor. Thus, it is easy to reconcile the paradox between a zero effective tax rate on the income from a marginal investment and the fact that the government collects tax revenue from the returns to the investment; the tax revenue received in Year 2 is exactly equal in present value terms to the tax revenue foregone in Year 1.

Of course, this interpretation of the effects of expensing implies that the investor's share in the investment is reduced by the amount of the government's share. That is, the tax reduction in Year 1 implies that the taxpayer effectively invests only $700 rather than the full $1,000. Since the after-tax return in Year 2 is $770, the investor realizes the full 10 percent rate of return on his original investment.

Note that the government does not play such a «risk-sharing» role under the income tax approach. In each year, a deduction is allowed only for the actual economic depreciation of the asset. Thus, although the government shares in the return to the investment, it provides none of the finance; this is in contrast to the expensing case, where the government effectively finances a share of the investment equal to the product of the tax rate and the «excess deduction», or the difference between expensing and economic depreciation.

Thus far, the analysis has considered the differences between income-based and consumption-based taxation only for a marginal investment. Suppose instead that the gross return on the investment is 20 percent rather than 10 percent, while the opportunity cost of funds remains at 10 percent. That is, the investment is an inframarginal one, where the return consists of a 10 percent normal rate of return and an additional 10 percent «above-normal» return. In the above example, this implies gross receipts of $1200. Under the income tax, gross receipts less economic depreciation yield taxable and economic income of $200 in Year 2, implying taxes of $60. The effective tax rate is again equal to the statutory rate of 30 percent ($0.30 = 60/200$).

Under the consumption-based approach with expensing, gross receipts of $1,200 result in taxes of $360 in Year 2. The present value in Year 2 pesos of the $300 tax reduction due to expensing of the investment in Year 1 is $330. Thus, the government collects $30 (360-330) of net revenue in present value terms. The effective tax rate on the investment can be viewed in three ways. First, the average effective tax rate, again defined as the net tax paid divided by total economic income, is 15 percent ($0.15 = 30/200$). Alternatively, a second interpretation is that the business tax can be viewed as assessing no tax in present value terms on marginal returns and assessing tax at the statutory rate on the inframarginal or above-normal returns; that is, the tax rate on the inframarginal return of $100 is 30 percent (0.30 = 30/100). Under this interpretation, the marginal effective tax rate on the normal returns to the investment is still zero, as in the case of the marginal investment with the 10 percent return.

However, a third interpretation, which uses the government risk-sharing analogy described above, provides the most instructive way to view the results when inframarginal returns are earned. Recall that under this interpretation the investor's share of the $1,000 investment is $700, with the government providing the remaining $300 in the form of a tax reduction in Year 1. The investor receives $840 in Year 2 ($1200 in gross receipts less $360 in taxes). This implies that the investor gets the full 20 percent return on his $700 investment (840 = 700x1.2). At the same time, the government, which receives $30 of net revenue in present value terms, earns only the inframarginal returns on its investment of $300 (30 = 300x0.1). Alternatively, the government does not merely receive the value of its original investment which is worth $330 in Year 2 pesos; it earns an additional $30 so that its net revenue increases by the amount of the inframarginal return.

Thus, under the government risk-sharing interpretation of the effects of a consumption-based business tax, private returns to investment are exempt from tax on inframarginal as well as marginal investments. The government receives positive net revenue in present value terms only if inframarginal returns are earned; the net revenue obtained equals the amount of the inframarginal returns on the government's share of the investment.

These simple examples demonstrate the sense in which a business tax that allows expensing of depreciable assets is a consumption-based tax. Specifically, such a tax imposes no tax burden in present value terms on either marginal or inframarginal returns on the individual's share of an investment. Thus, capital income is effectively exempt from tax, and the entire tax burden on individuals, again in present value terms, is due to the tax on personal consumption assessed at the individual level (to be considered below). This is in marked contrast to an income tax which allows deductions only for economic depreciation and thus taxes the return to capital investment at the statutory rate. Government revenue generated by the consumption-based business tax consists of two components. The first is the revenue earned from the taxation of normal returns to investment. This component does not contribute to net revenue in present value terms, since it is equal in present value to the revenue foregone due to the deduction for expensing rather than economic depreciation; this foregone revenue can be viewed as the government's share of the investment. The second component is the revenue earned from the taxation of above-normal or inframarginal returns to the investment. This does represent net positive revenue in present value terms, and is best viewed as the government simply receiving its share of the inframarginal returns generated by the investment which it partially financed.

Finally, note that the present value of government revenue will be positive only if positive inframarginal returns are earned on average. This will normally be the case if private investors are risk averse, as is assumed for the balance of the report. However, note that with sufficiently poor private investments, the government could lose revenue in present value terms under a consumption-based business tax.

B. The Treatment of Debt and Interest

The second major difference between an income-based and a consumption-based business tax is in the treatment of debt and interest. Under an income tax, interest payments are treated as a cost of obtaining income and are therefore deductible. Symmetrically, interest receipts are a form of income and are included in the tax base.

Consistent application of these income tax rules to a partially debt-financed investment yields results which are analogous to those in the case in which the investment is fully equity financed. Consider the first example above (with gross receipts of $1,100) when the investment is 80 percent debt-financed and the interest rate is 10 percent.[10] Gross receipts are still $1,100 in Year 2. However, the firm receives deductions in Year 2 for both economic depreciation ($1,000) and interest expense ($80). The taxable income of the firm ($20) is again equal to economic income, and the resulting tax burden is $6.

The result is that, under the income tax, the effective tax rate on the equity investment of the firm is again equal to the statutory rate of 30 percent. To see this, recall that the project is 80 percent debt-financed; thus, the firm's equity in the project is only $200. Accordingly, the after-tax return to the equity investment is 7 percent (0.07 = 14/200), and the effective tax rate on the equity investment is 30 percent (0.30 = 6/20). Recall, however, that this analysis considers only taxes at the firm level in calculating the effective tax rates in this section; the analysis thus neglects any additional individual taxes paid on interest income, dividends received and capital gains.

Consider next the treatment of debt under a consumption-based business tax. Two alternative methods of treating principal and interest on loans are consistent with the consumption approach. Under both methods, results analogous to those obtained in the case of a fully equity-financed investment are obtained.

The simplest method of treating debt under a consumption-based business tax is to ignore altogether interest payments and receipts, as well as loan proceeds and repayments. Thus interest expense is not deductible, interest income is not taxed, and borrowing and lending (and repayment of debt) have no tax consequences.[11] This method obviously has no effect on the calculations of effective tax rates presented above.

Such treatment of debt is consistent with the consumption tax treatment of investment in depreciable assets in the following sense. Recall that the effective tax rate on the income attributable to the share of an investment financed by a business is zero on both marginal and inframarginal investments under the consumption-based business tax. As noted above, this «government risk sharing» interpretation of expensing implies that such treatment is equivalent in present value terms to exempting capital income from tax. Accordingly, simply exempting interest income from tax is consistent with allowing expensing of depreciable assets. In addition, tax exemption of interest income implies that no deduction should be allowed for interest expense. Without such treatment, negative marginal effective tax rates at the firm level would result.[12]

Note that under such treatment of debt, financial institutions (and other businesses to the extent they lend money) are obviously untaxed since borrowing and lending transactions have no tax consequences. The above analysis indicates that such treatment effectively is also accorded to non-financial businesses on a present value basis, since they are allowed to expense their investments in depreciable assets. In both cases, marginal and inframarginal returns to investment are effectively exempt from tax; thus exempting interest income from taxation and disallowing all interest deductions does not result in a tax distortion favoring financial institutions. Whether perception problems are worse than for non-financial sectors depends on the degree that firms in the non-financial sector are able to avoid paying any tax or «zero out». This, in turn, depends on the rate of growth of investment, compared to the rate of return, and the prevalence of inframarginal returns in the non-financial sector.

The alternative treatment of debt under a consumption-based business tax is to include the proceeds of loans in the tax base, but to allow a deduction for both interest and the repayment of principal.[13]

Such treatment clearly has a zero net effect in present value terms on the business tax base; it is thus equivalent to the first consumption-based approach described above. In terms of the two-period example, $800 would be included in the business tax base in Year 1, but a deduction of $880 (principal plus interest) would be allowed in Year 2. These quantities are equal in present value terms, and thus have no net effect on the present value of tax burdens.

To summarize, the treatment of debt differs dramatically under the income-based and consumption-based business taxes. However, allowing debt finance has no effect on the results presented in the previous subsection, provided that debt is treated correctly. Under the income tax, capital income is still fully taxed. The effective tax rate on the income attributable to the share of an investment financed by a business is zero on both marginal and inframarginal investments under the consumption-based business tax. The latter result holds for both of the two alternative methods of treating debt available under the consumption-based business tax.

II. Individual Taxes

As noted above, the traditional Haig-Simons definition of income is annual consumption plus the change in net wealth. Under a consumption tax, changes in net wealth are excluded from the tax base. Thus, the major differences between income and consumption taxation at the individual level are in the treatment of transactions involving capital income and thus changes in net wealth; these differences are in the tax treatments of saving and dissaving, the return to saving, the proceeds of borrowing and lending, and interest income and expense.

This section compares income-based and consumption-based systems of individual taxation. Once again, there are two alternative ways of implementing the consumption tax approach; these are referred to as the individual cash flow approach and the individual tax prepayment approach. The cash flow approach is the one most commonly associated with taxation on the basis of consumption. Accordingly, the discussion begins by comparing the income tax and the individual cash flow tax approaches, and then turns to an exposition of the individual tax prepayment approach. A separate question, which raises similar issues in both the income and consumption tax contexts, is the treatment of gifts and bequests. The analysis in the section neglects gifts and bequests; such transfers are considered in the following chapter.

A. The Individual Cash Flow Approach

Under an income tax, the return to saving is included in the individual tax base, and interest expense is deducted from the tax base.[14/] Savings deposits and withdrawals, as well as the proceeds of loans and loan repayments, have no effect on the tax base.

In contrast, under a tax based on «individual cash flow» (hereafter, ICF), deductions are allowed for saving in any legitimate investment accounts, which are generally referred to as «qualified accounts». Symmetrically, all withdrawals from such accounts, including both interest and principal, are fully included in the tax base. Thus, interest, dividends, capital gains, and rents, as well as the initial amount of the investment (for which a deduction was allowed), are taxed only when withdrawn from a qualified account. Loans to the taxpayer are treated as withdrawals from a qualified account. Thus, the proceeds of loans are treated as dissaving and included in the tax base, while interest payments and repayment of principal are treated as saving and are fully deductible. Such a tax follows a «cash flow» approach because the individual tax base is net cash flow, or cash receipts less cash saving.

The tax base under such a cash flow approach is individual consumption. The deduction for saving implies that earned income is taxed only when actually consumed; similarly, the returns to capital are taxed only when withdrawn to finance consumption.[15]

The primary economic difference between income tax and cash flow consumption tax treatment of individuals is in the taxation of the return to saving. Under an income tax, such returns are subject to tax at the statutory rate. In contrast, an ICF consumption tax is commonly characterized as exempting capital income received by individuals from tax, or applying a zero effective tax rate to such capital income. The rationale underlying this characterization is analogous' to that presented above in the discussion of a business tax which allows expensing. Specifically, suppose that individual tax rates are constant over time. For a marginal investment, where the rate of return equals the individual discount rate, the revenue cost to the government of the deduction for individual saving is equal in present value terms to the revenues obtained from including both principal and interest in the tax base when savings are withdrawn. Thus, the government earns no net positive revenue in present value terms. For an inframarginal investment, the government earns positive net revenue in present value terms equal to the inframarginal return on the amount of its share of the investment, while the individual earns the full return on his share of the investment. As a result, the tax rate on capital income attributable to investment by the individual is effectively zero. These points can be illustrated with the following simple numerical examples.

Consider a two-period life-cycle model of individual behavior where consumption in the two periods is denoted as C1 and C2; in this model each of the two periods may consist of many years. (A «life-cycle» model is one that traces the economic behavior of an economic agent, such as the taxpayer in the following example, through two or more phases of life during which assets are accumulated and then spent during retirement.)

Individual wage earnings in the two periods are W1 = \$4,000 and W2 = \$2,000. The interest rate is assumed to equal the discount rate and to be one; it is relatively large to reflect the fact that the periods are relatively long rather than a single year. The tax rate is assumed to be constant and equal to 30 percent. In this example, period two values are discounted to period one present-value equivalents (by dividing them by one plus the discount rate, which equals two).

If consumption equals earnings in both periods, the present value of income tax paid (PVT) would simply be \$1,500, since

$$PVT = 0.3(4000) + 0.3 (2000)/2 = 1500.$$

In this case, the PVT under the income tax is equal to the product of the tax rate (t) and the present value of the individual's «lifetime endowment» (PVE), which is defined as the present value of earnings, or

$$PVE = 4000 + 2000/2 = 5000,$$
and
$$PVT = t (PVE) = 0.3 (5000) = 1500.$$

A tax in which the base equals the PVE is referred to as an endowment tax, and provides a convenient benchmark for the subsequent analysis. For the case where consumption equals earnings in each period and the individual saves nothing in the first period, the tax burdens under the income and consumption taxes are the same; thus, the actual tax equals the endowment tax in present value terms under both the income and consumption taxes.

The differences between the income and consumption taxes are brought out only when the individual saves. Suppose he wishes to consume $2,100 in period one and save the rest of after-tax earnings for period two consumption. Under the income tax, saving in the first period (S1) would be $700 (calculated as a residual, or $700 = 0.7 \times 4000 - 2100$). Period two consumption is thus the amount saved in period one, plus the sum of period two wage earnings and the return on savings, both after tax, or

$$C2 = 0.7(2000) + 700 + 0.7(700) = 2590,$$

where the first term is after-tax wages, the second term is return of principal saved in period one, and the last term is the after-tax return to period one saving. (Recall that the interest rate is one, so that the return to saving equals the principal amount saved.) Thus, the year one present value of taxes under the income tax in this case is

$$PVT = 0.3(4000) + 0.3(2000 + 700)/2 = 1605,$$

which represents a 7 percent greater tax burden than under the endowment tax of $1,500. The $105 difference in present value of taxes paid arises purely from the taxation of interest income in period two ($105 = 0.3 \times 700/2$). For simplicity, the discount rate is assumed to remain at one; the results would be qualitatively similar if the discount rate were reduced to the after-tax rate of 0.7.

Under the individual cash flow consumption tax, the individual again consumes $2,100, which implies he is able to save $1,000 in the first period ($C1 = 0.7(4000-1000) = 2100$). (Note that saving of $S1 = $1,000$ is deducted from the tax base.) Second period consumption is thus

$$C2 = 0.7(2000) + 0.7(2000) = 2800,$$

where the first term reflects after-tax wage earnings in period two and the second term reflects consumption funded from the after-tax proceeds of withdrawing gross savings of $2,000, consisting of $1,000 of principal and $1,000 of interest. The present value of ICF taxes paid is

$$PVT = 0.3(4000-1000) + 0.3(2000 + 2000)/2 = 1500.$$

This is equal to the value of the endowment tax.

Thus, in contrast to the income tax, the cash flow tax has the effect of exempting the yield from capital income from tax. This occurs because the value of the tax reduction resulting from the period one deduction for saving ($300 = 0.3 \times 1000$) is exactly equal in present value terms to the tax burden imposed by the taxation of the withdrawal of principal and interest in period two ($300 = 0.3 \times 2000/2$). Alternatively, the individual forgoes $700 of consumption in period one by saving $1,000 ($700 = 0.7 \times 1000$) in order to fund consumption of $1,400 in period two ($1400 = 0.7 \times 2000$). Because he realizes the full 100 percent return on his investment of foregone consumption of $700, the return to saving is said to be untaxed.

The fact that, under the appropriate assumptions, the ICF effectively exempts from tax the yield to capital income can be demonstrated in an even more straightforward fashion. Suppose that the yield to capital income is explicitly excluded from the tax base; that is, suppose no deduction is given for saving, but the return to saving is untaxed. The effects of such a «yield exemption» approach in the two-period example are straightforward. With no deduction for saving, $S1 = 0.7(4000) - 2100 = 700$. With no taxation of capital income, $C2 = 0.7(2000) + 1400 = 2800$. The present value of taxes paid is

$$PVT = 0.3(4000) + 0.3(2000)/2 = 1500,$$

or the value of the endowment tax. Thus consumption in both periods is the same as with the ICF tax, and the PVT is the same, although the time path of tax receipts is different. It is in this sense that an individual cash flow tax on a marginal investment is equivalent to a tax that exempts the yield from capital income. In addition, note that the individual pays tax equal in present value terms to the product of the amount of consumption in each period and his tax rate; that is,

$$PVT = 1500 = 0.3 \times 3000 + 0.3 \times 40010 / 2;$$

it is in this sense that the yield exemption approach is a tax on consumption.

The case of an inframarginal investment is analyzed as follows. Suppose the individual investment earns a 200 percent return while the discount rate remains at one. All period one quantities are unchanged. However, period one savings of $S1 = \$1,000$ generate earnings of $2,000. This implies a before-tax withdrawal of $3,000 in period two, so that period two consumption is

$$C2 = .7 (2000) + .7 (3000) = 3500.$$

The tax in period two is $900, which is $300 larger than the comparable figure for the marginal investment analyzed above. Thus, the government earns net positive revenue of $300 in present value terms.

It is once again instructive to separate the investment into its individual and «government risk-sharing» components. The government investment, which takes the form of revenue foregone in period one, is $300 while, as noted above, the individual investment is the $700 of foregone consumption in period one. Since the amount of period two individual consumption financed by the withdrawal of savings is $2,100, the individual receives the full 200 percent return on his investment of $700. At the same time, the government earns net positive revenue of $300, which equals the inframarginal return of 100 percent on its investment of $300. As in the case of the consumption-based business tax, capital income attributable to the individual's share of the investment is exempt from tax even in the case of the inframarginal investment; the net positive revenue obtained by the government reflects the inframarginal returns on its share of the investment. Finally, note that since the additional $300 paid in tax by the individual in the case of the inframarginal investment (relative to the marginal investment) should be viewed as a return on the government's share of the investment, the amount of tax attributable to the individual is unchanged. Thus, under the government risk-sharing interpretation, the cash flow tax still has the property of being equivalent to an endowment tax, and the equivalence between the cash flow and yield exemption approaches still obtains. (The expressions for PVT are the same as calculated above when the additional tax of $300 is treated as a return to the government's share of the investment rather than an additional individual tax, and $C2 = 3500$ under both the cash flow and yield exemption approaches).

B. The Individual Tax Prepayment Approach

The fact that the ICF approach effectively exempts capital income from tax for both marginal and inframarginal investments suggests that an alternative method of implementing a consumption-based tax at the individual level would be to exclude the yield to capital income from the tax base. That is, in contrast to the ICF approach, both saving and the receipt of capital income at the individual level would simply be ignored for tax purposes. Interest income, dividends, and capital gains would not be included in the individual tax base; symmetrically, interest payments would not be deductible. Loans would thus have no tax consequences. As a result, the individual tax base would consist of only labor income — wages, salaries, and other labor-related payments. (The following chapter discusses the treatment of gifts and bequests and of retirement benefits.) Such a method of implementing a consumption-based tax is referred to as an «individual tax prepayment» plan (hereafter, ITP), for reasons that will be made clear in the following paragraph.

In comparison to the ICF approach, no deduction is allowed for saving under the ITP approach, so that period one taxes are larger; on the other hand, no tax is assessed on the return to saving, so period two taxes are smaller. The tax that would be paid on the withdrawal from savings of principal and interest under the ICF tax is thus «prepaid» by virtue of the absence of a deduction for saving under the ITP approach. This can be seen by turning around the arguments made above. That is, for a marginal investment, the cost to the individual of the lost deduction is equal in present value terms to the benefit of the exemption of future capital earnings. For an inframarginal investment, the tax attributable to the inframarginal return on the government's share of the investment is not due simply because the government's share in the project is zero (and thus the scale of the investment is smaller for any given individual level of investment). The only difference is that the government neither shares in the investment nor obtains net positive revenue in present value terms from any inframarginal returns to investment.[16]

To summarize, an ICF tax differs from an income tax in that a deduction for saving is allowed, and all proceeds of dissaving are subject to tax. With constant individual tax rates over time, this is equivalent to exempting capital income from tax, except that under the yield exemption approach the government shares in neither the risks nor the returns to investment.[17] As a result, another way of achieving a tax base similar in present value terms to that under the ICF consumption tax is to exempt capital income from taxation at the individual level; this is the ITP approach to taxation on the basis of consumption.

Finally, it is interesting to note another implication of the result that both marginal and inframarginal returns to the individual's share of an investment are exempt from tax under both the ICF and ITP approaches. Specifically, early discussions of consumption tax options suggested that an ICF tax was inherently more equitable than the ITP approach.[18] The argument made was that the ICF tax was based on actual «outcomes» since the tax paid by the individual depended on the actual return to the investment, while the ITP tax was based on «opportunities» since the tax was prepaid and did not depend on actual investment performance. A tax based on opportunities rather than outcomes was viewed as a fairer tax. The above discussion indicates that this distinction is largely irrelevant. That is, in both cases, the returns to the individual's share of both marginal and inframarginal returns to the investment are exempt from tax; the additional revenue (in present value terms) that accrues to the government under the ICF approach is best viewed as the inframarginal return to the government's share of the investment. Accordingly, it is difficult to argue that the ICF approach is somehow inherently more equitable than an ITP tax.[19]

APPENDIX

Present Value Expensing

Most tax reform proposals that include a consumption-based business tax provide for expensing of purchases of depreciable assets. However, consideration has also been given to an alternative method of treating such purchases, which is referred to as «present value expensing». The primary difference between the two methods of accounting for purchases of depreciable assets is that present value expensing provides for deductions that are taken over a number of years while «normal» expensing allows a full deduction of the purchase price in the year of purchase; the present values of the deductions are the same in the two cases. Present value expensing is considered in this appendix.

As explained in Chapter 8, purchases of depreciable assets are generally fully deductible in the year of purchase (or «expensed») under a consumption-based business tax. However, the implementation of a tax system that allows expensing may result in the following three potential problems. First, during the switch from an income tax to a consumption tax, the replacement of depreciation allowances with expensing is likely to result in a relatively large reduction in revenue in the first few years after the enactment of reform. It may be desirable to spread this revenue loss over several years. Second, allowing expensing implies that many growing capital-intensive firms will have zero or negative cash flow; that is, they will «zero out» and have no tax liability.[20] It may be desirable for perception reasons to reduce the extent to which this occurs. Third, allowing expensing implies that the returns to various tax evasion or avoidance techniques is particularly large, relative to the returns obtained with the same techniques when deductions are spread out for several years. For example, the gains to purchasing a depreciable asset, holding it for a year or two, and then reselling it at an understated price (or simply neglecting to report the proceeds) are much larger with expensing than they are under a system that requires deductions to be spread out over several years.

All three of these problems arise from the fact that expensing allows a deduction for the full amount of a purchase in the year it is made; that is, expensing is very «front-loaded», in that it results in a time pattern of deductions that is very accelerated relative to that consistent with economic depreciation. An alternative approach that would mitigate these problems but still be consistent with a consumption-based business tax is «present value expensing». Present value expensing allows deductions that are spread out over several years but are equivalent in present value to expensing in the year of purchase.[21] The choice of the number of years and the time pattern of the deductions is somewhat arbitrary. A relatively long time period with greatly delayed deductions is desirable to mitigate the problems associated with «front-loaded» deductions described above. However, concerns with administrative and compliance costs suggest that a short time period and a simple time pattern of deductions is desirable. An «optimal» pattern of deductions would presumably balance these conflicting concerns.

A typical present value expensing plan would be constructed as follows. The nominal cost of the asset must be divided into components that are allocated to each year that deductions are to be taken; define these components as the «base» deductions under the plan. Suppose that the base deductions were to be uniformly spread out over a nominal three-year period, and that a «half-year» convention were adopted. In this case, the time path of base deductions (for a $1,000 investment) would be:

	Year 1	Year 2	Year 3	Year 4
«Base» deductions	167	333	333	167

Note that these base deductions sum to the purchase price and the half-year convention implies that one-third of the purchase price is divided between the deductions allowed in Years 1 and 4.

The actual deductions allowed under a system of present value expensing equal the base deductions indexed by a factor equal to one plus the nominal interest rate in each period.[22] Suppose the rate of inflation is 25 percent and the real interest rate is 4 percent in each period. Then the actual deductions allowed would equal the base deductions indexed by 1.3 (1.3=1.25x1.04). This would imply actual deductions of

	Year 1	Year 2	Year 3	Year 4
Actual deductions	167	434	564	367

Note that the present value of this stream of deductions is in fact equal to the value of expensing the $1,000 investment; that is

$$1000 = 167 + 434/1.30 + 564/1.69 + 367/2.20.$$

Thus, present value expensing is consistent with a consumption-based business tax. Since the present value of the allowed deductions is identical to that obtained with expensing, all of the results derived above related to the characteristics of a business tax that allows expensing apply in the case of present value expensing as well.

The benefits of present value expensing are that it mitigates the three problems related to expensing that were described above (early revenue losses, high probabilities of firms zeroing out, and large returns to certain tax evasion and avoidance techniques). The costs are that it adds complexity to the business component of a consumption-based tax system. This added complexity occurs in two forms. First, a system that requires deductions to be spread out over several years is clearly more complex for both taxpayers and tax administrators than one that simply allows expensing in the year of purchase. However, administration and enforcement may be easier to the extent that the use of tax evasion and avoidance techniques is reduced.

Second, the tax treatment of asset sales is more complicated. Under a system that allows expensing, all of the proceeds of asset sales are included in the gross receipts of the business. However, under a system that allows present value expensing, the inclusion of the proceeds of asset sales must be accompanied by a deduction for the «undeducted expense» of the asset. The calculation of the amount of this «undeducted expense» proceeds in two steps. First, in the year of purchase, the undeducted expense is simply the amount of the purchase less the actual deduction allowed. In each subsequent year, the undeducted expense is obtained by subtracting the actual deduction in that year from the undeducted expense in the previous year after it is indexed by a factor equal to one plus the nominal interest rate. Thus, in terms of the example above, the deduction for «undeducted expense» would be

	Year 1	Year 2	Year 3	Year 4
Actual deductions	167	434	564	367
Undeducted expense	833	649	280	0

For example, in Year 2, the undeducted expense equals 649 (649 = 1.3x833 — 434).

Note that this system of accounting for assets sold prior to the time deductions are exhausted is exactly analogous to that required under the system of inflation indexed economic depreciation described in Chapter 5, except that the indexing factor is related to the nominal interest rate rather than the inflation rate. Although this system would add complexity, it is fairly straightforward, and would have to be invoked only if an asset were sold prior to the time that the deductions specified under the system of present value expensing were exhausted. Note also that since the number of years over which deductions would be taken under a system of present value expensing would presumably be much smaller than under inflation indexed economic depreciation, taxpayers would have to perform such calculations relatively infrequently.

FOOTNOTES

1/ It is most closely related to the so-called «Plan X» proposed by Bradford (1986), which is in turn a multi-rate variant of the flat rate consumption-based tax advocated by Hall and Rabushka (1983, 1985).

2/ Much of the material in this chapter is based on McLure (1987) and Zodrow and McLure (1987).

3/ See the discussion of inflation indexing of interest income and expense in Chapter 7

4/ An alternative treatment of debt and interest under a consumption tax provides for inclusion of the proceeds of the loan in the tax base coupled with full deductibility of principal repayments and interest expense; as will be shown below, such treatment is roughly equivalent in present value terms to the treatment described in the text.

5/ It might be noted that strictly speaking in the literature on value added taxes the specified treatment of exports is consistent with an origin based system of taxation, that is, one on production, rather than consumption. Under a destination-based indirect tax on consumption, such as a value-added tax, sales of exports are excluded from the tax base and imports are included. Even so, the Simplified Alternative Tax is called a consumption-based tax, to distinguish it from the income tax. For further discussion, see Zodrow and McLure (1987).

6/ Note that the taxation of business receipts and expenditures on a «cash flow» basis deos not necessarily imply the «individual cash flow» tax treatment discussed below.

7/ The treatment of equity contributions is identical under the consumption-based and income-based taxes. The treatment of dividends at the firm level is similar to that in most countries, as firms do not receive a deduction for dividends paid. However, Colombia is quite unusual in that dividends are completely untaxed at the individual level; most countries that wish to grant shareholders relief from double taxation of dividends allow shareholders credits for corporate taxes paid on earnings attributable to them; see McLure (1979).

8/ This terminology follows from the notion that firms undertake investment projects in decreasing order of expected returns, and continue investing until the expected return to an investment is equal to the opportunity cost of funds. The final investment that is just profitable is the «marginal» one.

9/ Note that all returns are assumed to be real. Inflation is a separate issue which is ignored in the analysis below, but considered at length within the context of this model by McLure (1987).

10/ The interest rate is assumed to equal the gross rate of return. For an analysis of the effects of alternative assumptions, see Break (1987).

11/ To anticipate the discussion of consumption-based individual taxation in the following section, this method of treating debt corresponds to that under the individual tax prepayment approach.

12/ See McLure (1987) for a discussion of the undesirable effects of combining expensing with interest deductibility.

13/ This method of treating debt corresponds to the treatment of debt under the individual cash flow approach specified below.

14/ There is some disagreement among lawyers and economists as to whether interest on debt used to finance current consumption should be deductible under the Haig-Simons definition of the income tax base. In practice, most advisors on tax policy —and many income tax systems — attempt to limit interest deductions only to those cases in which the underlying debt is used to finance investment rather than consumption. Attempts to distinguish between «investment» interest and «consumption» interest add considerable complexity to an income tax system. In many countries interest is deductible from the business income tax, dividends paid are not deductible, and individuals are taxed on both interest income and dividends received. This results in an obvious incentive to recharacterize dividends paid as interest, which in turn increases the complexity of the tax system as tax administrators attempt to prevent such recharacterization. This incentive does not exist under current Colombian law, since dividends are not taxed at the individual level. Indeed, since interest is taxed only at the individual level while dividends are taxed only at the business level, Colombian firms face an incentive to recharacterize dividends as interest payments when the marginal tax rate of the recipient is lower than the tax rate of the firm. The following analysis ignores these complications.

15/ Note that the problem of distinguishing between loans used to finance consumption and those used to finance investment does not arise under the cash flow approach. The proceeds of a loan used to finance consumption are included in the tax base and thus result in a tax liability. In contrast, a loan used to finance an investment produces an offsetting deduction when the investment is made in a qualified account; thus, the loan has no immediate tax consequences.

16/ In anticipation of the discussion in the following chapter, note that the «tax prepayment» reasoning applies regardless of whether the funds saved are consumed or are used to fund the making of gifts and bequests.

17/ For this equivalence to hold universally, tax rates must be constant over time for all individuals; if rates change, the result holds only approximately. Specifically, if tax rates decline (increase) over time, lenders (borrowers) will bear a lower (higher) tax burden under the ICF tax than under the ITP approach. For example, if rates decline, lenders benefit because the deduction for a deposit in a qualified account is taken at a relatively high rate, while the associated withdrawal is subject to tax at a relatively low rate.

18/ See U.S. Treasury (1977) and Graetz (1979).

19/ This point is examined further in the appendix to Chapter 9.

20/ In the absence of inflation, firms will zero out if the growth rate of gross investment exceeds the before-tax rate of return; if interest payments are not fully indexed for inflation, the likelihood of zeroing out increases with the extent of debt finance and the rate of inflation. For further discussion, see McLure (1987).

21/ To avoid confusion, it should be noted that neither expensing nor present value expensing is equivalent to the «first-year write-off» plan advocated by Auerbach and Jorgenson (1980); under the Auerbach-Jorgenson plan, the first-year deduction is equal to the present value of economic depreciation rather than the full purchase price of the asset.

22/ Since interest is not taxed under a consumption-based tax system, the nominal before-tax and after-tax interest rates are equal.

9

The Simplified Alternative Tax

The Simplified Alternative Tax

The basic features of the Simplified Alternative Tax presented for consideration by the government of Colombia are summarized as follows. It is an integrated consumption-based system that consists of a business tax coupled with an individual tax. The business tax provides for cash flow treatment of receipts and expenditures, and treats debt and interest according to the «prepayment» approach described in the previous chapter.[1/] The business tax base generally includes all gross receipts of a business, including those from domestic and export sales, as well as sales of fixed assets previously expensed; the business tax base does not include equity contributions, the proceeds of loans, interest receipts, dividends received, or the proceeds from the disposition of debt instruments or ownership interests in another business such as stock or partnership interests.

Deductions from the business tax base are generally allowed for all business-related purchases (from either domestic or foreign sellers) in the year of cash disbursement. All labor-related payments, such as wages and salaries, severance payments, and lump-sum retirement payments, are deductible in the year payments are made. If contributions by a firm are made to a defined contribution pension fund, deductions from the business tax base are allowed at the time such contributions are made.[2/] For all other retirement benefits, deductions are not allowed to the firm until the time of the actual payment of the retirement benefit to the retiree. All other business-related expenditures, including those for depreciable assets, goods and materials, services, and intangibles (such as copyrights or good will), are deductible. (The treatment of land is discussed below.) No deductions are allowed for dividends paid, interest payments, or any other (non-wage) distributions to the owners of the business. In addition, no deductions are allowed for the purchase of debt instruments or the purchase of an equity interest in another business. The business tax has a single rate equal to the maximum individual rate, and applies to all businesses regardless of organizational form.

The individual tax is of the ITP type, and the fair market values of gifts and bequests received are included in the tax base. Retirement benefits are included in the individual tax base upon receipt.

This chapter consists of two sections. The first section considers several of the major issues involved in designing the consumption-based Simplified Alternative Tax for Colombia. It explains how each issue was resolved and provides the rationales underlying each resolution. The subsequent section provides the structural details of the Simplified Alternative Tax. In both sections, business and individual issues are considered in turn.

I. Major Design Issues

A. Business Tax Issues — Domestic

1. Taxing Businesses in a Consumption-Based Tax

The first and most obvious business tax issue is whether such a tax should even be included in a tax system which is based on the taxation of consumption. Some consumption tax proponents argue that a business tax is unnecessary and inappropriate in a consumption tax framework, since only individuals consume. According to this view, tax burdens should be solely a function of personal consumption levels; the only role for a business tax would be that of a withholding device.

This position has some theoretical merit. Nevertheless, the discussion in the previous chapter demonstrates that a business tax that includes receipts and allows deductions on a cash flow basis, including expensing of purchases of depreciable assets, is generally consistent with consumption tax principles. Such a «consumption-based» business tax provides an important and desirable complement to a consumption-based individual tax; such a business tax is included in the Simplified Alternative Tax for five reasons.

One important justification for including a business tax within a consumption tax framework in Colombia is that any reform which provided for complete elimination of business taxation would be very likely to be viewed as grossly unfair. Complete elimination of the taxation of businesses would be seen as an unjustifiable «give-away» to the rich and powerful and would probably encounter determined political opposition. Of course, similar concerns are likely to be expressed regarding a consumption-based business tax, since the analysis in Chapter 8 demonstrates that the effective tax rate on the income attributable to the private share of business investment is zero under such a tax. Nevertheless, even if such a tax would represent a reduction in the effective tax burden on business in Colombia, it would appear to be potentially much less controversial than complete elimination of a business-level tax; this is particularly likely to be the case since, as demonstrated in Chapter 8, the government would earn positive net revenue in present value terms on inframarginal investments under a consumption-based business tax and would not do so in the absence of such a tax. Moreover, it is not appropriate in the Colombian context to compare a consumption-based business tax with an income tax that would actually tax business income at the statutory rate. Indeed, the negative marginal effective tax rates under current law described in Chapter 4 suggest that, due to the elimination of deductions for interest expense, the business tax base of the Simplified Alternative Tax may actually be larger than it is under the current income tax.

Second, the business tax provides a potentially important means of preventing tax avoidance involving the purchase of personal consumption items disguised as tax deductible business expenditures. Such tax avoidance techniques are common under both income and consumption taxes; however, they would be more troublesome or offensive under the latter tax, since personal consumption expenditures are a larger share of the tax base under a consumption tax than under an income tax. Such abuses would be eliminated under the consumption tax to the extent deductions for personal expenditures were denied under the business tax. Of course, it is exceedingly difficult to devise workable rules that distinguish between business and personal use in an economically appropriate and administratively enforceable manner under either income or consumption-based taxes; a full discussion of this difficult issue is beyond the scope of this report. Nevertheless, the business tax provides an important vehicle for reducing opportunities for this form of abuse. In addition, employer-provided fringe benefits that are not taxable to the employee can be viewed as another form of the same sort of abuse. Full or partial denial of deductions for such fringe benefits under the business tax is a way to limit this form of tax avoidance.

Third, as noted above, under a consumption-based business tax, the government will collect revenue that is positive in present value terms on inframarginal investments. Thus, the business tax would provide a source of revenue to the Colombian government. This revenue source is potentially important, since it would not be surprising to observe above-normal returns in the petroleum and other natural resource industries as well as other industries which are characterized by some degree of monopoly power. Also, note that a consumption-based business tax is likely to be a fairly efficient source of revenue. This is true both because revenues represent only the government's share of inframarginal and not marginal returns, and because it reduces distortions by allowing lower rates on personal consumption.

Fourth, a consumption-based business tax provides a means of taxing foreign investors — an objective that presumably is generally accepted in Colombia. Note that application of consumption tax rules to foreign-owned branches and subsidiaries implies that the Colombian government would earn a share of the inframarginal returns to foreign investment; such returns are almost certainly quite important for foreign investment in Colombia.[3] Of course, if additional taxation of income from foreign investment were deemed desirable, the current withholding tax on dividends remitted from Colombia could be maintained. Indeed, as is argued in Chapter 5, a strong case can be made that Colombia should institute at least a relatively low rate of tax on interest payments to foreigners under either the income tax or the Simplified Alternative Tax.

Finally, a business tax is desirable at least as a transitional device during the switch from income to consumption taxation. Individuals making investments prior to the enactment of a consumption tax would have expected the returns to those investments to be subject to tax. If the business tax were simply eliminated, such investors would receive an arbitrary windfall gain. Thus, the business tax provides a means of assessing tax on the returns to capital existing at the time of enactment; the magnitude of this tax, relative to that expected under the income tax regime, would depend on the transition rules applied to capital extant at the time of enactment of reform.

The above discussion represents a compelling argument for including a business tax in any consumption tax framework. Accordingly, the Simplified Alternative Tax includes a separate consumption-based business tax.

2. The Treatment of Debt and Interest

As described in the previous chapter, two alternative methods of treating debt are consistent with a consumption-based business tax. The simpler method corresponds to the ITP treatment of debt; under it interest payments and receipts are ignored, as are the proceeds of loans and repayments of principal. The alternative method corresponds to the ICF approach, under which interest receipts and the proceeds of loans are included in the tax base, and interest payments and repayments of principal are deductible.

«Prepayment» treatment of debt is recommended under the Simplified Alternative Tax. This approach has two primary advantages. First, it is the simpler approach. Since neither interest payments and receipts nor loan proceeds and repayments have any effect on the tax base, compliance and administration are simplified considerably; in particular, administrative and enforcement problems associated with attempting to ensure that all interest receipts are included in the business tax base and that improper interest deductions are not claimed simply disappear. Note that business purchases of the bonds of another firm are simply treated as loans. Thus, such purchases are not deductible and interest receipts are not included in the tax base; this treatment is simple and consistent with the treatment of the borrowing firm, which does not include the proceeds of the loan in the tax base and gets no deduction for interest paid.

Second, debt and interest are treated the same way under the business tax as are equity and dividends.[4] As a result, there is no tax advantage to the firm in relabelling dividends as interest payments in order to make such payments deductible at the business level. This obviates the need for rules to differentiate dividends from interest payments, as well as the problems that would inevitably be associated with enforcing such rules.

However, it must be noted that the treatment of debt and interest on a tax-prepayment basis under the business tax component of the Simplified Alternative Tax raises two difficult tax avoidance problems.

Both problems are due to the simultaneous existence of prepayment treatment of debt coupled with cash flow treatment of business receipts and expenditures.

The first is the use of installment sales to defer tax liability when the purchaser is not a taxable Colombian business. From an economic perspective, an installment sale should be treated as a cash sale in the full amount of the transaction, coupled with a loan in the total amount of the deferred payment. Treating installment sales on such a basis would result in accurate tax liability for both the seller and the buyer under the Simplified Alternative Tax. However, under a strict cash flow approach, payments would be included in the taxable gross receipts of the seller only as received. If the buyer were a taxable Colombian business, this would not be a significant problem under the Simplified Alternative Tax (though there would be inconsistency with present rules under the value added tax), since the deferred receipts for the seller would be offset by deferred deductions for the buyer. However, suppose the buyer is an individual, a tax-exempt institution, an exempt government entity, or a foreigner. In this case, the deferral of receipts is not offset by a corresponding deferral of deductions, so that the only effect is a reduction in the tax liability of the seller.

Note that this problem arises only because loans receive tax prepayment treatment. Thus, only the «principal» portion of each installment payment is included in the gross receipts of the seller. If loans were treated on a cash flow basis, both the principal and the interest components of each installment payment would be included in the taxable receipts of the seller, and the tax paid would be correct in present value terms. In effect, the cash price of the sale would be included in the tax base, an offsetting deduction would be allowed for the implicit loan, and interest and principal repayments received would be included in the tax base.

The opportunity to defer taxes under the Simplified Alternative Tax using such installment sales would present a significant avoidance opportunity to Colombian businesses, and would likely result in greatly increased use of installment sales. Note that the buyers in the transaction described above would generally be indifferent between a cash sale and an installment sale on fair terms; individuals and tax-exempt institutions receive no deductions for purchases in any case, and foreigners on accrual accounting systems generally would receive a full deduction at the time of purchase on an installment sale.

To eliminate this opportunity, an exception to strict cash flow treatment of receipts and expenditures under the business tax should be provided for installment sales to entities other than taxable Colombian businesses. On such installment sales, the seller would include the cash price of the good or service in taxable receipts at the time of the sale; subsequent installment payments would not be included in taxable receipts. Such treatment clearly increases the complexity of the Simplified Alternative Tax. It requires special treatment of certain installment sales and it requires that firms identify installment sales made to entities other than taxable Colombian businesses. Nevertheless, this additional complexity seems worthwhile in order to eliminate the tax avoidance opportunity described above. Moreover, the special treatment recommended for installment sales to entities other than Colombian businesses is roughly similar to the income tax treatment of all installment sales proposed in Chapter 5.

The other problem caused by tax prepayment treatment of debt and interest is the avoidance opportunity that arises when a taxable Colombian business is simultaneously trading in goods and borrowing/lending money with an individual, a tax-exempt institution, or a foreigner.[5] The nature of the problem depends on whether the taxable Colombian business is a seller/lender or a buyer/borrower.

Suppose first that A is a taxable Colombian business that simultaneously sells a good or service and lends money to the purchaser B, who is an individual, tax-exempt institution or foreigner.[6] Firm A clearly has an incentive to strike a deal for an understated purchase price of the good, coupled with an above-market interest rate on the loan; the reduced purchase price would lower taxable receipts while the increased interest receipts would have no tax effects. Entity B is indifferent to such a substitution, provided that it is fair in present value terms; individuals and tax-exempt institutions get no deduction in any case, and the foreign firm (depending on tax treatment in its home country) is likely to be indifferent between deductions for purchases and deductions for interest payments. Once again, tax prepayment treatment results in an opportunity for tax avoidance. In contrast, under cash flow treatment of debt and interest, the Colombian firm would be indifferent between sales receipts and interest receipts.

Note that a similar if somewhat less severe problem arises under an income tax with inflation indexing of interest of the type described in Chapter 7. To the extent interest payments were subject to partial exclusion, Colombian firms would want to substitute such interest receipts for fully taxable receipts from sales; individuals, tax-exempt institutions and foreigners not subject to interest indexing would be indifferent to such a substitution.

The solution to this problem is problematical. One possibility is that Colombian businesses be required to include «excess interest payments» in taxable receipts; such payments would be defined on a loan-by-loan basis as interest payments in excess of a ceiling rate, such as the interest rate on credit card purchases. Such treatment would reduce, but certainly not eliminate, this opportunity for tax avoidance. Again, such special treatment adds complexity to the Simplified Alternative Tax in the interest of curbing opportunities for tax abuse.

The other version of this problem arises when the taxable Colombian business is a purchaser/borrower. Suppose Colombian firm A simultaneously borrows money and buys production inputs from the lender B, which is a tax-exempt institution or foreigner.[7] In this case, it is in the interest of A to agree to an overstated price of the good in exchange for a below-market interest rate; the price increase is deductible from the business tax base while the lower interest payments have no effect on the base. Entity B is indifferent to this substitution for the same reasons as in the previous example.

A solution to this problem is even more problematical. In the case of tax-exempt institutions, the need to prevent such avoidance techniques provides a reason to maintain the provisions of current law that subject such institutions to the business tax on all unrelated business activities. The problem is even more difficult for foreigners. One solution would be to establish an interest rate floor. Taxpayers that borrow money at rates below the floor could be required to include in taxable receipts the difference between actual interest payments and the payments that would be required at the floor rate. Such treatment is not recommended because it would be complex, would be difficult to administer and enforce, and would suffer from perception problems. Instead, it is recommended only that foreign transactions be monitored to determine if such avoidance techniques appear to be a significant problem. This area is one in which the Simplified Alternative Tax in fact would in fact be quite complex and would open an avenue for abuse that would be quite difficult to police. However, note again that a similar (if somewhat less severe) problem arises under an income tax with inflation indexing of interest; Colombian firms would have an incentive to substitute fully deductible purchases of goods and services for partially deductible interest payments.

3. The Use of Cash Flow Accounting

As noted above, many of the simplicity advantages of the Simplified Alternative Tax result from its use of cash flow rather than accrual accounting; a description of the relative advantages of cash flow accounting is provided in Chapter 10. However, adoption of a cash flow consumption-based business tax in Colombia would represent a significant departure from current practice in the calculation of the value added tax (VAT), where sales are generally deemed to occur at the time that property changes hands rather than when cash actually changes hands. The use of separate accounting systems for the VAT and the Simplified Alternative Tax would add complexity in both compliance and administration, and would be especially burdensome to small businesses subject to both taxes.

Ideally, the problem could be solved by calculating the value added tax on a cash flow basis. The rule specified above for installment sales to individuals, tax-exempt institutions, and foreigners would apply, so that VAT revenue loss due to the use of installment sales would not be a problem. Such an approach would extend the simplicity advantages of cash flow accounting to the VAT.

Alternatively, if such a switch is deemed impossible for administrative or other reasons, the Simplified Alternative Tax could be based on a «modified» cash flow approach. That is, the limited accrual rules used in the calculation of the VAT could be applied to the determination of the time that receipts are included in the tax base of the seller and deductions are allowed for purchases by the buyer. Such accrual-type accounting would apply only to the rules determining the simultaneous timing of realizations of sales and deductions for tax purposes. It would not greatly increase the complexity of the Simplified Alternative Tax, since no attempt would be made to use accrual accounting to measure all changes in the net wealth of firms; these attempts at totally accurate accrual accounting give rise to much of the complexity of the income tax reforms described in Chapter 5.[8/] However, the above discussion indicates that the differences between the Colombian VAT (which requires accrual accounting for sales and is calculated according to the so-called «credit method») and the Simplified Alternative Tax, a version of a subtraction method VAT, are significant.

4. The Treatment of Retirement Benefits

The appropriate treatment of retirement benefits under an ITP tax is that businesses are allowed a deduction for the payment of such benefits only when payment to the recipient is actually made; at that time, the benefits are included in the individual tax base of the recipient. There are no deductions for contributions to reserves established for the purpose of funding retirement benefits, and the earnings on such reserves are tax-free according to the general rules applicable to business investment under the Simplified Alternative Tax. Such treatment of retirement benefits is proposed generally under the Simplified Alternative Tax. It would apply, for example, to reserves set aside to fund severance payments and defined benefit pension plans.

However, it is recommended that an exception be provided under the Simplified Alternative Tax for defined contribution pension plans; this proposal follows Hall and Rabushka (1983, 1985) and Bradford (1986). In this case, firm contributions to pension funds would be deductible at the time of the contribution, earnings on such pensions funds would be tax-free following the general rules of the Simplified Alternative Tax, and that pension benefits received would be included in the individual tax base of the recipient. Under this approach, the firm effectively maintains ICF-type «qualified accounts» on behalf of its employees and pensioners. As demonstrated in Chapter 8, such treatment is equivalent, under certain conditions, to that called for under «strict» application of ITP tax principles. Such treatment would provide for business deductions for pension contributions, coupled with inclusion of the amount deducted in the individual tax base of the recipient, at the time of deduction; all subsequent earnings on pension fund investments would be tax exempt.

This approach is proposed because it is convenient from an administrative standpoint, and because the treatment of pension contributions and pension fund earnings (but not of pension benefits received) conforms with current practice. Note that both alternative treatments of retirement benefits provide a natural «averaging» mechanism not available under the «strict» ITP approach; that is, they permit an individual to defer taxation of current earnings to retirement years when marginal tax rates are likely to be lower. Such averaging provisions are generally desirable in a tax system with progressive marginal rates in order to avoid assessing relatively high taxes on individuals with earnings that fluctuate significantly over time.

The primary problem with implementing such treatment of retirement benefits in Colombia is a transitional one. Current law is even more generous than the recommended treatment. In particular, firms are allowed deductions for pension contributions, pension fund earnings are untaxed, and pension benefits and other retirement benefits received below a fairly generous exemption level are untaxed at the individual level. It is recommended that the proposed new treatment, the inclusion of all retirement benefits received in the taxable income of the individual recipient, be phased-in over time. For example, the current treatment could be maintained for five years, the exempt amount could be indexed for only half of inflation for another five years, and then the exemption could be eliminated.

Given the generous treatment of retirement benefits received under current law, subjecting retirement benefits to individual taxation under the Simplified Alternative Tax would be difficult from a political standpoint. An alternative treatment that might be politically more appealing would be to disallow business deductions for the costs of paying such benefits. Such treatment would be analogous to that proposed for personal expenditures disguised as business purchases and for fringe benefits. This alternative is an unattractive one. It would effectively tax retirement benefits at the business rate rather than the individual rate; it would thus over-tax all individuals other than those who are in the top individual rate bracket during their retirement years. Such tax treatment would provide a disincentive to the provision of retirement benefits, and would eliminate the natural averaging of tax burdens obtained under the treatment recommended above.

5. The Rate Structure

In many countries, the business tax schedule provides for a graduated rate structure; frequently, the lowest rates in the business tax structure are lower than the maximum rate of the individual tax. A graduated business rate structure is commonly justified as a means of stimulating small business activity or as an offset to market imperfections which result in relatively high costs of capital to small enterprises. Some observers also justify reduced rates for small businesses on the grounds that they have less «ability to pay» than larger firms. Finally, graduated rates may reduce the extent to which business income attributable to low-rate individuals is taxed at relatively high business rates.

These supposed advantages of a graduated business rate structure are highly suspect. It is unclear why the activities of small businesses should be encouraged at the expense of larger enterprises. The relatively high interest rates commonly paid by small firms may simply reflect the increased risk associated with investing in small and/or unproven companies. Since differential risk premiums serve the useful purpose of allocating scarce capital among investments of different risk, tax preferences designed to offset such higher costs would generally be expected to reduce the efficiency of the economy by distorting the market allocation of capital. In addition, it is clear that the notions of «ability to pay» that are commonly used to justify a progressive individual tax structure relate to individuals; that is, «ability to pay» refers to the capacity of an individual to finance public expenditures and progressivity is implied if this capacity is believed to rise more than proportionately with income (or consumption). This concept has no relevance for business income, and thus is inappropriate as a justification for a progressive business tax structure. Overtaxation of income attributable to low-rate individuals is not likely to be a serious problem in Colombia, where most owners of shares in businesses are (or should be) in the top rate bracket.

Moreover, a graduated business rate structure has several undesirable economic effects; some of these are common to both income-based and consumption-based business taxes. The most important under the income tax is that graduated rates create an opportunity for tax avoidance. High-bracket individuals can accumulate income within a «small» firm; this income is taxed at the firm's relatively low rate, and taxation at the individual's relatively high marginal tax rate is deferred. In many cases, the advantage of deferral outweighs the cost of any additional business tax the individual must pay, so that the small firm serves as a tax shelter. In addition, graduated rates encourage businesses to form multiple companies in order to increase the amount of income subject to tax at relatively low rates. Measures designed to limit these avoidance techniques and the inequities and economic distortions they cause are commonly ineffective and add complexity to the tax system.

On balance, the disadvantages of a graduated business rate structure far outweigh any advantages. The 1986 tax changes in Colombia that eliminated preferential rates for limited partnerships, and subjected all business income to tax at the maximum individual rate of 30 percent were positive ones; a reform that reversed this characteristic of the new Colombian tax structure would be highly undesirable. Accordingly, the Simplified Alternative Tax provides for a single business tax rate, which is equal to the maximum tax rate under the individual tax system.

6. Differentiation According to Organizational Form

The tax systems in many countries provide differential tax treatment to businesses according to their form of organization. The most common situation is where only corporations are subject to a business level tax (and dividends paid by corporations are taxed when received by shareholders), while partnerships and sole proprietorships are accorded «pass through» treatment with taxation only at the individual level. As in the case of differential rates, such treatment is commonly justified by dubious «ability to pay» arguments and as providing a tax incentive to small businesses; this assumes that small businesses are typically organized as partnerships or sole proprietorships.

The ability to pay arguments are clearly misplaced in this context, since the owners of partnerships and sole proprietorships may not be relatively low income individuals. Indeed, many wealthy individuals in Colombia have traditionally reduced their tax burdens through the use of limited partnerships. This practice is generally perceived to be highly inequitable. Preferential treatment of partnerships and sole proprietorships is also inefficient since it results in different tax burdens for activities that are economically similar or identical. Such treatment clearly distorts decisions regarding organizational form, and may discriminate against certain activities which, for economic reasons, are best organized in a particular form.

Moreover, preferential treatment of partnerships and sole proprietorships unnecessarily complicates the tax code in at least three ways. First, it creates a need to define and enforce rules which determine which businesses qualify for differential treatment. Second, allowing «pass through» treatment of losses permits individuals to use artificial accounting losses to shelter income which normally would be taxed under the individual tax system; such shelters generally increase the complexity of the tax system as administrators attempt to limit the extent to which individual income is sheltered from tax. Third, it greatly complicates the audit process in those cases where the partners of a firm must be audited, rather than a single firm. These complexities would appear to swamp any simplicity advantages gained from exempting certain firms from a business level tax.

For all of these reasons, the Simplified Alternative Tax should be applied uniformly to all forms of business organization. Such a rule would be consistent with current tax practice in Colombia.

B. Business Tax Issues — International

1. Treatment of Investment in Colombia by Foreigners

A consumption-based business tax would provide significantly lower marginal effective tax rates on new investment in Colombia than would the fully phased in version of the 1986 reform. For that reason the Simplified Alternative Tax would likely encourage investment in Colombia by foreigners as well as by domestic residents. A potentially important issue in such a policy change, though, is whether the consumption-based business tax would be creditable in the home country of the foreign investor. If it would not, policymakers may need to be concerned that adoption of the Simplified Alternative Tax would actually discourage investment in Colombia. Whether the consumption-based business tax would be creditable is evaluated in the first sub-section below. It is noted that the remittance tax levied on dividends paid to foreign parents of Colombian subsidiaries is likely to be creditable if and only if the consumption-based business tax is creditable. The importance of creditability is then discussed in the second sub-section. Because many foreign parents are likely to be in an excess foreign tax credit position, the creditability issue may not be as important as it first appears.

a. Creditability of the Simplified Alternative Tax

The United States, until recently the premier capital-exporting country in the world, has been extraordinarily zealous in attempting to guarantee that foreign tax credits are claimed only for income taxes paid to other countries. This concern has exhibited itself in complex and detailed statutory provisions and regulations specifying the conditions under which the credit is available in the United States. By comparison, some of the other capital-exporting countries that tax the worldwide income of their residents take a much more relaxed attitude, as evidenced by the use of much less exacting tests of creditability. (Though generalization is difficult in this area, it seems safe to say that the United States has been concerned until recently primarily with assuring that credit is allowed only for taxes judged to be income taxes, but has been less concerned with limiting the amount of credit taken for taxes judged to qualify for its foreign tax credit; by comparison, some foreign countries have been less concerned about whether credit should be allowed for a particular tax and more with limiting the amount of the credit.) For this reason, and because of the overwhelming importance of U.S. investment in Colombia, the following discussion focusses on whether the consumption-based business tax portion of the Simplified Alternative Tax is likely to be creditable in the United States.

As explained in Chapter 5, an important criterion in establishing the creditability of a foreign tax in the United States is that it be based on net income, and therefore that it allow for the deductibility of all significant business expenses. The base of the consumption-based business tax proposed in this Report for consideration by the Government of Colombia clearly differs from a noncreditable gross receipts tax, since payments for material inputs and labor are deductible expenses under the consumption-based business tax. The major point of controversy is the treatment of capital expenses. The Simplified Alternative Tax does not treat interest payments as deductible expenses, but it allows immediate expensing of all purchases. It is important to know a) whether the first of these features would, if considered by itself, render the consumption-based business tax ineligible for the U.S. foreign tax credit and b) whether the second is sufficient to compensate for the disallowance of the interest deduction and restore creditability.

The answer to these questions cannot be known with certainty, since the U.S. Internal Revenue Service (I.R.S.) has never ruled on the issue; nor does the I.R.S. commonly make rulings in advance of the actual passage of legislation by a foreign country, though it might be possible to obtain an informal judgement on the issue, perhaps by having a potentially affected taxpayer raise the issue. Clearly the denial of deductions for interest payments would raise major foreign tax credit issues.

The discussion that follows considers the following topics: the general issue of whether allowing foreign tax credits for a system of direct taxation based on consumption, rather than on income, would appear to be consistent with U.S. policy objectives that motivate restrictions on eligibility for the credit; the more specific issue of whether the allowance of expensing under the Simplified Alternative Tax would be considered adequate to compensate for the disallowance of deductions for interest expense if such disallowance would otherwise render the Simplified Alternative Tax ineligible for the foreign tax credit in the United States; and whether remittance taxes imposed on dividends as part of a system based on the Simplified Alternative Tax would be creditable in the United States.

i) General analysis

In attempting to understand the attitude the United States I.R.S. would take toward the consumption-based business tax it may be instructive to examine the reasons that presumably underlie the United States policy of allowing credit only for taxes on net income. The basic point is that no credit should be allowed for gross receipts taxes, for severance taxes, for royalties, or for levies that are economically equivalent to one of these, though called income taxes. As a result, it has been stressed that in order for a tax to be creditable, deductions must be allowed for costs of earning income; in short, for the purpose at hand it seems reasonable to say that emphasis has been placed on the word **net** in the term «net income», rather than on the word **income**. This leaves open the question of whether a direct tax based on consumption rather than on income would be creditable. Since the combination of deductions allowed under the consumption-based system are more generous (in present value terms) than those under the income tax, rather than less, the concerns that have traditionally motivated U.S. denial of creditability would be absent in the case of the consumption-based business tax. (This argument is developed further below in the discussion of whether expensing provides adequate compensation for the failure to allow deductions for interest expense.) This suggests that it would be reasonable for credit to be allowed for the business tax portion of the Simplified Alternative Tax.[9/]

This line of argumentation suggests that it is quite possible that the creditability of the consumption-based business tax would not be challenged by the I.R.S. After all, the disallowance of the interest deduction (accompanied by expensing) is an integral component of a consumption-based system of direct taxation, just as deduction of interest expense (accompanied by depreciation allowances) is an integral component of an income-based system; it is not even remotely similar to the disallowance of deductions for business purchases that characterize gross receipts taxes that are clearly not creditable. It would be applied in an even-handed manner to Colombian firms as well as to foreign firms, and it would not discriminate against U.S. investors. (In particular, it would not be structured in such a way as merely to «soak up» the U.S. foreign tax credit — a feature that would doom the creditability of any levy patently structured for that purpose.) From this perspective, then, a consumption-based business tax may appear sufficiently similar to an income tax that it would be creditable in the United States. (The Simplified Alternative Tax differs in an important way from the U.S. income tax system; it would include gifts and bequests received in the base of the tax on individuals. Since such transfers are not treated as part of income in the United States, it might be important to specify clearly that the individual and business components of the Simplified Alternative Tax are two distinct, though related, levies in order to avoid jeopardizing the creditability of the business portion, which would not involve gifts and bequests).

On the other hand, conceptually the two taxes are clearly different. The base of the consumption-based business tax is not current income but instead is cash flow. If the government allows immediate

304

expensing of capital when it is put into service, the government becomes a partner in the firm's operations. If the venture is successful, the government's «dividend» is the tax revenue collected from the additional cash flow. If the venture is unsuccessful the government receives no return (or a negative return, considering the initial loss of tax revenues) on the funds it committed by allowing the entire purchase price of capital to reduce immediately the firm's tax liability in the year the investment was made. By this line of reasoning, the tax collected in the event of a successful investment simply represents a return to the government's investment and should not be regarded as a creditable tax.

The consumption-based business tax can, however, be seen to be similar to an income tax in its taxation of above-average profits. A firm expenses its capital immediately, but when this investment gives rise to an above-average return, the payment to the government is greater than necessary simply to compensate it for its initial investment. Above-average profits appear likely in protected markets where firms may have significant market power. Both the income tax and the consumption-based business tax would tax this excess profit at the statutory tax rate.[10]

ii) Specific issues

It is possible that an overly strict interpretation would be given to the rules for creditability. It can be argued that the lack of deductibility of interest expense constitutes presumptive evidence that credit should not be allowed for the consumption-based business tax. In that case, one important consideration is the following stipulation contained in U.S. tax regulations:

> A foreign tax law that does not permit recovery of one or more significant costs or expenses, but that provides allowances that effectively compensate for nonrecovery of such significant costs or expenses, is considered to permit recovery of such costs or expenses. (26 Code of Federal Regulations, sect. 1.901-2(b)(4)(i)).

In a similar vein a tax will be regarded as a net income tax (and therefore be creditable) when it allows:

> recovery of such significant costs and expenses computed under a method that is likely to produce an amount that approximates, or is greater than, recovery of such costs and expenses.

Under the proposed consumption-based business tax, even though interest expenses are not deductible, a compensating benefit of considerable value is the opportunity to expense all investment immediately. Indeed, the consumption-based business tax would compensate investors more than adequately for the non-deductibility of interest payments, since the marginal effective tax rate on new investment is zero. (See Chapter 8, where it is noted that the benefit from expensing a new marginal investment matches the taxes paid on the discounted present value of future cash flow, taking into account the inability to deduct interest payments from future receipts.) By comparison, under an income tax with real economic depreciation allowances and deductions for the real component of interest expense, the marginal effective tax rate would be equal to the statutory tax rate. The consumption-based business tax is thus clearly much more generous than a tax on real economic income. It would be unreasonable for the United States or any other country to expect any further compensation, such as deductions for interest expense, since any further deductions or credits would result in negative marginal effective tax rates and create inequities and/or the sort of losses in economic efficiency discussed in Chapter 4.[11]

It is true, of course, that for some highly leveraged firms, especially those with substantial working capital and few assets eligible for the benefits of expensing, the non-deductibility of current interest payments may not be offset by the benefit of expensing new investments. (It is thus possible that the tax treatment of land might affect the extent to which it can be claimed that compensation occurs.) Indeed, in any one year many firms may find that the benefits of expensing do not match the costs of disallowing interest deductions. However, the fact that a compensating benefit is not received by all firms in all years should not be sufficient reason to rule that a tax is non-creditable. Rather, under U.S. law the character of a tax is judged by the predominant effect on those that pay it. Thus the expected average long-term effect across all firms appears to be the more appropriate standard to apply. From that standpoint, there is no doubt that expensing should be judged to be adequate compensation for not allowing the deduction for interest expense. Even so, if the Simplified Alternative Tax is to be adopted, it would be well to draft the statute with issues of creditability in mind and to stand ready to produce statistical evidence that compensation for the disallowance of interest expense is adequate, on average.

iii) Withholding tax on dividends

Given that the consumption-based business tax yields no revenue in present value terms, except from infra-marginal investments, there are important revenue advantages of relying on withholding taxes to reach the income of foreign multinationals earned in Colombia. Whether the tax imposed on foreign remittances as part of the consumption-based strategy would be eligible for credit in the United States is thus likely to be a potentially more important issue than the creditability of the consumption-based business tax. Unfortunately, the creditability of the withholding tax probably would depend on whether the consumption-based business tax is creditable, for reasons to be specified below.

Historically, withholding taxes have commonly been deemed to be creditable under Section 901 of the U.S. Internal Revenue Code on the grounds that they constitute part of systems of income taxation. Seen in this light a withholding tax levied as part of the consumption-based strategy of direct taxation would presumably continue to be creditable, though this cannot be known with certainty. Under this interpretation the fact that it is consumption, rather than income, which is being taxed by Colombia should not cause the credit to be disallowed.

Withholding taxes do not fit neatly into the pattern of Section 901, because they are levied on gross payments, rather than allowing a deduction for expenses incurred in earning the income. More recently regulations interpreting the provisions of Section 903 of the Internal Revenue Code have been applied to this issue; they would presumably be controlling in this case, in which event an appeal to the logic of Section 901 would probably be pointless. Dividends are generally regarded as creditable under this section if they are levied in lieu of a generally applicable income tax. (This rationale is most clearly seen in the case of a dividend withholding tax which is collected by the host country government in lieu of the recipient of the dividend filing an income tax return in the host country). This line of reasoning suggests that the creditability of the remittance tax is likely to depend on the creditability of the consumption-based business tax.

In short, whether Colombian withholding taxes on dividend remittances would continue to be creditable in the United States if Colombia were to adopt the Simplified Alternative Tax cannot be known with certainty. The answer appears to depend in large part on the creditability of the underlying consumption-based business tax. Because of the residual uncertainty that remains, the discussion that follows considers both the case in which the Colombian Simplified Alternative Tax and the accompanying remittance taxes would be creditable against home-country taxes and the case in which the taxes would not be creditable.

b. The Importance of Creditability

Given the uncertainty about the creditability of the consumption-based business tax, it is important to know the implications if creditability is not granted. The examples presented in Chapter 8 to distinguish between an income tax and a consumption-based business tax are extended here to include the foreign tax consequences for a U.S. parent. As before, an asset is assumed to be purchased for $1000 on the last day of the year. At the end of the next year, the asset yields a certain amount of gross receipts and also has fully depreciated, leaving a scrap value of zero. To simplify the example it is assumed that there is no inflation. Consideration is given first to a marginal investment that yields a 10 percent return (gross receipts of $1100) and then to an investment yielding inframarginal returns of 20 percent (gross receipts of $1200). Finally, the position of an investment existing at the time the Simplified Alternative Tax is introduced is examined. The results of this analysis are summarized in Tables 9-1 to 9-3.

i. Marginal investment

Under an income tax, economic depreciation is allowed; the corresponding deduction is $1000. Interest payments also can be deducted; the actual amount of deductible interest will depend upon the source of financing for this investment. Assume that the investment is financed 50 percent by equity and 50 percent by debt, and that the real interest rate paid on debt outstanding is 10 percent. (For purpose of the examples it is assumed that the debt is held by an unrelated Colombian lender, to avoid the necessity of considering the tax implications if there is a foreign lender.) The deduction for interest paid is thus $50, taxable income is $50, and the Colombian income tax paid (calculated at the rate of 30 percent) is $15. If the entire after-tax return of $35 is remitted to the U.S. parent, a 30 percent Colombian withholding tax of $10.50 must also be paid. Total Colombian taxes paid are thus $25.50. (See Table 9-1).

The U.S. tax liability on this dividend income is $17 (34 percent of $50). Both the Colombian income and withholding taxes are creditable against this liability. Since in total they exceed the U.S. liability, no additional tax is paid to the U.S. Treasury. If the parent is in an excess foreign tax credit position, the Colombian tax burden of $25.50 is the total tax burden, so the after-tax earnings of the U.S. parent are $24.50. The excess Colombian tax over the creditable amount of $17 has the potential of discouraging U.S. investment in Colombia, as discussed in chapter 5.

If the U.S. parent is in a deficit credit position, the situation is quite different. The excess credits earned in Colombia can be used to offset taxes paid to other foreign countries, so the total net burden of the Colombian tax is only $17, and after-tax income of the parent is $33. (See the top left entries in Table 9-1.)

Under a consumption-based business tax, the gross receipts of $1100 generated by a marginal investment are exactly matched in present value terms by the $1000 expenditure on the asset that was expensed the preceding year. This equivalence, which is inherent in the consumption-based business tax, distinguishes that tax from an income tax. From an administrative point of view the benefit from expensing could be achieved in several alternative ways. If the deduction allowed in the initial year can be applied against income from other sources, the $300 tax saving in the initial year is equal in present value terms to the $330 tax paid in the second year on revenue generated by the expensed asset. If expensing were to lead to an initial loss that resulted in a refund, the same result would occur. Most governments are unwilling to pay refunds in such cases, but it is common to allow losses to be carried forward and offset against future income. If amounts carried forward are to retain their present value, they must be augmented at the market return (assumed to be 10 percent). If this is done the deduction claimed in the second year will just equal the receipts generated then.[12] In the latter case the base of the consumption-based business tax in the second year is zero and no business tax is collected on the $100 of capital income.

It may appear that the creditability of the consumption-based business tax in not an issue in this situation, since no tax liability is incurred in present value terms. Nevertheless, the issue is important to the extent that a ruling on the creditability of the consumption-based business tax also affects the creditability of the Colombian withholding tax on dividend remittances.

The treatment of withholding taxes is considered below under four possible circumstances: (1) both Colombian taxes are creditable in the United States and the U.S. parent firm is in a deficit foreign tax credit position; (2) both Colombian taxes are creditable in the United States and the U.S. parent firm is in an excess foreign tax credit position; (3) neither Colombian tax is creditable in the United States and the U.S. parent firm is in an excess credit position; and (4) neither Colombian tax is creditable in the United States and the U.S. parent firm is in a deficit credit position.

In the example above, interest of $50 must be paid out of the $100 of capital income. If the remaining $50 (inclusive of withholding tax) is remitted to a U.S. parent, then a withholding tax of 30 percent, or $15, is imposed. If the Colombian withholding tax is creditable in the United States, the U.S. income tax liability on the $35 dividend received is $17 (.34 x $35/(1-.30) or .34 x $50). Under these circumstances a U.S. parent firm in a deficit credit position must pay an additional $2 to the U.S. Treasury (the difference between the $17 U.S. liability and the withholding tax of $15 paid to Colombia), and after-tax profits of the U.S. parent are $33, as in the income tax case. (See the top half of the second column of Table 9-1).

As discussed in Chapter 5, though, the large majority of U.S. parent firms are likely to be in excess credit positions as a result of the statutory rate reduction (and other provisions) of the U.S. 1986 tax reform; that is, the amounts paid to foreign governments and potentially creditable in the United States are likely to exceed U.S. liability on foreign-source income for many U.S. firms. For firms in that position no additional U.S. tax would be paid even if Colombian taxes fall short of U.S. tax on Colombian-source income, since excess tax credits would absorb the difference. In that case, the U.S. parent's after-tax profits from Colombian source income are $35, a figure 43 percent greater than in the income tax case. (See the bottom half of Table 9-1).

If the withholding tax is not creditable in the United States, then the tentative U.S. tax liability is $11.90 (.34 x $35). In other words, the Colombian tax paid is deductible and the U.S. liability is calculated on the basis of income received after payment of Colombian taxes; this treatment means that the withholding tax has an effect comparable to a Colombian property tax or any other noncreditable tax.[13] However, this additional liability need not result in more taxes being paid to the U.S. Treasury if the parent firm has sufficient excess foreign tax credits from other foreign-source income. In that case, the U.S. parent's after-tax profits still would be $35.

On the other hand the U.S. parent must actually pay the $11.90 U.S. liability if no credit is allowed for the $15 Colombian withholding tax and the firm is in a deficit foreign tax credit position. In that case its total tax payments on the Colombian- source income will be $26.90 and its after-tax profits $23.10. (See the top half of the third column in Table 9-1). The sharp decline in after-tax earnings, by 30 percent in comparison with the income tax scenario, demonstrates why creditability potentially is an important issue. Nevertheless, without a more accurate indication of the foreign tax credit position of foreign firms currently operating in Colombia (or contemplating future operations in the country), the appropriate weight to attach to this negative outcome is far from clear.

ii. Inframarginal investment

The possible loss of creditability under the Simplified Alternative Tax has somewhat different implications if the investment undertaken earns an above-average return. A simplified example again indicates the implications of shifting from an income tax to a noncreditable cash flow tax. (The results in this case are presented in Table 9-2).

Begin with the same $1000 investment discussed above, but now assume gross receipts are 20 percent of the amount invested, or $1200. In the case of an income tax, the taxable base will be gross receipts less economic depreciation and real interest paid: $1200–$1000–$50 = $150. Colombian income tax at a 30 percent rate will be $45. If all after-tax earnings are remitted to the United States, a withholding tax of $31.50 is collected (.30 x $105). Total Colombian taxes paid are thus $76.50. The U.S. tax liability is 34 percent of $150, or $51. If the U.S. parent is in an excess foreign tax credit position, this liability is less than the creditable Colombian tax; the firm pays no residual tax to the U.S. Treasury and is left with after-tax profits of $73.50. (See the bottom half of table 9-1, column one).

If the U.S. parent instead is in a deficit foreign tax credit position, the net additional taxes it pays on its Colombian source income is simply $51, the tentative U.S. liability on that income. Even though the income received from Colombia generates foreign tax credits that exceed the U.S. liability on that income, the excess credits can be used to offset U.S. tax due on other foreign source income. Because of this additional tax saving, the U.S. parent's after-tax profits in the situation depicted above are $99; the increase in profits of $25.50 represents a transfer from the U.S. Treasury to the firm. (See the top half of Table 9-2, column one.) As pointed out previously, this situation is likely to be observed for only a small minority of firms, given the 1986 changes in U.S. tax law. In the case of a consumption-based business tax the present value of the taxable base will be $100, a figure derived from gross receipts of $1200 less the value in year two of being able to expense immediately the purchase price of the asset, $1100. In present value terms a consumption-based business tax of $30 is collected. Also, interest of $50 must be paid. If the remaining cash flow of $120 is remitted to the U.S. parent, a withholding tax of $36 is imposed. Thus total Colombian taxes paid are $66.

In the case where both the consumption-based business tax and the withholding tax are creditable, the U.S. parent's tax liability on this remitted income is $51 (.34 x $150). That is, the relevant base for determining the U.S. liability is the cash dividend received, plus the creditable Colombian business tax, which is deemed to be paid by the recipient of the dividend.

When the U.S. parent is in an excess foreign tax credit position, it pays no additional tax to the U.S. Treasury on its Colombian-source income. Its after-tax income is $84, a figure 14 percent greater than obtained in the income tax example.

If the U.S. parent instead is in a deficit foreign tax credit position, its total tax burden on Colombian-source income is $51, as in the income tax case. Again, the income received from Colombia generates foreign tax credits that exceed the U.S. liability on the income, but the excess credits can be used to offset U.S. tax due on other foreign source income. The U.S. parent's after-tax profits are $99, but in this case the transfer from the U.S. Treasury to the firm is only $15. (See the second column in the top half of Table 9-2).

In the case where neither Colombian tax is creditable in the United States, the U.S. parent receives $84 net of all Colombian taxes, and that figure is the base on which its U.S. tax liability is determined. Consequently, the firm's U.S. liability is $28.56 (.34 x $84). If the parent has sufficient excess foreign tax credits, then no tax is actually paid to the U.S. Treasury as a result of earning income in Colombia; again, the parent's after-tax income of $84 exceeds the amount available under the income tax by 14 percent. (See the third column in the bottom half of Table 9-2).

If instead the parent is in a deficit foreign tax credit position, then its total tax payments are $94.56 (Colombian tax of $66 plus U.S. tax of $28.56) and its after-tax income is $55.44, 44 percent less than under the income tax. (See the third column in the top half of Table 9-2.) The benefit to U.S. firms of expensing is even less likely in the case of inframarginal investment than in the case of marginal investment to offset the loss of creditability of both the consumption-based business tax and the withholding tax.

iii. Existing investment

The two examples just considered apply to the situation where a new investment is made. Over the long run when all capital depreciates and must be replaced, this perspective is the appropriate one to use in evaluating the consequences of a change in tax policy. However, an important transition issue to consider is the effect of a shift from income to consumption-based business tax treatment on tax revenues from existing capital. With little remaining basis to expense in existing assets, firms will likely find that gross receipts are offset by fewer deductions than shown in the examples above. Owners of existing capital must pay a larger share of their gross receipts to the Colombian government, and if this Colombian tax is not creditable in the United States, foreign owners suffer a large windfall loss.

The following example illustrates this possibility. Suppose that $1100 of receipts are generated by an asset that has no remaining depreciable basis. (Depreciation has been taken in prior years, reducing income at that time.) Under the income tax real interest payments of $50 are deductible, giving taxable income of $1050 and Colombian income tax receipts of $315. If the after-tax income of $735 is remitted to the U.S. parent, a withholding tax of $220.50 is collected. If the U.S. parent firm is in an excess foreign tax credit position, total tax payments to the Colombian government, $535.50, exceed the U.S. tax liability of $357 (.34 x $1050). No additional taxes are paid to the U.S. Treasury, and after-tax earnings are $514.50. (See the bottom half of Table 9-3).

If the U.S. parent firm is in a deficit foreign tax credit position, the excess credits generated by the Colombian tax payments offset the parent's U.S. tax liability on other foreign source income. Given the latter tax saving, net additional taxes paid on Colombian source income are $357 and after-tax profits are $693. (See the top half of Table 9-3).

Applying the consumption-based business tax under the same economic circumstances results in a tax liability of $330 (.30 x $1100). (It is assumed in this example that deductions for interest expense are disallowed immediately; even if they are not, the result in this example would not be affected dramatically.) After payment of this tax and the $50 of interest expense, $720 is remitted to the U.S. parent, and a Colombian withholding tax of $216 is paid. If both Colombian taxes are creditable, the tentative tax liability of the U.S. parent is $357 (.34 x 1050). Total Colombian taxes paid are $546.

If the U.S. parent is in an excess foreign tax credit position, then total taxes paid are $546 and after-tax profits are $504. After-tax profits are lower than in the income tax case because real interest expenses are not a deductible expense in determining the consumption based business tax liability in Colombia and there is no offsetting benefit from expensing, as in Tables 9-1 and 9-2. (See the second column in the bottom half of Table 9-3).

310

If the U.S. parent is in a deficit foreign tax credit position, then the total tax burden on Colombian source income is $357, as determined by the U.S. tax rate. The parent firm's after-tax profits are $693, the same as in the income tax example. (See the second column in the top half of Table 9-3).

If both Colombian taxes are noncreditable, the U.S. firm receives $504 net of Colombian taxes. The tentative U.S. tax liability is $171.36 (.34 x $504). If the U.S. firm has sufficient excess foreign tax credits, no payment to the U.S. Treasury is made, and the parent firm's after-tax profits are $504. (See the third column in the bottom half of Table 9-3). When the U.S. firm is in a deficit foreign tax credit position, the total tax burden is $717.36 and the parent's after-tax profits are $332.64. (See the third column in the top half of Table 9-3). Compared to the examples of new investment presented above, the penalty that results from noncreditability is even larger, as after-tax profits are 52 percent less than under the income tax.

This particularly adverse short-term result rests on the rather extreme assumption that a determination of noncreditability would take effect immediately. In actuality, adoption of the proposal to phase in the implementation of the Simplified Alternative Tax would force a more difficult judgement by the United States. Specifically, if the creditability of the consumption-based business tax were to be challenged, the U.S. would have to determine the point at which the nondeductibility of interest payments would imply the disallowance of a significant enough cost element to warrant a ruling of noncreditability. The phased implementation of the Simplified Alternative Tax ensures that whenever a ruling of noncreditability might take place, a smaller share of the capital stock would be represented by assets that are fully depreciated and have derived no benefits from expensing.

In summary, it seems reasonable to expect the consumption-based business tax to be judged a creditable tax by the United States. This judgement is based in part on the fact that the tax clearly does not pose the type of problem that has traditionally motivated to United States to deny creditability and in part on the fact that it seems clearly to meet the compensation criterion discussed presented above. It should be emphasized, however, that under U.S. law, such a ruling cannot be guaranteed. It is likely that the creditability of the withholding tax applied to dividends would depend on the creditability of the consumption-based business tax, though again this cannot be known with certainty.

It is also important that not too much weight should be placed on the creditability issue. As noted earlier, many taxes paid to foreign governments by U.S. corporations will not be allowed as credits, even though they are creditable in principle, because of the 1986 changes in the U.S. tax law. For such taxpayers that are in an excess foreign tax credit position there is little practical difference between a tax being ineligible for the foreign tax credit and its being noncreditable because the firm has paid more foreign taxes than it can credit. In the case of U.S. parent firms in deficit foreign tax credit positions a finding of noncreditability would have its greatest effect on owners of existing capital, particularly if that capital were largely debt financed. Even in the case of new investment, the deterrent effect would be significant. Although firms that would owe residual tax liabilities in their home countries appear to represent a minority among foreigners investing in Colombia, the exact proportion cannot be established without access to confidential taxpayer information. If thought necessary, it might be possible to modify the applicability of the Simplified Alternative Tax to foreign firms, in a way which preserves creditability in foreign countries, but speculation about how this might be done appears premature.

2. Treatment of Investment Abroad by Colombians

Officially registered Colombian investment abroad is a small fraction of foreign investment by Colombians. Foreign exchange constraints have meant that only a few types of investments receive the necessary administrative approval from the Department of Planning and the Central Bank. For this limited approved activity, parallel treatment to the purchase of shares in a domestic firm suggests that the purchase of shares in a foreign firm be treated as a nondeductible expense under the Simplified Alternative Tax, and that any subsequent return on this investment be excluded from the Colombian firm's taxable base. Similar treatment would apply to the purchase of other financial assets such as bonds. However, if foreign transactions were to be treated identically to domestic investment in real assets, a purchase of plant or equipment in a foreign country would be expensed immediately. That situation potentially would result in foreign losses offsetting the tax liability on domestic receipts. While this result might seem appropriate under the Colombian system of taxing worldwide income, it opens the door to widespread abuse through the overstatement of foreign losses that can be audited only with great difficulty.

Countries with territorial systems of taxation, particularly France, have long been concerned about that latter situation. This concern, along with others, has caused them to choose a tax system in which foreign losses cannot flow through to reduce the tax liability on domestic income. Given its limited administrative ability to verify any losses claimed abroad, Colombia also should share this concern. Although it is not recommended that Colombia convert its tax system from its current worldwide basis to a territorial basis, it is proposed that Colombia establish a separate category or income basket for all foreign investment activity, and that it not distinguish between real and financial investment, as would be appropriate if totally parallel treatment instead were to be accorded domestic and foreign transactions. Under the proposed system, the purchase of any financial or real assets abroad results in a negative entry on the firm's cash flow account. If a loss results, it can be carried forward with interest to apply against future cash flow generated by those investments. However, such losses cannot be combined with domestic income at any time. By statute, income earned abroad would not escape Colombian taxation; this is perhaps a more attractive stand to take politically than ignoring both the initial expenditure and the subsequent income earned. In actuality, little revenue would be collected from Colombian investment abroad, due to the difficulty of ensuring that all foreign revenue is declared. Nevertheless, the creation of separate baskets avoids the situation in which foreign losses can be combined with domestic receipts to reduce the firm's business tax liability in Colombia. The latter outcome is particularly undesirable because such a loss in tax revenue requires higher taxes on domestic activity to make up the shortfall, a result that would be considered highly unfair and contrary to Colombian development strategy. Of course, administration of both the income tax and the Simplified Alternative Tax requires vigilant attention to transfer pricing and cost allocation practices that transfer income abroad while expenses are deducted against Colombian source income.

C. Individual Tax Issues

The major issues in the construction of the individual component of the Simplified Alternative Tax are the tax treatment of gifts and bequests, the choice between the ITP and ICF approaches to the taxation of individual consumption, the progressivity of the marginal tax rate structure, and the treatment of individual foreign investment. These issues are examined in turn.

1. The Treatment of Gifts and Bequests

The treatment of gifts and bequests to other individuals is a contentious issue under both income and consumption taxes. The questions raised are generally the same under both types of taxes; the essential question is whether gifts and bequests should be taxed to both the donor and the recipient. Yet, the issue is more critical under the consumption tax. One widely accepted purpose of the taxation of transfers is to reduce inequalities in the distribution of wealth. Under an income tax, this purpose is furthered by the taxation of capital income. In contrast, capital income is untaxed under a consumption tax (unless the consumption tax is supplemented by a net wealth tax). As a result, the tax treatment of gifts and bequests is more critical under a consumption tax than under an income tax, since it is relatively more important as a means of reducing inequalities in the distribution of wealth under the former.

Gifts and bequests can be treated in one of two ways under a consumption tax (as well as under an income tax). There is fairly wide agreement among tax experts that gifts and inheritances received represent additional ability to pay; this in turn implies that the fair market value of such transfers should, at least in principle, be included in the tax base of the recipient. However, the appropriate tax treatment of the individual making the gift or bequest is much less clear. There are two schools of thought on this issue.

According to one view, gifts and bequests should be taxed to the donor, as well as to the recipient. The rationale for this position is that the tax base over the lifetime of an individual should equal all of the resources at his command — earned income and gifts and inheritances received — irrespective of whether some of these resources are used to fund the making of gifts and bequests. Accordingly, this view is commonly referred to as the «lifetime endowment» view of tax equity. Note that it implies that for tax purposes gifts and bequests should be treated in the same way as consumption; that is, the donor should not receive a deduction for making such transfers any more than he should receive a deduction for other consumption expenditures.

The alternative view is that a deduction should in fact be allowed to the donor for the making of gifts and bequests to other individuals. According to this view, such transfers increase the potential to consume of the recipient, but do not represent consumption on the part of the donor. In the consumption tax context, this implies that the tax base over the lifetime of the individual should include gifts and inheritances received but should be reduced by the amount of gifts and bequests given. Thus, the tax base is consumption narrowly defined, with tax paid on gifts and bequests only when they are actually consumed by the recipient. Accordingly, this view is commonly referred to as the «dynastic» view of tax equity, since it implies that tax should be assessed only when resources are actually consumed by some member of a family that spans many generations.

The implications of these two views for the treatment of gifts and bequests under the ICF and ITP consumption taxes are profound. As noted above, the fair market value of gifts and bequests received is included in the tax base of the recipient in all cases. For the ICF tax, the lifetime endowment view clearly implies that amounts withdrawn from a qualified account and used to fund the making of a gift or bequest should be included in the tax base of the donor; that is, the amount withdrawn should be included in the tax base and no offsetting deduction should be allowed the donor for the transfer. In contrast, the dynastic view implies that such a deduction should in fact be allowed for amounts transferred, rather than consumed. Thus, withdrawals from a qualified account used to fund the making of gifts and bequests would be offset by the deduction, so that there would be no tax consequences to the donor.

The treatment under the ITP tax is determined by the fact that tax has been prepaid on both savings and the return to savings, so that withdrawals from savings do not result in tax liability; that is, relative to the ICF case, the tax on such withdrawals has been prepaid since no deduction for saving was allowed. Accordingly, the lifetime endowment view simply implies that no deduction should be allowed for the making of gifts and bequests, while the dynastic view implies that such a deduction should be allowed. In the latter case, such deductions would offset other receipts in the individual tax base, and refunds might be required.

An alternative means of constructing an ITP tax that is roughly consistent with the dynastic view of tax equity is also sometimes recommended. This approach takes account of two problems associated with the method of implementing the dynastic view under an ITP tax described above. First, the administrative and enforcement problems associated with including the fair market value of gifts and bequests received in the tax base of the recipient are significant. Second, granting tax deductions and perhaps refunds to big donors is unattractive from a political standpoint. In response to these problems, proponents of the dynastic view sometimes suggest that a «proxy» or «surrogate» tax approach be used under the ITP approach. Specifically, they recommend that no deduction be allowed for gifts and bequests made, and that gifts and inheritances received not be included in the tax base of the recipient. In this case, the tax paid by the donor is viewed as a proxy for the tax liability that should in theory be assessed on the recipient.[14] Of course, such a proxy tax will be inaccurate to the extent that the tax rates of the donor and recipient differ.

It is clear that the choice between these two alternative views of tax equity depends on a large number of factors, many of which are more philosophical than economic in nature. Nevertheless, the Government of Colombia should consider only those consumption (or income) tax reform alternatives that are consistent with the lifetime endowment view of tax equity. This recommendation is based on three considerations.

First, a tax system based on the lifetime endowment view will probably be more equitable than one based on the dynastic view; it certainly will be perceived as being fairer. Most tax experts in Colombia, as well as the general public, probably think about vertical equity in terms of annual individual tax burdens. As a result, even the lifetime perspective implicit in the lifetime view of equity represents a significant departure from conventional views. Such a perspective can plausibly be explained as a means of assuring that a tax system is characterized by horizontal equity between individuals with equal lifetime endowments, as well as vertical equity across individuals with differing lifetime endowments. Nevertheless, some prominent tax experts believe that a standard of equity based on a single year, or perhaps several years, is a more reasonable one.[15] Given the degree of disagreement about this point, it seems that the dynastic view of equity, which represents a much greater departure from conventional views, is unlikely to be acceptable as the underlying rationale for the tax treatment of gifts and bequests in Colombia.

This viewpoint is supported by the fact that the current individual income tax system of Colombia is characterized by progressive rates and is supplemented by an individual net wealth tax. This suggests that the social consensus regarding vertical equity requires a tax burden that is progressive with respect to annual income. (Note, however, that this conclusion must be qualified to the extent that Colombians accept tax evasion and poor administration as means to reduce the progressivity of the current income tax.) The construction of a consumption tax that has a tax burden across income classes that is similar to that of current law can be achieved much more easily if the lifetime endowment view is adopted. Indeed, it may be very difficult, as well as costly in terms of reduced economic incentives and increased tax avoidance and evasion due to higher tax rates on wealthy individuals, to achieve such a distributional result without adopting this viewpoint. Thus, vertical equity in Colombia is much more likely to be achieved if the reform proposal adopted is consistent with the lifetime endowment view of tax equity.

Second, the inclusion of gifts and inheritances as occasional gains under the Colombian individual income tax suggests that taxation of such transfers conforms with societal norms. It also suggests that allowing wealthy heirs to consume tax-free — under the «proxy tax» alternative version of the dynastic view — would not be widely acceptable. Moreover, it implies that the inclusion of gifts and bequests in the tax base of the recipient will not represent as drastic a change from the status quo as it would in many countries, and thus should be relatively easier to implement.

Third, income tax proponents frequently argue that the accumulation of wealth confers status, power, and peace of mind that should be included in measures of ability to pay. This argument is likely to be valid in Colombia where wealth differences are very great and an individual net wealth tax is already in place. Such reasoning supports the taxation of individual wealth — whether inherited, received as a gift, or accumulated from the taxpayer's own labor income — at least once during each generation.

These reasons provide a compelling rationale for evaluating tax reform proposals in Colombia from the perspective of the lifetime endowment view of tax equity.[16/] Accordingly, the Simplified Alternative-Tax is constructed to be consistent with that viewpoint. As noted above, this implies that the fair market value of gifts and inheritances received should be included in the tax base of the recipient and that donors should receive no deduction for giving gifts or leaving bequests.

Two important qualifications accompany this recommendation. First, as noted above, assuring the inclusion of gifts and bequests in the tax base of the recipient is very difficult from an administrative standpoint. Evasion is always a problem, as it is extremely difficult for tax administrators to uncover unreported transfers, especially between family members. Moreover, once gifts and bequests received are identified, they should be included in the tax base of the recipient at fair market value. Accurate valuations are frequently difficult to obtain, especially for interests in closely-held businesses and other items that are traded infrequently (such as art and other collectibles). For the Simplified Alternative Tax to be a fair tax from the perspective of the lifetime view of tax equity, serious efforts must be made to administer and enforce the recommended treatment of gifts and bequests as effectively as possible.[17/] This will increase the complexity of the tax system, add to administrative and compliance costs, and undoubtedly still result in a system that will leave many such transfers untaxed. However, note that it is recommended below that the Simplified Alternative Tax be supplemented with a reformed version of the current net wealth tax in Colombia. As a result, remaining deficiencies in administering and enforcing the taxation of gifts and bequests received will be at least partially offset in an indirect fashion through the improved taxation of the net wealth of the donors and recipients of such transfers (as occurs under the combination of the income tax and the net wealth tax).

Second, it should be noted that the equity gains obtained by structuring the Simplified Alternative Tax to be consistent with the lifetime endowment view will be partially offset by some efficiency costs, as well as by the administrative costs described above. For example, individual decisions regarding the making of gifts and bequests, as well as their nature (e.g., easily traceable transfers of real estate vs. more easily hidden transfers of cash or «in kind» transfers such as expensive educations that are unlikely to be taxable), will be distorted. In addition, the return to saving is reduced by taxation of gifts and bequests; this implies that some of the intertemporal neutrality benefits of reducing the taxation of capital income under a consumption-based tax (to be discussed in Chapter 10) will be reduced. Nevertheless, the arguments for the lifetime endowment view are compelling; thus it is recommended that the Government of Colombia consider only those tax reform options consistent with that view.

Given this decision, it may be useful to note that the numerical examples comparing consumption and income taxation in Chapter 8 are basically unchanged when gifts and bequests are considered. That is, as long as gifts and bequests received are included in the tax base and there are no deductions for gifts and bequests given (which are thus treated as consumption of the donor under the ICF tax), the numerical comparisons of the income and ICF and ITP consumption taxes are basically unchanged. To see this, note that gifts or bequests received would simply be included in the tax base and in the calculation of the present value of the individual's endowment. In terms of the two-period example analyzed above, gifts and inheritances received could be examined by separating W1 into $3,000 of wages and $1,000 of inheritance. Since no deduction is allowed for gifts and bequests made, the division of C2 into a consumption and a bequest component has no tax consequences. Thus, all results regarding the differences between income and consumption taxes, as well as the similarities between the ICF and ITP approaches, obtain when gifts and bequests are treated as specified above.

2. The Choice Between the ITP and ICF Approaches

The second major decision in the construction of the Simplified Alternative Tax is the choice between the cash flow and tax prepayment approaches at the individual level. This decision is perhaps the most difficult one in designing a tax based on consumption, and involves a host of primarily technical considerations. This section provides a brief summary of the rationale for choosing the ITP approach for the Simplified Alternative Tax; a detailed analysis appears in the appendix to this chapter.

The primary reason for choosing a tax based on the ITP approach over the ICF approach is that the former method avoids all of the complexity associated with the qualified accounts inherent in the ICF approach. This complexity takes many forms. The use of qualified accounts necessarily implies that saving (and dis-saving) and loans (and their repayment) have greater tax consequences than they would under either the ITP approach or an income tax. This adds complexity in and of itself; for example, estimated tax payments, and perhaps withholding, should reflect saving and loan transactions. Monitoring and compliance costs would be great, especially with large potential gains to reporting fraudulent saving and loans and not reporting withdrawals from qualified accounts. This would very likely increase the complexity of withholding. The treatment of the proceeds of loans under the ICF alternative would be completely new to Colombia. The treatment of interest under this approach would correspond to that under current law; it would thus involve all of the problems that currently plague the administration and enforcement of the taxation of interest under the Colombian income tax.

Moreover, the existence of qualified accounts opens avenues for abuse through loans and other forms of «tax base shifting» to lower-bracket relatives.[18/] Some of the problems associated with the ICF approach might be avoided if it included a provision that allowed some amount of outstanding debt to be treated on a tax prepayment basis; however, such an exception would give rise to a variety of administrative and enforcement problems as well. Finally, international considerations would complicate the administration of the ICF approach; however, as described above, potentially significant avoidance opportunities involving international transactions also exist under the ITP approach.

In addition to the simplicity argument, four additional factors argue for the adoption of the ITP rather than the ICF approach. First, the combination of an ICF tax with a consumption-based business tax results in some cases in the double taxation of the returns to entrepreneurship; this problem is avoided under an ITP tax.[19/] Second, the treatment of housing and consumer durables is somewhat simpler under the ITP approach. Third, transitional issues (which are problematical under either approach) are arguably more easily solved under an ITP tax. Finally, treatment of gifts and bequests which is consistent with the lifetime endowment view of equity is arguably more easily attainable from a political standpoint under the ITP approach.

Not surprisingly, several of the differences between the ITP and ICF approaches favor the latter; three of these are particularly significant. First, the ICF approach would be perceived as a more equitable tax, since the tax base would be actual consumption rather than «potential» consumption as under the tax prepayment approach. As noted above (and explained more fully in the appendix), this distinction is without economic significance in many cases; nevertheless it is valid under certain circumstances and would be perceived to be valid in virtually all cases. Second, recall that the ITP approach combines cash flow treatment of receipts and expenditures under the business tax with tax prepayment treatment of capital income at the individual level. This may result in some avoidance opportunities due to manipulation of business cash flow and individual tax prepayment accounts, which would be avoided entirely under the individual cash flow approach. However, this problem is minimized with broad coverage of the business tax. Finally, the ICF approach provides the taxpayer a natural mechanism for averaging that is absent with an ITP tax.

On balance, the argument for the ITP approach on simplicity grounds is a fairly strong one. The discussion above (and in the appendix) indicates that treatment of most transactions would be considerably simpler under the ITP approach that under an ICF tax. The other points considered either favor the ITP approach somewhat, or are not sufficiently important to outweigh its simplicity advantages. Accordingly, it is proposed that the Simplified Alternative Tax include an individual tax which follows the ITP approach; the remainder of the report focuses on this approach.

3. The Rate Structure

Some proponents of an ITP tax advocate applying a single tax rate to the individual tax base (which would allow personal exemptions and a standard deduction); this rate would equal the tax rate applied to the business tax base.[20] Such an approach has significant simplicity advantages. In particular, it allows generally accurate «proxy» taxation at the business level. For example, employer-provided consumption benefits and fringe benefits can be taxed by disallowing firms a deduction for such expenditures rather than by attributing them to employees for taxation under the individual tax; such a proxy tax would be accurate since the tax rates of the individual and of the firm would be identical. Moreover, a single individual rate greatly reduces opportunities for avoidance schemes based on «tax base shifting» to relatives with lower tax rates.[21]

However, adoption of a single rate individual tax structure would have extremely adverse effects on the vertical equity of the Colombian tax system; indeed, it would make it virtually impossible to achieve the goal of distributional neutrality described in Chapter 1 without net wealth tax rates that are so high as to be economically undesirable and politically unrealistic. Accordingly, it is recommended that the individual component of the Simplified Alternative Tax include a progressive rate structure. This follows the practice of current law, which suggests that a moderately progressive rate structure conforms with social norms in Colombia.[22]

4. The Treatment of Individual Investment Abroad

As discussed above, in considering the treatment of business investment abroad, a tax policy concern under the Simplified Alternative Tax is the possibility that negative cash flow from portfolio investment abroad will offset domestic tax liabilities. Under the current income tax, that result does not occur because many Colombians have avoided all domestic tax implications from foreign portfolio investment by not channeling their foreign investment through the Central Bank; neither their investments abroad, nor any income generated from them, have been reported to any branch of Colombian government (Banco de la República, DIN, etc). This current tax evasion results in an outcome under the income tax that is comparable to that under the tax prepayment form of the Simplified Alternative Tax, although at present this advantage accrues to foreign investment but not to all domestic investment. The tax prepayment approach does avoid the potential problem of a fall in Colombian tax revenue if negative foreign cash flow were to be consolidated with domestic receipts.

Although current practice may approximate tax prepayment on foreign portfolio investment because of extensive tax evasion, the Colombian government still may not want to signal publicly that it is giving up all claim to tax receipts of its residents that happen to be generated abroad. Such a position may be particularly premature before Colombian experience under the Simplified Alternative Tax shows whether the transfer of taxable income outside the country can be effectively controlled. Rejecting residence-based taxation also may seem outwardly inconsistent with the goal of promoting capital formation and development in Colombia. Perhaps advances in electronic record keeping and information exchanges between tax authorities of different countries may result in evasion of Colombian taxes becoming less feasible or attractive in the future than it is at present. (See McLure 1987 for a more pessimistic assessment of any prospects for improvement in this regard).

Therefore it is proposed that individuals also be required to report all foreign investment activity in a separate basket which will receive cash flow treatment. In this context purchases of foreign stocks and bonds are deductible expenditures that can create initial losses; those losses can be carried forward with interest, but can only be used to offset tax due on other foreign source income.

II. Details of the Simplified Alternative Tax

The major structural features of the Simplified Alternative Tax have been specified in the previous section. However, a wide variety of additional issues arise in the construction of this proposed alternative to income tax reform. This section considers these issues, and explains how each should be resolved in the construction of the Simplified Alternative Tax. It begins with business tax issues, focusing on the coverage of the business tax, the treatment of certain deductions, and various possibilities for tax avoidance. It then discusses several individual tax issues, including the need for averaging, the treatment of housing, consumer durables and collectibles, and the treatment of lottery winnings, prizes and awards. It also comments on the relationship between the Simplified Alternative Tax and the existing net wealth tax and the taxation of presumptive income in Colombia. Finally, it discusses the transition rules recommended for the proposal.

A. Coverage of the Business Tax and Withholding Rules

1. Defining a Business

Under the Simplified Alternative Tax, the sales receipts and expenditures of businesses are taxed on a cash flow basis, while the investment activities of individuals are treated on a tax prepayment basis. An implication of this differential treatment is that the definition of a «business» should be as broad as possible in order to reduce opportunities for tax avoidance techniques that take advantage of such differential treatment to reduce tax liability.

The essential nature of such avoidance schemes can be illustrated with the following example. Suppose a business and an individual are joint partners in a venture. (In the extreme case, the individual would be the owner of the business.) To reduce the joint tax burden of the individual and the company, the partnership could attempt to assign a disproportionate share of the expenses to the business in order to qualify for deductions from the cash flow tax; it would simultaneously attempt to attribute a disproportionate share of the receipts to the individual tax prepayment account where they would be free from tax.

The most effective way of eliminating such abuses is to define as narrowly as possible the activities which qualify for individual tax prepayment treatment, and to subject all other activities to cash flow treatment under the business tax. Accordingly, individual investment activities eligible for tax prepayment treatment should be limited to debt instruments, interests in taxable Colombian businesses, including all closely-held businesses (which would be subject to cash flow treatment at the business level), personal residences, and personal use property (including consumer durables). All other activities would be treated as businesses, and individuals engaging in such activities would be required to file business tax returns.[23/] Although this would result in a large number of business returns being filed, the limitation it places on the potential for tax abuse seems worth the additional complexity. Moreover, in many cases, the information required for filing the business return would be fairly minimal and would not result in significant compliance or administrative problems.

Several features of the recommended treatment are noteworthy. First, individual portfolio investment abroad would be treated on a cash flow basis. Of course, under such an approach, taxpayers would be much more likely to report deductions for making foreign portfolio investments than they would be to report the returns to such investments (or disinvestments). To limit the revenue loss from tax evasion in this area, it is recommended that losses on such investments should not be allowed to offset receipts generated by activities other than foreign portfolio investment under the individual tax.[24/] Thus, individuals would be required to keep a segregated cash flow account — or «basket» — for foreign portfolio investment. Such treatment is desirable primarily because the two alternatives of either tax prepayment treatment of foreign portfolio investment or allowing the use of foreign portfolio losses to reduce domestic tax liability under a cash flow approach would both suffer from severe perception problems.

Second, dealers in securities would be treated like any other business. That is, they would be subject to cash flow taxation of receipts and expenditures under the business tax component of the Simplified Alternative Tax.

Third, no special provisions requiring cash flow treatment for the individual investments of «large» or very wealthy investors are recommended. The theoretical case for such special treatment is weak, and any special provisions would be difficult to administer and enforce. Presumably, such a proposal would be recommended in response to the equity argument that individual tax prepayment treatment of wealthy investors is unfair. However, as will be discussed below, the Simplified Alternative Tax should be supplemented by a modified version of the existing Colombian net wealth tax. Such treatment should reduce any equity concerns about tax prepayment treatment of the individual investments of wealthy investors.

Fourth, the extent of aggregation of business activities on an individual's business tax return must be specified. In general, simplicity considerations suggest that any individual taxpayer engaged in one or more wholly-owned activities that qualify as a business for tax purposes should be allowed to aggregate all such business activities under the business tax component of the Simplified Alternative Tax. In this case, each taxpayer engaged in a business would have to file only a single business return; under such an approach, losses from one business would be allowed to offset income of another business.

However, two important problems would arise with such completely unlimited aggregation. First, the use of foreign business losses to offset domestic income would present significant perception problems. Moreover, in many cases, it would be relatively easy for businesses to understate foreign receipts and thereby generate losses; a significant tax avoidance opportunity would arise if such losses could be used to reduce domestic tax liability.[25/] Second, a common tax avoidance technique is the use of so-called «hobby farms» which generate losses but provide the owners with untaxed consumption benefits. Again, a significant tax avoidance opportunity would arise if such losses could be used to offset other business income.[26/]

In order to deal with these two avoidance problems, taxpayers should be required to segregate the profits and losses associated with foreign business investment and with agricultural investment from the profits and losses realized in other activities. That is, separate business cash flow returns would have to be filed for such activities, and losses incurred in these activities could not be used to offset the receipts generated by any other business activity. Thus, three activities would be required to use segregated cash flow accounts — individual foreign portfolio investment, all business investment abroad, and business investment in agriculture. Joint ventures abroad would be included in the business foreign investment basket. Again, such treatment adds complexity to the Simplified Alternative Tax in order to limit opportunities for tax avoidance; however, these provisions would affect relatively few individuals and firms. Note that similar problems arise under the income tax; as a result, such treatment of agriculture is already in place under current Colombian law.[27/]

Fifth, in the interest of simplicity, firms would generally be allowed to consolidate returns; thus, a firm and all of its wholly-owned subsidiaries chartered under Colombian law would be allowed to file a single return.[28/] However, to simplify administration, especially the auditing process, joint ventures and less than wholly-owned subsidiaries would be required to file a separate business tax return.

Finally, under current Colombian law, certain unincorporated partnerships are not treated as separate taxpayers; rather, receipts and expenses flow through to the joint owners of the enterprise. In general, uniform treatment of all business activities is appropriate; this implies that such businesses would be required to file a business tax return, and individual interests in the firms would be subject to taxation on a prepayment basis under the individual component of the Simplified Alternative Tax. However, if deemed desirable for administrative or other reasons, it would be possible to maintain the current law distinction that does not treat certain unincorporated partnerships as separate taxpayers; in this case, receipts and expenses related to such jointly-owned property would be allocated to the individual owners and would be subject to tax under the individual component of the Simplified Alternative Tax. Such treatment would reduce the number of business tax returns filed.

2. The Filing Threshold

A de minimis rule exempting small businesses and individuals who engage in business activities on only very rare occasions would clearly be desirable on simplicity grounds. Taxing such business activities would produce very little revenue while resulting in compliance and administrative costs (which quite conceivably could be greater than the revenue raised).

Nevertheless, exempting certain small businesses creates problems as well. Exempt businesses would effectively be on a tax prepayment basis; this would result in the avoidance problems associated with simultaneous use of cash flow and tax prepayment accounting described in the previous sub-section. Moreover, fraudulent tax evasion schemes involving fictitious purchases and sales of business assets would be difficult to monitor if the selling firm were a non-filing small business.

It is recommended that only those businesses that have gross receipts sufficiently large that they are required to file a return under the Colombian value added tax ($4,000,000) or that have fixed asset sales in a given year greater than some fixed peso amount (which could be indexed for inflation) be required to file a business tax return under the Simplified Alternative Tax. Such treatment balances the two concerns expressed above and is consistent with current Colombian practice. The fixed asset sales requirement will provide at least some deterrent to small taxpayers who expense an asset when they have enough receipts to be covered by the business tax, but resell it during a year when they would be exempt under the gross receipts component of the de minimis rule. Note that the additional compliance costs resulting from the fairly widespread coverage of the business tax under this de minimis rule should be small since the informational requirements for filing a return are likely to be quite small.

3. Withholding Rules

Under current Colombian law, sales of property and certain corporate payments are subject to the withholding rules described in Chapter 3. Such withholding provides an important limitation on tax evasion under the current income tax. Since the withholding rates are relatively low, and since the payments that are subject to withholding under current law would be included in gross receipts under the Simplified Alternative Tax, these rules should be maintained. In addition, non-corporate businesses should be subject to the same withholding rules applied to corporations.

It is also interesting to note that estimated tax payments by businesses may be somewhat more difficult to calculate under the Simplified Alternative Tax than under an income tax. This may occur because planned expenditures on depreciable assets would have a much larger effect on tax liability with expensing than with indexed economic depreciation. The extent to which this would be a serious problem is unclear. It seems to be a less important source of uncertainty than the difficulty of forecasting sales.

B. Treatment of Certain Deductions Under the Business Tax

Although the treatment of most business-related purchases is straightforward under the Simplified Alternative Tax, the treatment of certain transactions may be unclear or worthy of further elaboration; in addition, problems arise in several areas. The following subsections first address the issue of limits on the payment of wages and salaries under the Simplified Alternative Tax, and then discuss the recommended treatments of land, personal consumption and fringe benefits, business purchases and sales of collectibles, and business losses.

1. Limits on the Payment of Wages and Salaries

Limits on the wages and salaries paid by a business to owners or employees are generally unnecessary under the Simplified Alternative Tax. Thus, business cash flow, which is taxed at a rate equal to the maximum individual rate, can readily be converted into earned income, which is subject to taxation according to a progressive individual rate schedule. This «do-it-yourself» integration of the business and individual taxes is a positive feature of the Simplified Alternative Tax; it implies that low-bracket owners of small businesses can easily adjust their salary structures to avoid paying the maximum tax rate on business cash flow. This provides a simple way for small businesses to reduce the importance of the equity problem (discussed in Chapter 5 above) that occurs when business cash flow that is attributable to low-rate owners is taxed at a business tax rate that is equal to the maximum individual rate.[29]

In the case of large publicly held companies it is generally impossible to achieve integration in this way; business income would be taxed at the business rate (which, as noted above, would be equal to the top rate paid by individuals), regardless of the tax bracket of the owner. This does not seem to be a major defect, given the distribution of wealth in Colombia and the availability of the «do-it-yourself» integration for small firms discussed above; certainly, it is no more of a problem than under the existing income tax.

The only other problems arise when the owners of a business pay excessive wages and salaries to spouses, children, or other relatives in order to take advantage of their relatively low tax rates. Such abuses are common to both income and consumption taxes, and can be prevented only with careful administration and strict enforcement.

2. The Treatment of Land

The tax treatment of business purchases of land potentially poses some difficult problems under the Simplified Alternative Tax. The most straightforward approach is to allow expensing of land, and include the proceeds of land sales in the tax base. This would result in uniform tax treatment of land and depreciable assets, and would greatly simplify compliance and administration. Such treatment should also be accompanied by a requirement that the value of land claimed as a deduction for the business tax be used for purposes of local property taxes and for determining net wealth. This would improve taxpayer compliance with Colombian net wealth and property taxes. In particular, the buyer of land would face a smaller incentive to underreport the value of land purchases than under current law, since such purchases would be expensed under the business tax but are not deductible under current law.[30]

Implementation of this rule results in two problems. First, special transitional problems would have to be designed to prevent large reform-induced windfall losses. Purchases of land result in neither deductions nor depreciation allowances under current law; upon disposition, taxpayers are subject to tax only on the real capital gain. Under the Simplified Alternative Tax, taxpayers would be required to include all of the proceeds of land sales (with no deduction for basis) under the business tax. This problem is discussed in the transitional section below.

Second, taxing the income from land more heavily than that from capital may be an explicit goal of social policy in Colombia. Such taxation may be desirable on vertical equity grounds as a means of taxing wealthy landowners, although it is probably preferable to achieve this goal through the taxation of real property, if such is thought desirable. It may also be desirable on efficiency grounds; since the supply of land is relatively if not perfectly inelastic, the taxation of the income from land involves relatively little economic distortion. The necessity to pay the tax might induce more efficient use of land by owners who have not maximized its productivity.

Taxation of the annual flow of income (but not the capital gains) generated by land could be achieved by disallowing a deduction for purchases of land, excluding sales of land from the business tax base, and making no attempt to exempt from tax the portion of the firm's gross sales receipts that is attributable to land. The latter type of segregation would be virtually impossible on administrative grounds in any case.

Such treatment would involve serious problems. First, it would be administratively difficult to separate the purchase price of improved land into the value of improvements (deductible under the business tax) and the value of the unimproved land (which would not be deductible). Indeed, the definition of improvements would inevitably be somewhat arbitrary and difficult to enforce. There would be a strong incentive for buyers of improved land to understate the land portion of the purchase price and for sellers to overstate it. It would be difficult to ensure that the allocations of buyers and sellers were identical, despite the theoretical possibility of cross-checking returns.[31]

Third, firms in the business of buying and selling land presumably would be treated like all other firms; that is they would include sales of land in taxable receipts and deduct purchases of land from the business tax base on a cash flow basis. Rules to distinguish those firms that would qualify for consumption tax treatment of land purchases and sales as dealers in land from those subjected to the alternative treatment described above would be difficult to define, administer and enforce; the differential treatment of economically identical transactions would lead to inequities, allocative distortions, and opportunities for tax abuse.[32]

These problems are sufficiently troublesome that no attempt should be made to disallow deductions for land purchases while including in gross receipts the returns attributable to the land. Accordingly, purchases of land should be expensed under the business tax, subject to the transition rules described below.

3. Personal Consumption Benefits and Fringe Benefits

Since the Simplified Alternative Tax is a consumption-based tax, it is particularly critical that all elements of consumption be included in the tax base. This is important both to keep tax rates low and to avoid the inequities and distortions that result from allowing certain forms of consumption to be exempt from tax. Although a complete discussion of this difficult issue is beyond the scope of this report, as a general principle the Simplified Alternative Tax should be structured so as to allow no deduction for business expenditures to the extent such expenditures finance personal consumption on the part of the owners or employees of the business. For example, deductions generally should not be allowed for expenditures on business meals, entertainment, employer-provided housing, automobiles or computers with a significant personal use component, etc. Similar treatment should be applied to fringe benefits (other than contributions to defined contribution pension plans, which should be treated as described above). Rules identifying personal consumption benefits and determining which costs should be deemed to be expenditures on such benefits will, as always, be difficult to design, administer, and enforce.[33] Nevertheless, such rules would be an essential element of the Simplified Alternative Tax (as they would be under a reformed income tax).

Taxation of personal consumption and fringe benefits is generally desirable on both efficiency and equity grounds. Such treatment eliminates the distortion of consumption decisions that occurs when certain commodities are provided to employees on a tax-free basis. Moreover, it ensures that individuals with access to employer-provided benefits are not treated relatively favorably under the tax system. Note that disallowing business deductions for expenditures on personal consumption benefits and fringe benefits implies that such benefits are effectively taxed at the maximum individual rate. This generally is not problematical since the situation of a lower-rate employee paying tax at the maximum rate can be avoided simply by substituting cash payments for employer-provided benefits. However, taxing such benefits at the maximum individual rate is undesirable to the extent that employer provision of such benefits is economically efficient. This does not seem to be much of a problem in Colombia, where such benefits are a relatively unimportant form of compensation except among upper-income groups; certainly containing the abuses that can otherwise be expected to continue is more important than any problems of this type.

In addition, note that disallowing business deductions for expenditures on personal consumption benefits and fringe benefits does not deal with the inequities and inefficiencies that result from employer provision of consumption and fringe benefits by governments and tax-exempt institutions. These problems could be eliminated by assessing a special 30 percent tax on these two types of organizations on expenditures attributable to such benefits. All levels of government in Colombia should be required to pay this tax. (Such an approach has recently been implemented in New Zealand, but for all employers. Tax is levied at the company rate on most non-cash benefits of employees. The private use of automobiles, loans at concessionary interest rates, and free, subsidized, and discounted goods and services are among the items identified for this treatment).

Finally, note that one alternative to denying firms deductions for the costs of providing personal consumption benefits and fringe benefits to employees is to determine the cost of such benefits and attribute them to employees for inclusion in the individual tax base. In contrast to the denial of deductions at the firm level, this approach has the substantial advantage of ensuring that public employees and those employed by tax-exempt institutions are taxed on such benefits; it also implies that such benefits are subject to taxation at the marginal rate of the individual taxpayer, rather than the company rate. Nevertheless, such treatment is rejected under the Simplified Alternative Tax on complexity grounds. The difficulties of determining the cost of providing such benefits would be exacerbated by the complexities of allocating such costs among employees.

4. Business Purchases and Sales of Collectibles

Under the business tax component of the Simplified Alternative Tax, purchases and sales of art and other collectibles would be subject to the same cash flow treatment as other business purchases; that is, a deduction would be allowed for purchases of such items, with sales included in gross receipts. Such treatment opens an avenue for abuse in the form of business purchases of items with a significant personal consumption component. In addition, ensuring that sales of such items are included in the tax base at fair market value is difficult from an administrative standpoint. Nevertheless, cash flow treatment of business purchases and sales of art and other collectibles is recommended because the alternative of tax prepayment treatment would result in even greater problems.

Tax prepayment treatment of business transactions involving art and other collectibles would imply that deductions would be disallowed for purchases of such items, and sales would not be included in the tax base. Perhaps the most troublesome aspect of such treatment is that businesses, especially individuals providing professional services, could arrange for payment for goods or services sold to individuals or foreigners to be made in the form of purchases of «collectibles» at greatly inflated prices. The individuals would be indifferent between a cash payment and the purchase of the so-called collectible, while the firm would be able to obtain receipts that would not be included in the business tax base.

Several other problems would arise if business purchases and sales of collectibles were treated on a tax prepayment basis. Complex and somewhat arbitrary rules would have to be drawn defining which expenditures represented purchases of «collectibles» and thus would be non-deductible; in particular, it would be difficult to distinguish collectibles from pleasant office amenities. Segregating business sales of items deemed to be collectibles from other sales receipts would present monitoring and enforcement problems. Businesses that deal in collectibles presumably would be allowed to treat purchases and sales of such items on a cash flow basis; identifying such firms would also add complexity and result in somewhat arbitrary distinctions. Finally, it would be difficult to police avoidance techniques based on taking advantage of simultaneous cash flow and prepayment treatment of sales of collectibles. For example, a business subject to prepayment treatment and a «dealer» subject to cash flow treatment could arrange the following set of transactions. Each would buy a collectible from some seller; the price for the dealer would be overstated on the invoice while the price for the business would be understated. They then would arrange a joint sale, where the sales price for the dealer would be understated and the sales price for the business would be overstated. This set of transactions would generate a tax loss for the dealer, but would have no tax effects for the business; the other parties involved would be indifferent to the misstatements of prices described. For all of these reasons, cash flow treatment of business purchases of art and other collectibles is preferable to tax prepayment treatment.

5. The Treatment of Losses

Since the business tax component of the Simplified Alternative Tax provides for expensing of all purchases, including depreciable assets and additions to inventories, it is quite possible that many firms will be in a negative cash flow position; this is especially likely to be true of new and growing capital-intensive businesses. As a result, the tax treatment of such tax «losses» is critical. The Simplified Alternative Tax would allow unused business losses to be carried forward with interest at a market-based nominal interest rate. Such treatment has the effect of keeping the value of the deduction for the loss constant in present value terms. It is essential because it reduces a potential tax disadvantage for new firms, since such firms are more likely to be in a loss position than older and more established ones with positive cash flows. In addition, it reduces the tax-induced incentives for mergers, takeovers, and buyouts that arise without such indexing.[34/ 35/]

The individual and business tax components of the Simplified Alternative Tax are separate schedular taxes. In particular, business losses can not be used to offset earned income or gifts and bequests received that are taxable under the individual component of the Simplified Alternative Tax. Such treatment is desirable on simplicity grounds and to preclude sheltering opportunities and the inequities and perception problems they create; it is consistent with current practice in Colombia.

C. Additional Tax Avoidance Opportunities

As described above, tax prepayment treatment of interest, coupled with the opportunity to trade with and borrow from individuals, foreign firms or tax-exempt institutions, may cause serious avoidance problems under the Simplified Alternative Tax. Measures designed to limit such tax avoidance were described in the first section of this chapter. This subsection considers several other potential avoidance problem areas.

1. Leasing

Leasing generally would not cause problems under the Simplified Alternative Tax, even if lease payments included an interest component for a transaction implicitly involving simultaneous leasing and borrowing. This is true as long as both parties are taxable under the business tax. In this case, the borrower/lessee deducts the lease payments, including any interest component, and the lender/lessor must include the payments in gross receipts, including the interest component. Since the tax rates of the two businesses are equal, there is no tax advantage to the lease arrangement. However, if the lender/lessor were a foreign firm or financial institution or a tax-exempt institution, simultaneous lease/loan arrangements would result in the same kind of avoidance opportunities described in the first section of this chapter; that is, the borrower/lessee could arrange for inflated lease payments coupled with a loan at below-market interest rates.

2. Coupling Reduced Prices with Reduced Interest Rates

A difficult problem under the Simplified Alternative Tax, as well as under an ICF tax, the income tax, and the value-added tax, arises when a business firm lowers the price of its goods and services to individuals while simultaneously paying them below-market interest rates. Under the Simplified Alternative Tax, the firm's receipts are understated due to the price reduction, while the relatively low interest payments have no effect on the tax base. These linked transactions reduce the firm's tax liability, and have no effect on the tax base of the individual.[36/]

The most prominent example of this tax avoidance technique occurs when banks provide «free» financial services such as checking accounts to individuals while simultaneously paying a below-market (or zero) rate of interest on deposits. A similar problem arises with life insurance companies that charge relatively low premiums for life insurance policies but pay relatively low rate of interests on the cash value of the insurance policies.

In principle, this abuse can be prevented by imputing a market rate of interest to individual cash balances — deposits in the bank case and the cash value of policies in the insurance case. However, such treatment would dramatically increase the complexity of the Simplified Alternative Tax, and is therefore not recommended.

3. Sales of Assets Previously Expensed

The business tax base under the Simplified Alternative Tax includes the proceeds of sales of assets previously expensed. An obvious tax evasion technique is the purchase and deduction of an asset, followed in a subsequent year by a sale of the asset, which is omitted from the tax base or included at an understated value.[37/] Monitoring such transactions is clearly difficult from an administrative standpoint. In order to facilitate such monitoring, purchasers of assets should be required to keep invoice information specifying the name and taxpayer identification number of the seller on purchases exceeding some fixed peso amount. Such information is already required under the Colombian value added tax.

D. Individual Issues

The individual tax base is generally compensation, including all receipts arising from a current or former employee relationship including retirement benefits, plus the fair market value of gifts and inheritances received. However, the following issues are worthy of further clarification.

1. Averaging

With a progressive marginal rate structure and an individual tax base of earned income, retirement benefits, and gifts and bequests received, averaging may be desirable for some individuals under the Simplified Alternative Tax, especially over the life cycle. That is, in the absence of averaging individuals with a highly variable time pattern of earnings may pay more tax under a progressive tax than those with «smoother» earnings; this occurs because, relative to the tax paid on a smooth earnings stream, the increase in tax that occurs in high-earnings, high-rate years exceeds the reduction in tax that occurs in low-earnings, low-rate years.

Nevertheless, the need for averaging is not sufficiently great in Colombia to warrant the inclusion of special multi-year averaging provisions under the Simplified Alternative Tax. The relatively narrow range of tax rates reduces the need for averaging provisions. The proposed tax treatment of retirement benefits — taxation at the individual level when received — provides a natural averaging mechanism for the relatively small number of taxpayers in Colombia who receive them. Most importantly, averaging provisions greatly complicate the tax code. Compliance is usually difficult for the taxpayer, and averaging creates significant administrative problems in coping with monitoring multi-year records. Accordingly, the individual tax under the Simplified Alternative Tax provides for no explicit averaging provisions.

Finally, note that special averaging provisions could be provided only for individuals who receive large gifts or bequests. However, such treatment is not recommended, since it adds complexity and most recipients of such transfers are probably in the top rate bracket in any case (or should be).

2. Housing, Consumer Durables, and Collectibles

It is recommended that the tax treatment of individual investments in owner-occupied housing, consumer durables, and collectibles be identical to that of other individual investments; that is, no deduction would be allowed for expenditures and returns would not be included in the tax base. For owner-occupied housing and consumer durables, tax prepayment treatment is preferred to the cash flow alternative of allowing a deduction for purchases and attempting to calculate imputed returns and include them in the tax base; such an approach would be extremely difficult on both administrative and political grounds. Owner-occupied housing would be defined as under current law. Note that allowing a deduction for home mortgage interest under the Simplified Alternative Tax is undesirable on both efficiency and equity grounds. In principle, all interest deductions should be disallowed under the Simplified Alternative Tax. Allowing a deduction only for home mortgage interest distorts the allocation of capital away from non-residential investment and favors high-bracket homeowners. If political realities preclude elimination of the deduction for home mortgage interest, the Government of Colombia should at least adopt a rule (as described in Chapter 5) that would allow interest deductions only for mortgages on the taxpayer's principal residence.

For collectibles, tax prepayment treatment is also more attractive than cash flow treatment; evasion opportunities involving not reporting or under-reporting sales would be too great under the cash flow approach, and definitional issues as well as monitoring and enforcement under a separate individual cash flow tax on collectibles would be extraordinarily difficult. However, tax avoidance problems would arise due to the simultaneous individual tax prepayment treatment and business cash flow treatment of purchases and sales of collectibles. These avoidance problems are analogous to those described above in the discussion of the treatment of collectibles under the business tax.

Note that a capital gains tax on collectibles is conceptually unnecessary under the Simplified Alternative Tax, since the tax on the return, which consists partly of consumption benefits and partly of appreciation, has been prepaid. Additional tax on such gains would be desirable only if it were deemed desirable to discourage investment in collectibles. If so, one approach would be a special tax on capital gains on collectibles after an adjustment for inflation. Such a tax would be administratively infeasible because of the difficulty of taxing such gains, and is not recommended.

3. Lottery Winnings, Prizes and Awards

An arguably extreme interpretation of the logic underlying the tax prepayment approach is that lottery winnings and prizes that require an initial contribution of some sort can be seen as returns on «investments» that have been tax prepaid under the Simplified Alternative Tax and should not be subject to further tax. The economic rationale for this position (explained in the appendix to this chapter) is not totally convincing for such receipts, and exempting them from taxation would suffer from serious perception problems. Accordingly, the current Colombian withholding tax on lottery winnings should be maintained. In addition, all other prizes and awards, including those that are disguised payments for labor services, should be included in the individual tax base under the Simplified Alternative Tax (and subject to withholding, if provided by an employer). Besides being appropriate on policy grounds, this treatment would be desirable to avoid the need to distinguish between taxable and tax-free prizes.

4. Sheltering Labor Income

As noted above, business losses generally cannot be used to shelter labor income under the Simplified Alternative Tax. An exception to this rule occurs when individuals incorporate or otherwise form a business and receive payments for professional (or other) services which are included as gross receipts in the tax base of the business. Under the aggregation rules recommended above, such individuals could shelter the income attributable to the services they provide with sufficiently large investments in unrelated businesses (other than investments abroad or agricultural investments, which would be segregated in separate cash flow accounts).

Such sheltering could be eliminated by somehow defining the «labor income» component of a business owned by an individual or a small group of individuals; business losses would not be allowed to offset such income. Such a rule is not recommended under the Simplified Alternative Tax for tthree reasons. First, it would inevitably be somewhat arbitrary, complex and difficult to monitor and enforce. Second, the segregated cash flow treatment of foreign investment activities and agricultural investment, as well as individual tax prepayment treatment of individual investment, limit to some extent the sheltering opportunities available to such individuals. Third, the revenue losses due to such sheltering of labor income should subsequently be offset by revenue gains of the same magnitude (in present value terms), when the gross receipts attributable to the sheltering investments are included in the gross receipts of the business. However, it is certainly conceivable that such sheltering of labor income under the Simplified Alternative Tax would be perceived to be grossly unfair or would result in large short term revenue losses or dramatically increased tax avoidance opportunities; in this case, the Government of Colombia should consider a rule such as that described above in order to preclude this form of sheltering of labor income.

5. Trusts and Estates

The tax treatment of trusts and estates under the Simplified Alternative Tax is straightforward, as such entities would generally be subject to the same treatment accorded individuals without earned income. Thus, investments by trusts and estates that qualify for tax prepayment treatment under the individual tax would be treated as tax prepaid; for example, interest income, and dividends and capital gains attributable to investments in taxable Colombian businesses would not be subject to tax. Investments by trusts and estates in business activities (as defined above) would be subject to the business tax.

The primary complication arises in the treatment of disbursements by a trust or estate. As argued above, an important aspect of the Simplified Alternative Tax is that the fair market value of gifts and bequests should be included in the tax base of the recipient. However enforcement of this provisions will clearly be difficult. To curb evasion, it is recommended that tax be withheld at the maximum rate on transfers to individuals made by trusts and estates. Recipients would of course be credited for the tax paid on their behalf by the trust or estate.

E. Relationship to Net Wealth Tax and Presumptive Income

1. The Net Wealth Tax

The individual net wealth tax in Colombia can be viewed as a natural complement to the existing income tax, as it would be to a reformed income tax. However, the compatibility of the net wealth tax with the Simplified Alternative Tax is somewhat less clear, as the two taxes have very different properties. The net wealth tax represents a tax on the present discounted value of capital income, while the Simplified Alternative Tax exempts such income from taxation. The net wealth tax requires accurate measurement of capital for those individuals subject to the tax, as well as for all businesses so that, to the extent possible, the fair market value of all business holdings can be included in the individual net wealth tax base. In contrast, the fact that capital income is tax exempt under the Simplified Alternative Tax gives rise to most of its simplicity advantages.

Nevertheless, even if it adopts the Simplified Alternative Tax, Colombia should maintain its individual net wealth tax. The reforms in the calculation of the net wealth tax base recommended in Chapter 6 should also be adopted, with the modifications described below. The rationale for this recommendation follows.

The primary reason Colombia should consider the Simplified Alternative Tax is that it is simpler than the alternative of reforming the income tax system. Exempting capital income from tax is not an explicit tax reform goal; rather, it is an implication of expensing under the relatively simple consumption-based business component of the proposed reform. Accordingly, a net wealth tax that taxes the (discounted value of) capital income of only wealthy individuals is not inherently inconsistent with the Simplified Alternative Tax. Moreover, a net wealth tax is desirable in order to maintain the vertical equity of the Colombian tax system, to tax «ability to pay» not captured in the base of the Simplified Alternative Tax, and to reduce concentrations of wealth. Such a tax can also be justified as an indirect means of taxing gifts and inheritances that are not included in the individual tax base of the Simplified Alternative Tax due either to evasion or to exemptions made on administrative grounds.

A more difficult question is the nature of the net wealth tax that should be used in conjunction with the Simplified Alternative Tax. Two issues must be resolved. The first is the extent to which the reforms of the net wealth tax recommended in Chapter 6 should be adopted. These reforms are generally desirable, and would result in significantly more accurate measurement of net wealth regardless of whether the net wealth tax were used to supplement the Simplified Alternative Tax or a reformed income tax. This is particularly true of the proposals to adjust the values of capital assets, including land, depreciable assets, and inventories for inflation. Accordingly, these reforms should generally be adopted under the Simplified Alternative Tax.[38]

The second issue regarding the design of the net wealth tax is the extent to which businesses should be required to use the income measurement rules specified in Chapters 5 and 7. Recall from Chapter 8 that one component of the definition of Haig-Simons income is the annual change in net wealth. This implies that many of the complex rules required to measure annual income accurately should, in principle, also be used to calculate the base of the net wealth tax.

It is clear that requiring adoption of all of the income measurement rules recommended in Chapters 5 and 7 for purposes of measuring accurately the base of the tax on net wealth would eliminate much of the simplicity advantages of the Simplified Alternative Tax. Moreover, for virtually all individuals subject to the net wealth tax, the changes in net wealth experienced in any single year will be a relatively small component of the total net wealth tax base. Accordingly, income measurement errors generally are of less concern under the tax on net wealth than they are for purposes of the income tax. In addition, in the case of debts, understatements of the net wealth of one individual due to income mismeasurement should, at least to the extent that debts are reported consistently by borrowers and lenders, appear as overstatements of the net wealth of some other individual. (Note, however, that revenue from the net wealth tax would be affected adversely if the lender were subject to a lower rate of wealth taxation than the borrower). For these reasons, it is recommended that reforms in the measurement of net wealth that would increase the complexity of the net wealth tax be kept to a minimum if the net wealth tax is to be a supplement to the Simplified Alternative Tax. Specifically, it is recommended that none of the income tax reforms recommended in Chapter 5 (other than those related to inflation adjustment of the value of capital assets, including land, depreciable assets, and inventories, which are also described in Chapter 6) should be adopted for purposes of calculating net wealth if the net wealth tax is to be a supplement to the Simplified Alternative Tax rather than a reformed income tax.[39] A possible positive side effect of the adoption of such a change is that it would encourage the use of inflation-adjusted economic depreciation for purposes of financial accounting in Colombia; this would clearly represent a significant improvement in measuring real economic income over current financial accounting practices.[40]

2. Presumptive Income

The taxation of presumptive income in Colombia is effectively a minimum tax on the capital income of individuals and firms. Reforms which would make it more effective in this role are specified in Chapter 5. However, such a tax is, in principle, fundamentally inconsistent with the Simplified Alternative Tax, which exempts capital income from tax. Accordingly, there is no reasonable alternative to eliminating the taxation of presumptive income under the Simplified Alternative Tax.

This recommendation clearly implies that the Colombian tax system would no longer have a feature that would serve the function of a minimum tax. As argued above, this should not be viewed as a problem under the Simplified Alternative Tax to the extent that the existing taxation of presumptive income merely taxes capital income that would otherwise go unreported. However, tax avoidance will of course still be problematical under the Simplified Alternative Tax; in particular, firms that successfully under-report gross receipts will be able to evade tax liability. Since assets are in many cases more difficult to conceal from tax administrators than are receipts, some type of wealth-based minimum tax would seem to be desirable to limit tax avoidance possibilities. Unfortunately, there is no particular relationship between the value of the assets of a business and its gross receipts, so a «presumptive gross receipts tax» based on a firm's net wealth is also not a reasonable alternative as a minimum tax.

The most obvious way of mitigating the problem of under-reporting of gross receipts under the Simplified Alternative Tax is simply improved administration and enforcement. Since the Simplified Alternative Tax is simpler in terms of both compliance and administration, fewer resources need be devoted to interpreting, explaining and administering complex issues regarding measurement of the tax base. Accordingly, more resources can be devoted to the essential task of enforcing the reporting requirements of the Simplified Alternative Tax. Indeed, improved administration and enforcement is clearly a far superior way to attack evasion problems than rather indirect approaches such as the taxation of presumptive income.

Second, there will be at least some correspondence between those individuals who benefit from the under-reporting of gross receipts and those subject to the net wealth tax. This provides a rationale for making up any post-reform revenue shortfalls with higher tax rates under the net wealth tax rather than higher rates under the individual or business components of the Simplified Alternative Tax.[41/] Such an approach is clearly a very indirect method of attacking the evasion problem. Nevertheless, it does raise additional revenue from some of the same individuals who would be «caught» under the current law rules that provide for wealth-based taxation of presumptive income; of course, all owners of wealth, and not just those illegally evading taxes, would be subject to the increased rates of tax on net wealth.

It is interesting to note that a second rationale exists for an increase in net wealth tax rates during the transition from current law to the Simplified Alternative Tax. Specifically, the transition rules recommended above are quite generous to the owners of wealth existing at the time of enactment of a move to the Simplified Alternative Tax, who presumably expected income tax treatment to continue to be applied to such wealth. Accordingly, a temporary increase in tax rates on the net wealth of such taxpayers could be viewed as a transitional tool, that is, a means of reducing what would be perhaps the most significant windfall gain induced by the enactment of the Simplified Alternative Tax.

F. Transitional Issues

Implementation of a consumption tax is generally viewed as involving particularly difficult transitional problems. It is by no means clear in the Colombian context that the transitional problems involved in implementing the Simplified Alternative Tax would be more difficult than the transitional problems associated with implementing the proposed reform of the income tax system.

In any case, it seems clear that quite a few of the features of the current tax system imply that the transition to the Simplified Alternative Tax would be significantly less disruptive in Colombia than in most other countries. For example, at the individual level dividends and the inflationary component of interest receipts are already exempt from tax, and capital gains are taxed fairly lightly in practice. Gifts and bequests received are taxed as occasional gains under the individual income tax. An individual net wealth tax is in place and can be utilized as a supplement to the consumption-based Simplified Alternative Tax.

For businesses, depreciation allowances are accelerated and the elimination of the deductibility of the inflationary component of interest expense and the exclusion of the inflationary component of interest receipts is being phased in. All business activity is taxed at a single rate, equal to the maximum individual tax rate. All of these features would ease the transition to the Simplified Alternative Tax in Colombia. Nevertheless, the resolution of remaining transitional issues is critical to the implementation of the Simplified Alternative Tax.

A complete analysis of transitional issues would determine the net reform-induced changes in net wealth experienced throughout the economy. That is, it would identify all the gains and the losses experienced by each taxpayer or class of taxpayers as a result of the implementation of the entire reform proposal; such an analysis would determine the net effects of reform, rather than just the effects of a particular provision. Special transitional provisions could then be designed to reduce reform-induced net losses only in those cases where such net losses were sufficiently large to be deemed undesirable from a social standpoint; in particular, special transitional rules would not be required in situations in which taxpayers suffered losses due to certain reform proposals that were offset by gains attributable to other tax changes.

Unfortunately, such an analysis is far beyond the scope of this report. The analysis is limited to isolating the following major transitional effects of implementing the Simplified Alternative Tax, discussing the reform-induced gains and losses caused by each, and proposing special transitional rules in those areas where they seem warranted. A fairly extensive analysis of various business issues is followed by a discussion of transition issues in the tax treatment of capital gains realized by individuals.

1. Existing Business Assets and Debt

For business, the primary issues are the transitional rules to be applied to income and deductions attributable to «old» assets — those purchased under the Colombian income tax regime prior to the implementation of the Simplified Alternative Tax — and to the interest on pre-existing debt. It is clear that identifying those post-reform receipts attributable to old assets would be impossible from an administrative standpoint. Accordingly, all post-reform receipts should be included in the business cash flow tax base.[42]

The appropriate treatment of depreciation deductions on old assets and interest deductions (and receipts) on «old» loans — again, those entered into prior to enactment of the Simplified Alternative Tax — is a difficult issue. One possibility is the set of transitional rules proposed by Aaron and Galper (1985) for a movement toward a consumption-based business tax; these serve as a convenient benchmark in the subsequent analysis.

Aaron and Galper propose that the proceeds of all sales of «old» non-financial assets be fully included in the business tax base. In addition, at the time of sale of each such asset, taxpayers would receive a deduction related to the tax basis of the asset remaining in the year of enactment of reform. Old assets sold in the year of enactment would simply get a deduction for remaining basis. Old assets sold in later years would receive a deduction equal to the basis remaining in the year of enactment, indexed by a factor equal to one plus a market-related nominal interest rate each year. Such treatment would have the effect of keeping the deduction for basis constant in present value terms and equal to the basis remaining in the year of enactment of reform. In addition, they propose that this treatment of old assets be coupled with immediate disallowance of all interest deductions on all old loans.

The effect of the Aaron and Galper transitional rules would be to provide «old» non-financial assets and loans with consumption tax treatment in the year of enactment of the Simplified Alternative Tax. Cash flow treatment would be applied to old assets; that is, assets sold in the year of enactment would receive expensing of remaining basis in that year, with assets sold in later years receiving the same treatment in present value terms. The proceeds of all asset sales would be fully included in the tax base. At the same time, tax prepayment treatment would be applied to old loans; that is, repayments of interest and principal would not be deductible, and also would not be included in the tax base of the lender. As demonstrated in Chapter 8, these treatments are roughly equivalent, and both are consistent with a consumption tax. Thus, the owner of an old asset would experience a windfall gain from cash flow treatment of the basis of the asset remaining at the time of enactment; however, to the extent the asset were debt financed, he would experience a windfall loss from the denial of interest deductions for the outstanding debt.

The application of consumption tax rules to old non-financial assets and loans would have very different effects on different Colombian businesses; the magnitude and direction of these effects would depend on the relative magnitudes of remaining basis and outstanding debt. In the special case where the two magnitudes were just equal, the owners of the asset would be indifferent; the loss due to elimination of interest deductions would be exactly offset by the gain due to expensing of remaining basis. However, given the accelerated deductions for depreciation under current law, as well as the preponderance of debt finance, most owners of old assets in Colombia would be net losers; the loss due to the elimination of interest deductions would be only partially (if at all) offset by expensing of remaining basis.[43/] Moreover, complete elimination of interest deductibility would be viewed as an unfair repudiation of the commitment to a ten-year phase-out of the elimination of the inflationary component of interest deductions under the 1986 reform.

Accordingly, an alternative treatment is recommended. Rather than eliminating interest deductibility in the year of enactment, the elimination of deductibility of interest expense (and of inclusion of interest receipts) for businesses should follow the phase-out schedule for the inflationary component of interest described in Chapter 7. The only difference would be that the phase-out schedule would be applied to all interest rather than just the inflationary component of interest. Simultaneously, deductions for depreciation on old investments would simply follow those prescribed under law current at the time of acquisition of the asset. On balance, such treatment should generally be more favorable than the Aaron-Galper rules; the benefits of more generous treatment of old debt should in most cases exceed the costs of less generous treatment of old assets.

Note that proceeds of sales of old assets are included in the business tax base of the Simplified Alternative Tax; a deduction should be allowed for remaining basis on sales of such assets, following the same provisions for indexing of such basis available under current law. Such a rule is sufficiently harsh that churning of assets should not be a problem, and it causes no transitional problems since it represents no change relative to current law, which provides for full recapture and expensing if the funds obtained from the sale are used to buy new depreciable assets.

2. Inventories

Additions to inventories are expensed under the Simplified Alternative Tax; firms would be allowed to expense all such new additions. Transitional problems would arise only when a firm draws down inventories existing prior to the enactment of reform. In this case, the cost of goods sold should be based on the values used for purposes of calculating the net wealth tax base; rules that specify the calculation of these values during the transition from the existing net wealth tax to an inflation-adjusted one are specified in Chapter 7.

3. Dividends

The treatment of dividends under current law corresponds to that under the Simplified Alternative Tax; that is, firms do not receive a deduction for dividends paid and dividends are not taxed at the individual level. Thus, new transition issues do not arise in this area. Existing rules could be maintained initially for the taxation of dividends attributable to pre-1986 income; that is, such dividends would constitute taxable income of the shareholder receiving them. It would simplify administration and compliance if this distinction between pre-1986 income and post-1985 income were eventually eliminated. This could be done, for example, either by providing for the gradual conversion of income in the latter category to income that could be distributed without tax consequences for the recipient or by simply eliminating the distinction in one step. If either policy were enacted after the passage of an appreciable period (say five or, at most, ten years), it would have little consequences for either tax equity or revenues, due to the erosion of the real value of the amounts at issue by inflation.[44]

4. Land Sales

Transition rules must also be specified for land sales, assuming the Simplified Alternative Tax allows expensing of land purchases with inclusion of the proceeds of land sales in the tax base. Land sales should be subject to the Aaron-Galper rules specified above. Basis in the year of enactment would be equal to the smaller of the values used in the assessment of the net wealth tax or local property taxes. Taxpayers could revalue land holdings for purposes of determining basis for the business tax in the year of enactment, but the revaluation would apply for purposes of the net wealth tax and local property taxes. For land sales in years subsequent to the year of enactment, the deduction for basis would be indexed by a market interest rate, as described above.

5. Industry-Specific Transitional Relief

It might be argued that further transitional relief is justifiable for industries that are particularly tax-preferred under current Colombian law, since they would lose their relative advantage over industries that do not benefit from such preferences. For example, some industries already receive expensing, coupled with nearly full interest deductibility.[45] Such industries thus would only lose from the implementation of the Simplified Alternative Tax. Such requests for further transitional relief should be resisted. It is impossible to compensate for all windfall losses (or to tax away all windfall gains). They are an inevitable consequence of reform, and tax reform in Colombia historically has not been accompanied by comprehensive proposals for transitional relief. Moreover, the owners of existing wealth will generally benefit from the elimination of the taxation of capital income at the margin under the Simplified Alternative Tax. In particular, for the reasons discussed in Chapter 4, the Government of

Colombia should avoid any transitional provisions which result in negative marginal effective rates during the transition period. The introduction of such provisions would create later problems as special interests resisted the elimination of transitional provisions, would open the door for further subsidies, and would reduce or postpone if not eliminate many of the equity, efficiency, and simplicity advantages of the Simplified Alternative Tax.

6. Foreign Tax Creditability

An additional transitional issue will arise if, as discussed at length in Chapter 9, the United States (and/or other countries) determines that taxes paid by U.S. firms to Colombia under the Simplified Alternative Tax are not creditable against U.S. corporate income taxes. Such a decision would effectively impose a one-time windfall tax on the owners of existing U.S. investments in Colombia. However, no special transitional provisions to mitigate this windfall loss are recommended. Since the loss is indeed a one-time windfall loss (and additional windfall losses caused by similar policy changes are unlikely to occur in the future), it should have little effect on new foreign investment in Colombia, except as it creates a general sense of uncertainty about the tax treatment of foreign investors.

7. Intangibles

In addition, note that under the Simplified Alternative Tax the receipts from sales of intangibles such as goodwill, copyrights, and patents are fully included in the business tax base. Such treatment generally does not require a special transition rule, since the expenditures that gave rise to the intangible have already been fully deducted. However, under current law, Colombian companies have the option of deducting as a cost 70 percent of the sales price of intangibles. Anecdotal evidence suggests that this provision is seldom utilized; to the extent this is true, the elimination of the provision should not cause significant transitional problems. In any case, no special transitional rule for the sales of intangibles is recommended.

8. Revenue Losses Caused by Expensing

Finally, note that an additional transitional issue is the revenue loss due to switching from the deductions for depreciation allowed under current law to expensing. It may desirable to spread out this revenue loss over several years, especially in light of the potential revenue loss due to elimination of the presumptive income provisions of current law. One means of accomplishing this goal is to allow present value expensing rather actual expensing over a transition period.[46] For example, during the first few years following the enactment of the Simplified Alternative Tax, deductions equal in present value to expensing could be allowed over three years for equipment, and five or ten years for structures and land. At the end of the transition period, expensing would be allowed. Alternatively, present value expensing could be phased out at the cost of some additional complexity; for example, deductions for equipment could initially be spread out over three years, then two, and finally expensing could be allowed.

As is true of all special transition rules, allowing present value expensing would add complexity during the transition period. Taxpayers would have to take deductions for purchases of depreciable assets and land over several years instead of only one, and accounting for sales of assets that had not been fully deducted would be more complicated.[47] However, in addition to spreading out the revenue loss that would otherwise occur with a switch to expensing, the adoption of present value expensing during a transition period would have two other beneficial effects. First, the number of firms that would have sufficient deductions to eliminate their tax liability entirely during this period (when interest would still be partially deductible) would be reduced; such a reduction in the number of firms that can «zero out» is likely to be desirable on perception grounds. Second, a variety of tax evasion and avoidance schemes are particularly effective in reducing tax liability when expensing rather than deductions for economic or even accelerated depreciation is allowed. Present value expensing reduces the attractiveness of such schemes somewhat, since deductions are spread out over several years.

9. Capital Gains Realized by Individuals

The individual transitional issue that has received the most attention in the literature on the implementation of consumption taxes is the treatment of individual savings extant at the time of enactment. The primary problem associated with implementation of the Simplified Alternative Tax is that capital gains accrued under the income tax regime would, in the absence of special provisions, escape tax entirely. Some attempt could be made to tax such gains; for example, gains on old assets could be included in the individual tax base, with a deduction for basis along the lines of the Aaron-Galper proposal. However, capital gains are largely untaxed under the current Colombian tax on occasional gains, as a result sof evasion and generous treatment for assets transferred at death. Moreover, attempts to tax such gains would add complexity and probably yield fairly little revenue. Accordingly, no special transitional rule for capital gains is recommended.

Appendix

Details of the Choice Between the ITP and ICF Approaches

As noted above, the choice between the ITP (individual tax prepayment) and ICF (individual cash flow) approaches to an individual consumption-based tax hinges on a number of fairly technical considerations. Although most observers tend to think of consumption taxes in cash flow terms, the individual tax prepayment approach appears to be more appropriate for Colombia. This appendix, explains the rationale for this decision, discussing first the three major differences between the ICF and the ITP approaches — the use of so-called individual «qualified accounts» in the cash flow approach, the treatment of individual transitional problems, and the treatment of gifts and bequests — and then a wide variety of other issues.[48]

I. The Use of Individual Qualified Accounts

The most important difference between the two types of individual consumption-based taxes is that the ICF tax allows individuals deductions from the tax base for investments in so-called «qualified accounts» and taxes all withdrawals from such accounts. In contrast, since an ITP tax treats all individual transactions on a tax prepayment basis, saving and dis-saving are ignored for tax purposes, capital income is not taxed at the individual level, and no deduction is allowed for interest expense.

This results in dramatic simplicity advantages for the ITP tax. For example, all aspects of loans are simply ignored in the calculation of the individual tax under an ITP tax. In contrast, the inclusion of the proceeds of loans in the tax base as required under the ICF approach would probably be politically unpopular in Colombia, require an extensive informational and educational campaign, result in considerable additional record keeping requirements for all debt arrangements, and create opportunities for tax abuses within families in the form of loans to lower-bracket children.

Another potentially serious area for abuse under a consumption tax (as under most income taxes) is «tax base shifting» to lower bracket family members. Such problems might be quite serious under an ICF tax with progressive marginal rates and individual qualified accounts, as taxpayers could establish such accounts in the names of their children; this would be particularly troublesome to the extent gifts to children fell below under any lifetime gift/bequest exclusion under an ICF tax. Such problems should be minimized under an ITP tax, since all business income would be taxed at the top marginal rate, tax on earned income would be assessed on the earner, and no deductions would be allowed for saving. Owners of closely held firms could inflate the earnings of employed children, but this type of abuse is relatively easy to police and would pose similar problems under both ITP and ICF approaches.

Under the ICF tax, ensuring that all interest income is included in the individual tax base would present the same monitoring and enforcement problems that plague the income tax in Colombia; such problems disappear under the ITP approach since interest income is tax-exempt at the individual level.

Note that ITP treatment of interest would very likely raise revenue relative to income tax treatment for two reasons. First, even though lenders frequently avoid tax by not reporting interest receipts to the extent such receipts are not subject to withholding or are under-withheld, borrowers are very likely to report the associated interest deductions. Second, borrowers tend to be subject to higher tax rates than lenders, so that even in the absence of evasion the revenue loss due to deductions for interest payments is greater than the revenue gain from taxing interest receipts. Exempting capital income from tax would probably result in less revenue loss than the gain that would result from the disallowance of deductions for interest expense.

An exception to this general rule is interest on Colombian public debt held by taxable Colombian individuals or firms; interest on such debt issued after 1974 is taxable under the income tax (subject to the provisions for inflation indexing of interest receipts), with no associated deductions. Since such interest income would be excluded from the ITP tax base, this aspect of the ITP tax would lose revenue. Note that this effect could be eliminated with a special transition rule requiring interest on existing public debt to be taxed under the provisions of current law until retired. In the long run, the revenue lost from exempting from tax interest on public debt held by Colombian taxpayers might be offset at least partially by lower borrowing costs, since Colombian taxpayers would require a lower before-tax interest rate to achieve current after-tax rates of return. However, the extent of such interest rate adjustment is unclear, since one could also argue that interest rates would have to remain at roughly current levels to attract foreign lenders, who are not taxed on interest income under current law.

In addition, withholding would be much more complicated under the ICF approach. In principle, the rate of withholding applied to labor income should reflect capital transactions, since deposits in (withdrawals from) qualified accounts reduce (increase) tax liability. Note that this problem differs from that under an income tax, where withholding based on labor income is inaccurate if the individual receives capital income but not if he simply engages in a capital transaction; under an ICF tax, such inaccuracies arise as a result of capital transactions as well as capital income.

As a result, a system of withholding on loans used to finance consumption might need to be introduced in order to ensure timely payment of tax. In principle, withholding on loans should occur at the individual's marginal tax rate, although some type of average rate would likely be used to simplify administration. Such a system should theoretically also be accompanied by «negative withholding» on consumption loan repayments, since such repayments are deductible from the ICF tax base. Further complicating matters is the fact that tax should not be paid on loans used for investment purposes. But the financial institution making a loan cannot be expected to monitor the purpose to which proceeds of loans are put. All of these complexities are in marked contrast to a an ITP tax, where withholding would generally be much more accurate than under either an ICF tax or an income tax, since returns to capital would be excluded from the tax base and capital transactions would not affect withholding.

In order to avoid some of these problems, proponents of ICF taxes sometimes recommend that some amount of loans be treated on a tax prepayment basis; for example, in proposals made for the United States Aaron and Galper (1985) recommend that up to a total of US$20,000 (roughly the equivalent of $5 million) in outstanding loans be granted such treatment at the discretion of the taxpayer. This would simplify compliance for many taxpayers, although in principle records would still have to be kept to determine whether the limit was exceeded.

However, monitoring costs under such an approach would be increased in two ways. First, tax administrators would have to ensure that repayments of tax prepaid loans were not illegally deducted from the cash flow base. Second, the limit would have to be enforced. This would seem to be a difficult proposition even in a developed country, as it would require significant cross-checking capability across financial institutions. It would be significantly more difficult if not impossible to implement such a scheme in Colombia, which has considerably fewer administrative resources and cross-checking capabilities.

Individuals who could avoid the limit on prepayment-basis loans could defer tax liability to a significant degree by depositing the proceeds of such loans in qualified accounts. Moreover, they could reduce such liability if they could use prepayment-basis loans to take advantage of future lower rates. That is, a taxpayer could «average» or smooth taxable consumption by borrowing on a tax prepayment basis to make a deposit in a cash flow account during a relatively high-rate year, and then withdraw the proceeds from the qualified account to repay the loan during a relatively low-rate year. Of itself, allowing taxpayers to use techniques such as this to average is not undesirable; indeed, it has been advocated by proponents of consumption-based taxation.[49] But it would be inappropriate to enact legislation that is likely to favor those individuals able and willing to use illegal means to average taxable consumption relative to those unable or unwilling to engage in such efforts to reduce their tax liability.

Monitoring systems would generally have to be more comprehensive under an ICF tax with individual qualified accounts than under the ITP approach. The incentive to avoid reporting withdrawals would be great, since the principal amount withdrawn, as well as the return, would be subject to tax; monitoring systems would have to be sufficient to insure reporting of all withdrawals from all qualified accounts.

The use of individual qualified accounts also would result in additional opportunities for evasion and complexity in the international area. Individuals who could borrow funds abroad on a tax-prepaid basis to finance deposits in qualified accounts — like taxpayers who could avoid the limit on «tax prepayment» loans — would have significant opportunities to defer or reduce taxes; to the extent this was viewed as undesirable, complex restrictions and monitoring of such transactions or expansion of existing exchange controls would be required.

In addition, the opportunity to invest abroad through an individual qualified account as well as on a tax prepayment basis (either legally or illegally with little chance of apprehension) would provide opportunities for tax avoidance or evasion. A typical scheme would involve an investment that consists of two related and coordinated components, with one made through a qualified account and the other made on a tax prepaid basis. The investment would be structured so that a disproportionate share of the deductions would occur in qualified accounts, while a disproportionate share of the income would accrue in the tax prepaid account.[50] It might be possible to restrict investments from qualified accounts to the domestic market. Besides interfering with economic choices, measures taken to combat these avoidance or evasion strategies would add complexity. Indeed, all of the arguments presented above indicate that the use of qualified accounts under the ICF approach would result in more complexity than the ITP method, although the magnitude of the additional complexity is difficult to assess.

Another foreign sector issue raised by use of the ICF approach is the possibility that foreign losses would be used to offset Colombian-source income under the Simplified Alternative Tax. Since such a result is undesirable on revenue, equity, and perception grounds, it is necessary to limit possibilities for this type of evasion. Therefore, just as the proposed cash flow tax on business would include a separate basket to segregate international investment activity from domestic income, a similar measure would be desirable (and is proposed under the Simplified Alternative Tax) in treating the foreign investment activity of individuals.

Under the ICF approach, such treatment implies that buying stock in a foreign company or making a deposit in a foreign bank results in a deduction from cash flow, but this deduction can only be used to offset positive cash flow from foreign sources. Note that under the ITP approach, the purchase of stock or a deposit in a bank would not ordinarily create a deduction, nor would subsequent receipt of dividends or interest create a tax liability. However, from the standpoint of tax administration, it may be difficult to distinguish between investments where Colombian individuals are actively engaged in a business (and should file a business cash flow tax return) from those where Colombians are passive portfolio investors (and would not report foreign expenditures or receipts under the ITP approach). Joint ventures with foreign entities represent a situation where the ownership structure may be difficult to verify and to evaluate according to some standard rule. Such a situation would create opportunities for tax evasion using techniques similar to those described above. To limit such possibilities, segregated cash flow treatment of all individual foreign investment would be recommended even under the ITP approach. Accordingly, there is no distinction between the ICF and ITP approaches with respect to individual foreign investment activity.

Under the ICF approach, problems would also arise with respect to the treatment of individuals who migrate from Colombia.[51] Since an ITP tax would tax earnings on a prepayment basis and exempt the receipt of income, there would be no problems of deferral of tax and subsequent migration. In contrast, the cash flow approach would result in opportunities to avoid tax through emigration. As a result, transfers abroad from qualified accounts would likely have to be treated as taxable events. For example, Aaron and Galper recommend that all qualified accounts would have to be held in institutions with an established domestic residence and that a withholding tax should be imposed at the maximum individual tax rate on all transfers from qualified accounts to individuals or businesses with a foreign residence. Such measures would obviously increase the complexity of the ICF tax.

A final effect of using qualified accounts should be mentioned. To the extent deductions for deposits in qualified accounts were taken at higher tax rates than those applied to subsequent withdrawals, an ICF tax would subsidize saving rather than simply be neutral with respect to the consumption-saving decision. By comparison, the ITP tax would be neutral. As will be discussed in Chapter 10, the efficiency case for such tax treatment is unclear, and neutral treatment seems to be more likely to be optimal than policies which either tax or subsidize the return to saving.[52]

II. Transitional Issues

Implementation of a consumption tax is generally viewed as involving particularly difficult transitional problems. As noted above, it is by no means clear in the Colombian context that these would be significantly more difficult than the transitional problems associated with implementing the proposed reform of the income tax system.[53] Nevertheless, the resolution of transitional problems is critical to the implementation of any consumption tax.

In principle, transitional issues are important if the magnitudes of the changes in individual net wealth induced by implementing reform are sufficiently large. These changes must reflect all effects of reform and all special transitional provisions. Nevertheless, it is convenient to isolate several effects of implementing a consumption tax and discuss the reform-induced gains and losses caused by each; this approach is followed in the discussion below. Since the analysis assumes that both the ICF and ITP taxes would include a consumption-based business tax, their business transitional issues are the same and thus do not affect the comparison of the two approaches in this appendix.[54] Accordingly, the following considers only differences in the individual transitional issues associated with implementing the ICF and ITP taxes.

The transitional issue which has received the most attention is the treatment of individual savings extant at the time of enactment of a personal consumption tax. Two types of difficulties arise, which have been termed «price change» and «carryover» problems.[55]

Price change problems are unexpected net wealth changes that result from changes in the market prices of assets that are induced by changes in the tax structure; these occur because of reform-induced changes in the after-tax value of future returns attributable to an asset existing at the time of enactment of reform. For example, unless all factors are perfectly mobile, the elimination of favorable tax treatment for a business activity will lower after-tax returns to immobile assets employed in the activity and thus lower their values. Such price change problems would be broadly similar for both plans, and indeed for any reform including the income tax reform proposed in this report. They are generally mitigated with various sorts of delays, phase-ins, grandfathering, or compensation provisions, such as the provision for phasing out the deductibility of the inflationary component of interest expense described in Chapter 7. Since these issues are quite similar for both ITP and ICF taxes, they are not discussed further here.

Carryover problems occur when tax changes alter the tax treatment of income earned prior to the enactment of reform, relative to the treatment expected under the pre-reform tax structure. They arise in two forms. The first occurs when new rules imply that income earned under the old tax regime but untaxed due to deferral provisions will escape taxation under the new regime; for example, a switch from a realization-based income tax to an ITP tax would imply that capital gains accrued but untaxed under the income tax would escape tax entirely. The second form of carryover problem occurs when income which was fully taxed under the old system will be subject to a second tax under the new system; for example, adoption of rule that deemed all existing financial assets to be held in qualified accounts at the time of a switch from an income tax to an ICF tax would result in double taxation of savings which were subject to tax under the prior income tax regime. Such problems are frequently cited as one of the most disturbing features of switching to a consumption tax.

The two types of plans appear to face very different transitional problems of the carryover type. Under the ICF approach, any «old» assets — those existing at the time of enactment of reform — which would be newly classified at the time of enactment as qualified account assets would face double taxation to the extent they were accumulated out of after-tax income. The most straightforward approach of mitigating this double taxation is to allow a deduction related to the taxpayer's basis in the asset at the time the asset is withdrawn from the qualified account. An example of such an approach is the set of transitional rules proposed by Aaron and Galper (1985). Details of these rules were provided above. Briefly, they would attribute to old assets a deduction equal in present value terms to the remaining basis of the asset in the year of enactment of reform. This treatment of existing assets would be coupled with immediate disallowance of all interest deductions on all existing loans.[56]

Under an ITP tax, the carryover problem is the need to tax income accrued but untaxed under the income tax, such as unrealized capital gains. One approach, recommended by Hall and Rabushka (1983, 1985), is to provide for no special treatment, that is, to exempt such accrued pre-reform gains. This would be justifiable in Colombia to the extent that capital gains are largely untaxed under the current tax system; otherwise, it would confer a windfall gains on owners of existing capital assets. An alternative would be to require gains on pre-existing assets to be included in the ITP tax base on a cash flow basis as a transitional measure, calculating the amount to be included using an approach identical or similar to that proposed by Aaron and Galper.

Viewed in this way, the transitional problems (and perhaps the solutions) under the two reform plans are quite similar. The primary differences are two-fold. First, to the extent capital gains are lightly taxed under current Colombian law, no transition rule is necessary under the ITP approach; this is obviously much simpler than the basis calculation rules described above under the ICF approach. This is indeed the approach recommended above.

Second, applying the basis calculation rules described above to sales of old assets might cause significant revenue and equity problems in the first few years following the enactment of an ICF tax; only gain would be included in the base upon sale of an old asset, but the full amount of the proceeds could be reinvested and thus deducted from the ICF base. As a result, rules designed to limit the ability of taxpayers to roll existing assets over into deductible additions to qualified accounts might have to be devised; these would add considerable complexity during the transition period. In contrast, such rules would probably not be necessary under the ITP approach; the revenue loss and inequities associated with granting immediate deduction of basis (in present value terms) would be significantly smaller since reinvestment of funds would not reduce current tax liability.

III. The Tax Treatment of Bequests

As stressed above, Colombia should consider only consumption tax proposals consistent with the lifetime endowment interpretation of tax equity. As described earlier in this chapter, this criterion implies somewhat different treatment of gifts and bequests made under the ITP and ICF consumption taxes. But as demonstrated there, the two treatments are in fact roughly equivalent. However, to the extent the taxation of gifts and bequests to both donor and recipient generates political opposition in Colombia, questions of perception may favor the ITP approach. This point is valid only if the double taxation of gifts and bequests implied by the lifetime endowment view is less obvious under the ITP approach. This may be true, since the gift or bequest is simultaneously included in the tax base of the donor and the recipient at the time of transfer under the ICF tax; in contrast, only the recipient pays tax at the time of transfer under the ITP approach, since all forms of consumption funded by saving, including the making of gifts and bequests, are «tax prepaid».[57] As a result, there might be less sentiment for generous exclusions for gifts and inheritances received under the ITP approach. Note that Aaron and Galper recommend a lifetime gift/bequest exclusion of US$ 200,000 (the equivalent of roughly $50 million) under their version of the ICF tax.

IV. Additional Issues

A. Opportunities vs. Outcomes

As noted in Chapter 8, an interesting equity issue raised by the two plans is whether fairness across individuals should be judged on the basis of «opportunities» or on the basis of «outcomes.» The opportunities notion of fairness implies that individuals who face the same investment opportunities (have the same wealth and the same portfolio choices) should face the same tax burden regardless of the outcomes of their investment decisions; this view of fairness has been attributed to the ITP approach. In contrast, the outcomes notion of fairness implies that the actual outcomes of investment decisions are critical and should form the basis of taxation; this view has been attributed to the ICF approach and is sometimes phrased as the notion that ex post «winners» should pay higher taxes than «losers» who have the same opportunities.

Early discussions suggested that this difference was critical and that a system based on opportunities was likely to be perceived as fundamentally unfair.[58/] The examples described in Chapter 8 suggest that this difference is more apparent than real under many circumstances; in particular, as long as investments can be replicated, taxpayers are subject to tax rates that are constant across time periods, and the government can invest tax proceeds (which are received at an earlier point in time under the tax prepayment approach) at the average rate of return in the economy, both the after-tax returns to the investor and government receipts are the same under the two approaches.

An additional example may be useful in illustrating this point. Consider an investor in the 30 percent tax bracket who earns and invests $1,000. The investment has a 0.2 probability of a five-fold return and a 0.8 probability of becoming worthless after one «period»; the average gross rate of return in the economy, which is assumed to equal the government's discount rate, is thus 0.2 (i.e., 0.2 x 5 + 0.8 x (−1) = 0.2). Under the ITP approach (the «opportunities» approach where tax is prepaid), the investor pays tax of $300 in the first period, invests the remaining $700, and has period two consumption of either $4,200 (6 x 700) or zero, depending on the outcome of the investment. Under the ICF (the «outcomes» approach), the investor invests the full $1,000 but must pay tax at a rate of 70 percent on any returns. Depending on the outcome, the investor again has period two consumption of either $4,200 (6 x 1000 x 0.7) or zero, but pays tax in period two of either $1,800 (6 x 1000 x 0.3) or zero. Consumption possibilities are clearly the same under either approach for both «winners» and «losers». Moreover, as long as the government can invest at the average rate of return in the economy, the expected value of tax revenues in period two pesos is 360 in either case (300 x 1.2 for the ITP tax and 0.2 x 1800 + 0 for the ICF tax).

This argument must be qualified in several ways. First, situations in which investment opportunities can not be replicated, such as unique market opportunities identified by a single entrepreneur, are by no means trivial. Second, the government may be unwilling or unable to invest at the average gross rate of return in the economy, so that the present value as well as the time path of revenues would be different under the two approaches. Third, government revenues and private consumption would be larger under the ICF approach to the extent that individuals are risk averse and government risk-sharing encourages individual risk-taking. In this case the tax-induced increase in individual risk-taking yields positive returns on average.

Finally, the perception problems associated with the tax prepayment approach, especially within the context of a tax system with progressive marginal rates, could be significant. Such problems could arise for two reasons. First, some observers might feel that the above qualifications are sufficiently important that the equivalence result is of little policy significance. Second, and more likely, is that policy-makers in Colombia would either not understand or not be aware of the theoretical result just presented, but would certainly be aware of the intuitively appealing notion that «winners» should pay more tax than «losers.»

Nevertheless, these results suggest that, from an economic perspective, there is relatively little difference between basing a consumption tax on an opportunities rather than an outcomes approach. Moreover, this distinction is relatively unimportant in the context of the Simplified Alternative Tax for two reasons. First, it is important to note that most highly successful business investments, such as venture capital success stories and highly productive oil wells, would in fact be taxed on an «outcomes» or cash flow basis under the business tax component of the Simplified Alternative Tax. Second, for individuals, the main examples of highly successful outcomes that are not business related (and thus not subject to tax under the business tax) are items such as lottery winnings, prizes, and awards. It was recommended above that the current Colombian withholding tax on lottery winnings be maintained, and that all other prizes and awards be included in the individual tax base of the Simplified Alternative Tax. Accordingly, the distinction between the «opportunities» nature of the ITP tax and the «outcomes» nature of the ICF tax is almost certainly not of sufficient importance to be a critical factor in the choice between the two approaches.

B. Income Averaging

Income averaging is desirable on equity grounds from a lifetime perspective. However, explicit averaging is inappropriate in Colombia, since it introduces many problems, including complexity and administrative difficulties, especially those associated with the monitoring of multi-year records. As a result, any provisions in the tax structure that allow for implicit averaging may be important.

The ICF tax would provide more opportunities than the ITP approach for implicit averaging, since the timing of taxation would be determined by consumption rather than by earnings patterns, as under the ITP approach; Since the Colombian tax structure provides for relatively narrow rate differences, this problem is of relatively little importance. Moreover, the recommended treatment for retirement benefits provides an effective averaging mechanism for the relatively small fraction of the population in Colombia that can use such benefits to defer the receipt of labor income.

On a related point, some critics of the ICF consumption tax argue that it is, or would be perceived to be, unfair because it imposes relatively high tax burdens during the high-debt period of youth and the high-dissaving period of old age. This problem does not arise under the ITP approach, since tax burdens generally track earned income. Any problems of the ICF tax in this area could be mitigated by the provision discussed above that would allow some fixed amount of loans to be treated on a tax prepayment basis — but only at the cost of creating opportunities for tax abuses. Similar provisions could be made for housing purchases.

C. Housing and Other Consumer Durables

Apart from any subsidies (which could be applied under either approach), the tax treatment of owner-occupied housing would be similar under the two types of consumption taxes. It would be extraordinarily difficult, from both an administrative and a political standpoint, to impute the returns to investment in owner-occupied housing and include them in an individual cash flow base. As a result, both ITP and ICF plans would almost certainly treat housing on a tax-prepaid basis. For similar reasons, consumer durables and collectibles presumably would also be treated on a tax prepayment basis under both plans. That is, investments in owner-occupied housing would not be deductible, and no attempt would be made to impute rent to the owner.[59] The primary difference is that down payments withdrawn from a qualified account would result in a bulge in tax base under an ICF-based tax, since such funds would be withdrawn from a qualified account and included in the ICF tax base. One solution to this problem, if it were thought significant, would be to allow something like ten-year averaging for down payments for owner-occupied housing; this would add some complexity to the system.

D. The Taxation of Non-Wage Returns to Entrepreneurship

An ICF consumption tax couples cash flow treatment of receipts and expenditures at the business level with cash flow treatment at the individual level. Such an approach results in the double taxation of non-wage returns to entrepreneurship. This occurs because when an individual contributes entrepreneurial skills to a start-up venture neither the individual nor the firm gets a deduction for this risky «investment». Suppose that the venture is successful and the individual receives payment in the form of stock in the company. The result is that the returns to this entrepreneurship are taxed first at the company level, since there is no deduction for the «investment», and then at the individual level either as capital gains or as dividends.[60/] This problem does not arise under an ITP tax, since dividends and capital gains are not taxed at the individual level.

The double taxation of non-wage returns to entrepreneurship under a ICF tax would have several important and potentially undesirable effects in Colombia. To the extent such returns represent pure economic profits, double-taxing them would be efficient (although arguably inequitable) and would allow lower rates of tax on income from other activities where taxes are distortionary. However, to the extent such payments represent returns to risk-taking, a disincentive to risk-taking may arise, especially in the presence of a progressive rate structure and limitations on loss offsets and carryforwards. Such a result would be inconsistent with the goal of encouraging economic growth in Colombia. On balance, the absence of double taxation of the returns to entrepreneurship under the ITP tax seems to be a distinct advantage.

E. Defining Activities Subject to Business Taxation

It would be highly desirable for any consumption tax plan to be structured in such a way as to prevent abuses which involve «gaming the system» by assigning deductions and/or losses to cash flow accounts while receiving tax prepayment treatment (i.e., exclusion) for income and/or gains.[61/] This problem arises (leaving aside the possibility of manipulating international transactions) only under the combination of the consumption-based business tax and the ITP tax, where business receipts and purchases are included in the tax base on a cash flow basis, but individuals receive tax prepayment treatment. Accordingly, under an ITP tax, the definition of businesses, which are required to use cash flow treatment for receipts and purchases, would have to be quite broad (e.g., including speculative land purchases and the ownership of rights to royalties) in order to prevent opportunities for such schemes. Determining which activities would require the filing of a business return would be difficult and would inevitably require some arbitrary distinctions; administering such rules would also be difficult.

Note that a de minimis rule exempting small businesses from filing returns generally would be desirable on simplicity grounds. However, such a rule would open avenues for abuse of the type described in the text, since «small» firms qualifying for the tax exemption would effectively be treated on a tax prepayment basis. Finally, note also that monitoring international transactions to insure that similar techniques were not used to avoid or evade taxation would be difficult under both plans.

V. Conclusion

The above discussion presents a compelling argument in support of the ITP approach as the preferred method of structuring the individual component of a direct consumption-based tax in Colombia. Its primary advantage over the ICF approach is that it is much simpler in terms of compliance, monitoring and administration. In addition, structuring the tax to be consistent with the lifetime endowment view of tax equity would be marginally easier, while transitional problems would be broadly similar under the two approaches. All of the remaining points considered above either favor the ITP approach or are not sufficiently important to outweigh its simplicity advantages. Accordingly, if Colombia is considering a direct form of consumption taxation it should seriously consider only the ITP approach.

TABLE 9-1

Comparison of Tax Burdens and Profitability of Foreign Investment Alternative Foreign Tax Credit Treatment: New Marginal Investment

	Income Tax, Creditable in United States	Simplified Alternative Tax, Credit-able in U.S.	Simplified Alternative Tax, Not Creditable in U.S.
U.S. Parent Firm in Deficit Foreign Tax Credit Position			
Colombian Taxes Paid	25.50	15.00	15.00
U.S. Tax Liability	17.00	17.00	11.90
U.S. Tax Not Offset	—	2.00	11.90
Usable Excess Credits	8.50	—	—
Net Additional Tax	17.00	17.00	26.90
After-tax Profits	33.00	33.00	23.10
U.S. Parent Firm in Excess Foreign Tax Credit Position			
Colombian Taxes Paid	25.50	15.00	15.00
U.S. Tax Liability	17.00	17.00	11.90
U.S. Tax Not Offset	—	2.00	11.90
Other U.S. Tax Offset	—	2.00	11.90
Net Additional Tax	25.50	15.00	15.00
After-tax Profits	24.50	35.00	35.00

Notes: The example assumes a $1,000 expenditure on a capital good that yields $1,100 in one year, at which time the capital good is fully depreciated. The purchase of the good is financed 50 percent with debt and 50 percent with equity. The Colombian business-level tax and withholding tax are both 30 percent and the U.S. corporate income tax rate is 34 percent. After-tax profits are those of the U.S. parent. Creditability is assumed to be granted for the business-level tax (income tax or consumption-based tax) and for the withholding tax imposed on remitted dividends, or to be denied for both Colombian taxes.

Legend: Colombian Taxes Paid includes the business level tax and the withholding tax.
U.S. Tax Liability is the tentative U.S. liability on dividends received from Colombia.
U.S. Tax Not Offset is the remaining U.S. tax due after credit for Colombian taxes.
Other U.S. Tax Offset is the remaining tax liability on Colombian-source income offset by foreign tax credits generated by other (non-Colombian) foreign source income. Net Additional Tax is the combined additional Colombian and U.S. tax after all U.S. foreign tax credits.

TABLE 9-2

Comparison of Tax Burdens and Profitability of Foreign Investment Alternative Foreign Tax Credit Treatment: New Inframarginal Investment

	Income Tax, Creditable in United States	Simplified Alternative Tax, Creditable in U.S.	Simplified Alternative Tax, Not Creditable in U.S.
U.S. Parent Firm in Deficit Foreign Tax Credit Position			
Colombian Taxes Paid	76.50	66.00	66.00
U.S. Tax Liability	51.00	51.00	28.56
Usable Excess Credits	25.50	15.00	—
Net Additional Tax	51.00	51.00	94.56
After-tax Profits	99.00	99.00	55.44
U.S. Parent Firm in Excess Foreign Tax Credit Position			
Colombian Taxes Paid	76.50	66.00	66.00
U.S. Tax Liability	51.00	51.00	28.56
Usable Excess Credits	—	—	28.56
Other U.S. Tax Offset	—	—	28.56
Net Additional Tax	76.50	66.00	66.00
After-tax Profits	73.50	84.00	84.00

Notes: The example assumes a $1,000 expenditure on a capital good that yields $1,200 in one year, at which time the capital good is fully depreciated. The purchase of the good is financed 50 percent with debt and 50 percent with equity. The Colombian business-level tax and withholding tax are both 30 percent and the U.S. corporate income tax rate is 34 percent. After-tax profits are those of the U.S. parent. Creditability is assumed to be granted for the business-level tax (income tax or consumption-based tax) and for the withholding tax imposed on remitted dividends, or to be denied for both Colombian taxes.

Legend: Colombian Taxes Paid includes the business level tax and the withholding tax.
U.S. Tax Liability is the tentative U.S. liability on dividends received from Colombia.
U.S. Tax Not Offset is the remaining U.S. tax due after credit for Colombian taxes.
Other U.S. Tax Offset is the remaining tax liability on Colombian-source income offset by foreign tax credits generated by other (non-Colombian) foreign source income. Net Additional Tax is the combined additional Colombian and U.S. tax after all U.S. foreign tax credits.

TABLE 9-3

Comparison of Tax Burdens and Profitability of Foreign Investment Alternative Foreign Tax Credit Treatment: Receipts from Existing Capital

	Income Tax, Creditable in United States	Simplified Alternative Tax, Creditable in U.S.	Simplified Alternative Tax, Not Creditable in U.S.

U.S. Parent Firm in Deficit Foreign Tax Credit Position

Colombian Taxes Paid	535.50	546.00	546.00
U.S. Tax Liability	357.00	357.00	171.36
Usable Excess Credits	178.50	189.00	—
Net Additional Tax	357.00	357.00	717.36
After-tax Profits	693.00	693.00	332.64

U.S. Parent Firm in Excess Foreign Tax Credit Position

Colombian Taxes Paid	535.50	546.00	546.00
U.S. Tax Liability	357.00	357.00	171.36
U.S. Tax Not Offset	—	—	171.36
Other U.S. Tax Offset	—	—	171.36
Net Additional Tax	535.50	546.00	546.00
After-tax Profits	514.50	504.00	504.00

Notes: The example assumes that a fully depreciated capital good yields before-tax income of $1,100. The Colombian business-level tax and withholding tax are both 30 percent and the U.S. corporate income tax rate is 34 percent. After-tax profits are those of the U.S. parent. Creditability is assumed to be granted for the business-level tax (income tax or consumption-based tax) and for the withholding tax imposed on remitted dividends, or to be denied for both Colombian taxes.

Legend: Colombian Taxes Paid includes the business level tax and the withholding tax.
U.S. Tax Liability is the tentative U.S. liability on dividends received from Colombia.
U.S. Tax Not Offset is the remaining U.S. tax due after credit for Colombian taxes.
Other U.S. Tax Offset is the remaining tax liability on Colombian-source income offset by foreign tax credits generated by other (non-Colombian) foreign source income. Net Additional Tax is the combined additional Colombian and U.S. tax after all U.S. foreign tax credits.

FOOTNOTES

1/ Note that strict cash flow treatment of business receipts and expenditures under the Simplified Alternative Tax would imply different accounting rules than those currently used under the Colombian value added tax; the use of separate accounting systems for these two taxes would add complexity to the Colombian tax system. This issue is addressed in Section III.A.3 below.

2/ A «defined contribution» pension plan is one where the employer makes specified contributions to a pension fund, but the level of pension benefits paid to covered employees is determined by the earnings on the investments made by the pension fund. Thus, the employee bears the risk associated with uncertain investment returns. It is to be distinguished from a «defined benefit» pension plan, which is one where the employer has an obligation to pay retirement benefits at a specified level. Covered employees are guaranteed the benefits specified upon retirement, independently of the level of earnings of any reserves established to fund the payment of such benefits. Thus, the employer bears the risk associated with uncertain investment returns.

3/ A troublesome question that is discussed at length below is whether a tax patterned after the Simplified Alternative Tax would be allowed as a tax credit by capital-exporting countries, especially the United States.

4/ Equity contributions are not included in the tax base and no deduction is allowed for dividends paid.

5/ The foreigner can be subject either to no foreign taxation or to income taxation. The avoidance schemes described below are ineffective if the second party is also a taxable Colombian business; in this case, symmetric treatment of the transactions implies no net tax advantages to the two parties and thus no opportunity for tax avoidance.

6/ Thus the analysis also applies to the installment sales problem discussed above.

7/ Individuals selling production inputs would be treated as businesses under the Simplified Alternative Tax.

8/ This discussion points out an interesting feature of the Simplified Alternative Tax. Abstracting from the question of cash versus accrual accounting for sales described above, the Simplified Alternative Tax can be viewed as a form of a subtraction-type value added tax. That is, the calculation of the business tax base corresponds to that under a subtraction-type VAT (sales less expenditures other than wages and salaries), except that a deduction is allowed for wages. Wages and salaries deductible at the business level are taxed at the individual level, where personal exemptions and progressive marginal rates are easily included in the tax structure. For this reason, plans such as the Simplified Alternative Tax have been referred to as «personal exemption VATs.» See McLure (1987).

9/ The reasonableness of this conclusion is supported by the recent history of tax policy in the United States. In 1981 the United States adopted a combination of highly accelerated depreciation allowances and an investment credit (ITC) that in present value terms was roughly equivalent to expensing at the rate of inflation then prevailing. Thus marginal effective tax rates on income from equity-financed investments were roughly zero; because nominal interest expense remained fully deductible, marginal effective tax rates on income from debt-financed investments were quite negative. The Tax Reform Act of 1986 repealed the ITC and substituted much less generous depreciation allowances, in part because the decline in the rate of inflation in the interim had made this combination of allowances even more generous that expensing, creating negative marginal effective tax rates even on income from equity-financed investments and worsening the distortion of resource allocation. See U.S. Department of the Treasury (1984), vol. 2, chapter 8, for the Department's analysis of the negative effects of this policy.

Several points are noteworthy about this episode. First, it would be quite anomalous for the United States to object to a system of taxation that did explicitly what the United States did indirectly in 1981, introduce expensing. Second, during the years when this extremely generous system of allowances was in effect no foreign country threatened to deny its foreign tax credit for income tax paid to the United States. Similarly, the United States did not object when the United Kingdom employed expensing. There seems to be no general objection to tax systems that are more generous than an income tax. Finally, starting from a position that combined expensing or its present-value equivalent with full deduction of interest expense, the United States could have avoided negative marginal effective tax rates on income from debt-financed investments in either of two logically and economically consistent ways: by retaining the deduction for (inflation-adjusted) interest expense and decelerating depreciation allowances or by retaining expensing and eliminating the deduction of interest expense. The United States chose the former approach (but without indexing interest deductions), whereas the Simplified Alternative Tax would involve the latter. As noted above, the net effect of the consumption-based business tax is more generous treatment than provided by a tax on income, not less.

347

10/ It should be noted that this interpretation is somewhat different from that given to the application of the consumption-based business tax to infra-marginal returns in Chapter 8. Though this alternative interpretation was mentioned in Chapter 8, it was argued there that the government is simply a partner in all investments, sharing whatever returns they yield, whether equal, above, or below that on «marginal» projects. In the present interpretation the government is seen as a partner only to the extent of the return on marginal returns, but as a tax collector on infra-marginal returns. It helps to emphasize the similarity of the income and consumption-based business taxes where infra-marginal returns are concerned.

11/ It is conceivable that expensing could be interpreted as mere acceleration of depreciation allowances, rather than as a compensating benefit of the type required to offset the disallowance of interest deductions. To counter such hair-splitting, it would presumably be possible for legislation to break the expensing deduction into two components, the present-value equivalent of economic depreciation and an additional compensating benefit large enough that together the two would equal the total expenditure in question.

12/ If the government were to allow loss carry-forwards to be augmented at a rate less than the market return, then a cash flow tax liability would arise in the second scenario. As under the income tax, such a policy encourages business mergers between firms with current tax losses and those with positive cash flow. In the context of the consumption-based business tax this implies that the government is an asymmetric partner that shares fully in gains but not in losses.

13/ This calculation demonstrates that if a foreign tax is not creditable in the United States, it still may be a deductible expense; if a tax is not creditable, a firm does not face the restriction that creditable taxes must be either credited or deducted (but not partially deducted and partially credited).

14/ Recall that under the dynastic view the donor in principle owes no tax because it has been prepaid.

15/ See Goode (1980).

16/ This rationale applies to both consumption-based and income-based reforms; however, as argued above, the treatment of gifts and bequests is more critical under the former alternative.

17/ Recall that under the Colombian income tax, gifts and bequests received are in principle taxed as occasional gains. However compliance in this area is notoriously poor. Efforts to enforce and administer the taxation of such transfers should be increased under the Simplified Alternative Tax.

18/ «Tax base shifting» refers to attempts to lower tax burdens through transactions that shift tax base from a high-bracket taxpayer to one in a lower tax bracket. Such techniques are particularly common within families. For example, in the ICF tax context, a high-bracket parent could loan funds to a low-bracket child at an interest rate below the market rate, who would then make an investment yielding interest or dividends at a rate higher than the interest rate specified on the loan. As a result, the return to the investment in excess of the interest rate on the loan would be subject to taxation at the rate of the child rather than that of the parent.

19/ This point is explained in the appendix.

20/ See Hall and Rabushka (1983, 1985).

21/ Such opportunities are not entirely eliminated because a high bracket taxpayer can still shift some of his tax base to any relatives with income less than the amount that is not subject to tax due to personal exemptions and the standard deduction. Of course, the amount of tax that can be evaded in this way is quite limited.

22/ Within limits any revenue shortfalls that occur with implementation of this proposal could be offset by either increases in the tax rates on individual net wealth or increases in the withholding tax on foreign remittances, rather than increases in rates under the individual and business components of the Simplified Alternative Tax.

23/ Note that this implies that self-employed individuals offering professional services would be required to file a business tax return.

24/ This treatment is discussed further below.

25/ Alternatively, the same result could be achieved by establishing two related foreign firms, one of which would report realized losses while the other would not report realized profits.

26/ It is argued below that business losses should never be allowed to offset an individual's earned income; instead they should be carried forward with interest.

27/ Note also that the incentive to report deductions for foreign investment while understating or not reporting the associated receipts also exists under the income tax. However, in this case the gains to such evasion techniques are not as great as under the Simplified Alternative Tax, since expensing is not allowed.

28/ As noted above, receipts and expenses due to the foreign investment activities of a firm would be segregated in a separate cash flow account. It is unclear whether such wholly-owned subsidiaries are recognized as an important class of companies under Colombian law.

29/ It also implies that the relatively low-rate owners of a closely-held business can appropriate a portion of the government's share of inframarginal returns to investment by raising their own salaries when such returns are earned. In this case, the government's share of the inframarginal returns to the investment would be reduced. The importance of this problem is, however, quite limited, since it involves only the taxes that can be saved by paying less than the top marginal rate on such returns.

30/ In both cases, the buyer benefits from under-reporting the value of land since the base of the net wealth tax is understated.

31/ Moreover, it might be difficult to prevent attempts by buyers and sellers to use tax-exempt institutions as «middle men» to alter the allocations between buyers and sellers. (In the most blatant case, the tax-exempt institution would be affiliated with the buyer or seller.) For example, the seller could agree to sell to the tax-exempt institution with a relatively high allocation of the purchase price to the land portion in order to reduce the taxable amount attributable to improvements; the tax-exempt institution could then sell to the buyer with a relatively low allocation to the land portion in order to overstate the deductible amount attributable to improvements. Opportunities for such tax avoidance should not exist in principle since land transactions by tax-exempt institutions would be taxed as unrelated business activities; however, enforcement of such rules might be quite difficult.

32/ To avoid confusion, it should be noted that the distinction discussed above is not equivalent to that between cash flow and tax prepayment treatment. The cash flow and tax prepayment approaches are both accounting methods that yield results consistent with a consumption tax; that is, capital income is exempt from tax under both approaches. In contrast, disallowing deductions for land purchases while including in gross receipts the returns attributable to the land is equivalent to subjecting such returns to income taxation at the statutory rate. Such treatment clearly results in a much greater tax burden on income from land than that under a consumption tax.

33/ In particular, rules determining the treatment of mixed business/personal use assets would be difficult under the Simplified Alternative Tax. In principle, the taxpayer should be allowed to expense only part of the cost of a mixed business/personal use asset. Conceptually the amount eligible for expensing would equal the undiscounted sum of the estimated business use portion of economic depreciation in each year of the life of the asset; if the estimated fraction of business use during any year of the life of the asset changed from the taxpayer's initial estimate, a tax adjustment should be made that would ensure that the present value of the total deductions was correct. In practice, the best that can be hoped for is a rough estimate of the fraction of personal use at the time of purchase (with a corresponding reduction of the fraction of the cost of the asset that is expensed), with no subsequent adjustments. In order to limit the obvious potential for abuse, the rules that simply deny deductions for assets with a significant personal use component should be drawn tightly.

Note that the problem of determining the treatment of mixed business/personal use assets also arises under an income tax. However, the treatment of changes in the fraction of business use of the asset is straightforward in principle; the deductions for economic depreciation in each year of the life of the asset are multiplied by the fraction of business use in that year. Moreover, the taxpayer should not be allowed to deduct a fraction of interest expense incurred to purchase the asset in question equal to the percentage of personal use. In principle, this is the treatment required under current Colombian law. In fact, attempting to implement such a rule would lead to substantial complexity; due to the fungibility of money it would be necessary to make fairly arbitrary rules for the determination of whether the taxpayers's funds or borrowed funds were used to purchase the asset. In practice, it is also quite difficult to ensure taxpayer compliance in those situations in which the business use fraction is (or is alleged to be) large in the year of purchase but declines dramatically in subsequent years. The income tax approach does, however, have one important further advantage over the Simplified Alternative Tax. Under the income tax deductions for interest and depreciation must be taken over a period of years, whereas under the Simplified Alternative Tax (in the absence of disposition of the asseet or a change in the business/personal use fraction) only the initial purchase of an asset has relevance for tax purposes. Thus improper deductions for dual-use assets should, in principle, be more easily policed under the former approach than under the latter.

34/ Without indexing, the losses are less valuable to the firm that experiences them than they are to firms that can deduct them currently.

35/ Note also that indexing losses implies that there is little or no reason to worry about transactions between profitable firms and firms with losses that are designed solely to enable losses to be deducted currently. Such transactions are commonly considered to constitute tax avoidance under a system that does not allow indexation of losses. However, they cause few problems, if any, when indexing of losses is allowed since the present value of tax liability should generally be unchanged by such transactions. (The primary effect would be to ensure that losses can be utilized, even if the firm showing the loss never has a profit for tax purposes in the future; this does not seem problematical.)

36/ Note that such transactions generally do not reduce overall tax liability if the customer is another taxable business; the reduction in the price of services purchased from the financial institution implies smaller deductions for the firm, and interest receipts are not taxable in any event.

37/ Such tax avoidance is also a problem with the highly accelerated depreciation deductions provided under current law; it would be a less serious problem under the system of indexed economic depreciation allowances recommended in Chapters 5 and 7.

38/ However, as discussed below, the taxation of presumptive income should be eliminated under the Simplified Alternative Tax; accordingly, the provisions in Chapter 6 related to the adjustment of net wealth by the excess of presumptive income over income as ordinarily determined would be irrelevant.

39/ Note that this implies that real economic depreciation would be used in the calculation of the value of depreciable assets (following the procedures specified in Chapter 5). Such an approach is desirable to measure net wealth accurately, but it would be fairly complex. Accordingly, a simpler approximation to economic depreciation, such as a modified version of the system under current law, might be desirable for purposes of measuring net wealth. Further discussion of this point appears in Chapter 10 below.

40/ In addition, even if the Simplified Alternative Tax were adopted in Colombia, financial accounting procedures might change over time to reflect some of the other inflation accounting techniques described in Chapter 7; such changes would result in a more accurate representation of income for financial reporting purposes even if they would be unnecessary for reporting purposes under the Simplified Alternative Tax. If this were to occur, such changes should also be adopted for purposes of calculating the base of the net wealth tax.

41/ Such rate increases should be designed to meet the goal of distributional neutrality described in Chapter 1. They should initially be based on revenue estimates of the effects of the proposed reforms, and then revised when actual data on revenue effects are obtained. Note that adoption of the recommendations in Chapter 6 would result in a significant expansion of the net wealth tax base. As a result, it might be necessary to lower rather than raise wealth tax rates to achieve revenue neutrality. Note also that, in the event of a revenue shortfall, increases in the withholding tax on foreign remittances are an alternative source of revenue.

42/ The treatment of interest received by businesses is discussed below.

43/ Of course, investors with remaining basis greater than outstanding loans would gain from the application of these transition rules.

44/ Because of the way the «7/3» rule described in chapter 3 is structured, dividends are construed to be paid out of pre-1986 income only if dividends exceed 7/3 of income tax for the year. For this reason it would actually complicate tax compliance and administration under the income tax if the distinction between pre-1986 and post-1985 sources of dividends were eliminated, because it would necessitate creation of a distinction that is unnecessary under the 7/3 rule.

45/ Recall, however, that deductibility of the inflationary component of interest expense in being phased-out under current law.

46/ The details of present value expensing were presented in the appendix to Chapter 8.

47/ As described in Chapter 8, an allowance for «undeducted expense» would be required in the year of sale; the calculation of this deduction would be analogous to that under the system of inflation-indexed economic depreciation allowances described in Chapter 7.

48/ The material presented in this appendix draws on Zodrow and McLure (1987) and Zodrow (1987).

49/ See, for example, U.S. Department of the Treasury (1977).

50/ See Graetz (1979).

51/ The treatment of immigrants would probably be the same under both approaches — the assets and liabilities of an immigrant at the time of entry would be ignored for tax purposes. Of course, immigrants would have a greater opportunity to defer tax on income earned in Colombia under the ICF approach, since assets owned prior to entry could be sold with the proceeds being deposited in a qualified account.

52/ Subsidization of saving might be viewed as desirable in Colombia as a means of stimulating economic growth. However, this argument for subsidies to domestic saving is not compelling since such subsidies may have little effect on economic growth even if they are successful in stimulating saving; the additional saving may be invested abroad or may simply replace foreign savings invested in Colombia.

53/ See the transition rules recommended for the proposed income tax reform in Chapter 5.

54/ Business transitional issues were considered above.

55/ See U.S. Treasury (1977).

56/ Note that Hall and Rabushka (1983) recommend that no deductions be allowed for the remaining basis of «old» depreciable assets. Such treatment is sufficiently harsh that it is totally unrealistic from a political standpoint.

57/ Such treatment is similar to that under current law, except that the fair market value of the gift or bequest would be included in the tax base of the recipient rather than the basis of the donor and that there would be no special «occasional gains» treatment. It thus corresponds to the treatment recommended under the income tax reform proposals presented in Chapter 5.

58/ See Graetz (1979) and U.S. Treasury (1977).

59/ In principle, no deduction should be allowed for home mortgage interest; see the discussion in Chapter 9.

60/ Contracts that provided for large (deductible) wage payments contingent upon the success of new ventures could provide a partially satisfactory means of dealing with this problem.

61/ See Graetz (1979).

10

A Comparison of the Two Proposals

A Comparison of the two Proposals

Thus far, this Report has outlined two possible tax reform strategies for Colombia. The first is a restructuring of the current system to conform with income tax principles, coupled with thorough reform of the taxation of presumptive income and the net wealth tax; this will be referred to as the «income-based» proposal. The second is the introduction of the Simplified Alternative Tax, coupled with somewhat more modest reforms in the tax on net wealth and the elimination of the taxation of presumptive income; this will be referred to as the «consumption-based» proposal. This section compares the relative advantages and disadvantages of the two proposals.[1]

The issues discussed in this section are grouped according to the four criteria commonly used to evaluate tax structures – fairness, economic neutrality, simplicity, and consistency with economic growth.[2] To a large extent, the discussion focuses on the major components of the income-based and consumption-based tax reform strategies seen as «stand alone» taxes; that is, on the reformed income tax and the Simplified Alternative Tax. However, the implications of the net wealth tax (and the taxation of presumptive income under the income-based strategy) are also considered when appropriate.

I. Equity

It is essential that any tax reform undertaken by Colombia be perceived to be fair – by the general public, by decision makers in the public sector, and by those who mold public opinion in Colombia. Accordingly, the relative merits of the two proposals in terms of the equity criterion are a critical issue. Equity arguments for and against these two forms of taxation are presented below.

As noted in Chapter 1, the equity of a tax system is generally judged in both horizontal and vertical dimensions. Horizontal equity requires similar tax treatment of individuals who have a similar «ability to pay» taxes. Vertical equity requires larger tax payments by those individuals with a greater «ability to pay». This is commonly taken to imply tax payments that increase more rapidly than ability to pay – a progressive rate structure, although such a conclusion is not accepted universally. The following discussion considers each of these criteria in turn and then briefly examines several other related issues.

The primary distinction between the two tax reform strategies lies in the treatment of capital income.[3] The basic difference in this area between the reformed income tax and the Simplified Alternative Tax is clear; capital income is subject to tax only under the former alternative. However, a complete characterization of all aspects of the two reform strategies is more complex. Specifically, capital income is in fact indirectly subject to an important form of taxation under the consumption-based proposal, since wealth would be subject to a modified version of the current Colombian tax on net wealth. By comparison, capital income may be taxed under three different components of the income-based proposal – the business tax, the individual tax (as ordinary or presumptive income), and the net wealth tax. All of these aspects of the two proposals are considered in the discussion below.

A. Horizontal Equity

The definitions of horizontal and vertical equity suggest that the most fundamental question related to the equity properties of the two proposals is whether income or consumption is a better measure of the ability of an individual to pay taxes, that is, whether horizontal and vertical equity should be defined in terms of an individual's income or his consumption. This section focuses on two aspects of this question – the choice of the time period to be used in measuring ability to pay and the role of administrative considerations.

It is interesting (and perhaps somewhat surprising) to note that a critical issue in this debate is the length of the time period to be used in evaluating the individual's ability to pay. Income tax proponents rely on the argument that income – or the potential to consume – in a given relatively short period such as a year (or a few years with income averaging) is the appropriate measure of ability to pay taxes in that period; the exercise of that potential in the form of actual consumption is viewed as irrelevant. By excluding capital income from the individual tax base, consumption-based taxes exclude an important component of ability to pay, according to this view, and one that is highly concentrated among the wealthy.

Advocates of consumption-based taxes such as the Simplified Alternative Tax reply that a year (or even several years) is far too short a time period over which to evaluate ability to pay, and that ability to pay ideally should be evaluated according to a measure of lifetime potential to consume. The latter frame of reference implies that a consumption-based tax consistent with the lifetime view of tax equity, rather than an annual income tax, is the appropriate measure of ability to pay.[4] This follows from the fact that the present value of the tax base under the Simplified Alternative Tax is roughly invariant with respect to the time path of earnings and saving, and equal to the present value of the lifetime endowment (or lifetime potential to consume), as defined in Chapter 8.

In contrast, under an income tax the present value of taxes paid by individuals with the same lifetime potential to consume or lifetime endowment differs if the time path of either earnings or savings differs.[5] According to a lifetime perspective, the measure of ability to pay under the consumption-based Simplified Alternative Tax is quite appropriately «lifetime income», or the present value of all earned income and transfers received. In contrast, the base of an annual income tax mismeasures that base; it thus violates the principle of horizontal equity by overtaxing those who save unusually large fractions of income early in life either because they earn a disproportionate share of their income when young or because they elect to defer consumption.

The lifetime perspective has considerable intuitive appeal. The fact that most tax experts support averaging of income over several years in principle (even if they oppose it on administrative grounds) suggests acceptance of the general notion that a year is too short a time period to use when measuring an individual's ability to pay (even though it does not indicate agreement about the appropriate tax base over that multi-year period). To a certain extent, the logic that supports such a multi-period approach is theoretically applicable to the individual's lifetime as well.[6] However, there is considerably less agreement about the extent to which the fairness of a tax system should be evaluated in terms of lifetime tax burdens.

Income tax proponents make two general types of arguments against the use of the individual lifetime as the appropriate time period over which to measure ability to pay. First, they note that calculations which demonstrate that a tax such as the Simplified Alternative Tax is equivalent to a lifetime income tax are based on unrealistic assumptions. In particular, they argue that the assumptions that individuals systematically make lifetime consumption plans and that capital markets are perfect are unrealistic. Although these assumptions are indeed unrealistic, it is unclear that they bias the result toward a preference for consumption taxation over income taxation.

Second, income tax proponents sometimes argue that granting taxpayers the opportunity to engage in long-term averaging is undesirable. For example, it is sometimes argued that taxpayers with relatively high incomes in periods characterized by temporary tax rate increases should not be allowed to reduce their tax burdens through averaging. Alternatively, some argue that the marginal utility of income is lower during high-income years, even for taxpayers with typical lifetime incomes, so that relatively high taxes should be assessed during such periods without granting taxpayers the opportunity to reduce their tax burdens through averaging over long periods of time. Such arguments are difficult to resolve; however, both positions seem at least somewhat inconsistent with the multi-period approach used to justify short-term averaging.

A second aspect of the question of whether income or consumption represents a better measure of ability to pay on horizontal equity grounds is the role of administrative considerations. As noted above, the primary conceptual difference between the two proposals is that capital income is not taxed under the Simplified Alternative Tax component of the consumption-based proposal while, at least in principle, it would be nearly fully taxed under the reformed income tax component of the income-based plan. However, it could be noted that administration and enforcement of the provisions of the current Colombian income tax are significantly more comprehensive for labor income than for capital income; in particular, administration and enforcement of the taxation of interest income, capital gains, and income from foreign investment are relatively poor. This situation would be likely to continue under a reformed income tax; indeed, administration and enforcement might even be somewhat more difficult under the reformed income tax than under current law because the provisions for measuring capital income would be more complex.

Such a situation leads to problems of horizontal equity under the income tax. Specifically, the pattern of differential administration and enforcement described above implies that, at each income level, individuals with a disproportionately large share of capital income are more likely to be under-taxed than those with a larger share of labor income.

This line of reasoning indicates that a tax that can be administered and enforced uniformly is desirable on horizontal equity grounds. Such uniform administration and enforcement is probably more likely under the Simplified Alternative Tax than under the reformed income tax because taxation of capital income is eliminated; in particular, interest income and capital gains are excluded from the tax base and foreign investment income is effectively subject to a zero rate of tax. Advocates of an income tax object that eliminating the taxation of income from capital is a rather extreme way to eliminate horizontal inequities in the taxation of such income. Of course, if it were possible to improve administration and enforcement of the taxation of capital income under the reformed income tax, any advantages of the Simplified Alternative Tax in this area would be reduced. Yet experience in Colombia and elsewhere gives little reason for optimism in this regard.

The above discussion indicates that the Simplified Alternative Tax is superior to the income tax in terms of the criterion of horizontal equity if the lifetime endowment criterion is adopted and/or if administration and enforcement of the taxation of capital income are likely to be poor under the income tax; the opposite ranking results if ability to pay taxes is better measured over a shorter time period such as a year and the taxation of capital income can be administered and enforced effectively.

In addition, note the importance of taking administrative and enforcement measures to ensure that the fair market value of gifts and inheritances is in fact included in the tax base of the recipient. If this is not accomplished, horizontal equity is not achieved according to the lifetime endowment criterion, since individuals receiving such transfers are systematically under-taxed. This problem is common to both the income-based and the consumption-based proposals. In both cases, the existence of a net wealth tax indirectly compensates for evasion or avoidance of the taxation of gifts and bequests by reducing the net wealth of both donors and recipients. The taxation of capital income under the income tax provides an additional form of indirectly taxing the net wealth of such individuals; since this feature does not exist under the Simplified Alternative Tax, it is doubly important that gifts and inheritances be taxed effectively under the consumption-based strategy, and administrative problems are more troublesome than they would be under the reformed income tax.

B. Vertical Equity

Vertical equity questions are more difficult to resolve. Proponents of income taxation frequently stress the vertical equity problems that are likely to result from exempting capital income from tax, since capital income is highly concentrated among the wealthy; this is certainly true in Colombia. As noted in Chapter 1, a judgement on the proper degree of progressivity of the Colombian tax system is clearly beyond the scope of this Report. In the absence of policy guidance to the contrary, the presumption of the Report is that the implementation of either the income-based or the consumption-based reform packages should be distributionally neutral; that is, the current distribution of the burden of the income and complementary taxes across income classes should be maintained.[7]

Under the proposed income tax, tax rates must be adjusted to achieve distributional neutrality. Presumably adoption of all of the reforms recommended in this Report would result in broadening of both the income and net wealth tax bases; thus marginal tax rates under both taxes could be reduced on average while maintaining the existing distribution of tax burdens across income brackets.

A similar approach could, in principle, be utilized under the Simplified Alternative Tax; that is, marginal tax rates could be adjusted so that the total amount of tax paid by each income class under the Simplified Alternative Tax would be roughly the same as under the current Colombian income tax system. The result would be higher tax rates on the «income» of individuals in the higher income classes, who would receive the greatest benefit from the tax exemption of capital income. Alternatively, revenues under the Simplified Alternative Tax could be supplemented by revenues obtained from increases in the tax rates of the net wealth tax, if such increases are necessary for distributional neutrality after the broadening of the net wealth tax base. (Such base-broadening would be similar to that described in Chapter 6, but less ambitious, as noted in Chapter 9.) In this case, tax rates under the net wealth tax would be adjusted so that the combined burden of the Simplified Alternative Tax and the net wealth tax would be the same across income classes as under the income and complementary taxes of current Colombian law. Such an approach would permit the goal of distributional neutrality to be achieved with lower tax rates on wealthy individuals under the individual component of the Simplified Alternative Tax.

It is not clear, however, whether the problem of maintaining adequate progressivity can in fact be overcome simply by imposing higher tax rates on net wealth. For one thing, the political process may not produce a sufficiently high rate on net wealth to achieve this objective.

Moreover, a significant number of wealthy families may be able to evade the tax on donative transfers. This may have adverse effects on vertical equity, horizontal equity, or both. This potential problem deserves further explanation.

By exempting capital income from taxation, a «stand alone» tax on consumption tends to allow families to accumulate wealth without any payment of tax. This has undesirable effects on the long-run distribution of income, as well as on the short-run distribution of tax burdens. In principle the consumption-based alternative strategy offered in this Report does not suffer from this defect, since it does attempt to reach accumulated wealth, through both the net wealth tax and the inclusion of gifts and bequests received in the tax base of the recipient. However, given the history of tax compliance in Colombia, particularly with respect to the taxation of intra-family wealth transfers, it is questionable whether anything like full taxation of gifts and bequests can actually be achieved, even if required by law. Therefore, it is possible that in practice the consumption-based alternative will allow many wealthy families to pay less tax than under the income-based alternative. Even if the rates are sufficiently high so as to achieve rough overall distributional neutrality, this would still be cause for concern, since horizontal equity would be compromised. To the extent that this supposition is true and that this factor is considered important, the income-based alternative is more attractive.

The implications of the net wealth tax (and the taxation of presumptive income under the income tax) on the comparison of the relative equity properties of the two reform alternatives are difficult to ascertain. Under the consumption-based approach, capital income would be subject to tax only under the net wealth tax. In contrast, under the income-based strategy, various forms of capital or income therefrom would be subject to tax under the business income tax, the individual income tax (as ordinary or presumptive income), and the net wealth tax.

Suppose that some taxation of capital income is thought to be desirable, either because income (or consumption plus net wealth) is perceived to be a better measure of ability to pay than is consumption (alone) or because there are imperfections in the inclusion of gifts and bequests in the tax bases of recipients. In this case, multiple taxation of capital income improves the equity of the tax system to the extent that it compensates for tax evasion and to the extent that each separate tax captures different items of capital income. However, it is likely that to some (perhaps large) extent the same capital or capital income of the same taxpayers is subject to tax under the net wealth tax, the business income tax, and the individual income tax (as ordinary or presumptive income) and that to some extent certain kinds of capital or capital income avoid or evade all these taxes.[8] Whether multiple taxation of capital income, especially under the income and net wealth taxes, is equitable under these circumstances is open to debate. It would clearly be inequitable if one adopts either lifetime endowment or annual income as the sole appropriate measure of ability to pay. However, such multiple taxation of capital income would be equitable if wealth represents additional ability to pay – beyond the income earned on such wealth. (See the discussion in chapter 6.) To the extent such multiple taxation is undesirable, the use of a single, comprehensive and more easily enforceable tax on net wealth, coupled with the consumption-based Simplified Alternative Tax, is arguably a fairer way, if a more indirect way, to tax capital income than the multiple taxation approach proposed under the income-based strategy. In addition, one could argue that the multiple taxation of capital income under the income-based approach effectively assumes that taxpayeors are cheating systematically. That is, the combined tax burden on capital income under all elements of the reformed income tax could be viewed as punitive if taxpayers actually complied with all provisions, but more reasonable if widespread evasion were expected to occur. The troubling implication is that taxpayers will be forced to evade taxes to avoid punitive levels of taxation.

C. Additional Issues

Several additional but less important points are relevant to a comparison of the two strategies in terms of the equity criterion. Conspicuous consumption may dramatize inequity in a very obvious way, while the accumulation of wealth may be less offensive or even desirable to the extent it results in improved performance of the domestic economy. These considerations support a progressive consumption-based tax such as the Simplified Alternative Tax over an income-based tax, especially to the extent the stimulus to saving provided by the exemption of the return to saving results in additional domestic investment.

A related point is that any increases in domestic saving induced by a switch to a consumption-based tax would result in improved labor productivity and higher wages (to the extent such savings resulted in more domestic investment rather than more investment abroad or a substitution of domestic for foreign investment in Colombia). The resulting changes in the distribution of income might be perceived as an equitable tax-induced change. Moreover, more progressivity may be possible under the consumption-based approach than under the income-based strategy, since relatively high consumption tax rates would not result in disincentives to saving and investment. On the other hand, there would be some such disincentives if the net wealth tax rates were higher under the consumption-based strategy than under the income-based strategy. Moreover, the consumption-based alternative may have more adverse effects on work effort, since it is likely to entail higher marginal rates on earned income. Any resulting reduction in labor income would have uncertain effects on the distribution of income. To the extent that reductions in work effort would be disproportionately large for individuals at relatively high income levels, ability to pay – as measured by economic well-being rather than money income – would be more significantly understated for such individuals. (Reductions in work effort would likely be concentrated among high income individuals both because such individuals face the highest marginal tax rates and because they commonly have relatively more discretion in selecting the number of hours they work).

A final potentially important equity issue may favor the income-based tax strategy over the consumption-based approach. Businesses may pay less tax under the Simplified Alternative Tax than under current law. Such an outcome is likely to be subject to a criticism that is potentially significant politically, if difficult to define precisely; specifically, some may argue that business does not bear its «fair share» of the tax burden under the Simplified Alternative Tax. However, as noted previously, it is unclear whether businesses would in fact pay less tax under the Simplified Alternative Tax than under current law. The two major changes would be in the tax treatment of depreciable assets (and of land) and of interest income and expense. These changes would have opposing effects on the business tax base. Expensing under the Simplified Alternative Tax would result in more rapid deductions than the deductions for depreciation allowed under current law or under the system of real economic depreciation proposed in Chapter 5; in a growing economy this means that in a typical year this type of deductions would be greater under the Simplified alternative Tax than under the income tax. On the other hand, the elimination of deductions for interest expense, considered alone, would result in an increase in the business tax base relative to the system of inflation adjusted deductions for real interest expense in current law.

The net effect of these changes can be determined only with detailed revenue estimates that are beyond the scope of this Report. However, some insights can be obtained from the marginal effective tax rate calculations presented in Chapter 4. The results for the cases where capital income is not subject to tax at the saver level (e.g., those where the saver providing the investment funds is a tax-exempt institution) are the most relevant ones for analyzing business level taxation in isolation. The results for pre-1986 law indicate that marginal effective tax rates are quite negative on debt-financed investments and roughly equal to the statutory rate on equity-financed investment (at an inflation rate of 25 percent). As demonstrated in Chapter 8, the marginal effective tax rate on both debt-financed and equity-financed investment under the Simplified Alternative Tax is zero. As noted in Chapter 7, debt-financed investments have accounted for more than 70 percent of total investment by Colombian companies during the 1980s. Given the predominance of debt finance in the Colombian economy, these results suggest that it is quite possible that business tax revenues would actually increase (in present value terms), or at least not decline significantly, under the Simplified Alternative Tax relative to pre-1986 law.[9]

However, it should be noted that business tax revenues would be smaller even in present value terms under the Simplified Alternative Tax than under either the fully phased-in version of 1986 law or the reformed income tax proposed in Chapter 5, which would result in marginal effective tax rates roughly similar to those presented in Chapter 4 for a 25 percent inflation rate. For example, for the cases in which the saver is a tax-exempt institution and the inflation rate is 25 percent, the marginal effective tax rates under the fully phased-in 1986 law is approximately zero for a debt-financed investment and roughly equal to the statutory rate for an equity-financed investment; thus, revenues under this tax structure would always be greater in present value terms than those under the Simplified Alternative Tax, where the marginal effective tax rate is zero on both types of investments. Accordingly, to the extent that the increase in the business tax burden that will occur when the 1986 law is fully phased-in is perceived to be equitable, the reformed income tax would also be perceived to be fairer than the Simplified Alternative Tax.

Moreover, under the Simplified Alternative Tax, many growing, capital-intensive businesses will have zero tax liability; this will result primarily from the expensing of all purchases, including expenditures on depreciable equipment and additions to inventory. Although perfectly consistent with taxation on the basis of consumption, this aspect of the Simplified Alternative Tax could also result in political opposition to the plan. However, it is interesting to note that such «zeroing out» may actually be less of a problem under the Simplified Alternative Tax than under current law, since depreciation deductions are now highly accelerated and interest payments will remain nearly fully deductible for some time to come (since inflation indexing is being phased-in over a ten-year period).

II. Simplicity

The criterion of simplicity may be even more important than that of equity in evaluating reform of the Colombian tax system. The scarcity of administrative skills implies that the use of such resources to administer, monitor, and comply with an unnecessarily complex tax system is an extremely wasteful way to use a very valuable asset. Since many individuals and businesses are unable to comply with complex tax rules, an unnecessarily complex structure results in many filing errors and, by increasing compliance costs, provides another incentive for evasion. The result is inequity, as well as loss of revenue. In addition, a complex tax structure is likely to induce both individual and business taxpayers to alter their investment decisions in attempts to reduce compliance costs; such distortions of private decision-making impose efficiency costs on the economy. A further implication of a complex tax structure is that the total (or «social») cost of raising tax revenue is relatively high; that is, administrative and compliance costs, per dollar of tax revenue raised, are relatively high. Finally, a complex tax structure means that a great deal of administrative resources must be spent on monitoring honest taxpayers rather than searching out tax evaders. Accordingly, the relative merits of the two proposals in terms of the criterion of simplicity are critical.

The following discussion demonstrates that as a «stand alone» tax, the Simplified Alternative Tax is superior to the income tax in terms of the simplicity criterion in most areas. However, under the consumption-based strategy recommended in this Report, the relative simplicity advantages of the Simplified Alternative Tax would be reduced since it would be supplemented by a modified version of the tax on net wealth; as noted above, many of the calculations required for accurate measurement of net wealth tax are precisely the type that render implementation of an income tax difficult and that are avoided under the Simplified Alternative Tax. The additional complexity would be limited if filing thresholds under the net wealth tax were increased from their levels under current law; such a measure would reduce the number of individuals that would face the complexity of calculating net wealth under the consumption-based strategy. Note that raising filing thresholds for the net wealth tax would be less objectionable under the consumption-based approach than under the income-based strategy, since the calculation of net wealth for purposes of the taxation of presumptive income would not be necessary under the former alternative. (Restructuring of the measurement of net wealth and presumptive income along the lines suggested in Chapter 6 would add to complexity under the income-based strategy; eliminating the tax on presumptive income under the consumption-based strategy would be a simplification). Moreover, as noted above, less accurate but simpler approximations of the effects of transactions that give rise to income and to changes in ñet wealth are generally less problematical under a net wealth tax than under an income tax since the associated measurement errors have a relatively small effect on the accuracy of measurement of the net wealth tax base. Thus, rough approximations in the measurement of the base of the net wealth tax that are adopted to reduce complexity result in fewer inequities and distortions than would similar approximations under the income tax. Nevertheless, it is clear that the equity gains under the consumption-based reform strategy obtained by subjecting capital income to taxation through the net wealth tax (relative to a «stand alone» Simplified Alternative Tax) would be purchased at the cost of increased complexity due to the need to measure net wealth. Thus, the administrative advantages of the consumption-based strategy would be less than those of a «stand alone» Simplified Alternative Tax; while it seems clear that the consumption-based strategy would be superior to the income-based strategy on simplicity grounds, the degree of that superiority is less than in the comparison of the «stand alone» Simplified Alternative Tax and the «stand alone» income tax.

The following discussion of the relative simplicity properties of the income-based and consumption-based strategies focuses on: (a) timing issues; (b) the need for inflation adjustments; (c) compliance and administrative issues; (d) the treatment of capital gains; (e) relative opportunities for tax arbitrage; (f) the extent of integration of the individual and business taxes; (g) the relative number of returns; (h) consistency with financial accounting practices; and (i) transitional issues.

A. Timing Issues

Strict application of income tax principles requires that all changes in net wealth be included in the annual tax base; that is, an income tax requires general application of accrual accounting. As noted previously, this requirement raises a host of difficult timing issues.[10] Specifically, business expenses incurred in a given year should be deductible under an income tax in that year only to the extent that they result in business receipts in the same year. Expenses that give rise to receipts in later years should be capitalized and deducted in those years; that is, the deduction of expenses should be «matched» with the inclusion of the related receipts on a year-by-year basis. Thus, strict application of income tax principles implies that expenses that give rise to receipts in later years should be capitalized and recovered through subsequent deductions such as those for depreciation, depletion, amortization, and cost of goods sold from inventory. An income-based tax system that ignores these issues will be characterized by serious horizontal and vertical inequities and by allocative distortions. In addition, efforts to take advantage of timing advantages (and to police such efforts) can seriously complicate life for both the taxpayer and the tax administrator. However, dealing appropriately with such timing issues introduces considerable complexity into an income tax system. This is graphically demonstrated by the reforms of the Colombian tax system proposed in Chapter 5 that deal with various timing issues.

The proposed system for measuring economic depreciation for depreciable assets is probably the most prominent example. As described in Chapter 8, an income tax ideally allows deductions only for the real economic depreciation of a depreciable asset. However, the data required to obtain accurate measurements of the rate at which physical assets depreciate (in principle, by industry and by extent of use) are simply unavailable in Colombia.[11] The proposed income-based reform would require Colombian businesses to use U.S. estimates of economic depreciation for income and net wealth tax purposes. Although this approach is the best currently available, it is inevitably somewhat arbitrary and will no doubt result in overtaxation of some assets and industries and undertaxation of others; such treatment clearly implies inequities and allocative inefficiencies. Moreover, because the determination of allowances for economic depreciation is always fairly tenuous, such systems are particularly prone to be influenced by the exercise of political power.

In contrast, under the Simplified Alternative Tax, consumption tax principles allow purchases of depreciable assets simply to be deducted in the year of purchase or «expensed»; that is, cash flow accounting of such purchases is appropriate. Accordingly, the need for determining economic depreciation (and for inflation adjustment, to be considered in greater detail below) is eliminated, as are all of the other problems described above. Thus, the basic accounting system of the Simplified Alternative Tax component of the consumption-based reform strategy is significantly simpler than that required under the income-based proposal.

However, this conclusion is tempered by the fact that the consumption-based strategy under consideration in this Report includes a tax on net wealth; the real depreciated value of depreciable assets must still be determined for purposes of the net wealth tax. Recall that Chapter 9 recommends that inflation-adjusted economic depreciation be used to calculate such values. As a result, many taxpayers would still have to calculate inflation-indexed economic depreciation. However, the above analysis suggests that a simpler approximation to economic depreciation – such as a simple three or four asset system similar to that under current law, but with more realistic depreciable lives and adjustment for inflation – might be utilized for purposes of the net wealth tax under the consumption-based alternative. The resulting mismeasurement of the net wealth tax base would be relatively small, in comparison to the mismeasurement of the income tax base that would result from the adoption of a similar approximation under the reformed income tax. Such an approximation under the net wealth tax thus would result in relatively smaller errors in assessing tax liability and less serious distortions and inequities than it would under an income tax.

The tax treatment of a variety of other transactions is simpler under the Simplified Alternative Tax than under the proposed income tax reforms; in these cases, no changes in the current tax treatment under the net wealth tax are recommended if the Simplified Alternative Tax is adopted. For example, highly complex rules are recommended in Chapter 5 to deal with multi-period production processes; the receipts generated by such processes are simply included in the tax base on a cash flow basis under the Simplified Alternative Tax. Other income tax issues that disappear under the Simplified Alternative Tax are special tax rules for expenditures on goods placed in inventory, below-market business loans to owners or shareholders, capitalization of construction period interest and indirect production costs of self-constructed assets, bad debt reserves of financial institutions and other firms, and original issue discount obligations.

To summarize, much of the complexity of the reformed income tax proposed in this Report results from attempts to measure capital income accurately Since capital income is untaxed under the Simplified Alternative Tax, most of the complex issues related to capital income measurement disappear. This result is qualified under the consumption-based reform strategy recommended in this Report, since these same complex issues in principle should be addressed in measuring changes in the net wealth of those taxpayers subject to the net wealth tax. However, the method of calculating net wealth proposed under the consumption-based strategy is less complex (and therefore less accurate) than that proposed under the income-based approach; as argued above, such an approach is appropriate because approximate measures of changes in wealth that are used in the interest of simplicity are less inequitable and distortionary under a net wealth tax than under an income tax.

B. Inflation Adjustments

As described in Chapter 7, accurate measurement of real economic income under an income tax system requires systematic adjustments for the effects of inflation. Adjustment of the nominal amounts of exemption levels, deduction limits, bracket widths, etc. is straightforward, and would also be required under the Simplified Alternative Tax. However, the types of inflation adjustment required for the accurate measurement of real income from capital are quite complicated. This is demonstrated to some extent by the inflation adjustment provisions under current Colombian law. It is more fully illustrated by the two methods of inflation adjustment discussed in Chapter 7. Either of these approaches – an ad hoc approach involving inflation indexing of depreciation allowances, inventories, capital gains, and interest income and expense or the alternative approach of a Chilean-type integrated adjustment of all balance sheet items – would be quite complex.[12]

In marked contrast, consumption tax principles require only that all quantities included in or deducted from the tax base be measured accurately in monetary values of the current year. Thus, all of the problems of inflation adjustment, apart from the straightforward indexing of brackets, exemptions, etc., are eliminated under the Simplified Alternative Tax. However, once again the relative simplicity advantages of the consumption-based strategy are reduced when the existence of the net wealth tax is taken into account. Under the net wealth tax component of the consumption-based reform strategy detailed in Chapter 9, asset values would be indexed for inflation (as described in Chapters 6 and 7); in particular, land values would be indexed, the basis of depreciable assets would be indexed and subjected to real economic depreciation of the inflation-adjusted basis, and LIFO (or indexed-FIFO) inventory accounting would be allowed or required.[13] Accordingly, adoption of the consumption-based alternative would result in significant increases in simplicity only for taxpayers that would not be subject to the net wealth tax because their net wealth would be below the filing threshold.

C. Compliance and Administration

Given the scarcity of administrative resources at the government's disposal, as well as taxpayer attitudes and the relatively low level of compliance with the tax law, it is important to try to determine which alternative is likely to be administered in the more even-handed manner. The importance of administrability – in addition to the obvious implications for revenues – lies in the fundamental considerations that a tax system can be fair and economically neutral only if all sectors are taxed in roughly equivalent ways and all persons in similar positions pay roughly the same amount of tax. If some persons manage to pay substantially less tax than others with the same taxpaying ability, the tax system is seriously inequitable. A lack of even-handedness can also lead to economic inefficiency, insofar as it results in differential taxation of various activities. Prior Colombian experience with taxation suggests that any system of direct taxation will involve substantial unevenness. The question is whether the existing income tax, the reformed income tax, or the consumption-based alternative is likely to be significantly superior in this respect.

The elimination of the concept of the taxation of presumptive income must be counted as a substantial drawback of the consumption-based strategy. As noted in Chapter 9, this concept is simply incompatible with the Simplified Alternative Tax. However, its elimination runs the risk of revenue loss and an inequitable increase in the relative tax burden on taxpayers who are honest (or who receive income in forms that cannot be concealed). The benefits of taxing presumptive income come at very little expense in terms of compliance costs, since it is easy to calculate presumptive income, given the existence of the net wealth tax.

Under the proposed income-based strategy (and the current income tax system, to some extent), the net wealth tax, the system of presumptive income, the ordinary income tax, and financial accounting all tend to reinforce each other and thus strengthen administration of the income tax and the net wealth tax. For example, the taxation of interest income provides some assurance that debt instruments will be included in net wealth. It would be easier to avoid paying net wealth tax by failing to report the existence of such instruments if (as under the Simplified Alternative Tax) the income therefrom did not have to be reported. In the case of financial accounting, a company reporting large profits to its shareholders would find it difficult to understate blatantly its taxable income. By contrast, under the Simplified Alternative Tax, financial reports would be less useful in verifying tax liability. (This is discussed further below.) Moreover, under current law, taxpayers with assets that cannot readily be concealed (such as real property) pay at least some tax on the income of such assets because of the taxation of presumptive income. If the taxation of presumptive income were eliminated, such taxpayers could with greater impunity simply fail to report receipts from rental or other use of these properties.[14]

The structure of the Simplified Alternative Tax is also conducive to certain forms of abusive transactions. Under the income tax, it should be unusual for taxpayers that report significant amounts of income in some years to report zero taxable income in other years without arousing the suspicion of the tax administration (provided returns of different years are actually compared). Thus, a brazen attempt at cheating by understating receipts or overstating deductions in some years more than in others runs the risk of detection. (There is little difference in the ability of taxpayers simply to fail to file a return or to consistently underreport receipts or overstate deductions under the two systems.) In contrast, legitimately reporting a zero tax liability in particular years would not be unusual under the Simplified Alternative Tax. Since all capital expenditures would be immediately deductible, the deduction for investments could easily exceed net receipts for the year. Of course, in such a case, the tax liability under the Simplified Alternative Tax in future years would exceed that under the income tax. Such a situation implies that it would be more difficult under the Simplified Alternative Tax than under the income tax for an auditor to spot which returns are unusual. As a result, the temptation to cheat would be greater.

Apart from simply understating income or overstating deductions, taxpayers could purchase capital items, so that the deduction is legitimized, and then fail to report the proceeds of the sale of the capital item; alternatively, taxpayers could simply obtain a receipt from another person for purchase of an item that does not in fact exist. While this technique is fraudulent and could be precluded by hunting down the vendor of the capital item, in practice this is likely to be a difficult exercise for the tax administration, and some vendors (nonresident aliens or small businesses below the filing threshold) would be legally exempt from Colombian tax. These and similar abuses would be detected somewhat more easily under the income-based strategy, since the assets involved retain relevance for tax purposes throughout their depreciable lives.

Property that is acquired for both business and personal use poses problems under both the income tax and the Simplified Alternative Tax. In principle, under the income tax deductions for depreciation should be allowed only to the extent of business use in the tax year; similarly, only that percent of interest paid to buy the asset should be deductible. Under the Simplified Alternative Tax expensing should be allowed only for the business portion of the price of the asset; under the generally applicable rules no deduction would be allowed for interest.

On balance it is not clear which of these two approaches would be more problematical. In principle, it would be easier to adjust depreciation allowances and interest deductions under the income tax when the fraction of business use changes than to recapture (or increase) expensed amounts under the Simplified Alternative Tax. In fact, however, this is not likely to be the primary source of problems. The real issue is the identification of cases in which business use is greatly overstated even from the start. On this score the income tax probably has some advantage over the Simplified Alternative Tax, since under the former improper deductions must be taken over a period of years, rather than only in the year of acquisition, as under the Simplified Alternative Tax.

Tax evasion and avoidance through foreign transactions would result in compliance and administrative problems under both of the reform alternatives, as they do under current law. It can be argued that the effective exemption of foreign investment income under the Simplified Alternative Tax simply formalizes the situation that occurs in practice under current law and would very likely also occur under a reformed income tax. To the extent this is true, compliance and administrative problems are eased under the Simplified Alternative Tax, relative to the income tax, at fairly little revenue cost.[15/]

From an administrative standpoint, the above discussion suggests that the structure of the Simplified Alternative Tax is generally simpler than that of the reformed income tax, so that it should be relatively easier to administer. As a result, the inequities and inefficiencies that arise from poor administration should be relatively less severe under the consumption-based approach. However, tax prepayment treatment of interest at the business level under the Simplified Alternative Tax presents some potentially serious tax avoidance possibilities that are unique to this form of consumption-based business taxation. In particular, as described in detail in Chapter 9, installment sales and certain transactions that involve simultaneous selling/borrowing or buying/lending between taxable Colombian businesses and intdividuals, tax-exempt institutions or foreigners could be structured so as to reduce the tax liability of the Colombian firm. The measures recommended in Chapter 9 to limit these tax avoidance opportunities, as well as the need to monitor such transactions in order to detect abuse, increase the relative complexity of the Simplified Alternative Tax. The need to maintain a modified version of the tax on net wealth to complement the simplified Alternative Tax also adds complexity. As a result, the relative administrative advantages of the consumption-based approach are less than might appear from consideration of a «stand-alone» Simplified Alternative Tax in which these issues were not addressed.

In summary, then, without taking the presumptive income and net wealth taxes into account, it is probable that the consumption-based alternative should be judged superior to the income tax in terms of compliance and administration, despite the possibility of tax avoidance transactions and the somewhat greater problem posed by property that is used only in part for business purposes. The consumption-based alternative is likely to be administered in a more even-handed manner than the income tax, chiefly because it bypasses all the complicated problems of measuring income from business and capital. Even if all the proposed reforms of the income tax were to be adopted, the resulting system would not fully tax all forms of economic income accurately (for example, because many gains on assets would not be taxed until realized). Moreover, much income will go unreported, particularly income earned abroad. The extent of this problem is, however, difficult to assess, due to lack of relevant data (for example, on untaxed domestic income and unreported foreign-source income as a percentage of total capital income of Colombians). When the net wealth and presumptive income taxes are taken into account, the administrative dominance of the consumption-based strategy is much less clear.

D. Capital Gains

In principle, capital gains should be taxed on an accrual basis under a tax on real economic income; such gains represent a change in net wealth in the year they accrue. In practice, such accrual taxation is administratively difficult in many cases. Moreover, accrual taxation of capital gains only in those cases where it is administratively feasible, such as for equity securities traded on public exchanges, would distort investment away from such activities. As a result most countries that tax capital gains, including Colombia, do so on a realization basis. This results in opportunities for tax avoidance through deferral of tax obligations. Under current Colombian law, the taxation of capital gains under the separate tax on occasional gains implies that, in some cases, such gains are taxed at relatively low rates; the proposal for income tax reform recommends that such special treatment be repealed. In addition, capital gains on assets transferred by gift or at death are commonly excluded or given special treatment under most income tax systems. As noted in Chapter 3, under current Colombian law, the donor or testator is completely untaxed on such gains; again, such special treatment would be eliminated under the proposed income tax reforms, as the making of a gift or a bequest would be treated as a realization event.

These opportunities for tax avoidance create incentives to recharacterize ordinary income as capital gains. In addition to causing inequities and allocative distortions, this results in significant administrative and enforcement complexity as tax authorities attempt to design and enforce complex rules to limit the opportunities for such recharacterization. Note that an incentive to recharacterize ordinary income as capital gain would exist even under the income tax reforms proposed for Colombia in this Report; although the separate rate schedule for occasional gains would be eliminated, the deferral advantage created by taxation of capital gains upon realization rather than as accrued would remain. This incentive would be mitigated by the proposed reforms of the taxation of presumptive income which would to some extent represent accrual taxation. Thus, the incentive to recharacterize income as capital gains would be diminished for certain activities by those individuals subject to the taxation of presumptive income. These rules would add some complexity to the Colombian tax structure; moreover, they would complicate decision-making (and ultimately administration) as taxpayers attempt to arrange their affairs to avoid being subject to the taxation of presumptive income.

In contrast, capital gains that qualify for individual tax prepayment treatment under the consumption-based Simplified Alternative Tax are excluded from the individual tax base, while proceeds of sales of business assets are simply included in the receipts of the business on a cash flow basis. Such treatment is obviously simple. In particular, there is no need to keep track of the basis of assets qualifying for capital gains treatment. Moreover, since all forms of capital income are accorded identical treatment, the inequities, distortions, and incentives to convert ordinary income into capital gain described above are eliminated. But it would be appropriate to include such assets in the base of the net wealth; thus administrative benefits would be somewhat attenuated.

E. Tax Arbitrage

The income tax reforms proposed for Colombia in Chapter 5 would greatly reduce opportunities for tax arbitrage, such as borrowing with fully deductible interest to invest in activities where the income is exempt from tax or effectively taxed at preferential rates. However, such opportunities would not be eliminated. For example, capital gains would still be taxed on a realization basis and pensions would be treated favorably. Such opportunities for tax arbitrage result in inequities and inefficiencies, and generally result in complex rules designed to limit their use. Note however that the reformed tax on presumptive income to some extent represents an ad hoc attempt at accrual taxation; it would affect some individuals and some firms on some of their investments that generate capital gains. It thus would reduce some opportunities for tax arbitrage at the cost of some additional complexity as well as some inefficiencies and inequities due to its fairly arbitrary application.

In contrast, the Simplified Alternative Tax proposes uniform treatment of virtually all capital investments.[16] As a result, tax arbitrage should not be a problem under the Simplified Alternative Tax.[17]

Note also that opportunities to engage in tax arbitrage complicate saving and investment decisions. That is, individuals must consider the differential tax effects of such decisions in addition to analyzing their purely economic aspects. Under the proposed income tax reform, this aspect of complexity would be reduced significantly, but it would continue to face Colombian savers and investors to the extent that all tax arbitrage opportunities were not eliminated.

Again, such problems do not arise under the Simplified Alternative Tax, which results in a marginal effective tax rate of zero on all types of investments. However, it must be noted that this result obtains only if the Simplified Alternative Tax is in fact implemented without providing for explicit subsidies (or unwarranted deductions) to certain forms of saving and investment. Such investment subsidies would imply negative marginal effective tax rates. As noted in Chapter 4, such negative marginal effective tax rates result in particularly serious misallocations of resources, and should be avoided if at all possible.

F. Integration of Business and Individual Taxes

Integration of the business and individual level taxes is a difficult issue under most income taxes. Under the post-1985 Colombian system, an approximate form of integration is accomplished by exempting dividends from individual taxation. Such integration is not without problems; in particular, it is inequitable to the extent that corporate income attributable to lower-bracket individuals is effectively taxed at the business rate, which equals the top individual tax rate. Nevertheless, for the reasons specified in Chapter 5, the approach adopted in Law 75 of 1986 seems appropriate for Colombia, and no changes in this form of integration are recommended.

Under the Simplified Alternative Tax, integration of the business and individual taxes is generally not a problem as it is done «automatically» (or at the discretion of the taxpayer) and requires no special rules or administrative procedures.

G. Number of Returns

As noted in Chapter 9, the complexity of the Simplified Alternative Tax is increased by several provisions designed to limit tax avoidance possibilities. In particular, the types of investment activities that qualify for individual tax prepayment treatment are strictly limited, and segregated cash flow treatment is required for individual foreign portfolio investment and for foreign and agricultural investment by businesses. This implies that a relatively large number of business returns will be filed under the Simplified Alternative Tax. In particular, a fairly large number of individuals would be required to file business tax returns, although this number will be limited by the de minimis filing rule and the fairly generous aggregation rules recommended in Chapter 9.

It does not seem that the larger number of returns to be filed under the Simplified Alternative Tax represents much of an increase in complexity relative to the proposed income tax. In general, the same or more information would have to reported by the taxpayer under the income tax as under the Simplified Alternative Tax; the primary difference is that there would be fewer but more complicated returns under the income tax alternative. In particular, although a significant number of business tax forms would be filed by individuals under the Simplified Alternative Tax, these forms would be fairly straightforward since cash flow accounting would be used.

A related point is that withholding would generally be fairly accurate under the Simplified Alternative Tax, since individuals pay tax primarily on labor income. As a result, rules limiting the number of taxpayers required to file under the individual component of the Simplified Alternative Tax (similar to those in the 1986 reform) would be quite easy to devise. This contrasts with the situation under the income tax, where an accurate assessment of tax burden requires that tax on both individual labor and capital income be withheld accurately and that the rate at which tax on labor income is withheld ideally depends on the amount of capital income. Finally, the problems that give rise to the recommended «basket» treatment of certain forms of investment under the Simplified Alternative Tax also arise under the income tax; similar provisions designed to limit tax avoidance possibilities result in similar additional complexity.

H. Consistency with Financial Accounting

The proposed income tax reforms are designed to change tax accounting rules so that income for tax purposes more accurately reflects real economic income. As a result, the reforms recommended for tax accounting are equally relevant for financial accounting, although this Report stops short of recommending that tax rules must be used for financial accounting. If such reforms were adopted in both areas, tax and financial accounting procedures would be broadly similar if not identical. Such uniformity would generally simplify accounting procedures, would reduce the amount of scarce resources used to generate tax and financial accounting information, and would arguably improve economic decision-making. In addition, independently audited financial accounts would provide an important tool that could be used in tax audits of those businesses that maintain such accounts. Cross-checking financial accounts with tax accounts is simpler and discrepancies are somewhat easier to identify if both types of accounts are based on the same principles. This could occur under the income tax if the reforms proposed in Chapter 5 were adopted for both tax and financial accounting purposes.

These benefits would not materialize if the Simplified Alternative Tax were adopted in Colombia. Despite the complications detailed in Chapter 9, the primary advantage of the consumption-based proposal is the simplicity of the Simplified Alternative Tax, relative to a reformed income tax. The simplicity advantages of the Simplified Alternative Tax are achieved primarily by avoiding many of the complex issues involved in measuring real economic income properly. The tax base clearly is not income; as a result, the accounting information required to prepare returns under the Simplified Alternative Tax is not sufficient to determine income as required for financial purposes. In principle, financial accounting and accounting for purposes of the net wealth tax should be identical. However, the relatively modest changes in the net wealth tax proposed under the consumption-based strategy imply that the accounting information needed for purposes of the net wealth tax would also fall considerably short of the information required for accurate financial accounting.

This divergence between tax and financial accounting has several implications. It is clear that some of the simplicity gains obtained with the Simplified Alternative Tax are lost in the sense that financial accounting is still complex even if tax accounting is much simpler. However, the importance of this point is not clear for two reasons. First, all of the information required to prepare tax returns under the Simplified Alternative Tax is certainly included in the information required for accurate financial accounting; thus, introducing the tax would add little complexity to private accounting procedures while greatly simplifying tax procedures.

Second, in the absence of a government mandate of conformity it is certainly possible that financial accounting in Colombia will not conform to all of the complex income measurement proposals described in Chapter 5, even if such rules were required for tax purposes. In this case, the potential advantages of identical tax and financial accounting procedures under the income tax would not materialize. Indeed, it might be more difficult to complete income tax returns than to complete returns under the Simplified Alternative Tax if, in the former case, there were not substantial conformity of tax and financial accounting.

I. Transitional Issues

Transitional issues are always difficult for a comprehensive tax reform. However, the political need for complex special transitional provisions is reduced in Colombia by the historical fact that previous reforms have generally not been accompanied by comprehensive packages of transition rules designed to eliminate or reduce reform-induced losses. It is generally desirable to limit special transition rules (to the extent politically possible) only to those cases where reform would imply serious inequities or economic dislocations; such a practice reduces complexity and ensures that the benefits of reform are attained rapidly. It also avoids the legitimization of expectations that special transition rules will be utilized in subsequent reforms, so that future claims for transitional relief will receive less sympathy

In Colombia, the transitional problems associated with a movement to the Simplified Alternative Tax would probably be somewhat greater than they would be with a movement to the reformed income tax. However, the differences are fairly minor since, as noted above, quite a few of the features of the current tax system imply that the transition to the Simplified Alternative Tax would be significantly less disruptive in Colombia than in most other countries. Indeed, the transitional problems associated with moving to the Simplified Alternative Tax from current law (once fully phased in) as specified by Law 75 of 1986 would seem to be significantly less than those related to the movement from pre-1986 law to the current system (again, fully phased in).

The major transitional problems are in the following areas. Marginal effective tax rates on business investment would change from their current levels to roughly the statutory rate under the income tax and to zero under the Simplified Alternative Tax. For some industries, the income tax alternative would result in larger reform-induced losses (and gains), while for others larger losses (and gains) would be induced by implementation of the Simplified Alternative. The move to an income tax would generally result in larger losses for business and thus would spark more political opposition from this relatively well-organized and influential segment of the Colombian economy.

The proposed treatments of interest would be phased-in following similar rules under both the Simplified Alternative Tax and the reformed income tax; however, the magnitude of the problem is larger in the case of the Simplified Alternative Tax, since the transition rules apply to all interest rather than just the inflationary component of interest income and expense. It should be recognized, however, that a far greater fraction of nominal interest expense deductions are disallowed in moving from pre-1986 law to interest indexing than in moving from an indexed income tax to complete disallowance of interest expense. (If, for example, the inflation rate is 20 percent and the nominal interest rate is 25 percent, 80 percent of nominal interest deductions are disallowed in the first move and only the remaining 20 percent in the second).

The movement to expensing under the Simplified Alternative Tax would clearly represent a more dramatic change for new investments than the movement to indexed economic depreciation under the reformed income tax. However, this affects only new investments; the transition rules proposed for the tax treatment of existing investments are broadly similar under both proposals.

Recall that accrued capital gains on existing assets owned by individuals would not be taxed under the Simplified Alternative Tax.[18] Transition to such treatment is obviously simple, and it is appropriate to the extent that such gains were effectively taxed very lightly under current law. In contrast, realized real capital gains (and to some extent unrealized gains under the proposed rules for the taxation of presumptive income) would be fully taxed under the proposed income tax, with no transitional relief provided for gains accrued under the current tax system.

This brief discussion of the major transitional issues raised by adoption of either the Simplified Alternative Tax or the reformed income tax suggests that the transitional problems would be somewhat, but not significantly, greater under the former alternative. Indeed, the most severe transitional problems associated with the enactment of either the consumption-based or the income-based proposals would probably arise with the implementation of the new rules for calculating the base of the net wealth tax.

The revaluations of assets implied by these rules are likely to be very substantial and to vary widely across assets and individual taxpayers. Moreover, these increases in the net wealth tax base would likely be offset in a fairly haphazard fashion by any reductions in net wealth tax rates that would occur. Thus, the proposed changes in the net wealth tax are likely to result in the largest reform-induced changes in individual net wealth of any component of either the consumption-based or the income-based reform strategies. These are not likely to be very different, depending on which alternative is chosen.

J. Summary

It is rather difficult to draw a firm conclusion from this extended discussion of the relative simplicity properties of the consumption-based and income-based reform options. A systematic weighting of the economic importance of each aspect of the simplicity criterion discussed above is nearly impossible and beyond the scope of this Report. However, the following summarizes the major points that should be considered in determining whether the consumption-based or the income-based alternative represents the simpler tax reform option for Colombia.

The Simplified Alternative Tax has some very significant simplicity advantages relative to the reformed income tax. All of the complexity of adjusting for inflation under the income tax would disappear entirely under the Simplified Alternative Tax. Similarly, all of the timing issues that arise in the measurement of income do not exist under the Simplified Alternative Tax. In addition, the treatment of capital gains would be straightforward, opportunities for tax arbitrage would be eliminated in a systematic fashion, integration of the business and individual tax components of the Simplified Alternative Tax would be automatic, and withholding would be more accurate than under the income tax.

The proposed income tax also has some simplicity advantages relative to the Simplified Alternative Tax. The taxation of presumptive income would be maintained (and strengthened) only under the income tax; this provides the income tax with an important anti-evasion feature that strengthens administration. Cross-checking of financial accounts and tax accounts would be simpler under the income tax (especially if the methods of measuring real economic income recommended in this Report were adopted for purposes of financial accounting). In addition, as noted above, the Simplified Alternative Tax includes several measures designed to limit tax avoidance opportunities that arise due to tax prepayment treatment of interest at the business level; these particular measures are not necessary under the income tax.

Finally, some of the relative simplicity advantages of the Simplified Alternative Tax relative to the income tax are reduced because the consumption-based approach proposed in this Report would include an individual net wealth tax. However, the net wealth tax component of the consumption-based strategy would still be considerably simpler (though less accurate) than the net wealth tax proposed under the income-based strategy.

III. Economic Neutrality and Efficiency

Both the income-based and the consumption-based reform proposals would improve the efficiency of resource allocation in Colombia by reducing differential tax treatment of various industries. Such tax neutrality would result in more productive use of Colombia's scarce resources. Nevertheless, several distinctions between the two proposals can be drawn on efficiency grounds.

One important distinction is that the Simplified Alternative Tax eliminates taxation of the return to saving. As a result, it eliminates the distortion between current consumption and saving for future consumption that is inherent in the income tax. This is achieved at the cost of increasing the distortion of individual choices between current labor and leisure, since the tax rate on labor income would be higher under the Simplified Alternative Tax.[19/] The question of whether the consumption tax approach is the one that minimizes the efficiency costs of distortionary taxes has been hotly debated in the literature.[20/] One interpretation of the results of this literature is that excluding capital income from taxation under a consumption-based approach minimizes distortions under an «average» or «reasonable» set of assumptions regarding parameter values that describe individual behavior; under other assumptions, either taxation or subsidization of capital income can be optimal. In any case, the existence of the net wealth tax under the Simplified Alternative Tax implies that capital income would in fact be subject to tax under this proposal. Thus, the primary difference is that the level of taxation of capital income would be lower than under the proposed income tax reform.

A second major distinction arises from the fact that for political reasons adoption of either reform plan in Colombia might be partial; that is, certain forms of investment, including owner-occupied housing and perhaps certain other industries, might continue to receive preferential treatment, treatment perhaps as generous as (or even more generous than) that under a consumption-based approach. In addition, despite the 1986 reforms, it is likely that some of the business activities of tax-exempt institutions would not be subject to tax or would effectively be taxed at preferential rates. Under such so-called «second best» circumstances, the Simplified Alternative Tax, which would tax the income from all non-preferred investments at a zero marginal effective tax rate, is likely to be more nearly neutral than a reformed income tax, which would tax all such income at the statutory rate. That is, all investments by businesses and by tax-exempt institutions would effectively be treated identically under the Simplified Alternative Tax.[21/] In contrast, the income tax approach would result in much larger tax differentials between preferred and non-preferred activities, and between taxable businesses and tax-exempt institutions that were effectively taxed at zero or preferential rates. A similar argument can be made for the entire consumption-based strategy relative to the income-based strategy, since capital income would be taxed more heavily under the latter alternative.

Income and consumption taxes also differ in the extent to which they distort individual decisions regarding investment in human capital rather than in non-human or «physical» capital. The simplest models in this area are characterized by proportional taxation, exogenous labor supply, certain returns to investment, and the assumption that foregone earnings are the only cost of producing human capital; that is, direct costs such as tuition and books are ignored. In these models, both a consumption-based tax (of either the ITP or the ICF type) and an income tax reduce both the costs (foregone current earnings) and the benefits (increased future earnings) of investment in human capital proportionately. Under the consumption-based tax returns to investments in human and physical capital are thus treated equivalently. In contrast, under an income tax, investments in human capital effectively receive consumption tax treatment, but the return to investment is subject to tax. This taxation of the return to physical capital results in overinvestment in human capital. In such models, consumption taxes are preferable to income taxes on efficiency grounds; for example, in a model with investment in human and physical capital endogenous, Driffill and Rosen (1983) find that proportional income taxes result in much higher excess burdens than equal yield proportional consumption taxes.[22/]

These results must be qualified in a number of ways. For example, a progressive consumption tax of the ITP type discourages investment in human capital because future earnings are taxed at a relatively high rate; some taxation of the return to physical capital, as under a progressive income tax, may be desirable to offset this disincentive. Also, the return to investment in human capital may be relatively riskier than the return to investment in physical capital; again, some taxation of the return to physical capital may be desirable to offset under-investment in risky human capital by risk-averse individuals.[23/]

Thus, it is difficult to ascertain the relative efficiency properties of income and consumption taxes with respect to the allocation of investment across human and physical capital. In the absence of evidence to the contrary, the consumption tax would appear to be more efficient, especially if the range of marginal tax rates is not great. Once again, such a conclusion is obviously a tenuous one.[24/]

Two more minor points are relevant to the question of the relative efficiency properties of the two tax reform alternatives. First, the discussion of simplicity issues above demonstrates that application of the rules for accurate income measurement to various forms of capital income is considerably more difficult than the application of consumption-based rules to the same transactions. As a result, differential taxation due to mismeasurement of the appropriate tax base would be more prevalent under the reformed income tax than under the Simplified Alternative Tax. This implies that the latter approach should result in a somewhat more efficient allocation of resources.

Second, in light of the general neutrality of the Simplified Alternative Tax, it is interesting to note that it would alter individual and business decision-making in a way that would not occur under the reformed income tax. Recall from Chapter 8 that the government is «silent partner» in business investment only under the consumption-based approach, since it shares in both the risk and the return to investment. Under the Simplified Alternative Tax, which is characterized by a flat rate business tax and carry-forward of losses with interest, this is likely to result in an increase in private risk-taking. Suppose that investors in Colombia are generally risk-averse, so that in equilibrium the expected return to risky investments exceeds the «normal» risk-adjusted rate of return. In this case, a tax policy that encouraged risk-taking could be viewed as socially desirable to the extent that it encouraged taxpayers to make risky investments with expected returns in excess of the risk-adjusted normal return.

IV. Consistency with Economic Growth

The major difference between the two proposals in terms of affecting economic growth in Colombia lies in the effects of the alternative treatments of capital income. As noted above, under the income-based strategy (if effectively enforced, at least on new investments), various forms of capital or capital income originating in Colombia would be subject to the business income tax, to the individual income tax (as either ordinary or presumptive income), and to the net wealth tax. In particular, the intent of the some of the changes in the taxation of presumptive income is to subject certain forms of capital income to taxation on an accrual basis. In contrast, under the consumption-based approach, capital income originating in Colombia would be subject to taxation only under the net wealth tax.

The relative effect of the two proposals depends to a large degree on the extent to which domestic saving in Colombia is responsive to the after-tax rate of return. This response is theoretically ambiguous; some recent empirical and theoretical research suggests that the response in the U.S. would be positive.[25/] However, it is difficult to draw conclusions for Colombia from these results.

The fraction of domestic saving invested in Colombia is also a determinant of the effect on growth (to the extent such funds do not simply replace foreign funds). It seems likely that this fraction would be larger under the consumption-based strategy than under the income-based approach. Under the latter savings invested at home would be subject to the three layers of taxation described above.

By comparison, the proposed domestic income tax on foreign-source income is easily avoided, and foreign taxes on some types of income are likely to be quite small. For example, Colombian investors can choose from tax-free debt instruments in the U.S. or European bearer bonds, or they can channel their investments in developed countries through tax haven countries. As a result, saving abroad would be very attractive if the proposed income-based strategy were adopted and effectively enforced on new investments.[26/]

In contrast, under the consumption-based strategy, the effective exemption of the income from investment abroad would merely formalize practice under the income tax, while limiting the taxation of domestic capital income to that under the net wealth tax would represent a tax reduction. This should result in a larger fraction of domestic saving being invested in Colombia.

The relative effects of the two proposals on foreign investment in Colombia are also a critical factor in determining their relative effects on economic growth. The likely effects of the two proposals on foreign investment in Colombia are best seen by comparing the respective tax burdens on new investment. As shown in the examples presented in Chapter 8, the marginal tax burden faced by foreign investors, including both Colombian and home country taxes, is likely to be smaller under the Simplified Alternative Tax than under a reformed income tax. More foreign investment would thus be encouraged under that alternative. However, under those circumstances Colombian tax revenue raised from business sources would also be smaller under the Simplified Alternative Tax; as a result, the proposed compensating adjustment in the net wealth tax rate or in taxes on foreign remittances would need to be larger.

To the extent that increases in net wealth tax rates are relied on to make up any revenue shortfall, there would be no offsetting tendency for the cost of capital to rise in the Colombian economy as a whole. Because the net wealth tax is levied only on domestic individuals, the initial benefit foreigners would receive under the Simplified Alternative Tax would not be reduced by an increase in the net wealth tax. In the small country setting in which foreigners are the marginal source of funds – a description argued in Chapter 7 to be appropriate for analysis of effects of tax policy on the Colombian economy – higher net wealth taxes would not affect the cost of capital to the country.

If, on the other hand, any revenue shortfall were to be made up through higher remittance taxes on income paid to foreigners, or through a higher maximum Simplified Alternative Tax rate applied to individuals and companies (a possibility if distributional neutrality is to be maintained), the greater incentive to invest in Colombia under the Simplified Alternative Tax would be reduced.

An increase in tax collections from sources other than the Simplified Alternative Tax may not be necessary in the short run, if the business tax base expands sufficiently as a result of making interest expense nondeductible. In the examples presented in Chapter 8, Colombian taxes collected from existing foreign owned capital that already is fully depreciated appeared likely to rise slightly in comparison to what they would be under the income tax. Because the increase in burden is not particularly large, temporary measures to soften this impact do not seem necessary. Correspondingly, the creditability of the Simplified Alternative Tax against the U.S. income tax does not appear to be an issue of major importance, since most U.S. parent firms can be expected to be in excess foreign tax credit positions.

V. Concluding Remarks

The preceding discussion has summarized the advantages and disadvantages of the income-based and the consumption-based proposals in considerable detail, drawing together the analyses of previous chapters. As this discussion suggests, the choice between the two strategies is not a clear one. Each proposal has strong advantages and disadvantages, compared to the other. The relative importance that should be accorded each criterion is a matter of judgment over which reasonable analysts can differ. Moreover, the choice involves fundamental value judgments about the role of the tax system in Colombian society.

FOOTNOTES

1/ The debate regarding the relative merits of income and consumption taxes has a long history; for a collection of recent papers, see Pechman (1980).

2/ See Chapter 1. Revenue is not listed as a separate criterion, since it is assumed that tax rates would be adjusted to produce the same revenue under either alternative.

3/ Recall that there is no difference in the treatment of gifts and bequests under the two plans; that is that both reform alternatives provide for the inclusion of the fair market value of gifts and bequests received in the tax base of the recipient, with no deductions allowed to the donor for the making of gifts and bequests.

4/ Recall from Chapter 9 that the Simplified Alternative Tax is designed to be consistent with the lifetime view of tax equity, since gifts and inheritances received are included in the tax base of the recipient.

5/ See the numerical examples in Chapter 8.

6/ Indeed, the well-known «cumulative averaging» plan proposed by Vickrey (1947) would involve averaging income over the entire lifetime of the taxpayer.

7/ It might be objected that there is a logical inconsistency in appraising the progressivity of the consumption-based strategy in terms of taxes paid at each level of annual income (rather than at each level of consumption or lifetime income). Lack of data is likely to preclude any other assessment in Colombia. Note also that such an analysis in principle requires that taxes paid by businesses be imputed to individuals. Any such imputation would inevitably be controversial.

8/ Double taxation of capital income under the business and individual income taxes would be fairly minimal under the income-based reform strategy since dividends would not be taxed at the individual level. Double taxation would arise only in those cases in which retained earnings of companies were taxed at the business level and as capital gains at the individual level.

9/ A related point is the extent to which interest receipts are subject to taxation under pre-1986 law. It was noted in Chapter 4 that the average marginal tax rate on individual interest income receipts was roughly 22 percent in 1984, when the maximum individual rate was 49 percent. By comparison, interest deductions taken by companies reduced tax liabilities by either 40 percent of the amount deducted (for corporations) or 18 percent (for limited liability companies). This fact, coupled with the tax-free status of interest received by tax-exempt institutions and foreigners, suggests that, compared to pre-1986 law the revenue gain from eliminating business deductions for interest expense under the Simplified Alternative Tax would more than offset the revenue loss from eliminating the taxation of interest receipts; that this would be true at the rates enacted in 1986 is less certain. (Note that an exception to this general rule would occur if deductions for home mortgage interest were maintained under the Simplified Alternative Tax. There would be no revenue gain from disallowance of interest deductions to offset the revenue loss due to the elimination of the taxation of the interest income of mortgage lenders).

10/ This subsection focuses on problems of accurate income measurement caused by timing issues in a world without inflation; questions of inflation adjustment are generally left to the following subsection.

11/ Indeed, estimates of economic depreciation have only recently been made in the U.S. and other developed countries, and tax proposals for the United States based on these estimates have been highly controversial.

12/ The recent debate over tax reform in the United States suggests that coping with inflation is difficult in a developed country as well. The ad hoc indexing system proposed by the U.S. Treasury Department (1984) was highly controversial, and all of its elements were rejected in the reform package passed in 1986.

13/ Debt would not be indexed, except for debt where inflation adjustment is contractually specified and for obligations denominated in foreign currencies.

14/ Another matter of concern is that the proposed reform relating to adding the excess of presumptive over regular income to net wealth could not be implemented under the consumption-based alternative. This reform would help to conform the net wealth base to fair market value, and in its absence the taxation of net wealth will be less equitable, a matter of particular concern if greater reliance is being placed on the net wealth tax.

15/ Perhaps the most important difference between the two approaches is that the relative incentive to invest abroad in order to avoid the taxation of capital income is much smaller under the consumption-based alternative than under the income tax; this occurs because the income from domestic capital investment is not taxed under the Simplified Alternative Tax, although the capital is subject to the net wealth tax. This point is discussed further below.

16/ Owner-occupied housing would be the major exception if, contrary to the recommendations of this Report, home mortgage interest continues to be allowed as a deduction under the Simplified Alternative Tax. To the extent that political considerations dictate that such deductions be allowed, investment in owner-occupied housing will remain tax-preferred. However, the extent of tax arbitrage in this case is constrained by the limits on the deductibility of home mortgage interest. (Recall that Chapter 9 recommends that the existing limitations on home mortgage interest deductions be tightened by allowing such deductions only for mortgages on the taxpayer's principal residence.) Certainly mortgage deductions under the Simplified Alternative Tax should be subject to the same limitations as proposed under the reformed income tax, if they cannot be eliminated altogether.

17/ As noted above, several special rules would be required under the Simplified Alternative Tax to limit tax avoidance techniques involving businesses trading with individuals, tax-exempt institutions, or foreigners; such avoidance problems are a separate issue from the pure tax arbitrage problems discussed here.

18/ Capital gains on assets held by businesses (including individuals who file business returns) would be included in the receipts of the business; they thus would be included in the business tax base. Specifying which assets fall into the (taxable) business category and which would result in exempt gains of individuals would be troublesome, especially in transition.

19/ This occurs to the extent individual rates on labor income are higher under the Simplified Alternative Tax than under the reformed income tax because only the latter includes capital income in the individual tax base. Note that tax rates under the Simplified Alternative Tax could be maintained at current levels, with any revenue losses being made up through higher net wealth tax rates (if necessary after expansion of the net wealth tax base) or increased withholding taxes on remittances to foreigners. As a result, increased distortion of the labor-leisure choice should not be a problem, but the choice between current consumption and saving would be distorted even under the consumption-based alternative.

20/ See King (1980) and Bradford (1980).

21/ This is true in the sense that firms face a marginal effective tax rate of zero and are thus treated on a par with tax-exempt institutions. However, note that a marginal effective tax rate of zero is not identical to tax exemption. Rather than exemption from tax payments, such a tax rate implies that the present value of actual taxes paid on the income from an investment is offset by the present value of deductions attributable to that investment. The different treatments of certain transactions under a tax structure that yields a marginal effective tax rate of zero and under tax exemption give rise to certain tax avoidance problems. For examuple, a tax-exempt institution is indifferent between interest income and sales receipts and between interest payments and payments for goods purchased, while only sales receipts or purchases would have tax consequences for a firm subject to the business tax component of the Simplified Alternative Tax. As a result, opportunities for tax avoidance on transactions between these two types of entities arise, even though both can be described as facing a «zero» tax rate. See the discussion of tax avoidance problems under the Simplified Alternative Tax in Chapter 9.

22/ Driffill and Rosen (1983) include an assumption of endogenous labor supply without changing the basic results.

23/ Note that this discussion assumes that interest on student loans is deductible under the income tax; if this is not the case, there is no incentive for human capital accumulation under the income tax for individuals who borrow to finance their educations. Note that the direct expenses of producing human capital, such as tuition, books, etc., in principle should be deductible (or depreciable) under either an income or a consumption tax - to the extent that the purchase of inputs into the human capital production process is not subsidized and has no personal consumption component. In practice, such deductions are generally not allowed due to the difficulties of separating consumption from human capital investment expenditures, as well as the presence of significant educational subsidies. We would recommend that developing countries follow this practice, using the expenditure side of the budget to offset any disincentives to the production of human capital; note also that the absence of taxation of capital income under the consumption tax would facilitate saving to finance educational expenditures.

24/ Another issue that is important in the developing country context is the extent to which the tax system encourages emigration of highly-skilled individuals or «brain drain». Such emigration would be encouraged under a consumption tax to the extent that future consumption (or labor earnings) would be subject to relatively high tax rates in the developing country, but discouraged to the extent that the return to accumulated wealth would be subject to income taxation in the foreign country. The net effect is unclear and would likely be swamped by relative average rates of taxation and by non-tax factors.

25/ See Boskin (1978) and Summers (1981).

26/ For a discussion of the general problem of capital flight from Latin America induced by U.S. tax laws, see McLure (1987).

POSTSCRIPT

THE 1988 REFORMS

On December 26, 1988, acting under the extraordinary powers granted by Article 90 of the 1986 tax reform act, the government of Colombia issued decrees 2686 and 2687, laying out changes in the system of inflation adjustment introduced in 1986. In essence Colombia opted for a two-stage process in which the ad hoc approach to inflation adjustment, modified to include adjustment of depreciable assets, would continue to be used through 1991, with a switch to the integrated Chilean system of inflation adjustment in 1992. (Inflation adjustment is not extended to inventory accounting in the first stage; LIFO continues to provide an ad hoc substitute for income tax purposes.) These decrees, plus Law 84 and several other decrees issued at about the same time, also introduced several other modifications of the income and complementary taxes. This chapter briefly describes the most important of the 1988 changes, evaluates them, and then comments on the political considerations that presumably led to these choices.

I. The 1988 Legislation: Stage I

The changes that will be implemented during the period from 1989 through 1991 are relatively modest, especially when compared with the wide-ranging recommendations of the present Report. (They do, however, go beyond those recommendations in several respects.) These changes fall into three broad categories: inflation adjustment, presumptive taxation of income, and other provisions.[1]

Inflation adjustment

First, the basis of depreciable assets acquired after 1988 can be adjusted for inflation; net wealth tax and depreciation allowances on such assets will be based on inflation-adjusted values. Such adjustments can be made only when they are also used to calculate profits and loss for purposes of financial accounting. The inflation adjustment is based on the change in the consumer price index (CPI) over the period ending October 1 of the year prior to the taxable year in question; this definition of the rate of inflation to be used in making adjustments is carried over to stage II. The accelerated depreciation schedules of prior law are not modified.

Second, the use of LIFO inventory accounting will not be allowed after 1998. (Under the second stage of the 1988 reforms, replacement-cost accounting will be provided for companies and for some individuals; see below.) Until that time LIFO will continue to serve as a form of ad hoc adjustment for inflation for purposes of calculating taxable income. The difference in the value of inventories under LIFO and FIFO will be gradually reflected in net wealth, beginning in 1992; such differences will not be subject to income tax.

Third, beginning in 1989 owners of shares in open companies who have gross wealth of less than $20 million can use the market value of such shares in calculating capital gains on the disposal of such shares. In essence, this eliminates tax on capital gains from holding the shares.

Fourth, the portion of nominal income of companies representing inflation adjustment can either be distributed to shareholders as stock dividends (or their analog in the case of *limitadas*) or capitalized, without being taxed.

This chapter was prepared in early 1989. It was not part of the Report delivered to the government of Colombia.

Fifth, the phase-out of the deduction for the inflationary component of interest expense is frozen temporarily, with the fraction disallowed kept at its 1988 level of 30 percent through 1991; after that, the phase-out continues its previous pattern (with the fraction disallowed increasing by 10 percentage points per year).

Finally, beginning in 1989 leasing companies are subject to the general rules for inflation adjustment.

Presumptive taxation of income

First, the measure of presumptive income based on gross receipts will be phased out by 1990.

Second, the tax rate applied to net wealth in the calculation of presumptive income will be reduced from 8 percent to 7 percent.

Third, the value of real estate for purposes of the net wealth tax and the presumptive taxation of income will be increased to 100 percent of its cadastral value. In addition, for purpose of the presumptive income tax, the exemption of 60 percent of the value of beef and dairy cattle is repealed.

Fourth, to the extent that presumptive income exceeds income as calculated under the ordinary income tax system, the excess can be carried forward to the next two years as a deduction from taxable income as ordinarily determined, but not from presumptive income. That is, this deduction cannot be used to reduce the taxpayer's income to less than presumptive income for the year, determined as a percentage of net wealth.

Other issues [2]

First, Law 84 of 1988 provides emergency powers under which the net wealth tax can be reduced or eliminated.

Second, the same law also applies a 20 percent tax to the income of nonprofit organizations, to the extent such income is not employed for the social purpose of the organization. For these organizations there is no inflation adjustment in the measurement of income (including the taxation of nominal interest income and nominal capital gains), and immediate deductions are allowed for all (nonfinancial) outlays, including business investments.

II. The 1988 Legislation: Stage II

The second stage of the reforms introduced in 1988 deal almost exclusively with inflation adjustment; in particular, they define the technique by which the integrated system will be implemented. Since most such technical details are not of great interest for present purposes, they generally are not specified here. However, several details involving important policy decisions deserve mention. To the extent that changes described above carry over to stage II they generally are not mentioned in the following description. Only a few of the most important cases of governmental inaction—most notably the failure to introduce slower depreciation allowances—are discussed. Of course, the present Report contains many other proposals that were not adopted, some for reasons to be discussed below.

First, the integrated system is required for taxpayers who are required by law to keep books of account, except for (a) individuals who qualify for the use of the simplified regime under the sales tax and (b) nonprofit organizations. In short, most profit-seeking companies are required to use the system and most individuals are not, being left on the ad hoc system.[3/] The distinction between ordinary income and capital gains and losses was eliminated for taxpayers subject to the integrated system. Those not required to use the integrated system can do so at their option, or they can use the ad hoc system established in Stage I. Those using the integrated system must do so for purposes of both tax and commercial accounting.

The cost of fixed assets (including improvements made during the year and assets acquired before 1992) are to be adjusted for inflation, using the change in the CPI. If the cadastral value of real estate exceeds the inflation-adjusted cost, the former value is to be employed as the value of the asset. Depreciation allowances and gains and losses on the disposition of such assets are to be based on such inflation-adjusted values, except that depreciation is not allowed for land. No change is made in the accelerated depreciation schedules provided by prior law. Inventories are to be valued at replacement cost.[4/]

Shares in corporations traded on a stock exchange are valued at market prices. Shares in *limitadas* and corporations not traded on an exchange are valued on the basis of the "intrinsic" value of the shares certified by the company once it has revalued its assets.

Inflation adjustment is applied to net wealth and to real assets, including indexed monetary or financial assets; it is not applied to ordinary monetary assets (those fixed in nominal terms).[5/] In the case of assets and liabilities denominated in foreign currencies, the inflation adjustment is based on the change in the exchange rate for the relevant currency. Interest and similar expense incurred before an asset is placed in service (e.g., construction-period interest and the cost of acquiring inventories) is to be capitalized; only interest occurred after such time is to be subject to inflation adjustment and deducted in the year incurred.

III. Appraisal of the 1988 Changes

While generally consistent with the changes recommended in the present Report, the 1988 reforms are inconsistent in several significant respects. In several instances these inconsistencies raise important questions of policy. The most important of these changes—especially the inconsistencies—are discussed briefly.[6/]

Inflation Adjustment

First, the introduction of explicit inflation adjustment of depreciation allowances is an important improvement. But it is quite inconsistent to introduce inflation adjustment for depreciable assets without modifying the schedule of accelerated depreciation allowances to make it reflect economic depreciation more accurately. (See the system of real economic depreciation allowances described in chapter 5.) This can easily be seen in the changes in the marginal effective tax rates that result from the 1988 reforms. Under prior law, at an inflation rate of 25 percent, the acceleration of depreciation allowances roughly offset the failure to allow inflation adjustment, producing a METR for investments by tax-exempt organizations using the income for exempt purposes approximately equal to the statutory tax rate.[7/] By comparison, the uncompensated introduction of inflation adjustment reduces the METR on income resulting from depreciable assets to below the statutory rate, creating a tax distortion favoring investment in such assets.[8/] In addition, net wealth will continue to be understated due to the use of accelerated depreciation, though not by as much as in the absence of inflation adjustment.

Second, the 1988 law requires (a) that, during the 1989–91 transition period, inflation adjustment of depreciation allowances must be used for financial accounting if it is used for tax accounting and (b) that companies must use the integrated system for both purposes beginning in 1992. These "conformity requirements" are also an important step in the right direction. Their adoption will help to make financial accounting more accurate and to prevent the widespread (nontax, as well as tax) abuses based on questionable bookkeeping practices said to occur under prior law.

Third, the decision to base inflation adjustment on the change in the CPI during the year ending October 1 of the year before the tax year in question is debatable on policy grounds, though it may have some justification on grounds of certainty and administrative simplicity. At the very least, it means that real income will not be measured accurately during periods of changing inflation rates. Suppose, for argument's sake, that the real rate of interest is 5 percent, that the inflation rates over a three-year period are 10 percent, 25 percent, and 10 percent, and that the nominal interest rate reflects changes in inflation on a one-for-one basis; under such assumptions the nominal rate of interest in the three years will be 15 percent, 30 percent, and 15 percent.[9/] The conceptually correct interest exclusion/disallowance factors in the three years would be two-thirds ($^{10}/_{15}$), five-sixths ($^{25}/_{30}$), and two-thirds, respectively. But under the procedure of basing inflation adjustment on lagged values of the inflation rate, these factors will be two-thirds and five-sixths in the last two years. Thus, in these two years, instead of neglecting 10 and 25 percentage points of interest income and expense, as is conceptually correct, taxpayers would neglect 20 percentage points and 12.5 percentage points. Real income is not measured accurately in either year.

A potentially more serious problem is that this approach may lend itself to "game playing" by taxpayers. Under the conceptually correct approach, the exclusion/disallowance factors are known only after the year to which they apply; by comparison, under the lagged system they are known in advance. In the example this system provides artificial incentives to borrow during the second year and to lend during the third—and to engage in artificial transactions that produce this result for tax purposes.

The decisions (a) to base the valuation of inventories on replacement costs and (b) to base the calculation of exchange rate gains and losses on changes in the peso values of various currencies are a mixed blessing, at best. The use of replacement cost accounting for inventories and the use of currency-specific adjustments for changes in the relative value of the peso produce a more accurate measure of net wealth than do indexed FIFO and the use of a single measure of the fall in the value of the peso. But, as explained in chapter 7, they are far more complicated and they do not give as satisfactory a measure of taxable income. It seems quite puzzling that lagged values of inflation would be used on simplicity grounds, where there is loss of accuracy in the measurement of income and little actual gain in simplicity, while the much greater complication and inferior measure of income involved in replacement cost accounting and currency-specific adjustment of foreign assets and liabilities are accepted for no apparent or sound policy reason.

The integrated system clearly cannot be used for all individual taxpayers; it is necessary to use ad hoc methods for some. But this can create asymmetries in income measurement and opportunities for game-playing that were not fully recognized during the preparation of the Report.[10/] The root of the problem lies in the fact that the integrated system makes adjustments to the principal of indebtedness, while the ad hoc system adjusts interest. Suppose, for example, that a taxpayer using the integrated system were to make a loan at below-market interest rates to an affiliated taxpayer operating under the ad hoc system; the "integrated" adjustment to the principal of the loan (which would reduce taxable income) would exceed the ad hoc adjustment to the interest deduction. A loan at above market rates in the other direction would produce an ad hoc exemption of interest that would exceed the "integrated" adjustment to principal (an addition to income). Moreover, this is a "game" that can be played by unrelated parties through the use of reciprocal loans at different tax rates.

Prevention of such manipulation requires either very tight restrictions on eligibility to use the ad hoc system or effective administrative rules for presumptive interest rates. It would probably be difficult for both political and administrative reasons to implement tight eligibility rules, especially during the early years of inflation adjustment. On the other hand, Colombian law does not provide for presumptive interest rates, except in the case of transactions between affiliated parties. Nor does it seem likely that it would have been possible to introduce such rules under the extraordinary powers. Finding a solution in this area deserves further attention.

Other Measures

The elimination of the measure of presumptive income based on gross income, the full valuation of real estate and cattle, and the reduction of the presumed rate of return under the presumptive income tax are all appropriate reforms, for reasons given in the Report. Indeed, it can be argued, in principle, that the presumed rate of return should be reduced even further, given the more complete indexation of the measurement of income and the more accurate measurement of net wealth. On the other hand, it may be premature to do this, given the ease of tax evasion in Colombia.

The provision of emergency powers under which the net wealth tax might be eliminated is quite troubling, as the net wealth tax has long been a mainstay of progressive taxation in Colombia and has more recently also provided the basis for the presumptive taxation of income, an important anti-evasion backstop for the income tax. It would be anomalous from an administrative point of view to retain the presumptive income tax, while abandoning the net wealth tax. Yet to eliminate the presumptive income tax as well would further undermine the progressivity of the tax system. Thus eliminating the net wealth tax would be doubly undesirable.

The tightening of the taxation of nonprofit organizations is also appropriate, both to combat evasion and to prevent unfair competition with for-profit organizations.[11] But if this is the objective, it seems rather anomalous not to apply inflation adjustment to the income of these institutions, to allow them to expense investments, and to provide a preferential tax rate. Both fair competition with the for-profit private sector and the avoidance of abuse can be fully achieved only if the regular rules for determining taxable income (and the ordinary company tax rates) are applied to these organizations. The 1988 changes may represent only an intermediate step in a process that will see the continued refinement of this part of the Colombian income tax system.

The Agenda for Future Tax Reform

The 1988 changes just described and evaluated do not complete the task of tax reform in Colombia. Few substantive reforms were made in 1988 outside the area of inflation adjustment, presumably because of the perceived limitations on the types of changes that could be made under the extraordinary powers. The present Report has described many other needed changes in the measurement of income from business and capital and in the measurement of net wealth; it has thus defined the agenda—or at least some of the options—for future tax reform in Colombia. Pressures for these changes presumably will not be as great as those that led to the introduction of inflation adjustment. Yet the history of tax reform in Colombia makes it clear that in many cases reforms that once were thought too extreme to be viable have often been adopted after a gestation period.[12]

This conclusion is nowhere more relevant than in the case of the Simplified Alternative Tax (SAT). Too radical to be adopted on short notice in 1988, especially under the extraordinary powers, the SAT will undoubtedly continue to be studied in Colombia. It would not be surprising to see Colombia become one of the first countries to adopt such a tax system.

IV. Comments on the Politics of Tax Reform

This chapter is being written in early 1989, after the 1988 reforms described above, for inclusion in an English version of the Report to be published outside Colombia. It has thus provided the singular opportunity to see and evaluate the first installment of results the present Report has had on decisionmaking in Colombia. It is also possible—and presumably not inappropriate—to comment on political aspects of the basic decisions on tax reform taken in the closing days of 1988.

Rejection of the SAT

Much has been said recently about the apparent tendency for the design of Colombia's tax system to be affected strongly by the "conventional wisdom" prevailing in developed countries.[13] Since consumption-based direct taxes such as the SAT are the current "darling" of tax specialists, it is worthwhile to comment briefly on the Colombian government's decision not to adopt this new fiscal approach.

There were very good reasons for rejecting the SAT at this time. These include, but go well beyond, the technical concerns documented in the present Report (e.g., inconsistency with financial accounting and the net wealth tax). First, it is quite possible that introduction of the SAT under the extraordinary powers would have been ruled unconstitutional; certainly the threat of an adverse judicial ruling in this matter was an important factor in the minds of those responsible for rejecting the SAT.[14] Although the extraordinary powers appear to have provided the president of Colombia quite wide latitude in modifying the provisions for inflation adjustment, introduction of the SAT would have involved changes that could not reasonably be included under that rubric (e.g., complete elimination of both the taxation of interest income and the deduction for interest expense).

Even if there had been no such constitutional constraint, using the extraordinary powers to introduce the SAT would have been questionable on political grounds. Although the English version of the present Report had been available to the Director General of Internal Taxes since the spring of 1988—and in limited quantities to legislators and the general public since mid-September—the Spanish version of the Report was available in Colombia only in mid-November 1988. Thus, for the most part, Colombian taxpayers and policymakers had only about eight weeks in which to read and digest the Report, determine its likely consequences for themselves and the economy of the country, and react, since the government had to reach its decisions before the emergency powers expired at the end of the year.

To have attempted to introduce a change in the tax system as far-reaching as the SAT under these circumstances would have been unwise, if not foolhardy. It seems likely that introduction of the SAT could be accomplished smoothly, but only if the new system has been fully debated and is well understood; even so, it is likely to be bitterly opposed in some quarters. To attempt to introduce such a system quickly and without adequate discussion and preparation is a sure recipe for failure; merely drafting the legislation needed to replace the income tax with the SAT would have been a major undertaking. To have attempted to introduce the SAT in late 1988 under the extraordinary powers would almost certainly have spelled political disaster.

Another fact is important in understanding Colombia's decision not to introduce the SAT. Since no country currently uses the SAT, the first country to adopt this tax will be a fiscal pioneer. Thus introduction of the SAT will inevitably involve considerable political risk. That risk would be heightened if it appeared that the government had acted precipitously in choosing the SAT.

An abortive attempt to introduce the SAT could have cast a long shadow on tax policy in Colombia and elsewhere. Whether introduction of the SAT had been ruled unconstitutional, or had simply been politically infeasible, it is possible that the opponents of inflation adjustment could have seized the opportunity to gain the repeal of the 1986 provisions for interest indexing, leaving Colombia in the status quo ante as far as inflation adjustment is concerned. Even worse, it is likely that the experience would have caused policymakers both in and out of Colombia to be wary of the radical proposal embodied in the SAT; certainly the unsuccessful attempt to introduce the conceptually related expenditure tax in India and Sri Lanka (then Ceylon) a quarter century ago has caused others to be hesitant about repeating the experiment.

The Two-stage Transition to the Integrated System

As part of the government's attempt to assess the relative merits of the ad hoc and integrated or "Chilean" systems of inflation adjustment, Santiago Pardo, the most recent past Director General of Internal Taxes, visited Chile to meet with officials there and get a firsthand feel for the operation of their system. Contrary to the view expressed in this Report, Pardo concluded that the integrated system may not be more complicated than the ad hoc system for most taxpayers, especially those with reasonably sophisticated accounting systems. Indeed, in many respects the accuracy of the integrated system may make it simpler than the ad hoc system by eliminating opportunities for "game-playing" by taxpayers. On purely economic and administrative grounds, for such taxpayers an immediate shift to the integrated system may be preferable to a transition strategy of first gaining experience with the ad hoc system, contrary to the conclusion of the present Report.

Despite this view, the decision to opt for a two-stage transition to the integrated system—involving three years of continued reliance on the ad hoc system—can also be explained in part by constitutional and political concerns. It was (and is, as this is being written) far from clear that introduction of the integrated system under the emergency powers would pass constitutional muster. While less radical than the SAT, the integrated system involves changes that might be ruled not to be merely modifications in inflation adjustment (for example, adjustments to net wealth and the inclusion of the adjustments to net wealth, real assets, and real liabilities in taxable income). Moreover, as with the SAT, introduction of the integrated system probably should not be attempted without adequate advanced notice, study, and debate, especially since opposition to it might also have jeopardized the 1986 provisions for inflation adjustment. The two-stage approach will meet both these concerns, by providing time for discussion and by assuring that there will be a backstop (the ad hoc system) if the integrated system should be rejected by the judiciary.

NOTES

1/ The descriptions that follow focus on the most important changes in the taxation of income from business and capital; they are not intended to be exhaustive.

2/ In addition to the two provisions described here, the decrees deal with the treatment of business deductions for future pension payments, impose a tax of 2 percent on payments to foreigners for the rental of certain equipment, and eliminate the income tax on dividends received by Colombian branches of foreign corporations.

3/ There is a relief provision for taxpayers whose assets have a value of less than 50 percent of that resulting from the application of the regular rules for inflation adjustment.

4/ The decree specifies separate procedures for determining the replacement costs of inventories of unprocessed goods, finished goods, and goods in process. It might be noted that while net wealth tax is based on replacement costs, cost of goods sold in a given year is calculated before revaluing inventories to their replacement values.

5/ Article 24 of Decree 2687 contains transition provisions for the partial adjustment of interest during the period 1992–2002.

6/ The basis for most of these comments is provided at greater length in previous chapters, especially chapters 5 and 7.

7/ As explained in chapter 4, investment by tax-exempt investors provides a useful benchmark for the measurement of METRs, since there is no taxation at the investor level. The introduction of the 20 percent tax on tax-exempt institutions makes it necessary to specify that income is used for tax-exempt purposes if this benchmark is to be used.

8/ At an inflation rate of 20 percent, the two METRs under 1985 law were 35.4 percent and 42.2 percent, compared to a statutory rate of 40 percent. By comparison, the 1988 law reduced these METRs to 9.3 percent and 20.7 percent, respectively, compared to the statutory rate of 30 percent. See also McLure and Zodrow (1989).

9/ This "unmodified" version of "Fisher's Law" is employed for simplicity; see chapter 7 for further discussion of its shortcomings.

10/ This discussion is based on consultations with Luis Fernando Ramírez and Santiago Pardo, the present and immediate past Directors General of Internal Taxes.

11/ See McLure (1982).

12/ See Perry and Cárdenas (1986), Thirsk (1988), McLure (1989a), and McLure and Zodrow (1989).

13/ See Perry and Cárdenas (1986), Thirsk (1988), McLure (1989a), and McLure and Zodrow (1989).

14/ This impression, like others of a similar nature in this chapter, is based on the continued relationship between Charles McLure, the Director of this Study, and Luis Fernando Ramírez and Santiago Pardo, the present and immediate past Directors General of Internal Taxes.

Appendix

References to Colombian Law: Explanation of Terms

The following terms are used in this book to refer to Colombian law.

"Ley" refers to an Act of the Colombian legislature. For example, Ley 75/86 refers to Law 75 of 1986.

"D.L." is an abbreviation for Decreto Legislativo (legislative decree) and refers to an administrative regulation with the force of law.

"D.R." is an abbreviation for Decreto Reglamentario (regulatory decree) and refers to an interpretive regulation.

Translation of quotation on page 91:

Traditionally in this country, interest has been deductible while dividends have not been; the incoherence of the system stems from this.

Obviously, the State has thereby subsidized—in the case of corporations—40 percent of the interest costs incurred, while in the case of dividends the corporation itself must pay the taxes.

As a result of this state of affairs, in the last twenty years in this country—whenever enterprises have had to raise capital—the decision was always made to do so by means of debt.

Translation of quotation on page 196 (carrying over to page 197):

Between 1953, when double taxation was established, and 1985, the level of indebtedness of companies organized in this country increased from about 25 percent to about 85 percent; as a logical consequence, the concentration of share ownership increased greatly and the ownership of companies gradually began closing. . . . It was neither useful nor profitable to finance companies through equity. It was beyond question preferable to finance them by means of debt, among other things not only because of the existence of a tax burden at the level of both the company and the shareholder or partner, compared with the full deductibility of interest, but because the phenomenon was also aggravated to an even greater extent by the acceleration of inflation in Colombia starting in the seventies. . . . As a consequence, the portion of financing that was done via debt became completely abnormal in Colombia in the past several years, compared with that of countries with similar levels of per capita income. And the reason for this is quite logical: it was not profitable to raise equity capital, but rather to become indebted, both because of the problem of the double tax burden and because of the treatment of inflation in terms of the full deduction of interest, including its inflationary component. (Urdinola, 1987, pp. 58–59)

Translation of quotation on page 197:

Colombian corporations have undergone a process of progressive decapitalization and indebtedness at least since the fifties, accompanied, especially during the seventies, by a development of financial intermediaries. . . . These attracted the resources of households to lend them to enterprises, thereby providing a substitute for direct investment through share issuance. . . . Analyses performed for the Colombian situation point out a consistently lower cost for the debt finance alternative, which has become increasingly more favorable than the alternative of issuing shares, due to the increasing burden of direct taxation. (Carrizosa, 1986, p. 19)

Translation of first quotation in note 88, page 269:

It is necessary to begin to correct some of the phenomena that have been described, limiting the deductibility of the inflationary component of interest over a lengthy period of time, so as not to disturb the productive activity of the nation. (p. 10)

Translation of second quotation:

It is necessary to refer to the powers that the government has in the matter of inflation. . . . It seems to me that as a result of these powers, starting with taxable year 1987 or taxable year 1988, there will exist in this country, for income tax purposes, inflation adjustments to the depreciation schedules, inflation adjustments for inventories which would be capable of being deducted in the year in which they arise. This will permit an absolutely complete compensation for the elimination of the deductibility of the inflationary component of interest. (Pardo, 1987, p. 29)

Bibliography

Aaron, Henry J., ed., **Inflation and the Income Tax** (Washington, D.C.: Brookings Institution, 1976).

Aaron, Henry J., and Harvey Galper, **Assessing Tax Reform** (Washington, D.C.: Brookings Institution, 1985).

Adjustments for Tax Purposes in Highly Inflationary Economies, proceedings of a seminar held in Buenos Aires in 1984 during the 38th Congress of the International Fiscal Association.

Andrews, William D., "A Consumption-Type or Cash Flow Personal Income Tax," **Harvard Law Review** 87 (April 1974): 1113–88.

Asociación Nacional de Industriales (ANDI), **Memorias del Seminario sobre la Nueva Reforma Tributaria 1986** (Medellín, Colombia: Asociación Nacional de Industriales, 1987).

Atkinson, Anthony B., and Joseph E. Stiglitz, **Lectures on Public Economics** (New York: McGraw-Hill, 1980).

Auerbach, Alan J., "Wealth Maximization and the Cost of Capital," **Quarterly Journal of Economics** 93 (August 1979): 433–46.

Auerbach, Alan J., and Dale W. Jorgenson, "The First Year Capital Recovery System," **Tax Notes** 10, no. 15 (April 14, 1980): 515–23.

Auerbach, A. A., and L. Kotlikoff, "Investment versus Savings Incentives: The Size of the Bang for the Buck and the Potential for Self-Financing Tax Cuts," in L. H. Meyer, ed., **The Economic Consequences of Government Deficits** (Boston: Kluwer-Nijhoff, 1983).

Ayala, Horacio, "Tratamiento Fiscal a lo Intereses y Diferencias de Cambio sobre la Deuda del Sector Privado en Moneda Extranjera," **XII Jornadas Latinoamericanas de Derecho Tributario** (Bogotá, 1985).

———, "El Tratamiento Tributario a los Intereses," **Sintesis Economica** (Febrero 23, 1987), pp. 13–19.

———, "La Reforma Tributaria y Los Contribuyentes Extranjeros," xeroxed 1987.

Ayala, Horacio, ed., **Nueva Reforma Tributaria**, segunda edición (Bogotá: Cámara de Comercio de Bogotá, 1987).

Betancourt, Roger, and Christopher Clague, **Capacity Utilization: A Theoretical and Empirical Analysis** (New York: Cambridge University Press, 1981).

Bird, Richard M., "The Administrative Dimension of Tax Reform in Developing Countries," in Malcolm Gillis, ed., **Lessons from Fundamental Tax Reform in Developing Countries** (Durham, N.C.: Duke University Press, 1989), pp. 315–46.

Blejer, Mario, "Financial Market Taxation and International Capital Flows," in Vito Tanzi, **Taxation, Inflation and Interest Rates** (Washington, D.C.: International Monetary Fund, 1984), pp. 204–18.

Boskin, Michael J., "Taxation, Saving, and the Rate of Interest," **Journal of Political Economy** 86, no. 2 (April 1978, pt. 2): S3–S27.

Bossons, John, "Indexation After the Lortie Report," **Report of Proceedings of the Thirty-Fourth Tax Conference** (Canadian Tax Foundation, 1982), pp. 478–94.

————, "Indexing for Inflation and the Interest Deduction," **Wayne Law Review** (Spring 1984), pp. 945–68.

Bradford, David F., "The Economics of Tax Policy Toward Saving," in George M. von Furstenberg, ed., **The Government and Capital Formation** (Cambridge, Mass.: Ballinger, 1980), pp. 11–71.

————, "The Incidence and Allocation Effects of a Tax on Corporate Distributions," **Journal of Public Economics** 15, no.1 (February 1981): 1–22.

————, **Untangling the Income Tax** (Cambridge, Mass.: Harvard University Press, 1986).

Bradford, David F., and Don Fullerton, "Pitfalls in the Construction and Use of Effective Tax Rates," in Charles R. Hulten, ed., **Depreciation, Inflation, and the Taxation of Income From Capital** (Washington, D.C.: Urban Institute Press, 1981), pp. 251–78.

Bradford, David, and Charles Stuart, "Issues in the Measurement and Interpretation of Effective Tax Rates," **National Tax Journal** 39, no. 3 (September 1986): 307–16.

Break, George F., "Tax Reform, Investment Incentives, and Financial Market Efficiency," in George F. Break, Daniel Holland, and Charles E. McLure, Jr., "Private Sector Capital Investment and the Company Tax," Staff Paper 28, Jamaica Tax Structure Examination Project, Syracuse University, Syracuse, N.Y., 1986.

Carrizosa S., Mauricio, **Hacia La Recuperación del Mercado de Capitales en Colombia** (Bogotá: Editorial Presencia, Ltda., 1986).

Casanegra de Jantscher, Milka, "Chile," **Adjustments for Tax Purposes in Highly Inflationary Economies**, proceedings of a seminar held in Buenos Aires in 1984 during the 38th Congress of the International Fiscal Association, pp. 25–35, 88–104.

Chica A., Ricardo, "La Financiación de la Inversión en la Industria Manufacturera Colombiana: 1970–1980," **Desarrollo y Sociedad** 15–16 (Septiembre 1984, Marzo 1985): 193–285.

Cooper, George, **A Voluntary Tax? New Perspectives on Sophisticated Estate Tax Avoidance** (Washington, D.C.: Brookings Institution, 1979).

Davidson, Sidney, Clyde P. Stickney, and Roman L. Weil, **Inflation Accounting: A Guide for the Accountant and the Financial Analyst** (New York: McGraw-Hill, 1976).

Denison, Edward F., "Price Series for Indexing the Income Tax," in Henry J. Aaron, ed., **Inflation and the Income Tax** (Washington, D.C.: Brookings Institution, 1976), pp. 233–61.

Departamento Nacional de Planeación, República de Colombia, **Régimen Legal de la Inversión Extranjera**, segunda edición (Bogotá: Departmento Nacional de Planeación, 1985).

Dornbusch, Rudiger, **Open Economy Macroeconomics** (New York: Basic Books, 1980).

Driffill, E. John, and Harvey S. Rosen, "Taxation and Excess Burden: A Life Cycle Perspective," **International Economic Review** 24, no. 3 (October 1983): 671–83.

Economic Council of Canada, **Road Map for Tax Reform, The Taxation of Saving and Investment** (Ottawa: Economic Council of Canada, 1987).

Evans, Owen J., "Tax Policy, the Interest Elasticity of Savings, and Capital Accumulation: Numerical Analyses of Theoretical Models," **American Economic Review** 73, no. 3 (June 1983): 398–410.

Feldstein, Martin, "On the Theory of Tax Reform," **Journal of Public Economics** 6, nos. 1, 2 (July/August 1976): 77–104.

————, "Inflation, Income Taxes, and the Rate of Interest: A Theoretical Analysis," **American Economic Review** 66, no. 5 (December 1976): 809–20.

————, "The Welfare Cost of Capital Income Taxation," **Journal of Political Economy** 86, no. 2 (April 1978, pt. 2): S29–S51.

Feldstein, Martin, and Charles Horioka, "Domestic Savings and International Capital Flows," **Economic Journal** 90 (June 1980): 314–29.

Feldstein, Martin, and Joel Slemrod, "Inflation and the Excess Taxation of Capital Gains on Corporate Stock," **National Tax Journal** 31, no. 2 (June 1978): 107–18.

Financial Accounting Standards Board, "Financial Reporting and Changing Prices," Statement of Financial Accounting Standards No. 33 (September 1979).

Fullerton, Don, "The Indexation of Interest, Depreciation, and Capital Gains and Tax Reform in the United States," **Journal of Public Economics** 32, no. 1 (February 1987): 25–51.

Fullerton, Don, Robert Gillette, and James Mackie, "Investment Incentives under the Tax Reform Act of 1986," **OTA Compendium of Tax Research** (Washington, D.C.: U.S. Department of the Treasury, 1987), pp. 131–72.

Gillis, Malcolm, and Charles E. McLure, Jr., **La Reforma Tributaria Colombiana de 1974** (Bogotá: Banco Popular, 1977).

————, "Taxation and Income Distribution: The Colombian Tax Reform of 1974," **Journal of Development Economics** 5 (1978): 233–58.

Goode, Richard A., "New System of Direct Taxation in Ceylon," **National Tax Journal** 13 (December 1960): 329–40.

————, "The Economic Definition of Income," in Joseph A. Pechman, ed., **Comprehensive Income Taxation** (Washington, D.C.: Brookings Institution, 1977), pp. 1–30.

————, "The Superiority of the Income Tax," in Joseph A. Pechman, ed., **What Should be Taxed: Income or Expenditure?** (Washington, D.C.: Brookings Institution, 1980), pp. 49–73.

Gordon, R. H., J. R. Hines, Jr., and L. H. Summers, "Notes on the Tax Treatment of Structures," National Bureau of Economic Research Working Paper No. 1896, April 1986.

Graetz, Michael J., "Implementing a Progressive Consumption Tax," **Harvard Law Review** 92 (1979): 1575–1661.

————, "Expenditure Tax Design," in Joseph A. Pechman, ed., **What Should Be Taxed: Income or Expenditure?** (Washington, D.C.: Brookings Institution, 1980), pp. 161–76.

Gramlich, Edward M., "Comments" on John B. Shoven and Jeremy I. Bulow, "Inflation Accounting and Nonfinancial Corporate Profits: Physical Assets," **Brookings Papers on Economic Activity** 3 (1975): 604–8.

————, "Comments" on John B. Shoven and Jeremy I. Bulow, "Inflation Accounting and Nonfinancial Corporate Profits: Financial Assets and Liabilities," **Brookings Papers on Economic Activity** 1 (1976): 61–63.

Gravelle, Jane G., "Which Effective Tax Rate: A Comment and Extension," **National Tax Journal** 38, no. 1 (March 1985): 103–8.

Grubert, Harry, and Jack Mutti, "The Impact of the Tax Reform Act of 1986 on Trade and Capital Flows," in **Compendium of Tax Research: 1987** (Washington, D.C.: U.S. Department of the Treasury, 1987), pp. 229–52.

Hall, Robert E., and Alvin Rabushka, **Low Tax, Simple Tax, Flat Tax** (New York: McGraw-Hill, 1983).

————, **The Flat Tax** (Stanford, Calif.: Hoover Institution Press, 1985).

Halperin, Daniel, and Eugene Steuerle, "Indexing the Tax System for Inflation," in Henry J. Aaron, Harvey Galper, and Joseph A. Pechman, ed., **Uneasy Compromise** (Washington, D.C.: Brookings Institution, 1988), pp. 347–72.

Hansson, Ingemar, and Charles Stuart, "The Fisher Hypothesis and International Capital Markets," **Journal of Political Economy** 94, no. 6 (December 1986): 1330–37.

Harberger, Arnold C., "Vignettes on the World Capital Markets," **American Economic Review** 70, no. 2 (May 1980): 331–37.

————, "Notes on the Indexation of Income Taxes," memorandum prepared for the Ministry of Finance of Indonesia (August 1982), excerpted in "Comments" on Daniel Halperin and Eugene Steuerle, "Indexing the Tax System for Inflation," in Henry J. Aaron, Harvey Galper, and Joseph A. Pechman, eds., **Uneasy Compromise** (Washington, D.C.: Brookings Institution, 1988), pp. 380–83.

Hartman, David, "Tax Policy and Foreign Direct Investment in the United States," **National Tax Journal** 37, no. 4 (December 1984): 475–87.

Hicks, J. R., **Value and Capital**, 2d ed. (Oxford: Clarendon Press, 1946).

Howard, David, and Karen Johnson, "Interest Rates, Inflation, and Taxes: The Foreign Connection," **Economic Letters** 9 (1982): 181–84.

Hulten, Charles R., and Frank C. Wykoff, "The Measurement of Economic Depreciation and Accelerated Depreciation," in Charles R. Hulten, ed., **Depreciation, Inflation, and the Taxation of Income from Capital** (Washington, D.C.: Urban Institute Press, 1981), pp. 81–125.

Institute for Fiscal Studies, **The Structure and Reform of Direct Taxation** (London: Allen and Unwin, 1978).

Kay, John A., "Indexation of Tax and Securities in the United Kingdom," **Report of Proceedings of the Thirty-fourth Tax Conference** (Canadian Tax Foundation, 1982), pp. 520–31.

King, Mervyn A., **Public Policy and the Corporation** (New York: John Wiley and Sons, 1977).

————, "Savings and Taxation," in G. A. Hughes and G. M. Heal, eds., **Public Policy and the Tax System** (London: George Allen and Unwin, 1980), pp. 1–35.

King, Mervyn A., and Don Fullerton, eds., **The Taxation of Income from Capital** (Chicago: University of Chicago Press, 1984).

Largay, James A., III, and John Leslie Livingstone, **Accounting for Changing Prices: Replacement Cost and General Price Level Adjustments** (New York: John Wiley and Sons, 1976).

Lent, George E., "Adjusting Taxable Profits for Inflation: The Foreign Experience," in Henry J. Aaron, ed., **Inflation and the Income Tax** (Washington, D.C.: Brookings Institution, 1976), pp. 195–213.

————, **"Adjustment of Taxable Profits for Inflation," International Monetary Fund Staff Papers** 22, no. 3 (November 1978): 641–79.

Lodin, Sven-Olof, **Progressive Expenditure Tax – An Alternative?** (Stockholm: LiberFörlag, 1978).

Massone P., Pedro, "Adjustment of Profits for Inflation: Part I," **Bulletin of the International Bureau for Fiscal Documentation** (1981), pp. 3–15(a).

————, "Adjustment of Profits for Inflation: Part II," **Bulletin of the International Bureau for Fiscal Documentation** (1981), pp. 51–61(b).

McLure, Charles E., Jr., **Must Corporate Income Be Taxed Twice?** (Washington, D.C.: Brookings Institution, 1979).

————, "Income and Complementary Taxes," xeroxed 1982.

————, "Analysis and Reform of the Colombian Tax System," in Malcolm Gillis, ed., **Lessons from Fundamental Tax Reform in Developing Countries** (Durham, N.C.: Duke University Press, 1989), pp. 44–78(a).

————, "Lessons for LDCs of U.S. Income Tax Reform," in Malcolm Gillis, ed., **Lessons from Fundamental Tax Reform in Developing Countries** (Durham, N.C.: Duke University Press, 1989), pp. 347–90(b).

————, "U.S. Tax Laws and Capital Flight from Latin America," **Inter-American Law Review** 20, no. 2 (forthcoming).

McLure, Charles E., Jr., and George R. Zodrow, "Tax Reform in Colombia: Process and Results," xeroxed, 1989.

Menchik, Paul L., and Martin David, "The Incidence of a Lifetime Consumption Tax," **National Tax Journal** 35, no. 2 (June 1982): 189–220.

Mieszkowski, Peter, "The Cash Flow Version of an Expenditure Tax," Office of Tax Analysis, Paper No. 26 (U.S. Treasury Department, 1977).

———, "The Advisability and Feasibility of an Expenditure Tax System," in Henry J. Aaron and Michael J. Boskin, eds., **The Economics of Taxation** (Washington, D.C.: Brookings Institution, 1980), pp. 179–201.

Ministerio de Hacienda y Crédito Público, y Ministerio de Desarollo Económico, "Exposición de Motivos al Proyecto de Ley por medio de la cual Se Solicitan Facultades Extraordinarias Para Dictar Dispociónes Sobre Inversión Extranjera, Tecnología, Patentes y Marcas y Se Restructuran Algunos Organismos de la Administración" (Bogotá, no date).

Nueva Reforma Tributaria 1986 (Medellín, Colombia: Asociación Nacional de Industriales, 1986).

Pardo Ramirez, Santiago, "Fundamentos, Objectivos e Instrumentos de la Reforma," **Nueva Reforma Tributaria 1986** (Medellín, Colombia: Asociación Nacional de Industriales, 1986), pp. 19–43.

Pechman, Joseph A., ed., **What Should Be Taxed: Income or Expenditure?** (Washington, D.C.: Brookings Institution, 1980).

Peek, Joe, "Interest Rates, Income Taxes, and Anticipated Inflation," **American Economic Review** 72, no. 5 (December 1982): 980–91.

Perry R., Guillermo, and Cárdenas S., Mauricio, **Diez Años de Reformas Tributarios en Colombia** (Bogotá: Empresa Editorial, Universidad Nacional de Colombia, 1986).

Pigou, A. C., "Maintaining Capital Intact," **Economica** 8 (August 1941): 271–75.

Shoven, John B., and Jeremy I. Bulow, "Inflation Accounting and Nonfinancial Corporate Profits: Physical Assets," **Brookings Papers on Economic Activity** 3 (1975): 557–98.

———, "Inflation Accounting and Nonfinancial Corporate Profits: Financial Assets and Liabilities," **Brookings Papers on Economic Activity** 1 (1976): 15–57.

Siegel, Stanley, "Accounting and Inflation: An Analysis and a Proposal," **UCLA Law Review** 29 (December 1981): 271–329.

Simons, Henry C., **Personal Income Taxation** (Chicago: University of Chicago Press, 1938).

———, **Federal Tax Reform** (Chicago: University of Chicago Press, 1950).

Sterling, Robert R., **Theory of the Measurement of Enterprise Income** (Lawrence: University Press of Kansas, 1970).

Steuerle, C. E., "Equity and the Taxation of Wealth Transfers," **Tax Notes** 11, no. 10 (September 9, 1980): 459–64.

Stiglitz, J. E., and P. S. Dasgupta, "Differential Taxation, Public Goods, and Economic Efficiency," **Review of Economic Studies** 8 (1971): 151–74.

Summers, L. H., "Capital Taxation and Accumulation in a Life Cycle Growth Model," **American Economic Review** 71, no. 4 (1981): 533–44.

Surrey, Stanley S., **Pathways to Tax Reform** (Cambridge, Mass.: Harvard University Press, 1973).

Surrey, Stanley S., and Paul R. McDaniel, **Tax Expenditures** (Cambridge, Mass.: Harvard University Press, 1985).

Swanson, Edward P., "Accounting for Changing Prices: Some Mid-Course Corrections," **Journal of Accountancy** (April 1984), pp. 78–93.

Thirsk, Wayne, "Some Lessons from the Colombian Experience," xeroxed, Public Economics Department, World Bank, 1988.

Thompson, A. E. John, "The Desirability and Feasibility of Indexing Business Profits for Tax Purposes," **Report of Proceedings of the Thirty-Fourth Tax Conference** (Canadian Tax Foundation, 1982), pp. 495–519.

Urdinola U., Antonio, "Tributación y Deuda: Aspectos de la Reforma Tributaria de 1986," **Nueva Reforma Tributaria 1986** (Medellín, Colombia: Asociación Nacional de Industriales, 1986), pp. 55–62.

U.S. Department of the Treasury, **Tax Reform for Fairness, Simplicity, and Economic Growth** (Washington, D.C., November 1984).

U.S. Department of the Treasury, **Blueprints for Basic Tax Reform** (Washington, D.C.: U.S. Government Printing Office, 1977), also available as David F. Bradford and the U.S. Treasury Department Staff, **Blueprints for Basic Tax Reform** (Arlington, Va.: Tax Analysts, 1984).

Vickrey, William, **Agenda for Progressive Taxation** (New York: Ronald Press, 1947).

Wanless, P. T., and Forrester, D. A. R., eds., **Readings in Inflation Accounting** (New York: John Wiley and Sons), 1979.

Zodrow, George R., "Implementing Tax Reform," **National Tax Journal** 34 (1981): 401–18.

———, "Optimal Tax Reform in the Presence of Adjustment Costs," **Journal of Public Economics** 27 (1985): 211–30.

———, "Implementing Tax Reform: The Intergenerational Carryover Problem," **National Tax Journal** 39 (1986): 419–34.

———, "Alternative Approaches to Progressive Expenditure Taxation," **1986 Proceedings of the Seventy-Ninth Annual Conference on Taxation**, National Tax Association-Tax Institute of America (1987), pp. 125–34.

Zodrow, George R., and Charles E. McLure, Jr., "Implementing Direct Consumption Taxes in Developing Countries," World Bank Working Paper WPS 131, December 1988.

INDEX

Aaron, Henry J., 259n.5, 261n.20, 261–62n.21, 265–66n.55, 266n.57, 272n.113, 331–35, 339–40

Aaron-Galper transition rules, 331–35

Ability to pay: concept of, 355–56; measure of, 6–7

Accounting. *See* Accrual accounting; Cash flow accounting; Financial accounting; Inventory accounting; Realization accounting; Replacement cost accounting; Tax accounting

Accounting methods, 33, 37, 98–102

Accrual accounting: advantage of, 33; for capital gains, 136; compared with business cash flow accounting, 278–79; compared with realization accounting for inflation adjustment, 256–58; economic and straightline methods, 103–4

Additional-shift rule. *See* Depreciation

Ad hoc system of inflation adjustment. *See* Inflation adjustment

Administration: comparison of income- and consumption-based tax system, 364–66

Agriculture: and investment losses, 178; proposed changes in tax base for, 182; special rules, 40–41; tax accounting for, 101–2, 118

Amortization: and capital cost recovery, 36–37; timing of, 111

Andean Pact countries: Cartagena Agreement, 123, 134; effect of competing tax policy in, 132; and source-based income taxation, 119

Arms-length price, 43

Assets: allocation of debt under net wealth tax, 168–71; depreciation, 150, 180, 279–82; inflation adjustment calculation for depreciation, 21; and measurement of net wealth, 173; real, 238–39; sale of fixed, 44; transfer of, 138–39; valuation under net wealth tax, 48.

See also Depreciation; Inflation adjustment

Auerbach, Alan J., 86n.34, 267n.72

Ayala, Horacio, 267n.72

Bad debt deductions: timing for tax purposes, 38–39, 116

Banco de la Republica. *See* Central Bank, Colombia

Belgium, 119

Bequests, 45; and taxation of accrued gains, 138; tax treatment under Simplified Alternative Tax (SAT), 312–18. *See also* Gifts

Betancourt, Roger R., 217–18

Blejer, Mario, 227, 269n.84

Boskin, Michael J., 377n.25

Bossons, John, 269n.89, 270n.98

Bradford, David F., 26n.1, 86n.34, 87n.39, 265n.50, 291n.1, 300, 376n.20

Break, George F., 291n.10

Bulow, Jeremy I., 264n.45, 265n.53, 265–66n.55, 266n.57

Business entity: seller/lender or purchaser/borrower tax avoidance opportunity, 298–99; tax treatment under Simplified Alternative Tax (SAT), 302

Business taxation: and cash flow basis for receipts and expenditures, 278–82; comparison of income- and consumption-based tax system, 278–82, 297; for domestic entities under consumption-based tax, 295–302; for foreign investment, 41–42; for international entities under Simplified Alternative Tax (SAT), 303–12

Cadastral value. *See* Property; Real estate: cadastral value

Capital cost: debt finance in open and closed economies, 211–18; recovery of, 16–17; *See also* Depreciation

Capital gains: and accrual accounting, 136; and ad hoc and inte-

grated inflation adjustment, 240; basis for computing gain or loss, 138; in calculation of marginal effective tax rates, 62–64; comparison of treatment under income- and consumption-based tax system, 366–67; deduction of losses against, 137; effect of integrated and ad hoc inflation adjustment systems, 240; taxation, 135–39; tax on foreign business for, 42; treatment of debt instrument, 104–5

Capital income: treatment under income- and consumption-based tax system, 363

Capital losses. *See* Capital gains

Cardenas S., Mauricio, 386nn.12, 13

Carrizosa S., Mauricio, 197, 262n.25, 263nn.27, 28, 387–88

Casanegra de Jantscher, Milka, 200, 201, 262n.23, 263–64n.42, 271n.102, 271n.105, 271–72n.106

Cash flow accounting: for consumption-based business tax, 278–82; under Simplified Alternative Tax (SAT), 299. *See also* Individual cash flow (ICF)

Cash holdings: under ad hoc and integrated inflation adjustment, 241

Cattle raising: and proposed changes for taxation, 182; and taxation rules, 40; and tax credits, 118

Central Bank, Colombia: remittance and withholding tax data from, 124–28

CERT (Certificado de Reembolso Tributario) program, 43

CFC. *See* Controlled foreign corporations (CFC)

Chica A., Ricardo, 262n.25

Chile: and integrated system of inflation adjustment, 189–90, 200–201, 208, 236–42, 263n.42, 264n.43

Churning, 74, 222

Clague, Christopher, 217–18

Closed economy: and debt-financed capital costs, 211–14

Comision Nacional de Valores, 36

397

Commission of the Cartagena Agreement: Decisions 24 and 220, 123
Commissions: tax on foreign business for, 42, 43
Complementary taxes, 44–49. *See also* Net wealth tax; Occasional gains; Presumptive income; Remittance tax; Withholding tax
Compliance, 25–26. *See also* Tax avoidance
Conformity, 206–8
Consumption, personal: taxation under Simplified Alternative Tax (SAT), 323–24
Consumption-based tax system, 4–5, 10, 12–13; business taxes under, 278; compared with income-based tax system, 278–90; creditability, 304–7; debt and interest under, 282–84; definition, 277; depreciable assets under, 279–82; individual cash flow (ICF) approach, 284–87; individual tax prepayment (ITP) approach, 287–88; rationale for taxation of business, 295–98; tax treatment of gifts and bequests, 312–13. *See also* Simplified Alternative Tax (SAT)
Contracts, long-term, 37–38, 181; calculation of taxable income from, 147–50, 181; timing of taxable income from, 111–13
Controlled foreign corporations (CFC): taxation of earnings, 121–22
Corporate payments withholding tax, 40
Corporate shares taxation, 177
Cost capitalization of production, 113–15
Creditability: of Colombian income tax, 219–20; under Simplified Alternative Tax (SAT), 303–12; of withholding tax, 306, 308

Data sources: DIN and Central Bank in Colombia, 124–25, 126, 128; US Department of Commerce and Internal Revenue Service, 125–26
Davidson, Sidney, 264n.46
Debt: allocation to assets, 168–71; definition under net wealth tax, 48–49; of foreign companies, 43; in measurement of net wealth,

168–71; bad timing of taxation for, 38–39, 116; treatment under Simplified Alternative Tax (SAT), 297; treatment under income- and consumption-based tax system, 282–84
Debt, below-market. *See* Loans, below-market
Debt finance: comparison of effect of integrated and ad hoc inflation adjustment, 237–38; and marginal effective tax rate calculation, 64
Debt instruments: publicly traded, 48, 104–5, 179
Deductions: for capital losses, 137–38; for income losses, 33; limits on interest income and expense, 35; using present value expensing, 288–90
Denison, Edward, 259n.4
Depletion, 37, 111
Depreciation, 36–37, 44, 221–23; and assets classes, 150, 180–81; economic and straightline methods of accounting, 103–4; expensing as alternative to deduction, 280; in marginal effective tax rate calculations, 63; percentage-of-basis and straightline methods for calculating, 108–11; and present value expensing, 288–90
DIN. *See* National Tax Administration (Direccion de Impuestos Nacionales, DIN)
Distributional neutrality: in tax system, 7, 8
Dividends: calculation of exempt income from, 93; definition, 95; exemption at shareholder level, 32; and taxation, 67; withholding tax rate on, 39. *See also* Financial accounting; Law 75 of 1986; Profits, inflationary; Seven-thirds (7/3) rule
Dornbusch, Rudiger, 227
Driffill, E. John, 376n.22
Dynastic view of tax equity, 313–14

Economic development, 8–9
Economic neutrality, 7–10, 59, 65, 221, 371–72
Equity finance: comparison of effect of integrated and ad hoc inflation adjustment, 237

Evasion. *See* Tax avoidance
Exchange rate: effect of inflation adjustment phase-in, 227–28; and rate of inflation in Colombia, 205
Exemptions, 93
Expensing, 98, 102–8, 198–99, 223–27; compared under income- and consumption-based business tax, 307; outside Colombia, 43; present value, 288–90. *See also* Interest/income expense
Exports: tax credits for free trade zone income, 118; tax incentives for nontraditional, 43

Fairness, 6–7, 340–42
Family wealth, 185–86. *See also* Husband, wife, and children; Net wealth
Feldstein, Martin, 259n.9, 269n.83
FIFO (first-in, first-out) accounting. *See* Inventory accounting
Financial accounting: and conformity of tax accounting, 206–8; limitation on exemption of dividend income, 93–94, 177; revaluation of assets, 173, 186
Fisher's Law, 27n.8, 74, 75, 271n.104; modified, 75, 212, 268n.81
Foreign currency: debt from exchange rate changes, 49; and exchange losses, 178; and treatment of debt denominated, 204–6, 241
Foreign entities tax rate, 42
Foreign investment: in Colombia, 123–24; consumption-based business tax as means to tax, 297; non-tax elements of control, 123; taxation of income from, 41–43; and treatment of individual under Simplified Alternative Tax (SAT), 317–18
Foreign parent company: taxation of payments to, 43
Foreign tax credit, 119–22; of capital exporting countries, 9; and proposals for public policy in Colombia, 128–35; treatment under Simplified Alternative Tax (SAT), 303; and United States and Colombian policy strategy, 126–28; and United States policy, 119–22. *See*

AUTHORS

Charles E. McLure, Jr., the Director of this study for the government of Colombia, is a Senior Fellow at the Hoover Institution at Stanford University, California. He has served as Deputy Assistant Secretary of the U. S. Treasury for Tax Analysis and as Vice President of the National Bureau of Economic Research. He has been an advisor on tax policy to the World Bank, the International Monetary Fund, and the United Nations, as well as to a number of foreign governments, including those of Jamaica, Venezuela, New Zealand, and Canada.

John Mutti is the Sydney Meyer Professor of International Economics at Grinnell College. He has served on the staffs of the president's Council of Economic Advisors and the U.S. Treasury Department's Office of International Tax Analysis.

Victor Thuronyi is Associate Professor of Law at the State University of New York at Buffalo. He has been on the staff of the Office of Tax Legislative Counsel of the U.S. Treasury Department.

George R. Zodrow is Associate Professor of Economics at Rice University. He has served on the staff of the U.S. Treasury Department's Office of Tax Analysis and as a consultant to the World Bank.

Mutti, Thuronyi, and Zodrow participated in the preparation of *Tax Reform for Fairness, Simplicity, and Economic Growth*, the U.S. Treasury Department's 1984 Tax Reform Proposals to President Ronald Reagan, for which Charles McLure had primary responsibility.